SO-AEK-016

PENGUIN BOOKS

THE ISRAEL-ARAB READER

WALTER LAQUEUR, a professor of history and a commentator and expert on international affairs, is chairman of the International Research Council of the Center for Strategic and International Studies at Georgetown University in Washington, D.C., and director of the Institute of Contemporary History and Wiener Library in London. He has written and edited more than twenty-five books—among them, *Europe in Our Time*, *The Terrible Secret*, and *Terrorism*.

BARRY RUBIN is a professor at Hebrew University's Rothberg School and a Senior Fellow at the Bar-Ilan University BESA Center, Hebrew University Truman Center, and University of Haifa Jewish-Arab Center. His books include *Assimilation and Its Discontents*; *Revolution Until Victory?: The Politics and History of the PLO*; *Cauldron of Turmoil: America in the Middle East*; *Islamic Fundamentalism in Egyptian Politics*; *Istanbul Intrigues*; *Modern Dictators: Third World Coupmakers, Strongmen, and Populist Tyrants*; *Secrets of State: The State Department and the Struggle over U.S. Foreign Policy*; *The Arab States and the Palestine Conflict*; *Paved with Good Intentions: The American Experience and Iran*; *The Great Powers in the Middle East 1941–1947: The Road to Cold War*; and, as co-editor, *Iraq's Road to War*.

The Israel-Arab Reader

A Documentary History of the Middle East Conflict

FIFTH REVISED AND
UPDATED EDITION

**Walter Laqueur and
Barry Rubin, editors**

PENGUIN BOOKS

PENGUIN BOOKS
Published by the Penguin Group
Penguin Books USA Inc., 375 Hudson Street, New York, New York 10014, U.S.A.
Penguin Books Ltd, 27 Wrights Lane, London W8 5TZ, England
Penguin Books Australia Ltd, Ringwood, Victoria, Australia
Penguin Books Canada Ltd, 10 Alcorn Avenue, Toronto, Ontario, Canada M4V 3B2
Penguin Books (N.Z.) Ltd, 182–190 Wairau Road, Auckland 10, New Zealand

Penguin Books Ltd, Registered Offices: Harmondsworth, Middlesex, England

The Israel-Arab Reader, edited by Walter Laqueur, first published 1969
Revised edition published 1970
Third revised edition published 1976
Fourth revised and updated edition, edited by Walter Laqueur and Barry Rubin, published in
Pelican Books 1984
Published in Penguin Books 1991
This fifth revised and updated edition published in Penguin Books 1995

1 3 5 7 9 10 8 6 4 2

LIBRARY OF CONGRESS CATALOGING IN PUBLICATION DATA
Main entry under title:
The Israel-Arab reader.
Bibliography: p.
1. Jewish-Arab relations—1917– —Sources.
I. Laqueur, Walter, 1921– . II. Rubin, Barry M.
DS119.7.I8256 1984b 956 84-10992
ISBN 0 14 02.45621 6

Printed in the United States of America
Set in Times Roman
Designed by Paula Szafranski

Contents

PART IV: *FROM WAR TO WAR*

PART V: *CAMP DAVID AND WAR IN LEBANON*

Introduction

This collection of documents aims to provide a better understanding of the background, history, and efforts to resolve the Arab-Israeli conflict. The story is traced from the origins of Zionism and Arab nationalism, into the struggles both preceding and following Israel's independence in 1948, the wars and hostilities characterizing the following decades, and finally through the long diplomatic process and many initiatives made to resolve the issue.

We thank the Institute of Contemporary History (the Wiener Library) in London—especially Christa Wichmann and Ze'ev Ben Shlomo—and also Eric Fredell for help in preparing earlier editions. Yohai Sella assisted greatly in preparing the current edition.

Walter Laqueur

Barry Rubin

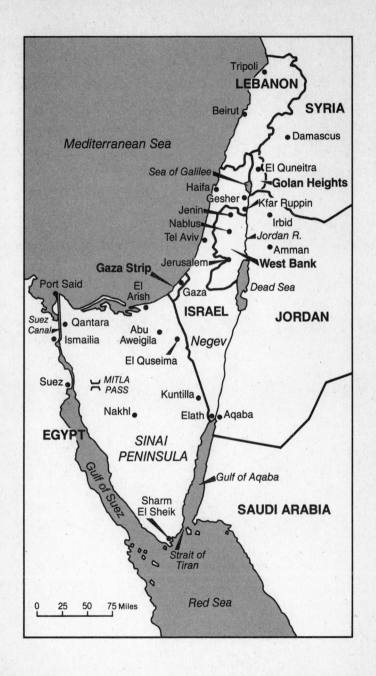

Tripoli
LEBANON
SYRIA
Beirut
Damascus
Mediterranean Sea
Sea of Galilee
El Quneitra
Golan Heights
Haifa
Gesher
Kfar Ruppin
Jenin
Irbid
Nablus
Jordan R.
Tel Aviv
Amman
Jerusalem
West Bank
Gaza Strip
El Arish
Gaza
Dead Sea
Port Said
ISRAEL
JORDAN
Suez Canal
Qantara
Abu Aweigila
Negev
Ismailia
El Quseima
MITLA PASS
Suez
Kuntilla
Nakhl
Elath
Aqaba
EGYPT
SINAI PENINSULA
Gulf of Suez
Gulf of Aqaba
Sharm El Sheik
SAUDI ARABIA
Strait of Tiran
0 25 50 75 Miles
Red Sea

Part I

From the Bilu to the British Mandate

Part I of the Reader covers the period from the first stirrings of the Jewish and Arab national movements to 1917, the date of the Balfour Declaration. The tie between the Jewish communities in what was still commonly defined as the diaspora had been submerged but never entirely severed; it survived, for instance, in the traditional prayer ("Next year in Jerusalem") and found its political expression in the emergence of the Zionist movement in the last decade of the nineteenth century. There was no specific Arab Palestinian national consciousness, but among the leaders of the Arab population of the Ottoman Empire the demand for national self-determination gained ground. After the defeat of the Turks in 1918, this movement quickly gathered momentum.

The Manifesto of the Bilu

Bilu are the first letters of a passage in Isaiah, Chapter 2, Verse 5: "House of Jacob, come, let us go." The Biluim, about five hundred young people mainly from the Kharkov region, were part of the wider movement of the "Lovers of Zion" (*Hovevei Zion*) which had developed in Russia in the early eighteen-eighties mainly under the impact of the pogroms of 1881. This manifesto was issued by a Bilu group in Constantinople in 1882.

To our brothers and sisters in Exile!
'If I help not myself, who will help me?'
Nearly two thousand years have elapsed since, in an evil hour, after a heroic struggle, the glory of our Temple vanished in fire and our kings and chieftains changed their crowns and diadems for the chains of exile. We lost our country where dwelt our beloved sires. Into the Exile we took with us, of all our glories, only a spark of the fire by which our Temple, the abode of our Great One, was engirdled, and this little spark kept us alive while the towers of our enemies crumbled into dust, and this spark leapt into celestial flame and shed light on the heroes of our race and inspired them to endure the horrors of the dance of death and the tortures of the *autos-da-fé*. And this spark is again kindling and will shine for us, a true pillar of fire going before us on the road to Zion, while behind us is a pillar of cloud, the pillar of oppression threatening to destroy us. Sleepest thou, O our nation? What hast thou been doing until 1882? Sleeping, and dreaming the false dream of Assimilation. Now, thank God, thou art awakened from thy slothful slumber. The Pogroms have awakened thee from thy charmed sleep. Thine eyes are open to recognise the cloudy delusive hopes. Canst thou listen silently to the taunts and mockeries of thine enemies? . . . Where is thy ancient pride, thine olden spirit? Remember that thou wast a nation possessing a wise religion, a law, a con-

3

stitution, a celestial Temple whose wall* is still a silent witness to the glories of the past; that thy sons dwelt in palaces and towers, and thy cities flourished in the splendour of civilisation, while these enemies of thine dwelt like beasts in the muddy marshes of their dark woods. While thy children were clad in purple and fine linen, they wore the rough skins of the wolf and the bear. Art thou not ashamed?

Hopeless is your state in the West; the star of your future is gleaming in the East. Deeply conscious of all this, and inspired by the true teaching of our great master, Hillel, 'If I help not myself, who will help me?' we propose to form the following society for national ends.

1. The Society will be named 'BILU', according to the motto 'House of Jacob, come, let us go'. It will be divided into local branches according to the numbers of its members.

2. The seat of the Committee shall be Jerusalem.

3. Donations and contributions shall be unfixed and unlimited.

WE WANT:

1. A home in our country. It was given us by the mercy of God; it is ours as registered in the archives of history.

2. To beg it of the Sultan himself, and if it be impossible to obtain this, to beg that we may at least possess it as a state within a larger state; the internal administration to be ours, to have our civil and political rights, and to act with the Turkish Empire only in foreign affairs, so as to help our brother Ishmael in the time of his need.

We hope that the interests of our glorious nation will rouse the national spirit in rich and powerful men, and that everyone, rich or poor, will give his best labours to the holy cause.

Greetings, dear brothers and sisters!

HEAR, O ISRAEL! The Lord our God, the Lord is one, and our land Zion is our one hope.

GOD be with us! THE PIONEERS OF BILU.

* The Wailing Wall.

Negib Azouri: Program of the
League of the Arab Fatherland*

N. Azouri, a Christian Arab, edited the journal *L'Indépendance Arabe* in Paris before the first world war. His *"Réveil de la Nation Arabe dans l'Asie Turque . . ."* (1905) from which this excerpt is drawn was the "first open demand for the secession of the Arab lands from the Ottoman Empire." (Sylvia G. Haim: *Arab Nationalism*)

. . . There is nothing more liberal than the league's program. The league wants, before anything else, to separate the civil and the religious power, in the interest of Islam and the Arab nation, and to form an Arab empire stretching from the Tigris and the Euphrates to the Suez Isthmus, and from the Mediterranean to the Arabian Sea.

The mode of government will be a constitutional sultanate based on the freedom of all the religions and the equality of all the citizens before the law. It will respect the interests of Europe, all the concessions and all the privileges which had been granted to her up to now by the Turks. It will also respect the autonomy of the Lebanon, and the independence of the principalities of Yemen, Nejd, and Iraq.

The league offers the throne of the Arab Empire to that prince of the Khedivial family of Egypt who will openly declare himself in its favor and who will devote his energy and his resources to this end.

It rejects the idea of unifying Egypt and the Arab Empire under the same monarchy, because the Egyptians do not belong to the Arab race; they are of the African Berber family and the language which they spoke before Islam bears no similarity to Arabic. There exists, moreover, between Egypt and the Arab Empire a natural frontier which must be respected in order to avoid the introduction, in the new state, of the germs of discord and destruction. Never, as a matter of fact, have the ancient Arab caliphs succeeded for any length of time in controlling the two countries at the same time. . . .

Theodor Herzl: The Jewish State

Theodor Herzl (1860–1904) was the founder of modern political Zionism. In the preface to *Der Judenstaat* (published in 1896) he says:

* Translated by Sylvia G. Haim.

"The Idea which I have developed in this pamphlet is a very old one: it is the restoration of the Jewish State."

. . . The Jewish question still exists. It would be foolish to deny it. It is a remnant of the Middle Ages, which civilized nations do not even yet seem able to shake off, try as they will. They certainly showed a generous desire to do so when they emancipated us. The Jewish question exists wherever Jews live in perceptible numbers. Where it does not exist, it is carried by Jews in the course of their migrations. We naturally move to those places where we are not persecuted, and there our presence produces persecution. This is the case in every country, and will remain so, even in those highly civilized—for instance, France—until the Jewish question finds a solution on a political basis. The unfortunate Jews are now carrying the seeds of Anti-Semitism into England; they have already introduced it into America.

I believe that I understand Anti-Semitism, which is really a highly complex movement. I consider it from a Jewish standpoint, yet without fear or hatred. I believe that I can see what elements there are in it of vulgar sport, of common trade jealousy, of inherited prejudice, of religious intolerance, and also of pretended self-defence. I think the Jewish question is no more a social than a religious one, notwithstanding that it sometimes takes these and other forms. It is a national question, which can only be solved by making it a political world-question to be discussed and settled by the civilized nations of the world in council.

We are a people—one people.

We have honestly endeavored everywhere to merge ourselves in the social life of surrounding communities and to preserve the faith of our fathers. We are not permitted to do so. In vain are we loyal patriots, our loyalty in some places running to extremes; in vain do we make the same sacrifices of life and property as our fellow-citizens; in vain do we strive to increase the fame of our native land in science and art, or her wealth by trade and commerce. In countries where we have lived for centuries we are still cried down as strangers, and often by those whose ancestors were not yet domiciled in the land where Jews had already had experience of suffering. The majority may decide which are the strangers; for this, as indeed every point which arises in the relations between nations, is a question of might. I do not here surrender any portion of our prescriptive right, when I make this statement merely in my own name as an individual. In the world as it now is and for an indefinite period will probably remain, might precedes right. It is useless, therefore, for us to be loyal patriots, as were the Huguenots who were forced to emigrate. If we could only be left in peace. . . .

But I think we shall not be left in peace.

Oppression and persecution cannot exterminate us. No nation on earth has survived such struggles and sufferings as we have gone through. Jew-baiting has merely stripped off our weaklings; the strong among us were invariably true to their race when persecution broke out against them. This attitude was most clearly apparent in the period immediately following the emancipation of the Jews. Those Jews who were advanced intellectually and materially entirely lost the feeling of belonging to their race. Wherever our political well-being has lasted for any length of time, we have assimilated with our surroundings. I think this is not discreditable. Hence, the statesman who would wish to see a Jewish strain in his nation would have to provide for the duration of our political well-being; and even a Bismarck could not do that.

For old prejudices against us still lie deep in the hearts of the people. He who would have proofs of this need only listen to the people where they speak with frankness and simplicity: proverb and fairy-tale are both Anti-Semitic. A nation is everywhere a great child, which can certainly be educated; but its education would, even in most favorable circumstances, occupy such a vast amount of time that we could, as already mentioned, remove our own difficulties by other means long before the process was accomplished.

Assimilation, by which I understood not only external conformity in dress, habits, customs, and language, but also identity of feeling and manner—assimilation of Jews could be effected only by intermarriage. But the need for mixed marriages would have to be felt by the majority; their mere recognition by law would certainly not suffice. . . .

No one can deny the gravity of the situation of the Jews. Wherever they live in perceptible numbers, they are more or less persecuted. Their equality before the law, granted by statute, has become practically a dead letter. They are debarred from filling even moderately high positions, either in the army, or in any public or private capacity. And attempts are made to thrust them out of business also: "Don't buy from Jews!"

Attacks in Parliaments, in assemblies, in the press, in the pulpit, in the street, on journeys—for example, their exclusion from certain hotels—even in places of recreation, become daily more numerous. The forms of persecutions vary according to the countries and social circles in which they occur. In Russia, imposts are levied on Jewish villages; in Rumania, a few persons are put to death; in Germany, they get a good beating occasionally; in Austria, Anti-Semites exercise terrorism over all public life; in Algeria, there are travelling agitators; in Paris, the Jews are shut out of the so-called best social circles and excluded from clubs. Shades of anti-Jewish feeling are innumerable. But this is not to be an attempt to make out a doleful category of Jewish hardships.

I do not intend to arouse sympathetic emotions on our behalf. That would be a foolish, futile, and undignified proceeding. I shall content myself with putting the following questions to the Jews: Is it not true that, in countries where we live in perceptible numbers, the position of Jewish lawyers, doctors, technicians, teachers, and employees of all descriptions becomes daily more intolerable? Is it not true, that the Jewish middle classes are seriously threatened? Is it not true, that the passions of the mob are incited against our wealthy people? Is it not true, that our poor endure greater sufferings than any other proletariat? I think that this external pressure makes itself felt everywhere. In our economically upper classes it causes discomfort, in our middle classes continual and grave anxieties, in our lower classes absolute despair.

Everything tends, in fact, to one and the same conclusion, which is clearly enunciated in that classic Berlin phrase: *"Juden Raus!"* (Out with the Jews!)

I shall now put the Question in the briefest possible form: Are we to "get out" now and where to?

Or, may we yet remain? And, how long?

Let us first settle the point of staying where we are. Can we hope for better days, can we possess our souls in patience, can we wait in pious resignation till the princes and peoples of this earth are more mercifully disposed towards us? I say that we cannot hope for a change in the current of feeling. And why not? Even if we were as near to the hearts of princes as are their other subjects, they could not protect us. They would only feel popular hatred by showing us too much favor. By "too much," I really mean less than is claimed as a right by every ordinary citizen, or by every race. The nations in whose midst Jews live are all either covertly or openly Anti-Semitic.

The common people have not, and indeed cannot have, any historic comprehension. They do not know that the sins of the Middle Ages are now being visited on the nations of Europe. We are what the Ghetto made us. We have attained pre-eminence in finance, because mediaeval conditions drove us to it. The same process is now being repeated. We are again being forced into finance, now it is the stock exchange, by being kept out of other branches of economic activity. Being on the stock exchange, we are consequently exposed afresh to contempt. At the same time we continue to produce an abundance of mediocre intellects who find no outlet, and this endangers our social position as much as does our increasing wealth. Educated Jews without means are now rapidly becoming Socialists. Hence we are certain to suffer very severely in the struggle between classes, because we stand in the most exposed position in the camps of both Socialists and capitalists. . . .

The Plan

The whole plan is in its essence perfectly simple, as it must necessarily be if it is to come within the comprehension of all.

Let the sovereignty be granted us over a portion of the globe large enough to satisfy the rightful requirements of a nation; the rest we shall manage for ourselves.

The creation of a new State is neither ridiculous nor impossible. We have in our day witnessed the process in connection with nations which were not largely members of the middle class, but poorer, less educated, and consequently weaker than ourselves. The Governments of all countries scourged by Anti-Semitism will be keenly interested in assisting us to obtain the sovereignty we want.

The plan, simple in design, but complicated in execution, will be carried out by two agencies: The Society of Jews and the Jewish Company.

The Society of Jews will do the preparatory work in the domains of science and politics, which the Jewish Company will afterwards apply practically.

The Jewish Company will be the liquidating agent of the business interests of departing Jews, and will organize commerce and trade in the new country.

We must not imagine the departure of the Jews to be a sudden one. It will be gradual, continuous, and will cover many decades. The poorest will go first to cultivate the soil. In accordance with a preconceived plan, they will construct roads, bridges, railways and telegraph installations; regulate rivers; and build their own dwellings; their labor will create trade, trade will create markets and markets will attract new settlers, for every man will go voluntarily, at his own expense and his own risk. The labor expended on the land will enhance its value, and the Jews will soon perceive that a new and permanent sphere of operation is opening here for that spirit of enterprise which has heretofore met only with hatred and obloquy.

If we wish to found a State today, we shall not do it in the way which would have been the only possible one a thousand years ago. It is foolish to revert to old stages of civilization, as many Zionists would like to do. Supposing, for example, we were obliged to clear a country of wild beasts, we should not set about the task in the fashion of Europeans of the fifth century. We should not take spear and lance and go out singly in pursuit of bears; we would organize a large and active hunting party, drive the animals together, and throw a melinite bomb into their midst.

If we wish to conduct building operations, we shall not plant a mass of stakes and piles on the shore of a lake, but we shall build as men build now. Indeed, we shall build in a bolder and more stately style than was ever adopted before, for we now possess means which men never yet possessed.

The emigrants standing lowest in the economic scale will be slowly followed by those of a higher grade. Those who at this moment are living in despair will go first. They will be led by the mediocre intellects which we produce so superabundantly and which are persecuted everywhere.

This pamphlet will open a general discussion on the Jewish Question, but that does not mean that there will be any voting on it. Such a result would ruin the cause from the outset, and dissidents must remember that allegiance or opposition is entirely voluntary. He who will not come with us should remain behind.

Let all who are willing to join us, fall in behind our banner and fight for our cause with voice and pen and deed.

Those Jews who agree with our idea of a State will attach themselves to the Society, which will thereby be authorized to confer and treat with Governments in the name of our people. The Society will thus be acknowledged in its relations with Governments as a State-creating power. This acknowledgment will practically create the State.

Should the Powers declare themselves willing to admit our sovereignty over a neutral piece of land, then the Society will enter into negotiations for the possession of this land. Here two territories come under consideration, Palestine and Argentine. In both countries important experiments in colonization have been made, though on the mistaken principle of a gradual infiltration of Jews. An infiltration is bound to end badly. It continues till the inevitable moment when the native population feels itself threatened, and forces the Government to stop a further influx of Jews. Immigration is consequently futile unless we have the sovereign right to continue such immigration.

The Society of Jews will treat with the present masters of the land, putting itself under the protectorate of the European Powers, if they prove friendly to the plan. We could offer the present possessors of the land enormous advantages, assume part of the public debt, build new roads for traffic, which our presence in the country would render necessary, and do many other things. The creation of our State would be beneficial to adjacent countries, because the cultivation of a strip of land increases the value of its surrounding districts in innumerable ways.

The Basle Declaration

This official statement of Zionist purpose was adopted by the first Zionist Congress in Basle in August 1897.

The aim of Zionism is to create for the Jewish people a home in Palestine secured by public law.

The Congress contemplates the following means to the attainment of this end:

1. The promotion, on suitable lines, of the colonization of Palestine by Jewish agricultural and industrial workers.

2. The organization and binding together of the whole of Jewry by means of appropriate institutions, local and international, in accordance with the laws of each country.

3. The strengthening and fostering of Jewish national sentiment and consciousness.

4. Preparatory steps towards obtaining government consent, where necessary, to the attainment of the aim of Zionism.

The Sykes–Picot Agreement

Sir Mark Sykes (1873–1919), a distinguished British orientalist, and Charles Georges-Picot, formerly French Consul in Beirut, prepared a draft agreement in 1915–16 about the post-war division of the Middle East, which was also approved in principle by Russia.

1. Sir Edward Grey to Paul Cambon,
15 May 1916

I shall have the honour to reply fully in a further note to your Excellency's note of the 9th instant, relative to the creation of an Arab State, but I should meanwhile be grateful if your Excellency could assure me that in those regions which, under the conditions recorded in that communication, become entirely French, or in which French interests are recognised as predominant, any existing British concessions, rights of navigation or development, and the rights and privileges of any British religious, scholastic, or medical institutions will be maintained.

His Majesty's Government are, of course, ready to give a reciprocal assurance in regard to the British area.

2. Grey to Cambon, 16 May 1916

I have the honour to acknowledge the receipt of your Excellency's note of the 9th instant, stating that the French Government accept the limits of a future Arab State, or Confederation of States, and of those parts of Syria where French interests predominate, together with certain conditions attached thereto, such as they result from recent discussions in London and Petrograd on the subject.

I have the honour to inform your Excellency in reply that the acceptance of the whole project, as it now stands, will involve the abdication of considerable British interests, but, since His Majesty's Government recognise the advantage to the general cause of the Allies entailed in producing a more favourable internal political situation in Turkey, they are ready to accept the arrangement now arrived at, provided that the cooperation of the Arabs is secured, and that the Arabs fulfil the conditions and obtain the towns of Homs, Hama, Damascus, and Aleppo.

It is accordingly understood between the French and British Governments—

1. That France and Great Britain are prepared to recognize and protect an independent Arab State or a Confederation of Arab States in the areas (A) and (B) marked on the annexed map (*map not reproduced: Ed.*), under the suzerainty of an Arab chief. That in area (A) France, and in area (B) Great Britain, shall have priority of right of enterprise and local loans. That in area (A) France, and in area (B) Great Britain, shall alone supply advisers or foreign functionaries at the request of the Arab State or Confederation of Arab States.

2. That in the blue area France, and in the red area Great Britain, shall be allowed to establish such direct or indirect administration or control as they desire and as they may think fit to arrange with the Arab State or Confederation of Arab States.

3. That in the brown area there shall be established an international administration, the form of which is to be decided upon after consultation with Russia, and subsequently in consultation with the other Allies, and the representatives of the Shereef of Mecca.

4. That Great Britain be accorded (1) the ports of Haifa and Acre, (2) guarantee of a given supply of water from the Tigris and Euphrates in area (A) for area (B). His Majesty's Government, on their part, undertake that they will at no time enter into negotiations for the cession of Cyprus to any third Power without the previous consent of the French Government.

5. That Alexandretta shall be a free port as regards the trade of the British Empire, and that there shall be no discrimination in port charges or facilities as regards British shipping and British goods; that there shall be freedom of transit for British goods through Alexandretta and by railway through the blue area, whether those goods are intended for or originate in the red area, or (B) area, or area (A); and there shall be no discrimination, direct or indirect against British goods on any railway or against British goods or ships at any port serving the areas mentioned.

That Haifa shall be a free port as regards the trade of France, her dominions and protectorates, and there shall be no discrimination in port charges or facilities as regards French shipping and French goods. There shall be freedom of transit for French goods through Haifa and by the British railway through the brown area, whether those goods are intended for or originate in the blue area, area (A), or area (B), and there shall be no discrimination, direct or indirect, against French goods on any railway, or against French goods or ships at any port serving the areas mentioned.

6. That in area (A) the Baghdad Railway shall not be extended southwards beyond Mosul, and in area (B) northwards beyond Samarra, until a railway connecting Baghdad with Aleppo via the Euphrates Valley has been completed, and then only with the concurrence of the two Governments.

7. That Great Britain has the right to build, administer, and be sole owner of a railway connecting Haifa with area (B), and shall have a perpetual right to transport troops along such a line at all times.

It is to be understood by both Governments that this railway is to facilitate the connexion of Baghdad with Haifa by rail, and it is further understood that, if the engineering difficulties and expense entailed by keeping this connecting line in the brown area only make the project unfeasible, that the French Government shall be prepared to consider that the line in question may also traverse the polygon Banias-Keis Marib-Salkhab Tell Otsda-Mesmie before reaching area (B).

8. For a period of twenty years the existing Turkish customs tariff shall remain in force throughout the whole of the blue and red areas, as well as in areas (A) and (B), and no increase in the rates of duty or conversion from *ad valorem* to specific rates shall be made except by agreement between the two Powers.

There shall be no interior customs barriers between any of the above-mentioned areas. The customs duties leviable on goods destined for the interior shall be collected at the port of entry and handed over to the administration of the area of destination.

9. It shall be agreed that the French Government will at no time enter into any negotiations for the cession of their rights and will not cede such rights in the blue area to any third Power, except the Arab State or Confederation of Arab States without the previous agreement of His Majesty's Government, who, on their part, will give a similar undertaking to the French Government regarding the red area.

10. The British and French Governments, as the protectors of the Arab State, shall agree that they will not themselves acquire and will not consent to a third Power acquiring territorial possessions in the Arabian peninsula, nor consent to a third Power installing a naval base either on the east coast, or on the islands, of the Red Sea. This, however, shall not prevent such adjustment of the Aden frontier as may be necessary in consequence of recent Turkish aggression.

11. The negotiations with the Arabs as to the boundaries of the

Arab State or Confederation of Arab States shall be continued through the same channel as heretofore on behalf of the two Powers.

12. It is agreed that measures to control the importation of arms into the Arab territories will be considered by the two Governments.

I have further the honour to state that, in order to make the agreement complete, His Majesty's Government are proposing to the Russian Government to exchange notes analogous to those exchanged by the latter and your Excellency's Government on the 26th April last. Copies of these notes will be communicated to your Excellency as soon as exchanged.

I would also venture to remind your Excellency that the conclusion of the present agreement raises, for practical consideration, the question of the claims of Italy to a share in any partition or rearrangement of Turkey in Asia, as formulated in article 9 of the agreement of the 26th April, 1915, between Italy and the Allies.

His Majesty's Government further consider that the Japanese Government should be informed of the arrangement now concluded.

The McMahon Letter

Sir Henry McMahon (1862–1949), British High Commissioner in Cairo, negotiated in 1915–16 with Husain Ibn Ali, the Sherif of Mecca. The British government promised to support his bid for the restoration of the Caliphate (and leadership in the Arab world) if Husain supported the British war effort against Turkey. Palestine was not mentioned by name in this exchange: the Arabs subsequently claimed that it had been included in the promise of an independent Arab state. The British denied this—as evidenced by McMahon's letter published in the London *Times* in 1937.

October 24, 1915.

I have received your letter of the 29th Shawal, 1333, with much pleasure and your expression of friendliness and sincerity have given me the greatest satisfaction.

I regret that you should have received from my last letter the impression that I regarded the question of limits and boundaries with coldness and hesitation; such was not the case, but it appeared to me that the time had not yet come when that question could be discussed in a conclusive manner.

I have realised, however, from your last letter that you regard this question as one of vital and urgent importance. I have, therefore, lost no time in informing the Government of Great Britain of the contents of your letter, and it is with great pleasure that I communicate to you on their behalf the following statement, which I am confident you will receive with satisfaction.

The two districts of Mersina and Alexandretta and portions of Syria lying to the west of the districts of Damascus, Homs, Hama and Aleppo cannot be said to be purely Arab, and should be excluded from the limits demanded.

With the above modification, and without prejudice to our existing treaties with Arab chiefs, we accept those limits.

As for those regions lying within those frontiers wherein Great Britain is free to act without detriment to the interests of her ally, France, I am empowered in the name of the Government of Great Britain to give the following assurances and make the following reply to your letter:

(1) Subject to the above modifications, Great Britain is prepared to recognise and support the independence of the Arabs in all the regions within the limits demanded by the Sherif of Mecca.

(2) Great Britain will guarantee the Holy Places against all external aggression and will recognise their inviolability.

(3) When the situation admits, Great Britain will give to the Arabs her advice and will assist them to establish what may appear to be the most suitable forms of government in those various territories.

(4) On the other hand, it is understood that the Arabs have decided to seek the advice and guidance of Great Britain only, and that such European advisers and officials as may be required for the formation of a sound form of administration will be British.

(5) With regard to the *vilayets* of Bagdad and Basra, the Arabs will recognise that the established position and interests of Great Britain necessitate special administrative arrangements in order to secure these territories from foreign aggression to promote the welfare of the local populations and to safeguard our mutual economic interests.

I am convinced that this declaration will assure you beyond all possible doubt of the sympathy of Great Britain towards the aspirations of her friends the Arabs and will result in a firm and lasting alliance, the immediate results of which will be the expulsion of the Turks from the Arab countries and the freeing of the Arab peoples from the Turkish yoke, which for so many years has pressed heavily upon them.

I have confined myself in this letter to the more vital and important questions, and if there are any other matters dealt with in your letters which I have omitted to mention, we may discuss them at some convenient date in the future.

It was with very great relief and satisfaction that I heard of the safe arrival of the Holy Carpet and the accompanying offerings which, thanks to the clearness of your directions and the excellence of your arrangements, were landed without trouble or mishap in spite of the dangers and difficulties occasioned by the present sad war. May God soon bring a lasting peace and freedom of all peoples.

I am sending this letter by the hand of your trusted and excellent messenger, Sheikh Mohammed ibn Arif ibn Uraifan, and he will inform you of the various matters of interest, but of less vital importance, which I have not mentioned in this letter.

(Compliments).

(Signed): A. HENRY McMAHON.

The Balfour Declaration

British policy during the war years became gradually committed to the idea of the establishment of a Jewish home in Palestine. After discussions on cabinet level and consultation with Jewish leaders, the decision was made known in the form of a letter by Arthur James Lord Balfour (1848–1930) to Lord Rothschild.

Foreign Office
November 2nd, 1917.

Dear Lord Rothschild,

I have much pleasure in conveying to you, on behalf of His Majesty's Government, the following declaration of sympathy with Jewish Zionist aspirations which has been submitted to, and approved by, the Cabinet.

"His Majesty's Government view with favour the establishment in Palestine of a national home for the Jewish people, and will use their best endeavours to facilitate the achievement of this object, it being clearly understood that nothing shall be done which may prejudice the civil and religious rights of existing non-Jewish communities in Palestine, or the rights and political status enjoyed by Jews in any other country."

I should be grateful if you would bring this declaration to the knowledge of the Zionist Federation.

Yours sincerely,

ARTHUR JAMES BALFOUR.

The Feisal–Weizmann agreement and Feisal–Frankfurter letters

During the peace conference Emir Feisal (1855–1933), the son of Husain, the Sherif of Mecca, met various Jewish leaders and signed an agreement with Dr. Chaim Weizmann (1877–1952), leader of the Zionist movement. Feisal, who in 1921 became King of Iraq, had it announced ten years later that "His Majesty does not remember having written anything of that kind with his knowledge."

Agreement Between Emir Feisal and Dr. Weizmann January 3, 1919

His Royal Highness the Emir Feisal, representing and acting on behalf of the Arab Kingdom of Hedjaz, and Dr. Chaim Weizmann, representing and acting on behalf of the Zionist Organisation, mindful of the racial kinship and ancient bonds existing between the Arabs and the Jewish people, and realising that the surest means of working out the consummation of their national aspirations is through the closest possible collaboration in the development of the Arab State and Palestine, and being desirous further of confirming the good understanding which exists between them, have agreed upon the following Articles:

ARTICLE I

The Arab State and Palestine in all their relations and undertakings shall be controlled by the most cordial goodwill and understanding, and to this end Arab and Jewish duly accredited agents shall be established and maintained in the respective territories.

ARTICLE II

Immediately following the completion of the deliberations of the Peace Conference, the definite boundaries between the Arab State and Palestine shall be determined by a Commission to be agreed upon by the parties hereto.

ARTICLE III

In the establishment of the Constitution and Administration of Palestine all such measures shall be adopted as will afford the fullest guarantees for carrying into effect the British Government's Declaration of the 2d of November, 1917.

ARTICLE IV

All necessary measures shall be taken to encourage and stimulate immigration of Jews into Palestine on a large scale, and as quickly as possible to settle Jewish immigrants upon the land through closer settlement and intensive cultivation of the soil. In taking such measures the Arab peasant and tenant farmers shall be protected in their rights, and shall be assisted in forwarding their economic development.

ARTICLE V

No regulation nor law shall be made prohibiting or interfering in any way with the free exercise of religion; and further the free exercise and enjoyment of religious profession and worship without discrimination or reference shall forever be allowed. No religious test shall ever be required for the exercise of civil or political rights.

ARTICLE VI

The Mohammedan Holy Places shall be under Mohammedan control.

ARTICLE VII

The Zionist Organisation proposes to send to Palestine a Commission of experts to make a survey of the economic possibilities of the country, and to report upon the best means for its development. The Zionist Organisation will place the aforementioned Commission at the disposal of the Arab State for the purpose of a survey of the economic possibilities of the Arab State and to report upon the best means for its development. The Zionist Organisation will use its best efforts to assist the Arab State in providing the means for developing the natural resources and economic possibilities thereof.

ARTICLE VIII

The parties hereto agree to act in complete accord and harmony on all matters embraced herein before the Peace Congress.

ARTICLE IX

Any matters of dispute which may arise between the contracting parties shall be referred to the British Government for arbitration.

Given under our hand at London, England, the third day of January, one thousand nine hundred and nineteen.

CHAIM WEIZMANN.
FEISAL IBN-HUSSEIN.

RESERVATION BY THE EMIR FEISAL

If the Arabs are established as I have asked in my manifesto of January 4th addressed to the British Secretary of State for Foreign Affairs, I will carry out what is written in this agreement. If changes are made, I cannot be answerable for failing to carry out this agreement.

FEISAL IBN-HUSSEIN.

Feisal–Frankfurter Correspondence

DELEGATION HEDJAZIENNE, *Paris, March 3, 1919.*

DEAR MR. FRANKFURTER: I want to take this opportunity of my first contact with American Zionists to tell you what I have often been able to say to Dr. Weizmann in Arabia and Europe.

We feel that the Arabs and Jews are cousins in race, having suffered similar oppressions at the hands of powers stronger than themselves, and by a happy coincidence have been able to take the first step towards the attainment of their national ideals together.

We Arabs, especially the educated among us, look with the deepest sympathy on the Zionist movement. Our deputation here in Paris is fully acquainted with the proposals submitted yesterday by the Zionist Organization to the Peace Conference, and we regard them as moderate and proper. We will do our best, in so far as we are concerned, to help them through: we will wish the Jews a most hearty welcome home.

With the chiefs of your movement, especially with Dr. Weizmann, we have had and continue to have the closest relations. He has been a great helper of our cause, and I hope the Arabs may soon be in a position to make the Jews some return for their kindness. We are working together for a reformed and revived Near East, and our two movements complete one another. The Jewish movement is national and not imperialist. Our movement is national and not imperialist, and there is room in Syria for us both. Indeed I think that neither can be a real success without the other.

People less informed and less responsible than our leaders and yours, ignoring the need for cooperation of the Arabs and Zionists have been trying to exploit the local difficulties that must necessarily arise in Palestine in the early stages of our movements. Some of them have, I am afraid, misrepresented your aims to the Arab peasantry, and our aims to the Jewish peasantry, with the result that interested parties have been able to make capital out of what they call our differences.

I wish to give you my firm conviction that these differences are not on questions of principle, but on matters of detail such as must inevitably occur in every contact of neighbouring peoples, and as are easily adjusted by mutual goodwill. Indeed nearly all of them will disappear with fuller knowledge.

I look forward, and my people with me look forward, to a future in which we will help you and you will help us, so that the countries in which we are mutually interested may once again take their places in the community of civilised peoples of the world.

Believe me,

Yours sincerely,

(*Sgd.*) FEISAL.

5TH MARCH, 1919.

ROYAL HIGHNESS:

Allow me, on behalf of the Zionist Organisation, to acknowledge your recent letter with deep appreciation.

Those of us who come from the United States have already been gratified by the friendly relations and the active cooperation maintained between you and the Zionist leaders, particularly Dr. Weizmann. We knew it could not be otherwise; we knew that the aspirations of the Arab and the Jewish peoples were parallel, that each aspired to reestablish its nationality in its own homeland, each making its own distinctive contribution to civilisation, each seeking its own peaceful mode of life.

The Zionist leaders and the Jewish people for whom they speak have watched with satisfaction the spiritual vigour of the Arab movement. Themselves seeking justice, they are anxious that the just national aims of the Arab people be confirmed and safeguarded by the Peace Conference.

We knew from your acts and your past utterances that the Zionist movement—in other words the national aims of the Jewish people—had your support and the support of the Arab people for whom you speak. These aims are now before the Peace Conference as definite proposals by the Zionist Organisation. We are happy indeed that you consider these proposals "moderate and proper," and that we have in you a staunch supporter for their realisation. For both the Arab and the Jewish peoples there are difficulties ahead—difficulties that challenge the united statesmanship of Arab and Jewish leaders. For it is no easy task to rebuild two great civilisations that have been suffering oppression and misrule for centuries. We each have our difficulties we shall work out as friends, friends who are animated by similar purposes, seeking a free and full development for the two neighbouring peoples. The Arabs and Jews are neighbours in territory; we cannot but live side by side as friends.

Very respectfully,

(Sgd.) FELIX FRANKFURTER.

Recommendations of the King–Crane Commission

The King–Crane Commission was appointed by President Wilson, following a suggestion by Dr. Howard Bliss, President of the American University in Beirut and a sympathizer with the Arab cause. Its main function was to determine which of the Western nations should act as the mandatory power for Palestine.

August 28, 1919

The Commissioners make to the Peace Conference the following recommendations for the treatment of Syria:

1. We recommend, as most important of all, and in strict harmony with our instructions, that whatever foreign administration (whether of one or more powers) is brought into Syria, should come in, not at all as a colonization Power in the old sense of that term, but as a Mandatory under the League of Nations, with the clear consciousness that "the well-being and development" of the Syrian people form for it a "sacred trust".

(1) To this end the mandate should have a limited term, the time of expiration to be determined by the League of Nations, in the light of all the facts as brought out from year to year, in the annual reports of the Mandatory to the League or in other ways.

(2) The Mandatory Administration should have, however, a period and power sufficient to ensure the success of the new State; and especially to make possible carrying through important educational and economic undertakings, essential to secure founding of the State.

(3) The Mandatory Administration should be characterized from the beginning by a strong and vital educational emphasis in clear recognition of the imperative necessity of education for the citizens of a democratic state, and the development of a sound national spirit. This systematic cultivation of national spirit is particularly required in a country like Syria, which has only recently come to self-consciousness.

(4) The Mandatory should definitely seek, from the beginning of its trusteeship, to train the Syrian people to independent self-government as rapidly as conditions allow, by setting up all the institutions of a democratic state, and by sharing with them increasingly the work of administration and so forming gradually an intelligent citizenship, interested unselfishly in the progress of the country, and forming at the same time a large group of disciplined civil servants.

(5) The period of "tutelage" should not be unduly prolonged, but independent self-government should be granted as soon as it can safely

be done; remembering that the primary business of government is not the accomplishment of certain things, but the development of citizens.

(6) It is peculiarly the duty of the Mandatory in a country like Syria, and in this modern age, to see that complete religious liberty is ensured, both in the constitution and in the practice of the state, and that a jealous care is exercised for the rights of all minorities. Nothing is more vital than this for the enduring success of the new Arab State.

(7) In the economic development of Syria, a dangerous amount of indebtedness on the part of the new State should be avoided, as well as any entanglements financially with the affairs of the Mandatory Power. On the other hand the legitimate established privileges of foreigners such as rights to maintain schools, commercial concessions, etc., should be preserved, but subject to review and modification under the authority of the League of Nations in the interest of Syria. The Mandatory Power should not take advantage of its position to force a monopolistic control at any point to the detriment either of Syria or of other nations; but it should seek to bring the new State as rapidly as possible to economic independence as well as to political independence. Whatever is done concerning the further recommendations of the Commission, the fulfillment of at least the conditions now named should be assured, if the Peace Conference and the League of Nations are true to the policy of mandatories already embodied in "The Covenant of the League of Nations". This should effectively guard the most essential interests of Syria, however the machinery of administration is finally organized. The Damascus Congress betrayed in many ways their intense fear that their country would become, though under some other name, simply a colonial possession of some other Power. That fear must be completely allayed.

2. We recommend, in the second place that the unity of Syria be preserved, in accordance with the earnest petition of the great majority of the people of Syria.

(1) The territory concerned is too limited, the population too small, and the economic, geographic, racial and language unity too manifest to make the setting up of independent states within its boundaries desirable, if such division can possibly be avoided. The country is very largely Arab in language, culture, traditions, and customs.

(2) This recommendation is in line with important "general considerations" already urged, and with the principles of the League of Nations, as well as in answer to the desires of the majority of the population concerned.

(3) The precise boundaries of Syria should be determined by a special commission on boundaries, after the Syrian territory has been in general allotted. The Commissioners believe, however, that the claim of the Damascus Conference to include Cilicia in Syria is not justified, either historically or by commercial or language relations. The line between the

Arabic-speaking and the Turkish-speaking populations would quite certainly class Cilicia with Asia Minor rather than with Syria. Syria, too, has no such need of further sea coast as the large interior sections of Asia Minor.

(4) In standing thus for the recognition of the unity of Syria, the natural desires of regions like the Lebanon, which have already had a measure of independence, should not be forgotten. It will make for real unity, undoubtedly, to give a large measure of local autonomy, and especially in the case of strongly unified groups. Even the "Damascus Program" which presses so earnestly the unity of Syria, itself urges a government "on broad decentralization principles".

Lebanon has achieved a considerable degree of prosperity and autonomy within the Turkish Empire. She certainly should not find her legitimate aspirations less possible within a Syrian national State. On the contrary, it may be confidently expected that both her economic and political relations with the rest of Syria would be better if she were a constituent member of the State, rather than entirely independent of it.

As a predominantly Christian country, too, Lebanon naturally fears Moslem domination in a unified Syria. But against such domination she would have a four-fold safeguard: her own large autonomy; the presence of a strong Mandatory for the considerable period in which the constitution and practice of the new State would be forming; the oversight of the League of Nations, with its insistence upon religious liberty and the rights of minorities; and the certainty that the Arab Government would feel the necessity of such a state, if it were to commend itself to the League of Nations. Moreover, there would be less danger of reactionary Moslem attitude, if Christians were present in the state in considerable numbers, rather than largely segregated outside the state, as experience of the relations of different religious faiths in India suggests.

As a predominantly Christian country, it is also to be noted that Lebanon would be in a position to exert a stronger and more helpful influence if she were within the Syrian State, feeling its problems and needs, and sharing all its life, instead of outside it, absorbed simply in her own narrow concerns. For the sake of the larger interests, both of Lebanon and of Syria, then, the unity of Syria is to be urged. It is certain that many of the more thoughtful Lebanese themselves hold this view. A similar statement might be made for Palestine; though, as "the Holy Land" for Jews and Christians and Moslems alike, its situation is unique, and might more readily justify unique treatment, if such treatment were justified anywhere. This will be discussed more particularly in connection with the recommendation concerning Zionism.

3. We recommend, in the third place, that Syria be placed under an (e) Mandatory Power, as the natural way to secure real and efficient unity.

(1) To divide the administration of the provinces of Syria among sev-

eral mandatories, even if existing national unity were recognized; or to attempt a joint mandatory of the whole on the commission plan:—neither of these courses would be naturally suggested as the best way to secure and promote the unity of the new State, or even the general unity of the whole people. It is conceivable that circumstances might drive the Peace Conference to some such form of divided mandate; but it is not a solution to be voluntarily chosen, from the point of view of the larger interests of the people, as considerations already urged indicate.

(2) It is not to be forgotten, either, that, however they are handled politically, the people of Syria are there, forced to get on together in some fashion. They are obliged to live with one another—the Arabs of the East and the people of the Coast, the Moslems and the Christians. Will they be helped or hindered, in establishing tolerable and finally cordial relations, by a single mandatory? No doubt the quick mechanical solution of the problem of different relations is to split the people up into little independent fragments. And sometimes, undoubtedly, as in the case of the Turks and Armenians, the relations are so intolerable as to make some division imperative and inevitable. But in general, to attempt complete separation only accentuates the differences and increases the antagonism. The whole lesson of the modern social consciousness points to the necessity of understanding "the other half", as it can be understood only by close and living relations. Granting reasonable local autonomy to reduce friction among groups, a single mandatory ought to form a constant and increasingly effective help to unity of feeling throughout the state, and ought to steadily improve group relations.

The people of Syria, in our hearings, have themselves often insisted that, so far as unpleasant relations have hitherto prevailed among various groups, it has been very largely due to the direct instigation of the Turkish Government. When justice is done impartially to all; when it becomes plain that the aim of the common government is the service of all classes alike, not their exploitation, decent human relations are pretty certain to prevail, and a permanent foundation for such relations to be secured—a foundation which could not be obtained by dividing men off from one another in antagonistic groups.

The Commissioners urge, therefore, for the largest future good of all groups and regions alike, the placing of the whole of Syria under a single mandate.

4. We recommend, in the fourth place, that Emir Feisal be made the head of the new united Syrian State.

(1) This is expressly and unanimously asked for by the representative Damascus Congress in the name of the Syrian people, and there seems to be no reason to doubt that the great majority of the population of Syria sincerely desire to have Emir Feisal as ruler.

(2) A constitutional monarchy along democratic lines, seems naturally

adapted to the Arabs, with their long training under tribal conditions, and with their traditional respect for their chiefs. They seem to need, more than most people, a King as the personal symbol of the power of the State.

(3) Emir Feisal has come, too, naturally into his present place of power, and there is no one else who could well replace him. He had the great advantage of being the son of the Sherif of Mecca, and as such honored throughout the Moslem world. He was one of the prominent Arab leaders who assumed responsibility for the Arab uprising against the Turks, and so shared in the complete deliverance of the Arab-speaking portions of the Turkish Empire. He was consequently hailed by the "Damascus Congress" as having "merited their full confidence and entire reliance". He was taken up and supported by the British as the most promising candidate for the headship of the new Arab State—as Arab of the Arabs, but with a position of wide appeal through his Sherifian connection, and through his broad sympathies with the best in the Occident. His relations with the Arabs to the east of Syria are friendly, and his kingdom would not be threatened from that side. He undoubtedly does not make so strong an appeal to the Christians of the West Coast, as to the Arabs of the East; but no man can be named who would have a stronger general appeal. He is tolerant and wise, skilful in dealing with men, winning in manner, a man of sincerity, insight, and power. Whether he has the full strength needed for his difficult task it is too early to say; but certainly no other Arab leader combines so many elements of power as he, and he will have invaluable help throughout the mandatory period.

The Peace Conference may take genuine satisfaction in the fact that an Arab of such qualities is available for the headship of this new state in the Near East.

5. We recommend, in the fifth place, serious modification of the extreme Zionist program for Palestine of unlimited immigration of Jews, looking finally to making Palestine distinctly a Jewish State.

(1) The Commissioners began their study of Zionism with minds predisposed in its favor, but the actual facts in Palestine, coupled with the force of the general principles proclaimed by the Allies and accepted by the Syrians have driven them to the recommendation here made.

(2) The Commission was abundantly supplied with literature on the Zionist program by the Zionist Commission to Palestine; heard in conferences much concerning the Zionist colonies and their claims and personally saw something of what had been accomplished. They found much to approve in the aspirations and plans of the Zionists, and had warm appreciation for the devotion of many of the colonists, and for their success, by modern methods, in overcoming great natural obstacles.

(3) The Commission recognized also that definite encouragement had been given to the Zionists by the Allies in Mr. Balfour's often quoted statement, in its approval by other representatives of the Allies. If, how-

ever, the strict terms of the Balfour Statement are adhered to—favoring "the establishment in Palestine of a national home for the Jewish people," "it being clearly understood that nothing shall be done which may prejudice the civil and religious rights of existing non-Jewish communities in Palestine"—it can hardly be doubted that the extreme Zionist Program must be greatly modified. For "a national home for the Jewish people" is not equivalent to making Palestine into a Jewish State; nor can the erection of such a Jewish State be accomplished without the gravest trespass upon the "civil and religious rights of existing non-Jewish communities in Palestine". The fact came out repeatedly in the Commission's conference with Jewish representatives, that the Zionists looked forward to a practically complete dispossession of the present non-Jewish inhabitants of Palestine, by various forms of purchase.

In his address of July 4, 1918, President Wilson laid down the following principle as one of the four great "ends for which the associated peoples of the world were fighting": "The settlement of every question, whether of territory, of sovereignty, of economic arrangement, or of political relationship upon the basis of the free acceptance of that settlement by the people immediately concerned, and not upon the basis of the material interest or advantage of any other nation or people which may desire a different settlement for the sake of its own exterior influence or mastery". If that principle is to rule, and so the wishes of Palestine's population are to be decisive as to what is to be done with Palestine, then it is to be remembered that the non-Jewish population of Palestine—nearly nine-tenths of the whole—are emphatically against the entire Zionist program. The tables show that there was no one thing upon which the population of Palestine were more agreed than upon this. To subject a people so minded to unlimited Jewish immigration, and to steady financial and social pressure to surrender the land, would be a gross violation of the principle just quoted, and of the peoples' rights, though it kept within the forms of law.

It is to be noted also that the feeling against the Zionist program is not confined to Palestine, but shared very generally by the people throughout Syria, as our conferences clearly showed. More than 72 per cent—1350 in all—of all the petitions in the whole of Syria were directed against the Zionist program. Only two requests—those for a united Syria and for independence—had a larger support. This general feeling was only voiced by the "General Syrian Congress," in the seventh, eighth and tenth resolutions of their statement.

The Peace Conference should not shut its eyes to the fact that the anti-Zionist feeling in Palestine and Syria is intense and not lightly to be flouted. No British officer, consulted by the Commissioners, believed that the Zionist program could be carried out except by force of arms. The officers generally thought that a force of not less than fifty thousand soldiers would be required even to initiate the program. That of itself is evidence of a strong sense of the injustice of the Zionist program, on the part of the non-Jewish populations of Palestine and Syria. Decisions, requiring armies to carry them out, are sometimes necessary, but they are surely not gratuitously to be taken in the interests of a serious injustice. For the initial claim, often submitted by Zionist representatives, that they have a "right" to Palestine, based on an occupation of two thousand years ago, can hardly be seriously considered.

There is a further consideration that cannot justly be ignored, if the world is to look forward to Palestine becoming a definitely Jewish state, however gradually that may take place. That consideration grows out of the fact that Palestine is "the Holy Land" for Jews, Christians, and Moslems alike. Millions of Christians and Moslems all over the world are quite as much concerned as the Jews with conditions in Palestine, especially with those conditions which touch upon religious feelings and rights. The relations in these matters in Palestine are most delicate and difficult. With the best possible intentions, it may be doubted whether the Jews could possibly seem to either Christians or Moslems proper guardians of the holy places, or custodians of the Holy Land as a whole. The reason is this: the places which are most sacred to Christians—those having to do with Jesus—and which are also sacred to Moslems, are not only not sacred to Jews, but abhorrent to them. It is simply impossible, under those circumstances, for Moslems and Christians to feel satisfied to have these places in Jewish hands, or under the custody of Jews. There are still other places about which Moslems must have the same feeling. In fact, from this point of view, the Moslems, just because the sacred places of all three religions are sacred to them, have made very naturally much more satisfactory custodians of the holy places than the Jews could be. It must be believed that the precise meaning, in this respect, of the complete Jewish occupation of Palestine has not been fully sensed by those who urge the extreme Zionist program. For it would intensify, with a certainty like fate, the anti-Jewish feeling both in Palestine and in all other portions of the world which look to Palestine as "the Holy Land".

In view of all these considerations, and with a deep sense of sympathy for the Jewish cause, the Commissioners feel bound to recommend that only a greatly reduced Zionist program be attempted by the Peace Conference and even that, only very gradually initiated. This would have to mean that Jewish immigration should be definitely limited, and that the project for making Palestine distinctly a Jewish commonwealth should be given up.

There would then be no reason why Palestine could not be included in a united Syrian State, just as other portions of the country, the holy places being cared for by an International and Inter-religious Commission, somewhat as at present, under the oversight and approval of the Mandatory and of the League of Nations. The Jews, of course, would have representation upon this Commission.

[The remaining part of this document recommended that the United States be asked to undertake the single Mandate for all Syria. Ed.]

Memorandum Presented to the King–Crane Commission by the General Syrian Congress

This is one of the first Arab statements on record opposing Jewish migration to Palestine.

July 2, 1919

We the undersigned members of the General Syrian Congress, meeting in Damascus on Wednesday, July 2nd, 1919, made up of representatives from the three Zones, viz., the Southern, Eastern, and Western, provided with credentials and authorizations by the inhabitants of our various districts, Moslems, Christians, and Jews, have agreed upon the following statement of the desires of the people of the country who have elected us to present them to the American Section of the International Commission; the fifth article was passed by a very large majority; all the other articles were accepted unanimously.

1. We ask absolutely complete political independence for Syria within these boundaries: the Taurus System on the North; Rafah and a line running from Al Jauf to the south of the Syrian and the Hejazian line to Akaba on the south; the Euphrates and Khabur Rivers and a line extending east of Abu Kamal to the east of Al Jauf on the east; and the Mediterranean on the west.

2. We ask that the Government of this Syrian country should be a democratic civil constitutional Monarchy on broad decentralization principles, safeguarding the rights of minorities, and that the King be the Emir Feisal, who carried on a glorious struggle in the cause of our liberation and merited our full confidence and entire reliance.

3. Considering the fact that the Arabs inhabiting the Syrian area are not naturally less gifted than other more advanced races and that they are by no means less developed than the Bulgarians, Serbians, Greeks, and Roumanians at the beginning of their independence, we protest against Article 22 of the Covenant of the League of Nations, placing us among the nations in their middle stage of development which stand in need of a mandatory power.

4. In the event of the rejection by the Peace Conference of this just

protest for certain considerations that we may not understand, we, relying on the declarations of President Wilson that his object in waging war was to put an end to the ambition of conquest and colonization, can only regard the mandate mentioned in the Covenant of the League of Nations as equivalent to the rendering of economical and technical assistance that does not prejudice our complete independence. And desiring that our country should not fall a prey to colonization is farthest from any thought of colonization and has no political ambition in our country, we will seek the technical and economical assistance from the United States of America, provided that such assistance does not exceed 20 years.

5. In the event of America not finding herself in a position to accept our desire for assistance, we will seek this assistance from Great Britain, also provided that such assistance does not infringe the complete independence and unity of our country and that the duration of such assistance does not exceed that mentioned in the previous article.

6. We do not acknowledge any right claimed by the French Government in any part whatever of our Syrian country and refuse that she should assist us or have a hand in our country under any circumstances and in any place.

7. We oppose the pretensions of the Zionists to create a Jewish commonwealth in the southern part of Syria, known as Palestine, and oppose Zionist migration to any part of our country; for we do not acknowledge their title but consider them a grave peril to our people from the national, economical, and political points of view. Our Jewish compatriots shall enjoy our common rights and assume the common responsibilities.

8. We ask that there should be no separation of the southern part of Syria, known as Palestine, nor of the littoral western zone, which includes Lebanon, from the Syrian country. We desire that the unity of the country should be guaranteed against partition under whatever circumstances.

9. We ask complete independence for emancipated Mesopotamia and that there should be no economical barriers between the two countries.

10. The fundamental principles laid down by President Wilson in condemnation of secret treaties impel us to protest most emphatically against any treaty that stipulates the partition of our Syrian country and against any private engagement aiming at the establishment of Zionism in the southern part of Syria; therefore we ask the complete annulment of these conventions and agreements.

The noble principles enunciated by President Wilson strengthen our confidence that our desires emanating from the depths of our hearts, shall be the decisive factor in determining our future; and that President Wilson and the free American people will be our supporters for the realization of our hopes thereby proving their sincerity and noble sympathy with the aspiration of the weaker nations in general and our Arab people in particular.

We also have the fullest confidence that the Peace Conference will realize that we would not have risen against the Turks, with whom we had participated in all civil, political, and representative privileges, but for their violation of our national rights, and so will grant us our desires in full in order that our political rights may not be less after the war than they were before, since we have shed so much blood in the cause of our liberty and independence.

We request to be allowed to send a delegation to represent us at the Peace Conference to defend our rights and secure the realization of our aspirations.

The British Mandate

The San Remo Conference decided on April 24, 1920 to assign the Mandate under the League of Nations to Britain. The terms of the Mandate were also discussed with the United States which was not a member of the League. An agreed text was confirmed by the Council of the League of Nations on July 24, 1922, and it came into operation in September 1923.

"The Council of the League of Nations:

Whereas the Principal Allied Powers have agreed, for the purpose of giving effect to the provisions of Article 22 of the Covenant of the League of Nations, to entrust to a Mandatory selected by the said Powers the administration of the territory of Palestine, which formerly belonged to the Turkish Empire, within such boundaries as may be fixed by them; and

Whereas the Principal Allied Powers have also agreed that the Mandatory should be responsible for putting into effect the declaration originally made on November 2nd, 1917, by the Government of His Britannic Majesty, and adopted by the said Powers, in favour of the establishment in Palestine of a national home for the Jewish people, it being clearly understood that nothing should be done which might prejudice the civil and religious rights of existing non-Jewish communities in Palestine, or the rights and political status enjoyed by Jews in any other country; and

Whereas recognition has thereby been given to the historical connexion of the Jewish people with Palestine and to the grounds for reconstituting their national home in that country; and

Whereas the Principal Allied Powers have selected His Britannic Majesty as the Mandatory for Palestine; and

Whereas the mandate in respect of Palestine has been formulated in the following terms and submitted to the Council of the League for approval; and

Whereas His Britannic Majesty has accepted the mandate in respect of Palestine and undertaken to exercise it on behalf of the League of Nations in conformity with the following provisions; and

Whereas by the aforementioned Article 22 (paragraph 8), it is provided that the degree of authority, control or administration to be exercised by the Mandatory, not having been previously agreed upon by the Members of the League, shall be explicitly defined by the Council of the League of Nations;

Confirming the said Mandate, defines its terms as follows:

ARTICLE 1.

The Mandatory shall have full powers of legislation and of administration, save as they may be limited by the terms of this mandate.

ARTICLE 2.

The Mandatory shall be responsible for placing the country under such political, administrative and economic conditions as will secure the establishment of the Jewish national home, as laid down in the preamble, and the development of self-governing institutions, and also for safeguarding the civil and religious rights of all the inhabitants of Palestine, irrespective of race and religion.

ARTICLE 3.

The Mandatory shall, so far as circumstances permit, encourage local autonomy.

ARTICLE 4.

An appropriate Jewish agency shall be recognized as a public body for the purpose of advising and cooperating with the Administration of Palestine in such economic, social and other matters as may affect the establishment of the Jewish national home and the interests of the Jewish population in Palestine, and, subject always to the control of the Administration, to assist and take part in the development of the country.

The Zionist Organization, so long as its organization and constitution are in the opinion of the Mandatory appropriate, shall be recognized as such agency. It shall take steps in consultation with His Britannic Majesty's Government to secure the cooperation of all Jews who are willing to assist in the establishment of the Jewish national home.

ARTICLE 5.

The Mandatory shall be responsible for seeing that no Palestine territory shall be ceded or leased to, or in any way placed under the control of, the Government of any foreign Power.

ARTICLE 6.

The Administration of Palestine, while ensuring that the rights and position of other sections of the population are not prejudiced, shall facilitate Jewish immigration under suitable conditions and shall encourage, in cooperation with the Jewish agency referred to in Article 4, close settlement by Jews on the land, including State lands and waste lands not required for public purposes.

ARTICLE 7.

The Administration of Palestine shall be responsible for enacting a nationality law. There shall be included in this law provisions framed so as to facilitate the acquisition of Palestinian citizenship by Jews who take up their permanent residence in Palestine.

ARTICLE 8.

The privileges and immunities of foreigners, including the benefits of consular jurisdiction and protection as formerly enjoyed by Capitulation or usage in the Ottoman Empire, shall not be applicable in Palestine.

Unless the Powers whose nationals enjoyed the aforementioned privileges and immunities on August 1st, 1914, shall have previously renounced the right to their re-establishment, or shall have agreed to their non-application for a specified period, these privileges and immunities shall, at the expiration of the mandate, be immediately re-established in their entirety or with such modifications as may have been agreed upon between the Powers concerned.

ARTICLE 9.

The Mandatory shall be responsible for seeing that the judicial system established in Palestine shall assure to foreigners, as well as to natives, a complete guarantee of their rights.

Respect for the personal status of the various peoples and communities and for their religious interests shall be fully guaranteed. In particular, the control and administration of Waqfs shall be exercised in accordance with religious law and the dispositions of the founders.

ARTICLE 10.

Pending the making of special extradition agreements relating to Palestine, the extradition treaties in force between the Mandatory and other foreign Powers shall apply to Palestine.

ARTICLE 11.

The Administration of Palestine shall take all necessary measures to safeguard the interests of the community in connexion with the development of the country, and, subject to any international obligations accepted by the Mandatory, shall have full power to provide for public ownership or control of any of the natural resources of the country or of the public works, services and utilities established or to be established therein. It shall introduce a land system appropriate to the needs of the country having regard, among other things, to the desirability of promoting the close settlement and intensive cultivation of the land.

The Administration may arrange with the Jewish agency mentioned in Article 4 to construct or operate, upon fair and equitable terms, any public works, services and utilities, and to develop any of the natural resources of the country, in so far as these matters are not directly undertaken by the Administration. Any such arrangements shall provide that no profits distributed by such agency, directly or indirectly, shall exceed a reasonable rate of interest on the capital, and any further profits shall be utilized by it for the benefit of the country in a manner approved by the Administration.

ARTICLE 12.

The Mandatory shall be entrusted with the control of the foreign relations of Palestine, and the right to issue exequaturs to consuls appointed by foreign Powers. He shall also be entitled to afford diplomatic and consular protection to citizens of Palestine when outside its territorial limits.

ARTICLE 13.

All responsibility in connexion with the Holy Places and religious buildings or sites in Palestine, including that of preserving existing rights and of securing free access to the Holy Places, religious buildings and sites and the free exercise of worship, while ensuring the requirements of public order and decorum, is assumed by the Mandatory, who shall be responsible solely to the League of Nations in all matters connected herewith, provided that nothing in this article shall prevent the Mandatory from entering into such arrangements as he may deem reasonable with the Administration for the purpose of carrying the provisions of this article into effect; and provided also that nothing in this Mandate shall be construed as conferring upon the Mandatory authority to interfere with the fabric or the management of purely Moslem sacred shrines, the immunities of which are guaranteed.

ARTICLE 14.

A special Commission shall be appointed by the Mandatory to study, define and determine the rights and claims in connexion with the Holy Places and the rights and claims relating to the different religious communities in Palestine. The method of nomination, the composition and the functions of this Commission shall be submitted to the Council of the League for its approval, and the Commission shall not be appointed or enter upon its functions without the approval of the Council.

ARTICLE 15.

The Mandatory shall see that complete freedom of conscience and the free exercise of all forms of worship, subject only to the maintenance of public order and morals, are ensured to all. No discrimination of any kind shall be made between the inhabitants of Palestine on the ground of race, religion or language. No person shall be excluded from Palestine on the sole ground of his religious belief.

The right of each community to maintain its own schools for the education of its own members in its own language, while conforming to such educational requirements of a general nature as the Administration may impose, shall not be denied or impaired.

ARTICLE 16.

The Mandatory shall be responsible for exercising such supervision over religious or eleemosynary bodies of all faiths in Palestine as may be required for the maintenance of public order and good government. Subject to such supervision, no measures shall be taken in Palestine to obstruct or interfere with the enterprise of such bodies or to discriminate against any representative or member of them on the ground of his religion or nationality.

ARTICLE 17.

The Administration of Palestine may organize on a voluntary basis the forces necessary for the preservation of peace and order, and also for the defence of the country, subject, however, to the supervision of the Mandatory, but shall not use them for purposes other than those above specified save with the consent of the Mandatory. Except for such purposes, no military, naval or air forces shall be raised or maintained by the Administration of Palestine.

Nothing in this article shall preclude the Administration of Palestine from contributing to the cost of the maintenance of the forces of the Mandatory in Palestine.

The Mandatory shall be entitled at all times to use the roads, railways and ports of Palestine for the movement of armed forces and the carriage of fuel and supplies.

ARTICLE 18.

The Mandatory shall see that there is no discrimination in Palestine against the nationals of any State Member of the League of Nations (including companies incorporated under its laws) as compared with those of the Mandatory or of any foreign State in matters concerning taxation, commerce or navigation, the exercise of industries or professions, or in the treatment of merchant vessels or civil aircraft. Similarly, there shall be no discrimination in Palestine against goods originating in or destined for any of the said States, and there shall be freedom of transit under equitable conditions across the mandated area.

Subject as aforesaid and to the other provisions of this mandate, the Administration of Palestine may, on the advice of the Mandatory, impose such taxes and customs duties as it may consider necessary, and take such steps as it may think best to promote the development of the natural resources of the country and to safeguard the interests of the population. It may also, on the advice of the Mandatory, conclude a special customs agreement with any State the territory of which in 1914 was wholly included in Asiatic Turkey or Arabia.

ARTICLE 19.

The Mandatory shall adhere on behalf of the Administration of Palestine to any general international conventions already existing, or which may be concluded hereafter with the approval of the League of Nations, respecting the slave traffic, the traffic in arms and ammunition, or the traffic in drugs, or relating to commercial equality, freedom of transit and navigation, aerial navigation and postal, telegraphic and wireless communication or literary, artistic or industrial property.

ARTICLE 20.

The Mandatory shall co-operate on behalf of the Administration of Palestine, so far as religious, social and other conditions may permit, in the execution of any common policy adopted by the League of Nations for preventing and combating disease, including diseases of plants and animals.

ARTICLE 21.

The Mandatory shall secure the enactment within twelve months from this date, and shall ensure the execution of a Law of Antiquities based on the following rules. This law shall ensure equality of treatment in the matter of excavations and archaeological research to the nationals of all States Members of the League of Nations. . . .

ARTICLE 22.

English, Arabic and Hebrew shall be the official languages of Palestine. Any statement or inscription in Arabic on stamps or money in Palestine shall be repeated in Hebrew and any statement or inscription in Hebrew shall be repeated in Arabic.

ARTICLE 23.

The Administration of Palestine shall recognize the holy days of the respective communities in Palestine as legal days of rest for the members of such communities.

ARTICLE 24.

The Mandatory shall make to the Council of the League of Nations an annual report to the satisfaction of the Council as to the measures taken during the year to carry out the provisions of the mandate. Copies of all laws and regulations promulgated or issued during the year shall be communicated with the report.

ARTICLE 25.

In the territories lying between the Jordan and the eastern boundary of Palestine as ultimately determined, the Mandatory shall be entitled, with the consent of the Council of the League of Nations, to postpone or withhold application of such provisions of this mandate as he may consider inapplicable to the existing local conditions, and to make such provision for the administration of the territories as he may consider suitable to those conditions, provided that no action shall be taken which is inconsistent with the provisions of Articles 15, 16 and 18.

ARTICLE 26.

The Mandatory agrees that if any dispute whatever should arise between the Mandatory and another Member of the League of Nations relating to the interpretation or the application of the provisions of the mandate, such dispute, if it cannot be settled by negotiation, shall be submitted to the Permanent Court of International Justice provided for by Article 14 of the Covenant of the League of Nations.

ARTICLE 27.

The consent of the Council of the League of Nations is required for any modification of the terms of this mandate.

ARTICLE 28.

In the event of the termination of the mandate hereby conferred upon the Mandatory, the Council of the League of Nations shall make such arrangements as may be deemed necessary for safeguarding in perpetuity, under guarantee of the League, the rights secured by Articles 13 and 14, and shall use its influence for securing, under the guarantee of the League, that the Government of Palestine will fully honour the financial obligations legitimately incurred by the Administration of Palestine during the period of the mandate, including the rights of public servants to pensions or gratuities.

The present instrument shall be deposited in original in the archives of the League of Nations and certified copies shall be forwarded by the Secretary General of the League of Nations to all Members of the League.

DONE AT LONDON the twenty-fourth day of July, one thousand nine hundred and twenty-two.''

Part II

Palestine 1920–1947

Part II of the Reader deals with the unhappy history of the British Mandate, from the Balfour Declaration promising the establishment of a Jewish Home in Palestine to the British decision to return the Mandate to the United Nations, and the U.N. resolution about partition and the establishment of an Arab and a Jewish state in Palestine. During this period Arab opposition grew against Jewish colonization and immigration; there was frequent unrest (in 1920–21, 1928, 1933, 1936–39) and the various suggestions for a solution to the conflict were rejected as impractical.

The Churchill White Paper—1922

In view of growing opposition to Zionism, a new statement of policy was drafted in 1922 by the then British Colonial Secretary, which, while not explicitly opposing the idea of a Jewish state, "redeemed the Balfour promise in depreciated currency" to quote a contemporary British source.

STATEMENT OF BRITISH POLICY IN PALESTINE ISSUED BY MR. CHURCHILL IN JUNE, 1922.

The Secretary of State for the Colonies has given renewed consideration to the existing political situation in Palestine, with a very earnest desire to arrive at a settlement of the outstanding questions which have given rise to uncertainty and unrest among certain sections of the population. After consultation with the High Commissioner for Palestine the following statement has been drawn up. It summarizes the essential parts of the correspondence that has already taken place between the Secretary of State and a Delegation from the Moslem Christian Society of Palestine, which has been for some time in England, and it states the further conclusions which have since been reached.

The tension which has prevailed from time to time in Palestine is mainly due to apprehensions, which are entertained both by sections of the Arab and by sections of the Jewish population. These apprehensions, so far as the Arabs are concerned, are partly based upon exaggerated interpretations of the meaning of the Declaration favouring the establishment of a Jewish National Home in Palestine, made on behalf of His Majesty's Government on 2nd November, 1917. Unauthorized statements have been made to the effect that the purpose in view is to create a wholly Jewish Palestine. Phrases have been used such as that Palestine is to become "as Jewish as England is English." His Majesty's Government regard any such expectation as impracticable and have no such aim in view.

Nor have they at any time contemplated, as appears to be feared by the Arab Delegation, the disappearance or the subordination of the Arabic population, language, or culture in Palestine. They would draw attention to the fact that the terms of the Declaration referred to do not contemplate that Palestine as a whole should be converted into a Jewish National Home, but that such a Home should be founded *in Palestine.* In this connection it has been observed with satisfaction that at the meeting of the Zionist Congress, the supreme governing body of the Zionist Organization, held at Carlsbad in September, 1921, a resolution was passed expressing as the official statement of Zionist aims "the determination of the Jewish people to live with the Arab people on terms of unity and mutual respect, and together with them to make the common home into a flourishing community, the upbuilding of which may assure to each of its peoples an undisturbed national development."

It is also necessary to point out that the Zionist Commission in Palestine, now termed the Palestine Zionist Executive, has not desired to possess, and does not possess, any share in the general administration of the country. Nor does the special position assigned to the Zionist Organization in Article IV of the Draft Mandate for Palestine imply any such functions. That special position relates to the measures to be taken in Palestine affecting the Jewish population, and contemplates that the Organization may assist in the general development of the country, but does not entitle it to share in any degree in its Government.

Further, it is contemplated that the status of all citizens of Palestine in the eyes of the law shall be Palestinian, and it has never been intended that they, or any section of them, should possess any other juridical status.

So far as the Jewish population of Palestine are concerned it appears that some among them are apprehensive that His Majesty's Government may depart from the policy embodied in the Declaration of 1917. It is necessary, therefore, once more to affirm that these fears are unfounded, and that that Declaration, re-affirmed by the Conference of the Principal Allied Powers at San Remo and again in the Treaty of Sèvres, is not susceptible of change.

During the last two or three generations the Jews have recreated in Palestine a community, now numbering 80,000, of whom about one-fourth are farmers or workers upon the land. This community has its own political organs; an elected assembly for the direction of its domestic concerns; elected councils in the towns; and an organization for the control of its schools. It has its elected Chief Rabbinate and Rabbinical Council for the direction of its religious affairs. Its business is conducted in Hebrew as a vernacular language, and a Hebrew Press serves its needs. It has its distinctive intellectual life and displays considerable economic activity. This community, then, with its town and country population, its political, religious, and social organizations, its own language, its own customs, its own life, has in fact "national" characteristics. When it is asked what is meant by the development of the Jewish National Home in Palestine, it may be answered that it is not the imposition of a Jewish nationality upon the inhabitants of Palestine as a whole, but the further development of the existing Jewish community, with the assistance of Jews in other parts of the world, in order that it may become a centre in which the Jewish people as a whole may take, on grounds of religion and race, an interest and a pride. But in order that this community should have the best prospect of free development and provide a full opportunity for the Jewish people to display its capacities, it is essential that it should know that it is in Palestine as of right and not on sufferance. That is the reason why it is necessary that the existence of a Jewish National Home in Palestine should be internationally guaranteed, and that it should be formally recognized to rest upon ancient historic connection.

This, then, is the interpretation which His Majesty's Government place upon the Declaration of 1917, and, so understood, the Secretary of State is of opinion that it does not contain or imply anything which need cause either alarm to the Arab population of Palestine or disappointment to the Jews.

For the fulfilment of this policy it is necessary that the Jewish community in Palestine should be able to increase its numbers by immigration. This immigration cannot be so great in volume as to exceed whatever may be the economic capacity of the country at the time to absorb new arrivals. It is essential to ensure that the immigrants should not be a burden upon the people of Palestine as a whole, and that they should not deprive any section of the present population of their employment. Hitherto the immigration has fulfilled these conditions. The number of immigrants since the British occupation has been about 25,000.

It is necessary also to ensure that persons who are politically undesirable are excluded from Palestine, and every precaution has been and will be taken by the Administration to that end.

It is intended that a special committee should be established in Palestine, consisting entirely of members of the new Legislative Council elected by the people, to confer with the administration upon matters relating to the regulation of immigration. Should any difference of opinion arise between this committee and the Administration the matter will be referred to His Majesty's Government, who will give it special consideration. In addition, under Article 81 of the draft Palestine Order in Council, any religious community or considerable section of the population of Palestine will have a general right to appeal, through the High Commissioner and the Secretary of State, to the League of Nations on any matter on which they may consider that the terms of the Mandate are not being fulfilled by the Government of Palestine.

With reference to the Constitution which it is now intended to establish in Palestine, the draft of which has already been published, it is desirable to make certain points clear. In the first place, it is not the case, as has been represented by the Arab Delegation, that during the war His Majesty's Government gave an undertaking that an independent national government should be at once established in Palestine. This representation mainly rests upon a letter dated the 24th October, 1915, from Sir Henry McMahon, then His Majesty's High Commissioner in Egypt, to the Sherif of Mecca, now King Hussein of the Kingdom of the Hejaz. That letter is quoted as conveying the promise to the Sherif of Mecca to recognise and support the independence of the Arabs within the territories proposed by him. But this promise was given subject to a reservation made in the same letter, which excluded from its scope, among other territories, the portions of Syria lying to the west of the district of Damascus. This reservation has always been regarded by His Majesty's Government as covering the vilayet of Beirut and the independent Sanjak of Jerusalem. The whole of Palestine west of the Jordan was thus excluded from Sir H. McMahon's pledge.

Nevertheless, it is the intention of His Majesty's Government to foster the establishment of a full measure of self-government in Palestine. But they are of opinion that, in the special circumstances of that country, this should be accomplished by gradual stages and not suddenly. The first step was taken when, on the institution of a Civil Administration, the nominated Advisory Council, which now exists, was established. It was stated at the time by the High Commissioner that this was the first step in the development of self-governing institutions, and it is now proposed to take a second step by the establishment of a Legislative Council containing a large proportion of members elected on a wide franchise. It was proposed in the published draft that three of the members of this Council should be non-official persons nominated by the High Commissioner, but representations having been made in opposition to this provision, based on cogent considerations, the Secretary of State is prepared to omit it. The Legislative Council would then consist of the High Commissioner as President and twelve elected and ten official members. The Secretary of State is of opinion that before a further measure of self-government is extended to Palestine and the Assembly placed in control over the Executive, it would be wise to allow some time to elapse. During this period the institutions of the country will have become well established; its financial credit will be based on firm foundations, and the Palestinian officials will have been enabled to gain experience of sound methods of government. After a few years the situation will be again reviewed, and if the experience of the working of the constitution now to be established so warranted, a larger share of authority would then be extended to the elected representatives of the people.

The Secretary of State would point out that already the present Administration has transferred to a Supreme Council elected by the Moslem community of Palestine the entire control of Moslem religious endowments (Wakfs), and of the Moslem religious Courts. To this Council the Administration has also voluntarily restored considerable revenues derived from ancient endowments which had been sequestrated by the Turkish Government. The Education Department is also advised by a committee representative of all sections of the population, and the Department of Commerce and Industry has the benefit of the co-operation of the Chambers of Commerce which have been established in the principal centres. It is the intention of the Administration to associate in an increased degree similar representative committees with the various Departments of the Government.

The Secretary of State believes that a policy upon these lines, coupled with the maintenance of the fullest religious liberty in Palestine and with scrupulous regard for the rights of each community with reference to its Holy Places, cannot but commend itself to the various sections of the population, and that upon this basis may be built up that spirit of cooperation upon which the future progress and prosperity of the Holy Land must largely depend.

The MacDonald Letter

Following the Arab riots of 1929, the British Labor government published a new statement of policy (the Passfield White Paper), which urged the restriction of immigration and of land sales to Jews. It was bitterly denounced by Zionist leaders as a violation of the letter and the spirit of the Mandate. The MacDonald letter, while not openly repudiating the Passfield report, gave assurances that the terms of the Mandate would be fulfilled. It was rejected by the Arabs as the ''Black Letter''. James Ramsay MacDonald (1866–1937) was Prime Minister in 1931; Lord Passfield (Sidney Webb, 1859–1947) was Colonial Secretary in the Labor cabinet.

Premier MacDonald's Letter
Addressed to Dr. Chaim Weizmann
nFebruary 13, 1931

DEAR DR. WEIZMANN:

In order to remove certain misconceptions and misunderstandings which have arisen as to the policy of his Majesty's Government with regard to Palestine, as set forth in the White Paper of October, 1930, and which were the subject of a debate in the House of Commons on Nov. 17, and also to meet certain criticisms put forward by the Jewish Agency, I have pleasure in forwarding you the following statement of our position, which will fall to be read as the authoritative interpretation of the White Paper on the matters with which this letter deals.

It has been said that the policy of his Majesty's Government involves a serious departure from the obligations of the mandate as hitherto understood; that it misconceives the mandatory obligations, and that it foreshadows a policy which is inconsistent with the obligations of the mandatory to the Jewish people.

His Majesty's Government did not regard it as necessary to quote in extenso the declarations of policy which have been previously made, but attention is drawn to the fact that, not only does the White Paper of 1930 refer to and endorse the White Paper of 1922, which has been accepted by the Jewish Agency, but it recognizes that the undertaking of the mandate is an undertaking to the Jewish people and not only to the Jewish population of Palestine. The White Paper places in the foreground of its statement my speech in the House of Commons on the 3d of April, 1930, in which I announced, in words that could not have been made more plain, that it was the intention of his Majesty's Government to continue to administer Palestine in accordance with the terms of the mandate as approved by the Council of the League of Nations. That position has been reaffirmed and again made plain by my speech in the House of Commons on the 17th of November. In my speech on the 3d of April I used the following language:

His Majesty's Government will continue to administer Palestine in accordance with the terms of the mandate as approved by the Council of the League of Nations. This is an international obligation from which there can be no question of receding.

Under the terms of the mandate his Majesty's Government are responsible for promoting the establishment of a national home for the Jewish people, it being clearly understood that nothing shall be done which might prejudice the civil and religious rights of existing non-Jewish communities in Palestine or the rights and political status enjoyed by Jews in any other country.

A double undertaking is involved, to the Jewish people on the one hand and to the non-Jewish population of Palestine on the other; and it is the firm resolve of his Majesty's Government to give effect, in equal measure, to both parts of the declaration and to do equal justice to all sections of the population of Palestine. That is a duty from which they will not shrink and to discharge of which they will apply all the resources at their command.

That declaration is in conformity not only with the articles but also with the preamble of the mandate, which is hereby explicitly reaffirmed.

In carrying out the policy of the mandate the mandatory cannot ignore the existence of the differing interests and viewpoints. These, indeed, are not in themselves irreconcilable, but they can only be reconciled if there is a proper realization that the full solution of the problem depends upon an understanding between the Jews and the Arabs. Until that is reached, considerations of balance must inevitably enter into the definition of policy.

A good deal of criticism has been directed to the White Paper upon the assertion that it contains injurious allegations against the Jewish people and Jewish labor organizations. Any such intention on the part of his Majesty's Government is expressly disavowed. It is recognized that the Jewish Agency have all along given willing cooperation in carrying out the policy of the mandate and that the constructive work done by the Jewish people in Palestine has had beneficial effects on the development and well-being of the country as a whole. His Majesty's Government also recognizes the value of the services of labor and trades union organizations in Palestine, to which they desire to give every encouragement.

A question has arisen as to the meaning to be attached to the words 'safeguarding the civil and religious rights of all inhabitants of Palestine irrespective of race and religion' occurring in Article II, and the words 'insuring that the rights and position of other sections of the population are not prejudiced' occurring in Article VI of the mandate. The words 'safeguarding the civil and religious rights' occurring in Article II cannot be read as meaning that the civil and religious rights of individual citizens are unalterable. In the case of Suleiman Murra, to which reference has been made, the Privy Council, in construing these words of Article II said 'It does not mean . . . that all the civil rights of every inhabitant of Palestine which existed at the date of the mandate are to remain unaltered throughout its duration; for if that were to be a condition of the mandatory jurisdiction, no effective legislation would be possible.' The words, accordingly, must be read in another sense, and the key to the true purpose and meaning of the sentence is to be found in the concluding words of the article, 'irrespective of race and religion.' These words indicate that in respect of civil and religious rights the mandatory is not to discriminate between persons on the ground of religion or race, and this protective provision applies equally to Jews, Arabs and all sections of the population.

The words 'rights and position of other sections of the population,' occurring in Article VI, plainly refer to the non-Jewish community. These rights and position are not TO BE prejudiced; that is, are not to be impaired or made worse. The effect of the policy of immigration and settlement on the economic position of the non-Jewish community cannot be excluded from consideration. But the words are not to be read as implying that existing economic conditions in Palestine should be crystallized. On the contrary, the obligation to facilitate Jewish immigration and to encourage close settlement by Jews on the land remains a positive obligation of the mandate and it can be fulfilled without prejudice to the rights and position of other sections of the population of Palestine.

We may proceed to the contention that the mandate has been interpreted in a manner highly prejudicial to Jewish interests in the vital matters of land settlement and immigration. It has been said that the policy of the White Paper would place an embargo on immigration and would suspend, if not indeed terminate, the close settlement of the Jews on the land, which is a primary purpose of the mandate. In support of this contention particular stress has been laid upon the passage referring to State lands in the White Paper, which says that 'it would not be possible to make available for Jewish settlement in view of their actual occupation by Arab cultivators and of the importance of making available suitable land on which to place the Arab cultivators who are now landless.'

The language of this passage needs to be read in the light of the policy as a whole. It is desirable to make it clear that the landless Arabs, to whom it was intended to refer in the passage quoted, were such Arabs as can be shown to have been displaced from the lands which they occupied in consequence of the land passing into Jewish hands, and who have not obtained other holdings on which they can establish themselves, or other equally satisfactory occupation. The number of such displaced Arabs must be a matter for careful inquiry. It is to landless Arabs within this category that his Majesty's Government feels itself under an obligation to facilitate their settlement upon the land. The recognition of this obligation in no way detracts from the larger purposes of development which his Majesty's Government regards as the most effectual means of furthering the establishment of a national home for the Jews. . . .

Further, the statement of policy of his Majesty's Government did not imply a prohibition of acquisition of additional land by Jews. It contains no such prohibition, nor is any such intended. What it does contemplate is such temporary control of land disposition and transfers as may be necessary not to impair the harmony and effectiveness of the scheme of land settlement to be undertaken. His Majesty's Government feels bound to point out that it alone of the governments which have been responsible for the administration of Palestine since the acceptance of the mandate has declared its definite intention to initiate an active policy of development, which it is believed will result in a substantial and lasting benefit to both Jews and Arabs.

Cognate to this question is the control of immigration. It must first of all be pointed out that such control is not in any sense a departure from previous policy. From 1920 onward, when the original immigration ordinance came into force, regulations for the control of immigration have been issued from time to time, directed to prevent illicit entry and to define and facilitate authorized entry. This right of regulation has at no time been challenged.

But the intention of his Majesty's Government appears to have been represented as being that 'no further immigration of Jews is to be permitted so long as it might prevent any Arab from obtaining employment.' His Majesty's Government never proposed to pursue such a policy. They were concerned to state that, in the regulation of Jewish immigration, the following principles should apply: viz., that 'it is essential to insure that the immigrants should not be a burden on the people of Palestine as a whole, and that they should not deprive any section of the present population of their employment.' (White Paper 1922.)

In one aspect, his Majesty's Government have to be mindful of their obligations to facilitate Jewish immigration under suitable conditions, and to encourage close settlement by Jews on the land; in the other aspect, they have to be equally mindful of their duty to insure that no prejudice results to the rights and position of the non-Jewish community. It is because of this apparent conflict of obligations that his Majesty's Government have felt bound to emphasize the necessity of the proper application of the absorptive principle.

That principle is vital to any scheme of development, the primary purpose of which must be the settlement both of Jews and of displaced Arabs on the land. It is for that reason that his Majesty's Government have insisted, and are compelled to insist, that government immigration regulations must be properly applied. The considerations relevant to the limits of absorptive capacity are purely economic considerations.

His Majesty's Government did not prescribe and do not contemplate any stoppage or prohibition of Jewish immigration in any of its categories. The practice of sanctioning a labor schedule of wage-earning immigrants will continue. In each case consideration will be given to anticipated labor requirements for works which, being dependent upon Jewish or mainly Jewish capital, would not be or would not have been undertaken unless Jewish labor was available. With regard to public and municipal works failing to be financed out of public funds, the claim of Jewish labor to a due share of the employment available, taking into account Jewish contributions to public revenue, shall be taken into consideration. As regards other kinds of employment, it will be necessary in each case to take into account the factors bearing upon the demand for labor, including the factor of unemployment among both the Jews and the Arabs.

Immigrants with prospects of employment other than employment of a purely ephemeral character will not be excluded on the sole ground that the employment cannot be guaranteed to be of unlimited duration.

In determining the extent to which immigration at any time may be permitted it is necessary also to have regard to the declared policy of the Jewish Agency to the effect that 'in all the works or undertakings carried out or furthered by the Agency it shall be deemed to be a matter of principle that Jewish labor shall be employed.' His Majesty's Government do not in any way challenge the right of the Agency to formulate or approve and endorse this policy. The principle of preferential, and indeed exclusive, employment of Jewish labor by Jewish organizations is a principle which the Jewish Agency are entitled to affirm. But it must be pointed out that if in consequence of this policy Arab labor is displaced or existing unemployment becomes aggravated, that is a factor in the situation to which the mandatory is bound to have regard.

His Majesty's Government desire to say, finally, as they have repeatedly and unequivocally affirmed, that the obligations imposed upon the mandatory by its acceptance of the mandate are solemn international obligations from which there is not now, nor has there been at any time, any intention to depart. To the tasks imposed by the mandate, his Majesty's Government have set their hand, and they will not withdraw it. But if their efforts are to be successful, there is need for coöperation, confidence, readiness on all sides to appreciate the difficulties and complexities of the problem, and, above all, there must be a full and unqualified recognition that no solution can be satisfactory or permanent which is not based upon justice, both to the Jewish people and to the non-Jewish communities of Palestine.

RAMSAY MACDONALD

From the Report of the Palestine Royal Commission (Peel Commission)—1937

A Royal Commission headed by Lord Peel was appointed in 1936, following the outbreak of fresh Arab riots earlier that year. Its report, published in July 1937, stated that the desire of the Arabs for national independence and their hatred and fear of the establishment of the Jewish National Home were the underlying causes of the disturbances. It found that Arab and Jewish interests could not be reconciled under the Mandate and it suggested, therefore, the partition of Palestine. The Jewish state was to comprise Galilee, the Yezreel Valley and the Coastal Plain to a point midway between Gaza and Jaffe, altogether about twenty per cent of the area of the country. The rest, Arab Palestine, was to be united with Transjordan. Jerusalem, Bethlehem, a corridor linking them to the Sea, and, possibly, Nazareth and the Sea of Genezareth would remain a British mandatory zone. The Arab leadership rejected the plan, the Zionist Congress accepted it with qualifications—against the wish of a substantial minority. The British government which had initially favored partition eventually rejected it in November 1938. (See page 53.)

. . . To foster Jewish immigration in the hope that it might ultimately lead to the creation of a Jewish majority and the establishment of a Jewish State with the consent or at least the acquiescence of the Arabs was one thing. It was quite another to contemplate, however remotely, the forcible conversion of Palestine into a Jewish State against the will of the Arabs. For that would clearly violate the spirit and intention of the Mandate System. It would mean that national self-determination had been withheld when the Arabs were a majority in Palestine and only conceded when the Jews were a majority. It would mean that the Arabs had been denied the opportunity of standing by themselves: that they had, in fact, after an interval of conflict, been bartered about from Turkish sovereignty to Jewish sovereignty. It is true that in the light of history Jewish rule over Palestine could not be regarded as foreign rule in the same sense as Turkish; but the international recognition of the right of the Jews to return to their old homeland did not involve the recognition of the right of the Jews to govern the Arabs in it against their will. The case stated by Lord Milner against an Arab control of Palestine applies equally to a Jewish control. . . .

An irrepressible conflict has arisen between two national communities within the narrow bounds of one small country. About 1,000,000 Arabs are in strife, open or latent, with some 400,000 Jews. There is no common ground between them. The Arab community is predominantly Asiatic in character, the Jewish community predominantly European. They differ in religion and in language. Their cultural and social life, their ways of thought and conduct, are as incompatible as their national aspirations. These last are the greatest bar to peace. Arabs and Jews might possibly learn to live and work together in Palestine if they would make a genuine effort to reconcile and combine their national ideals and so build up in time a joint or dual nationality. But this they cannot do. The War and its sequel have inspired all Arabs with the hope of reviving in a free and united Arab world the traditions of the Arab golden age. The Jews similarly are inspired by their historic past. They mean to show what the Jewish nation can achieve when restored to the land of its birth. National assimilation between Arabs and Jews is thus ruled out. In the Arab picture the Jews could only occupy the place they occupied in Arab Egypt or Arab Spain. The Arabs would be as much outside the Jewish picture as the Canaanites in the old land of Israel. The National Home, as we have said before, cannot be half-national. In these circumstances to maintain that Palestinian citizenship has any moral meaning is a mischievous pretense. Neither Arab nor Jew has any sense of service to a single State. . . .

V. Jabotinsky: A Jewish State Now: Evidence Submitted to the Palestine Royal Commission*

Vladimir Ze'ev Jabotinsky (1880–1940) was the leader of the Zionist–Revisionists advocating the establishment of a Jewish state in its historic borders.

The conception of Zionism which I have the honour to represent here is based on what I should call the humanitarian aspect. By that I do not mean to say that we do not respect the other, the purely spiritual aspects of Jewish nationalism, such as the desire for self-expression, the rebuilding of a Hebrew culture, or creating some "model community of which the Jewish people could be proud." All that, of course, is most important; but as compared with our actual needs and our real position in the world to-day, all that has rather the character of luxury. The Commission have already heard a description of the situation of World Jewry especially in Eastern Europe, and I am not going to repeat any details, but you will allow me to quote a recent reference in *The New York Times* describing the position of Jewry in Eastern Europe as "a disaster of historic magnitude." I only wish to add that it would be very naïve, and although many Jews make this mistake I disapprove of it—it would be very naïve to ascribe that state of disaster, permanent disaster, only to the guilt of men, whether it be crowds and multitudes, or whether it be Governments. The thing goes much deeper than that. I am very much afraid that what I am going to say will not be popular with many among my co-religionists, and I regret that, but the truth is the truth. We are facing an elemental calamity, a kind of social earthquake. Three generations of Jewish thinkers and Zionists among whom there were many great minds—I am not going to fatigue you by quoting them—three generations have given much thought to analysing the Jewish position and have come to the conclusion that the cause of our suffering is the very fact of the "Diaspora," the bedrock fact that we are everywhere a minority. It is not the anti-Semitism of men; it is, above all, the anti-Semitism of things, the inherent xenophobia of the body social or the body economic under which we suffer. Of course, there are ups and downs; but there are moments, there are whole periods in history when this "xenophobia of Life itself" takes dimensions which no people can stand, and that is what we are facing now. I do not mean to suggest that I would recognise that all the Gov-

---

* V. Jabotinsky, House of Lords, London: February 11, 1937.

ernments concerned have done all they ought to have done; I would be the last man to concede that. I think many Governments, East and West, ought to do much more to protect the Jews than they do; but the best of Governments could perhaps only soften the calamity to quite an insignificant extent, but the core of the calamity is an earthquake which stands and remains. I want to mention here that, since one of those Governments (the Polish Government) has recently tried what amounts to bringing to the notice of the League of Nations and the whole of humanity that it is humanity's duty to provide the Jews with an area where they could build up their own body social undisturbed by anyone, I think the sincerity of the Polish Government, and of any other Governments who, I hope, will follow, should not be suspected, but on the contrary it should be recognised and acknowledged with due gratitude.—Perhaps the greatest gap in all I am going to say and in all the Commission have heard up to now is the impossibility of really going to the root of the problem, really bringing before you a picture of what that Jewish hell looks like, and I feel I cannot do it. I do hope that the day may come when some Jewish representative may be allowed to appear at the Bar of one of these two Houses just to tell them what it really is, and to ask the English people: "What are you going to advise us? Where is the way out? Or, standing up and facing God, say that there is no way out and that we Jews have just to go under." But unfortunately I cannot do it, so I will simply assume that the Royal Commission are sufficiently informed of all this situation, and then I want you to realise this: the phenomenon called Zionism may include all kinds of dreams—a "model community", Hebrew culture, perhaps even a second edition of the Bible—but all this longing for wonderful toys of velvet and silver is nothing in comparison with that tangible momentum of irresistible distress and need by which we are propelled and borne. We are not free agents. We cannot "concede" anything. Whenever I hear the Zionist, most often my own Party, accused of asking for too much— Gentlemen, I really cannot understand it. Yes, we do want a State; every nation on earth, every normal nation, beginning with the smallest and the humblest who do not claim any merit, any role in humanity's development, they all have States of their own. That is the normal condition for a people. Yet, when we, the most abnormal of peoples and therefore the most unfortunate, ask only for the same condition as the Albanians enjoy, to say nothing of the French and the English, then it is called too much. I should understand it if the answer were, "It is impossible," but when the answer is, "It is too much" I cannot understand it. I would remind you (excuse me for quoting an example known to every one of you) of the commotion which was produced in that famous institution when Oliver Twist came and asked for "more." He said "more" because he did not know how to express it; what Oliver Twist really meant was this: "Will you just give me that normal portion which is necessary for a boy of my age to be able to live." I assure you that you face here to-day, in the Jewish people with its demands, an Oliver Twist who has, unfortunately, no concessions to make. What can be the concessions? We have got to save millions, many *millions*. I do not know whether it is a question of re-housing one-third of the Jewish race, half of the Jewish race, or a quarter of the Jewish race; I do not know; but it is a question of millions. Certainly the way out is to evacuate those portions of the Diaspora which have become no good, which hold no promise of any possibility of a livelihood, and to concentrate all those refugees in some place which should *not* be Diaspora, not a repetition of the position where the Jews are an unabsorbed minority within a foreign social, or economic, or political organism. Naturally, if that process of evacuation is allowed to develop, as it ought to be allowed to develop, there will very soon be reached a moment when the Jews will become a majority in Palestine. I am going to make a "terrible" confession. Our demand for a Jewish majority is not our maximum—it is our minimum: it is just an inevitable stage if only we are allowed to go on salvaging our people. The point when the Jews will reach a majority in that country will not be the point of saturation yet—because with 1,000,000 more Jews in Palestine to-day you could already have a Jewish majority, but there are certainly 3,000,000 or 4,000,000 in the East who are virtually knocking at the door asking for admission, i.e., for salvation.

I have the profoundest feeling for the Arab case, in so far as that Arab case is not exaggerated. This Commission have already been able to make up their minds as to whether there is any individual hardship to the Arabs of Palestine as men, deriving from the Jewish colonisation. We maintain unanimously that the economic position of the Palestinian Arabs, under the Jewish colonisation and owing to the Jewish colonisation, has become the object of envy in all the surrounding Arab countries, so that the Arabs from those countries show a clear tendency to immigrate into Palestine. I have also shown to you already that, in our submission, there is no question of ousting the Arabs. On the contrary, the idea is that Palestine on both sides of the Jordan should hold the Arabs, their progeny, *and* many millions of Jews. What I do not deny is that in that process the Arabs of Palestine will necessarily become a minority in the country of Palestine. What I do deny is that *that* is a hardship. It is not a hardship on any race, any nation, possessing so many National States now and so many more National States in the future. One fraction, one branch of that race, and not a big one, will have to live in someone else's State: well, that is the case with all the mightiest nations of the world. I could hardly mention one of the big nations, having their States, mighty and powerful, who had not one branch living in someone else's State. That is only normal and there is no "hardship" attached to that. So when we hear the Arab claim confronted with the Jewish claim; I fully understand that any minority would prefer to be a majority, it is quite understandable that the Arabs of

Palestine would also prefer Palestine to be the Arab State No. 4, No. 5, or No. 6—that I quite understand; but when the Arab claim is confronted with our Jewish demand to be saved, it is like the claims of appetite versus the claims of starvation. No tribunal has ever had the luck of trying a case where all the justice was on the side of one Party and the other Party had no case whatsoever. Usually in human affairs any tribunal, including this tribunal, in trying two cases, has to concede that both sides have a case on their side and, in order to do justice, they must take into consideration what should constitute the basic justification of all human demands, individual or mass demands—the decisive terrible balance of Need. I think it is clear.

Against Partition: British Statement of Policy—November, 1938

. . . 3. His Majesty's Government have now received the report of the Palestine Partition Commission who have carried out their investigations with great thoroughness and efficiency, and have collected material which will be very valuable in the further consideration of policy. Their report is now published, together with a summary of their conclusions. It will be noted that the four members of the Commission advise unanimously against the adoption of the scheme of partition outlined by the Royal Commission. In addition to the Royal Commission's scheme, two other schemes described as plans B and C are examined in the report. One member prefers plan B. Two other members, including the Chairman, consider that plan C is the best scheme of partition which, under the terms of reference, can be devised. A fourth member, while agreeing that plan C is the best that can be devised under the terms of reference, regards both plans as impracticable. The report points out that under either plan, while the budget of the Jewish State is likely to show a substantial surplus, the budgets of the Arab State (including Trans-Jordan) and of the Mandated Territories are likely to show substantial deficits. The Commission reject as impracticable the Royal Commission's recommendation for a direct subvention from the Jewish State to the Arab State. They think that, on economic grounds, a customs union between the States and the Mandated Territories is essential and they examine the possibility of finding the solution for the financial and economic problems of partition by means of a scheme based upon such a union. They consider that any such scheme would be inconsistent with the grant of fiscal independence to the Arab and Jewish States. Their conclusion is that, on a strict interpretation of their terms of reference, they have no alternative but to report that they are unable to recommend boundaries for the proposed areas which will afford a reasonable prospect of the eventual establishment of self-supporting Arab and Jewish States.

4. His Majesty's Government, after careful study of the Partition Commission's report, have reached the conclusion that this further examination has shown that the political, administrative and financial difficulties involved in the proposal to create independent Arab and Jewish States inside Palestine are so great that this solution of the problem is impracticable.

5. His Majesty's Government will therefore continue their responsibility for the government of the whole of Palestine. They are now faced with the problem of finding alternative means of meeting the needs of the difficult situation described by the Royal Commission which will be consistent with their obligations to the Arabs and the Jews. His Majesty's Government believe that it is possible to find these alternative means. They have already given much thought to the problem in the light of the reports of the Royal Commission and of the Partition Commission. It is clear that the surest foundation for peace and progress in Palestine would be an understanding between the Arabs and the Jews, and His Majesty's Government are prepared in the first instance to make a determined effort to promote such an understanding. With this end in view, they propose immediately to invite representatives of the Palestinian Arabs and of neighbouring States on the one hand and of the Jewish Agency on the other, to confer with them as soon as possible in London regarding future policy, including the question of immigration into Palestine. As regards the representation of the Palestinian Arabs, His Majesty's Government must reserve the right to refuse to receive those leaders whom they regard as responsible for the campaign of assassination and violence.

6. His Majesty's Government hope that these discussions in London may help to promote agreement as to future policy regarding Palestine. They attach great importance, however, to a decision being reached at an early date. Therefore, if the London discussions should not produce agreement within a reasonable period of time, they will take their own decision in the light of their examination of the problem and of the discussions in London, and announce the policy which they propose to pursue.

7. In considering and settling their policy His Majesty's Government will keep constantly in mind the international character of the Mandate with which they have been entrusted and their obligations in that respect.

The White Paper of 1939

After the failure of the partition scheme and a subsequent attempt to work out an agreed solution at a Conference in London (February–March, 1939), the British government announced its new policy in a White Paper published on May 17, 1939. The Arab demands were largely met: Jewish immigration was to continue at a maximum rate of 15,000 for another five years. After that it was to cease altogether unless the Arabs would accept it. Purchase of land by Jews would be prohibited in some areas, restricted in others. Jewish reaction was bitterly hostile (see page 64), but the Arab leaders also rejected the White Paper: according to their demands, Palestine was to become an Arab state immediately, no more Jewish immigrants were to enter the country, the status of every Jew who had immigrated since 1918 was to be reviewed.

May 17, 1939

In the Statement on Palestine, issued on 9th November, 1938, His Majesty's Government announced their intention to invite representatives of the Arabs of Palestine, of certain neighbouring countries and of the Jewish Agency to confer with them in London regarding future policy. It was their sincere hope that, as a result of full, free and frank discussion, some understanding might be reached. Conferences recently took place with Arab and Jewish delegations, lasting for a period of several weeks, and served the purpose of a complete exchange of views between British Ministers and the Arab and Jewish representatives. In the light of the discussions as well as of the situation in Palestine and of the Reports of the Royal Commission and the Partition Commission, certain proposals were formulated by His Majesty's Government and were laid before the Arab and Jewish delegations as the basis of an agreed settlement. Neither the Arab nor the Jewish delegation felt able to accept these proposals, and the conferences therefore did not result in an agreement. Accordingly His Majesty's Government are free to formulate their own policy, and after careful consideration they have decided to adhere generally to the proposals which were finally submitted to, and discussed with, the Arab and Jewish delegations.

2. The Mandate for Palestine, the terms of which were confirmed by the Council of the League of Nations in 1922, has governed the policy of successive British Governments for nearly 20 years. It embodies the Balfour Declaration and imposes on the Mandatory four main obligations. These obligations are set out in Article 2, 6 and 13 of the Mandate. There is no dispute regarding the interpretation of one of these obligations, that touching the protection of and access to the Holy Places and religious building or sites. The other three main obligations are generally as follows:—

(i) To place the country under such political, administrative and economic conditions as will secure the establishment in Palestine of a national home for the Jewish people, to facilitate Jewish immigration under suitable conditions, and to encourage, in co-operation with the Jewish Agency, close settlement by Jews on the land.

(ii) To safeguard the civil and religious rights of all the inhabitants of

Palestine irrespective of race and religion, and, whilst facilitating Jewish immigration and settlement, to ensure that the rights and position of other sections of the population are not prejudiced.

(iii) To place the country under such political, administrative and economic conditions as will secure the development of self-governing institutions.

3. The Royal Commission and previous Commissions of Enquiry have drawn attention to the ambiguity of certain expressions in the Mandate, such as the expression "a national home for the Jewish people", and they have found in this ambiguity and the resulting uncertainty as to the objectives of policy a fundamental cause of unrest and hostility between Arabs and Jews. His Majesty's Government are convinced that in the interests of the peace and well-being of the whole people of Palestine a clear definition of policy and objectives is essential. The proposal of partition recommended by the Royal Commission would have afforded such clarity, but the establishment of self-supporting independent Arab and Jewish States within Palestine has been found to be impracticable. It has therefore been necessary for His Majesty's Government to devise an alternative policy which will, consistently with their obligations to Arabs and Jews, meet the needs of the situation in Palestine. Their views and proposals are set forth below under the three heads, (I) The Constitution, (II) Immigration, and (III) Land.

I.—THE CONSTITUTION

4. It has been urged that the expression "a national home for the Jewish people" offered a prospect that Palestine might in due course become a Jewish State or Commonwealth. His Majesty's Government do not wish to contest the view, which was expressed by the Royal Commission, that the Zionist leaders at the time of the issue of the Balfour Declaration recognised that an ultimate Jewish State was not precluded by the terms of the Declaration. But, with the Royal Commission, His Majesty's Government believe that the framers of the Mandate in which the Balfour Declaration was embodied could not have intended that Palestine should be converted into a Jewish State against the will of the Arab population of the country. That Palestine was not to be converted into a Jewish State might be held to be implied in the passage from the Command Paper of 1922 which reads as follows:—

"Unauthorized statements have been made to the effect that the purpose in view is to create a wholly Jewish Palestine. Phrases have been used such as that 'Palestine is to become as Jewish as England is English.' His Majesty's Government regard any such expectation as impracticable and have no such aim in view. Nor have they at any time contemplated . . . the disappearance or the subordination of the Arabic population, language or culture in Palestine. They would draw attention to the fact that the terms of the (Balfour) Declaration referred to do not contemplate that

Palestine as a whole should be converted into a Jewish National Home, but that such a Home should be founded *in Palestine.*"

But this statement has not removed doubts, and His Majesty's Government therefore now declare unequivocally that it is not part of their policy that Palestine should become a Jewish State. They would indeed regard it as contrary to their obligations to the Arabs under the Mandate, as well as to the assurances which have been given to the Arab people in the past, that the Arab population of Palestine should be made the subjects of a Jewish State against their will.

5. The nature of the Jewish National Home in Palestine was further described in the Command Paper of 1922 as follows:

"During the last two or three generations the Jews have recreated in Palestine a community, now numbering 80,000, of whom about one-fourth are farmers or workers upon the land. This community has its own political organs; an elected assembly for the direction of its domestic concerns; elected councils in the towns; and an organisation for the control of its schools. It has its elected Chief Rabbinate and Rabbinical Council for the direction of its religious affairs. Its business is conducted in Hebrew as a vernacular language, and a Hebrew press serves its needs. It has its distinctive intellectual life and displays considerable economic activity. This community, then, with its town and country population, its political, religious and social organisations, its own language, its own customs, its own life, has in fact 'national' characteristics. When it is asked what is meant by the development of the Jewish National Home in Palestine, it may be answered that it is not the imposition of a Jewish nationality upon the inhabitants of Palestine as a whole, but the further development of the existing Jewish community, with the assistance of Jews in other parts of the world, in order that it may become a centre in which the Jewish people as a whole may take, on grounds of religion and race, an interest and a pride. But in order that this community should have the best prospect of free development and provide a full opportunity for the Jewish people to display its capacities, it is essential that it should know that it is in Palestine as of right and not on sufferance. That is the reason why it is necessary that the existence of a Jewish National Home in Palestine should be internationally guaranteed, and that it should be formally recognised to rest upon ancient historic connection."

6. His Majesty's Government adhere to this interpretation of the Declaration of 1917 and regard it as an authoritative and comprehensive description of the character of the Jewish National Home in Palestine. It envisaged the further development of the existing Jewish community with the assistance of Jews in other parts of the world. Evidence that His Majesty's Government have been carrying out their obligation in this respect is to be found in the facts that, since the statement of 1922 was published, more than 300,000 Jews have immigrated to Palestine, and that the population of the National Home has risen to some 450,000, or approaching

a third of the entire population of the country. Nor has the Jewish community failed to take full advantage of the opportunities given to it. The growth of the Jewish National Home and its achievements in many fields are a remarkable constructive effort which must command the admiration of the world and must be, in particular, a source of pride to the Jewish people.

7. In the recent discussions the Arab delegations have repeated the contention that Palestine was included within the area in which Sir Henry McMahon, on behalf of the British Government, in October, 1915, undertook to recognise and support Arab independence. The validity of this claim, based on the terms of the correspondence which passed between Sir Henry McMahon and the Sharif of Mecca, was thoroughly and carefully investigated by British and Arab representatives during the recent conferences in London. Their Report, which has been published, states that both the Arab and the British representatives endeavoured to understand the point of view of the other party but that they were unable to reach agreement upon an interpretation of the correspondence. There is no need to summarize here the arguments presented by each side. His Majesty's Government regret the misunderstandings which have arisen as regards some of the phrases used. For their part they can only adhere, for the reasons given by their representatives in the Report, to the view that the whole of Palestine west of Jordan was excluded from Sir Henry McMahon's pledge, and they therefore cannot agree that the McMahon correspondence forms a just basis for the claim that Palestine should be converted into an Arab State.

8. His Majesty's Government are charged as the Mandatory authority "to secure the development of self-governing institutions" in Palestine. Apart from this specific obligation, they would regard it as contrary to the whole spirit of the Mandate system that the population of Palestine should remain forever under Mandatory tutelage. It is proper that the people of the country should as early as possible enjoy the rights of self-government which are exercised by the people of neighbouring countries. His Majesty's Government are unable at present to foresee the exact constitutional forms which government in Palestine will eventually take, but their objective is self-government, and they desire to see established ultimately an independent Palestine State. It should be a State in which the two peoples in Palestine, Arabs and Jews, share authority in government in such a way that the essential interests of each are secured.

9. The establishment of an independent State and the complete relinquishment of Mandatory control in Palestine would require such relations between the Arabs and the Jews as would make good government possible. Moreover, the growth of self-governing institutions in Palestine, as in other countries, must be an evolutionary process. A transitional period will be required before independence is achieved, throughout which ultimate responsibility for the Government of the country will be retained by His

Majesty's Government as the Mandatory authority, while the people of the country are taking an increasing share in the Government, and understanding and co-operation amongst them are growing. It will be the constant endeavour of His Majesty's Government to promote good relations between the Arabs and the Jews.

10. In the light of these considerations His Majesty's Government make the following declaration of their intentions regarding the future government of Palestine:—

(1) The objective of His Majesty's Government is the establishment within ten years of an independent Palestine State in such treaty relations with the United Kingdom as will provide satisfactorily for the commercial and strategic requirements of both countries in the future. The proposal for the establishment of the independent State would involve consultation with the Council of the League of Nations with a view to the termination of the Mandate.

(2) The independent State should be one in which Arabs and Jews share in government in such a way as to ensure that the essential interests of each community are safeguarded.

(3) The establishment of the independent State will be preceded by a transitional period throughout which His Majesty's Government will retain responsibility for the government of the country. During the transitional period the people of Palestine will be given an increasing part in the government of their country. Both sections of the population will have an opportunity to participate in the machinery of government, and the process will be carried on whether or not they both avail themselves of it.

(4) As soon as peace and order have been sufficiently restored in Palestine steps will be taken to carry out this policy of giving the people of Palestine as increasing part in the government of their country, the objective being to place Palestinians in charge of all the Departments of Government, with the assistance of British advisers and subject to the control of the High Commissioner. With this object in view His Majesty's Government will be prepared immediately to arrange that Palestinians shall be placed in charge of certain Departments, with British advisers. The Palestinian heads of Departments will sit on the Executive Council which advises the High Commissioner. Arab and Jewish representatives will be invited to serve as heads of Departments approximately in proportion to their respective populations. The number of Palestinians in charge of Departments will be increased as circumstances permit until all heads of Departments are Palestinians, exercising the administrative and advisory functions which are at present performed by British officials. When that stage is reached consideration will be given to the question of converting the Executive Council into a Council of Ministers with a consequential change in the status and functions of the Palestinian heads of Departments.

(5) His Majesty's Government make no proposals at this stage regarding the establishment of an elective legislature. Nevertheless they would

regard this as an appropriate constitutional development, and, should public opinion in Palestine hereafter show itself in favour of such a development, they will be prepared, provided that local conditions permit, to establish the necessary machinery.

(6) At the end of five years from the restoration of peace and order, an appropriate body representative of the people of Palestine and of His Majesty's Government will be set up to review the working of the constitutional arrangements during the transitional period and to consider and make recommendations regarding the constitution of the independent Palestine State.

(7) His Majesty's Government will require to be satisfied that in the treaty contemplated by sub-paragraph (1) or in the constitution contemplated by sub-paragraph (6) adequate provision has been made for:—

(a) the security of, and freedom of access to, the Holy Places, and the protection of the interests and property of the various religious bodies.

(b) the protection of the different communities in Palestine in accordance with the obligations of His Majesty's Government to both Arabs and Jews and for the special position in Palestine of the Jewish National Home.

(c) such requirements to meet the strategic situation as may be regarded as necessary by His Majesty's Government in the light of the circumstances then existing.

His Majesty's Government will also require to be satisfied that the interests of certain foreign countries in Palestine, for the preservation of which they are at present responsible, are adequately safeguarded.

(8) His Majesty's Government will do everything in their power to create conditions which will enable the independent Palestine State to come into being within ten years. If, at the end of ten years, it appears to His Majesty's Government that, contrary to their hope, circumstances require the postponement of the establishment of the independent State, they will consult with representatives of the people of Palestine, the Council of the League of Nations and the neighbouring Arab States before deciding on such a postponement. If His Majesty's Government come to the conclusion that postponement is unavoidable, they will invite the co-operation of these parties in framing plans for the future with a view to achieving the desired objective at the earliest possible date.

11. During the transitional period steps will be taken to increase the powers and responsibilities of municipal corporations and local councils.

II. — IMMIGRATION

12. Under Article 6 of the Mandate, the Administration of Palestine, "while ensuring that the rights and position of other sections of the population are not prejudiced," is required to "facilitate Jewish immigration under suitable conditions." Beyond this, the extent to which Jewish im-

migration into Palestine is to be permitted is nowhere defined in the Mandate. But in the Command Paper of 1922 it was laid down that for the fulfilment of the policy of establishing a Jewish National Home

"it is necessary that the Jewish community in Palestine should be able to increase its numbers by immigration. This immigration cannot be so great in volume as to exceed whatever may be the economic capacity of the country at the time to absorb new arrivals. It is essential to ensure that the immigrants should not be a burden upon the people of Palestine as a whole, and that they should not deprive any section of the present population of their employment.''

In practice, from that date onwards until recent times, the economic absorptive capacity of the country has been treated as the sole limiting factor, and in the letter which Mr. Ramsay MacDonald, as Prime Minister, sent to Dr. Weizmann in February 1931 it was laid down as a matter of policy that economic absorptive capacity was the sole criterion. This interpretation has been supported by resolutions of the Permanent Mandates Commission. But His Majesty's Government do not read either the Statement of Policy of 1922 or the letter of 1931 as implying that the Mandate requires them, for all time and in all circumstances, to facilitate the immigration of Jews into Palestine subject only to consideration of the country's economic absorptive capacity. Nor do they find anything in the Mandate or in subsequent Statements of Policy to support the view that the establishment of a Jewish National Home in Palestine cannot be effected unless immigration is allowed to continue indefinitely. If immigration has an adverse effect on the economic position in the country, it should clearly be restricted; and equally, if it has a seriously damaging effect on the political position in the country, that is a factor that should not be ignored. Although it is not difficult to contend that the large number of Jewish immigrants who have been admitted so far have been absorbed economically, the fear of the Arabs that this influx will continue indefinitely until the Jewish population is in a position to dominate them has produced consequences which are extremely grave for Jews and Arabs alike and for the peace and prosperity of Palestine. The lamentable disturbances of the past three years are only the latest and most sustained manifestation of this intense Arab apprehension. The methods employed by Arab terrorists against fellow-Arabs and Jews alike must receive unqualified condemnation. But it cannot be denied that fear of indefinite Jewish immigration is widespread amongst the Arab population and that this fear has made possible disturbances which have given a serious setback to economic progress, depleted the Palestine exchequer, rendered life and property insecure, and produced a bitterness between the Arab and Jewish populations which is deplorable between citizens of the same country. If in these circumstances immigration is continued up to the economic absorptive capacity of the country, regardless of all other considerations, a fatal enmity between the two peoples will be perpetuated, and the situation in Palestine may become a permanent source of friction amongst all peoples in the Near and Middle East. His Majesty's Government cannot take the view that either their obligations under the Mandate, or considerations of common sense and justice, require that they should ignore these circumstances in framing immigration policy.

13. In the view of the Royal Commission the association of the policy of the Balfour Declaration with the Mandate system implied the belief that Arab hostility to the former would sooner or later be overcome. It has been the hope of British Governments ever since the Balfour Declaration was issued that in time the Arab population, recognizing the advantages to be derived from Jewish settlement and development in Palestine, would become reconciled to the further growth of the Jewish National Home. This hope has not been fulfilled. The alternatives before His Majesty's Government are either (i) to seek to expand the Jewish National Home indefinitely by immigration, against the strongly expressed will of the Arab people of the country; or (ii) to permit further expansion of the Jewish National Home by immigration only if the Arabs are prepared to acquiesce in it. The former policy means rule by force. Apart from other considerations, such a policy seems to His Majesty's Government to be contrary to the whole spirit of Article 22 of the Covenant of the League of Nations, as well as to their specific obligations to the Arabs in the Palestine Mandate. Moreover, the relations between the Arabs and the Jews in Palestine must be based sooner or later on mutual tolerance and goodwill; the peace, security and progress of the Jewish National Home itself require this. Therefore His Majesty's Government, after earnest consideration, and taking into account the extent to which the growth of the Jewish National Home has been facilitated over the last twenty years, have decided that the time has come to adopt in principle the second of the alternatives referred to above.

14. It has been urged that all further Jewish immigration into Palestine should be stopped forthwith. His Majesty's Government cannot accept such a proposal. It would damage the whole of the financial and economic system of Palestine and thus affect adversely the interests of Arabs and Jews alike. Moreover, in the view of His Majesty's Government, abruptly to stop further immigration would be unjust to the Jewish National Home. But, above all, His Majesty's Government are conscious of the present unhappy plight of large numbers of Jews who seek a refuge from certain European countries, and they believe that Palestine can and should make a further contribution to the solution of this pressing world problem. In all these circumstances, they believe that they will be acting consistently with their Mandatory obligations to both Arabs and Jews, and in the manner best calculated to serve the interests of the whole people of Palestine, by adopting the following proposals regarding immigration:—

(1) Jewish immigration during the next five years will be at a rate

which, if economic absorptive capacity permits, will bring the Jewish population up to approximately one-third of the total population of the country. Taking into account the expected natural increase of the Arab and Jewish populations, and the number of illegal Jewish immigrants now in the country, this would allow of the admission, as from the beginning of April this year, of some 75,000 immigrants over the next five years. These immigrants would, subject to the criterion of economic absorptive capacity, be admitted as follows:—

(*a*) For each of the next five years a quota of 10,000 Jewish immigrants will be allowed on the understanding that a shortage in any one year may be added to the quotas for subsequent years, within the five-year period, if economic absorptive capacity permits.

(*b*) In addition, as a contribution towards the solution of the Jewish refugee problem, 25,000 refugees will be admitted as soon as the High Commissioner is satisfied that adequate provision for their maintenance is ensured, special consideration being given to refugee children and dependants.

(2) The existing machinery for ascertaining economic absorptive capacity will be retained, and the High Commissioner will have the ultimate responsibility for deciding the limits of economic capacity. Before each periodic decision is taken, Jewish and Arab representatives will be consulted.

(3) After the period of five years no further Jewish immigration will be permitted unless the Arabs of Palestine are prepared to acquiesce in it.

(4) His Majesty's Government are determined to check illegal immigration, and further preventive measures are being adopted. The numbers of any Jewish illegal immigrants who, despite these measures, may succeed in coming into the country and cannot be deported will be deducted from the yearly quotas.

15. His Majesty's Government are satisfied that, when the immigration over five years which is now contemplated has taken place, they will not be justified in facilitating, nor will they be under any obligation to facilitate, the further development of the Jewish National Home by immigration regardless of the wishes of the Arab population.

III.—LAND

16. The Administration of Palestine is required, under Article 6 of the Mandate, "while ensuring that the rights and position of other sections of the population are not prejudiced," to encourage "close settlement by Jews on the land," and no restriction has been imposed hitherto on the transfer of land from Arabs to Jews. The Reports of several expert Commissions have indicated that, owing to the natural growth of the Arab population and the steady sale in recent years of Arab land to Jews, there is now in certain areas no room for further transfers of Arab land, whilst in some other areas such transfers of land must be restricted if Arab cultivators are to maintain their existing standard of life and a considerable

landless Arab population is not soon to be created. In these circumstances, the High Commissioner will be given general powers to prohibit and regulate transfers of land. These powers will date from the publication of this statement of policy and the High Commissioner will retain them throughout the transitional period.

17. The policy of the Government will be directed towards the development of the land and the improvement, where possible, of methods of cultivation. In the light of such development it will be open to the High Commissioner, should he be satisfied that the "rights and position" of the Arab population will be duly preserved, to review and modify any orders passed relating to the prohibition or restriction of the transfer of land.

18. In framing these proposals His Majesty's Government have sincerely endeavoured to act in strict accordance with their obligations under the Mandate to both the Arabs and the Jews. The vagueness of the phrases employed in some instances to describe these obligations has led to controversy and has made the task of interpretation difficult. His Majesty's Government cannot hope to satisfy the partisans of one party or the other in such controversy as the Mandate has aroused. Their purpose is to be just as between the two peoples in Palestine whose destinies in that country have been affected by the great events of recent years, and who, since they live side by side, must learn to practice mutual tolerance, goodwill and co-operation. In looking to the future, His Majesty's Government are not blind to the fact that some events of the past make the task of creating these relations difficult; but they are encouraged by the knowledge that at many times and in many places in Palestine during recent years the Arab and Jewish inhabitants have lived in friendship together. Each community has much to contribute to the welfare of their common land, and each must earnestly desire peace in which to assist in increasing the well-being of the whole people of the country. The responsibility which falls on them, no less than upon His Majesty's Government, to co-operate together to ensure peace is all the more solemn because their country is revered by many millions of Moslems, Jews and Christians throughout the world who pray for peace in Palestine and for the happiness of her people.

The Zionist Reaction to the White Paper

*Statement by the Jewish Agency
for Palestine (1939)*

1. The new policy for Palestine laid down by the Mandatory in the White Paper now issued denies to the Jewish people the right to rebuild their

national home in their ancestral country. It transfers the authority over Palestine to the present Arab majority and puts the Jewish population at the mercy of that majority. It decrees the stoppage of Jewish immigration as soon as the Jews form a third of the total population. It puts up a territorial ghetto for Jews in their own homeland.

2. The Jewish people regard this policy as a breach of faith and a surrender to Arab terrorism. It delivers Britain's friends into the hands of those who are biting her and must lead to a complete breach between Jews and Arabs which will banish every prospect of peace in Palestine. It is a policy in which the Jewish people will not acquiesce. The new regime now announced will be devoid of any moral basis and contrary to international law. Such a regime can only be established and maintained by force.

3. The Royal Commission invoked by the White Paper indicated the perils of such a policy, saying it was convinced that an Arab Government would mean the frustration of all their (Jews') efforts and ideals and would convert the national home into one more cramped and dangerous ghetto. It seems only too probable that the Jews would fight rather than submit to Arab rule. And repressing a Jewish rebellion against British policy would be as unpleasant a task as the repression of the Arab rebellion has been. The Government has disregarded this warning.

4. The Jewish people have no quarrel with the Arab people. Jewish work in Palestine has not had an adverse effect upon the life and progress of the Arab people. The Arabs are not landless or homeless as are the Jews. They are not in need of emigration. Jewish colonization has benefited Palestine and all its inhabitants. Insofar as the Balfour Declaration contributed to British victory in the Great War, it contributed also, as was pointed out by the Royal Commission, to the liberation of the Arab peoples. The Jewish people has shown its will to peace even during the years of disturbances. It has not given way to temptation and has not retaliated to Arab violence. But neither have the Jews submitted to terror nor will they submit to it even after the Mandatory has decided to reward the terrorists by surrendering the Jewish National Home.

5. It is in the darkest hour of Jewish history that the British Government proposes to deprive the Jews of their last hope and to close the road back to their Homeland. It is a cruel blow, doubly cruel because it comes from the government of a great nation which has extended a helping hand to the Jews, and whose position must rest on foundations of moral authority and international good faith. This blow will not subdue the Jewish people. The historic bond between the people and the land of Israel cannot be broken. The Jews will never accept the closing to them of the gates of Palestine nor let their national home be converted into a ghetto. The Jewish pioneers who, during the past three generations, have shown their strength in the upbuilding of a derelict country, will from now on display the same

strength in defending Jewish immigration, the Jewish home and Jewish freedom.

Towards a Jewish State: The Biltmore Program (1942)

During a visit to the United States by David Ben Gurion, Chairman of the Executive of the Jewish Agency, Zionist policy was reformulated. At a conference at the Biltmore Hotel in New York, in May 1942, the establishment of a Jewish state was envisaged to open the doors of Palestine to Jewish refugees escaping from Nazi terror and to lay the foundations for the establishment of a Jewish majority.

Declaration Adopted by the Extraordinary Zionist Conference, Biltmore Hotel, New York City, May 11, 1942

1. American Zionists assembled in this Extraordinary Conference reaffirm their unequivocal devotion to the cause of democratic freedom and international justice to which the people of the United States, allied with the other United Nations, have dedicated themselves, and give expression to their faith in the ultimate victory of humanity and justice over lawlessness and brute force.

2. This Conference offers a message of hope and encouragement to their fellow Jews in the Ghettos and concentration camps of Hitler-dominated Europe and prays that their hour of liberation may not be far distant.

3. The Conference sends its warmest greetings to the Jewish Agency Executive in Jerusalem, to the Va'ad Leumi, and to the whole Yishuv in Palestine, and expresses its profound admiration for their steadfastness and achievements in the face of peril and great difficulties. The Jewish men and women in field and factory, and the thousands of Jewish soldiers of Palestine in the Near East who have acquitted themselves with honor and distinction in Greece, Ethiopia, Syria, Libya and on other battlefields, have shown themselves worthy of their people and ready to assume the rights and responsibilities of nationhood.

4. In our generation, and in particular in the course of the past twenty years, the Jewish people have awakened and transformed their ancient homeland; from 50,000 at the end of the last war their numbers have increased to more than 500,000. They have made the waste places to bear fruit and the desert to blossom. Their pioneering achievements in agricul-

ture and in industry, embodying new patterns of cooperative endeavor, have written a notable page in the history of colonization.

5. In the new values thus created, their Arab neighbors in Palestine have shared. The Jewish people in its own work of national redemption welcomes the economic, agricultural and national development of the Arab peoples and states. The Conference reaffirms the stand previously adopted at Congresses of the World Zionist Organization, expressing the readiness and the desire of the Jewish people for full cooperation with their Arab neighbors.

6. The Conference calls for the fulfilment of the original purpose of the Balfour Declaration and the Mandate which *"recognizing the historical connection of the Jewish people with Palestine"* was to afford them the opportunity, as stated by President Wilson, to found there a Jewish Commonwealth.

The Conference affirms its unalterable rejection of the White Paper of May 1939 and denies its moral or legal validity. The White Paper seeks to limit, and in fact to nullify Jewish rights to immigration and settlement in Palestine, and, as stated by Mr. Winston Churchill in the House of Commons in May 1939, constitutes "a breach and repudiation of the Balfour Declaration." The policy of the White Paper is cruel and indefensible in its denial of sanctuary to Jews fleeing from Nazi persecution; and at a time when Palestine has become a focal point in the war front of the United Nations, and Palestine Jewry must provide all available manpower for farm and factory and camp, it is in direct conflict with the interests of the allied war effort.

7. In the struggle against the forces of aggression and tyranny, of which Jews were the earliest victims, and which now menace the Jewish National Home, recognition must be given to the right of the Jews of Palestine to play their full part in the war effort and in the defense of their country, through a Jewish military force fighting under its own flag and under the high command of the United Nations.

8. The Conference declares that the new world order that will follow victory cannot be established on foundations of peace, justice and equality, unless the problem of Jewish homelessness is finally solved.

The Conference urges that the gates of Palestine be opened; that the Jewish Agency be vested with control of immigration into Palestine and with the necessary authority for upbuilding the country, including the development of its unoccupied and uncultivated lands; and that Palestine be established as a Jewish Commonwealth integrated in the structure of the new democratic world.

Then and only then will the age-old wrong to the Jewish people be righted.

Adolf Hitler, Zionism and the Arab Cause*

Haj Amin al Husaini, the most influential leader of Palestinian Arabs, lived in Germany during the Second World War. He met Hitler, Ribbentrop and other Nazi leaders on various occasions and attempted to coordinate Nazi and Arab policies in the Middle East.

BERLIN, NOVEMBER 30, 1941.

Record of the Conversation Between the Führer and the Grand Mufti of Jerusalem on November 28, 1941, in the Presence of Reich Foreign Minister and Minister Grobba in Berlin

The Grand Mufti began by thanking the Führer for the great honor he had bestowed by receiving him. He wished to seize the opportunity to convey to the Führer of the Greater German Reich, admired by the entire Arab world, his thanks for the sympathy which he had always shown for the Arab and especially the Palestinian cause, and to which he had given clear expression in his public speeches. The Arab countries were firmly convinced that Germany would win the war and that the Arab cause would then prosper. The Arabs were Germany's natural friends because they had the same enemies as had Germany, namely the English, the Jews, and the Communists. They were therefore prepared to cooperate with Germany with all their hearts and stood ready to participate in the war, not only negatively by the commission of acts of sabotage and the instigation of revolutions, but also positively by the formation of an Arab Legion. The Arabs could be more useful to Germany as allies than might be apparent at first glance, both for geographical reasons and because of the suffering inflicted upon them by the English and the Jews. Furthermore, they had had close relations with all Moslem nations, of which they could make use in behalf of the common cause. The Arab Legion would be quite easy to raise. An appeal by the Mufti to the Arab countries and the prisoners of Arab, Algerian, Tunisian, and Moroccan nationality in Germany would produce a great number of volunteers eager to fight. Of Germany's victory the Arab world was firmly convinced, not only because the Reich possessed a large army, brave soldiers, and military leaders of genius, but

* *Documents on German Foreign Policy 1918–45*, Series D, Vol. XIII, London, 1964, pp. 881 *ff.*

also because the Almighty could never award the victory to an unjust cause.

In this struggle, the Arabs were striving for the independence and unity of Palestine, Syria, and Iraq. They had the fullest confidence in the Führer and looked to his hand for the balm on their wounds which had been inflicted upon them by the enemies of Germany.

The Mufti then mentioned the letter he had received from Germany, which stated that Germany was holding no Arab territories and understood and recognized the aspirations to independence and freedom of the Arabs, just as she supported the elimination of the Jewish national home.

A public declaration in this sense would be very useful for its propagandistic effect on the Arab peoples at this moment. It would rouse the Arabs from their momentary lethargy and give them new courage. It would also ease the Mufti's work of secretly organizing the Arabs against the moment when they could strike. At the same time, he could give the assurance that the Arabs would in strict discipline patiently wait for the right moment and only strike upon an order from Berlin.

With regard to the events in Iraq, the Mufti observed that the Arabs in that country certainly had by no means been incited by Germany to attack England, but solely had acted in reaction to a direct English assault upon their honor.

The Turks, he believed, would welcome the establishment of an Arab government in the neighboring territories because they would prefer weaker Arab to strong European governments in the neighboring countries, and, being themselves a nation of 7 millions, they had moreover nothing to fear from the 1,700,000 Arabs inhabiting Syria, Transjordan, Iraq, and Palestine.

France likewise would have no objections to the unification plan because she had conceded independence to Syria as early as 1936 and had given her approval to the unification of Iraq and Syria under King Faisal as early as 1933.

In these circumstances he was renewing his request that the Führer make a public declaration so that the Arabs would not lose hope, which is so powerful a force in the life of nations. With such hope in their hearts the Arabs, as he had said, were willing to wait. They were not pressing for immediate realization of their aspirations; they could easily wait half a year or a whole year. But if they were not inspired with such a hope by a declaration of this sort, it could be expected that the English would be the gainers from it.

The Führer replied that Germany's fundamental attitude on these questions, as the Mufti himself had already stated, was clear. Germany stood for uncompromising war against the Jews. That naturally included active opposition to the Jewish national home in Palestine, which was nothing other than a center, in the form of a state, for the exercise of destructive influence by Jewish interests. Germany was also aware that the assertion that the Jews were carrying out the function of economic pioneers in Palestine was a lie. The work there was done only by the Arabs, not by the Jews. Germany was resolved, step by step, to ask one European nation after the other to solve its Jewish problem, and at the proper time direct a similar appeal to non-European nations as well.

Germany was at the present time engaged in a life and death struggle with two citadels of Jewish power: Great Britain and Soviet Russia. Theoretically there was a difference between England's capitalism and Soviet Russia's communism; actually, however, the Jews in both countries were pursuing a common goal. This was the decisive struggle; on the political plane, it presented itself in the main as a conflict between Germany and England, but ideologically it was a battle between National Socialism and the Jews. It went without saying that Germany would furnish positive and practical aid to the Arabs involved in the same struggle, because platonic promises were useless in a war for survival or destruction in which the Jews were able to mobilize all of England's power for their ends.

The aid to the Arabs would have to be material aid. Of how little help sympathies alone were in such a battle had been demonstrated plainly by the operation in Iraq, where circumstances had not permitted the rendering of really effective, practical aid. In spite of all the sympathies, German aid had not been sufficient and Iraq was overcome by the power of Britain, that is, the guardian of the Jews.

The Mufti could not but be aware, however, that the outcome of the struggle going on at present would also decide the fate of the Arab world. The Führer therefore had to think and speak coolly and deliberately, as a rational man and primarily as a soldier, as the leader of the German and allied armies. Everything of a nature to help in this titanic battle for the common cause, and thus also for the Arabs, would have to be done. Anything, however, that might contribute to weakening the military situation must be put aside, no matter how unpopular this move might be.

Germany was now engaged in very severe battles to force the gateway to the northern Caucasus region. The difficulties were mainly with regard to maintaining the supply, which was most difficult as a result of the destruction of railroads and highways as well as of the oncoming winter. If at such a moment, the Führer were to raise the problem of Syria in a declaration, those elements in France which were under de Gaulle's influence would receive new strength. They would interpret the Führer's declaration as an intention to break up France's colonial empire and appeal to their fellow countrymen that they should rather make common cause with the English to try to save what still could be saved. A German declaration regarding Syria would in France be understood to refer to the French colonies in general, and that would at the present time create new troubles in western Europe, which means that a portion of the German armed forces would be immobilized in the west and no longer be available for the campaign in the east.

The Führer then made the following statement to the Mufti, enjoining him to lock it in the uttermost depths of his heart:

1. He (the Führer) would carry on the battle to the total destruction of the Judeo-Communist empire in Europe.

2. At some moment which was impossible to set exactly today but which in any event was not distant, the German armies would in the course of this struggle reach the southern exit from Caucasia.

3. As soon as this had happened, the Führer would on his own give the Arab world the assurance that its hour of liberation had arrived. Germany's objective would then be solely the destruction of the Jewish element residing in the Arab sphere under the protection of British power. In that hour the Mufti would be the most authoritative spokesman for the Arab world. It would then be his task to set off the Arab operations which he had secretly prepared. When that time had come, Germany could also be indifferent to French reaction to such a declaration.

Once Germany had forced open the road to Iran and Iraq through Rostov, it would be also the beginning of the end of the British world empire. He (the Führer) hoped that the coming year would make it possible for Germany to thrust open the Caucasian gate to the Middle East. For the good of their common cause, it would be better if the Arab proclamation were put off for a few more months than if Germany were to create difficulties for herself without being able thereby to help the Arabs.

He (the Führer) fully appreciated the eagerness of the Arabs for a public declaration of the sort requested by the Grand Mufti. But he would beg him to consider that he (the Führer) himself was the Chief of State of the German Reich for 5 long years during which he was unable to make to his own homeland the announcement of its liberation. He had to wait with that until the announcement could be made on the basis of a situation brought about by the force of arms that the Anschluss had been carried out.

The moment that Germany's tank divisions and air squadrons had made their appearance south of the Caucasus, the public appeal requested by the Grand Mufti could go out to the Arab world.

The Grand Mufti replied that it was his view that everything would come to pass just as the Führer had indicated. He was fully reassured and satisfied by the words which he had heard from the Chief of the German State. He asked, however, whether it would not be possible, secretly at least, to enter into an agreement with Germany of the kind he had just outlined for the Führer.

The Führer replied that he had just now given the Grand Mufti precisely that confidential declaration.

The Grand Mufti thanked him for it and stated in conclusion that he was taking his leave from the Führer in full confidence and with reiterated thanks for the interest shown in the Arab cause.

SCHMIDT

The Anglo-American Committee of Inquiry—1946

An Anglo-American Inquiry Committee was appointed in November, 1945, to examine the status of the Jews in former Axis-occupied countries and to find out how many were impelled by their conditions to migrate. Britain, weakened by the war, found itself under growing pressure from Jews and Arabs alike and the Labor Government decided, therefore, to invite the United States to participate in finding a solution. The Report of the Committee was published on May 1, 1945 (below). President Truman welcomed its recommendation that the immigration and land laws of the 1939 White Paper were to be rescinded. Prime Minister Attlee, on the other hand, declared that the report would have to be "considered as a whole in all its implications." Arab reaction was hostile (see page 80); the Arab League announced that Arabs would not stand by with their arms folded. The Ihud (Association) group led by Dr. J. L. Magnes and Professor M. Buber (who submitted the document on page 89 to the Committee), favored a binational solution, equal political rights for Arabs and Jews, and a Federative Union of Palestine and the neighboring countries. Ihud found little support among the Jewish Community. It had, in the beginning, a few Arab sympathizers, but some of them were assassinated by supporters of the Mufti and the others dropped out.

Recommendations and Comments

THE EUROPEAN PROBLEM

Recommendation No. 1. We have to report that such information as we received about countries other than Palestine gave no hope of substantial assistance in finding homes for Jews wishing or impelled to leave Europe.

But Palestine alone cannot meet the emigration needs of the Jewish victims of Nazi and Fascist persecution; the whole world shares responsibility for them and indeed for the resettlement of all "displaced persons."

We therefore recommend that our Governments together, and in association with other countries, should endeavor immediately to find new homes for all such "displaced persons," irrespective of creed or nationality, whose ties with their former communities have been irreparably broken.

Though emigration will solve the problems of some victims of persecution, the overwhelming majority, including a considerable number of Jews, will continue to live in Europe. We recommend therefore that our Governments endeavor to secure that immediate effect is given to the provision of the United Nations Charter calling for "universal respect for, and observation of, human rights and fundamental freedoms for all without distinction as to race, sex, language or religion."

Comment. In recommending that our Governments, in association with other countries, should endeavor to find new homes for "displaced persons," we do not suggest that any country should be asked to make a permanent change in its immigration policy. The conditions which we have seen in Europe are unprecedented and so unlikely to arise again that we are convinced that special provision could and should be made in existing immigration laws to meet this unique and peculiarly distressing situation. Furthermore, we believe that much could be accomplished—particularly in regard to those "displaced persons," including Jews, who have relatives in countries outside Europe—by a relaxation of administrative regulations.

Our investigations have led us to believe that a considerable number of Jews will continue to live in most European countries. In our view the mass emigration of all European Jews would be of service neither to the Jews themselves nor to Europe. Every effort should be made to enable the Jews to rebuild their shattered communities, while permitting those Jews who wish to do so to emigrate. In order to achieve this, restitution of Jewish property should be effected as soon as possible. Our investigations showed us that the Governments chiefly concerned had for the most part already passed legislation to this end. A real obstacle, however, to individual restitution is that the attempt to give effect to this legislation is frequently a cause of active anti-Semitism. We suggest that, for the reconstruction of the Jewish communities, restitution of their corporate property, either through reparations payments or through other means, is of the first importance.

Nazi occupation has left behind it a legacy of anti-Semitism. This cannot be combatted by legislation alone. The only really effective antidotes are the enforcement by each Government of guaranteed civil liberties and equal rights, a program of education in the positive principles of democracy, the sanction of a strong world public opinion—combined with economic recovery and stability.

Refugee Immigration into Palestine

Recommendation No. 2. We recommend (a) that 100,000 certificates be authorized immediately for the admission into Palestine of Jews who have been the victims of Nazi and Fascist persecution; (b) that these certificates be awarded as far as possible in 1946 and that actual immigration be pushed forward as rapidly as conditions will permit.

Comment. The number of Jewish survivors of Nazi and Fascist persecution with whom we have to deal far exceeds 100,000: indeed there are more than that number in Germany, Austria and Italy alone. Although nearly a year has passed since their liberation, the majority of those in Germany and Austria are still living in assembly centers, the so-called "camps," island communities in the midst of those at whose hands they suffered so much.

In their interests and in the interests of Europe, the centers should be closed and their camp life ended. Most of them have cogent reasons for wishing to leave Europe. Many are the sole survivors of their families and few have any ties binding them to the countries in which they used to live.

Since the end of hostilities, little has been done to provide for their resettlement elsewhere. Immigration laws and restrictions bar their entry to most countries and much time must pass before such laws and restrictions can be altered and effect given to the alterations.

Some can go to countries where they have relatives; others may secure inclusion in certain quotas. Their number is comparatively small.

We know of no country to which the great majority can go in the immediate future other than Palestine. Furthermore, that is where almost all of them want to go. There they are sure that they will receive a welcome denied them elsewhere. There they hope to enjoy peace and rebuild their lives.

We believe it is essential that they should be given an opportunity to do so at the earliest possible time. Furthermore, we have the assurances of the leaders of the Jewish Agency that they will be supported and cared for.

We recommend the authorization and issue of 100,000 certificates for these reasons and because we feel that their immediate issue will have a most salutary effect upon the whole situation.

In the awarding of these certificates priority should, as far as possible, be given to those in the centers and to those liberated in Germany and Austria who are no longer in the centers but remain in those countries. We do not desire that other Jewish victims who wish or will be impelled by their circumstances to leave the countries where they now are or that those who fled from persecution before the outbreak of war should be excluded. We appreciate that there will be difficulty in deciding questions of priority, but none the less we urge that so far as possible such a system should be adhered to, and that, in applying it, primary consideration should be given to the aged and infirm, to the very young and also to skilled workmen whose services will be needed for many months on work rendered necessary by the large influx.

It should be made clear that no advantage in the obtaining of a certificate is to be gained by migrating from one country to another or by entering Palestine illegally.

Receiving so large a number will be a heavy burden on Palestine. We feel sure that the authorities will shoulder it and that they will have the full cooperation of the Jewish Agency.

Difficult problems will confront those responsible for organizing and carrying out the movement. The many organizations—public and private—working in Europe will certainly render all the aid they can; we mention UNRRA especially. Cooperation by all throughout is necessary.

We are sure that the Government of the United States, which has shown such keen interest in this matter, will participate vigorously and generously with the Government of Great Britain in its fulfillment. There are many ways in which help can be given.

Those who have opposed the admission of these unfortunate people into Palestine should know that we have fully considered all that they have put before us. We hope that they will look upon the situation again, that they will appreciate the considerations which have led us to our conclusion, and that above all, if they cannot see their way to help, at least they will not make the position of these sufferers more difficult.

PRINCIPLES OF GOVERNMENT: NO ARAB, NO JEWISH STATE

Recommendation No. 3. In order to dispose, once and for all, of the exclusive claims of Jews and Arabs to Palestine, we regard it as essential that a clear statement of the following principles should be made:

(I) That Jew shall not dominate Arab and Arab shall not dominate Jew in Palestine. (II) That Palestine shall be neither a Jewish state nor an Arab state. (III) That the form of government ultimately to be established, shall, under international guarantees, fully protect and preserve the interests in the Holy Land of Christendom and of the Moslem and Jewish faiths.

Thus Palestine must ultimately become a state which guards the rights and interests of Moslems, Jews and Christians alike and accords to the inhabitants, as a whole, the fullest measure of self-government consistent with the three paramount principles set forth above.

Comment. Throughout the long and bloody struggle of Jew and Arab for dominance in Palestine, each crying fiercely: ''This land is mine''—except for the brief reference in the Report of the Royal Commission (Hereinafter referred to as the Peel Report) and the little evidence, written and oral, that we received on this point—the great interest of the Christian world in Palestine has been completely overlooked, glossed over or brushed aside.

We therefore emphatically declare that Palestine is a Holy Land, sacred to Christian, to Jew and to Moslem alike; and because it is a Holy Land, Palestine is not, and can never become, a land which any race or religion can justly claim as its very own.

We further, in the same emphatic way, affirm that the fact that it is the Holy Land sets Palestine completely apart from other lands and dedicates it to the precepts and practices of the brotherhood of man, not those of narrow nationalism.

For another reason, in the light of its long history, and particularly its history of the last thirty years, Palestine cannot be regarded as either a purely Arab or a purely Jewish land.

The Jews have a historic connection with the country. The Jewish National Home, though embodying a minority of the population, is today a reality established under international guarantee. It has a right to continued existence, protection and development.

Yet Palestine is not, and never can be a purely Jewish land. It lies at the crossroads of the Arab world. Its Arab population, descended from long-time inhabitants of the area, rightly look upon Palestine as their homeland.

It is, therefore, neither just nor practicable that Palestine should become either an Arab state, in which an Arab majority would control the destiny of a Jewish minority, or a Jewish state, in which a Jewish majority would control that of an Arab minority. In neither case would minority guarantees afford adequate protection for the subordinated group.

A Palestinian put the matter thus: "In the hearts of us Jews there has always been a fear that some day this country would be turned into an Arab state and the Arabs would rule over us. This fear has at times reached the proportions of terror . . . Now this same feeling of fear has started up in the hearts of Arabs . . . fear lest the Jews acquire the ascendancy and rule over them."

Palestine, then, must be established as a country in which the legitimate national aspirations of both Jews and Arabs can be reconciled without either side fearing the ascendancy of the other. In our view this cannot be done under any form of constitution in which a mere numerical majority is decisive, since it is precisely the struggle for a numerical majority which bedevils Arab-Jewish relations. To ensure genuine self-government for both the Arab and the Jewish communities, this struggle must be made purposeless by the constitution itself.

MANDATE AND
UNITED NATIONS TRUSTEESHIP

Recommendation No. 4. We have reached the conclusion that the hostility between Jews and Arabs and, in particular, the determination of each to achieve domination, if necessary by violence, make it almost certain that, now and for some time to come, any attempt to establish either an independent Palestinian state or independent Palestinian states would result in civil strife such as might threaten the peace of the world. We therefore recommend that, until this hostility disappears, the Government of Palestine be continued as at present under mandate pending the execution of a trusteeship agreement under the United Nations.

Comment. We recognize that in view of the powerful forces both Arab and Jewish, operating from outside Palestine, the task of Great Britain, as mandatory, has not been easy. The Peel Commission declared in 1937 that the mandate was unworkable, and the Permanent Mandates Commission of the League of Nations thereupon pointed out that it became almost unworkable once it was publicly declared to be so by such a body. Two years later the British Government, having come to the conclusion that the alternative of partition proposed by the Peel Commission was also unworkable, announced their intention of taking steps to terminate the mandate by establishment of an independent Palestine state.

Our recommendations are based on what we believe at this stage to be as fair a measure of justice to all as we can find in view of what has gone before and of all that has been done. We recognize that they are not in accord with the claims of either party, and furthermore that they involve a departure from the recent policy of the mandatory.

We recognize that, if they are adopted, they will involve a long period of trusteeship, which will mean a very heavy burden for any single Government to undertake, a burden which would be lightened if the difficulties were appreciated and the trustee had the support of other members of the United Nations.

EQUALITY OF STANDARDS

Recommendation No. 5. Looking toward a form of ultimate self-government consistent with the three principles laid down in Recommendation No. 3, we recommend that the mandatory or trustee should proclaim the principle that Arab economic, educational and political advancement in Palestine is of equal importance with that of the Jews; and should at once prepare measures designed to bridge the gap which now exists and raise the Arab standard of living to that of the Jews; and to bring the two peoples to a full appreciation of their common interest and common destiny in the land where both belong.

Comment. Our examination of conditions in Palestine led us to the conclusion that one of the chief causes of friction is the great disparity between the Jewish and Arab standards of living. Even under conditions of war, which brought considerable financial benefits to the Arabs, this disparity has not been appreciably reduced. Only by a deliberate and carefully planned policy on the part of the mandatory can the Arab standard of living be raised to that of the Jews. In stressing the need for such a policy we would particularly call attention to the discrepancies between the social services, including hospitals, available in Palestine for Jews and Arabs.

SOCIAL AID

We fully recognize that the Jewish social services are financed to a very great extent by the Jewish community in Palestine, with the assistance of outside Jewish organizations; and we would stress that nothing should be done which would bring these social services down to the level of those provided for the Arabs, or halt the constant improvements now being made in them.

We suggest that consideration be given to the advisability of encouraging the formation by the Arabs of an Arab community on the lines of the Jewish community which now largely controls and finances Jewish social services. The Arabs will have to rely, to a far greater extent than the Jews, on financial aid from the Government. But the Jews of Palestine should accept the necessity that taxation, raised from both Jews and Arabs, will have to be spent very largely on the Arabs in order to bridge the gap which now exists between the standard of living of the two peoples.

FURTHER IMMIGRATION POLICY

Recommendation No. 6. We recommend that pending the early reference to the United Nations and the execution of a trusteeship agreement, the mandatory should administer Palestine according to the mandate, which declares, with regard to immigration, that ''the administration of Palestine, while insuring that the rights and position of other sections of the population are not prejudiced, shall facilitate Jewish immigration under suitable conditions.''

Comment. We have recommended the admission of 100,000 immigrants, victims of Nazi persecution, as soon as possible. We now deal with the position after the admission of that number. We cannot look far into the future. We cannot construct a yardstick for annual immigration. Until a trusteeship agreement is executed it is our clear opinion that Palestine should be administered in accordance with the terms of the mandate quoted above.

Further than that we cannot go in the form of a recommendation. In this disordered world speculation as to the economic position of any country a few years ahead would be a hazardous proceeding. It is particularly difficult to predict what, after a few years have passed, will be the economic and political condition of Palestine. We hope that the present friction and turbulence will soon die away and be replaced by an era of peace, absent so long from the Holy Land; that the Jew and Arab will soon realize that collaboration is to their mutual advantage, but no one can say how long this will take.

The possibility of the country sustaining a largely increased population at a decent standard of living depends largely on whether or not plans referred to in Recommendation No. 8 can be brought to fruition.

The Peel Commission stated that political as well as economic considerations have to be taken into account in regard to immigration, and recommended a "political high level" of 12,000 a year. We cannot recommend the fixing of a minimum or of a maximum for annual immigration in the future. There are too many uncertain factors.

We desire, however, to state certain considerations which we agree should be taken into account in determining what number of immigrants there should be in any period. It is the right of every independent nation to determine in the interests of its people the number of immigrants to be admitted to its lands. Similarly it must, we think, be conceded that it should be the right of the Government of Palestine to decide, having regard to the well-being of all the people of Palestine, the number of immigrants to be admitted within any given period.

In Palestine there is the Jewish National Home, created in consequence of the Balfour Declaration. Some may think that that declaration was wrong and should not have been made; some that it was a conception on a grand scale and that effect can be given to one of the most daring and significant colonization plans in history. Controversy as to which view is right is fruitless. The national home is there. Its roots are deep in the soil of Palestine. It cannot be argued out of existence; neither can the achievements of the Jewish pioneers.

The Government of Palestine in having regard to the well-being of all the people of Palestine cannot ignore the interests of so large a section of the population. It cannot ignore the achievements of the last quarter of a century. No Government of Palestine doing its duty to the people of that land can fail to do its best not only to maintain the national home but also to foster its proper development and such development must, in our view, involve immigration.

The well-being of all the people of Palestine, be they Jews, Arabs or neither, must be the governing consideration. We reject the view that there shall be no further Jewish immigration into Palestine without Arab acquiescence, a view which would result in the Arab dominating the Jew. We also reject the insistent Jewish demand that forced Jewish immigration must proceed apace in order to produce as quickly as possible a Jewish majority and a Jewish State. The well-being of the Jews must not be subordinated to that of the Arabs; nor that of the Arabs to the Jews. The well-being of both, the economic situation of Palestine as a whole, the degree of execution of plans for further development, all have to be carefully considered in deciding the number of immigrants for any particular period.

Palestine is a land sacred to three faiths and must not become the land of any one of them to the exclusion of the others, and Jewish immigration for the development of the national home must not become a policy of discrimination against other immigrants. Any person, therefore, who desires and is qualified under applicable laws to enter Palestine must not be refused admission or subjected to discrimination on the ground that he is not a Jew. All provisions respecting immigration must be drawn, executed and applied with that principle always firmly in mind.

Further, while we recognize that any Jew who enters Palestine in accordance with its laws is there of right, we expressly disapprove of the position taken in some Jewish quarters that Palestine has in some way been ceded or granted as their state to the Jews of the world, that every Jew everywhere is, merely because he is a Jew, a citizen of Palestine and therefore can enter Palestine as of right without regard to conditions imposed by the Government upon entry and that therefore there can be no illegal immigration of Jews into Palestine. We declare and affirm that any immigrant Jew who enters Palestine contrary to its laws is an illegal immigrant.

[Recommendations 7–9 deal with land policy, economic development, and education. Ed.]

The Arab Case for Palestine: Evidence Submitted by the Arab Office, Jerusalem, to the Anglo–American Committee of Inquiry, March, 1946

THE PROBLEM OF PALESTINE

1. The whole Arab people is unalterably opposed to the attempt to impose Jewish immigration and settlement upon it, and ultimately to establish a Jewish State in Palestine. Its opposition is based primarily upon right. The Arabs of Palestine are descendants of the indigenous inhabitants of the country, who have been in occupation of it since the beginning of history; they cannot agree that it is right to subject an indigenous population against its will to alien immigrants, whose claim is based upon a historical connection which ceased effectively many centuries ago. Moreover they form the majority of the population; as such they cannot submit to a policy of immigration which if pursued for long will turn them from a majority into a minority in an alien state; and they claim the democratic right of a majority to make its own decisions in matters of urgent national concern. . . .

2. In addition to the question of right, the Arabs oppose the claims of political Zionism because of the effects which Zionist settlement has already had upon their situation and is likely to have to an even greater extent in the future. Negatively, it has diverted the whole course of their national development. Geographically Palestine is part of Syria; its indigenous inhabitants belong to the Syrian branch of the Arab family of nations; all their culture and tradition link them to the other Arab peoples; and until 1917 Palestine formed part of the Ottoman Empire which included also several of the other Arab countries. The presence and claims of the Zionists, and the support given them by certain Western Powers have resulted in Palestine being cut off from the other Arab countries and subjected to a regime, administrative, legal, fiscal and educational, different from that of the sister-countries. Quite apart from the inconvenience to individuals and the dislocation of trade which this separation has caused, it has prevented Palestine participating fully in the general development of the Arab world.

First, while the other Arab countries have attained or are near to the attainment of self-government and full membership of the U.N.O., Palestine is still under Mandate and has taken no step towards self-government; not only are there no representative institutions, but no Palestinian can rise to the higher ranks of the administration. This is inacceptable on grounds of principle, and also because of its evil consequence. It is a hardship to individual Palestinians whose opportunities of responsibility are thus curtailed; and it is demoralizing to the population to live under a government which has no basis in their consent and to which they can feel no attachment or loyalty.

Secondly, while the other Arab countries are working through the Arab League to strengthen their ties and coordinate their policies, Palestine (although her Arab inhabitants are formally represented in the League's Council) cannot participate fully in this movement so long as she has no indigenous government; thus the chasm between the administrative system and the institutions of Palestine and those of the neighbouring countries is growing, and her traditional Arab character is being weakened.

Thirdly, while the other Arab countries have succeeded in or are on the way to achieving a satisfactory definition of their relations with the Western Powers and with the world-community, expressed in their treaties with Great Britain and other Powers and their membership of the United Nations Organization, Palestine has not yet been able to establish any definite status for herself in the world, and her international destiny is still obscure.

3. All these evils are due entirely to the presence of the Zionists and the support given to them by certain of the Powers; there is no doubt that had it not been for that, Arab Palestine would by now be a self-governing member of the U.N.O. and the Arab League. Moreover, in addition to the

obstacles which Zionism has thus placed in the way of Palestine's development, the presence of the Zionists gives rise to various positive evils which will increase if Zionist immigration continues.

The entry of incessant waves of immigrants prevents normal economic and social development and causes constant dislocation of the country's life; in so far as it reacts upon prices and values and makes the whole economy dependent upon the constant inflow of capital from abroad it may even in certain circumstances lead to economic disaster. It is bound moreover to arouse continuous political unrest and prevent the establishment of that political stability on which the prosperity and health of the country depend. This unrest is likely to increase in frequency and violence as the Jews come nearer to being the majority and the Arabs a minority.

Even if economic and social equilibrium is re-established, it will be to the detriment of the Arabs. The superior capital resources at the disposal of the Jews, their greater experience of modern economic technique and the existence of a deliberate policy of expansion and domination have already gone far toward giving them the economic mastery of Palestine. The biggest concessionary companies are in their hands; they possess a large proportion of the total cultivable land, and an even larger one of the land in the highest category of fertility; and the land they possess is mostly inalienable to non-Jews. The continuance of land-purchase and immigration, taken together with the refusal of Jews to employ Arabs on their lands or in their enterprises and the great increase in the Arab population, will create a situation in which the Arab population is pushed to the margin of cultivation and a landless proletariat, rural and urban, comes into existence. This evil can be palliated but not cured by attempts at increasing the absorptive capacity or the industrial production of Palestine; the possibility of such improvements is limited, they would take a long time to carry out, and would scarcely do more than keep pace with the rapid growth of the Arab population; moreover in present circumstances they would be used primarily for the benefit of the Jews and thus might increase the disparity between the two communities.

Nor is the evil economic only. Zionism is essentially a political movement, aiming at the creation of a state: immigration, land-purchase and economic expansion are only aspects of a general political strategy. If Zionism succeeds in its aim, the Arabs will become a minority in their own country; a minority which can hope for no more than a minor share in the government, for the state is to be a Jewish state, and which will find itself not only deprived of that international status which the other Arab countries possess but cut off from living contact with the Arab world of which it is an integral part.

It should not be forgotten too that Palestine contains places holy to Moslems and Christians, and neither Arab Moslems nor Arab Christians would willingly see such places subjected to the ultimate control of a Jewish Government.

4. These dangers would be serious enough at any time, but are particularly so in this age, when the first task of the awakening Arab nation is to come to terms with the West; to define its relationship with the Western Powers and with the westernized world community on a basis of equality and mutual respect, and to adapt what is best in Western civilization to the needs of its own genius. Zionist policy is one of the greatest obstacles to the achievement of this task: both because Zionism represents to the Arabs one side of the Western spirit and because of the support given to it by some of the Western Powers. In fact Zionism has become in Arab eyes a test of Western intentions towards them. So long as the attempt of the Zionists to impose a Jewish state upon the inhabitants of Palestine is supported by some or all of the Western Governments, so long will it be difficult if not impossible for the Arabs to establish a satisfactory relationship with the Western world and its civilization, and they will tend to turn away from the West in political hostility and spiritual isolation; this will be disastrous both for the Arabs themselves and for those Western nations which have dealings with them.

5. There are no benefits obtained or to be expected from Zionism commensurate with its evils and its dangers. The alleged social and economic benefits are much less than is claimed. The increase in the Arab population is not primarily due to Zionist immigration, and in any case would not necessarily be a sign of prosperity. The rise in money wages and earnings is largely illusory, being offset by the rise in the cost of living. In so far as real wages and the standard of living have risen, this is primarily an expression of a general trend common to all Middle Eastern countries. The inflow of capital has gone largely to raising money prices and real estate values. The whole economy is dangerously dependent upon the citrus industry. The benefits derived from the establishment of industries and the exploitation of the country's few natural resources have been largely neutralized by the failure of Jewish enterprises to employ Arabs.

The Zionist contention that their social organizations provide health and social services for the Arab population is exaggerated; only a minute proportion of the Arabs, for example, are looked after by Jewish health organizations. Even if true it would prove nothing except that the Government was neglecting its responsibilities in regard to the welfare of the population. Arab voluntary social organizations have grown up independently of Jewish bodies and without help from them. Even in so far as social and economic benefits have come to the Arabs from Zionist settlement, it remains true on the one hand that they are more than counterbalanced by the dangers of that settlement, and on the other that they are only incidental and are in no way necessary for the progress of the Arab people. The main stimulus to Arab economic and social progress does not come from the example or assistance of the Zionists but from the natural tendency of the whole Middle Eastern areas, from the work of the Government and above all from the newly awakened will to progress of the

Arabs themselves. The Arabs may have started later than the Jews on the road of modern social and economic organization, but they are now fully awake and are progressing fast. This is shown in the economic sphere for example by the continued development of the Arab citrus industry and financial organizations, in the social sphere by the growth of the labour movement and the new Land Development Scheme.

If any proof were needed of this, it could be found in the progress made during the last three decades by the neighbouring countries. None of the Arab countries is stagnant today: even without the example and capital of the Zionists, they are building up industries, improving methods and extending the scope of agriculture, establishing systems of public education and increasing the amenities of life. In some countries and spheres the progress has been greater than among the Arabs of Palestine, and in all of them it is healthier and more normal.

The Zionists claim further that they are acting as mediators of Western civilization to the Middle East. Even if their claim were true, the services they were rendering would be incidental only: the Arab world has been in direct touch with the West for a hundred years, and has its own reawakened cultural movement, and thus it has no need of a mediator. Moreover the claim is untrue: so long as Jewish cultural life in Palestine expresses itself through the medium of the Hebrew language, its influence on the surrounding world is bound to be negligible; in fact, Arab culture today is almost wholly uninfluenced by the Jews, and practically no Arabs take part in the work of Jewish cultural or educational institutions. In a deeper sense the presence of the Zionists is even an obstacle to the understanding of Western civilization, in so far as it more than any other factor is tending to induce in the Arabs an unsympathetic attitude towards the West and all its works.

6. Opposition to the policy of the Zionists is shared by all sections of the Palestinian Arab people. It is not confined to the townspeople but is universal among the rural population, who stand to suffer most from the gradual alienation of the most fertile land to the Jewish National Fund. It is felt not only by the landowners and middle class but by the working population, both for national reasons and for reasons of their own. It is not an invention of the educated class; if that class have seen the danger more clearly and sooner than others, and if they have assumed the leadership of the opposition, that is no more than their duty and function.

Moreover not only the Arab Moslem majority are opposed to Zionism but also and equally the Arab Christian minority who reject Zionism both because they share to the full in the national sentiments of other Arabs and because as Christians they cannot accept that their Holy Places should be subject to Jewish control, and cannot understand how any Christian nation could accept it.

7. The sentiments of the Palestinian Arabs are fully shared by the other

Arab countries, both by their Government and their peoples. Their support has shown itself in many ways: in Pan-Arab Conferences, in the moral and material support given by the whole Arab world to the revolt of 1936–39, in the diplomatic activities of Arab Governments, and most recently in the formation of the Arab League, which has taken the defense of Palestine as one of its main objectives. The members of the Arab League are now taking active measures to prevent the alienation of Arab lands to the Zionists and Jewish domination of the economic life of the Middle East. . . .

8. In the Arab view, any solution of the problem created by Zionist aspirations must satisfy certain conditions:

(i) It must recognize the right of the indigenous inhabitants of Palestine to continue in occupation of the country and to preserve its traditional character.

(ii) It must recognize that questions like immigration which affect the whole nature and destiny of the country, should be decided in accordance with democratic principles by the will of the population.

(iii) It must accept the principle that the only way by which the will of the population can be expressed is through the establishment of responsible representative government. (The Arabs find something inconsistent in the attitude of Zionists who demand the establishment of a free democratic commonwealth in Palestine and then hasten to add that this should not take place until the Jews are in a majority.)

(iv) This representative Government should be based upon the principle of absolute equality of all citizens irrespective of race and religion.

(v) The form of Government should be such as to make possible the development of a spirit of loyalty and cohesion among all elements of the community, which will override all sectional attachments. In other words it should be a Government which the whole community could regard as their own, which should be rooted in their consent and have a moral claim upon their obedience.

(vi) The settlement should recognize the fact that by geography and history Palestine is inescapably part of the Arab world; that the only alternative to its being part of the Arab world and accepting the implications of its position is complete isolation, which would be disastrous from every point of view; and that whether they like it or not the Jews in Palestine are dependent upon the goodwill of the Arabs.

(vii) The settlement should be such as to make possible a satisfactory definition within the framework of U.N.O. of the relations between Palestine and the Western Powers who possess interests in the country.

(viii) The settlement should take into account that Zionism is essentially a political movement aiming at the creation of a Jewish state and should therefore avoid making any concession which might encourage Zionists in the hope that this aim can be achieved in any circumstances.

9. In accordance with these principles, the Arabs urge the establishment in Palestine of a democratic government representative of all sections of the population on a level of absolute equality; the termination of the Mandate once the Government has been established; and the entry of Palestine into the United Nations Organization as a full member of the working community.

Pending the establishment of a representative Government, all further Jewish immigration should be stopped, in pursuance of the principle that a decision on so important a matter should only be taken with the consent of the inhabitants of the country and that until representative institutions are established there is no way of determining consent. Strict measures should also continue to be taken to check illegal immigration. Once a Palestinian state has come into existence, if any section of the population favours a policy of further immigration it will be able to press its case in accordance with normal democratic procedure; but in this as in other matters the minority must abide by the decision of the majority.

Similarly, all further transfer of land from Arabs to Jews should be prohibited prior to the creation of self-governing institutions. The Land Transfer Regulations should be made more stringent and extended to the whole area of the country, and severer measures be taken to prevent infringement of them. Here again once self-government exists matters concerning land will be decided in the normal democratic manner.

10. The Arabs are irrevocably opposed to political Zionism, but in no way hostile to the Jews as such nor to their Jewish fellow-citizens of Palestine. Those Jews who have already entered Palestine, and who have obtained or shall obtain Palestinian citizenship by due legal process will be full citizens of the Palestinian state, enjoying full civil and political rights and a fair share in government and administration. There is no question of their being thrust into the position of a "minority" in the bad sense of a closed community, which dwells apart from the main stream of the State's life and which exists by sufferance of the majority. They will be given the opportunity of belonging to and helping to mould the full community of the Palestinian state, joined to the Arabs by links of interest and goodwill, not the goodwill of the strong to the powerless, but of one citizen to another.

It is to be hoped that in course of time the exclusiveness of the Jews will be neutralized by the development of loyalty to the state and the emergence of new groupings which cut across communal divisions. This however will take time; and during the transitional period the Arabs recognize the need for giving special consideration to the peculiar position and the needs of the Jews. No attempt would be made to interfere with their communal organization, their personal status or their religious observances. Their schools and cultural institutions would be left to operate unchecked except for that general control which all governments exercise over education. In the districts in which they are most closely settled they would possess municipal autonomy and Hebrew would be an official language of administration, justice and education.

11. The Palestinian State would be an Arab state not (as should be clear from the preceding paragraph) in any narrow racial sense, nor in the sense that non-Arabs should be placed in a position of inferiority, but because the form and policy of its government would be based on a recognition of two facts: first that the majority of the citizens are Arabs, and secondly that Palestine is part of the Arab world and has no future except through close co-operation with the other Arab states. Thus among the main objects of the Government would be to preserve and enrich the country's Arab heritage, and to draw closer the relations between Palestine and the other Arab countries. The Cairo Pact of March, 1945, provided for the representation of Palestine on the Council of the Arab League even before its independence should be a reality; once it was really self-governing, it would participate fully in all the work of the League, in the cultural and economic no less than the political sphere. This would be of benefit to the Jewish no less than the Arab citizens of Palestine, since it would ensure those good relations with the Arab world without which their economic development would be impossible.

12. The state would apply as soon as possible for admission into U.N.O., and would of course be prepared to bear its full share of the burdens of establishing a world security-system. It would willingly place at the disposal of the Security Council whatever bases or other facilities were required, provided those bases were really used for the purpose for which they were intended and not in order to interfere in the internal affairs of the country, and provided also Palestine and the other Arab states were adequately represented on the controlling body.

The state would recognize also the world's interest in the maintenance of a satisfactory regime for the Moslem, Christian and Jewish Holy Places. In the Arab view however the need for such a regime does not involve foreign interference in or control of Palestine; no opportunity should be given to Great Powers to use the Holy Places as instruments of policy. The Holy Places can be most satisfactorily and appropriately guarded by a Government representative of the inhabitants, who include adherents of all three faiths and have every interest in preserving the holy character of their country.

Nor in the Arab view would any sort of foreign interference or control be justified by the need to protect the Christian minorities. The Christians are Arabs, who belong fully to the national community and share fully in its struggle. They would have all the rights and duties of citizens of a Palestinian state, and would continue to have their own communal organizations and institutions. They themselves would ask for no more, having learnt from the example of other Middle Eastern countries the dangers of an illusory foreign ''protection'' of minorities.

13. In economic and social matters the Government of Palestine would

follow a progressive policy with the aim of raising the standard of living and increasing the welfare of all sections of the population, and using the country's natural resources in the way most beneficial to all. Its first task naturally would be to improve the condition of the Arab peasants and thus to bridge the economic and social gulf which at present divides the two communities. Industry would be encouraged, but only in so far as its economic basis was sound and as part of a general policy of economic development for the whole Arab world; commercial and financial ties with the other Arab countries would so far as possible be strengthened, and tariffs decreased or abolished.

14. The Arabs believe that no other proposals would satisfy the conditions of a just and lasting settlement. In their view there are insuperable objections of principle or of practice to all other suggested solutions of the problem.

(1) The idea of partition and the establishment of a Jewish state in a part of Palestine is inadmissible for the same reasons of principle as the idea of establishing a Jewish state in the whole country. If it is unjust to the Arabs to impose a Jewish state on the whole of Palestine, it is equally unjust to impose it in any part of the country. Moreover, as the Woodhead Commission showed, there are grave practical difficulties in the way of partition; commerce would be strangled, communications dislocated and the public finances upset. It would also be impossible to devise frontiers which did not leave a large Arab minority in the Jewish state. This minority would not willingly accept its subjection to the Zionists, and it would not allow itself to be transferred to the Arab state. Moreover, partition would not satisfy the Zionists. It cannot be too often repeated that Zionism is a political movement aiming at the domination at least of the whole of Palestine; to give it a foothold in part of Palestine would be to encourage it to press for more and to provide it with a base for its activities. Because of this, because of the pressure of population and in order to escape from its isolation it would inevitably be thrown into enmity with the surrounding Arab states and this enmity would disturb the stability of the whole Middle East.

(2) Another proposal is for the establishment of a bi-national state, based upon political parity, in Palestine and its incorporation into a Syrian or Arab Federation. The Arabs would reject this as denying the majority its normal position and rights. There are also serious practical objections to the idea of a bi-national state, which cannot exist unless there is a strong sense of unity and common interest overriding the differences between the two parties. Moreover, the point made in regard to the previous suggestion may be repeated here: this scheme would in no way satisfy the Zionists, it would simply encourage them to hope for more and improve their chances of obtaining it. . . .

The Case for a Bi-national State*

THE ARAB CONTENTION

The Arabs say that "the existence of the Jewish National Home, whatever its size, bars the way to the attainment by the Arabs of Palestine of the same national status as that attained, or soon to be attained, by all the other Arabs of Asia" (Royal Commission, p. 307). That is so. And they ask if they are not as fit for self-government as the Arabs of other countries. They are.

ARAB CONCESSIONS

But the whole history of Palestine shows that it just has not been made for uni-national sovereign independence. This is an inescapable fact which no one can disregard. Although the Arabs cannot have a uni-national independent Arab Palestine, they can enjoy independence in a bi-national Palestine together with their Jewish fellow-citizens. This will afford them a maximum of national freedom. What the bi-national State will take away from them is sovereign independence in Palestine. There are other Arab States with sovereign independence. But we contend that the sovereign independence of tiny Palestine, whether it be Jewish sovereignty or Arab sovereignty, is a questionable good in this post-war period, when even great States must relinquish something of their sovereignty and seek union, if the world is not to perish. We contend that for this Holy Land the idea of a bi-national Palestine is at least as inspiring as that of an Arab sovereign Palestine or a Jewish sovereign Palestine.

JEWISH CONCESSIONS

On the other hand, the bi-national Palestine would deprive the Jews of their one chance of a Jewish State. But this bi-national Palestine would be the one State in the world where they would be a constituent nation, i.e. an equal nationality within the body politic, and not a minority as everywhere else. The absence of a Jewish State would make more difficult direct access by the Jewish people to U.N.O. To compensate for this, some form should be devised for giving the Jewish people a recognised place within the structure of the United Nations Organisation.

Nevertheless, the concessions the Jews would have to make on these matters are, we think, more far-reaching than the concessions the Arabs of Palestine would have to make. But the hard facts of the situation are that this is not a Jewish land and it is not an Arab land—it is the Holy Land, a bi-national country—and it is in the light of such hard facts that the problem must be approached.

* Reprinted from M. Buber and J. L. Magnes, *Arab-Jewish Unity*, London: Victor Gollancz Ltd., 1947.

THE ADVANTAGES OF A BI-NATIONAL PALESTINE

Before proceeding to outline our suggestions as to the political structure of the bi-national Palestine, we should like finally to point out some of the advantages of bi-nationalism based on parity in a country which has two nationalities.

Failure of Minority Guarantees

1. The breakdown of the minority guarantees provided for in the Versailles Peace treaties is proof that in a bi-national country the only safeguard for a minority is equality with the majority. There is no prospect of peace in a country where there is a dominant people and a subordinate people. The single nation-State is a proper form for a country where there is but one legally recognised nationality, as, for example, the United States. But in countries with more than one recognised nationality—and they are numerous in Europe and in Asia—bitterness is engendered among the minority because the civil service, the military, the economic key positions, foreign affairs, are in the hands of the ruling class of the majority nation. Parity in a multi-national country is the only just relationship between the peoples.

Switzerland

2. The multi-national state is an effective method of affording full protection for the national languages, cultures and institutions of each nationality. That there can be full cultural autonomy combined with full allegiance to the multi-national political state is proven in Switzerland's history for more than 100 years. The Swiss are divided by language, religion and culture; nor do the linguistic and religious groupings coincide in the various cantons. Yet all of these divergencies have not been obstacles to political unity. This is a newer form of democracy which is as important for multi-national states as the more familiar form of democracy is for uni-national states. The Swiss example is most relevant to Palestine, although there are, of course, many points of difference.

Other Multi-national Countries

The Soviet Union is a newer example of a multi-national State. The new Yugoslav State is an attempt at multi-national federalism. Professor Seton Watson outlines a bi-national solution of the age-long problem of Transylvania. Roumanian domination, Hungarian domination, partition had all been tried without success.

Bi-nationalism a High Ideal

3. In many senses the multi-national state represents a higher, more modern and more hopeful ideal than the uni-national sovereign independent State. The old way of having a major people and a minor people in a State of various nationalities is reactionary. The progressive conception is parity among the peoples of the multi-national State. The way of peace in the world to-day and tomorrow is through federation, union. Dividing up the world into tiny nationalistic sovereign units has not been the success the advocates of self-determination had hoped for at the end of the First World War. (Cobban, *National Self-Determination.*) The peoples who have been placed by fate or by history in the same country have warred with one another for domination throughout the centuries. The majority have tried to make the State homogeneous through keeping down the minority nationalities. The federal multi-national State, based on the parity of the nationalities, is a most hopeful way of enabling them to retain their national identity, and yet of coalescing in a larger political framework. It results in separate nationalities, yet a single citizenship. This is a noble goal to which the youth of multi-national countries can be taught to give their enthusiasm and their energies. It is a modern challenge to the intelligence and the moral qualities of the peoples constituting multi-national lands.

The United Nations Takes Over

British Foreign Secretary Ernest Bevin announced on February 14, 1947, that His Majesty's Government had decided to refer the Palestine problem to the United Nations. Tension inside Palestine had risen, illegal Jewish immigration continued, there was growing restiveness in the Arab countries: Palestine, Bevin said, could not be so divided as to create two viable states, since the Arabs would never agree to it, the Mandate could not be administered in its present form, and Britain was going to ask the United Nations how it could be amended.

The United Nations set up a U.N. Special Committee on Palestine (U.N.S.C.O.P.) composed of representatives of eleven member states. Its report and recommendations were published on August 31, 1947 (below). The Jewish Agency accepted the partition plan as the "indispensable minimum," the Arab governments and the Arab Higher Executive rejected it. On November 29, 1947, the U.N. General Assembly endorsed the partition plan by a vote of thirty-three to thirteen (see page 95). The two-thirds majority included the United States and the Soviet Union but not Britain.

Summary of the Report of U.N.S.C.O.P.
(U.N. Special Committee on Palestine)

August 31, 1947

(A) GENERAL RECOMMENDATIONS OF THE COMMITTEE

The eleven unanimously-adopted resolutions of the Committee were:

That the Mandate should be terminated and Palestine granted independence at the earliest practicable date (recommendations I and II);

That there should be a short transitional period preceding the granting of independence to Palestine during which the authority responsible for administering Palestine should be responsible to the United Nations (recommendations III and IV);

That the sacred character of the Holy Places and the rights of religious communities in Palestine should be preserved and stipulations concerning them inserted in the constitution of any state or states to be created and that a system should be found for settling impartially any disputes involving religious rights (recommendation V);

That the General Assembly should take steps to see that the problem of distressed European Jews should be dealt with as a matter of urgency so as to alleviate their plight and the Palestine problem (recommendation VI);

That the constitution of the new state or states should be fundamentally democratic and should contain guarantees for the respect of human rights and fundamental freedoms and for the protection of minorities (recommendation VII);

That the undertakings contained in the Charter whereby states are to settle their disputes by peaceful means and to refrain from the threat or use of force in international relations in any way inconsistent with the purposes of the United Nations should be incorporated in the constitutional provisions applying to Palestine (recommendation VIII);

That the economic unity of Palestine should be preserved (recommendation IX);

That states whose nationals had enjoyed in Palestine privileges and immunities of foreigners, including those formerly enjoyed by capitulation or usage in the Ottoman Empire, should be invited to renounce any rights pertaining to them (recommendation X);

That the General Assembly should appeal to the peoples of Palestine to cooperate with the United Nations in its efforts to settle the situation there and exert every effort to put an end to acts of violence (recommendation XI);

In addition to these eleven unanimously approved recommendations, the Special Committee, with two members (Uruguay and Guatemala) dissenting, and one member recording no opinion, also approved the following twelfth recommendation:

"*Recommendation XII. The Jewish Problem in General*

"It is recommended that

"In the appraisal of the Palestine question, it be accepted as incontrovertible that any solution for Palestine cannot be considered as a solution of the Jewish problem in general."

(B) MAJORITY PROPOSAL: PLAN OF PARTITION WITH ECONOMIC UNION

According to the plan of the majority (the representatives of Canada, Czechoslovakia, Guatemala, Netherlands, Peru, Sweden and Uruguay), Palestine was to be constituted into an Arab State, a Jewish State and the City of Jerusalem. The Arab and the Jewish States would become independent after a transitional period of two years beginning on September 1, 1947. Before their independence could be recognized, however, they must adopt a constitution in line with the pertinent recommendations of the Committee and make to the United Nations a declaration containing certain guarantees, and sign a treaty by which a system of economic collaboration would be established and the economic union of Palestine created.

The plan provided, *inter alia*, that during the transitional period, the United Kingdom would carry on the administration of Palestine under the auspices of the United Nations and on such conditions and under such supervision as the United Kingdom and the United Nations might agree upon. During this period a stated number of Jewish immigrants was to be admitted. Constituent Assemblies were to be elected by the populations of the areas which were to comprise the Arab and Jewish States, respectively, and were to draw up the constitutions of the States.

These constitutions were to provide for the establishment in each State of a legislative body elected by universal suffrage and by secret ballot on the basis of proportional representation and an executive body responsible to the legislature. They would also contain various guarantees, e.g., for the protection of the Holy Places and religious buildings and sites, and of religious and minority rights.

The Constituent Assembly in each State would appoint a provisional government empowered to make the declaration and sign the Treaty of Economic Union, after which the independence of the State would be recognized. The Declaration would contain provisions for the protection of the Holy Places and religious buildings and sites and for religious and minority rights. It would also contain provisions regarding citizenship.

A treaty would be entered into between the two States, which would contain provisions to establish the economic union of Palestine and to provide for other matters of common interest. A Joint Economic Board would be established consisting of representatives of the two States and members appointed by the Economic and Social Council of the United Nations to organize and administer the objectives of the Economic Union.

The City of Jerusalem would be placed, after the transitional period, under the International Trusteeship System by means of a Trusteeship Agreement, which would designate the United Nations as the Administering Authority. The plan contained recommended boundaries for the city and provisions concerning the governor and the police force.

The plan also proposed boundaries for both the Arab and Jewish States.

(c) Minority Proposal: Plan of a Federal State

Three U.N.S.C.O.P. members (the representatives of India, Iran and Yugoslavia) proposed an independent federal state. This plan provided, *inter alia*, that an independent federal state of Palestine would be created following a transitional period not exceeding three years, during which responsibility for administering Palestine and preparing it for independence would be entrusted to an authority to be decided by the General Assembly.

The independent federal state would comprise an Arab State and a Jewish State. Jerusalem would be its capital.

During the transitional period a Constituent Assembly would be elected by popular vote and convened by the administering authority on the basis of electoral provisions which would ensure the fullest representation of the population.

The Constituent Assembly would draw up the constitution of the federal state, which was to contain, *inter alia*, the following provisions:

The federal state would comprise a federal government and governments of the Arab and Jewish States, respectively.

Full authority would be vested in the federal government with regard to national defence, foreign relations, immigration, currency, taxation for federal purposes, foreign and inter-state waterways, transport and communications, copyrights and patents.

The Arab and Jewish States would enjoy full powers of local self-government and would have authority over education, taxation for local purposes, the right of residence, commercial licenses, land permits, grazing rights, inter-state migration, settlement, police, punishment of crime, social institutions and services, public housing, public health, local roads, agriculture and local industries.

The organs of government would include a head of state, an executive body, a representative federal legislative body composed of two chambers, and a federal court. The executive would be responsible to the legislative body.

Election to one chamber of the federal legislative body would be on the basis of proportional representation of the population as a whole, and to the other on the basis of equal representation of the Arab and Jewish citizens of Palestine. Legislation would be enacted when approved by majority votes in both chambers; in the event of disagreement between the two chambers, the issue would be submitted to an arbitral body of five members including not less than two Arabs and two Jews.

The federal court would be the final court of appeal regarding constitutional matters. Its members who would include not less than four Arabs and three Jews, would be elected by both chambers of the federal legislative body.

The constitution was to guarantee equal rights for all minorities and fundamental human rights and freedoms. It would guarantee, *inter alia*, free access to the Holy Places and protect religious interests.

The constitution would provide for an undertaking to settle international disputes by peaceful means.

There would be a single Palestinian nationality and citizenship.

The constitution would provide for equitable participation of representatives of both communities in delegations to international conferences.

A permanent international body was to be set up for the supervision and protection of the Holy Places, to be composed of three representatives designated by the United Nations and one representative of each of the recognized faiths having an interest in the matter, as might be determined by the United Nations.

For a period of three years from the beginning of the transitional period Jewish immigration would be permitted into the Jewish State in such numbers as not to exceed its absorptive capacity, and having due regard for the rights of the existing population within that State and their anticipated natural rate of increase. An international commission, composed of three Arab, three Jewish and three United Nations representatives, would be appointed to estimate the absorptive capacity of the Jewish State. The commission would cease to exist at the end of the three-year period mentioned above.

The minority plan also laid down the boundaries of the proposed Arab and Jewish areas of the federal state.

U.N. General Assembly Resolution on the Future Government of Palestine (Partition Resolution)

November 29, 1947

The General Assembly,

Having met in special session at the request of the mandatory Power to constitute and instruct a special committee to prepare for the consideration of the question of the future government of Palestine at the second regular session;

Having constituted a Special Committee and instructed it to investigate all questions and issues relevant to the problem of Palestine, and to prepare proposals for the solution of the problem, and

Having received and examined the report of the Special Committee (document A/364) including a number of unanimous recommendations and a plan of partition with economic union approved by the majority of the Special Committee,

Considers that the present situation in Palestine is one which is likely to impair the general welfare and friendly relations among nations;

Takes note of the declaration by the mandatory Power that it plans to complete its evacuation of Palestine by 1 August 1948;

Recommends to the United Kingdom, as the mandatory Power for Palestine, and to all other Members of the United Nations the adoption and implementation, with regard to the future government of Palestine, of the Plan of Partition with Economic Union set out below;

Requests that

(a) The Security Council take the necessary measures as provided for in the plan for its implementation;

(b) The Security Council consider, if circumstances during the transitional period require such consideration, whether the situation in Palestine constitutes a threat to the peace. If it decides that such a threat exists, and in order to maintain international peace and security, the Security Council should supplement the authorization of the General Assembly by taking measures, under Articles 39 and 41 of the Charter, to empower the United Nations Commission, as provided in this resolution, to exercise in Palestine the functions which are assigned to it by this resolution;

(c) The Security Council determine as a threat to the peace, breach of the peace or act of aggression, in accordance with Article 39 of the Charter, any attempt to alter by force the settlement envisaged by this resolution;

(d) The Trusteeship Council be informed of the responsibilities envisaged for it in this plan;

Calls upon the inhabitants of Palestine to take such steps as may be necessary on their part to put this plan into effect;

Appeals to all Governments and all peoples to refrain from taking any action which might hamper or delay the carrying out of these recommendations, and

Authorizes the Secretary-General to reimburse travel and subsistence expenses of the members of the commission referred to in Part I, Section B, paragraph 1 below, on such basis and in such form as he may determine most appropriate in the circumstances, and to provide the Commission with the necessary staff to assist in carrying out the functions assigned to the Commission by the General Assembly.

*Plan of Partition with Economic Union
Part I—Future Constitution and
Government of Palestine*

A. TERMINATION OF MANDATE PARTITION AND INDEPENDENCE

1. The Mandate for Palestine shall terminate as soon as possible but in any case not later than 1 August 1948.

2. The armed forces of the mandatory Power shall be progressively withdrawn from Palestine, the withdrawal to be completed as soon as possible but in any case not later than 1 August 1948.

The mandatory Power shall advise the Commission, as far in advance as possible, of its intention to terminate the Mandate and to evacuate each area.

The mandatory Power shall use its best endeavours to ensure that an area situated in the territory of the Jewish State, including a seaport and hinterland adequate to provide facilities for a substantial immigration, shall be evacuated at the earliest possible date and in any event not later than 1 February 1948.

3. Independent Arab and Jewish States and the Special International Regime for the City of Jerusalem, set forth in part III of this plan, shall come into existence in Palestine two months after the evacuation of the armed forces of the mandatory Power has been completed but in any case not later than 1 October 1948. The boundaries of the Arab State, the Jewish State, and the City of Jerusalem shall be described in parts II and III below.

4. The period between the adoption by the General Assembly of its recommendation on the question of Palestine and the establishment of the independence of the Arab and Jewish States shall be a transitional period.

B. STEPS PREPARATORY TO INDEPENDENCE

1. A Commission shall be set up consisting of one representative of each of five Member States. The Members represented on the Commission shall be elected by the General Assembly on as broad a basis, geographically and otherwise, as possible.

2. The administration of Palestine shall, as the mandatory Power withdraws its armed forces, be progressively turned over to the Commission, which shall act in conformity with the recommendations of the General Assembly, under the guidance of the Security Council. The mandatory Power shall to the fullest possible extent co-ordinate its plans for withdrawal with the plans of the Commission to take over and administer areas which have been evacuated.

In the discharge of this administrative responsibility the Commission shall have authority to issue necessary regulations and take other measures as required.

The mandatory Power shall not take any action to prevent, obstruct or delay the implementation by the Commission of the measures recommended by the General Assembly.

3. On its arrival in Palestine the Commission shall proceed to carry out measures for the establishment of the frontiers of the Arab and Jewish States and the City of Jerusalem in accordance with the general lines of the recommendations of the General Assembly on the partition of Palestine. Nevertheless, the boundaries as described in part II of this plan are to be modified in such a way that village areas as a rule will not be divided by state boundaries unless pressing reasons make that necessary.

4. The Commission, after consultation with the democratic parties and other public organizations of the Arab and Jewish States, shall select and establish in each State as rapidly as possible a Provisional Council of Government. The activities of both the Arab and Jewish Provisional Councils of Government shall be carried out under the general direction of the Commission.

If by 1 April 1948 a Provisional Council of Government cannot be selected for either of the States, or, if selected, cannot carry out its functions, the Commission shall communicate that fact to the Security Council for such action with respect to that State as the Security Council may deem proper, and to the Secretary-General for communication to the Members of the United Nations.

5. Subject to the provisions of these recommendations, during the transitional period the Provisional Councils of Government, acting under the Commission, shall have full authority in the areas under their control, including authority over matters of immigration and land regulation.

6. The Provisional Council of Government of each State, acting under the Commission, shall progressively receive from the Commission full responsibility for the administration of that State in the period between the termination of the Mandate and the establishment of the State's independence.

7. The Commission shall instruct the Provisional Councils of Government of both the Arab and Jewish States, after their formation, to proceed to the establishment of administrative organs of government, central and local.

8. The Provisional Council of Government of each State shall, within the shortest time possible, recruit an armed militia from the residents of that State, sufficient in number to maintain internal order and to prevent frontier clashes.

This armed militia in each State shall, for operational purposes, be under the command of Jewish or Arab officers resident in that State, but general political and military control, including the choice of the militia's High Command, shall be exercised by the Commission.

9. The Provisional Council of Government of each State shall, not later than two months after the withdrawal of the armed forces of the mandatory Power, hold elections to the Constituent Assembly which shall be conducted on democratic lines.

The election regulations in each State shall be drawn up by the Provisional Council of Government and approved by the Commission.

Qualified voters for each State for this election shall be persons over eighteen years of age who are: (*a*) Palestinian citizens residing in that State and (*b*) Arabs and Jews residing in the State, although not Palestinian citizens, who, before voting, have signed a notice of intention to become citizens of such State.

Arabs and Jews residing in the City of Jerusalem who have signed a notice of intention to become citizens, the Arabs of the Arab State and the Jews of the Jewish State, shall be entitled to vote in the Arab and Jewish States respectively.

Women may vote and be elected to the Constituent Assemblies.

During the transitional period no Jew shall be permitted to establish residence in the area of the proposed Arab State, and no Arab shall be permitted to establish residence in the area of the proposed Jewish State, except by special leave of the Commission.

10. The Constituent Assembly of each State shall draft a democratic constitution for its State and choose a provisional government to succeed the Provisional Council of Government appointed by the Commission. The constitutions of the States shall embody chapters 1 and 2 of the Declaration provided for in section C below and include *inter alia* provisions for:

(*a*) Establishing in each State a legislative body elected by universal suffrage and by secret ballot on the basis of proportional representation, and an executive body responsible to the legislature;

(*b*) Settling all international disputes in which the State may be involved by peaceful means in such a manner that international peace and security, and justice, are not endangered;

(*c*) Accepting the obligation of the State to refrain in its international relations from the threat or use of force against the territorial integrity or political independence of any State, or in any other manner inconsistent with the purposes of the United Nations;

(*d*) Guaranteeing to all persons equal and non-discriminatory rights in civil, political, economic and religious matters and the enjoyment of human rights and fundamental freedoms, including freedom of religion, language, speech and publication, education, assembly and association;

(*e*) Preserving freedom of transit and visit for all residents and citizens of the other State in Palestine and the City of Jerusalem, subject to considerations of national security, provided that each State shall control residence within its borders.

11. The Commission shall appoint a preparatory economic commission of three members to make whatever arrangements are possible for economic co-operation, with a view to establishing, as soon as practicable, the Economic Union and the Joint Economic Board, as provided in section D below.

12. During the period between the adoption of the recommendations on the question of Palestine by the General Assembly and the termination of the Mandate, the mandatory Power in Palestine shall maintain full responsibility for administration in areas from which it has not withdrawn its armed forces. The Commission shall assist the mandatory Power in the carrying out of these functions. Similarly the mandatory Power shall co-operate with the Commission in the execution of its functions.

13. With a view to ensuring that there shall be continuity in the functioning of administrative services and that, on the withdrawal of the armed forces of the mandatory Power, the whole administration shall be in charge of the Provisional Councils and the Joint Economic Board, respectively, acting under the Commission, there shall be a progressive transfer, from the mandatory Power to the Commission, of responsibility for all the functions of government, including that of maintaining law and order in the areas from which the forces of the mandatory Power have been withdrawn.

14. The Commission shall be guided in its activities by the recommendations of the General Assembly and by such instructions as the Security Council may consider necessary to issue.

The measures taken by the Commission, within the recommendations of the General Assembly, shall become immediately effective unless the Commission has previously received contrary instructions from the Security Council.

The Commission shall render periodic monthly progress reports, or more frequently if desirable, to the Security Council.

15. The Commission shall make its final report to the next regular session of the General Assembly and to the Security Council simultaneously.

C. DECLARATION

A declaration shall be made to the United Nations by the provisional government of each proposed State before independence. It shall contain *inter alia* the following clauses:

General Provision

The stipulations contained in the declaration are recognized as fundamental laws of the State and no law, regulation or official action shall conflict or interfere with these stipulations, nor shall any law, regulation or official action prevail over them.

Chapter 1.—Holy Places, Religious Buildings and Sites
1. Existing rights in respect of Holy Places and religious buildings or sites shall not be denied or impaired.

2. In so far as Holy Places are concerned, the liberty of access, visit and transit shall be guaranteed, in conformity with existing rights, to all residents and citizens of the other State and of the City of Jerusalem, as well as to aliens, without distinction as to nationality, subject to requirements of national security, public order and decorum.

Similarly, freedom of worship shall be guaranteed in conformity with existing rights, subject to the maintenance of public order and decorum.

3. Holy Places and religious buildings or sites shall be preserved. No act shall be permitted which may in any way impair their sacred character. If at any time it appears to the Government that any particular Holy Place, religious building or site is in need of urgent repair, the Government may call upon the community or communities concerned to carry out such repair. The Government may carry it out itself at the expense of the community or communities concerned if no action is taken within a reasonable time.

4. No taxation shall be levied in respect of any Holy Place, religious building or site which was exempt from taxation on the date of the creation of the State.

No change in the incidence of such taxation shall be made which would either discriminate between the owners or occupiers of Holy Places, religious buildings or sites, or would place such owners or occupiers in a position less favourable in relation to the general incidence of taxation than existed at the time of the adoption of the Assembly's recommendation.

5. The Governor of the City of Jerusalem shall have the right to determine whether the provisions of the Constitution of the State in relation to Holy Places, religious buildings and sites within the borders of the State and the religious rights appertaining thereto, are being properly applied and respected, and to make decisions on the basis of existing rights in cases of disputes which may arise between the different religious communities or the rites of a religious community with respect to such places, buildings and sites. He shall receive full cooperation and such privileges and immunities as are necessary for the exercise of his functions in the State.

Chapter 2.—Religious and Minority Rights
1. Freedom of conscience and the free exercise of all forms of worship, subject only to the maintenance of public order and morals, shall be ensured to all.

2. No discrimination of any kind shall be made between the inhabitants on the ground of race, religion, language or sex.

3. All persons within the jurisdiction of the State shall be entitled to equal protection of the laws.

4. The family law and personal status of the various minorities and their religious interests, including endowments, shall be respected.

5. Except as may be required for the maintenance of public order and good government, no measure shall be taken to obstruct or interfere with the enterprise of religious or charitable bodies of all faiths or to discriminate against any representative or member of these bodies on the ground of his religion or nationality.

6. The State shall ensure adequate primary and secondary education for the Arab and Jewish minority, respectively, in its own language and its cultural traditions.

The right of each community to maintain its own schools for the education of its own members in its own language, while conforming to such educational requirements of a general nature as the State may impose, shall not be denied or impaired. Foreign educational establishments shall continue their activity on the basis of their existing rights.

7. No restriction shall be imposed on the free use by any citizen of the State of any language in private intercourse, in commerce, in religion, in the Press or in publications of any kind, or at public meetings.[1]

8. No expropriation of land owned by an Arab in the Jewish State (by a Jew in the Arab State)[2] shall be allowed except for public purposes. In all cases of expropriation full compensation as fixed by the Supreme Court shall be paid previous to dispossession.

Chapter 3.—Citizenship, International Conventions and Financial Obligations

1. *Citizenship.* Palestinian citizens residing in Palestine outside the City of Jerusalem, as well as Arabs and Jews who, not holding Palestinian citizenship, reside in Palestine outside the City of Jerusalem shall, upon the recognition of independence, become citizens of the State in which they are resident and enjoy full civil and political rights. Persons over the age of eighteen years may opt, within one year from the date of recognition of independence of the State in which they reside, for citizenship of the other State, providing that no Arab residing in the area of the proposed Arab State shall have the right to opt for citizenship in the proposed Jewish State and no Jews residing in the proposed Jewish State

[1] The following stipulation shall be added to the declaration concerning the Jewish State: "In the Jewish State adequate facilities shall be given to Arabic-speaking citizens for the use of their language, either orally or in writing, in the legislature, before the Courts and in the administration."

[2] In the declaration concerning the Arab State, the words "by an Arab in the Jewish State" should be replaced by the words "by a Jew in the Arab State."

shall have the right to opt for citizenship in the proposed Arab State. The exercise of this right of option will be taken to include the wives and children under eighteen years of age of persons so opting.

Arabs residing in the area of the proposed Jewish State and Jews residing in the area of the proposed Arab State who have signed a notice of intention to opt for citizenship of the other State shall be eligible to vote in the elections to the Constituent Assembly of that State, but not in the elections to the Constituent Assembly of the State in which they reside.

2. *International conventions.* (*a*) The State shall be bound by all the international agreements and conventions, both general and special, to which Palestine has become a party. Subject to any right of denunciation provided for therein, such agreements and conventions shall be respected by the State throughout the period for which they were concluded.

(*b*) Any dispute about the applicability and continued validity of international conventions or treaties signed or adhered to by the mandatory Power on behalf of Palestine shall be referred to the International Court of Justice in accordance with the provisions of the Statute of the Court.

3. *Financial obligations.* (*a*) The State shall respect and fulfil all financial obligations of whatever nature assumed on behalf of Palestine by the mandatory Power during the exercise of the Mandate and recognized by the State. This provision includes the right of public servants to pensions, compensation or gratuities.

(*b*) These obligations shall be fulfilled through participation in the Joint Economic Board in respect of those obligations applicable to Palestine as a whole, and individually in respect of those applicable to, and fairly apportionable between, the States.

(*c*) A Court of Claims, affiliated with the Joint Economic Board, and composed of one member appointed by the United Nations, one representative of the United Kingdom and one representative of the State concerned, should be established. Any dispute between the United Kingdom and the States respecting claims not recognized by the latter should be referred to that Court.

(*d*) Commercial concessions granted in respect of any part of Palestine prior to the adoption of the resolution by the General Assembly shall continue to be valid according to their terms, unless modified by agreement between the concession-holder and the State.

[Section D has been deleted: "Economic Union and Transit." Part II of the Resolution deals with the borders of the new State; Part III with "Capitulations." Ed.]

Part III

Israel and the Arab World 1948–1967

Part III of the Reader extends from the establishment of the State of Israel in May, 1948 to the aftermath of the third Arab–Israeli war in 1967. The United Nations resolution about the partition of Palestine was bitterly resented by the Palestinian Arabs and their supporters in the neighboring countries who tried to prevent with the force of arms the establishment of a Zionist state by the "Jewish usurpers." This attempt failed and Israel, as a result, seized areas beyond those defined in the U.N. resolution. The armistice of 1949 did not restore peace; an Arab refugee problem came into being, guerrilla attacks, Israel retaliation and Arab blockage of the Suez Canal and the Gulf of Aqaba led to the second and third Arab–Israeli Wars.

State of Israel Proclamation of Independence

The Proclamation of Independence was published by the Provisional State Council in Tel Aviv on May 14, 1948. The Provisional State Council was the forerunner of the Knesset, the Israeli parliament. The British Mandate was terminated the following day and regular armed forces of Transjordan, Egypt, Syria and other Arab countries entered Palestine.

The Land of Israel was the birthplace of the Jewish people. Here their spiritual, religious and national identity was formed. Here they achieved independence and created a culture of national and universal significance. Here they wrote and gave the Bible to the world.

Exiled from the Land of Israel the Jewish people remained faithful to it in all the countries of their dispersion, never ceasing to pray and hope for their return and the restoration of their national freedom.

Impelled by this historic association, Jews strove throughout the centuries to go back to the land of their fathers and regain their statehood. In recent decades they returned in their masses. They reclaimed the wilderness, revived their language, built cities and villages, and established a vigorous and ever-growing community, with its own economic and cultural life. They sought peace, yet were prepared to defend themselves. They brought the blessings of progress to all inhabitants of the country and looked forward to sovereign independence.

In the year 1897 the First Zionist Congress, inspired by Theodor Herzl's vision of the Jewish State, proclaimed the right of the Jewish people to national revival in their own country.

This right was acknowledged by the Balfour Declaration of November 2, 1917, and re-affirmed by the Mandate of the League of Nations, which gave explicit international recognition to the historic connection of the Jewish people with Palestine and their right to reconstitute their National Home.

The recent holocaust, which engulfed millions of Jews in Europe, proved anew the need to solve the problem of the homelessness and lack of independence of the Jewish people by means of the re-establishment of the Jewish State, which would open the gates to all Jews and endow the Jewish people with equality of status among the family of nations.

The survivors of the disastrous slaughter in Europe, and also Jews from other lands, have not desisted from their efforts to reach Eretz-Yisrael, in face of difficulties, obstacles and perils; and have not ceased to urge their right to a life of dignity, freedom and honest toil in their ancestral land.

In the second World War the Jewish people in Palestine made their full contribution to the struggle of the freedom-loving nations against the Nazi evil. The sacrifices of their soldiers and their war effort gained them the right to rank with the nations which founded the United Nations.

On November 29, 1947, the General Assembly of the United Nations adopted a Resolution requiring the establishment of a Jewish State in Palestine. The General Assembly called upon the inhabitants of the country to take all the necessary steps on their part to put the plan into effect. This recognition by the United Nations of the right of the Jewish people to establish their independent State is unassailable.

It is the natural right of the Jewish people to lead, as do all other nations, an independent existence in its sovereign State.

ACCORDINGLY WE, the members of the National Council, representing the Jewish people in Palestine and the World Zionist Movement, are met together in solemn assembly today, the day of termination of the British Mandate for Palestine; and by virtue of the natural and historic right of the Jewish people and of the Resolution of the General Assembly of the United Nations.

WE HEREBY PROCLAIM the establishment of the Jewish State in Palestine, to be called Medinath Yisrael (The State of Israel).

WE HEREBY DECLARE that, as from the termination of the Mandate at midnight, the 14th–15th May, 1948, and pending the setting up of the duly elected bodies of the State in accordance with a Constitution, to be drawn up by the Constituent Assembly not later than the 1st October, 1948, the National Council shall act as the Provisional State Council, and that the National Administration shall constitute the Provisional Government of the Jewish State, which shall be known as Israel.

THE STATE OF ISRAEL will be open to the immigration of Jews from all countries of their dispersion; will promote the development of the country for the benefit of all its inhabitants; will be based on the principles of liberty, justice and peace as conceived by the Prophets of Israel; will uphold the full social and political equality of all its citizens, without distinction of religion, race, or sex; will guarantee freedom of religion, conscience, education and culture; will safeguard the Holy Places of all religions; and will loyally uphold the principles of the United Nations Charter.

THE STATE OF ISRAEL will be ready to co-operate with the organs and representatives of the United Nations in the implementation of the Resolution of the Assembly of November 29, 1947, and will take steps to bring about the Economic Union over the whole of Palestine.

We appeal to the United Nations to assist the Jewish people in the building of its State and to admit Israel into the family of nations.

In the midst of wanton aggression, we yet call upon the Arab inhabitants of the State of Israel to preserve the ways of peace and play their part in the development of the State, on the basis of full and equal citizenship and due representation in all its bodies and institutions—provisional and permanent.

We extend our hand in peace and neighbourliness to all the neighbouring states and their peoples, and invite them to co-operate with the independent Jewish nation for the common good of all. The State of Israel is prepared to make its contribution to the progress of the Middle East as a whole.

Our call goes out to the Jewish people all over the world to rally to our side in the task of immigration and development, and to stand by us in the great struggle for the fulfilment of the dream of generations for the redemption of Israel.

With trust in the Rock of Israel, we set our hand to this Declaration, at this Session of the Provisional State Council, on the soil of the Homeland, in the city of Tel-Aviv, on this Sabbath eve, the fifth of Iyar, 5708, the fourteenth of May, 1948.

The Law of Return

The "Law of Return" was passed unanimously by the Knesset on July 5, 1950 and written into the State Legislation.

The Law of Return states:

1. Every Jew has the right to immigrate to the country.
2. (*a*) Immigration shall be on the basis of immigration visas.
   (*b*) Immigrant visas shall be issued to any Jew expressing a desire to settle in Israel, except if the Minister of Immigration is satisfied that the applicant:
   (i) acts against the Jewish nation; or
   (ii) may threaten the public health or State security.
3. (*a*) A Jew who comes to Israel and after his arrival expresses a desire to settle there may, while in Israel, obtain an immigrant certificate.
   (*b*) The exceptions listed in Article 2 (*b*) shall apply also with respect to the issue of an immigrant certificate, but a person

shall not be regarded as a threat to public health as a result of an illness that he contracts after his arrival in Israel.

4. Every Jew who migrated to the country before this law goes into effect, and every Jew who was born in the country either before or after the law is effective enjoys the same status as any person who migrated on the basis of this law.

5. The Minister of Immigration is delegated to enforce this law and he may enact regulations in connection with its implementation and for the issue of immigrant visas and immigrant certificates.

The Manifesto of the United Arab Republic (Preamble)

The manifesto concerning the principles to govern the new Federal State of the United Arab Republic was published in April 1963. It was prepared in connection with an abortive attempt to establish federal union in the Arab world. Signed by Gamal Abdel Nasser and the presidents of Iraq and Syria, it is of interest mainly in view of the reference to Palestine.

In the name of the Merciful Compassionate God,
In the name of the Almighty God,
The three delegations representing the United Arab Republic, Syria and Iraq met in Cairo and in response to the will of the Arab people in the three regions and the great Arab fatherland, brotherly talks began between the three delegations on Saturday, April 6, and ended on Wednesday, April 17, 1963.

The delegations in all their discussions were inspired by faith that Arab unity was an inevitable aim deriving its principles from the oneness of language bearing culture and thought, common history-making sentiment and conscience, common national struggle deciding and defining destiny, common spiritual values stemming from Divine messages and common social and economic understanding based on liberty and socialism.

The delegations were guided by the will of the masses of the Arab peoples, demanding unity, struggling to attain it and sacrificing in its defence, and realising that the hard core of the union is to be formed by the unification of the parts of the homeland which have acquired their freedom and independence and in which nationalist, progressive governments have emerged with the determination to destroy the alliance of feudalism, capital, reaction and imperialism, and to liberate the working forces of the people in order to join them in alliance and to express their genuine will.

The revolution of July 23 was a historical turning point at which the

Arab people in Egypt, discovering their identity and regaining their free will, set out on their quest for freedom, Arabism and union. The revolution of the 14th of Ramadan (February 8) illuminated the true Arab face of Iraq, and the path leading it to the horizons of unity, envisaged by the zealous elements of the July 14 revolution. The revolution of March 8 put Syria back into the line of the union destroyed by the setback of reactionary secession, having destroyed all the obstacles which the reactionaries and imperialism had determinedly put up in the path of union.

The three Revolutions thus met which affirmed again that unity is a revolutionary action deriving its conceptions from the people's faith, its power from their will, and its objectives from their aspirations for freedom and socialism.

Unity is a revolution—a revolution because it is popular, a revolution because it is progressive, and a revolution because it is a powerful tide in the current of civilisation.

Unity is especially a revolution because it is profoundly connected with the Palestine cause and with the national duty to liberate that country. It was the disaster of Palestine that revealed the conspiracy of the reactionary classes and exposed the treacheries of the hired regional parties and their denial of the people's objectives and aspirations. It was the disaster of Palestine that showed the weakness and backwardness of the economic and social systems that prevailed in the country, released the revolutionary energies of our people and awakened the spirit of revolt against imperialism, injustice, poverty and underdevelopment. It was the disaster of Palestine that clearly indicated the path of salvation, the path of unity, freedom and socialism. This was kept in mind by the delegations during their talks. If unity is a sacred objective, it is also the instrument of the popular struggle and its means to achieve its major objectives of freedom and security in liberating all the parts of the Arab homeland and in establishing a society of sufficiency and justice, a society of socialism, in continuing the revolutionary tide without deviation or relapse and its extension to embrace the greater Arab homeland, and in contributing to the progress of human civilisation and consolidation of world peace.

It was unanimously agreed that unity between the three regions would be based, as required by the Arab people, on the principles of democracy and socialism, would be a real and strong unity which would consider the regional circumstances to consolidate the ties of unity on a basis of practical understanding, not ignore the reasons for partitioning and separation, and make the power of each region a power for the Federal State of the Arab Nation, and make the Federal State a power for each of its regions as well as for the whole Arab Nation.

The Draft Constitution of the "Palestine Liberation Organisation"

The charter of the Palestine Liberation Organisation (PLO) was prepared under Egyptian auspices following an agreement at the Arab Summit Conference in 1963 by Ahmed Shukairy, a lawyer born in Palestine who represented Saudi Arabia and later Syria in the U.N. and ultimately became President of the PLO. The role of the PLO on the eve of the Arab-Israeli war was later criticized in the Arab capitals and Shukairy forced to resign in December 1967.

1. In accordance with this constitution, an organisation known as "The Palestine Liberation Organisation" shall be formed, and shall launch its responsibilities in accordance with the principles of the National Charter and clauses of this constitution.

2. All the Palestinians are natural members in the Liberation Organisation exercising their duty in the liberation of their homeland in accordance with their abilities and efficiency.

3. The Palestinian people shall form the larger base for this Organisation; and the Organisation, after its creation, shall work closely and constantly with the Palestine people for the sake of their organisation and mobilisation so they may be able to assume their responsibility in the liberation of their country.

4. Until suitable conditions are available for holding free general elections among all the Palestinians and in all the countries in which they reside, the Liberation Organisation shall be set up in accordance with the rules set in this constitution.

5. Measures listed in this constitution shall be taken for the convocation of a Palestinian General Assembly in which shall be represented all Palestinian factions, emigrants and residents, including organisations, societies, unions, trade unions and representatives of (Palestinian) public opinions of various ideological trends; this assembly shall be called The National Assembly of the Palestine Liberation Organisation.

6. In preparation and facilitation of work of the assembly, the Palestinian representative at the Arab League (i.e., Ahmed Shukairy), shall, after holding consultations with various Palestinian factions, form:

a)—A Preparatory Committee in every Arab country hosting a minimum of 10,000 Palestinians; the mission of each one of these committees is to prepare lists according to which Palestinian candidates in the respective Arab country will be chosen as members of the assembly; these committees shall also prepare studies and proposals which may help the assembly carry out its work; these studies and proposals shall be presented to the Coordination Committee listed below.

b)—A Coordination Committee, with headquarters in Jerusalem; the mission of this committee shall be to issue invitations to the assembly, adopt all necessary measures for the holding of the assembly, and coordinate all proposals and studies as well as lists of candidates to the assembly, as specified in the clause above; also the committee shall prepare a provisional agenda—or as a whole, undertake all that is required for the holding and success of the assembly in the execution of its mission.

7. The National Assembly shall be held once every two years; its venue rotates between Jerusalem and Gaza; the National Assembly shall meet for the first time on May 14, 1964, in the city of Jerusalem.

8. To facilitate its work, the Assembly shall form the following committees:

a)—The Political Committee: shall be in charge of studying the political sides of the Palestine question in the Arab and international fields.

b)—The Charter By-laws and Lists Committee: shall consider the National Charter as well as the various by-laws and lists required by the Organisation in the execution of its duties.

c)—The Financial Committee: shall formulate a complete plan for the National Palestinian Fund required for financing the Organisation.

d)—Information Committee: shall work out a complete scheme for information and offices to be established in various parts of the world.

e)—The Juridical Committee: shall study the various legal aspects of the Palestine question, be it in relation to principles of International Law, U.N. Charter, or international documents pertaining to the Palestine question.

f)—Proposals and Nomination Committee: shall coordinate proposals and nominations submitted to the Assembly.

g)—Awakening Committee: shall study ways and means for the upbringing of the new generations both ideologically and spiritually so they may serve their country and work for the liberation of their homeland.

h)—The National Organisation Committee: shall lay down general plans pertaining to trade unions, federations, sports organisations and scouts groups; this is in accordance with rules and laws in effect in Arab countries.

9. The National Assembly shall have a Presidency Office composed of the president, two vice presidents, a secretary, and a secretary general; these officers shall be elected by the National Assembly when it meets.

10. These (above-listed eight committees) shall submit their reports and recommendations to the National Assembly which, in turn, shall discuss them and issue the necessary resolutions.

11. The National Assembly shall have an executive apparatus to be called 'The Executive Committee of the Liberation Organisation' which

shall practice all responsibilities of the Liberation Organisation in accordance with the general plans and resolutions issued by the National Assembly.

12. The Executive Committee shall be formed of fifteen members elected by the National Assembly; the Committee shall in its turn elect a President, two Vice Presidents and a Secretary General.

13. The Executive Committee can be called to a meeting in the time and place decided by the President, or by a proposal submitted by five members of the Committee.

14. The President of the Executive Committee shall represent the Palestinians at the Arab League; therefore, his office shall be in Cairo since the Arab League Headquarters is there.

15. The Executive Committee shall establish the following departments:

a)—Department of Political and Information Affairs.

b)—Department of the National Fund.

c)—Department of General Affairs.

Each one of these departments shall have a Director General and the needed number of employees. Duties of each one of these departments shall be defined by special by-laws prepared by the Executive Committee.

16. The Executive Committee has the right of calling the National Assembly to meet in a place and time it specifies; it has the right also to call to a meeting any committee of the National Assembly to study certain subjects.

17. The Executive Committee shall have a consultative council to be known as 'The Shura (Consultative) Council'; the Executive Committee shall select the president and members of this council from people of opinion and prestige among the Palestinians; prerogatives of the Consultative Council are in matters proposed to it by the Executive Committee.

18. The Arab states shall avail the sons of Palestine the opportunity of enlisting in their regular armies on the widest scale possible.

19. Private Palestinian contingents shall be formed in accordance with the military needs and plans decided by the Unified Arab Military Command in agreement and cooperation with the concerned Arab states.

20. A Fund, to be known as 'The National Palestinian Fund', shall be established to finance operations of the Executive Committee: the Fund shall have a Board of Directors whose members shall be elected by the National Assembly.

21. Sources of the Fund are to be from:

a)—Fixed taxes levied on Palestinians and collected in accordance with special laws.

b)—Financial assistance offered by the Arab governments and people.

c)—A 'Liberation Stamp' to be issued by the Arab states and be used in postal and other transactions.

d)—Donations on national occasions.

e)—Loans and assistance given by the Arabs or by friendly nations.

22. Committees, to be known as 'Support Palestine Committees', shall be established in Arab and friendly countries to collect donations and to support the Liberation Organisation.

23. The Executive Committee shall have the right to issue by-laws for fulfillment of provisions of this constitution.

24. This draft constitution shall be submitted to the National Assembly for consideration; what is ratified of it cannot be changed except by a two-thirds majority of the National Assembly.

United Nations General Assembly Resolution on the Internationalization of Jerusalem

This U.N. Resolution (No. 303[IV]) and the following one—Resolution 619[VII])—are among those most frequently quoted in the discussions about the Arab-Israeli conflict.

December 9, 1949

The General Assembly,

Having regard to its resolution 181 (II) of 29 November 1947 and 194 (III) of 11 December 1948,

Having studied the reports of the United Nations Conciliation Commission for Palestine set up under the latter resolution,

I. Decides

In relation to Jerusalem,

Believing that the principles underlying its previous resolutions concerning this matter, and in particular its resolution of 29 November 1947, represent a just and equitable settlement of the question,

1. To restate, therefore, its intention that Jerusalem should be placed under a permanent international regime, which should envisage appropriate guarantees for the protection of the Holy Places, both within and outside Jerusalem and to confirm specifically the following provisions of General Assembly resolution 181 (II):

(1) The City of Jerusalem shall be established as a *corpus separatum* under a special international régime and shall be administered by the United Nations; (2) The Trusteeship Council shall be designated to discharge the responsibilities of the Administering Authority . . . ; and (3) The City of Jerusalem shall include the present municipality of Jerusalem plus the surrounding villages and towns, the most eastern of which shall be Abu Dis; the most southern, Bethlehem; the most western, Ein Karim (including also the built-up area of Motsa); and the most northern, Shu'fat, as indicated on the attached sketch-map; (*map not reproduced: Ed.*)

2. To request for this purpose that the Trusteeship Council at its next session, whether special or regular, complete the preparation of the Statute of Jerusalem, omitting the now inapplicable provisions, such as articles 32 and 39, and, without prejudice to the fundamental principles of the international régime for Jerusalem set forth in General Assembly resolution 181 (II) introducing therein amendments in the direction of its greater democratization, approve the Statute, and proceed immediately with its implementation. The Trusteeship Council shall not allow any actions taken by any interested Government or Governments to divert it from adopting and implementing the Statute of Jerusalem;

II. Calls upon the States concerned, to make formal undertakings, at an early date and in the light of their obligations as Members of the United Nations, that they will approach these matters with good will, and be guided by the terms of the present resolution.

U.N. Security Council Resolution Concerning Restrictions on the Passage of Ships through the Suez Canal

September 1, 1951

The Security Council

1. *Recalling* that in its resolution of 11 August 1949 (S/1376) relating to the conclusion of Armistice Agreements between Israel and the neighbouring Arab States, it drew attention to the pledges, in these Agreements "against any further acts of hostility between the Parties";

2. *Recalling* further that in its resolution of 17 November 1950 (S/1907) it reminded the States concerned that the Armistice Agreements to which they were parties contemplated "the return of permanent peace in Palestine," and therefore urged them and the other States in the area to take all such steps as would lead to the settlement of the issues between them;

3. *Noting* the report of the Chief of Staff of the Truce Supervision Organization to the Security Council of 12 June 1951 (S/2194);

4. *Further noting* that the Chief of Staff of the Truce Supervision Organization recalled the statement of the senior Egyptian delegate in Rhodes on 13 January 1949, to the effect that his delegation was "inspired with every spirit of co-operation, conciliation and a sincere desire to restore peace in Palestine," and that the Egyptian Government has not complied with the earnest plea of the Chief of Staff made to the Egyptian delegate on 12 June 1951, that it desist from the present practice of interfering with the passage through the Suez Canal of goods destined for Israel;

5. *Considering* that since the Armistice regime, which has been in existence for nearly two and a half years, is of a permanent character, neither party can reasonably assert that it is actively a belligerent or re-

quires to exercise the right of visit, search, and seizure for any legitimate purpose of self-defence;

6. *Finds* that the maintenance of the practice mentioned in paragraph 4 above is inconsistent with the objectives of a peaceful settlement between the parties and the establishment of a permanent peace in Palestine set forth in the Armistice Agreement;

7. *Finds further* that such practice is an abuse of the exercise of the right of visit, search and seizure;

8. *Further finds* that that practice cannot in the prevailing circumstances be justified on the ground that it is necessary for self-defence;

9. *And further noting* that the restrictions on the passage of goods through the Suez Canal to Israel ports are denying to nations at no time connected with the conflict in Palestine valuable supplies required for their economic reconstruction, and that these restrictions together with sanctions applied by Egypt to certain ships which have visited Israel ports represent unjustified interference with the rights of nations to navigate the seas and to trade freely with one another, including the Arab States and Israel;

10. *Calls upon* Egypt to terminate the restrictions on the passage of international commercial shipping and goods through the Suez Canal wherever bound and to cease all interference with such shipping beyond that essential to the safety of shipping in the Canal itself and to the observance of international conventions in force.

President Nasser on Zionism and Israel

The following excerpts are from Nasser's "The Philosophy of the Revolution," and speeches on various occasions between 1960 and 1963. Nasser served as an army officer in the Palestine War of 1948. The liberation of Palestine has been one of the chief planks of his political program, but there have been conflicting statements as to whether there was a definitive plan for the liberation. On several occasions, he announced that his army would soon be ready to enter Palestine on "a carpet of blood," on others that the time was not ripe yet.

As far as I am concerned I remember that the first elements of Arab consciousness began to filter into my mind as a student in secondary schools, wherefrom I went out with my fellow schoolboys on strike on December 2nd of every year as a protest against the Balfour Declaration whereby England gave the Jews a national home usurped unjustly from its legal owners.

When I asked myself at that time why I left my school enthusiastically and why I was angry for this land which I never saw I could not find an answer except the echoes of sentiment. Later a form of comprehension of this subject began when I was a cadet in the Military College studying the Palestine campaigns in particular and the history and conditions of this region in general which rendered it, throughout the last century, an easy prey ravaged by the claws of a pack of hungry beasts.

My comprehension began to be clearer as the foundation of its facts stood out when I began to study, as a student in the Staff College, the Palestine campaign and the problems of the Mediterranean in greater detail.

And when the Palestine crisis loomed on the horizon I was firmly convinced that the fighting in Palestine was not fighting on foreign territory. Nor was it inspired by sentiment. It was a duty imposed by self-defense.

Address by President Gamal Abdel Nasser in Aleppo (February 17, 1960)

Yesterday, the elderly Foreign Minister of Israel threatened the U.A.R. and said that Israel would not tolerate the ban on Israeli ships transiting the Suez Canal.

I would like to tell her and her master, Ben Gurion, as well as the Israeli people, that Israeli ships and cargoes will not, under any circumstances, transit the Canal.

Once these cargoes arrive in Port-Said or in any other port in the U.A.R. they become the property of the people of Palestine against whom Zionism and imperialism have conspired.

Eleven years after this tragedy, the people of Palestine have not changed. They, and we, are working for the restoration of their rights in their homeland. The rights of the people of Palestine are Arab rights above all. We feel it is our sacred duty to regain those rights for the people of Palestine.

By this unity which is binding you and the power of Arab unity and Arab nationalism, we can march along the road of freedom and liberation in order to get back the usurped rights of the Palestine Arabs.

Speech by President Gamal Abdel Nasser at a Mass Rally of the Youth Organisations in Damascus (October 18, 1960)

Now for the Palestinian issue. Wherever I have been in this or the Southern Region I hear the strong call for the liberation of this Arab territory of Palestine, and I would like to tell you, Brethren, that all that we are now doing is just a part of the battle for Palestine. Once we are fully emancipated from the shackles of colonialism and the intrigues of colonialist agents, we shall take a further step forward towards the liberation of Palestine.

When we have brought our armed forces to full strength and made our own armaments we will take another step forward towards the liberation of Palestine, and when we have manufactured jet aircraft and tanks we will embark upon the final stage of this liberation.

*Address by President Gamal Abdel Nasser on the 11th Anniversary
of the Revolution at the Republican Square, Cairo
(July 22, 1963)*

Work and readiness are the only means to protect the Arab's right in
Palestine.

Arab unity is our hope of liberating Palestine and restoring the rights
of the people of Palestine.

Arab unity is a sort of preparation, a human and national preparation
as well as a preparation with weapons and plans in all fields. It is not
enough to deliver speeches declaring that we would liberate Palestine and
liberate it just on paper for political consumption. As I said before, we do
not have any defined plan for the liberation of Palestine. I mention this
because I find it my duty to say it. But we have a plan to be implemented
in case of any Israeli aggression against us or against any Arab country.

In this case, we know well what to do. We have to be prepared. We have a
plan for this preparation and for the unification of the Arab world which is the
only means to protect the Arab land and safeguard Arab Nationalism.

God be with you and may his peace and mercy be upon you.

*Speech Delivered by President Gamal Abdel Nasser at Alexandria
on the Return of Another Contingent of U.A.R. Troops in Yemen
(August 11, 1963)*

The Armed Forces are getting ready for the restoration of the rights of the Palestine people because the Palestine battle was a smear on the entire Arab nation. No one can forget the shame brought by the battle of 1948. The rights of
the Palestine people must be restored. Therefore, we must get ready to
face Israel and Zionism as well as Imperialism which stands behind them.

Ahmed Shukairy: The Palestine Refugees

Excerpts from a speech at the United Nations by Shukairy in 1958
when serving as a member of the Saudi Arabian mission.

The Five Principles

Having portrayed the refugees' problem against its lengthy background of
United Nations' action, of the Conciliation Commission and the relief
Agency, we come to the crucial question. What is next? What is the solu-
tion?

In my submission, this is the question which must engage our attention and call for our action; and I shall endeavor to answer the question in a manner devoid of any decoration. For when the destiny of a whole people is involved, when the fundamental human rights are in question, and lastly when the peace of the world is at stake, there should be no fineness in our approach. The need calls for plain talking characterized with frankness, and sharp frankness indeed.

It is for these reasons that it becomes our duty to answer the question in all the candour under our command. In this spirit, Mr. Chairman, I propose now to deal with three matters: The solution of the problem, the fundamental principles of the solution, and the measures and sanctions to implement the solution.

Beginning with the fundamental principle of the solution, I must reiterate, even to the point of redundance, that these fundamental principles constitute the only basis for the solution to the refugee question. No matter how we view the problem, no solution can offer a chance for a peaceful settlement unless it takes full cognizance of the following five principles:

FIRST: The *de facto* situation created by Israel is entirely unacceptable as a basis for the solution of the Palestine problem in general, or the refugee question in particular. This *de facto* situation is the *fait accompli* of military action that does not vest rights non existing, or divest rights already existing.

SECOND: The rights of the refugees to their homes and homeland are not related to, or in any way dependent upon, the consent or refusal of Israel. These rights are natural, inherent and self-existing. They are not bestowed even by the United Nations, let alone Israel. They cannot be denied even by the United Nations, let alone Israel. They are vested in the refugees; they reside with the refugees. Thus, consent or no consent, these rights are theirs imprescriptible, irresistible and indivisible.

THIRD: Resettlement, reintegration, rehabilitation or any similar projects, no matter what their connotation may be, are not a solution by themselves. They should be planned or implemented not as aims, but merely as a means to meet the legitimate aspirations of the refugees and to the extent of giving effect to their inherent right to their homeland.

FOURTH: The relief program of the refugees is no solution to the problem, neither is it a substitute, no matter for how long it is continued. It is a humanitarian measure having no political implications.

FIFTH: Works projects, and self-support programs are not a solution; nor a solution to avoid the solution. Self-supporting or dependent, a refugee remains a refugee and his status remains an international problem until it is finally and satisfactorily solved.

To recast such a background has become the more necessary after we heard yesterday the statement on behalf of the United States. The Distinguished Representative of the United States, in his outline of the background of the refugee question, has omitted certain truths entirely, related half truths on certain aspects and finally arrived at wrongful conclusions on the substance of the problem.

As to the termination of the mandate of the Agency in favor of a better system as implied in the statement of the United States, we have serious misgivings of paramount nature. I must assure the Distinguished Representative of the United States that no Arab State, and no refugee, to use the words of the Distinguished Representative of the United States, feels it "best to let matters ride as in the past." To the refugees, continuation of relief is a source of great humiliation. To the Arab Governments it is a source of distress. If "some" feel differently, I assure the Distinguished Representative of the United States, it is not the Arabs anyhow. These refugees who are costing you 7 cents a day per head, have properties, revenues, fortunes in their homeland. The minute they lay hand on their properties they will be the first to thank you and plead the discontinuation of relief. It is only then that the U.N. responsibility ends, but not before.

I must, therefore, make it quite clear to the Committee in general and to the Distinguished Representative of the United States in particular, that we shall resist any attempt which directly or indirectly reduces in any degree the right of the refugees to repatriation. At a later stage of the debate, I will show the flaw in the reasoning underlying the position of the United States on the question. I simply wish to say here and now that any measure that might be in the direction of even scratching the right to repatriation or absolving the United Nations from its responsibility will be resisted in the Committee and in the Arab World.

With these five principles in mind, I can turn now to the solution of the problem. Here I would say that we need not look for a solution. The solution is there. It is repatriation and nothing but repatriation. It is the only solution that does not dishonour, but certainly does honour the Charter. It is the only solution that does not defeat, but rather does endorse the resolution of the United Nations. It is the only solution that does not defame the bill of human rights, but surely gives it a worthy fame. Lastly, it is the only solution that constitutes an investment of peace, and an asset of confidence in this organization.

After all, repatriation is one of those principles that cannot be questioned by the United Nations. It does not stand by our acceptance, nor does it lapse by our non-acceptance. To borrow a legal term, repatriation is a right *In Rem*, that can be exercised against the whole world, if need be. It springs from the right to a homeland, which is not subject to waiver, surrender, or compensation. Compensation is one remedy open for individual property rights, but a homeland does not submit to compensation even for the most precious possessions of this planet, and indeed the whole universe with all its fabulous riches. This is no exaggeration, unless I exaggerate your feelings towards your respective homelands.

Erskine Childers: The Other Exodus*

Erskine Childers, an Irish journalist, has published articles bitterly critical of Israeli policies. The present article was originally published in the London weekly *The Spectator* (May 12, 1961) and provoked a great deal of controversy. Childers, the grandson of a well known Irish patriot and writer, also worked for the British Broadcasting Corporation and subsequently became a leading official in Irish television.

The Palestine Arab refugees wait, and multiply, and are debated at the United Nations. In thirteen years, their numbers have increased from 650,000 to 1,145,000. Most of them survive only on rations from the U.N. agency, UNRWA. Their subsistence has already cost L.S. 110,000,000. Each year, UNRWA has to plead at New York for the funds to carry on, against widespread and especially Western lack of sympathy. There is one reason for this impatience: the attitude created towards these refugees by Israeli argument. For over ten years, Israeli spokesmen have claimed that:

> Unless we understand how this problem was caused we cannot rightly judge how it should be solved. . . . The responsibility of the Arab Governments is threefold. Theirs is the initiative for its creation. Theirs is the onus for its endurance. Above all—theirs is the capacity for its solution.
>
> (Abba Eban to the U.N. 1957).

In this inquiry, I propose only briefly to examine the last two of these three claims. The last, about a "solution," is that if the Arab host governments were willing, they could resettle the refugees quite easily outside Palestine—where, as Israel claims and as President Kennedy's 1960 election platform also had it, "there is room and opportunity for them." This is not even remotely true. UNRWA's new chief, Dr. John Davis, has now bluntly and bravely warned against "facile assumptions that it rests with the host governments to solve the problem . . . the simple truth is that the jobs . . . do not exist today within the host countries." Nor can the jobs be created, Dr. Davis reports, because most of the refugees are unskilled peasants—precisely the host countries' worst problem among their own rapidly expanding populations.

These Arabs, in short, are displaced persons in the fullest, most tragic meaning of the term—an economic truth cruelly different from the myth.

* Reprinted by permission of *The Spectator* Limited.

But there is also the political myth, and it too has been soothing our highly pragmatic Western conscience for thirteen years. This is the Israeli charge, solemnly made every year and then reproduced around the world, that these refugees are—to quote a character in Leon Uris's *Exodus*—"kept caged like animals in suffering as a deliberate political weapon."

This, again, Dr. Davis has now bravely called a "misconception." The reality here is that the refugees themselves fanatically oppose any resettlement outside Palestine. UNRWA even had to persuade them that concrete huts, even in the U.N. camps, replacing their squalid tents and hovels, would not be the thin end of a resettlement wedge. Unlike other refugees, these refuse to move; they insist on going home.

Why? The answer, I believe, lies in the third of the three issues Israel argues—in the cause itself of the mass exodus. The very fact that cause is argued by both sides is significant. Israel claims that the Arabs left because they were ordered to, and deliberately incited into panic, by their own leaders who wanted the field cleared for the 1948 war. It is also argued that there would today be no Arab refugees if the Arab States had not attacked the new Jewish State on May 15, 1948 (though 800,000 had already fled before that date). The Arabs charge that their people were evicted at bayonet-point and by panic deliberately incited by the Zionists.

Examining every official Israeli statement about the Arab exodus, I was struck by the fact that no primary evidence of evacuation orders was ever produced. The charge, Israel claimed, was "documented"; but where were the documents? There had allegedly been Arab radio broadcasts ordering the evacuation; but no dates, names of stations, or texts of messages were ever cited. In Israel in 1958, as a guest of the Foreign Office and therefore doubly hopeful of serious assistance, I asked to be shown the proofs, I was assured they existed, and was promised them. None had been offered when I left, but I was again assured. I asked to have the material sent on to me. I am still waiting.

While in Israel, however, I met Dr. Leo Kohn, professor of political science at Hebrew University and an ambassador-rank adviser to the Israeli Foreign Office. He had written one of the first official pamphlets on the Arab refugees. I asked him for concrete evidence of the Arab evacuation orders. Agitatedly, Dr. Kohn replied: "Evidence? Evidence? What more could you want than this?" and he took up his own pamphlet. "Look at this 'Economist' report," and he pointed to a quotation. "You will surely not suggest that the 'Economist' is a Zionist journal?"

The quotation is one of about five that appear in every Israeli speech and pamphlet, and are in turn used by every sympathetic analysis. It seemed very impressive: it referred to the exodus from Haifa, and to an Arab broadcast order as one major reason for that exodus.

I decided to turn up the relevant (October 2) 1948 issue of the 'Economist.' The passage that has literally gone around the world was certainly there, but I had already noticed one curious word in it. This was a description of the massacre at Deir Yassin as an "incident." No impartial observer of Palestine in 1948 calls what happened at this avowedly non-belligerent, unarmed Arab village in April, 1948, an "incident"—any more than Lidice is called an "incident." Over 250 old men, women and children were deliberately butchered, stripped and mutilated or thrown into a well, by men of the Zionist Irgun Zvai Leumi.

Seen in its place in the full 'Economist' article, it was at once clear that Dr. Kohn's quotation was a second-hand account, inserted as that of an eye-witness at Haifa, by the journal's own correspondent who had not been in that city at the time. And in the rest of the same article, written by the Economist correspondent himself, but never quoted by Israel, the second great wave of refugees were described as "all destitute, as the Jewish troops gave them an hour in which to quit, but simultaneously requisitioned all transport."

It was now essential to check all other, even secondary, Israeli "evidence." Another stock quotation down the years has been that, supposedly, of the Greek-Catholic Archbishop of Galilee. For example, Israel's Abba Eban told the U.N. Special Political Committee in 1957 that the Archbishop had "fully confirmed" that the Arabs were urged to flee by their own leaders.

I wrote to His Grace, asking for his evidence of such orders. I hold signed letters from him, with permission to publish, in which he has categorically denied ever alleging Arab evacuation orders; he states that no such orders were ever given. He says that his name has been abused for years; and that the Arabs fled through panic and forcible eviction by Jewish troops.

As none of the other stock quotations in Israeli propaganda are worth comment, I next decided to test the undocumented charge that the Arab evacuation orders were broadcast by Arab radio—which could be done thoroughly because the BBC monitored all Middle Eastern broadcasts throughout 1948. The records, and companion ones by a U.S. monitoring unit, can be seen at the British Museum.

There was not a single order, or appeal, or suggestion about evacuation from Palestine from any Arab radio station, inside or outside Palestine, in 1948. There is repeated monitored record of Arab appeals, even flat orders, to the civilians of Palestine to stay put. To select only two examples: on April 4, as the first great wave of flight began, Damascus Radio broadcast an appeal to everyone to stay at their homes and jobs. On April 24, with the exodus now a flood, Palestine Arab leaders warned that:

Certain elements and Jewish agents are spreading defeatist news to create chaos and panic among the peaceful population. Some cowards are deserting their houses, villages or cities. . . . Zionist agents and corrupt cowards will be severely punished (Al-Inqaz, the Arab Liberation Radio, at 12.00 hours).

Even Jewish broadcasts (in Hebrew) mentioned such Arab appeals to stay put. Zionist newspapers in Palestine reported the same: none so much as hinted at any Arab evacuation orders.

The fact is that Israel's official charges, which have vitally influenced the last ten years of Western thought about the refugees, are demonstrably and totally hollow. And from this alone, suspicion is justified. Why make such charges at all? On the face of it, this mass exodus might have been entirely the result of "normal" panic and wartime dislocation.

We need not even touch upon Arab evidence that panic was quite deliberately incited. The evidence is there, on the Zionist record. For example, on March 27, four days before the big offensive against Arab centres by the official Zionist (Haganah) forces, the Irgun's radio unit broadcast in Arabic. Irgun, a terrorist organisation like the Stern Gang, was officially disowned by Ben Gurion and the Haganah. Yet just four days before the Haganah offensive Irgun warned "Arabs in urban agglomerations" that typhus, cholera and similar diseases would break out "heavily" among them "in April and May."

The effect may be imagined. Two weeks later, it was this same Irgun, apparently so solicitous of Arab welfare, that butchered the people of Deir Yassin. Irgun then called a press conference to announce the deed; paraded other captured Arabs through Jewish quarters of Jerusalem to be spat upon; then released them to tell their kin of the experience. Arthur Koestler called the "bloodbath" of Deir Yassin "the psychologically decisive factor in this spectacular exodus." But this was only Irgun, it may be said. Is there evidence that official Zionist forces—the Haganah under Ben Gurion and the Jewish Agency—were inciting panic? An Israeli Government pamphlet of 1958 states that "the Jews tried, by every means open to them, to stop the Arab evacuation" (this same 1958 pamphlet has diluted Deir Yassin to "the one and only instance of Jewish high-handed (sic) action in this war").

There is one recorded instance of such an appeal. It is beyond dispute even by Arabs, that in Haifa the late gentle Mayor, Shabeitai Levi, with the tears streaming down his face, implored the city's Arabs to stay. But elsewhere in Haifa, Arthur Koestler wrote in his book that Haganah loudspeaker vans and the Haganah radio promised that city's Arabs escort to "Arab territory," and "hinted at terrible consequences if their warning were disregarded." There are many witnesses of this loudspeaker method elsewhere. In Jerusalem the Arabic warning from the vans was, "The road to Jericho is open! Fly from Jerusalem before you are all killed!" (Meyer Levin in *Jerusalem Embattled*). Bertha Vester, a Christian missionary, reported that another theme was, "Unless you leave your homes, the fate of Deir Yassin will be your fate.'' The Haganah radio station also broadcast, in Arabic, repeated news of Arabs fleeing ''in terror and fear'' from named places.

Still, however, we have plumbed this exodus only so far as panic is concerned. There are U.N. and Economist reports of forcible expulsion, which is something else. How much evidence is there for this? And were only the ''unofficial'' Irgun and Stern forces responsible? This is what Nathan Chofshi, one of the original Jewish pioneers in Palestine, wrote in an ashamed rebuttal of an American Zionist rabbi's charges of evacuation orders:

> If Rabbi Kaplan really wanted to know what happened, we old Jewish settlers in Palestine who witnessed the fight could tell him how and in what manner we, Jews, forced the Arabs to leave cities and villages . . . some of them were driven out by force of arms; others were made to leave by deceit, lying and false promises. It is enough to cite the cities of Jaffa, Lydda, Ramleh, Beersheba, Acre from among numberless others. (in 'Jewish Newsletter,' New York, February 9, 1959).

Were official Zionist troops involved at any of these places? I propose to select, for the sake of brevity, only the Lydda-Ramleh area. It was about the exodus from this area, among others, that the Economist reported. ''Jewish troops gave them an hour to quit.''

In their latest book, which has been publicly endorsed by Ben Gurion, Jon Kimche and his brother devoted considerable detail to the Zionist offensive against Lydda and Ramich. It was undertaken by official Israeli forces under Yigael Alon. And the immediately responsible officer was Moshe Dayan, commander of the 1956 Sinai attack, now a Cabinet Minister. Kimche has described how, on July 11, 1948, Dayan with his columns:

> . . . drove at full speed into Lydda, shooting up the town and creating confusion and a degree of terror among the population . . . its Arab population of 30,000 either fled or were herded on the road to Ramallah. The next day Ramleh also surrendered and its Arab population suffered the same fate. Both towns were sacked by the victorious Israelis.

Ramallah, on the road to which these particular Arabs—numbering over 60,000 from this one area alone—were herded, was up in the Judean hills, outside Zionist-held territory. The ''road to Jericho,'' which Arabs in Jerusalem were warned to take, brought them into the Jordan Valley. Some 85,000 are still there in one U.N. camp alone, under the Mount of Temptation. The Arab population of Acre, mentioned by Chofshi, exceeded 45,000: Acre was attacked by official Zionist troops.

From this analysis of only some of the sources of the Arab exodus, then, it is clear beyond all doubt that official Zionist forces were responsible for expulsion of thousands upon thousands of Arabs, and for deliberate incitement to panic. Seen from the viewpoint of the Arab refugees themselves, little more would need to be said. And needless to say, even those Arabs expelled or who fled through "unofficially" incited panic can hardly be asked to look differently on the Israeli Government today. It pays former Irgunists and Sternists the same war pensions as former Haganah troops; its denial of expulsion is total.

But is it conceivable that Ben Gurion and his colleagues could have deliberately contemplated an "emptying" of Palestine? That a motive existed is beyond doubt. The U.N. partition scheme had in no way solved the "Arab problem" that a Jewish State would face. It would have given Zionism what its leaders publicly called the "irreducible minimum" of territory in a Palestine they claimed should entirely belong to them. And we know that the official Zionist movement had in fact no intention of accepting the U.N. territorial award. Six weeks before the British Mandate ended, before the Israeli State was proclaimed, and before the Arab States sent in their armies, an all-out Zionist military offensive was launched. Later, Ben Gurion publicly said of this offensive:

> As fighting spread, the (Arab) exodus was joined by Bedouin and fellahin (peasants), but not the remotest Jewish homestead was abandoned and nothing a tottering (British) administration could unkindly do stopped us from reaching our goal on May 14, 1948, in a State made larger and Jewish by the Haganah (cf. Rebirth and Destiny of Israel).

The Jewish State envisaged by the U.N. would have contained a 45 per cent Arab population: the extra territory attacked by the Zionists before May 14 would have increased that ratio—for example, by more than 80,000 Arabs in Jaffa alone. But it was not just a question of numbers. The Arabs owned and occupied far too much of the territory's productive and social facilities to enable anything like the mass Jewish immigration of which Zionists dreamed.

What this meant in terms of motive can be seen in the statistics that followed the Arab exodus. More than 80 per cent of the entire land area of Israel is land abandoned by the Arab refugees. Nearly a quarter of all the standing buildings in Israel had been occupied by those Arabs. Ten thousand shops, stores and other firms inside new Israel had been Arab. Half of all the citrus fruit holdings in the new State had belonged to the Arabs now made refugees. By 1954, more than one-third of the entire Jewish population of Israel was living on "absentee property"—most of it now "absorbed" into the Israeli economy, and unilaterally sequestered by Israeli legislation against a "global" compensation offer.

It is, then, little wonder that old Chaim Weizmann, Israel's first President, described the Arab exodus as a "miraculous simplification of Israel's tasks." But was it "miraculous"? Unexpected? In no way part of combined military and economic planning of nascent Israel's leaders?

We come to perhaps the most grave evidence of all. The mass exodus began in April, 1948. By June, the U.N. Mediator was fully seized of it. He formally demanded a statement of policy from the new Israeli Government about the refugees. At first, he could get no satisfaction. Then, in an official letter dated: August 1, 1948, Israeli's Foreign Minister replied.

It was only four months since the first waves of flight; only eleven weeks since Israel had been proclaimed, ostensibly calling on the Arabs to "play their part in the development of the State." And it was at this time that a Government since claiming that this whole exodus was unexpected and despite its implorings, formally denied the refugees the right of return. Israel did not merely plead "security," but told the United Nations:

> On the economic side, the reintegration of the returning Arabs into normal life, and even their mere sustenance, would present an insuperable problem. The difficulties of accommodation, employment, and ordinary livelihood would be insuperable.

The case rests. This is not the place to discuss a "solution," and no summary conclusion is needed, save perhaps to recall the words of an official Israeli spokesman, though in rather different import:

> Unless we understand how this problem was caused, we cannot rightly judge how it should be solved.

The Arabs of Palestine now enter their fourteenth year of exile. If you go among them in the hills of Judea, they will take you by the arm to a crest of land and point downwards, across the rusty skeins of barbed wire. "Can you see it—over there beside those trees? That is my home."

It is shaming beyond all brief descriptions to move among these million people, as a Westerner. It is shaming for many Jews, and some speak out as Nathan Chofshi has bravely done:

> We came and turned the native Arabs into tragic refugees. And still we dare to slander and malign them, to besmirch their name. Instead of being deeply ashamed of what we did and trying to undo some of the evil we committed . . . we justify our terrible acts and even attempt to glorify them.

Abba Eban: The Refugee Problem

Excerpts from a speech (Nov. 17, 1958) by the Chief Israeli representative to the United Nations who subsequently became Foreign Minister of Israel.

How Was the Refugee Problem Caused?

AGGRESSION BY ARAB STATES CREATED REFUGEE PROBLEM

The Arab refugee problem was caused by a war of aggression, launched by the Arab States against Israel in 1947 and 1948. Let there be no mistake. If there had been no war against Israel, with its consequent harvest of bloodshed, misery, panic and flight, there would be no problem of Arab refugees today. Once you determine the responsibility for that war, you have determined the responsibility for the refugee problem. Nothing in the history of our generation is clearer or less controversial than the initiative of Arab governments for the conflict out of which the refugee tragedy emerged. The historic origins of that conflict are clearly defined by the confessions of Arab governments themselves: "This will be a war of extermination," declared the Secretary General of the Arab League speaking for the governments of six Arab States; "It will be a momentous massacre to be spoken of like the Mongolian massacre and the Crusades."

PALESTINE ARABS URGED TO FLEE BY ARAB LEADERS

The assault began on the last day of November 1947. From then until the expiration of the British Mandate in May 1948 the Arab States, in concert with Palestine Arab leaders, plunged the land into turmoil and chaos. On the day of Israel's Declaration of Independence, on May 14, 1948, the armed forces of Egypt, Jordan, Syria, Lebanon and Iraq, supported by contingents from Saudi Arabia and the Yemen, crossed their frontiers and marched against Israel. The perils which then confronted our community; the danger which darkened every life and home; the successful repulse of the assault and the emergence of Israel into the life of the world community are all chapters of past history, gone but not forgotten. But the traces of that conflict still remain deeply inscribed upon our region's life. Caught up in the havoc and tension of war; demoralized by the flight of their leaders; urged on by irresponsible promises that they would return to inherit the spoils of Israel's destruction—hundreds of thousands of Arabs sought the shelter of Arab lands. A survey by an international body in 1957 described these violent events in the following terms:

As early as the first months of 1948 the Arab League issued orders exhorting the people to seek a temporary refuge in neighboring countries, later to return to their abodes in the wake of the victorious Arab armies and obtain their share of abandoned Jewish property (Research Group for European Migration Problems Bulletin, Vol. V—No. 1, 1957, p. 10).

Contemporary statements by Arab leaders fully confirm this version. On 16 August 1948 Msgr. George Hakim, the Greek Catholic Archbishop of Galilee, recalled:

The refugees had been confident that their absence from Palestine would not last long; that they would return within a few days—within a week or two; their leaders had promised them that the Arab armies would crush the "Zionist gangs" very quickly and that there would be no need for panic or fear of a long exile.

A month later on September 15, 1948, Mr. Emile Ghoury who had been the Secretary of the Arab Higher Committee at the time of the Arab invasion of Israel declared:

I do not want to impugn anyone but only to help the refugees. The fact that there are these refugees is the direct consequence of the action of the Arab States in opposing partition and the Jewish State. The Arab States agreed upon this policy unanimously and they must share in the solution of the problem.

MISERY IS RESULT OF UNLAWFUL RESORT TO FORCE BY ARABS

No less compelling than these avowals by Arab leaders are the judgments of United Nations organs. In April 1948, when the flight of the refugees was in full swing, the United Nations Palestine Commission inscribed its verdict on the tablets of history:

Arab opposition to the plan of the Assembly of 29 November 1947 has taken the form of organized efforts by strong Arab elements, both inside and outside Palestine, to prevent its implementation and to thwart its objectives by threats and acts of violence, including repeated armed incursions into Palestine territory. The Commission has had to report to the Security Council that powerful Arab interests, both inside and outside Palestine, are defying the resolution of the General Assembly and are engaged in a deliberate effort to alter by force the settlement envisaged therein.

This is a description of the events between November 1947 and May 1948 when the Arab exodus began. Months later, when the tide of battle rolled away, its consequences of bereavement, devastation and panic were left behind. At the General Assembly meetings in 1948 the United Nations Acting Mediator recorded a grave international judgment:

> The Arab States had forcibly opposed the existence of the Jewish State in Palestine in direct opposition to the wishes of two-thirds of the members of the Assembly. Nevertheless their armed intervention proved useless. The [Mediator's] report was based solely on the fact that the Arab States had no right to resort to force and that the United Nations should exert its authority to prevent such a use of force.

The significance of the Arab assault upon Israel by five neighboring States had been reflected in a letter addressed by the Secretary General of the United Nations to representatives of the permanent members of the Security Council on 16 May 1948:—

"The Egyptian Government," wrote the Secretary-General, "has declared in a cablegram to the President of the Security Council on 15 May that Egyptian armed forces have entered Palestine and it has engaged in 'armed intervention' in that country. On 16 May I received a cablegram from the Arab League making similar statements on behalf of the Arab States. I consider it my duty to emphasize to you that *this is the first time since the adoption of the Charter that Member States have openly declared that they have engaged in armed intervention outside their own territory.*"

Arab Governments Must Accept Responsibility

These are only a few of the documents which set out the responsibility of the Arab Governments for the warfare of which the refugees are the main surviving victims. Even after a full decade it is difficult to sit here with equanimity and listen to Arab representatives disengaging themselves from any responsibility for the travail and anguish which they caused. I recall this history not for the purpose of recrimination, but because of its direct bearing on the Committee's discussion. Should not the representatives of Arab States, as the authors of this tragedy, come here in a mood of humility and repentance rather than in shrill and negative indignation? Since these governments have, by acts of policy, created this tragic problem, *does it not follow that the world community has an unimpeachable right to claim their full assistance in its solution?* How can governments create a vast humanitarian problem by their action—then wash their hands of all responsibility for its alleviation? The claim of the world community on the cooperation of Arab governments is all the more compelling when we reflect that these States, in their vast lands, command all the resources and conditions which would enable them to liberate the refugees from their plight, in full dignity and freedom.

With this history in mind the Committee should not find it difficult to reject the assertion that the guilt for the refugee problem lies with the United Nations itself. The refugee problem was not created by the General Assembly's recommendation for the establishment of Israel. It was created by the attempts of Arab governments to destroy that recommendation by force. The crisis arose not as Arab spokesmen have said because the United Nations adopted a resolution eleven years ago; it arose because Arab governments attacked that resolution by force. If the United Nations proposal had been peacefully accepted, there would be no refugee problem today hanging as a cloud upon the tense horizons of the Middle East.

The next question is—why has the problem endured?

Why Does the Refugee Problem Endure?

REFUGEE PROBLEM CANNOT BE SOLVED BY REPATRIATION

In his statement to the Committee on November 10, 1958, the representative of the United States said:

> In our view it is not good enough consciously to perpetuate for over a decade the dependent status of nearly a million refugees.

Other speakers in this debate have echoed a similar sense of frustration.

Apart from the question of its origin, the perpetuation of this refugee problem is an unnatural event, running against the whole course of experience and precedent. Since the end of the Second World War, problems affecting forty million refugees have confronted Governments in various parts of the world. In no case, except that of the Arab refugees, amounting to less than two percent of the whole, has the international community shown constant responsibility and provided lavish aid. In every other case a solution has been found by the integration of refugees into their host countries. Nine million Koreans; 900,000 refugees from the conflict in Viet Nam; 8½ million Hindus and Sikhs leaving Pakistan for India; 6½ million Moslems fleeing India to Pakistan; 700,000 Chinese refugees in Hong Kong; 13 million Germans from the Sudetenland, Poland and other East European States reaching West and East Germany; thousands of Turkish refugees from Bulgaria; 440,000 Finns separated from their homeland by a change of frontier; 450,000 refugees from Arab lands arrived destitute in Israel; and an equal number converging on Israel from the remnants of the Jewish holocaust in Europe—these form the tragic procession of the world's refugee population in the past two decades. *In every case but that of the Arab refugees now in Arab lands the countries in which the refugees sought shelter have facilitated their integration.* In this case alone has integration been obstructed.

The paradox is the more astonishing when we reflect that the kinship of language, religion, social background and national sentiment existing between the Arab refugees and their Arab host countries has been at least as intimate as those existing between any other host countries and any other refugee groups. It is impossible to escape the conclusion that the integration of Arab refugees into the life of the Arab world is an objectively feasible process which has been resisted for political reasons.

In a learned study on refugee problems published by the Carnegie Endowment for International Peace in November 1957 under the title "Century of the Homeless Man" Dr. Elfan Rees, Advisor on Refugees to the World Council of Churches, sums up the international experience in the following terms:

> No large scale refugee problem has ever been solved by repatriation, and there are certainly no grounds for believing that this particular problem can be so solved. Nothing can bring it about except wars which in our time would leave nothing to go back to. War has never solved a refugee problem and it is not in the books that a modern war would.

ARAB LEADERS BLOCK SOLUTION FOR POLITICAL REASONS

Those words should be compared with Mr. Shukairy's peroration, in which he seems to look forward to a settlement of the refugee problem by a war launched for the extinction of Israel's independence. Such a war, whose result would not be that envisaged by Mr. Shukairy, would be more likely to create new refugee problems than to solve the existing ones.

Dr. Rees' Report continues:

> This then is not a case of a refugee rejecting a particular solution but of the international community having to reject it as dangerous and impossible. It is time this was done with more frankness and force than has been used hitherto. Until it is—real danger remains, and these refugee problems will be unnecessarily perpetuated by the rejection of other and viable solutions.

The Carnegie Endowment publication concludes:

> The facts we must face force us to the conclusion that for most of the world refugees the only solution is integration where they are.

Another important study on refugee problems carried out last year has been published by the Research Group for European Migration. This study reaches the following grave conclusion:

The official attitude of the [Arab] host countries is well known. It is one of seeking to prevent any sort of adaptation and integration because the refugees are seen as a political means of pressure to get Israel wiped off the map or to get the greatest possible number of concessions.

It is painfully evident that this refugee problem has been artificially maintained for political motives against all the economic, social and cultural forces which, had they been allowed free play, would have brought about a solution.

Recent years have witnessed a great expansion of economic potentialities in the Middle East. The revenues of the oil bearing countries have opened up great opportunities of work and development, into which the refugees by virtue of their linguistic and national background could fit without any sense of dislocation. The expansion in the areas of Arab sovereignty has also created opportunities of employment which did not exist in the days of colonial tutelage. There cannot be any doubt that if free movement had been granted to the refugees there would have been a spontaneous absorption of thousands of them into these expanded Arab economies. It is precisely this that Arab Governments have obstructed. In his report to the Eighth session of the General Assembly the Director of UNRWA describes Arab policies on free movement in a highly significant passage:

The full benefit of the spread of this large capital investment [in Arab countries] will be felt only if restrictions on the movement of refugees are withdrawn. This is a measure which was proposed in the original three-year plan but little has been done so far to give effect to it. Such freedom of movement would enable refugees to take full advantage of the opportunities for work arising in countries such as Iraq, Saudi Arabia and the Persian Gulf Sheikhdoms where economic development has already taken place.

There has, of course, been some movement of refugees into the new labor opportunities of the region. The force of economic attraction has sometimes prevailed. But these potentialities can only be fully realized if political resistance to integration is overcome. There are broad opportunities in the Arab world for refugees to build new lives; but the governments concerned have so far sought to debar refugees from using them. In the survey published by the Carnegie Endowment the obstructive record of Arab governments is set out in graphic words:

The history of UNRWA has been a clinical study in frustration. No Agency has been better led or more devoutly served but the organized intransigence of the refugees and the calculated indifference of the Arab States concerned have brought all its plans to nought. By chicanery it is feeding the dead, by political pressure it is feeding non-refugees, its relief supplies have been subjected in some instances to import duty, its personnel policies are grossly interfered with and its "constructive measures," necessarily requiring the concurrence of governments, have been pigeon-holed. The net result is that relief is being provided in 1957 to refugees who could have been rehabilitated in 1951 with "home and jobs," without prejudice to their just claims.

In a survey on "Social Forces in the Middle East 1956," Dr. Channing B. Richardson of Hamilton University writes:

Towards UNRWA the attitudes of the Arab Governments vary between suspicion and obstruction. It cannot be denied that the outside observer gains the impression that the Arab governments have no great desire to solve the refugee problem.

In June, 1957 the Chairman of the Near Eastern Sub-Committee of the United States Senate Foreign Relations Committee reported at the end of an illuminating survey:

The fact is that the Arab States have for ten years used the Palestine refugees as political hostages in their struggle with Israel. While Arab delegates in the United Nations have condemned the plight of their brothers in the refugee camps nothing has been done to assist them in a practical way lest political leverage against Israel be lost.

450,000 JEWISH REFUGEES FROM ARAB LANDS ABSORBED BY ISRAEL

The failure or refusal of Arab governments to achieve a permanent economic integration of refugees in their huge lands appears all the more remarkable when we contrast it with the achievements of other countries when confronted by the challenge and opportunity of absorbing their kinsmen into their midst. Israel with her small territory, her meager water resources and her hardpressed finances, has found homes, work and citizenship in the past ten years for nearly a million newcomers arriving in destitution no less acute than those of Arab refugees. These refugees from Arab lands left their homes, property and jobs behind. Their standards of physique and nutrition were in many cases pathetically low. They have had to undergo processes of adaptation to a social, linguistic and national ethos far removed from any that they had known before. Thus, integration in this case has been far more arduous than it would be for Arab refugees in Arab lands, where no such differences exist between the society and culture of the host country and those with which the refugees are already familiar. If Israel in these conditions could assimilate nearly one million refugees—450,000 of them from Arab lands—how much more easily could the vast Arab world find a home for a similar number of Arab refugees if only the same impulse of kinship asserted itself.

This is concisely described in the report published by the Carnegie Endowment:

> There is another aspect of the Middle East refugee problem that is also frequently ignored. It is necessary to remember that concurrently with the perpetuation of the Arab refugee problem more than 400,000 Jews have been forced to leave their homes in Iraq, the Yemen, and North Africa. They have not been counted as refugees because they were readily and immediately received as new immigrants into Israel. Nevertheless they were forced to leave their traditional homes against their will and to abandon, in the process, all that they possessed. The latest addition to their number are the 20,000 Jews for whom life has become impossible in Egypt. Fifteen thousand of them have sought asylum in Israel while the remainder are in Europe seeking other solutions to their problem.

Nor is this an isolated example of what can be achieved by Governments in circumstances much less favorable than those which the Arab States command. Less than two weeks ago the representative of Finland, in the Third Committee of this Assembly, gave the following moving account of what a small country can achieve in refugee integration:

> In 1944 the 3,300,000 people who lived within the present boundaries of Finland had to receive in a couple of weeks' time around 440,000 displaced persons, all Finnish citizens who had left their homesteads after the new frontier line had cut off some 13 percent of our territory from the rest of Finland. . . .
>
> As in 1944 practically no emigration of the displaced persons was possible and none of them could be sent back to their earlier home region, complete integration was the only solution. It was an extremely heavy economic burden taking into consideration that there was no international aid, that the reparation of war destruction and the payment of war indemnities all came simultaneously and that the displaced persons came practically empty handed.

I will not ask the Committee to consider the other numerous precedents. Enough has been said to prove the crucial point that there is no objective difficulty in solving such problems provided the will for a solution exists.

Indeed, compared with other problems, the Arab refugee problem is one of the easiest to solve.

REFUGEES CLOSELY AKIN TO ARABS IN HOST COUNTRIES

The Research Group for European Migration points out in its report (pps. 25–26) that

> The Palestine refugees have the closest possible affinities of national sentiment, language, religion and social organization with the Arab host countries and the standard of living of the majority of the refugee population is little different from those of the inhabitants of the countries that have given them refuge or will do so in the future.

The same point is made in the report of a Special Study Commission to the Near East and Africa despatched by the Committee on Foreign Affairs of the United States House of Representatives, the source of a great proportion of U.N. relief funds:

> Unlike refugees in other parts of the world the Palestine refugees are no different in language and social organization from the other Arabs. Resettlement therefore would be in familiar environment. If the local governments are unwilling to tackle the problem except on their own terms there is little incentive for outside governments to continue financial support. Original humanitarian impulse which led to the creation and perpetuation of UNRWA is gradually being perverted into a political weapon. (May 19, 1958).

REGIONAL ECONOMIC DEVELOPMENT BLOCKED BY ARAB GOVERNMENTS

Most of the recent literature describes Arab resistance to integration by two methods—political opposition to integration; and careful scrutiny of UNRWA's activities to ensure that they do not develop into permanent solutions. The policy of obstruction however also has a third heading. I refer to the rejection of economic development proposals which seemed to hold the promise of a refugee solution. The thinking behind these plans was simple but imaginative. The international community was willing to create special opportunities of livelihood by irrigating new areas of land, establishing new farms or, in some cases, new village communities with industrial as well as agricultural activity. Refugees were to be placed into these newly created labor opportunities. The result would be a reduction of the number of refugees receiving relief and progress towards lightening the international burden.

None of these schemes has won Arab acceptance. Many of them have been rejected precisely because their implementation would help solve the refugee problem. A typical and spectacular instance is to be found in the long negotiations conducted between 1953 and 1956 on a project for the coordinated use of the Jordan and Yarmuk Rivers. Israel was prepared, despite certain disavowal—indeed is still prepared—to cooperate in this plan. Ambassador Eric Johnston has summed up his experience in the following words:

> Between 1953 and 1956, at the request of President Eisenhower, I undertook to negotiate with these States a comprehensive Jordan Valley development plan that would have provided for the irrigation of some 225,000 acres. . . . After two years of discussion, technical experts of Israel, Jordan, Lebanon and Syria agreed upon every important detail of a unified Jordan plan. But in October 1956 it was rejected for political reasons at a meeting of the Arab League. . . . Three years have passed and no agreement has yet been reached on developing the Jordan. Every year a billion cubic meters of precious water still roll down the ancient stream, wasted, to the Dead Sea.

ARAB GOVERNMENTS PREFER REFUGEE STATUS QUO

In the light of these experiences it cannot be doubted that Arab Governments have been determined that the refugees shall remain refugees; and that the aim of wrecking any alternative to "repatriation" has been pursued by these governments with an ingenuity worthy of a better cause. With an international agency working for integration; with millions of dollars expended every year to move refugees away from a life of dependence, the Arab governments have brought us to a point where there are more refugees on United Nations rolls than ever before.

How to Solve the Arab Refugee Problem

RESETTLEMENT AMONG HOST COUNTRIES THE ONLY SOLUTION

Any discussion of this problem revolves around the two themes of resettlement, and what is called "repatriation." There is a growing skepticism about the feasibility of repatriation. These hundreds of thousands of Arab refugees are now in Arab lands on the soil of their kinsmen. They have been nourished for ten years on one single theme—hatred of Israel; refusal to recognize Israel's sovereignty; resentment against Israel's existence; the dream of securing Israel's extinction. All these implacable sentiments found expression in the address by the representative of Saudi Arabia.

REPATRIATION A THREAT TO SECURITY

Repatriation would mean that hundreds of thousands of people would be introduced into a State whose existence they oppose, whose flag they despise and whose destruction they are resolved to seek. The refugees are all Arabs; and the countries in which they find themselves are Arab countries. Yet the advocates of repatriation contend that these Arab refugees should be settled in a non-Arab country, in the only social and cultural environment which is alien to their background and tradition. The Arab refugees are to be uprooted from the soil of nations to which they are akin and loyal—and placed in a State to which they are alien and hostile. Israel, whose sovereignty and safety are already assailed by the States surrounding her, is invited to add to its perils by the influx from hostile territories of masses of people steeped in the hatred of her existence. All this is to happen in a region where the Arab nations possess unlimited opportunities for resettling their kinsmen, and in which Israel has already contributed to a solution of the refugee problems of Asia and Africa by receiving 450,000 refugees from Arab lands among its immigrants.

Surely the Committee will not find it difficult to understand why this solution finds such little favor. In discussing the rights and duties of individuals let us not forget the rights and duties of States. Israel is a small sovereign State whose primary preoccupation is that of its safety. It cannot in conscience entertain a solution which would involve its own disruption, and bring misery and disillusionment to refugees who have surely suffered enough from false hopes and vain illusions. While every State is entitled to respect for its security needs, Israel is surely unique in the acuteness of the threats which surround her. No other State on the face of the globe is surrounded, as we are, by hostile neighbors who openly avow its destruction. To suggest that in addition to facing external perils from the north, south and east, we should import a massive quantity of hatred and rancor into our midst is to demand something beyond prudence or reason.

ARAB COUNTRIES TRUE ''PATRIA'' FOR ARAB REFUGEES

There are three other considerations which must be placed on the scale against repatriation. First the word itself is not accurately used in this context. Transplanting an Arab refugee from an Arab land to a non-Arab land is not really ''repatriation.'' ''Patria'' is not a mere geographical concept. Resettlement of a refugee in Israel would be not repatriation, but alienation from Arab society; a true repatriation of an Arab refugee would be a process which brought him into union with people who share his conditions of language and heritage, his impulses of national loyalty and cultural identity.

Second, the validity of the ''repatriation'' concept is further undermined when we examine the structure of the refugee population. More than 50% of the Arab refugees are under 15 years of age. This means that at the time of Israel's establishment many of those, if born at all at that time, were under 5 years of age. We thus reach the striking fact that a majority of the refugee population can have no conscious memory of Israel at all.

Thirdly those who speak of repatriation to Israel might not always be aware of the measure of existing integration of refugees into countries of their present residence. In the Kingdom of Jordan, refugees have full citizenship and participate fully in the Government of the country. They are entitled to vote and be elected to the Jordanian parliament. Indeed many of them hold high rank in the government of the kingdom. Thousands of refugees are enrolled in the Jordanian army and its National Guard. It is, to say the least, eccentric to suggest that people who are citizens of another land and are actually or potentially enrolled in the armed forces of a country at war with Israel are simultaneously endowed with an optional right of Israel citizenship.

In the Syrian region of Egypt refugees have not been granted citizenship; but by virtue of a law of July 1956, their status is, to a large degree, assimilated to that of citizens. This is especially so in respect of the right to work and to establish commercial enterprises. According to the law of July 1956, refugees are subject to compulsory military service in the Syrian army. Here again, to adduce an unconditional right "repatriation" would signify that those who are citizens of a state foreign and hostile to Israel have a simultaneous right to be regarded as Israel citizens! Is there any state represented here which would acknowledge a right of entry to those who having left its shores have become the citizens of a foreign and hostile state, and have taken military service under Governments which proclaim a state of war against it?

This is merely a striking example of the sharp paradox which we enter if we try to reconcile the slogan of "repatriation" with the actual context, the hard facts of Arab Israel relations.

I do not believe it necessary to speak at any length on the point that resettlement in Arab countries is free from all the disadvantages which adhere to "repatriation." Every condition which has ever contributed to a solution of refugee problems by integration is present in this case. With its expanse of territory, its great rivers, its resources of mineral wealth, its accessibility to international aid, the Arab world is easily capable of absorbing an additional population, not only without danger to itself, but with actual reinforcement of its security and welfare. . . .

Golda Meir: A Call for Disarmament

From an address by the then Israeli Foreign Minister before the U.N. General Assembly on October 9, 1962.

The small and new countries, emerging into a world of armed camps, suffer twofold. Our immediate aim is rapid development, but since the danger of war still looms over every dispute, we are constantly burdened with defense expenditures to the detriment of our development needs. We too quickly learn the bitter lesson that those who threaten others must be deterred by some equilibrium, and let not those whose declared policy is to attack their neighbour cry out in mock indignation when the latter seeks some means of defense.

My Government rejects war as a means of settling disputes. From the day that the State of Israel was established, my Government has called for settling all outstanding differences by direct negotiations.

We do not rest content with calling upon the Great Powers to find a way to disarmament, and to settle outstanding problems by negotiation and conciliation between them. We are prepared to put this into practice in the dispute in which we are involved with our neighbours. As we have done in the past, we call again upon the Arab States to agree to complete disarmament with mutual inspection, covering all types of weapons, and to accept that method of direct negotiations as the only means for solving all differences between them and Israel . . .

There are many that are misled by two fallacies regarding the Middle East. The first is that it is an Arab region. In fact there are in it more non-Arabs than Arabs—Moslems, Christians and Jews. This composite pattern of peoples of various faiths and cultures has always been the pattern of the Middle East, each people with its historic continuity, past, present and future.

The second fallacy is that all would be well in that region if it were not for the tension between the Arab States and Israel. I would be the last to underrate the difficulties and dangers which arise from that conflict. But this is only one source of tension in a part of the world which is, unhappily, the scene of so much political instability, economic and social backwardness, rivalry and friction between different countries and regions and the pressures of the cold war. Anyone who follows the affairs of the Middle East knows that during this last year the focus of trouble in the area has been the bitter struggles within the Arab world which have made of the Arab League no longer even a façade of unity.

Israel longs for the day when the political independence and territorial integrity of every single State in the area—Arab and non-Arab—will be assured and when we can all concentrate on the welfare of our people. When I refer to the turmoil in the Arab world, it is because we are a Middle Eastern country and therefore affected by all that affects the peace of our area.

As far as the Israel-Arab dispute itself is concerned, it is well to see clearly what is the basic problem. It is the denial by the Arab States of Israel's right to exist. If this attitude were to change, and if the Arab States and Israel were to discuss their differences at the conference table in a frank and open manner, I am positive that solutions could be found on all the specific issues.

Year after year Israel has come on this rostrum with one demand— peace between it and its Arab neighbours. May I say here that we were grateful to the distinguished Deputy Foreign Minister of Ghana when he drew our attention again to the important statement of President Nkrumah during the 15th General Assembly, in which he called for recognition of the political realities in the Middle East and for insurance against non-aggression. We are entirely in agreement with that view.

The Arab denial of Israel's right of existence has a direct bearing on the distressing refugee problem. We are willing, and always have been willing, to discuss with the Arab Governments what can best be done to secure the future of the refugees in the light of the political and economic realities in the region. But a natural solution to the problem is frustrated by the Arab dream of destroying Israel and openly-proclaimed Arab intention of using the refugees for this purpose.

This design has been openly propagated even from the rostrum of this Assembly. This small spot of land, in which the Jewish people have revived their ancient home and nationhood, must again be wrested from them and they again be scattered to the four corners of the earth. Our neighbours have tried to achieve this by various means, open or guerilla warfare, economic boycott, propaganda and threats.

Negotiations and conciliation are proclaimed from this rostrum as the method to solve all other problems in the world except this one, which must, according to these spokesmen, be resolved by force. For every other nation, they claim co-existence, practised in peace. For Israel, non-existence, to be achieved by war. This doctrine not only runs counter to the basic principles of the United Nations Charter; its acceptance strikes at the very roots of our organization.

The world of today is overwhelmed by ideological disputes, international conflicts and economic controversies. In face of this situation, the basic concepts of the Charter, on the eschewing of force, on the unremitting search for peace, on international co-operation, on negotiation as the means to solve problems, have gained a new depth and significance. As long as negotiation is sought, there is hope. Those who rule out negotiation in the Middle East, those who year after year engage in sterile and stereotyped speeches of hostility, should know that their attitude is irrelevant to the basic theme of the international community and can have no echo in an organization which has proclaimed peace to be synonymous with human survival: that they are assaulting the foundations of human progress.

The policy of the Israel Government has been and continues to be peace. It is peace, not only for the world, but also between us and our neighbours. We believe in co-existence and co-operation everywhere and we shall do everything in our power towards that end . . .

Despite all the speeches which we have heard from Arab representatives, we are convinced that for us and for our neighbours the day must come when we shall live in amity and co-operation. Then will the entire Middle East become a region where the tens of millions of people will dwell in peace and then will its economic potentialities and rich cultural heritage achieve fulfilment. This Israel believes and towards this end we shall devote all our efforts.

Fayez A. Sayegh:
Zionist Colonialism in Palestine

This statement is from a booklet published in Beirut in 1965 by a leading spokesman of the Palestinian refugees maintaining that the Liberation of Palestine from the Zionist usurpers was the only possible solution of the problem.

In 1948, the Palestinian Arab people was forcibly dispossessed. Most Palestinians were evicted from their country. Their unyielding resistance and their costly sacrifices over three decades had failed to avert the national catastrophe.

But those sacrifices were not in vain. For they safeguarded the Palestinian national rights and underscored the legitimacy of the Arabs' claim to their national heritage. Rights undefended are rights surrendered. Unopposed and acquiesced in, usurpation is legitimized by default. For forfeiture of its patrimony, the Palestinian generation of the Inter-War era will be indicted by the Palestinian generations to come. It lost indeed—but not without fighting. It was dislodged indeed—but not for want of the will to defend its heritage.

Nor has the people of Palestine retroactively bestowed undeserved legitimacy upon the Zionist colonization of Palestine by recognizing the *fait accompli* after the fact. Many have been the self-appointed counselors of "realism", urging upon Palestinians acknowledgement of the new *status quo* in Palestine and acceptance of their exile "in good grace"; and many have been the lucrative offers of economic aid for "resettlement" and "rehabilitation" outside Palestine. But the people which had remained for thirty years undaunted by the combined power of British Imperialism and Zionist Colonialism, and which subsequently refused to allow the seizure of its land and the dispersal of its body to conquer its soul also, knew very well how to resist those siren-calls.

The Zionist settler-state, therefore, has remained a usurper, lacking even the semblance of legitimacy—because the people of Palestine has remained loyal to its heritage and faithful to its rights . . .

The people of Palestine, notwithstanding all its travails and misfortunes, still has undiminished faith in its future.

And the people of Palestine knows that the pathway to that future is the liberation of its homeland.

It was in this belief that the Palestinian people—after sixteen years of dispersion and exile, during which it had reposed its faith in its return to its country in world conscience and international public opinion, in the United Nations, and/or in the Arab states—chose at last to seize the initiative. In 1964, it reasserted its corporate personality by creating the Palestine Liberation Organization.

Only in the liberation of Palestine, spearheaded by Palestinians prepared to pay the price, can the supreme sacrifices of past generations of Palestinians be vindicated, and the visions and hopes of living Palestinians be transformed into reality.

Towards the Third Round

The Arab-Israeli conflict again escalated with the Egyptian decision in mid-May, 1967 to concentrate troops in Sinai and the announcement that the Straits of Tiran would be closed to Israeli shipping. In his speech on May 25, Nasser said that "under no circumstances" would he allow the Israeli flag to pass the Straits. On the day after: "Recently we felt we are strong enough, that if we were to enter a battle with Israel, with God's help, we could triumph" (see page 149). On the 29th: "The issue now at hand is not the Gulf of Aqabah but the rights of the Palestinian people" (see page 158). Meanwhile Hassanain Haykal, Egypt's leading spokesman, had explained (on May 26—see page 152) why a war with Israel was inevitable. On June 9, after the Egyptian defeat, Nasser announced his resignation (see page 160), but several hours after, following demonstrations in Cairo, withdrew it.

Nasser's Speech at UAR Advanced Air Headquarters,
May 25, 1967

The entire country looks up to you today. The entire Arab nation supports you. It is clear that in these circumstances the entire people support you completely and consider the armed forces as their hope today. It is also a fact that the entire Arab nation supports our armed forces in the current situation through which the entire Arab nation is passing.

What I wish to say is that we are now in 1967 and not in 1956 after the tripartite aggression. A great deal was said then and all the secrets revealed had a double interpretation. Israel, its commanders and rulers, boasted a great deal after 1956. I have read every word written about the 1956 events and I also know exactly what happened in 1956.

On the night of 29th October 1956 the Israeli aggression against us began. Fighting began on 30th October. We received the Anglo-French ultimatum which asked us to withdraw several miles west of the Suez Canal. On 31st October the Anglo-French attack on us began. The air raids began at sunset on 31st October. At the same time all our forces in Sinai were withdrawn completely to inside Egypt.

Thus in 1956 we did not have an opportunity to fight Israel. We decided to withdraw before the actual fighting with Israel began. Despite our decision to withdraw Israel was unable to occupy any of our positions except after we left them. Yet Israel created a major uproar, boasted and said a great deal about the Sinai campaign and the Sinai battle. Everyone of you knows all the rubbish that was said. They probably believed what they said themselves.

Today, more than 10 years after Suez all the secrets have been exposed. The most important secret concerns when they brought Ben Gurion to France to employ him as a dog for imperialism, to begin the operation. Ben Gurion refused to undertake anything unless he was given a written guarantee that they would protect him from the Egyptian bombers and the Egyptian Air Force. All this is now no longer secret. The entire world knows. It was on this basis that France sent fighter aircraft to Ben Gurion, and it was also on this basis that Britain pledged to Ben Gurion to bomb Egyptian airfields within 24 hours after the aggression began.

This goes to show how much they took into account the Egyptian forces. Ben Gurion himself said he had to think about the Haifa-Jerusalem-Tel Aviv triangle, which holds one-third of Israel's population. He could not attack Egypt out of fear of the Egyptian air force and bombers. At that time we had a few Ilyushin bombers. We had just acquired them to arm ourselves. Today we have many Ilyushins and other aircraft. There is a great difference between yesterday and today, between 1956 and 1967. Why do I say all this? I say it because we are in a confrontation with Israel. Israel today is not backed by Britain and France as was the case in 1956. It has the United States supporting it and supplying it with arms. But the world cannot again accept the plotting which took place in 1956.

Israel has been clamouring since 1956. They spoke of Israel's competence and high standard of training. It was backed in this by the West and the Western press. They capitalised on the Sinai campaign where no fighting actually took place because we withdrew to confront Britain and France.

Today we have a chance to prove the fact. We have, indeed, a chance to make the world see matters in their true perspective. We are now face to face with Israel. In recent days Israel has been making aggressive threats and boasting. On 12th May a very impertinent statement was made. Anyone reading this statement must believe that these people are so boastful and deceitful that one simply cannot remain silent. The statement said that the Israeli commanders announced they would carry out military operations against Syria in order to occupy Damascus and overthrow the Syrian Government. On the same day the Israeli Premier, Eshkol, made a very threatening statement against Syria. At the same time the commentaries said that Israel believed that Egypt could not make a move because it was bogged down in Yemen.

Of course they say that we are bogged down in Yemen and have problems there. We are in Yemen but they seem to have believed the lies they have been saying all these years about our being in Yemen. It is very possible that the Israelis themselves believed such lies. We are capable of carrying out our duties in Yemen and at the same time doing our national duty here in Egypt, both in defending our borders and in attacking if Israel attacks any Arab country.

On 13th May we received accurate information that Israel was concentrating on the Syrian border huge armed forces of about 11 to 13 brigades. These forces were divided into two fronts, one south of Lake Tiberias and the other north of the Lake. The decision made by Israel at this time was to carry out an attack against Syria starting on 17th May. On 14th May we took action, discussed the matter and contacted our Syrian brothers. The Syrians also had this information. Based on the information Lt-Gen. Mahmud Fawzi left for Syria to co-ordinate matters. We told them that we had decided that if Syria was attacked Egypt would enter the battle right from the start. This was the situation on 14th May; forces began to move in the direction of Sinai to take up their normal positions.

News agencies reported yesterday that these military movements must have been the result of a previously well laid plan. I say that the sequence of events determined the plan. We had no plan prior to 13th May because we believed that Israel would not have dared to make such an impertinent statement.

On 16th May we requested the withdrawal of the United Nations Emergency Force [UNEF] in a letter from Lt-Gen. Mahmud Fawzi. We requested the complete withdrawal of the UNEF. A major world wide campaign, led by the United States, Britain and Canada, began opposing the withdrawal of the UNEF from Egypt. Thus we felt that attempts were being made to turn the UNEF into a force serving neo-imperialism. It is obvious that the UNEF entered Egypt with our approval and therefore cannot continue to stay in Egypt except with our approval. Until yesterday a great deal was said about the UNEF. A campaign is also being mounted against the UN Secretary-General because he made a faithful and honest decision and could not surrender to the pressure brought to bear upon him by the United States, Britain and Canada to make the UNEF an instrument for implementing imperialism's plans.

It is quite natural, and I say this quite frankly, that had the UNEF ignored its basic task and turned to working for the aims of imperialism we would have regarded it as a hostile force and forcibly disarmed it. We are definitely capable of doing such a job. I say this now not to discredit the UNEF but to those who have neo-imperialist ideas and who want the UN to achieve their neo-imperialist aims—that there is not a single nation which respects itself and enjoys full sovereignty which could accept these methods in any shape or form. At the same time I say that the UNEF has honourably and faithfully carried out its duties. The UN Secretary-General refused to succumb to pressure. He issued immediate orders to the UNEF to withdraw. Consequently we praise the UNEF which has stayed 10 years in our country serving peace. And when they left—at a time when we found that the neo-imperialist force wanted to divert them from their basic task—we gave them a cheerful send-off and saluted them.

Our forces are now in Sinai and we are fully mobilised both in Gaza and Sinai. We notice that there is a great deal of talk about peace these days. Peace, peace, international peace, international security, UN intervention, and so on and so forth, all appears daily in the press. Why is it that no one spoke about peace, the UN and security when on 12th May the Israeli premier and the Israeli commanders made their statements that they would occupy Damascus, overthrow the Syrian regime, strike vigorously at Syria, and occupy a part of Syria? It was obvious that the press approved of the statements made by the Israeli premier and commanders.

There is talk about peace now. What peace? If there is a true desire for peace we say that we also work for peace. But does peace mean ignoring the rights of the Palestinian people because of the passage of time? Does peace mean that we should concede our rights because of the passage of time? Nowadays they speak about a UN presence in the region for the sake of peace. Does a UN presence in the region for peace mean that we should close our eyes to everything? The UN has adopted a number of resolutions in favour of the Palestinian people. Israel has implemented none of these resolutions. This brought no reaction from the UN.

Today US Senators, members of the House of Representatives, the press and the entire world speak in favour of Israel, of the Jews. But nothing is said in the Arabs' favour. The UN resolutions which favour the Arabs have not been implemented. What does this mean? No one is speaking in the Arabs' favour. How does the UN stand with regard to the Palestinian people? How does it stand with regard to the rights of the Palestinian people? How does it stand with regard to the tragedy which has continued since 1948? Talk of peace is heard only when Israel is in danger. But when Arab rights and the rights of the Palestinian people are lost, no one speaks about peace, rights, or anything like this.

It is clear, therefore, that an alliance exists between the Western powers, chiefly represented by the United States and Britain, with Israel. There is a political alliance. This political alliance prompts the Western powers to give military equipment to Israel. Yesterday and the day before yesterday the entire world was speaking about Sharm ash-Shaykh, navigation in the Gulf of Aqabah, and Eilat Port. This morning I heard the BBC say that in 1956 Abd an-Nasir promised to open the Gulf of Aqabah.

Of course, this is not true. It was copied from a British paper called the 'Daily Mail.' No such thing happened. Abd an-Nasir would never forfeit any UAR right. As I said, we would never give away a grain of sand from our soil or our country.

The armed forces' responsibility is now yours. The armed forces yesterday occupied Sharm ash-Shaykh. What does this mean? It is affirmation of our rights and our sovereignty over the Gulf of Aqabah which constitutes Egyptian territorial waters. Under no circumstances will we allow the Israeli flag to pass through the Gulf of Aqabah.

The Jews threaten war. We tell them you are welcome, we are ready for war. Our armed forces and all our people are ready for war, but under no circumstances will we abandon any of our rights. This water is ours. War might be an opportunity for the Jews, for Israel and Rabin, to test their forces against ours and to see that what they wrote about the 1956 battle and the occupation of Sinai was all a lot of nonsense.

With all this there is imperialism, Israel and reaction. Reaction casts doubt on everything and so does the Islamic alliance. We all know that the Islamic alliance is now represented by three states: the Kingdom of Saudi Arabia, the Kingdom of Jordan and Iran. They are saying that the purpose of the Islamic alliance is to reunite the Muslim against Israel. I would like the Islamic alliance to serve the Palestine question in only one way—by preventing the supply of oil to Israel. The oil which now reaches Israel, which reaches Eilat, comes from some of the Islamic alliance states. It goes to Eilat from Iran. Who then is supplying Israel with oil? The Islamic alliance—Iran, an Islamic alliance state. Such is the Islamic alliance. It is an imperialist alliance and this means it sides with Zionism because Zionism is the main ally of imperialism.

The Arab world, which is now mobilised to the highest degree, knows all this. It knows how to deal with the imperialist agents, the allies of Zionism and the fifth column.

They say they want to co-ordinate their plans with us. We cannot co-ordinate our plans in any way with Islamic alliance members because it would mean giving our plans to the Jews and to Israel. This is a vital battle. When we said that we were ready for the battle we meant that we would surely fight if Syria or any other Arab state was subjected to aggression.

The armed forces are now everywhere. The army and all the forces are now mobilised and so are the people. They are all behind you, praying for you day and night and believing that you are the pride of their nation, of the Arab nation. This is the feeling of the Arab people in Egypt and outside Egypt. We are confident that you will honour the trust. Everyone of us is ready to die and not give away a grain of his country's sand. This for us is the greatest honour. It is the greatest honour for us to defend our country. We are not scared by the imperialist, Zionist or reactionary campaigns. We are independent and we know the taste of freedom. We have built a strong national army and achieved our aims. We are building our country. There is currently a propaganda campaign, a psychological campaign, and a campaign of doubt against us. We leave all this behind us and follow the course of duty and victory. May God be with you.

Nasser's Speech to Arab Trade Unionists,
May 26, 1967

Thank you for this initiative. You have provided me with an opportunity to see you. I have actually heard your speeches and resolutions, there is nothing to add during this meeting to what you have already said. You, the Arab workers' federation, represent the biggest force in the Arab world.

We can achieve much by Arab actions, which is a main part of our battle. We must develop and build our countries to face the challenge of our enemies. The Arab world now is very different from what it was 10 days ago. Israel is also different from what it was 10 days ago. Despair has never found its way into Arab hearts and never will. The Arabs insist on their rights and are determined to regain the rights of the Palestinian people. The Arabs must accomplish this set intention and this aim. The first elements of this aim appeared in the test of Syria and Egypt in facing the Israeli threat. I believe that this test was a major starting point and basis from which to achieve complete cohesion in the Arab world. What we see today in the masses of the Arab people everywhere is their desire to fight. The Arab people want to regain the rights of the people of Palestine.

For several years, many people have raised doubts about our intentions towards Palestine. But talk is easy and action is difficult, very difficult. We emerged wounded from the 1956 battle. Britain, Israel and France attacked us then. We sustained heavy losses in 1956. Later, union was achieved. The 1961 secession occurred when we had only just got completely together and had barely begun to stand firmly on our feet.

Later the Yemeni revolution broke out. We considered it our duty to rescue our brothers, simply because of the principles and ideals which we advocated and still advocate.

We were waiting for the day when we would be fully prepared and confident of being able to adopt strong measures if we were to enter the battle with Israel. I say nothing aimlessly. One day two years ago, I stood up to say that we have no plan to liberate Palestine and that revolutionary action is our only course to liberate Palestine. I spoke at the summit conferences. The summit conferences were meant to prepare the Arab states to defend themselves.

Recently we felt we are strong enough, that if we were to enter a battle with Israel, with God's help, we could triumph. On this basis, we decided to take actual steps.

A great deal has been said in the past about the UN Emergency Force (UNEF). Many people blamed us for UNEF's presence. We were not strong enough. Should we have listened to them, or rather built and trained our Army while UNEF still existed? I said once that we could tell UNEF to leave within half an hour. Once we were fully prepared we could ask UNEF to leave. And this is what actually happened.

The same thing happened with regard to Sharm al Shaykh. We were also attacked on this score by some Arabs. Taking Sharm al Shaykh meant confrontation with Israel. Taking such action also meant that we were ready to enter a general war with Israel. It was not a separate operation. Therefore we had to take this fact into consideration when moving to Sharm al Shaykh. The present operation was mounted on this basis.

Actually I was authorised by the [Arab Socialist Union's] Supreme Executive Committee to implement this plan at the right time. The right time came when Syria was threatened with aggression. We sent reconnaissance aircraft over Israel. Not a single brigade was stationed opposite us on the Israeli side of the border. All Israeli brigades were confronting Syria. All but four brigades have now moved south to confront Egypt. Those four are still on the border with Syria. We are confident that once we have entered the battle we will triumph, God willing.

With regard to military plans, there is complete co-ordination of military action between us and Syria. We will operate as one army fighting a single battle for the sake of a common objective—the objective of the Arab nation.

The problem today is not just Israel, but also those behind it. If Israel embarks on an aggression against Syria or Egypt the battle against Israel will be a general one and not confined to one spot on the Syrian or Egyptian borders. The battle will be a general one and our basic objective will be to destroy Israel. I probably could not have said such things five or even three years ago. If I had said such things and had been unable to carry them out my words would have been empty and worthless.

Today, some 11 years after 1956, I say such things because I am confident. I know what we have here in Egypt and what Syria has. I also know that other states—Iraq, for instance, has sent its troops to Syria; Algeria will send troops; Kuwait also will send troops. They will send armoured and infantry units. This is Arab power. This is the true resurrection of the Arab nation, which at one time was probably in despair.

Today people must know the reality of the Arab world. What is Israel? Israel today is the United States. The United States is the chief defender of Israel. As for Britain, I consider it America's lackey. Britain does not have an independent policy. Wilson always follows Johnson's steps and says what he wants him to say. All Western countries take Israel's view.

The Gulf of Aqabah was a closed waterway prior to 1956. We used to search British, US, French and all other ships. After the tripartite aggression—and we all know the tripartite plot—we left the area to UNEF which came here under a UN resolution to make possible the withdrawal of Britain, France and Israel. The Israelis say they opened the maritime route. I say they told lies and believed their own lies. We withdrew because the British and the French attacked us. This battle was never between us and Israel alone.

I have recently been with the armed forces. All the armed forces are ready for a battle face to face between the Arabs and Israel. Those behind Israel are also welcome.

We must know and learn a big lesson today. We must actually see that in its hypocrisy and in its talks with the Arabs, the United States sides with Israel 100 per cent and is partial in favour of Israel. Why is Britain biased towards Israel? The West is on Israel's side. Gen. de Gaulle's personality caused him to remain impartial on this question and not to toe the US or the British line; France therefore did not take sides with Israel.

The Soviet Union's attitude was great and splendid. It supported the Arabs and the Arab nation. It went to the extent of stating that, together with the Arabs and the Arab nation, it would resist any interference or aggression.

Today every Arab knows foes and friends. If we do not learn who our enemies and our friends are, Israel will always be able to benefit from this behaviour. It is clear that the United States is an enemy of the Arab because it is completely biased in favour of Israel. It is also clear that Britain is an enemy of the Arabs because she, too, is completely biased in favour of Israel. On this basis we must treat our enemies and those who side with our enemies as our actual enemies. We can accord them such treatment. In fact we are not states without status. We are states of status, occupying an important place in the world. Our states have thousands of years of civilisation behind them—7,000 years of civilisation. Indeed, we can do much; we can expose the hypocrisy—the hypocrisy of our enemies if they try to persuade us that they wish to serve our interests. The United States seeks to serve only Israel's interests. Britain also seeks to serve only Israel's interests.

The question is not one of international law. Why all this uproar because of the closure of the Gulf of Aqabah? When Eshkol and Rabin threatened Syria, nobody spoke about peace or threats to peace. They actually hate the progressive regime in Syria. The United States, Britain and reaction—which is the friend of the United States and Britain—do not favour the national progressive regime in Syria. Israel, of course, shares their feelings. Israel is an ally of the United States and Britain. When Israel threatened Syria, they kept quiet and accepted what it said. But when we exercise one of our legitimate rights, as we always do, they turn the world upside down and speak about threats to peace and about a crisis in the Middle East. They fabricate these matters and threaten us with war.

We shall not relinquish our rights. We shall not concede our right in the Gulf of Aqabah. Today, the people of Egypt, the Syrian Army, and the Egyptian Army comprise one front. We want the entire front surrounding Israel to become one front. We want this. Naturally there are obstacles at present. Of course, Wasfi at-Tall is a spy for the Americans and the British. We cannot co-operate with these spies in any form, because the battle is one of destiny and the spies have no place in this battle. We want the front to become one united front around Israel. We will not relinquish the rights of the people of Palestine, as I have said before. I was told at the time that I might have to wait 70 years. During the crusader's occupation, the Arabs waited 70 years before a suitable opportunity arose and they drove away the crusaders. Some people commented that Abd an-Nasir said we should shelve the Palestinian question for 70 years. I do not mean exactly 70 years, but I say that as a people with an ancient civilisation, as an Arab people, we are determined that the Palestine question will not be liquidated or forgotten. The whole question then, is the proper time to achieve our aims. We are preparing ourselves constantly.

You are the hope of the Arab nation and its vanguard. As workers, you are actually building the Arab nation. The quicker we build, the quicker we will be able to achieve our aim. I thank you for your visit and wish you every success. Please convey my greetings and best wishes to the Arab workers in every Arab country.

Hassanain Haykal: An Armed Clash with
Israel Is Inevitable—Why?

Al Ahram, May 26, 1967.

It is extremely difficult to write about current events, particularly when such events are as swift and violent as a hurricane. But it is easy to write about what has already happened, to give an account and analysis of facts. It is also safe to write about what could take place in the future, because the future is boundless. Tomorrow never comes because every day has a tomorrow. The real problem is to speak about what is taking place while it happens. Then every interpretation may endure only a few minutes or even seconds.

There are two considerations which make the problem even more difficult: the topic is one of destiny and life, and there is the need for rational, intelligent writing without indulging in a long composition or platitudes.

What I am going to say after this introduction will in fact be no more than a collection of observations which I think are important at present. The first observation is that I believe an armed clash between the UAR and Israel is inevitable. This armed clash could occur at any moment, at any place along the line of confrontation between the Egyptian forces and the enemy Israeli forces—on land, air or sea along the area extending from Gaza in the North to the Gulf of Aqabah at Sharm ash-Shaykh in the South. But why do I emphasise this in such a manner? There are many reasons, particularly the psychological factor and its effect on the balance of power in the Middle East.

Passage through the Gulf of Aqabah is economically important to Israel at a time when it is suffering the symptoms a man has on waking up after a long, boisterous and drunken party. The fountains of German reparations are drying up. Israel has also drained the sources of contributions and gifts. Although emergency sources will emerge as a result of the present crisis, particularly with the help of Western propaganda trumpets, people in the West, at least many of them, are getting tired of an entity which has been unable to lead a normal life, like a child who does not want to grow up, who cannot depend on himself and does not want to take on any responsibility. Israel is suffering from an economic crisis. There are over 100,000 unemployed, nearly one quarter of Israel's manpower. The new blow had added to the economic plight. Israel attached great importance to its trade with East Africa and Asia. This trade depended on one route: the Red Sea via the Gulf of Aqabah, to Eilat. There were many projects for enlarging the port of Eilat, which at present can handle 400,000 tons a year. In addition, there were the oil lines. Israel has built two pipelines to carry Iranian oil from Eilat to the Haifa oil refinery. Israel has also dreamed of digging a canal from Eilat to Ashdod to compete with or replace the Suez Canal.

In my personal opinion all these important economic matters and questions are not the decisive factor which will influence or dictate the Israeli reaction to the closure of the Gulf of Aqabah. The decisive factor in my opinion is the psychological factor. The economic aspect swings back and forth between yes and no. From this aspect the challenge of war can be either accepted or put off. But the psychological factor cannot swing back and forth. From this aspect there is one answer: Yes. It is in the light of the compelling psychological factor that the needs of security, of survival itself, make acceptance of the challenge of war inevitable.

One thing is clear: The closure of the Gulf of Aqabah to Israeli navigation and the ban on the import of strategic goods, even when carried by non-Israeli ships, means first and last that the Arab nation represented by the

UAR has succeeded for the first time, *vis-à-vis* Israel, in changing by force a *fait accompli* imposed on it by force. This is the essence of the problem, regardless of the complications surrounding it and future contingencies.

As for the complications, we can find in the past ample justification for Arab resistance. We could say that the British mandate in Palestine had sold Palestine to Zionism in accordance with a resolution adopted by the League of Nations. This is true. We could say that the UN betrayed Palestine, and this is true. We could say Arab reaction from the Jordanian King Abdullah to the Saudi King Faysal connived at the plot against Palestine, and this is true. We could say about the Gulf of Aqabah that in 1956 imperialism, represented by the British and French forces, imposed a *fait accompli* during this period from autumn 1956 to spring 1967. It was imperialist not Israeli arms which imposed this *fait accompli*. We could say all this is seeking to justify Arab resistance. But the naked and rocky truth which remains after all this is that the accomplished fact was aggressively imposed by force. The Arabs did not have the force to resist the accomplished fact, let alone to change it by force and to impose a substitute consistent with their rights and interests.

As for the contingencies which may be precipitated by this new development, I do not think I need go into detail.

Israel has built its existence, security and future on force. The prevalent philosophy of its rulers has been that the Arab quakes before the forbidding glance, and that nothing deters him but fear. Thus Israeli intimidation reached its peak. Provocation went beyond tolerable bounds. But all of this, from the Israeli point of view, had the psychological aim of convincing the Arabs that Israel could do anything and that the Arabs could do nothing; that Israel was omnipotent and could impose any accomplished fact, while the Arabs were weak and had to accept any accomplished fact. Despite the error and danger in this Israeli philosophy—because two or even three million Israelis cannot by military force or by myth dominate a sea of 80 million Arabs—this philosophy remained a conviction deeply embedded in Israeli thinking, planning and action for many disturbing years, without any Arab challenge capable of restoring matters to their proper perspective.

Now this is the first time the Arabs have challenged Israel in an attempt to change an accomplished fact by force and to replace it by force with an alternative accomplished fact consistent with their rights and interests. The opening of the Gulf of Aqabah to Israel was an accomplished fact imposed by the force of imperialist arms. This week the closure of the Gulf of Aqabah to Israel was an alternative accomplished fact imposed and now being protected by the force of Arab arms. To Israel this is the most dangerous aspect of the current situation . . . Therefore it is not a matter of the Gulf of Aqabah but of something bigger. It is the whole philosophy of Israeli security. It is the philosophy on which Israeli existence has pivoted since its birth and on which it will pivot in the future.

Hence I say that Israel must resort to arms. Therefore I say that an armed clash between UAR and the Israeli enemy is inevitable.

As from now, we must expect the enemy to deal us the first blow in the battle. But as we wait for that first blow, we should try to minimise its effect as much as possible. The second blow will then follow. But this will be the blow we will deliver against the enemy in retaliation and deterrence. It will be the most effective blow we can possibly deal. Why do I say this now? My point of view is as follows:

When one studies the strategy of the Egyptian action of the 10 great days from 14th to 23rd May in which the positions and balance in the Middle East changed, one will immediately perceive two factors which at first sight may appear contradictory: The first factor: Egypt was ready and prepared. The second factor: the Egyptian action was a complete surprise, even to Egypt in so far as it was a reaction to a specific situation, namely, Israel's threat to and readiness to invade Syria.

By analysing the first factor in the strategy of the Egyptian action during the 10 great days which changed the positions and balance in the Middle East we find that there are roots extending from the spring of 1967 back to the time when the UAR called for the Arab summit conferences. The first summit conference was convened in January 1964. The first item submitted by the UAR to that conference was the Jordan headwaters. At that time the anti-Egyptian Western propaganda which was backed by the reactionary elements sought, discreetly at times but most of the time shamelessly, to hamper Egyptian policy at that time by two propaganda themes: (1) that Egypt's whole aim in the summit conferences policy was to settle the Yemeni issue with Saudi Arabia; (2) that when Egypt called for the summit conferences it wanted to abandon the responsibility of action for Palestine, in accordance with the traditional method which says that when you face a problem for which you cannot find a solution the only way to bury and get rid of it is to form a commission to discuss and study it. All this, of course, was untrue, since Egypt at the time imagined that the Arab summit conferences could draw up the policy of the liberation battle and could prepare for it. Egypt wanted unified action to be the front of a broad movement which might have world-wide political influence serving the strategy of battle. Besides, unified Arab action might be beneficial in providing possibilities for defending Arab countries which at that time did not have reassuring defences. At the same time Egypt believed that when the time came for earnest action, loyalty and fidelity to the trust dictated that it should primarily depend on itself.

Accordingly the summit conferences were a broad front suitable for world-wide political influence. It was also possible for them to help strengthen the defence of Arab countries surrounding Israel. Behind this broad front and the consolidation of the other Arab countries surrounding Israel Egypt could prepare and mobilise its own effective forces.

The remainder of the story of the summit conferences is known and I do not propose to repeat it. It ended in utter failure because of Arab reactionary rancour, and because reaction had greater hatred for Arab social progress than for the Israeli enemy, which wants to humiliate all the Arabs whatever their social views. The broad front for unified Arab action therefore collapsed with the failure of the summit conferences. The possibilities of strengthening the defence of the other Arab countries surrounding Israel did not sufficiently materialise as they should have done. Egypt was unable to control all those circumstances but it was able to control the third objective, namely, to prepare and mobilise its effective forces.

Anti-Egyptian Western propaganda, backed by the Arab reactionary elements, continued to attack Egypt fiercely. The attack went to the length of spreading the belief that the entire Egyptian Army had perished in Yemen, had been scattered into aimless groups, and that the remainder had been killed, wounded or captured. Similarly it was said that the Egyptian economy was collapsing and could not stand on its feet, let alone bear the weight of any bold venture and carry on with it. But Egypt knew the truth and was confident that the truth would appear to the entire Arab nation one day when the time was ripe for serious action.

Egypt, then, was prepared and ready. This is the first fact about the strategy of Egyptian action during the 10 great days.

I will now come to the second factor in the crisis. This factor is that the Egyptian action was a complete surprise. It appears, and it is now almost certain, that the forces hostile to Egypt, that is imperialism, Arab reaction and Israel, had come in the end to believe their own propaganda. People sometimes fall prey to the lies they themselves fabricate. Something of that sort must certainly have happened, otherwise Israel would not have persisted in its threats against Syria and gone to the length of the cry of 'March on Damascus.' It must have felt certain that there would be no decisive Egyptian reaction, because there were insufficient forces for any initiative or retaliatory action.

It was this Israeli threat to Syria and information confirming it concerning intentions and plans that precipitated the emergency situation to which Egypt had to react immediately, even though it came as a surprise to it. There was preparation and mobilisation of the effective Egyptian forces. There was national consciousness and abidance by its principles. There was creative leadership. What I mean to say is that Egypt was not prepared for this specific contingency but was prepared for all contingencies including such a one.

Now, to turn to the march of events during the 10 great days which changed the situation and the balance of the Middle East. Events began to move. One calculated and effective step followed another: the decision was taken to implement the joint defence agreement with Syria—this is the decision which Lt-Gen. Muhammad Fawzi, the Chief of Staff of the

Egyptian Armed Forces, carried on the five-hour visit to Damascus. Then followed the message addressed by Lt-Gen. Muhammad Fawzi to the Commander of the UN Emergency Force to withdraw his forces from the Egyptian borders with Israel. The Egyptian Armed Forces then, without waiting, actually began occupying all the border positions. The Foreign Minister Mahmud Riyad then then sent his message to the UN Secretary-General U Thant on the withdrawal and evacuation of the Emergency Forces in the UAR and Gaza. Then followed the advance on Sharm al Shaykh, the entrance to the Gulf of Aqabah; the order was issued to close the Gulf of Aqabah to Israeli shipping and to strategic goods for Israel even if transported aboard non-Israeli ships; and all the US initiatives were rejected. All these actions were backed by a massive, ready force enjoying a morale brimming over with a fighting spirit the like of which the Middle East has never seen.

Two results were thus achieved, that is to say: (1) The plan against Syria collapsed; the invasion of Syria became impossible because all of the enemy forces streamed into the South to confront the Egyptian concentration. (2) The accomplished fact which the British-French invasion, and not the Israeli Army, had imposed in 1956 to the benefit of Israel, was changed.

In other words the strategy of this stage achieved its first objective by frustrating the plot to invade Syria, and moreover, it achieved another longed-for and precious objective: the return of the armed forces to direct confrontation with Israel and the closing once again of the door to the Gulf of Aqabah in Israel's face.

Is this, then, the end of the matter? I would answer that I have explained—or rather tried to explain—with the first observation in this inquiry that the problem has not ended but rather has hardly begun. This is because I am confident that for many reasons, chiefly the psychological, Israel cannot accept or remain indifferent to what has taken place. In my opinion it simply cannot do so. This means, and that is what I intend to say in the second observation of this inquiry that the next move is up to Israel. Israel has to reply now. It has to deal a blow. We have to be ready for it, as I said, to minimise its effect as much as possible. Then it will be our turn to deal the second blow, which we will deliver with the utmost possible effectiveness.

In short, Egypt has exercised its power and achieved the objectives of this stage without resorting to arms so far. But Israel has no alternative but to use arms if it wants to exercise power. This means that the logic of the fearful confrontation now taking place between Egypt, which is fortified by the might of the masses of the Arab nation, and Israel, which is fortified by the illusion of American might, dictates that Egypt, after all it has now succeeded in achieving must wait, even though it has to wait for a blow. This is necessitated also by the sound conduct of the battle, particularly from the international point of view. Let Israel begin. Let our second blow then be ready. Let it be a knockout.

Nasser's Speech to National Assembly Members on May 29, 1967

Brothers, when Brother Anwar as Sadat informed me of your decision to meet me I told him that I myself was prepared to call on you at the National Assembly, but he said you were determined to come. I therefore responded to this and I thank you heartily for your consideration.

I was naturally not surprised by the law which Brother Anwar as Sadat read because I was notified of it before I came here. However, I wish to thank you very much for your feelings and for the powers given me. I did not ask for such powers because I felt that you and I were as one, that we could co-operate and work for the sublime interest of this country giving a great example of unselfishness and of work for the welfare of all. Thanks be to God, for four years now the National Assembly has been working and has given great examples. We have given great examples in co-operation and unselfishness and in placing before us the sublime and highest objective—the interest of this nation.

I am proud of this resolution and law. I promise you that I will use it only when necessary. I will, however, send all the laws to you. Thank you once again. The great gesture of moral support represented by this law is very valuable to my spirit and heart. I heartily thank you for this feeling and this initiative.

The circumstances through which we are now passing are in fact difficult ones because we are not only confronting Israel but also those who created Israel and who are behind Israel. We are confronting Israel and the West as well—the West, which created Israel and which despised us Arabs and which ignored us before and since 1948. They had no regard whatsoever for our feelings, our hopes in life, or our rights. The West completely ignored us, and the Arab nation was unable to check the West's course.

Then came the events of 1956—the Suez battle. We all know what happened in 1956. When we rose to demand our rights. Britain, France and Israel opposed us, and we were faced with the tripartite aggression. We resisted, however, and proclaimed that we would fight to the last drop of our blood. God gave us success and God's victory was great.

Subsequently we were able to rise and to build. Now, 11 years after 1956, we are restoring things to what they were in 1956. This is from the material aspect. In my opinion this material aspect is only a small part, whereas the spiritual aspect is the great side of the issue. The spiritual aspect involves the renaissance of the Arab nation, the revival of the Palestine question, and the restoration of confidence to every Arab and to every Palestinian. This is on the basis that if we are able to restore conditions to what they were before 1956 God will surely help and urge us to restore the situation to what it was in 1948 [prolonged applause].

Brothers, the revolt, upheaval and commotion which we now see taking place in every Arab country are not only because we have returned to the Gulf of Aqabah or rid ourselves of the UNEF, but because we have restored Arab honour and renewed Arab hopes.

Israel used to boast a great deal, and the Western powers, headed by the United States and Britain, used to ignore and even despise us and consider us of no value. But now that the time has come—and I have already said in the past that we will decide the time and place and not allow them to decide—we must be ready for triumph and not for a recurrence of the 1948 comedies. We shall triumph, God willing.

Preparations have already been made. We are now ready to confront Israel. They have claimed many things about the 1956 Suez war, but no one believed them after the secrets of the 1956 collusion were uncovered—that mean collusion in which Israel took part. Now we are ready for the confrontation. We are now ready to deal with the entire Palestine question.

The issue now at hand is not the Gulf of Aqabah, the Straits of Tiran, or the withdrawal of the UNEF, but the rights of the Palestine people. It is the aggression which took place in Palestine in 1948 with the collaboration of Britain and the United States. It is the expulsion of the Arabs from Palestine, the usurpation of their rights, and the plunder of their property. It is the disavowal of all the UN resolutions in favour of the Palestinian people.

The issue today is far more serious than they say. They want to confine the issue to the Straits of Tiran, the UNEF and the right of passage. We demand the full rights of the Palestinian people. We say this out of our belief that Arab rights cannot be squandered because the Arabs throughout the Arab world are demanding these Arab rights.

We are not afraid of the United States and its threats, of Britain and her threats, or of the entire Western world and its partiality to Israel. The United States and Britain are partial to Israel and give no consideration to the Arabs, to the entire Arab nation. Why? Because we have made them believe that we cannot distinguish between friend and foe. We must make them know that we know who our foes are and who our friends are and treat them accordingly.

If the United States and Britain are partial to Israel, we must say that our enemy is not only Israel but also the United States and Britain and treat them as such. If the Western Powers disavow our rights and ridicule and despise us, we Arabs must teach them to respect us and take us seriously. Otherwise all our talk about Palestine, the Palestine people, and Palestinian rights will be null and void and of no consequence. We must treat enemies as enemies and friends as friends.

I said yesterday that the States that champion freedom and peace have supported us. I spoke of the support given us by India, Pakistan, Afghanistan, Yugoslavia, Malaysia, the Chinese People's Republic and the Asian and African States.

After my statements yesterday I met the War Minister Shams Badran and learned from him what took place in Moscow. I wish to tell you today that the Soviet Union is a friendly Power and stands by us as a friend. In all our dealings with the Soviet Union—and I have been dealing with the USSR since 1955—it has not made a single request of us. The USSR has never interfered in our policy or internal affairs. This is the USSR as we have always known it. In fact, it is we who have made urgent requests of the USSR. Last year we asked for wheat and they sent it to us. When I also asked for all kinds of arms they gave them to us. When I met Shams Badran yesterday he handed me a message from the Soviet Premier Kosygin saying that the USSR supported us in this battle and would not allow any Power to intervene until matters were restored to what they were in 1956.

Brothers, we must distinguish between friend and foe, friend and hypocrite. We must be able to tell who is making requests, who has ulterior motives, and who is applying economic pressure. We must also know those who offer their friendship to us for no other reason than a desire for freedom and peace.

In the name of the UAR people, I thank the people of the USSR for their great attitude, which is the attitude of a real friend. This is the kind of attitude we expect. I said yesterday that we had not requested the USSR or any other state to intervene, because we really want to avoid any confrontation which might lead to a world war and also because we really work for peace and advocate world peace. When we voiced the policy of non-alignment, our chief aim was world peace.

Brothers, we will work for world peace with all the power at our disposal, but we will also hold tenaciously to our rights with all the power at our disposal. This is our course. On this occasion, I address myself to our brothers in Aden and say: Although occupied with this battle, we have not forgotten you. We are with you. We have not forgotten the struggle of Aden and the occupied South for liberation. Aden and the occupied South must be liberated and colonialism must end. We are with them; present matters have not taken our minds from Aden.

I thank you for taking the trouble to pay this visit. Moreover, your presence is an honour to the Qubbah Palace, and I am pleased to have met you. Peace be with you.

Nasser's Resignation Broadcast, June 9, 1967

Brothers, at times of triumph and tribulation, in the sweet hours and bitter hours, we have become accustomed to sit together to discuss things, to speak frankly of facts, believing that only in this way can we always find the right path however difficult circumstances may be.

We cannot hide from ourselves the fact that we have met with a grave setback in the last few days, but I am confident that we all can and, in a short time, will overcome our difficult situation, although this calls for much patience and wisdom as well as moral courage and ability to work on our part. Before that, brothers, we need to cast a glance back over past events so that we shall be able to follow developments and the line of our march leading to the present conditions.

All of us know how the crisis started in the Middle East. At the beginning of last May there was an enemy plan for the invasion of Syria and the statements by his politicians and all his military leaders openly said so. There was plenty of evidence concerning the plan. Sources of our Syrian brothers were categorical on this and our own reliable information confirmed it. Add to this the fact that our friends in the Soviet Union warned the parliamentary delegation, which was on a visit to Moscow, at the beginning of last month, that there was a premeditated plan against Syria. We considered it our duty not to accept this silently. This was the duty of Arab brotherhood, it was also the duty of national security. Whoever starts with Syria will finish with Egypt.

Our armed forces moved to our frontiers with a competence which the enemy acknowledged even before our friends. Several steps followed. There was the withdrawal of the United Nations Emergency Force and the return of our forces to the Sharm al Shaykh post, the controlling point in the Straits of Tiran, which had been used by the Israeli enemy as one of the after-effects of the tripartite aggression against us in 1956. The enemy's flag passing in front of our forces was intolerable, apart from other reasons connected with the dearest aspirations of the Arab nation.

Accurate calculations were made of the enemy's strength and showed us that our armed forces, at the level of equipment and training which they had reached, were capable of repelling the enemy and deterring him. We realised that the possibility of an armed clash existed and accepted the risk.

Before us were several factors—national, Arab and international. A message from the US President Lyndon Johnson was handed to our Ambassador in Washington 26th May asking us to show self-restraint and not to be the first to fire, or else we should have to face grave consequences. On the very same night, the Soviet Ambassador asked to have an urgent meeting with me at 05.30 [as broadcast] after midnight. He informed me of an urgent request from the Soviet Government not to be the first to open fire.

In the morning of last Monday, 5th June, the enemy struck. If we say now it was a stronger blow than we had expected, we must say at the same time, and with complete certainty that it was bigger than the potential at his disposal. It became very clear from the first moment that there were other powers behind the enemy—they came to settle their accounts with the Arab national movement. Indeed, there were surprises worthy of note:

(1) The enemy, whom we were expecting from the east and north, came from the west—a fact which clearly showed that facilities exceeding his own capacity and his calculated strength had been made available to him.

(2) The enemy covered at one go all military and civilian airfields in the UAR. This means that he was relying on some force other than his own normal strength to protect his skies against any retaliatory action from our side. The enemy was also leaving other Arab fronts to be tackled with outside assistance which he had been able to obtain.

(3) There is clear evidence of imperialist collusion with the enemy— an imperialist collusion, trying to benefit from the lesson of the open collusion of 1956, by resorting this time to abject and wicked concealment. Nevertheless, what is now established is that American and British aircraft carriers were off the shores of the enemy helping his war effort. Also, British aircraft raided, in broad daylight, positions on the Syrian and Egyptian fronts, in addition to operations by a number of American aircraft reconnoitering some of our positions. The inevitable result of this was that our land forces, fighting most violent and brave battles in the open desert, found themselves at the difficult time without adequate air cover in face of the decisive superiority of the enemy air forces. Indeed it can be said without emotion or exaggeration, that the enemy was operating with an air force three times stronger than his normal force.

The same conditions were faced by the forces of the Jordanian Army, fighting a brave battle under the leadership of King Husayn who—let me say for the sake of truth and honesty—adopted an excellent stand; and I admit that my heart was bleeding while I was following the battles of his heroic Arab Army in Jerusalem and other parts of the West Bank on the night when the enemy and his plotting forces massed no less than 400 aircraft over the Jordanian front.

There were other honourable and marvellous efforts. The Algerian people, under their great leader Hawwari Bumedien, gave without reservation and without stinting for the battle. The people of Iraq and their faithful leader Abd ar-Rahman Arif gave without reservation or stinting for the battle. The Syrian Army fought heroically, consolidated by the forces of the great Syrian people and under the leadership of their national Government. The peoples and governments of Sudan, Kuwait, Yemen, Lebanon, Tunisia and Morocco adopted honourable stands. All the peoples of the Arab nation, without exception, adopted a stand of manhood and dignity all along the Arab homeland; a stand of resolution and determination that Arab right shall not be lost, shall not be humiliated, and that the war in its defence is advancing, regardless of sacrifice and setbacks, on the road of the sure and inevitable victory. There were also great nations outside the Arab homeland who gave us invaluable moral support.

But the plot, and we must say this with the courage of men, was bigger and fiercer. The enemy's main concentration was on the Egyptian front which he attacked with all his main force of armoured vehicles and infantry, supported by air supremacy the dimensions of which I have outlined for you. The nature of the desert did not permit a full defence especially, in face of the enemy's air supremacy. I realised that the armed battle might not go in our favour. I, with others, tried to use all sources of Arab strength. Arab oil came in to play its part. The Suez Canal came in to play its part. A great role is still reserved for general Arab action. I am fully confident that it will measure up to its task. Our Armed Forces in Sinai were obliged to evacuate the first line of defence. They fought fearful tank and air battles on the second line of defence.

We then responded to the cease-fire resolution, in view of assurances contained in the latest Soviet draft resolution, to the Security Council, as well as French statements to the effect that no one must reap any territorial expansion from the recent aggression, and in view of world public opinion, especially in Asia and Africa, which appreciates our position and feels the ugliness of the forces of international domination which pounced on us.

We now have several urgent tasks before us. The first is to remove the traces of this aggression against us and to stand by the Arab nation resolutely and firmly; despite the setback, the Arab nation, with all its potential and resources, is in a position to insist on the removal of the traces of the aggression.

The second task is to learn the lesson of the setback. In this connection there are three vital facts, (1) The elimination of imperialism in the Arab world will leave Israel with its own intrinsic power; yet, whatever the circumstances, however long it may take, the Arab intrinsic power is greater and more effective. (2) Redirecting Arab interests in the service of Arab rights is an essential safeguard: the American Sixth Fleet moved with Arab oil, and there are Arab bases, placed forcibly and against the will of the peoples, in the service of aggression. (3) The situation now demands a united word from the entire Arab nation; this, in the present circumstances, is irreplaceable guarantee.

Now we arrive at an important point in this heartsearching by asking ourselves: does this mean that we do not bear responsibility for the consequences of the setback? I tell you truthfully and despite any factors on which I might have based my attitude during the crisis, that I am ready to bear the whole responsibility. I have taken a decision in which I want you all to help me. I have decided to give up completely and finally every official post and every political role and return to the ranks of the masses and do my duty with them like every other citizen.

The forces of imperialism imagine that Jamal Abd al-Nasser is their enemy. I want it to be clear to them that their enemy is the entire Arab nation, not just Jamal Abd al-Nasser. The forces hostile to the Arab national movement try to portray this movement as an empire of Abd al-Nasser. This is not true, because the aspiration for Arab unity began before Abd al-Nasser and will remain after Abd al-Nasser. I always used to tell you that the nation remains, and that the individual—whatever his role and however great his contribution to the causes of his homeland—is only a tool of the popular will, and not its creator.

In accordance with Article 110 of the Provisional Constitution promulgated in March 1964 I have entrusted my colleague, friend and brother Zakariya Muhiedin with taking over the point of President and carrying out the constitutional provisions on this point. After this decision, I place all I have at his disposal in dealing with the grave situation through which our people are passing.

In doing this I am not liquidating the revolution—indeed the revolution is not the monopoly of any one generation of revolutionaries. I take pride in the brothers of this generation of revolutionaries. It has brought to pass the evacuation of British imperialism, has won the independence of Egypt and defined its Arab personality, and has combated the policy of spheres of influence in the Arab world; it has led the social revolution and created a deep transformation in the Egyptian reality by establishing the people's control over the sources of their wealth and the result of Arab action; it recovered the Suez Canal and laid down the foundation of industrial upsurge in Egypt; it built the High Dam to bring fertile greenness to the barren desert; it laid down a power network over the whole of the north of the Nile Valley; it made oil resources gush out after a long wait. More important still, it gave the leadership of political action to the alliance of the people's working forces, the constant source of renewed leaderships carrying the banners of Egyptian and Arab struggle through its successive stages, building socialism, succeeding and triumphing.

I have unlimited faith in this alliance as the leader of national action: the peasants, the workers, the soldiers, the intellectuals and national capital. Its unity and cohesion and creative response within the framework of this unity are capable of creating—through work, serious work, difficult work, as I have said more than once—colossal miracles for this country in order to be a strength for itself, for its Arab nation, for the movement of national revolution and for world peace based on justice.

The sacrifices made by our people and their burning spirit during the crisis and the glorious pages of heroism written by the officers and soldiers of our armed forces with their blood will remain an unquenchable torch in our history and a great inspiration for the future and its great hopes. The people were splendid as usual, noble as their nature, believing, sincere and loyal. The members of our armed forces were an honourable example of Arab man in every age and every place. They defended the grains of sand in the desert to the last drop of their blood. In the air, they were, despite enemy supremacy, legends of dedication and sacrifice, of courage and willingness to perform the duty in the best way.

This is an hour for action; not an hour for sorrow. It is a situation calling for ideals and not for selfishness or personal feelings. All my heart is with you, and I want all your hearts to be with me. May God be with us all, a hope in our hearts, a light and guidance. Peace and the blessing of God be with you.

The Six Days War:

Abba Eban's Speech at the Special Assembly of the United Nations, June 19, 1967*

Our Watchword Is 'Forward to Peace'

The subject of our discussion is the Middle East, its past agony and its future hope. We speak of a region whose destiny has profoundly affected the entire human experience. In the heart of that region, at the very centre of its geography and history, lives a very small nation called Israel. This nation gave birth to the currents of thought which have fashioned the life of the Mediterranean world and of vast regions beyond. It has now been re-established as the home and sanctuary of a people which has seen six million of its sons exterminated in the greatest catastrophe ever endured by a family of the human race.

In recent weeks the Middle East has passed through a crisis whose shadows darken the world. This crisis has many consequences but only one cause. Israel's rights to peace, security, sovereignty, economic development and maritime freedom—indeed its very right to exist—has been forcibly denied and aggressively attacked. This is the true origin of the tension which torments the Middle East. All the other elements of the conflict are the consequences of this single cause. There has been danger, there is still peril in the Middle East because Israel's existence, sovereignty and vital interests have been and are violently assailed.

The threat to Israel's existence, its peace, security, sovereignty and development has been directed against her in the first instance by the neighbouring Arab states. But all the conditions of tension, all the impulses of aggression in the Middle East have been aggravated by the policy of one of the Great Powers which under our Charter bear primary responsi-

---

* Reprinted from *The Jerusalem Post*.

bilities for the maintenance of international peace and security. I shall show how the Soviet Union has been unfaithful to that trust. The burden of responsibility lies heavy upon her.

I come to this rostrum to speak for a united people which, having faced danger to the national survival, is unshakably resolved to resist any course which would renew the perils from which it has emerged.

The General Assembly is chiefly pre-occupied by the situation against which Israel defended itself on the morning of June 5. I shall invite every peace-loving state represented here to ask itself how it would have acted on that day if it faced similar dangers. But if our discussion is to have any weight or depth, we must understand that great events are not born in a single instant of time. It is beyond all honest doubt that between May 14 and June 5, Arab governments led and directed by President Nasser, methodically prepared and mounted an aggressive assault designed to bring about Israel's immediate and total destruction. My authority for that conviction rests on the statements and actions of Arab governments themselves. There is every reason to believe what they say and to observe what they do.

The Pattern of Aggression 1957–1967

During Israel's first decade, the intention to work for her destruction by physical violence has always been part of the official doctrine and policy of Arab states. But many members of the United Nations hoped and believed that relative stability would ensue from the arrangements discussed in the General Assembly in March 1957. An attempt has been made to inaugurate a period of non-belligerency and co-existence in the relations between the UAR and Israel. A United Nations emergency force was to separate the armies in Sinai and Gaza. The Maritime Powers were to exercise free and innocent passage in the Gulf of Akaba and the Straits of Tiran. Terrorist attacks against Israel were to cease. The Suez Canal was to be opened to Israel shipping, as the Security Council had decided six years before.

In March 1957, these hopes and expectations were endorsed in the General Assembly by the United States, France, the United Kingdom, Canada and other states in Europe, the Americas, Africa, Asia and Australia. These assurances, expressed with special solemnity by the four governments which I have mentioned, induced Israel to give up positions which she then held at Gaza and at the entrance to the Straits of Tiran and in Sinai. Non-belligerency, maritime freedom and immunity from terrorist attack were henceforth to be secured, not by Israel's own pressure but by the concerted will of the international community. Egypt expressed no opposition to these arrangements. Bright hopes for the future illuminated this hall ten years ago.

There were times during the past decade when it really seemed that a certain stability had been achieved. As we look back it becomes plain that the Arab governments regarded the 1957 arrangements merely as a breathing space enabling them to gather strength for a later assault. At the end of 1962, President Nasser began to prepare Arab opinion for an armed attack that was to take place within a few brief years. As his armaments grew his aggressive designs came more into light. On December 23, 1962, Nasser said:

> We feel that the soil of Palestine is the soil of Egypt, and of the whole Arab world. Why do we all mobilize? Because we feel that the land of Palestine is part of our land, and are ready to sacrifice ourselves for it.

The present Foreign Minister of Egypt, Mahmoud Riad, echoed his master's voice:

> The sacred Arab struggle will not come to an end until Palestine is restored to its owners.

In March 1963, the official Cairo radio continued the campaign of menace:

> Arab unity is taking shape towards the great goal—i.e. the triumphant return to Palestine with the banner of unity flying high in front of the holy Arab march.

The newspaper *Al-Gumhuriya* published an official announcement on the same day:

> The noose around Israel's neck is tightening gradually . . . Israel is mightier than the empires which were vanquished in the Arab East and West . . . The Arab people will take possession of their full rights in their united homeland.

Egypt is not a country in which the press utters views and opinions independently of the official will. There is thus significance in the statement of *Al-Akhbar* on April 4, 1963:

> The liquidation of Israel will not be realized through a declaration of war against Israel by Arab states, but *Arab unity and inter-Arab understanding will serve as a hangman's rope for Israel.*

The Assembly will note that the imagery of a hangman's rope or of a tightening noose occurs frequently in the macabre vocabulary of Nasserism. He sees himself perpetually presiding over a scaffold. In June 1967 the metaphor of encirclement and strangulation was to come vividly to life, in Israel's hour of solitude and danger.

In February 1964 Nasser enunciated in simple terms what was to become his country's policy during the period of preparation:

The possibilities of the future will be war with Israel. It is we who will dictate the time. It is we who will dictate the place.

A similar chorus of threats arose during this period from other Arab capitals. President Aref of Iraq and President Ben-Bella of Algeria were especially emphatic and repetitive in their threat to liquidate Israel. The Syrian attitude was more ominous because it affected a neighbouring frontier. Syrian war propaganda has been particularly intense in the past few years. In 1964 the Syrian Defence Minister, General Abdulla Ziada, announced:

The Syrian army stands as a mountain to crush Israel and demolish her. This army knows how to crush its enemies.

Early last year Syria began to proclaim and carry out what it called a "popular war" against Israel. The Syrian concept of "popular war" expressed itself in the dispatch of trained terrorist groups into Israel territory to blow up installations and communication centres, to kill, maim, cripple and terrorise civilians in peaceful homes and farms. Sometimes the terrorists, trained in Syria, were dispatched through Jordan or Lebanon. The terrorist war was formally declared by President Al-Atassi on May 22, 1966, when he addressed soldiers on the Israel-Syrian front:

We raise the slogan of the people's liberation war. We want total war with no limits, a war that will destroy the Zionist base.

The Syrian Defence Minister, Hafiz Asad, said two days later:

We say: We shall never call for, nor accept peace. We shall only accept war and the restoration of the usurped land. We have resolved to drench this land with our blood, to oust you, aggressors, and throw you into the sea for good. We must meet as soon as possible and fight a single liberation war on the level of the whole area against Israel, Imperialism and all the enemies of the people.

Mr. President, from that day to this, not a week passed without Syrian officials adding to this turgid stream of invective and hate. From that day to this, there has not been a single month without terrorist acts, offensive to every impulse of human compassion and international civility, being directed from Syria against Israel citizens and territory. I would have no difficulty in filling the General Assembly's records with a thousand official statements by Arab leaders in the past two years announcing their intention to destroy Israel by diverse forms of organized physical violence. The Arab populations have been conditioned by their leaders to the anticipation of a total war, preceded by the constant harassment of the prospective victim.

Israel's Policy 1957–1967

From 1948 to this very day there has not been one statement by any Arab representative of a neighbouring Arab state indicating readiness to respect existing agreements or the permanent renunciation of force to recognize Israel's sovereign right of existence or to apply to Israel any of the central provisions of the United Nations Charter.

For some time Israel showed a stoic patience in her reaction to these words of menace. This was because the threats were not accompanied by a capacity to carry them into effect. But the inevitable result of this campaign of menace was the burden of a heavy race of arms. We strove to maintain an adequate deterrent strength and the decade beginning in March 1957 was not monopolized by security considerations alone. Behind the wall of a strong defence, with eyes vigilantly fixed on dangerous borders, we embarked on a constructive era in the national enterprise. These were years of swift expansion in our agriculture and industry, of intensive progress in the sciences and arts, of a widening international vocation, symbolized in the growth of strong links with the developing world. At the end of this first decade, Israel had established relations of commerce and culture with all the Americas, and with most of the countries of Western, Central and Eastern Europe. In her second decade she built constructive links with the emerging countries of the developing world with whom we are tied by a common aspiration to translate national freedom into creative economic growth and progress.

Fortified by friendships in all five continents, inspired by its role in the great drama of developments, intensely preoccupied by tasks of spiritual cooperation with kindred communities in various parts of the world, and in the efforts to assure the Jewish survival after the disastrous blows of Nazi oppressions, tenaciously involved in the development of original social ideas, Israel went on with its work. We could not concern ourselves exclusively with the torrent of hatred pouring in upon us from Arab governments. In the era of modern communication a nation is not entirely dependent on its regional context. The wide world is open to the voice of friendship. Arab hostility towards Israel became increasingly isolated, while our position in the international family became more deeply entrenched. Many in the world drew confidence from the fact that a very small nation could, by its exertion and example, rise to respected levels in social progress, scientific progress and the human arts, and so our policy was to deter the aggression of our neighbours so long as it was endurable, to resist it only when failure to resist would have invited its intensified renewal, to withstand Arab violence without being obsessed by it, and even to search patiently here and there for any glimmer of moderation and realism in the Arab mind. We also pursued the hope of bringing all the great powers to a harmonious policy in support of the security and sovereignty of Middle Eastern states. It was not easy to take this course. The sacrifice imposed upon our population by Arab violence was cumulative in its effects, but as it piled up month by month the toll of death and bereavement was heavy and in the last few years it was evident that this organized murder was directed by a central hand.

We were able to limit our response to this aggression so long as its own scope appeared to be limited. President Nasser seemed for some years to be accumulating inflammable material without an immediate desire to set it alight. He was heavily engaged in domination and conquest elsewhere. His speeches were strong against Israel, but his bullets, guns and poison gases were for the time being used to intimidate other Arab states and to maintain a colonial war against the villagers of the Yemen and the peoples of the Arabian Peninsula.

But Israel's danger was great. The military build-up in Egypt proceeded at an intensive rate. It was designed to enable Egypt to press its war plans against Israel while maintaining its violent adventures elsewhere. In the face of these developments, Israel was forced to devote an increasing part of its resources to self-defence. With the declaration by Syria of the doctrine of a "day by day military confrontation," the situation in the Middle East grew darker. The Palestine Liberation Organization, the Palestine Liberation Army, the Unified Arab Command, the intensified expansion of military forces and equipment in Egypt, Syria, Lebanon, Jordan and more remote parts of the Arab continent—these were the signals of a growing danger to which we sought to alert the mind and conscience of the world.

The War Design, 1967

In three tense weeks between May 14, and June 5, Egypt, Syria and Jordan, assisted and incited by more distant Arab states, embarked on a policy of immediate and total aggression.

June 1967 was to be the month of decision. The "final solution" was at hand.

There was no convincing motive for the aggressive design which was now unfolded. Egyptian and Soviet sources had claimed that a concentrated Israeli invasion of Syria was expected during the second or third week in May. No claim could be more frivolous or far-fetched. It is true that Syria was sending terrorists into Israel to lay mines on public roads and, on one occasion, to bombard the Israeli settlement at Manara from the Lebanese border. The accumulation of such actions had sometimes evoked Israeli responses always limited in scope and time. All that Syria had to do to ensure perfect tranquility on her frontier with Israel was to discourage the terrorist war. Not only did she not discourage these actions—she encouraged them, she gave them every moral and practical support. But the picture of Israeli troop concentrations in strength for an invasion of Syria was a monstrous fiction. Twice Syria refused to cooperate with suggestions by the U.N. authorities, and accepted by Israel, for a simultaneous and reciprocal inspection of the Israel-Syrian frontier. On one occasion the Soviet Ambassador complained to my Prime Minister of heavy troop concentrations in the North of Israel. When invited to join the Prime Minister that very moment in a visit to any part of Israel which he would like to see, the distinguished envoy brusquely refused. The prospect of finding out the truth at first hand seemed to fill him with a profound disquiet. But by May 9, the Secretary-General of the United Nations from his own sources on the ground had ascertained that no Israeli troop concentration existed. This fact had been directly communicated to the Syrian and Egyptian Governments. The excuse had been shattered, but the allegations still remained. The steps which I now describe could not possibly have any motive or justification if an Israeli troop concentration, as both Egypt and Syria knew, did not exist. Indeed the Egyptian build-up ceased to be described by its authors as the result of any threat to Syria.

On May 14, Egyptian forces began to move into Sinai.

On May 16, the Egyptian Command ordered the United Nations Emergency Force to leave the border. The following morning the reason became clear. For on May 17, 1967, at 6 in the morning, Radio Cairo broadcast that Field-Marshal Amer had issued alert orders to the Egyptian armed forces. Nor did he mention Syria as the excuse. This announcement reads:

1. The state of preparedness of the Egyptian armed forces will increase to the full level of preparedness for war, beginning 14.30 hours last Sunday.

2. Formations and units allocated in accordance with the operational plans will advance from their present locations to the designated positions.

3. The armed forces are to be in full preparedness to carry out

any combat tasks on the Israel front in accordance with developments.

On May 18, Egypt called for the total removal of the United Nations Emergency Force. The Secretary-General of the United Nations acceded to this request and moved to carry it out, without reference to the Security Council or the General Assembly, without carrying out the procedures indicated by Secretary-General Hammerskjold in the event of a request for a withdrawal being made, without heeding the protesting voices of some of the permanent members of the Security Council and of the government at whose initiative the force had been established, without consulting Israel on the consequent prejudice to her military security and her vital maritime freedom, and without seeking such delay as would enable alternative measures to be concerted for preventing belligerency by sea and a dangerous confrontation of forces by land.

It is often said that United Nations procedures are painfully slow. This decision was disastrously swift. Its effect was to make Sinai safe for belligerency from North to South, to create a sudden disruption of the local security balance, and to leave an international maritime interest exposed to almost certain threat. I have already said that Israel's attitude to the peace-keeping functions of the United Nations has been traumatically affected by its experience. What is the use of a fire brigade which vanishes from the scene as soon as the first smoke and flames appear? Is it surprising that we are firmly resolved never again to allow a vital Israel interest and our very security to rest on such a fragile foundation?

The clouds now gathered thick and fast. Between May 14 and May 23, Egyptian concentrations in Sinai increased day by day. Israel took corresponding measures. In the absence of an agreement to the contrary it is, of course, legal for any state to place its armies wherever it chooses in its territory. It is equally true that nothing could be more uncongenial to the prospect of peace than to have large armies facing each other across a narrow space, with one of them clearly bent on an early assault. For the purpose of the concentration was not in doubt. On May 18, at 24.00 hours, the Cairo radio, Saut el-Arab, published the following order of the day by Abdul Mushin Murtagi, the General then commanding Sinai:

The Egyptian forces have taken up positions in accordance with a definite plan.

Our forces are definitely ready to carry the battle beyond the borders of Egypt.

Morale is very high among the members of our armed forces because this is the day for which they have been waiting—to make a holy war in order to return the plundered land to its owners.

In many meetings with army personnel they asked when the holy war would begin—the time has come to give them their wish.

On May 21 General Amer gave the order to mobilize reserves. Now came the decisive step. All doubt that Egypt had decided upon immediate or early war was now dispelled. Appearing at an Air Force Base at 6 o'clock in the morning, President Nasser announced that he would blockade the Gulf of Akaba to Israeli ships, adding: "The Jews threaten war and we say: by all means, we are ready for war."

But the Jews were not threatening war. Prime Minister Eshkol was calling for a de-escalation of forces. Nasser treated this as a sign of weakness.

On May 25, Cairo Radio announced:

The Arab people is firmly resolved to wipe Israel off the map and to restore the honour of the Arabs of Palestine.

On the following day, May 26, Nasser spoke again:

The Arab people wants to fight. We have been waiting for the right time when we will be completely ready. Recently we have felt that our strength has been sufficient and that if we make battle with Israel we shall be able, with the help of God, to conquer. Sharm e-Sheikh implies a confrontation with Israel. Taking this step makes it imperative that we be ready to undertake a total war with Israel.

Writing in Al-Ahram, on May 26, Nasser's mouthpiece, Hasanein Heikal, wrote, with engaging realism:

I consider that there is no alternative to armed conflict between the United Arab Republic and the Israeli enemy. This is the first time that the Arab challenge to Israel attempts to change an existing fact in order to impose a different fact in its place.

On May 28, Nasser had a press conference. He was having them every day. He said:

We will not accept any possibility of co-existence with Israel.

And on the following day:

If we have succeeded to restore the situation to what it was before 1956, there is no doubt that God will help us and will inspire us to restore the situation to what it was prior to 1948.

There are various ways of threatening Israel's liquidation. Few ways could be clearer than this.

The troop concentrations and blockade were now to be accompanied by encirclement. The noose was to be fitted around the victim's neck. Other Arab states were closing the ring. On May 30 Nasser signed the Defence Agreement with Jordan, and described its purpose in these terms:

> The armies of Egypt, Jordan, Syria and Lebanon are stationed on the borders of Israel in order to face the challenge. Behind them stand the armies of Iraq, Algeria, Kuwait, Sudan and the whole of the Arab nation.
>
> This deed will astound the world. Today they will know that the Arabs are ready for the fray. The hour of decision has arrived.

On June 4 Nasser made a statement on Cairo Radio after signing the protocol associating Iraq with the Egyptian-Jordanian Defence Pact. Here are his words:

> . . . We are facing you in the battle and are burning with desire for it to start, in order to obtain revenge. This will make the world realize what the Arabs are and what Israel is . . .

Mr. President, nothing has been more startling in recent weeks than to read discussions about who planned, who organized, who initiated, who wanted and who launched this war. Here we have a series of statements, mounting in crescendo from vague warning through open threat, to precise intention.

Here we have the vast mass of the Egyptian armies in Sinai with seven infantry and two armoured divisions, the greatest force ever assembled in that Peninsula in all its history. Here we have 40,000 regular Syrian troops poised to strike at the Jordan Valley from advantageous positions in the hills. Here we have the mobilized forces of Jordan, with their artillery and mortars trained on Israel's population centres in Jerusalem and along the vulnerable narrow coastal plain. Troops from Iraq, Kuwait and Algeria converge towards the battle-front at Egypt's behest. 900 tanks face Israel on the Sinai border, while 200 more are poised to strike the isolated town of Eilat at Israel's southern tip. The military dispositions tell their own story. The Northern Negev was to be invaded by armour and bombarded from the Gaza Strip. From May 27 onward, Egyptian air squadrons in Sinai were equipped with operation orders instructing them in detail on the manner in which Israeli airfields, pathetically few in number, were to be bombarded, thus exposing Israel's crowded cities to easy and merciless assault. Egyptian air sorties came in and out of Israel's southern desert to reconnoitre, inspect and prepare for the assault. An illicit blockade had cut Israel off from all her commerce with the eastern half of the world.

Blockade on Tiran Straits

Those who write this story in years to come will give a special place in their narrative to Nasser's blatant decision to close the Straits of Tiran in Israel's face. It is not difficult to understand why this outrage had a drastic impact. In 1957 the maritime nations, within the framework of the United Nations General Assembly, correctly enunciated the doctrine of free and innocent passage to the Straits. When that doctrine was proclaimed—and incidentally, not challenged by the Egyptian Representative at that time —it was little more than an abstract principle for the maritime world. For Israel it was a great but still unfulfilled prospect, it was not yet a reality. But during the ten years in which we and the other states of the maritime community have relied upon that doctrine and upon established usage, the principle had become a reality consecrated by hundreds of sailings under dozens of flags and the establishment of a whole complex of commerce and industry and communication. A new dimension has been added to the map of the world's communication. And on that dimension we have constructed Israel's bridge towards the friendly states of Asia and Africa, a network of relationships which is the chief pride of Israel in the second decade of its independence and on which its economic future depends.

All this, then, had grown up as an effective usage under the United Nations' flag. Does Mr. Nasser really think that he can come upon the scene in ten minutes and cancel the established legal usage and interests of ten years?

There was in his wanton act a quality of malice. For surely the closing of the Straits of Tiran gave no benefit whatever to Egypt except the perverse joy of inflicting injury on others. It was an anarchic act, because it showed a total disregard for the law of nations, the application of which in this specific case had not been challenged for ten years. And it was, in the literal sense, an act of arrogance, because there are other nations in Asia and East Africa that trade with the port of Eilat, as they have every right to do, through the Straits of Tiran and across the Gulf of Akaba. Other sovereign states from Japan to Ethiopia, from Thailand to Uganda, from Cambodia to Madagascar, have a sovereign right to decide for themselves whether they wish or do not wish to trade with Israel. These countries are not colonies of Cairo. They can trade with Israel or not trade with Israel as they wish, and President Nasser is not the policeman of other African and Asian States.

Here then was a wanton intervention in the sovereign rights of other states in the eastern half of the world to decide for themselves whether or not they wish to establish trade relations with either or both of the two ports at the head of the Gulf of Akaba.

An Act of War

When we examine, then, the implications of this act, we have no cause to wonder that the international shock was great. There was another reason, too, for that shock. Blockades have traditionally been regarded, in the pre-Charter parlance, as acts of war. To blockade, after all, is to attempt strangulation—and sovereign states are entitled not to have their State strangled.

The blockade is by definition an act of war, imposed and enforced through violence.

Never in history have blockade and peace existed side by side. From May 24 onward, the question of who started the war or who fired the first shot became momentously irrelevant. There is no difference in civil law between murdering a man by slow strangulation or killing him by a shot in the head. From the moment at which the blockade was imposed, active hostilities had commenced and Israel owed Egypt nothing of her Charter rights. If a foreign power sought to close Odessa, or Copenhagen or Marseilles or New York Harbour by the use of force, what would happen? Would there be any discussion about who had fired the first shot? Would anyone ask whether aggression had begun? Less than a decade ago the Soviet Union proposed a draft resolution in the General Assembly on the question of defining aggression. The resolution reads:

> In an international conflict, that State shall be declared an attacker which first commits one of the following acts:
> a. Naval blockade of the coastal ports of another State.

This act constituted in the Soviet view aggression as distinguished from other specific acts designated in the Soviet draft as indirect aggression. In this particular case the consequences of Nasser's action had been fully announced in advance. On March 1, 1967, my predecessor announced that:

> Interference, by armed force, with ships of the Israel flag exercising free and innocent passage in the Gulf of Akaba and through the Straits of Tiran, will be regarded by Israel as an attack entitling it to exercise its inherent right of self-defence under Article 51 of the United Nations Charter and to take all such measures as are necessary to ensure the free and innocent passage of its ships in the Gulf and in the Straits.

The representative of France declared that any obstruction of free passage in the Straits or Gulf was contrary to international law "entailing a possible resort to the measures authorized by Article 51 of the Charter."

The United States, inside and outside of the United Nations, gave specific endorsement to Israel's right to invoke her inherent right of self-defence against any attempt to blockade the Gulf. Nasser was speaking with acute precision when he stated that Israel now faced the choice either between being choked to death in her southern maritime approaches or to await the death blow from Northern Sinai.

Nobody who lived through those days in Israel, between May 23 and June 5, will ever forget the air of doom that hovered over our country. Hemmed in by hostile armies ready to strike, affronted and beset by a flagrant act of war, bombarded day and night by predictions of her approaching extinction, forced into a total mobilization of all her manpower, her economy and commerce beating with feeble pulse, her main supplies of vital fuel choked by a belligerent act, Israel faced the greatest peril of her existence that she had known since her resistance against aggression 19 years before, at the hour of her birth. There was peril wherever she looked and she faced it in deepening solitude. On May 24 and on succeeding days, the Security Council conducted a desultory debate which sometimes reached a point of levity. The Soviet Representative asserted that he saw no reason for discussing the Middle Eastern situation at all. The Bulgarian delegate uttered these unbelievable words.

At the present moment there is really no need for an urgent meeting of the Security Council.

A crushing siege bore down upon us. Multitudes throughout the world trembled for Israel's fate. The single consolation lay in the surge of public opinion which rose up in Israel's defence. From Paris to Montevideo, from New York to Amsterdam, tens of thousands of persons of all ages, peoples and affiliations marched in horrified protest at the approaching stage of genocide. Writers and scientists, religious leaders, trade union movements and even the Communist parties in France, Holland, Switzerland, Norway, Austria and Finland asserted their view that Israel was a peace-loving State, whose peace was being wantonly denied. In the history of our generation it is difficult to think of any other hour in which progressive world opinion rallied in such tension and agony of spirit.

To understand the full depth of pain and shock, it is necessary to grasp the full significance of what Israel's danger meant. A small sovereign State had its existence threatened by lawless violence. The threat to Israel was a menace to the very foundations of the international order. The State thus threatened bore a name which stirred the deepest memories of civilized mankind and the people of the remnant of millions, who, in living memory had been wiped out by a dictatorship more powerful, through scarcely more malicious, than Nasser's Egypt. What Nasser had predicted, what he had worked for with undeflecting purpose, had come to pass—the noose was tightly drawn.

On the fateful morning of June 5, when Egyptian forces moved by air and land against Israel's western coast and southern territory, our country's choice was plain. The choice was to live or perish, to defend the national existence or to forfeit it for all time.

From these dire moments Israel emerged in five heroic days from awful peril to successful and glorious resistance. Alone, unaided, neither seeking nor receiving help, our nation rose in self-defence. So long as men cherish freedom, so long as small states strive for the dignity of existence, the exploits of Israel's armies will be told from one generation to another with the deepest pride. The Soviet Union has described our resistance as aggression and sought to have it condemned. We reject this accusation with all our might. Here was armed force employed in a just and righteous cause, as righteous as the defenders at Valley Forge, as just as the expulsion of Hitler's bombers from the British skies, as noble as the protection of Stalingrad against the Nazi hordes, so was the defence of Israel's security and existence against those who sought our nation's destruction.

What should be condemned is not Israel's action, but the attempt to condemn it. Never have freedom, honour, justice, national interest and international morality been so righteously protected. While fighting raged on the Egyptian-Israel frontier and on the Syrian front, we still hoped to contain the conflict. Jordan was given every chance to remain outside the struggle. Even after Jordan had bombarded and bombed Israel territory at several points we still proposed to the Jordanian monarch that he abstain from general hostilities. A message to this effect reached him several hours after the outbreak of hostilities on the southern front on June 5.

Jordan answered not with words but with shells. Artillery opened fire fiercely along the whole front with special emphasis on the Jerusalem area. Thus Jordan's responsibility for the second phase of the concerted aggression is established beyond doubt. This responsibility cannot fail to have its consequences in the peace settlement. As death and injury rained on the city, Jordan had become the source and origin of Jerusalem's fierce ordeal. The inhabitants of the city can never forget this fact, or fail to draw its conclusions.

Soviet Role in the Middle East Crisis

Mr. President, I have spoken of Israel's defence against the assaults of neighbouring states. This is not the entire story. Whatever happens in the Middle East for good or ill, for peace or conflict, is powerfully affected by what the Great Powers do or omit to do. When the Soviet Union initiates a discussion here, our gaze is inexorably drawn to the story of its role in recent Middle Eastern history. It is a sad and shocking story, it must be frankly told.

Since 1955 the Soviet Union has supplied the Arab States with 2,000 tanks, of which more than 1,000 have gone to Egypt. The Soviet Union has supplied the Arab States with 700 modern fighter aircraft and bombers, more recently with ground missiles, and Egypt alone has received from the U.S.S.R. 540 field guns, 130 medium guns, 200 120 mm mortars, anti-aircraft guns, 175 rocket launchers, 650 anti-tank guns, seven destroyers, a number of Luna M and SPKA 2 ground-to-ground missiles, 14 submarines and 46 torpedo boats of various types including missile-carrying boats. The Egyptian Army has been trained by Soviet experts. This has been attested to by Egyptian officers captured by Israel. Most of this equipment was supplied to the Arab States after the Cairo Summit Conference of Arab leaders in January 1964 had agreed on a specific programme for the destruction of Israel, after they had announced and hastened to fulfil this plan by accelerating their arms purchases from the Soviet Union. The proportions of Soviet assistance are attested to by the startling fact that in Sinai alone the Egyptians abandoned equipment and offensive weapons of Soviet manufacture whose value is estimated at two billion dollars.

Together with the supply of offensive weapons, the Soviet Union has encouraged the military preparations of the Arab States.

Since 1961, the Soviet Union has assisted Egypt in its desire to conquer Israel. The great amount of offensive equipment supplied to the Arab States strengthens this assessment.

A Great Power which professes its devotion to peaceful settlement and the rights of states has for 14 years afflicted the Middle East with a headlong armaments race, with the paralysis of the United Nations as an instrument of security and against those who defend it.

The constant increase and escalation of Soviet armaments in Arab countries has driven Israel to a corresponding, though far smaller, procurement programme. Israel's arms purchases were precisely geared to the successive phases of Arab, and especially Egyptian, rearmament. On many occasions in recent months we and others have vainly sought to secure Soviet agreement for a reciprocal reduction of arms supplies in our region. These efforts have borne no fruit. The expenditure on social and economic progress of one half of what has been put into the purchase of Soviet arms would have been sufficient to redeem Egypt from its social and economic ills. A corresponding diversion of resources from military to social expenditure would have taken place in Israel. A viable balance of forces could have been achieved at a lower level of armaments, while our region could have moved forward to higher standards of human and social welfare. For Israel's attitude is clear. We should like to see the arms race slowed down. But if the race is joined, we are determined not to lose it. A fearful waste of economic energy in the Middle East is the direct result of the Soviet role in the constant stimulation of the race in arms.

It is clear from Arab sources that the Soviet Union has played a provocative role in spreading alarmist and incendiary reports of Israel intentions amongst Arab Governments.

On June 9 President Nasser said:

Our friends in the U.S.S.R. warned the visiting parliamentary delegation in Moscow at the beginning of last month, that there exists a plan of attack against Syria.

Similarly an announcement by Tass of May 23 states:

The Foreign Affairs and Security Committee of the Knesset have accorded the Cabinet special powers to carry out war operations against Syria. Israeli forces concentrating on the Syrian border have been put in a state of alert for war. General mobilization has also been proclaimed in the country . . .

There was not one word of truth in this story. But its diffusion in the Arab countries could only have an incendiary result.

Cairo Radio broadcast on May 28 (0500 hours) an address by Marshal Gretchko at a farewell party in honour of the former Egyptian Minister of Defence, Shams ed-Din Badran:

The U.S.S.R., her armed forces, her people and Government will stand by the Arabs and will continue to encourage and support them. We are your faithful friends and we shall continue aiding you because this is the policy of the Soviet nation, its Party and Government. On behalf of the Ministry of Defence and in the name of the Soviet nation we wish you success and victory.

This promise of military support came less than a week after the illicit closing of the Tiran Straits, an act which the U.S.S.R. has done nothing to condemn.

U.S.S.R. Attitudes at the U.N.

The U.S.S.R. has exercised her veto right in the Security Council five times. Each time a just and constructive judgment has been frustrated. On January 22, 1964, France, the United Kingdom and the United States presented a Draft Resolution to facilitate work on the West Bank of the River Jordan in the B'not Ya'akov Canal Project. The Soviet veto held up regional water development for several years. On March 29, 1954, a New Zealand resolution simply reiterating U.N. policy on blockade along the Suez Canal was frustrated by Soviet dissent. On August 19, 1963, a United Kingdom and United States Resolution on the murder of two Israelis at Almagor was denied adoption by Soviet opposition. On December 21, 1964, the U.S.S.R. vetoed a United Kingdom and United States Resolution on incidents at Tel Dan, including the shelling of Dan, Dafna and Sha'ar

Yashuv. On November 2, 1966, Argentina, Japan, the Netherlands, New Zealand and Nigeria joined to express regret at "infiltration from Syria and loss of human life caused by the incidents in October and November 1966." This was one of the few resolutions sponsored by member-States from five continents.

The Soviet use of veto has had a dual effect. First, it prevented any resolution which an Arab State has opposed, from being adopted by the Council. Secondly, it has inhibited the Security Council from taking constructive action in disputes between an Arab State and Israel because of the certain knowledge that the veto would be applied in what was deemed to be the Arab interest. The consequences of the Soviet veto policy have been to deny Israel any possibility of just and equitable treatment in the Security Council, and to nullify the Council as a constructive factor in the affairs of the Middle East.

Does all this really add up to a constructive intervention by the U.S.S.R. in the Arab-Israel tension? The position becomes graver when we recall the unbridled invective against the Permanent Representative of Israel in the Security Council. In its words and in the letter to the Israel Government, the U.S.S.R. has formulated an obscene comparison between the Israel Defence Forces and the Hitlerite hordes which overran Europe in the Second World War. There is a flagrant breach of international morality and human decency in this comparison. Our nation never compromised with Hitler Germany. It never signed a pact with it as did the U.S.S.R. in 1939.

To associate the name of Israel with the accursed tyrant who engulfed the Jewish people in a tidal wave of slaughter is to violate every canon of elementary taste and fundamental truth.

In the light of this history, the General Assembly will easily understand Israel's reaction to the Soviet initiative in convening this Special Session for the purpose of condemning our country and recommending a withdrawal to the position that existed before June 5.

Your (the Soviet) Government's record in the stimulation of the arms race, in the paralysis of the Security Council, in the encouragement throughout the Arab World of unfounded suspicion concerning Israel's intentions, your constant refusal to say a single word of criticism at any time of declarations threatening the violent overthrow of Israel's sovereignty and existence—all this gravely undermines your claims to objectivity. You come here in our eyes not as a judge or as a prosecutor, but rather as a legitimate object of international criticism for the part that you have played in the sombre events which have brought our region to a point of explosive tension.

If the Soviet Union had made an equal distribution of the friendship amongst the peoples of the Middle East, if it had refrained from exploiting regional rancours and tensions for the purpose of its own global policy, if it had stood in even-handed devotion to the legitimate interests of all states, the crisis which now commands our attention and anxiety would never have occurred. To the charge of aggression I answer that Israel's resistance at the lowest ebb of its fortunes will resound across history, together with the uprising of our battered remnants in the Warsaw Ghetto, as a triumphant assertion of human freedom. From the dawn of its history the people now rebuilding a State in Israel has struggled often in desperate conditions against tyranny and aggression. Our action on June 5 falls nobly within that tradition. We have tried to show that even a small state and a small people have the right to live. I believe that we shall not be found alone in the assertion of that right, which is the very essence of the Charter of the United Nations. Similarly, the suggestion that everything goes back to where it was before the 5th of June is totally unacceptable. The General Assembly cannot ignore the fact that the Security Council, where the primary responsibility lay, has emphatically rejected such a course. It was not Israel, but Syria, Egypt and Jordan, who violently shattered the previous situation to smithereens. It cannot be recaptured. It is a fact of technology that it is easier to fly to the moon than to reconstruct a broken egg. The Security Council acted wisely in rejecting the backward step, advocated by the Soviet Union. To go back to the situation out of which the conflict arose would mean that all the conditions for renewed hostilities would be brought together again. I repeat what I said to the Security Council. Our watchword is not "backward to belligerency" but "forward to peace."

What the Assembly should prescribe is not a formula for renewed hostilities, but a series of principles for the construction of a new future in the Middle East. With the cease-fire established, our progress must be not backward to an armistice regime which has collapsed under the weight of years and the brunt of hostility. History summons us forward to permanent peace and the peace that we envisage can only be elaborated in frank and lucid dialogue between Israel and each of the states which have participated in the attempt to overthrow her sovereignty and undermine her existence. We dare not be satisfied with intermediate arrangements which are neither war nor peace. Such patchwork ideas carry within themselves the seeds of future tragedy. Free from external pressures and interventions, imbued with a common love for a region which they are destined to share, the Arab and Jewish nations must now transcend their conflicts in dedication to a new Mediterranean future in concert with a renascent Europe and an Africa and Asia which have emerged at last to their independent role on the stage of history.

The Vision of Peace

In free negotiation with each of our neighbours we shall offer durable and just solutions redounding to our mutual advantage and honour. The Arab states can no longer be permitted to recognize Israel's existence only for the purpose of plotting its elimination. They have come face to face with us in conflict. Let them now come face to face with us in peace.

In peaceful conditions we could imagine communications running from Haifa to Beirut and Damascus in the north, to Amman and beyond in the east, and to Cairo in the south. The opening of these blocked arteries would stimulate the life, thought and commerce in the region beyond any level otherwise conceivable. Across the southern Negev, communication between the Nile Valley and the fertile crescent could be resumed without any change in political jurisdiction. What is now often described as a wedge between Arab lands would become a bridge. The Kingdom of Jordan, now cut off from its maritime outlet, could freely import and export its goods on the Israeli coast. On the Red Sea, cooperative action could expedite the port developments at Eilat and Akaba, which give Israel and Jordan their contact with a resurgent East Africa and a developing Asia.

The Middle East, lying athwart three continents, could become a busy centre of air communications, which are now impeded by boycotts and the necessity to take circuitous routes. Radio, telephone and postal communications, which now end abruptly in mid-air, would unite a divided region. The Middle East, with its historic monuments and scenic beauty, could attract a vast movement of travellers and pilgrims if existing impediments were removed. Resources which lie across national frontiers— the minerals of the Dead Sea and the phosphates of the Negev and the Arava—could be developed in mutual interchange of technical knowledge. Economic cooperation in agricultural and industrial development could lead to supranational arrangements like those which mark the European community. The United Nations could establish an economic commission for the Middle East, similar to the commissions now at work in Europe, Latin America and the Far East. The specialized agencies could intensify their support of health and educational development with greater efficiency if a regional harmony were attained. The development of arid zones, the desalination of water and the conquest of tropical disease are common interests of the entire region, congenial to a sharing of knowledge and experience.

In the institutions of scientific research and higher education of both sides of the frontiers, young Israelis and Arabs could join in a mutual discourse of learning. The old prejudices could be replaced by a new comprehension and respect, born of a reciprocal dialogue in the intellectual domain. In such a Middle East, military budgets would spontaneously find a less exacting point of equilibrium. Excessive sums devoted to security could be diverted to development projects.

Thus, in full respect of the region's diversity, an entirely new story, never known or told before, would unfold across the Eastern Mediterranean. For the first time in history, no Mediterranean nation is in subjection. All are endowed with sovereign freedom. The challenge now is to use this freedom for creative growth. There is only one road to that end. It is the road of recognition, of direct contact, of true cooperation. It is the road of peaceful co-existence. This road, as the ancient prophets of Israel foretold, leads to Jerusalem.

Jerusalem, now united after her tragic division, is no longer an arena for gun emplacements and barbed wire. In our nation's long history there have been few hours more intensely moving than the hour of our reunion with the Western Wall. A people had come back to the cradle of its birth. It has renewed its link with the memories which that reunion evokes. For 20 years there has not been free access by men of all faiths to the shrines which they hold in unique reverence. This access now exists. Israel is resolved to give effective expression, in cooperation with the world's great religions, to the immunity and sanctity of all the Holy Places. The prospect of a negotiated peace is less remote than it may seem. Israel waged her defensive struggle in pursuit of two objectives—security and peace. Peace and security, with their territorial, economic and demographic implications, can only be built by the free negotiation which is the true essence of sovereign responsibility. A call to the recent combatants to negotiate the conditions of their future co-existence is the only constructive course which this Assembly could take.

We ask the great powers to remove our tormented region from the scope of global rivalries, to summon its governments to build their common future themselves, to assist it, if they will, to develop social and cultural levels worthy of its past.

We ask the developing countries to support a dynamic and forward-looking policy and not to drag the new future back into the out-worn past.

To the small nations, which form the bulk of the international family, we offer the experience which teaches us that small communities can best secure their interests by maximal self-reliance. Nobody will help those who will not help themselves; we ask the small nations in the solidarity of our smallness, to help us stand firm against intimidation and threat such as those by which we are now assailed. We ask world opinion, which rallied to us in our plight, to accompany us faithfully in our new opportunity. We ask the United Nations, which was prevented from offering us security in our recent peril, to respect our independent quest for the peace and security which are the Charter's higher ends. We shall do what the Security Council decided should be done—and reject the course which the Security Council emphatically and wisely rejected. It may seem that Israel stands alone against numerous and powerful adversaries. But we have faith in the undying forces in our nation's history which have so often given the final victory to spirit over matter, to inner truth over mere quantity. We believe in the vigilance of history which has guarded our steps. The Guardian of Israel neither slumbers nor sleeps.

The Middle East, tired of wars, is ripe for a new emergence of human vitality. Let the opportunity not fall again from our hands.

The Right of Israel

By Yizhak Rabin*

Your Excellency, President of the State, Mr. Prime Minister, President of the Hebrew University, Rector of the University; Governors, Teachers, Ladies and Gentlemen:

I stand in awe before you, leaders of the generation, here in this venerable and impressive place overlooking Israel's eternal capital and the birth-place of our Nation's earliest history.

Together with other distinguished personalities who are no doubt worthy of this honour, you have chosen to do me great honour in conferring upon me the title of Doctor of Philosophy. Permit me to express to you here my feelings on this occasion. I regard myself, at this time, as a representative of the entire Israel Forces, of its thousands of officers and tens of thousands of soldiers who brought the State of Israel its victory in the six-day war. It may be asked why the University saw fit to grant the title of Honorary Doctor of Philosophy to a soldier in recognition of his martial activities. What is there in common to military activity and the academic world which represents civilisation and culture? What is there in common between those whose profession is violence and spiritual values? I, however, am honoured that through me you are expressing such deep appreciation to my comrades in arms and to the uniqueness of the Israel Defence Forces, which is no more than extension of the unique spirit of the entire Jewish People.

The world has recognised the fact that the Israel Defence Forces are different from other armies. Although its first task is the military task of ensuring security, the Israel Defence Forces undertakes numerous tasks of peace, tasks not of destruction but of construction and of the strengthening of the Nation's cultural and moral resources.

Our educational work has been praised widely and was given national recognition, when in 1966 it was granted the Israel Prize for Education, The Nahal, which combines military training and agricultural settlement, teachers in border villages contributing to social and cultural enrichment; these are but a few small examples of the Israel Defence Forces' uniqueness in this sphere.

However, today, the University has conferred this honorary title on us

* The text of an address by Rabin, formerly Israeli chief of staff and at present Israeli Ambassador in the United States, on the occasion of receiving an honorary doctorate from the Hebrew University, June 28, 1967.

in recognition of our Army's superiority of spirit and morals as it was revealed in the heat of war, for we are standing in this place by virtue of battle which though forced upon us was forged into a victory astounding the world.

War is intrinsically harsh and cruel, bloody and tear-stained, but particularly this war, which we have just undergone, brought forth rare and magnificent instances of heroism and courage, together with humane expressions of brotherhood, comradeship, and spiritual greatness.

Whoever has not seen a tank crew continue its attack with its commander killed and its vehicle badly damaged, whoever has not seen sappers endangering their lives to extricate wounded comrades from a minefield, whoever has not seen the anxiety and the effort of the entire Air Force devoted to rescuing a pilot who has fallen in enemy territory, cannot know the meaning of devotion between comrades in arms.

The entire Nation was exalted and many wept upon hearing the news of the capture of the Old City. Our Sabra Youth and most certainly our soldiers do not tend to sentimentality and shy away from revealing it in public. However, the strain of battle, the anxiety which preceded it, and the sense of salvation and of direct participation of every soldier in the forging of the heart of Jewish history cracked the shell of hardness and shyness and released well-springs of excitement and spiritual emotion. The paratroopers, who conquered the Wailing Wall, leaned on its stones and wept, and as a symbol this was a rare occasion, almost unparalleled in human history. Such phrases and cliches are not generally used in our Army but this scene on the Temple Mount beyond the power of verbal description revealed as though by a lightning flash deep truths. And more than this, the joy of triumph seized the whole nation. Nevertheless we find more and more and more a strange phenomenon among our fighters. Their joy is incomplete, and more than a small portion of sorrow and shock prevails in their festivities. And there are those who abstain from all celebration. The warriors in the front lines saw with their own eyes not only the glory of victory but the price of victory. Their comrades who fell beside them bleeding. And I know that even the terrible price which our enemies paid touched the hearts of many of our men. It may be that the Jewish People never learned and never accustomed itself to feel the triumph of conquest and victory and therefore we receive it with mixed feelings.

The six-day war revealed many instances of heroism far beyond the single attack which dashes unthinkingly forward. In many places desperate and lengthy battles raged. In Rafiah, in El Arish, in Um Kataf, in Jerusalem, and in Ramat Hagollan, there, and in many other places, the soldiers of Israel were revealed as heroic in spirit, in courage, and in persistence which cannot leave anyone indifferent once he has seen this great and exalting human revelation. We speak a great deal of the few against the many. In this war perhaps for the first time since the Arab invasions of the spring of 1948 and the battles of Negba and Degania, units of the Israel Forces stood in all sectors, few against many. This means that relatively small units of our soldiers, often entered seemingly endless networks of fortification, surrounded by hundreds and thousands of enemy troops and faced with the task of forcing their way, hour after hour, in this jungle of dangers, even after the momentum of the first attack has passed and all that remains is the necessity of belief in our strength, the lack of alternative and the goal for which we are fighting, to summon up every spiritual resource in order to continue the fight to its very end.

Thus our armoured Forces broke through on all fronts, our paratroopers fought their way into Rafiah and Jerusalem, our sappers cleared minefields under enemy fire. The units which broke the enemy lines and came to their objectives after hours upon hours of struggle continuing on and on, while their comrades fell right and left and they continued forward, only forward. These soldiers were carried forward by spiritual values, by deep spiritual resources, far more than by their weapons or the technique of warfare.

We have always demanded the cream of our youth for the Israel Defence Forces when we coined the slogan "Hatovim l'Tayis"—The Best to Flying, and this was a phrase which became a value. We meant not only technical and manual skills. We meant that if our airmen were to be capable of defeating the forces of four enemy countries within a few short hours, they must have moral values and human values.

Our airmen, who struck the enemies' planes so accurately that no one in the world understands how it was done and people seek technological explanations of secret weapons; our armoured troops who stood and beat the enemy even when their equipment was inferior to his; our soldiers in all various branches of the Israel Defence Forces who overcame our enemies everywhere, despite their superior numbers and fortifications; all these revealed not only coolness and courage in battle but a burning faith in their righteousness, an understanding that only their personal stand against the greatest of dangers could bring to their country and to their families victory, and that if the victory was not theirs the alternative was destruction.

Furthermore, in every sector our Forces' commanders, of all ranks, far outshone the enemies' commanders. Their understanding, their will, their ability to improvise, their care for soldiers and above all, their leading troops into battle, these are not matters of material or of technique. They have no rational explanation, except in terms of a deep consciousness of the moral justice of their fight.

All of this springs from the soul and leads back to the spirit. Our warriors prevailed not by their weapons but by the consciousness of a mission, by a consciousness of righteousness, by a deep love for their homeland and an understanding of the difficult task laid upon them; to ensure the existence of our people in its homeland, to protect, even at the price of their lives, the right of the Nation of Israel to live in its own State, free, independent and peaceful.

This Army, which I had the privilege of commanding through these battles, came from the people and returns to the people, to the people which rises in its hour of crisis and overcomes all enemies by virtue of its moral values, its spiritual readiness in the hour of need.

As the representative of the Israel Defence Forces, and in the name of everyone of its soldiers, I accept with pride your recognition.

"We Shall Triumph"

**President Nasser's speech at the National
Congress of the Arab Socialist Union at
Cairo University, Cairo, July 23, 1968. (The
first part of the speech, which is omitted,
was devoted to questions of domestic policy.)**

The Middle East crisis: I do not want to go back to the circumstances which led to the Middle East crisis. All the details are known, starting with the premeditated aggression against Arab territory, to the imperialist collusion with the Israeli enemy, to the 5th June setback and its serious and sad results for our Arab nation. As you know, we lost the major part of our military power. We accepted the political solution experiment for several reasons. At that time we had no alternative to talking about a political solution; we had no armed forces to depend on. At the same time we are not advocates of war for the sake of war—not at all. If we can obtain our rights through political action, as happened in 1957, fine; if not, we have no alternative but to struggle for our rights and to liberate our land.

Furthermore, we want world public opinion to be on our side and really to know our position. At the same time, we must consider our present friends and our possible friends before we consider our enemies. A major part of the battle is taking place on an international level and under the eyes of public opinion throughout the entire world, which wants to live in peace.

We realised from the beginning, as we were trying a political solution, that it was a difficult and thorny road because the enemy was drunk with victory. We know that the principle that what has been taken by force cannot be regained by anything but force is a sound and correct principle in all circumstances. But we tried sincerely and are still trying sincerely on a basis from which we do not deviate. This basis is clear and definite in UAR policy: no negotiations with Israel, no peace with Israel, no recognition of Israel, and no deals at the expense of Palestinian soil or the Palestinian people.

These are the foundations on which we proceeded in regard to solving the Middle East crisis peacefully. However, since 23rd November and until now, give and take has been going on with the UN representative. Have we achieved anything? We have achieved nothing. We co-operated to the maximum with the UN Secretary-General's representative. We accepted the Security Council resolution, but Israel did not.

No projects exist now for a peaceful solution, and it does not seem to me that there will be any in the future. We hear what the representative of the UN Secretary-General says, and we express our opinion on what we hear. So far our opinion has been clear.

With regard to a political solution, we will not in any way agree to give away one inch of Arab territory in any Arab country.

It is clear that Israel, which rejected the Security Council resolution, has many aims. The first is to achieve a political objective, because it won a military victory but did not achieve a political gain. Israel wants direct negotiations and wants a peace treaty signed. We reject this. Israel thus won a military victory but has so far been unable to achieve the political objective—signing a peace treaty with any of the Arab States surrounding it.

Therefore Israel will not withdraw. Why should it withdraw from the territory it occupied after achieving a crushing military victory? Israel, as they say, will remain in this territory hoping that conditions or regimes will be changed and replaced by regimes which will agree to the conclusion of a peace treaty with Israel [shouts of "God forbid" from audience].

How would the conditions change? Israel knows that the occupation burdens the hearts of all the sons of the Arab nation. Occupation represents fragmentation. Occupation is something out of the ordinary and is like a nightmare to all of us. Israel and the imperialist forces working behind it would be able to influence the domestic fronts and might be able to change the regimes and replace them with others which would agree to the conclusion of peace with Israel. As long as Israel knows that we have not yet attained a crushing offensive military strength, it will remain where it is, hoping to achieve political victory through a changing of regimes.

Israel continues to refuse the Security Council resolution. Israel refuses to discuss the Security Council resolution. Israel says: We will remain in our places along the cease-fire lines until you agree to negotiate with us and conclude a peace treaty. Naturally we counter this by rebuilding our armed forces. A year ago after the defeat, we had no armed forces. We now have armed forces which may be greater than those existing before the battle. We are working for the development of the armed forces in order to attain supremacy because our enemy is a cunning enemy backed by a force which gives him everything—money and arms.

After this, we shall discuss the possibilities of the military and political solutions. Because of its nature, the crisis cannot last long. We have been waiting for one year. Our area is a sensitive one. The status quo cannot be accepted. This status quo is against nature and creates a situation conducive to quick ignition and explosion at any time.

There exists a basic and principal commitment which is a question of life or death: the liberation of the land inch by inch if necessary even if one martyr must fall on every inch of land. That is clear. A war to regain a right is a legal war. However, we shall allow no one to provoke us. We shall decide, prepare and arrange things. This is a lengthy matter which demands our patience and endurance. We must be patient and stand fast in order to triumph and attain supremacy. Having attained supremacy, we shall triumph.

Life will be meaningless and worthless to us however, until every inch of Arab soil is liberated. To us the liberation of Arab soil represents an indivisible whole. In no circumstances is there an alternative to the departure of the occupation forces from all occupied territory. Prior to this departure, there can be no peace in the Middle East in any circumstances. If there is no peace in the Middle East, it is very doubtful that the repercussions will be restricted to borders of the Middle East.

We do not address ourselves to Israel alone but to the whole world. We have nothing to say as far as Israel is concerned. Israel's role has been exposed. Its role as a stooge of world imperialism and colonialism has been fully exposed. However, our talk today is addressed to the world, which is anxious for peace and adheres to peace. We add that peace in this part of the world will not be achieved by the mere elimination of the consequences of the 5th June aggression. Real peace should take into consideration the legal rights of the Palestinian people.

The third subject is the armed forces. When we study the causes of the defeat—I have studied the causes of the defeat and attended command meetings which discussed everything that took place—when we study the causes of the defeat, it becomes clear to us that there was no deficiency among the officers and soldiers. We must know this well. A mistake was made and it is painful to go back over its details.

Four-fifths of our forces did not encounter the enemy and had no opportunity to fight. They were placed in extremely bad conditions. It is not advantageous to talk now about the past except within the limits necessary to reassess matters and to benefit from the lessons of the battle. Our soldiers and officers who entered the battles proved that they could stand firm and die. The Egyptian soldier is a fighting soldier who does not fear death. I fought with the Egyptian peasant soldier in 1948 and saw how he welcomes death.

We should therefore be doing our soldiers and officers an injustice if we looked at them on the basis of what has taken place. The fact is that a very large part of the army did not enter battle. Each of us knows that during the withdrawal operation the hostile forces were finally able to inflict the heaviest losses on us. We have now learned and benefited from the lessons of the battle. We have compensated for much of the loss our armed forces suffered last year. As I said before, we have attained defence capability. We shall now strive to transform our army into a strong offensive army supplied with the most up-to-date weapons.

I witnessed an exercise before leaving for the Soviet Union. I saw our armed forces that participated in it. I can say that in the past year they achieved as much as five years of work. One can say that we now have capable armed forces. However it is all-essential that we understand that the officers and soldiers are doing a very difficult job. They are now working day and night. Every officer and NCO feels that the whole country is watching him and assigning him a duty which will determine our fate and future. Each of them feels that the nation is giving him the responsibility. They are therefore carrying out this duty. However, our armed forces must bide their time and be ready to take the opportunity to achieve what they are duty bound to achieve.

We, as a people, fully support our armed forces and have full faith in them because when the people lose confidence in their armed forces, they also lose confidence in themselves and in their destiny. The people must give to their armed forces because there is no alternative. It is my duty to say that the people have given. What have they given? They have given their sons. The best of their sons are now members of the armed forces. The soldiers and officers of the armed forces are our sons. The people feel and live with them constantly. The people feel that the armed forces are living under difficult psychological and physical conditions as a result of their hard work, great efforts, training and exhausting conditions. To live under such conditions day after day is painful to the soul and to our armed forces, who see the enemy on the other bank of the Canal.

The fourth question is my recent visit to the Soviet Union and to Yugoslavia. Brothers, I mainly went to thank the leaders and people of the Soviet Union for everything they have given us and to discuss the situation. However, there is a fact which we must realise and know: Had it not been for the Soviet Union, we would now find ourselves facing the enemy without any weapons and compelled to accept his conditions. The United States would not have given us a single round of ammunition. It has given us and will give us nothing, but it gives Israel everything from guns to aircraft and missiles.

In reality, we have so far paid not one millieme for the arms we obtained from the Soviet Union to equip our armed forces. Actually, were it a question of payment, we have no money to buy arms. We all know the situation. We took part of the Soviet weapons as a gift and concluded a contract for the remainder for which we shall pay in the future in long-term installments. Had it not been for the Soviet Union and its agreement to supply us with arms, we should now be in a position similar to our position a year ago. We should have no weapons and should be compelled to accept Israel's condition under its threat.

At the same time, there exists a question which we must fully realise and understand: Why does the Soviet Union give us all these things? Why? We have one common aim with the Soviet Union—to resist imperialism. We do not want foreign influence in our part of the world. For its part, the Soviet Union is most anxious to oppose imperialism and to liquidate the imperialist concentrations to the south of its borders. Our ideological and national interest is against imperialism; the Soviet Union's ideological interest and strategy are against imperialism. I wish to tell you frankly and clearly that the Soviet Union has never tried, not even in our most crucial times, to dictate conditions to us or to ask anything of us. On the contrary, it has always been we who have asked.

Naturally, I did not pay my recent visit to the Soviet Union to express gratitude only, but to ask for things as well. After expressing my gratitude, I asked for things and after asking, I told them that I was ashamed. Do you not want anything from us? We ask you for things. But they answered: We have nothing to ask of you. I am actually telling this to you and to history so we may know who our friends and enemies are.

We went on asking for hours but they did not make one request of us. Even when I told them I felt ashamed that we were making many demands while they had asked nothing of us—I wish they had a request which we could fulfil—I asked if they had nothing to ask of us. They told us: We take this stand on the basis of our ideology—the ideology of national liberation and the peoples' struggle. We have nothing to ask.

The Soviet Union did not try to dictate any conditions to us. In our constant dealings with it, the Soviet Union has not tried to dictate any conditions—not even when we differed and we differed with the Soviet Union in 1959. At that time there was agreement on the first stage of the High Dam, the first industrialisation agreement and the arms deal agreement. Despite this, despite the difference which reached such extent that it was published in the newspapers, no attempt was made to apply pressure and no word of threat was uttered by the Soviet Union. Sincerity prompts me to say this.

There is another point. This is the element of the Soviet Navy and its appearance in the Mediterranean. I say that the States of the region, all the liberated States in the region, welcome the appearance of the Soviet Navy in the Mediterranean Sea as an element to balance the US Sixth Fleet, which sought to turn the Mediterranean into an American sea. The Soviet Navy did not threaten us. The Sixth Fleet is a strategic reserve for

Israel, according to the Israel Premier himself. When the US Navy leaves the Mediterranean, then those who wonder about the danger of the presence of the Soviet Navy will be able to speak and be heard.

On this occasion, I may make a quick reference to our attitude towards the United States. US policy has failed rapidly in this region. No one other than an obvious agent can openly declare friendship for the United States. The entire Arab world is aware of what the United States has done. We expected something different from the United States, or at least we did not expect all that has happened. However, that is the United States' business.

Giving arms to Israel while it is occupying Arab territory means that the United States supports Israel in the occupation of the Arab territory. Giving aircraft to Israel while it is occupying Arab territory means that the United States supports Israel in the occupation of the Arab territory. The complete US support for Israel at the United Nations and the adoption and defence of the Israeli point of view means that the United States supports Israel's occupation of the Arab territory. The US refusal to make a statement stipulating the need for the withdrawal of the Israeli forces to the positions they occupied before 5th June is proof that the United States supports Israel and, indeed, colludes with Israel in what it has done and is doing. Every member of the Arab nation is aware of this.

This matter is not confined to the Arab nation but also includes other States. Last year, it appeared that some CENTO member-States wanted to absolve themselves of CENTO, which was formerly called the Baghdad Pact. Yesterday we read that the Turkish students were throwing Sixth Fleet crews into the sea. Why? No sensible man in the United States asks himself why this has happened in the Arab world and in other States.

The United States, which possesses means of power that no other State has had the chance to possess throughout history or in our era, should really ask itself what the people want of it. The people want the United States to adopt an attitude based on justice, an attitude based on equality, for as a great Power the United States should also have great principles which reject aggression and occupation and in no circumstances agree to support the aggressor and give him arms.

I shall now refer to my visit to Yugoslavia. I visited Yugoslavia for a short time. Maybe we stayed two nights there. The purpose of the visit was to prove our appreciation for President Tito's visit to us last August. He decided to come in August, the warmest time, last year. Such a gesture on his part deserves great appreciation. President Tito is our friend. After the setback, he actually played a very great role everywhere and in all States against aggression, occupation and Israel's methods. At the same time we discussed the new conference of non-aligned States.

We shall now speak about the economic situation. Despite all the conditions of war, the Egyptian economic situation is sound in its entirety.

Industry has obtained investments, new factories are being opened daily, and agricultural products are setting records. This does not mean that we have no economic problems. No. We have economic problems. We have problems in respect of hard currency, the balance of payments and investments required for development. We want to employ the largest number of people and therefore we need a large amount of money. However, despite these problems, the economy is proceeding on its course. There were hopes that economic pressure would make us hungry and would place us in a situation so that we could not import wheat or food. Now, one year later, we are able to stand fast. There is wheat, flour and corn. There are no crises involving supplies, all this despite the fact that we have made an unprecedented allocation for the defence budget this year —over £E300 million.

The next point I wish to discuss concerns youth and its role. Concern about youth is one of the most important phenomena in our homeland. We must develop this concern. The worst thing that can happen to any country is to have its youth feel indifferent. We want our youth to be interested in everything. The condition of youth must be one of our most important subjects, because youth is the hope of the homeland. Young people participating in public affairs is a healthy sign and a guarantee of hope for the future. This is the reason for the concern about the representation of youth at this Congress.

We also believe that the university's positive participation in forming concepts is necessary. I have spoken, perhaps in this very hall, of this many times in past years. The university must be the stronghold protecting national social development and opening the way before it. I never cease to say that the guarantees for the future are the universities, concern about the universities, and democracy.

The next point is Arab action. The battle against the enemy must have priority over everything else. The battle demands a single Arab nation. Up to now we have been trying by all means to attain this aim.

A meeting was held at Khartoum. I have spoken previously about the Khartoum meeting and its importance. We called for another summit conference but did not insist on it and substituted bilateral co-ordination instead. We are not about to be side-tracked. Some have tried to drag us along, but we are not prepared to be dragged.

There is one battle which is absorbing all our efforts in preparing for it; we have no time for anything else. It is the battle against the enemy. Our attitude towards any Arab State depends on that State's attitude towards the battle. Naturally, some states have sent us forces, Sudan and Algeria for instance. Their forces are with us. Other Arab countries such as Iraq and Kuwait have forces with us too. Some States have helped us to resist economically and have adhered to the Arab support agreement such as Saudi Arabia, Libya and Kuwait. I believe that Arab action can progress day after day in spite of the slow rate of progress.

The next point concerns Palestinian fida'i activity. We are fully committed to offering all help to the Palestinian fida'i action. We consider that the Palestinian struggle last year was a big sign of change in the whole Arab situation. Not only we but the entire world senses this indication that the Palestinian people have risen to champion their own cause by themselves and to defend their rights by themselves.

The ninth point concerns psychological warfare. Psychological warfare means an attempt to arouse doubt about everything. Its aim is to strike at the domestic front. But attempts to cast suspicion are not new to us. As we have said, in 1957 there were 11 clandestine radios broadcasting against us. Attempts to arouse suspicions are useless so far as the masses of the Arab nation are concerned.

Suspicion campaigns act in various directions. Firstly, they try to distort the essential widescale diplomatic activity of the UAR and to depict it as accepting suspect plans. Of course, it is our duty to launch a diplomatic offensive and expose Israel throughout the world. Of course, psychological warfare is being used in an effort to depict this diplomatic offensive as acceptance of suspicious plans.

Psychological warfare also seeks to speak of the Soviet Union and holds that our relations with the USSR have expanded and become closer and that this will drive us into communism and embroil us in subservience. All of us know these points and I do not have to repeat them.

There is a big difference between co-operation and subservience. When we concluded the 1955 arms deal with the Soviet Union they said there was danger in the arms deal because it would drag us into subservience. They cited examples. When we began to conclude the High Dam agreement with the Soviet Union, they said Soviet experts would come to work at the High Dam and that this would lead to some sort of subservience. More than 5,000 Soviet experts came to the High Dam, but none of them interfered in our domestic affairs and none of them tried to convert any of the people of Aswan to communism. Nothing of the sort happened.

Today they are saying the same thing. For example, they say the Soviet experts in the Army mean domination of the army and subservience. I have said before that we asked the Soviet Union for these experts and that the Soviet Union was not receptive to giving us experts, saying it would expose us to attack. But in fact, after the 5th June events, anyone with insight who could evaluate things felt that we needed training and that we had a great deal to learn about war. Thus we asked for and got the military experts. They are helping us. We have, in fact, benefited from them; we have benefited from them in all fields.

What the psychological warfare suggested when we received arms in 1955 and when we concluded the High Dam agreement in 1960 may again be suggested this time.

Brothers, we feel that the entire Arab nation must feel grateful to the Soviet Union. Had it not been for the Soviet Union, as I have already said, we should now find ourselves with no arms in the face of the Israeli militarism, which has been blinded by its victory of June 1967. Egypt's independence—and I say this to all people—is not for sale, is not for anyone to buy and is not for mortgage. This will continue to be the case. It is this attitude that has placed us in the difficult situations we are experiencing. Had we agreed to subservience, such as that represented by the Baghdad Pact which we were asked under threats to join, we should have accepted subservience some years ago, long ago and there would have been no need for us to wage all these battles. We have not accepted subservience, we will never accept it and for this reason we have been struggling and fighting for freedom, independence and the building of a free homeland and free citizens.

There has also been the psychological war—poisoned news. It was reported in recent dispatches that demonstrations had been started in Alexandria and that travellers were the source of this information. Our country is an open, not a closed, country. Our country is not a closed country—people can come and go. Thousands of people enter and leave our country every hour. These reports reflect a form of psychological war involving false reports to influence us and to prove that the domestic front is not strong and is not steadfast and, at the same time, to influence the domestic front and shake it so that imperialism, Israel and those who stand behind Israel can achieve their purpose.

Our enemies have succeeded in winning a military victory, but our country has not fallen, has not accepted defeat, but has decided to stand fast. They have applied economic pressure to us and, despite this pressure, we have not surrendered but have marched on. We have imposed restrictions on ourselves and have accepted these restrictions. Our enemies have failed to destroy us economically. Hence, there remains one thing for them to do—to strike at the domestic front and to break up the alliance of the people's working forces because if the domestic front collapses the hostile imperialist forces and Israel will achieve the aims they have so far been unable to achieve.

The 10th and last point is the inevitability of victory and the conditions for victory. Brothers, there is no alternative to victory for our nation. The nation is capable of achieving victory provided it mobilises its forces and benefits properly from its energy and conditions, and also if we can build up and safeguard our domestic front according to the needs of the battle. The domestic front is the pillar of the fighting front. We must expose, defeat and crush all enemy attempts to influence the domestic front.

Now comes your role, brothers, comrades in the struggle, and members of the ASU National Congress. You are the command of the alliance of the people's working forces. You are the more capable of cohesion with these forces. You are the more capable of guiding them through work, struggle, clarity and truth. The battle is all the people's battle. It is the battle for the people's lives, and all the people must participate in it. It must be a victory for life and for the people. May God grant you success. Peace be with you.

UN Resolution 242: A Common Denominator

By Gideon Rafael*

A variety of attributions and interpretations have been bestowed upon Resolution 242, depending upon the party which invoked its blessings. Some see in it a magic formula to dispel the Israel-Arab conflict; others regard it as a means of perpetuating it. But the real significance of that Resolution is that it has been accepted as a common denominator by the warring camps despite their differing views. In fact, Resolution 242 was never contemplated to be an act of revelation. It was the outcome of six months of passionate on-stage United Nations debates and arduous backstage diplomatic wrangling.

When, at five o'clock in the afternoon of 22 November 1967, Ambassador Mamadou Boubacar Kante, representative of the Republic of Mali, pounded his Presidential gavel to announce that all the fifteen members of the Security Council had voted in favour of the British draft resolution—from now on to figure as Resolution 242—its adoption was not greeted with hymns of Hallelujah but rather with a sigh of relief that the United Nations had at long last acquitted itself of a tedious task. What the Security Council had achieved was to formulate a set of guide-lines for the establishment of a just and lasting peace between the Arab States and Israel, to be translated into treaty terms through agreement by the States themselves. What it had not accomplished was to reconcile the parties to the conflict.

Before the meeting rose for adjournment Mahmoud Riad, then Foreign Minister of Egypt, asked for the floor and enunciated the three articles of Egypt's political faith:

a) Israel is the aggressor and responsible for the war;

b) As the first step towards peace Israel must withdraw all its forces from all the territories occupied since 5 June;

c) The United Nations must recognise and respect the inalienable rights of the Palestine people.

---

* Israel Permanent Representative to the United Nations in 1967. Former Director-General of the Israeli Ministry for Foreign Affairs; Israeli ambassador in London. This article was originally published in *New Middle East* (June, 1973).

Israel aggression, total withdrawal and the restoration of the rights of the Palestinian people have remained until this day the three pillars of Egypt's proclaimed policy. It may have changed occasionally its diplomatic tactics, but so far it has not deviated from its strategic objective.

At that same meeting, Foreign Minister Abba Eban summarised Israel's basic position, which has remained the cornerstone of its policy:

We shall respect and fully maintain the situation embodied in the cease-fire agreement until it is succeeded by peace treaties between Israel and the Arab States ending the state of war, establishing agreed, recognised and secure territorial boundaries, guaranteeing free navigation for all shipping, including that of Israel, in all the waterways leading to and from the Red Sea, committing all signatories to the permanent and mutual recognition and respect of the sovereignty, security and national identity of all Middle Eastern States and ensuring a stable and mutually guaranteed security. Such a peace settlement, directly negotiated and contractually confirmed, would create conditions in which refugee problems could be justly and effectively solved through international and regional cooperation. . . .

The Lessons of 1956 and the Objectives of 1962

To assess the essence and significance, the purpose and value of Resolution 242, one has to retrace the course of the political struggle which was waged in the United Nations during six tense months. It opened at the end of May 1967 when Egypt's preparations for offensive military action became manifest by the expulsion of the United Nations Emergency Force, the massive concentration of its forces in Sinai and the re-imposition of the blockade in the Straits of Tiran.

At the end of May, Foreign Minister Eban visited Paris, London and Washington in order to acquaint the heads of Governments with the full weight of the impending peril. Israel's Permanent Representative to the United Nations not only scornfully repudiated the slander and abuse with which the Arab and Soviet delegates were inundating the Security Council, but called upon that highest organ of the United Nations to stand up and to be counted in the face of a grave and imminent threat to international peace and security. Israel's envoys in the capitals of the world toiled to enlist understanding and support for it in its hour of destiny. Yet the Powers shirked their undertakings and the United Nations drowned in a flood of words with not a single drop of action in them.

In the wake of the armies clashing on the battlefield the diplomats took up the cudgels in the United Nations arena. When the curtain rose at the Security Council in the early hours of Monday, 5 June, the Israel representative defined the main political objectives he was determined to pursue with the lessons of the 1956–57 political struggle well in mind:

To permit the momentum gained by Israel's Army in cutting through the formidable Egyptian build-up, to take its full course;

To prevent the adoption of any resolution calling for the withdrawal of forces prior to the establishment of peace, meaning that the Israel forces would remain on the cease-fire lines until replaced by agreed boundaries of peace;

To oppose any resurrection of the collapsed armistice régime and insist on the erection of a new structure of complete and lasting peace;

To cooperate closely with the United States to avoid the reactivation of that fatal Soviet-American vise whose closing jaws cracked in 1956 the position of America's friends and enabled its opponents to regroup and to recuperate their strength.

The Arab States on the other hand, staunchly supported by their Soviet allies, were guided by three diametrically opposite objectives:

The immediate unconditional and total withdrawal of Israel's forces from all the territories evacuated by the retreating Arab armies; in other words to return to the old armistice lines as the first step for the continued onslaught against Israel's very existence;

Condemnation of Israel as aggressor;

Full compensation to the Arab States for all war damages.

As soon as it became evident to the Soviet Government that contrary to the claims of Arab propaganda, the Israeli forces were advancing on that 5 June towards the Suez Canal, and not Egypt's armies towards Tel Aviv, the Soviet representatives hastened to secure United States support for a resolution that would call for a ceasefire and the immediate withdrawal of all forces to their previous positions. Encouraged by their experience of 1956 they believed that this exercise could be successfully repeated in 1967. The Arab Governments hoped that joint American-Soviet action would extricate them from the political and territorial consequences of their military debacle, that an American-Soviet salvage tug would tow their stranded ship back to the breached breakwaters of the old armistice lines.

But the United States had also learned from its 1956–57 experience. It had recognised that its policy then had helped the design of the Soviet Union to deepen its penetration into the Mediterranean area, to consolidate its position in the Middle East, had humiliated and estranged America's allies, and resurrected Nasser, the West's implacable adversary. Thus in 1967, American policy did not hasten to restore a dilapidated armistice régime which had broken down under the constant batterings of Arab assault and subversion, but insisted on a complete termination of the state of war and its replacement by a just and lasting peace.

From the very outset of the deliberations in the Security Council, and throughout their multiple stages, Israel's UN delegation maintained close contacts with the United States mission, in order to protect its political front line exposed to a constant assault by a formidable array of political forces commanding in the United Nations vast reserves of voting power. This cooperation was imperative to ensure the attainment of Israel's main objective: the transformation of the hostile Arab-Israel confrontation into a state of peaceful coexistence.

Arab Objectives

The debate in the Security Council ended with a resounding set-back for the Soviet and Arab delegations on every one of their claims. None of their proposals contained in a variety of draft resolutions calling for the withdrawal of the Israel forces, for its condemnation and for payment for war damages was adopted. In the United Nations forum the Arab Governments manifested an unusual measure of tenacity matched by an equal standard of obduracy. Undaunted by defeat in the Security Council, they carried their fight into the General Assembly. There they command the support of the entire Communist bloc from Cuba in the West to Mongolia in the East, of a dozen or so Muslim states and of a number of developing countries that traditionally side with them.

Upon the initiative of the Soviet Union, an Emergency Session of the General Assembly convened on 19 June. Moscow decided to send to New York its national diplomatic team captained by Prime Minister Kosygin, coached by veteran "pro" Gromyko and composed of top flight diplomats, seasoned propagandists and master tacticians. Most of the Soviet bloc countries followed suit and despatched delegations also led by their Prime Ministers. Against this redoubtable striking force Israel put into the field a small but closely knit delegation of a handful of experienced career diplomats, led by Foreign Minister Abba Eban and assisted by a group of parliamentary advisers.

In the General Assembly the Arab-Soviet coalition renewed its offensive which had been repelled in the Security Council, determined to attain its three objectives: condemnation, compensation and evacuation. When they failed to muster the necessary votes for their extremist proposals, they sent their strategic reserves into the field: Yugoslavia together with a number of States traditionally aligned with the Arab countries, introduced a new draft resolution which though watered-down in its style and wording pursued in its meaning the same principal aim: unconditional Israel withdrawal without an equivalent Arab advance towards peace.

Another move was initiated by a group of Latin American states which linked the withdrawal clause to a change in Arab-Israel relations. Their central plea was that the termination of the state of war was a prior condition to withdrawal.

By mid-July the debates of the Emergency Session and the behind-the-scenes diplomatic haggling had reached a deadlock. Two opposing concepts were in conflict with no chance of compromise in sight. Neither side could whip up the necessary voting majority. The Arab-Soviet bloc insisted on the restoration of the pre-June situation. On the other side, a powerful group of delegations, led by the United States, and composed mainly of pro-Western States and a number of developing countries, refuted the false allegations of Israel's responsibility for the outbreak of the war and urged a new constructive approach which would bring the Israel-Arab conflict to an end. This group drafted its proposals with caution and restraint. It did not explicitly call for the establishment of peace. It confined itself to the demand that the state of war be terminated once and for all. On the question of the withdrawal of forces the resolution which was prepared by a number of Latin American states, did not differ substantially from Arab-Soviet formulations except that it linked it to the termination of belligerency.

The Gromyko-Goldberg Connection

When it became clear to the Soviet delegation that its massive diplomatic and propaganda offensive designed to extricate the Arab States from their self-inflicted predicament had bogged down, and that the Emergency Session was about to disperse without any results, the Soviet Ambassador in Washington, Anatoly Dobrynin, contacted Secretary of State Dean Rusk, to break the deadlock. He suggested a new formula which abandoned the demands for condemnation of Israel and payment of compensation to the Arab States. He concentrated on one principal objective: the immediate withdrawal by Israel from all the territories in exchange for a vague and noncommittal undertaking by the Arab States to relinquish their hostility. Rusk, well versed in the art of diplomacy in general and Soviet negotiating practices in particular, replied: "What you are suggesting, Mr. Ambassador, is to trade a horse for a rabbit." "What do you mean by that, Mr. Secretary?" asked Dobrynin. Rusk explained: "The horse is the withdrawal of the Israel forces and the rabbit is the trifle that you are offering in exchange." But American diplomacy is also guided by the rule, which is always good diplomacy: never slam the door in the face of your interlocutor. Never cut off a probing exercise until you know exactly what the other side really is aiming at. Dean Rusk, therefore, agreed that Ambassador Goldberg, the United States representative to the United Nations, should be available for further contacts with Soviet representatives.

Ambassador Dobrynin hurried to New York. Intensive talks between him and Ambassador Goldberg began on 18 July. Their objective was to find a mutually acceptable formula. Their main difference centred around the "horse-rabbit" equation. The principal issue remained the American position that withdrawal must be accompanied by a definite termination of the state of war. The Soviet representatives argued deviously that they too favoured this objective but that their Arab friends refused to accept a draft which would explicitly stipulate the cessation of belligerence. In an attempt to overcome this "semantic allergy," Ambassador Goldberg suggested the following wording:

The Arab States must recognise Israel's right to maintain its own national State and to live in peace and security, and, furthermore, the Arab States must give up all demands and actions that contradict this.

But even this meek and involved formula did not satisfy Dobrynin. He objected to any wording which would require the Arab States to give unequivocal recognition of Israel's right to national independence. He answered with a counterformulation:

All States in the Middle East have a right to independence.

The Israel delegation viewed with growing concern the gradual erosion of the American position. Foreign Minister Eban assisted by Israel's Permanent Representative to the United Nations and the Ambassador in Washington intervened strongly with the representatives of the United States to arrest this ominous drift. The American desire, however, to reach with the Soviet Union a parliamentary understanding in the United Nations was in this case a stronger motivating force for the State Department than to take a firm stand on a position designed to promote lasting peace between Israel and the Arab States.

To bolster its negotiating strength, the Soviet Government circulated through "reliable channels" repeated hints that it would not remain indifferent to the continued occupation of Arab territories and would take appropriate steps if the political efforts were to fail. The United States, deeply and painfully involved in Vietnam, pursued at the time a cautious course in other international crises. It preferred a dubious diplomatic compromise to avoid further foreign complications. Moreover, some of the American policy experts believed that an accommodation with the Soviet Union would curb its ambitions to expand its influence in the Mediterranean.

These considerations seemed to have guided the State Department in directing Ambassador Goldberg to work for an American-Soviet compromise formula. When the talks with Ambassador Dobrynin failed to produce results, Foreign Minister Gromyko personally took over. He invited Ambassador Goldberg for a cup of Russian tea to gain American sympathy. Eventually both sides agreed on a compromise draft which was far closer to the Soviet position than to the policy enunciated by President

Johnson in his speech of 19 June. Both parties to the bargain were fully aware that their real differences had simply been papered over. In parting, Gromyko suggested to Goldberg, true to classical Soviet diplomacy: "Let's agree on the wording and differ on its interpretation."

The Israel delegation learnt the full measure of the United States retreat only on the morrow of the Soviet–United States transaction when it was shown the text of the agreed draft resolution which read:

The General Assembly. . . .

1. Declares that peace and final solutions of this problem can be achieved within the framework of the Charter of the United Nations.

2. Affirms the principles under the Charter of:

A. Withdrawal without delay by the parties to the conflict of their forces from territories occupied by them, in keeping with the inadmissibility of conquest of territory by war.

B. Acknowledgment without delay by all member-States of the United Nations in the area; that each enjoys the right to maintain an independent national State of its own and to live in peace and security; and renunciation of all claims and acts inconsistent therewith.

3. Requests the Security Council to continue examining the situation in the Middle East with a sense of urgency, working directly with the parties and utilising a United Nations presence to achieve an appropriate and just solution of all aspects of the problem, in particular bringing to an end the long-deferred problem of the refugees and guaranteeing freedom of transit through international waterways.

The reversal of the United States position was perhaps the most hazardous of all the many ups and downs which had occurred since the beginning of the United Nations deliberations in the Security Council on 5 June. The United States, in its attempt to close the gap between the differing American and Soviet positions on the question of withdrawal, retreated itself from its proclaimed policies. It was on the point of creating a situation as dangerous to Israel's future as it was detrimental to the prospects of peace in the Middle East. It abandoned in the American-Soviet draft not only the call for a lasting peace but even the demand for the termination of the state of war, while supporting a precipitate withdrawal by Israel. In effect, the United States had come very close to buying Dobrynin's rabbit, after all.

Everything was ready, then, for a grand finale of the Emergency Session. The Soviets undertook to secure the assent of the Arab delegations to the terms of the draft. But, Mr. Gromyko was in for a major surprise, when he learnt the result of their consultations. They rejected the draft resolution. The Algerians and Syrians led the opposition and Egypt felt obliged to follow suit. Its negative stand doomed the Soviet-American initiative and relieved Israel from Big Power diplomatic encirclement.

Emergency Session Recessed

When this last effort to pass a resolution had failed, it was decided to wind up the Emergency Session without further delay. At the end of two months of this parliamentary tug-of-war, the situation presented itself as follows. The determined and unrelenting efforts made by the Soviet and Arab Governments since the military debacle in June, to mobilise international support for the immediate and unconditional withdrawal of the Israel forces, had failed. The United Nations organs declined to hold Israel responsible for the outbreak of the hostilities. All claims for the payment of war damages to the Arab States had been dismissed and dropped even by their sponsors. The Soviet-American accord had floundered on the rocks of Arab obstinacy. This was the optimum Israel could expect to achieve in the United Nations. The composition of the General Assembly, where the pro-Arab voting bloc can defeat any resolution not to its liking, makes it virtually impossible for Israel to marshal sufficient support for any of its objectives and in particular not for its central aim: the establishment of peace by negotiation.

Behind the scenes, however, diplomatic activity did not cease. Lord Caradon, Great Britain's permanent representative, led the group of activists. Early in October, he presented to the Israel delegation a draft resolution, a kind of see-saw puzzle, which he had pieced together from bits of the defunct Gromyko-Goldberg formula, seasoning it with ingredients from a previous Latin-American draft, and adding to it a new idea of appointing a special United Nations representative to act as mediator. Yet Lord Caradon's new model was a nonstarter. It did not commend itself to the Israel and other like-minded delegations. Israel agreed to consider a draft which would limit itself to the appointment of a special representative confined to the task of assisting the parties to enter into peace negotiations.

The diplomatic probings proceeded in an unhurried and relaxed atmosphere, until the calm was broken on 21 October by the stirring news that the Israel destroyer *Eilat* had been sunk by Soviet-made Egyptian missiles. In the wake of the shelling by Israel artillery of the refineries at Port Suez, on 24 October, the Security Council was called into urgent session. The international community was seized with anxiety that the cease-fire was about to collapse. The two incidents raised the Middle Eastern temperatures to a degree which the Big Powers considered perilously inflammable. The representative of the Soviet Union attacked Israel in his usual manner while completely disregarding the Egyptian aggression committed against the Israel naval vessel. To heighten the dramatic effect of their performance, the Soviets again circulated rumours of a possibility of their military intervention in case Israeli forces intended to operate on the Egyptian side of the Canal. The United States Government counselled caution and restraint, but in the Security Council it did not yield to Soviet fulminations. Thanks to the strenuous efforts of Ambassador Arthur Goldberg, a balanced resolution was adopted, calling upon both parties to cease all hostile acts and to observe scrupulously the cease-fire.

The military incidents on the Egyptian front expedited from now on the diplomatic activity. The pace of consultations was accelerated. The Soviet Union sent to New York its First Deputy Foreign Minister, Kusnetsov, a competent and skilled negotiator and a diplomat highly respected by his Western colleagues. His opening gambit was a conversation with Secretary Dean Rusk in Washington, where again he warned of the dangers of a Middle Eastern conflagration to which the Soviet Union could not remain indifferent. He indicated that the Arab Governments were now ready to accept the Gromyko-Goldberg formula which they had rejected only a few weeks ago. The permanent members of the Security Council —the Big Powers—incapable of reaching an agreement among themselves, encouraged the other ten members of the Council to try expeditiously their hand in drafting a resolution. But the ten equally could not reach agreement. Denmark and Canada stuck to their position that the central aim of any resolution should be the establishment of secure and recognised boundaries within the framework of a lasting and just peace. Opposing them was a group comprising India, Mali and Nigeria that tried to blend the Latin American principles of the termination of the state of war and the inadmissibility of acquisition of territory by war with the Arab demand of the unconditional withdrawal of the Israel forces from all the occupied territories. On 3 November, the ten non-permanent members of the Security Council informed their permanent colleagues of their failure to reach agreement.

Egypt; Surprise Move

The United States delegation, undeterred by the failure of other members of the Security Council to reach agreement, pursued its independent efforts to enlist support for a resolution of its own drafting. On 7 November while the American diplomatic activity was in full swing, the Egyptian delegation made a surprise move. It called for an urgent meeting of the Security Council. In his explanatory memorandum, the Representative of Egypt claimed that the meeting was necessary, ''because of the explosive situation in the Middle East resulting from Israel's refusal to withdraw its forces.'' Yet he did not explain where it had been decided that Israel must withdraw, nor did he point to any resolution in this regard on which he could base his contention, because nothing of the kind had ever been ruled by any United Nations body.

Concurrently with the Egyptian sortie, India presented its own draft resolution. The United States countered by introducing their own proposal. In precipitating the convening of the Council, Egypt apparently was under the impression that it could muster a majority in favour of the Indian draft resolution. By taking this unexpected step it did not only surprise the United States representatives, but also antagonised them. For, in these critical weeks, while the delegates of the ten non-permanent members were consulting together, the United States representatives were engaged in secret and searching talks of clarification with the Egyptian Foreign Minister, Mahmoud Riad, and with King Husain, who was in New York at the time. They had obtained the consent of the King to the principles and formulations of the American draft which they presented to the Council on 7 November. Moreover, King Husain affirmed that his position had been endorsed by Nasser when they coordinated their moves at the United Nations at a meeting in Cairo on 17 September. The American representatives, in their conversations with Foreign Minister Riad, did not reach complete Egyptian consent to all the proposed wording but they were led to believe that Egypt had an interest in continuing the dialogue and was anxious to reach an agreement with them on a draft resolution. However the United States delegation realised later that while they were holding talks with Foreign Minister Riad, he was at the same time, urging the Indian delegation to proceed with the preparation of their own draft and to introduce it forthwith. Their proposal ran counter in its principal provisions to the United States position. The United States representatives did not conceal from Foreign Minister Riad their dismay at his double-dealing.

When the Council met on 9 November, it had before it two rival draft resolutions—the American and the Indian. The sponsors launched brisk campaigns to mobilise the required majority. India's prospects seemed to be far brighter than America's. At that time, the United States was not yet prepared to employ the ultimate United Nations diplomatic weapon, the veto, as a means of blocking undesirable draft resolutions. It relied on its power of persuasion in discussions with the delegates at the United Nations and with the Governments in the capitals. It was clear to all delegations, the Soviet Union and Egypt included, that any resolution unacceptable to the United States and rejected by Israel, would even if pushed through, carry no real political weight and have no influence on the situation in the Middle East.

The British Draft Resolution

In the face of this dilemma, Lord Caradon decided that the time was ripe to expedite his own efforts. He exerted considerable diplomatic skill and zeal to bridge the gap between the two draft resolutions. He now produced a proposal based in its essentials on the objectives of the American draft, adding to it formulations from earlier texts and some adaptations from the Indian draft.

Intrinsically, the new design "made in Britain" was not much different from the American draft. It contained, however, two important modifications. Lord Caradon inserted into the preambular part a provision concerning the "inadmissibility of the acquisition of territory by war"; and added to the one and only operative paragraph of the draft resolution which defined the terms of reference of the Special United Nations Representative, two essential provisions: agreement and acceptability. The Special Representative was to promote *agreement* between the parties concerned: and the peace settlement must be *acceptable* to them.

The preamble was altered in order to obtain Latin American support. While all this complicated backstage diplomacy was proceeding, Argentina and Brazil championed a draft of their own making which also was intended to be a compromise between the Indian and American proposals. It was based on the concepts of the proposal which the Latin American group had submitted unsuccessfully to the Emergency Session. The United States did not spare any effort to persuade the Governments of Argentina and Brazil to abandon their separate initiative which jeopardised Lord Caradon's endeavours to work out a unanimously acceptable compromise. He himself apparently felt that the only way to make Argentina and Brazil yield was to compensate them by incorporating into his own draft their peculiar doctrine of the inadmissibility of the acquisition of territory. But to lessen its significance and to indicate that this was not an operational provision but an abstract principle, he put it into the preamble and, for good measure, balanced it by adding another provision: "The need to work for a just and lasting peace in which every State in the area can live in security."

The change in the operational paragraph emphasising the need for agreement between the parties and the acceptability of a negotiated peace agreement was the result of arduous and sometimes tense discussions between Lord Caradon and the representatives of Israel who insisted, and won their point, that the resolution must reflect five guiding principles:

a) The central objective is the establishment of a just and lasting peace between Israel and the Arab States.

b) The withdrawal of Israel forces from the cease-fire lines would take place only after secure and recognised boundaries had been agreed upon within the terms of a peace treaty.

c) Peace must be the outcome of an agreement between the parties, achieved through free negotiations and not by outside imposition. Refuting the views of the French Representative expressed in one of his statements that it was unrealistic to expect negotiations without prior withdrawal, Mr. Eban answered, "I invite the Council to understand that it is unrealistic to believe that withdrawal is possible without negotiation."

d) Guaranteed freedom of navigation through all the international waterways in the area without limitations or reservations.

e) The United Nations Special Representative would be authorised to render good offices to the parties and not to act as a mediator presenting them with proposals of his own.

One difference between the American and British drafts was a curious omission in the British text of a provision contained in the United States draft, namely, to halt the arms race in the Middle East. The reason for its elimination is not clear. The first impression was that it was excluded out of consideration for the Soviet large-scale supplies of military equipment to the Arab countries, to replenish their arsenals depleted by combat losses. However, a Soviet draft resolution presented at the final stage of the Security Council debates included a similar call to halt the arms race couched in almost identical terms used in the United States text.

At the meeting of the Security Council on 15 November Ambassador Goldberg made a lucid and forceful presentation of his Government's policy in regard to the main issues to be embodied in the resolution:

To seek withdrawal without secure and recognised boundaries, for example, would be just as fruitless as to seek secure and recognised boundaries without withdrawal. Historically there have never been secure and recognised boundaries in the area. Neither the Armistice lines of 1949 nor the cease-fire lines of 1967 have answered that description. Now such boundaries have yet to be agreed upon. An agreement on that point is an essential to a just and lasting peace, just as withdrawal is. Such boundaries cannot be determined by force. They cannot be imposed from the outside. For history shows that imposed boundaries are not secure and secure boundaries must be mutually worked out and recognised as part of the peace-making process.

The next day Lord Caradon submitted formally the British draft resolution. The Arab representatives were still holding out on two points. They objected to "recognised boundaries," since they were prepared to recognise only the 1949 Armistice lines. They insisted that the wording on evacuation of forces should state explicitly: "Withdrawal of the Israel forces from *all* the territories occupied in the recent conflict." The behind-the-scenes diplomatic activities reached a new high pitch. Lord Caradon tried without avail to obtain Israel's consent to dispense with the term "recognised boundaries" and content itself with "secure boundaries." He also urged it to accept the insertion of a single little word, the definite article "the" before the word "territories," so that the text would read: "withdrawal of Israeli forces from *the* territories." He appeared to be disappointed when he encountered a resolute rejection of these changes which would have altered the very significance of the resolution in two of its most essential points. He tried to enlist the influence of the United States delegation to make Israel yield. However, it declined and made it clear that the United States would withdraw its support from the British draft, if it were to be changed by the omission or addition of even one single word.

The Withdrawal Formula Death at Summit Talks

When the Security Council met again on 17 November, the Soviet Representative, Deputy Foreign Minister Kusnetsov, took everybody by surprise with a brief and carefully worded statement. To gain his main objective, namely, a change in the withdrawal paragraph, he stressed that the Soviet Union supported the inalienable right of every State in the Middle East, including Israel, to national and independent existence. At the same time he urged that the resolution should express in unequivocal terms that Israel must withdraw its forces from all the occupied territories. When he eventually realised that the Western delegations were determined to resist even the slightest change in the British draft, he arranged for the Bulgarian representative to ask for an adjournment of the meeting until 20 November.

A well-tested feature of Soviet diplomacy is to wear their opponents down by prolonging the negotiating process until every political, tactical, psychological and propaganda device has been brought into full play. There was good reason for believing that in the end the Soviet Union would not veto the British draft resolution. A high-ranking and authoritative source close to the Soviet delegation expressed his opinion that, in the final analysis, the Soviets would vote for the British draft as it stood. All the same, Soviet diplomacy customarily does not yield until it has exhausted all its means. Even when it was evident that Egypt and Jordan were prepared as a result of an agreement reached in mid-November between King Husain and President Nasser, to accept the British draft without any changes, the Soviet delegation continued its parliamentary war of attrition in an endeavour to erode the text.

The evening before the meeting at which the decisive vote was to be taken, Kusnetsov sprang a new surprise. He informed the American delegation that he had been instructed by Moscow to present a new draft resolution—this time in the name of the Soviet Union alone. At the meeting of the Council, on 20 November, he tabled his proposal. Its main provisions reflected the defunct Gromyko-Goldberg formula, embellished by meaningless additions concerning the termination of the state of war and the need to restore peace and the establishment of normal conditions in the Middle East. It was obvious that this was a still-born initiative; but the adoption of the draft was not the purpose of the Soviet exercise. It was merely designed to serve as a delaying device. Once again Bulgaria's representative, the Soviet delegation's man Friday, asked for another adjournment of two days.

During that interval the Soviet Government made a concerted effort to press the United States to accept the wording. ''Withdrawal of Israel forces from *all* the territories.'' They were so determined to achieve their purpose that they decided to carry their fight for the definite article to the highest level in Washington. During these two days Prime Minister Kosygin exchanged messages with President Johnson pleading for the acceptance of the Soviet change in return for their vote in favour of the amended British text. When President Johnson sternly declined Kosygin proposed a compromise: Instead of ''withdrawal from *all the* territories,'' he was ready to content himself with the wording ''from *the* territories occupied.'' The summit correspondence ended, when the United States informed the Soviet Union in final and unmistakable terms that it would not agree to change even an iota in the British draft. It is established Soviet negotiating practice to yield once they become convinced that they are up against a stone wall which can be neither breached nor by-passed.

When the Security Council met for its crucial session on 22 November after hectic last minute negotiations, the Soviet delegate raised his hand in unison with his American colleague and all the other delegates in favour of the unaltered original British draft. The resolution was passed unanimously and became Security Council Resolution 242. All the members had voted for the same text, but not all of them were prepared to recite it with the same incantation. Foreign Minister Eban in summarising the Israel position declared that only the original British text was the authorised version and the Government of Israel would refer to it alone in determining its position towards the resolution.

With American backing, the British delegate who had sponsored and presented the draft opposed last-minute attempts to confuse and distort the meaning of the resolution. Lord Caradon stated that the resolution:

> Opens the way to agreement and to action. It is the result of close and prolonged consultations with both sides and with all members of this Council. The draft resolution is a balanced whole. To add to it or to detract from it would destroy the balance and also destroy the wide measure of agreement we have reached together. It must be considered as a whole and as it stands. We have reached the stage when we want the resolution, the whole resolution and nothing but the resolution. The draft resolution does not belong to one side or the other or to any one delegation, it belongs to us all and that is the only resolution that will bind us and we regard its wording as clear.

The Balance Sheet

The adoption of the resolution brought to an end the political struggle which began in May 1967, with the aim to prevent the outbreak of war. Because of its ineffectuality and lethargy to face the aggressive designs of the Arab States, the United Nations failed in this task. The contest ended in November, after Israel's successful resistance to the military threat, with a United Nations decision calling for the establishment of a lasting peace between the Arab States and Israel, the first call since 1953 by a United Nations organ categorically stating that nothing but the conclusion of a negotiated peace could solve the Israel-Arab conflict.

During the long months of the debates in the United Nations, Israel's opponents were compelled to abandon one demand after another, whereas Israel gained support for its positions. The Security Council did not call for immediate, unconditional and total withdrawal of the Israel forces; it called, instead, for qualified withdrawal to secure and recognised boundaries; it rejected all attempts to saddle Israel with the responsibility for the outbreak of the hostilities; it insisted on the termination of the state of war imposed by the Arab States and the cessation of all hostile acts such as blockade and boycott conducted by them against Israel for more than 20 years; it did not adopt a formula concerning itself with the "rights of the Palestinian people," but recommended a just settlement of the refugee problem; it did not advocate the imposition of a settlement, but favoured a negotiated peace agreement. Though it mentioned an abstract principle of inadmissibility of non-acquisition of territory by war, it also spelt out the fundamental principle of the Charter of the inadmissibility of war itself. It stressed the main Charter clause which outlawed the use of force or even the threat to resort to force—a situation to which Israel had been exposed from the very first day of its independent statehood. On these basic principles Resolution 242 is founded. Its purpose and significance is its insistence that the parties should withdraw from hostility and belligerency and advance towards a system of peaceful and good neighbourly relations.

For over five years now, Resolution 242 has served a variety of purposes: many a Government, hesitant to take an independent stand on the Israel-Arab conflict, has found it a useful noncommittal political hide-out. Arab Governments have used it as a barrier behind which they entrenched themselves in their refusal to negotiate a peace treaty with Israel. But it also had served as an agreed basis for Israel and the Arab States to enter into the Jarring talks, until the UN Representative brought them to a standstill by departing from his terms of reference. And perhaps one day it will serve again as a platform for true negotiations, when the Arab states have reached the conclusion that it is more beneficial to live in peace with Israel than to fight it.

Over the years various Arab States have claimed that peace depends on the implementation of that Resolution—to be effected without negotiations or agreement between the parties. Only those who believe that it is possible for the three pillars of unwisdom of the resolution adopted in Khartoum in summer 1967: "No recognition of Israel, no negotiations, no peace"—to co-exist with the positive provisions of Resolution 242: The establishment of peace by agreement, the recognition of each State's right to independence and the establishment of a system of relations guaranteeing to all States of the region to dwell in peace and security—can maintain the fictitious view that Resolution 242 is a self-implementing proposition. To this day, the most agile performers of diplomatic acrobatics have failed to reconcile the abysmal contradiction of Resolution 242's positive principles with the continued adherence to the sterile negations of the Khartoum position. . . .

Since its adoption, Resolution 242 has remained the principal workhorse of the diplomatic ploughmen. Its wording, principles and provisions are sign-posts pointing the way to the negotiating table. It is not a detailed blue-print for peace, but rather an outline to guide the peace-makers. The sooner the parties to the conflict meet around the drawing board to draft the terms of peace, the earlier they will be able to move into a new, safe and comfortable dwelling of peaceful relations.

Part IV

From War to War

The documents and articles contained in the present section refer to developments since the Six Day War in 1967, with the exception of the National Covenant of the Palestine Liberation Organization. This manifesto, drawn up in May 1964, superseded the earlier Draft Constitution. The Palestine Liberation Organization is the biggest of the Palestinian refugee organizations; its manifesto has been modified since in various points. The Fatah *"Seven Points" and the interview with the leader of the organization, YasIr Arafat, both published in 1969, offer more recent interpretations of the aims of this movement. The* Arab National Movement *(the predecessor of the* Popular Front*) was founded in the Lebanon in 1948. It did not join* Fatah *which in its view was not radical enough and it has since split into two factions led by Dr. George Habbash and Naif Hawatme respectively. The Platform of the Popular Front for the Liberation of Palestine was formulated by the latter, the extreme left-wing faction of the movement. General Harkabi, the author of several studies on Arab-Israeli problems, taught at the Hebrew University, Jerusalem. The essay on Fatah Doctrine is taken from a more detailed study: "Fedayeen Action and Arab Strategy" published by the Institute of Strategic Studies in London in December 1968. Nasser's speech at the Arab Socialist Union Congress in March 1969 and the Syrian Ba'th Party Resolution of April 1969 reflect the stand* *taken by the Egyptian and Syrian governments in the dispute since the armistice of June 1967. The excerpts from articles by Hassanain Haykal, the leading Egyptian journalist, define in more detail the objectives of the war of attrition against Israel as seen from Cairo. Ahmad Baha Ed-Dine is another prominent Egyptian journalist, editor of the weekly* Mussawar; *the ideas expressed in his article were later discussed at greater length in a book by the same author which attracted much attention in Arab circles. "Two Years Later" written by Foreign Minister Abba Eban and General Dayan's speech present Israeli points of view on both the short-term issues involved in the Arab-Israeli dispute and the long-term perspectives. Yehoshua Arieli is professor of history at the Hebrew University, Jerusalem; his speech reflecting the opinions of the anti-annexationist movement in Israel was made at an international symposium in Tel Aviv in March 1969 sponsored by the monthly* New Outlook. *"Sartre looks at the Middle East again" is based on an interview with Arturo Schwartz, editor of the* Quaderni del Medio Oriente. *Sartre had visited the Middle East shortly before the Six Day War. Prof. Bernard Lewis argues in his essay, originally written for* Foreign Affairs, *that the two main problems of the area—the East-West rivalry and the Arab-Israeli conflict—while likely to persist are not necessarily connected. Prof. Uri Ra'anan of the Fletcher School of Law and Diplomacy discusses in his contribution first published in* Midstream *in May 1969 Soviet interest in the Middle East and the possibilities of U.S.–Soviet agreement.*

Security Council Resolution on the Middle East, November 22, 1967

THE SECURITY COUNCIL,

Expressing its continuing concern with the grave situation in the Middle East,

Emphasizing the inadmissibility of the acquisition of territory by war and the need to work for a just and lasting peace in which every state in the area can live in security.

Emphasizing further that all member states in their acceptance of the Charter of the United Nations have undertaken a commitment to act in accordance with Article 2 of the Charter,

1. *Affirms* that the fulfillment of Charter principles requires the establishment of a just and lasting peace in the Middle East which should include the application of both the following principles:

(i) Withdrawal of Israeli armed forces from territories occupied in the recent conflict;

(ii) Termination of all claims or states of belligerency and respect for and acknowledgment of the sovereignty, territorial integrity and political independence of every state in the area and their right to live in peace within secure and recognized boundaries free from threats or acts of force;

2. *Affirms further* the necessity

(a) For guaranteeing freedom of navigation through international waterways in the area;

(b) For achieving a just settlement of the refugee problem;

(c) For guaranteeing the territorial inviolability and political independence of every state in the area, through measures including the establishment of demilitarized zones;

3. *Requests* the Secretary General to designate a special representative to proceed to the Middle East to establish and maintain contacts with the states concerned in order to promote agreement and assist efforts to achieve a peaceful and accepted settlement in accordance with the provisions and principles in this resolution.

4. *Requests* the Secretary General to report to the Security Council on the progress of the efforts of the special representative as soon as possible.

The Palestinian National Charter: Resolutions of the Palestine National Council

*Charter**

1. Palestine is the homeland of the Arab Palestinian people; it is an indivisible part of the Arab homeland, and the Palestinian people are an integral part of the Arab nation.

2. Palestine, with the boundaries it had during the British Mandate, is an indivisible territorial unit.

3. The Palestinian Arab people possess the legal right to their homeland and have the right to determine their destiny after achieving the liberation of their country in accordance with their wishes and entirely of their own accord and will.

4. The Palestinian identity is a genuine, essential, and inherent characteristic; it is transmitted from parents to children. The Zionist occupation and the dispersal of the Palestinian Arab people, through the disasters which befell them, do not make them lose their Palestinian identity and their membership in the Palestinian community, nor do they negate them.

5. The Palestinians are those Arab nationals who, until 1947, normally resided in Palestine regardless of whether they were evicted from it or have stayed there. Anyone born, after that date, of a Palestinian father— whether inside Palestine or outside it—is also a Palestinian.

6. The Jews who had normally resided in Palestine until the beginning of the Zionist invasion will be considered Palestinians.

7. That there is a Palestinian community and that it has material, spiritual, and historical connection with Palestine are indisputable facts. It is a national duty to bring up individual Palestinians in an Arab revolutionary manner. All means of information and education must be adopted in order to acquaint the Palestinian with his country in the most profound manner,

* Decisions of the National Congress of the Palestine Liberation Organization held in Cairo July 1–17, 1968.

both spiritual and material, that is possible. He must be prepared for the armed struggle and ready to sacrifice his wealth and his life in order to win back his homeland and bring about its liberation.

8. The phase in their history, through which the Palestinian people are now living, is that of national struggle for the liberation of Palestine. Thus the conflicts among the Palestinian national forces are secondary, and should be ended for the sake of the basic conflict that exists between the forces of Zionism and of imperialism on the one hand, and the Palestinian Arab people on the other. On this basis the Palestinian masses, regardless of whether they are residing in the national homeland or in diaspora, constitute—both their organizations and the individuals—one national front working for the retrieval of Palestine and its liberation through armed struggle.

9. Armed struggle is the only way to liberate Palestine. Thus it is the overall strategy, not merely a tactical phase. The Palestinian Arab people assert their absolute determination and firm resolution to continue their armed struggle and to work for an armed popular revolution for the liberation of their country and their return to it. They also assert their right to normal life in Palestine and to exercise their right to self-determination and sovereignty over it.

10. Commando action constitutes the nucleus of the Palestinian popular liberation war. This requires its escalation, comprehensiveness, and the mobilization of all the Palestinian popular and educational efforts and their organization and involvement in the armed Palestinian revolution. It also requires the achieving of unity for the national struggle among the different groupings of the Palestinian people, and between the Palestinian people and the Arab masses, so as to secure the continuation of the revolution, its escalation, and victory.

11. The Palestinians will have three mottoes: national unity, national mobilization, and liberation.

12. The Palestinian people believe in Arab unity. In order to contribute their share toward the attainment of that objective, however, they must, at the present stage of their struggle, safeguard their Palestinian identity and develop their consciousness of that identity, and oppose any plan that may dissolve or impair it.

13. Arab unity and the liberation of Palestine are two complementary objectives, the attainment of either of which facilitates the attainment of the other. Thus, Arab unity leads to the liberation of Palestine, the liberation of Palestine leads to Arab unity; and work toward the realization of one objective proceeds side by side with work toward the realization of the other.

14. The destiny of the Arab nation, and indeed Arab existence itself, depend upon the destiny of the Palestine cause. From this interdependence spring the Arab nation's pursuit of, and striving for, the liberation of Pal-

estine. The people of Palestine play the role of the vanguard in the realization of this sacred national goal.

15. The liberation of Palestine, from an Arab viewpoint, is a national duty and it attempts to repel the Zionist and imperialist aggression against the Arab homeland, and aims at the elimination of Zionism in Palestine. Absolute responsibility for this falls upon the Arab nation—peoples and governments—with the Arab people of Palestine in the vanguard. Accordingly, the Arab nation must mobilize all its military, human, moral, and spiritual capabilities to participate actively with the Palestinian people in the liberation of Palestine. It must, particularly in the phase of the armed Palestinian revolution, offer and furnish the Palestinian people with all possible help, and material and human support, and make available to them the means and opportunities that will enable them to continue to carry out their leading role in the armed revolution, until they liberate their homeland.

16. The liberation of Palestine, from a spiritual point of view, will provide the Holy Land with an atmosphere of safety and tranquility, which in turn will safeguard the country's religious sanctuaries and guarantee freedom of worship and of visit to all, without discrimination of race, color, language, or religion. Accordingly, the people of Palestine look to all spiritual forces in the world for support.

17. The liberation of Palestine, from a human point of view, will restore to the Palestinian individual his dignity, pride, and freedom. Accordingly the Palestinian Arab people look forward to the support of all those who believe in the dignity of man and his freedom in the world.

18. The liberation of Palestine, from an international point of view, is a defensive action necessitated by the demands of self-defense. Accordingly, the Palestine people, desirous as they are of the friendship of all people, look to freedom-loving, and peace-loving states for support in order to restore their legitimate rights in Palestine, to re-establish peace and security in the country, and to enable its people to exercise national sovereignty and freedom.

19. The partition of Palestine in 1947 and the establishment of the state of Israel are entirely illegal, regardless of the passage of time, because they were contrary to the will of the Palestinian people and to their natural right in their homeland, and inconsistent with the principles embodied in the Charter of the United Nations, particularly the right to self-determination.

20. The Balfour Declaration, the Mandate for Palestine, and everything that has been based upon them, are deemed null and void. Claims of historical or religious ties of Jews with Palestine are incompatible with the facts of history and the true conception of what constitutes statehood. Judaism, being a religion, is not an independent nationality. Nor do Jews constitute a single nation with an identity of its own; they are citizens of the states to which they belong.

21. The Arab Palestinian people, expressing themselves by the armed Palestinian revolution, reject all solutions which are substitutes for the total liberation of Palestine and reject all proposals aiming at the liquidation of the Palestinian problem, or its internationalization.

22. Zionism is a political movement organically associated with international imperialism and antagonistic to all action for liberation and to progressive movements in the world. It is racist and fanatic in its nature, aggressive, expansionist, and colonial in its aims, and fascist in its methods. Israel is the instrument of the Zionist movement, and a geographical base for world imperialism placed strategically in the midst of the Arab homeland to combat the hopes of the Arab nation for liberation, unity, and progress. Israel is a constant source of threat *vis-à-vis* peace in the Middle East and the whole world. Since the liberation of Palestine will destroy the Zionist and imperialist presence and will contribute to the establishment of peace in the Middle East, the Palestinian people look for the support of all the progressive and peaceful forces and urge them all, irrespective of their affiliations and beliefs, to offer the Palestinian people all aid and support in their just struggle for the liberation of their homeland.

23. The demands of security and peace, as well as the demands of right and justice, require all states to consider Zionism an illegitimate movement, to outlaw its existence, and to ban its operations, in order that friendly relations among peoples may be preserved, and the loyalty of citizens to their respective homelands safeguarded.

24. The Palestinian people believe in the principles of justice, freedom, sovereignty, self-determination, human dignity, and in the right of all peoples to exercise them.

25. For the realization of the goals of this Charter and its principles, the Palestine Liberation Organization will perform its role in the liberation of Palestine in accordance with the Constitution of this Organization.

26. The Palestine Liberation Organization, representative of the Palestinian revolutionary forces, is responsible for the Palestinian Arab people's movement in its struggle—to retrieve its homeland, liberate and return to it and exercise the right to self-determination in it—in all military, political, and financial fields and also for whatever may be required by the Palestine case on the inter-Arab and international levels.

27. The Palestine Liberation Organization shall cooperate with all Arab states, each according to its potentialities; and will adopt a neutral policy among them in the light of the requirements of the war of liberation; and on this basis it shall not interfere in the internal affairs of any Arab state.

28. The Palestinian Arab people assert the genuineness and independence of their national revolution and reject all forms of intervention, trusteeship, and subordination.

29. The Palestinian people possess the fundamental and genuine legal right to liberate and retrieve their homeland. The Palestinian people de-

termine their attitude toward all states and forces on the basis of the stands they adopt *vis-à-vis* the Palestinian case and the extent of the support they offer to the Palestinian revolution to fulfill the aims of the Palestinian people.

30. Fighters and carriers of arms in the war of liberation are the nucleus of the popular army which will be the protective force for the gains of the Palestinian Arab people.

31. The Organization shall have a flag, an oath of allegiance, and an anthem. All this shall be decided upon in accordance with a special regulation.

32. Regulations, which shall be known as the Constitution of the Palestine Liberation Organization, shall be annexed to this Charter. It shall lay down the manner in which the Organization, and its organs and institutions, shall be constituted; the respective competence of each; and the requirements of its obligations under the Charter.

33. This Charter shall not be amended save by [vote of] a majority of two-thirds of the total membership of the National Congress of the Palestine Liberation Organization [taken] at a special session convened for that purpose.

*Resolutions**

1. The PLO reaffirms its previous attitude concerning Security Council Resolution 242 which obliterates the patriotic and national rights of our people and treats our national cause as a refugee problem. It therefore refuses categorically any negotiations on the basis of this Resolution at any level of inter-Arab or international negotiation including the Geneva Conference.

2. The PLO will struggle by all possible means and foremost by means of armed struggle for the liberation of the Palestinian lands and the setting up of a patriotic, independent, fighting peoples' regime in every part of the Palestine territory which will be liberated. It affirms that this will only be accomplished through major changes in the balance of forces to the advantage of our people and their struggle.

3. The PLO will struggle against any proposal to set up a Palestine entity at the price of recognition, peace and secure boundaries, giving up the historic right and depriving our people of its right to return and to self-determination on its national soil.

4. The PLO will consider any step toward liberation which is accomplished as a stage in the pursuit of its strategy for the establishment of a democratic Palestinian state, as laid down in the decisions of previous National Council meetings.

* Cairo (June, 1974).

5. The PLO will struggle together with patriotic Jordanian forces for the creation of a Jordanian-Palestinian patriotic front, the object of which will be the establishment of a patriotic, democratic regime in Jordan which will make common cause with the Palestinian entity which will arise as a result of struggle and conflict.

6. The PLO will struggle for the establishment of a fighting union between the Palestinian and Arab peoples and between all Arab liberation forces agreed on this program.

7. The Palestine national authority will strive to call on the Arab states in confrontation [with Israel] to complete the liberation of the whole of the soil of Palestine as a step on the way to comprehensive Arab unity.

8. The PLO will strive to strengthen its solidarity with the socialist countries and world forces of liberation and progress to thwart all Zionist, reactionary, and imperialist designs.

9. In the light of this program, the PLO will strive to strengthen patriotic unity and raise it to the level at which it will be able to fulfill its patriotic and national tasks and duties.

10. In the light of this program, the revolutionary command will prepare tactics which will serve and make possible the realization of these objectives.

Fatah

The Seven Points,
Passed by the Central Committee of Fatah
January, 1969

1. *Fatah*, the Palestine National Liberation Movement, is the expression of the Palestinian people and of its will to free its land from Zionist colonisation in order to recover its national identity.

2. *Fatah*, the Palestine National Liberation Movement, is not struggling against the Jews as an ethnic and religious community. It is struggling against Israel as the expression of colonisation based on a theocratic, racist and expansionist system and of Zionism and colonialism.

3. *Fatah*, the Palestine National Liberation Movement, rejects any solution that does not take account of the existence of the Palestinian people and its right to dispose of itself.

4. *Fatah*, the Palestine National Liberation Movement, categorically rejects the Security Council Resolution of 22 November 1967 and the Jarring Mission to which it gave rise.

This resolution ignores the national rights of the Palestinian people— failing to mention its existence. Any solution claiming to be peaceful which ignores this basic factor, will thereby be doomed to failure.

In any event, the acceptance of the resolution of 22 November 1967, or any pseudo-political solution, by whatsoever party, is in no way binding upon the Palestinian people, which is determined to pursue mercilessly its struggle against foreign occupation and Zionist colonisation.

5. *Fatah*, the Palestine National Liberation Movement, solemnly proclaims that the final objective of its struggle is the restoration of the independent, democratic State of Palestine, all of whose citizens will enjoy equal rights irrespective of their religion.

6. Since Palestine forms part of the Arab fatherland, *Fatah*, the Palestine National Liberation Movement, will work for the State of Palestine to contribute actively towards the establishment of a progressive and united Arab society.

7. The struggle of the Palestinian People, like that of the Vietnamese people and other peoples of Asia, Africa and Latin America, is part of the historic process of the liberation of the oppressed peoples from colonialism and imperialism.

An Interview with "Abu Ammar" (Yasir Arafat)*

Q.—*Fatah* has offered an alternative to the Jews in Palestine—that is the creation of a progressive, democratic State for all. How do you reconcile this with the slogan "Long live Palestine Arab and Free?"

Abu Ammar.—A democratic, progressive State in Palestine is not in contradiction to that State being Arab. The social, geographical and historical factors play a major role in determining the nature and identity of any State. Anyone who has tried to look at the Palestinian problem in its historic perspective would realise that the Zionist State has failed to make itself acceptable because it is an artificially created alien state in the midst of an Arab world.

Palestine has acquired its identity through the historical development of the area. It is impossible for any Palestinian State to isolate itself from its geographical surroundings. It has been proved historically that any State, created on the land of Palestine which had been alien to the area, was unable to survive.

It is claimed that the main reason for the establishment of the State of Israel was to find a solution to the Jewish problem, but the experience of the past twenty years has proved that the absorbing capacity of the State has been insufficient to solve the problem of the 16 million Jews in the world.

The Zionist Movement has, as a result, to face one of two alternatives: either to carry on an expansionist policy which will enable it to absorb all

* Text of an interview with the leader of *Fatah*, published in *Free Palestine,* August, 1969.

the Jews of the world or to admit the failure of its experience and try and find a solution for those Jews who have been uprooted from their countries of origin to be settled on the land of Palestine.

We have offered our solution: that is the creation of a democratic Palestinian State for all those who wish to live in peace on the land of peace. Such a State can only acquire stability and viability by forming a part of the surrounding area, which is the Arab area. Otherwise this State with its Jewish, Christian and Moslem citizens would be another alien and temporary phenomenon in the area, which will arouse the antagonism of its neighbours, exactly as did the first Jewish State and the Crusaders' State. Neither of these States lasted for more than 70 years.

The word Arab implies a common culture, a common language and a common background. The majority of the inhabitants of any future State of Palestine will be Arab, if we consider that there are at present 2,500,000 Palestinian Arabs of the Moslem and Christian faiths and another 1,250,000 Arabs of the Jewish faith who live in what is now the State of Israel.

Q.—The immediate objective of your Movement is the liberation of your occupied homeland. What are your long-term objectives after achieving liberation? How do you envisage the future State of Palestine?

Abu Ammar.—As you have rightly mentioned, the immediate objective of Fatah is the total liberation of Palestine from Zionism and the destruction of any racial or sectarian notion which might exist among the Arabs.

Accordingly, we believe the only way to realise our objective is by overcoming our differences and achieving national unity. Our struggle in its present stage is a struggle for survival and for recovering our national identity. We aim ultimately at the establishment of an independent, progressive, democratic State in Palestine, which will guarantee equal rights to all its citizens, regardless of race or religion.

We wish to liberate the Jews from Zionism, and to make them realise that the purpose behind the creation of the State of Israel, namely to provide a haven for the persecuted Jews, has instead thrown them into a ghetto of their own making.

We wish to help build a progressive society based on liberty and equality for all. We also aim at participating actively in any struggle led by any Arab nation to achieve freedom and independence and to help build the united progressive Arab society of the future.

We support the struggle of all oppressed peoples in the world and we believe in the right for self-determination to all nations. We do not know for how long our struggle will go on until the liberation of our homeland is achieved. It might be a few years, or perhaps tens of years. It will be up to the generation that will finally liberate Palestine to decide upon the structure of their State.

Q.—The Palestine National Liberation Movement has certainly been able to achieve a break-through in what used to be a Zionist domain: the Western Leftist movements. Fatah has become to many synonymous with freedom fighting and an expression of struggle against oppression everywhere. Yet the new Zionist propaganda tactic is to smear it, by accusing it of accepting help from what is termed by them as "reactionary sources." What have you to say to this?

Abu Ammar.—Our Revolution accepts help, whether technological, material or military, from all sources. We seek the support of all those who wish to see Palestine liberated from Zionism, provided it is unconditional. We address ourselves equally to those who wish to offer help because they wish to see the Holy places liberated or to those revolutionaries in Africa, Asia and Latin America who consider our struggle as part of the struggle against oppression everywhere.

We have formed very strong ties with the liberation movements all over the world—in Cuba, in China, in Algeria and in Vietnam. We must not forget that in a war of liberation we should make use of every available source and means that will help us reach our ultimate goal—that is the liberation of our homeland.

I would also like to point out that other nations who have entered a war of liberation have adopted the same methods: for example in Vietnam the National Liberation Front includes 23 different organisations ranging from the Catholics and Buddhists to the Communists.

Can anyone accuse the Vietnamese Revolution of being a reactionary force? Add to this that the Palestinian Revolution in undertaking to lead the struggle against the Zionists, and to prevent any further aggression against the rest of the Arab world is entitled to use all the resources available in the Arab area.

Q.—Plans for a "peaceful settlement" of what is termed as an "Arab-Israeli" conflict seem to be speeding up, with the Four Power talks going ahead. Both the United States and the Soviet Union are eager to impose such a solution. How will Fatah react or rather act?

Abu Ammar.—The United Nations Security Council and the Big Powers have chosen to call their solutions "peaceful", whereas, in fact they are political solutions which are in no way related to peace as they all aim at safeguarding the state of Israel and ignoring the Palestinian Revolution. As such we declare that we will not under any circumstances accept any so-called peaceful solution which is being concocted by either the "Big" States or the "Small" States. We regard any such settlement as a document of self-humiliation which our people are forcibly asked to accept.

I believe that if our generation is unable to liberate its homeland, it should not commit the crime of accepting a fait accompli, which will prevent the future generations from carrying on the struggle for liberation.

What seems strange is that the call for a peaceful settlement started to be heard only when the Zionist enemy began to feel the blows dealt him by our Revolution.

I would like to mention here that immediately following the June War 1967, when President Johnson was asked about the problem in the Middle East, he replied, "is there a problem?" This goes to prove that a problem exists only when Israel considers it as existing. We, the Palestinian people, refuse to capitulate or to give legality to usurpation. As long as Israel is an invading, racialist, fascist State, it will be rejected. Let no one think that any resolution taken outside the will of the Palestinians will ever acquire viability or legality.

We have waited twenty years for world conscience to awaken, but it was at the cost of more dispersion. And here I would like to state that in this we do not only have the support of the Palestinian masses, but also of the whole Arab masses. We must also not forget that our Movement started before the 5th of June 1967, with the purpose of liberating Palestine and we will not throw our arms until victory, no matter who stands in our way.

Q.—Your Movement has on more than one occasion declared that it will not interfere in the affairs of other Arab countries. Don't you think that owing to recent developments in certain neighbouring Arab countries, this policy should be revised, especially as these developments aim at threatening the Palestinian Revolution?

Abu Ammar.—We will not interfere in the internal affairs of any Arab country that will not in its turn put obstacles in the way of our Revolution or threaten its continuation.

Q.—During her last visit to Britain, Golda Meir denied the existence of a Palestinian people or a Palestinian resistance movement. What is your answer?

Abu Ammar.—Her predecessor, Levi Eshkol, also denied our existence for a very long time. Yet before his death, in an interview with the American magazine *Newsweek*, he had to admit that we do exist. In 1967 Moshe Dayan claimed that the Palestinian resistance was like an egg in his hand, which he could crush any time. Yet in 1969 he was quoted as advising the Israelis to "deepen their graves." Our answer therefore to Golda Meir and to anyone who doubts our existence can be found in our actions inside the occupied territories, whether in Haifa or Jerusalem or Tel Aviv or Eilat or elsewhere. Besides, you are now living amongst us and you can judge whether a Palestinian Resistance Movement exists or not.

Q.—Besides the military field, what are Fatah's achievements, for example, in other fields such as the emancipation of women, the education of children, social services and so on?

Abu Ammar.—As a progressive revolution, we consider that all members of our society, whether men or women, should enjoy equal rights. We therefore encourage the total emancipation of all our women and we endeavour to give them every opportunity to participate actively in our struggle. The Palestinian woman has since the days of the Mandate fought side by side with our men. In the occupied territories at present, it is our valiant sisters who are leading the civilian resistance against the occupying forces.

We do not place any obstacles or restrictions in the face of any woman who wishes to join in our Movement. In fact, we are encouraging them to join both our military and political ranks.

As for the education of children, we have established schools for both girls and boys; we have the "Cubs" training centers, we have organizations for caring for the families of our martyrs. We have founded our own hospitals and clinics which provide free medical treatment to the displaced persons in their camps. In fact, we know that our struggle is a long-term one and we are preparing ourselves accordingly.

Q.—How many times did you personally cross the Jordan since 1967?

Abu Ammar.—I do not answer personal questions, but I have entered the occupied territories every time that my military command has asked me to do so.

Q.—Do you consider your struggle as part of the struggle against imperialism and colonialism everywhere and why?

Abu Ammar.—Our struggle is part and parcel of every struggle against imperialism, injustice and oppression in the world. It is part of the world revolution which aims at establishing social justice and liberating mankind. Outside the Palestinian and Arab masses our greatest support comes from all freedom-loving people who have realised the true nature of Zionism and its association with imperialism and neo-colonialism. Israel's natural allies are sufficient proof of this. We only have to look at the support it receives from the United States, at its close links with the racist Republics of South Africa and Rhodesia.

As for its ties with the puppet regime of South Vietnam, let us only remember that its defence minister Moshe Dayan found it necessary and useful to spend a few months there learning their methods. The 1956 aggression against Egypt is another very clear example of the reasons for the creation of a Zionist state in the area. To sum up, we consider Israel as playing the new role of the East India Company in the Middle East.

Q.—Do you accept non-Palestinians in your fighting forces?

Abu Ammar.—We have at present both Arab and non-Arab freedom fighters in our ranks.

Q.—Why do you think Fatah has had such an appeal on both the national and international levels?

Abu Ammar.—Fatah has revolutionised the approach to the Palestinian problem. It has been the active force behind the resurgence of the Palestinian entity, which has established itself as the major element in the conflict. It is a true expression of the new Arab determination to resist invasion and oppression. Above all, it is part of the world movements for liberation and as such must attract freedom-loving people everywhere. Fatah was the first movement which translated the Palestinian aspirations into actions and which by its nature represents the true Palestinian determination.

Platform of the Popular Front for the Liberation of Palestine

*1. Conventional War Is the War of the Bourgeoisie.
Revolutionary War Is People's War*

The Arab bourgeoisie has developed armies which are not prepared to sacrifice their own interests or to risk their privileges. Arab militarism has become an apparatus for oppressing revolutionary socialist movements within the Arab states, while at the same time it claims to be staunchly anti-imperialist. Under the guise of the national question, the bourgeoisie has used its armies to strengthen its bureaucratic power over the masses, and to prevent the workers and peasants from acquiring political power. So far it has demanded the help of the workers and peasants without organising them or without developing a proletarian ideology. The national bourgeoisie usually comes to power through military coups and without any activity on the part of the masses, as soon as it has captured power it reinforces its bureaucratic position. Through widespread application of terror it is able to talk about revolution while at the same time it suppresses all the revolutionary movements and arrests everyone who tries to advocate revolutionary action.

The Arab bourgeoisie has used the question of Palestine to divert the Arab masses from realising their own interests and their own domestic problems. The bourgeoisie always concentrated hopes on a victory outside the state's boundaries, in Palestine, and in this way they were able to preserve their class interests and their bureaucratic positions.

The war of June 1967 disproved the bourgeois theory of conventional war. The best strategy for Israel is to strike rapidly. The enemy is not able to mobilise its armies for a long period of time because this would intensify its economic crisis. It gets complete support from US imperialism and for these reasons it needs quick wars. Therefore for our poor people the best strategy in the long run is a people's war. Our people must overcome their weaknesses and exploit the weaknesses of the enemy by mobilising the Palestinian and Arab peoples. The weakening of imperialism and Zionism in the Arab world demands revolutionary war as the means to confront them.

*2. Guerrilla Struggle as a Form of Pressure
for the "Peaceful Solution"*

The Palestinian struggle is a part of the whole Arab liberation movement and of the world liberation movement. The Arab bourgeoisie and world imperialism are trying to impose a peaceful solution on this Palestinian problem but this suggestion merely promotes the interests of imperialism and of Zionism, doubt in the efficacy of people's war as a means of liberation and the preservation of the relations of the Arab bourgeoisie with the imperialist world market.

The Arab bourgeoisie is afraid of being isolated from this market and of losing its role as a mediator of world capitalism. That is why the Arab oil-producing countries broke off the boycott against the west (instituted during the June war) and for this reason McNamara, as head of the World Bank, was ready to offer credits to them.

When the Arab bourgeoisie strive for a peaceful solution, they are in fact striving for the profit which they can get from their role as mediator between the imperialist market and the internal market. The Arab bourgeoisie are not yet opposed to the activity of the guerrillas, and sometimes they even help them; but this is because the presence of the guerrillas is a means of pressure for a peaceful solution. As long as the guerrillas don't have a clear class affiliation and a clear political stand they are unable to resist the implication of such a peaceful solution; but the conflict between the guerrillas and those who strive for a peaceful solution is unavoidable. Therefore the guerrillas must take steps to transform their actions into a people's war with clear goals.

3. No Revolutionary War Without a Revolutionary Theory

The basic weakness of the guerrilla movement is the absence of a revolutionary ideology, which could illuminate the horizons of the Palestinian fighters and would incarnate the stages of a militant political programme. Without a revolutionary ideology the national struggle will remain imprisoned within its immediate practical and material needs. The Arab bourgeoisie is quite prepared for a limited satisfaction of the needs of the national struggle, as long as it respects the limits that the bourgeoisie sets. A clear illustration of this is the material help that Saudi Arabia offers *Fatah* while *Fatah* declares that she will not interfere in the internal affairs of any Arab countries.

Since most of the guerrilla movements have no ideological weapons, the Arab bourgeoisie can decide their fate. Therefore, the struggle of the Palestinian people must be supported by the workers and peasants, who will fight against any form of domination by imperialism, Zionism or the Arab bourgeoisie.

4. The War of Liberation Is a Class War
Guided by a Revolutionary Ideology

We must not be satisfied with ignoring the problems of our struggle, saying that our struggle is a national one and not a class struggle. The national struggle reflects the class struggle. The national struggle is a struggle for land and those who struggle for it are the peasants who were driven away from their land. The bourgeoisie is always ready to lead such a movement, hoping to gain control of the internal market. If the bourgeoisie succeeds in bringing the national movement under its control, which strengthens its position, it can lead the movement under the guise of a peaceful solution into compromises with imperialism and Zionism.

Therefore, the fact that the liberation struggle is mainly a class struggle emphasises the necessity for the workers and peasants to play a leading role in the national liberation movement. If the small bourgeoisie take the leading role, the national revolution will fall as a victim of the class interests of this leadership. It is a great mistake to start by saying that the Zionist challenge demands national unity for this shows that one does not understand the real class structure of Zionism.

The struggle against Israel is first of all a class struggle. Therefore the oppressed class is the only class which is able to face a confrontation with Zionism.

5. The Main Field of Our Revolutionary Struggle Is Palestine

The decisive battle must be in Palestine. The armed people's struggle in Palestine can help itself with the simplest weapons in order to ruin the economies and the war machinery of their Zionist enemy. The moving of the people's struggle into Palestine depends upon agitating and organising the masses, more than depending upon border actions in the Jordan valley, although these actions are of importance for the struggle in Palestine.

When guerrilla organisations began their actions in the occupied areas, they were faced with a brutal military repression by the armed forces of Zionism. Because these organisations had no revolutionary ideology and so no programme, they gave in to demands of self-preservation and retreated into eastern Jordan. All their activity turned into border actions. This presence of the guerrilla organisations in Jordan enables the Jordanian bourgeoisie and their secret agents to crush these organisations when they are no longer useful as pressure for a peaceful solution.

6. Revolution in Both Regions of Jordan

We must not neglect the struggle in east Jordan for this land is connected with Palestine more than with the other Arab countries. The problem of the revolution in Palestine is dialectically connected with the problem of the revolution in Jordan. A chain of plots between the Jordanian monarchy, imperialism and Zionism have proved this connection.

The struggle in east Jordan must take the correct path, that of class struggle. The Palestinian struggle must not be used as a means of propping up the Jordanian monarchy, under the mask of national unity, and the main problem in Jordan is the creation of a Marxist-Leninist party with a clear action programme according to which it can organise the masses and enable them to carry out the national and class struggle. The harmony of the struggle in the two regions must be realised through co-ordinating organs whose tasks will be to guarantee reserves inside Palestine and to mobilise the peasants and soldiers in the border-territories.

This is the only way in which Amman can become an Arab Hanoi:— a base for the revolutionaries fighting inside Palestine.

Fatah's Doctrine

by Y. Harkabi*

Fatah's Major Conceptions

Fatah's prescription for facing the challenge inherent in [its] dilemma was Revolutionary War waged on guerrilla warfare lines. Its merit is that it does not require such long and tedious preparations as a conventional war, for it can be launched with small forces. Revolutions, *Fatah* reasons, once set in motion, generate their own forces and acquire momentum. "The armed struggle is the basic factor for expanding the revolution and its continuation; in short, causing a revolution in the life of this society. Such historic changes are usually achieved by wars, calamities and uncontrollable economic fluctuations. The nearest means of producing such a convulsion and a great historic change in the course of the national development of the Arab nation is by creating an appropriate environment for a decisive fateful battle between the Arabs and the Zionist enemy."

Arab politicians usually subordinated the Palestinian issue to their interests and policy, and manipulated it accordingly. *Fatah* signifies an attempt to reverse this trend and subordinate all other Arab problems to the goal of liberating Palestine. Before, the Palestinians orbited round the Arab state; now, *Fatah* tries to stage a Copernican revolution, and reverse the relationship.

The Objective of War

Fatah sets out the objective of the war against Israel in bold type: "The liberation action is not only the wiping out of an Imperialist base but, what is more important, the extinction of a society [*Inqirad mujtama*]. Therefore armed violence will necessarily assume diverse forms in addition to the

* Reprinted by special permission from *Adelphi Papers* No. 53 (December, 1968), "Fedayeen Action and Arab Strategy." Institute of Strategic Studies, London.

liquidation of the armed forces of the Zionist occupying state, namely, it should turn to the destruction of the factors sustaining the Zionist society in all their forms: industrial, agricultural, and financial. The armed violence necessarily should also aim at the destruction of the various military, political, economic, financial and intellectual institutions of the Zionist occupation state, to prevent any possibility of a re-emergence of a new Zionist society. Military defeat is not the sole goal in the Palestinian Liberation War, but it is the blotting out of the Zionist character of the occupied land, be it human or social.'' Or: ''The Jewish state is an aberrant mistaken phenomenon in our nation's history and therefore there is no alternative but to wipe out the existential trace [*Alathar alwujudi*] of this artificial phenomenon.''

Lt.-Col. Sha'ir, an officer in the command of the PLO Army, also expresses the objective in unmistakable terms: ''The chief objective and the fundamental effort for the Popular War concerning the liberation of Palestine is the reoccupation of the usurped land regardless of the method, be it smashing or annihilation [*Ibada*], because the enemy when he usurped Palestine did not think of the fate of our people, of things holy to it and its lawful rights, in the lands of his forefathers.''

Arab declarations of objectives frequently used extreme expressions like ''throwing the Jews into the sea'' which implied genocide. *Fatah* endeavours in its publications to avoid such notorious expressions, stressing that the purpose is limited to the destruction of the state, not of its people. The formula most frequently used in its writings is ''liquidation, or the uprooting of the Zionist existence or entity.'' However, when the implications of this objective come to be spelled out, it is realised that Zionism is not only a political regime or a superstructure of sorts, but is embodied in a *society*. Therefore, this *society* has to be liquidated, which underlines that achieving it will require a great deal of killing. The Arabs' objective of destroying the state of Israel (what may be called a ''politicide'') drives them to genocide. Since the existence of Israel is founded on the existence of a concentration of Jews so their dispersion should precede the demise of the state. Thus, despite *Fatah*'s efforts, it comes back to the Arab objective in its extremist version.

Fatah stresses that Jews will be allowed to live in a democratic Arab Palestine after Israel's extinction. In order for the country to become Arab again, the sheer numerical predominance of Jews over Palestinian Arabs requires part of the Jewish population to disappear. How?

Fatah's recognition of the right of a Jewish minority to exist is nothing new. It recalls the fundamental Islamic position, which grants the Jews security on the condition of their subordination as a tolerated minority.

The Arab position is enmeshed in this complexity arising from the impossibility of destroying Israel as a state without destroying a considerable part of her inhabitants. To escape from this dilemma the Arab objective is sometimes expressed in another formula showing perhaps improved articulation without changing the issue: "the de-Zionization of Israel." Since the basic meaning of Zionism was the achievement of Jewish statehood, de-Zionizing Israel has only one implication, that Israel will cease being a Jewish state; not Israel but Palestine. Israel and Zionism are organically connected. De-Zionizing Israel is only a contradiction in terms.

Fatah senses the difficulties in the Arab position: "Examining the Palestinian issue from all its aspects, we realize the necessity to satisfy many parties by our solution. For instance, if we consider world public opinion has some weight and influence, we must put out a solution which will satisfy public opinion or be acceptable to it, even be it with difficulty. Of course, when we speak about the need for satisfying world opinion, we do not mean in the kind of solution to the Palestine issue, but in its method. Public opinion has no right to dispute the imperative necessity of its solution [i.e. by destruction of the state], but its right to know the method, so that public opinion will not castigate us with Fascism, anti-Semitism or other inhuman epithets."

What is more important for the present discussions is the influence of the objective on the nature of the war by which *Fatah* hopes to achieve its aim. Such a war is different from one directed towards a change of the political regime, or towards harassment of the representatives of a remote country until the government prefers to relinquish its rule in that area. In order to achieve the purpose of liquidating a society or wiping out its "existential trace," war must be of great extent and intensity and become really total.

The question that is crucial to any evaluation of *Fatah*'s position is the degree to which guerrilla warfare can suit such an objective. This will be taken up at the conclusion of this paper.

Palestinian Activism

Fatah exhorted the Palestinians to become the driving force in the conflict, not by agitation in the Arab countries as they had previously, not by pushing the Arab states to action, but by starting actual fighting themselves. *Fedayeen* action should be developed into a fully fledged War of National Liberation. Only by what *Fatah* terms an "armed struggle" can the Palestinians solve their problems and regain Palestine.

Fatah stressed its disbelief in the possibility of a political solution. Arab politics are treated, especially before the six-day war, with marked disapproval. Politics are sickening when juxtaposed with the sublimity of the "armed struggle." The Palestinians will be able to concentrate on their conflict only if they extricate themselves from inter-Arab rivalries and exercise neutrality. If they take sides in any Arab issue, they will antagonize the opponents of the side they support, who will then try to make things difficult for them. The Palestinian problem should be put above Arab politics. Only by freeing themselves from Arab rivalries will the Palestinians be able to acquire liberty of action in their affairs.

There are inconsistencies in the writings and pronouncements of *Fatah* on how far the Palestinians are capable of accomplishing by themselves the liberation of Palestine. On the one hand, there are announcements that the forces of the Palestinian masses are irresistible and can achieve this goal. On the other hand, there is recognition that the last stroke will have to be dealt by the concerted forces of the Arab armies.

The war *Fatah* aspires to wage is called, in its parlance, the "Palestinian Revolution," to signify as well the transformation it will cause in the Palestinians themselves who from passive onlookers will become dynamic fighters.

This trend towards Palestinian activism and the Palestinization of the conflict has to be seen against its historical background. Its psychological aspects should also be tackled, otherwise the human dimension of such developments will evade us. However, in offering psychological explanations, it should always be borne in mind how tentative they are so long as they are based on intuition, and how corrupting they may be by inspiring in the writer, and even the reader, a false sense of clairvoyance.

The mid-1960s saw the re-emergence of the Palestinians as contestants in the Arab-Israel conflict, after about seventeen years in which the confrontation was mainly at states level. The entry of the Arab armies into the war in 1948 transformed the conflict from a civil one between Jews and Arabs in Palestine, or an intra-state war, to an inter-state war. The activities surrounding the setting up of the Palestine Liberation Organization and the *Fedayeen* organizations signify in some respects an attempt to revert to the previous state of affairs. This development of the Palestinians' reassertion embodied elements of both protest and reproach towards the Arab states for their failure to fulfil their obligation towards the Palestinians. *Fatah*, by emphasizing that the "Palestinian people is the only true available stock [*Rasid*] for the war of return," insinuates that the others are not so trustworthy.

On the other hand, the Arab states handing over to the Palestinians the leading role in the conflict implied an abdication of sorts by the Arab states and an avowal of their failure. It is not mere coincidence that the Summit Meetings which established the PLO were convened as a result of, presumably, the most dismal of Arab failures between 1948 and the six-day war. All the Arab leaders had committed themselves to preventing Israel from completing her project of pumping water from Lake Tiberias (what Arabs called "the diversion of the Jordan"). When the time came, they realized their helplessness.

The relationship between the Palestinians and the Arabs has always been ambivalent, each accused the other of being responsible for their inadequacies in the conflict. The Arab states blamed the Palestinians for selling land to the Jews, for their feeble resistance during the Mandate, and for their acting as agents for Israel Intelligence. Their existence epitomized the calamities that befell the Arab world as a result of the Arab-Israel conflict, and the Palestinians were blamed for them.

The Palestinians blamed the Arab states for their half-hearted activities in the conflict, their irresolution, internal bickerings, the restrictions they imposed on the Palestinians, and their manipulation of the conflict to their narrow interests.

Despite that element of protest against the Arab states embodied in the Palestinians' organizations, they could be created only with the help of some Arab official quarters. The PLO did not come into being only by Palestinian spontaneity. It was established from above by the Summit Meetings and derived its authority and part of its finances from them. The *Fatah* acted under the aegis of the Syrian radical Baath. Thus protest and dependence intermingled.

Palestinian activism came in the early 1960s to be cherished widely in Palestinian circles. Palestinian initiative seemed vital after the Arab states' failure. Mr. Nashashibi ends his book as follows: "Oh Palestinians, if you do not restore the land, you will not return to it, and it will not return to you."

An important factor in the Palestinian move for the "re-Palestinization" of the conflict was the influence of the Algerian War. It was a source of both pride and inspiration. If the Algerians prevailed over a great power such as France, so it was argued, there was hope in defeating small Israel.

Hence the effort to draw analogies between Algeria and Palestine and the effort to describe Israel as only another colonialist case, whose fate is doomed as part of the general historical trend of the liquidation of colonies.

Palestinian ideologists argued that previous presentation of the conflict as an inter-state one was erroneous. It was an Imperialist ruse aimed at excluding the Palestinians from their natural role, thus "liquidating" the conflict. This argument was, too, an apologia for the Arabs themselves as they too described the conflict as international. They were only deluded and their failing was only naïvety. Both Israel and the Imperialists conspired to blur the "liberation" aspect of the conflict.

Naming the conflict a "War of National Liberation" after it had already reached a mature age, and the identification of "War of National Liberation" with guerrilla warfare, produced among Palestinians an inclination to project it backwards and describe the conflict as if the Palestinians had waged continuous popular guerrilla warfare against the Jews. The history of the events in Palestine from World War I is being rewritten to appear as a continuous popular resistance and heroic uprisings. The blame for failure is focused on the leadership. Naji Alush in his book *Arab*

Resistance in Palestine 1917–1948 gives a Marxist explanation for this failing. Because of its class interests the Palestinian leadership tied its destiny to colonialism, and betrayed the national cause.

Palestinian radio programmes abound with plays and descriptions of brave resistance against the Jews in Palestine. Small ambushes or attacks on Jewish settlers are elevated into heroic acts of guerrilla warfare. Thus, heroism anticipated in the future is reinforced by inspiration drawn from the past, and if the real past cannot be a source of such inspiration, some retouching is done. Such an account may have another merit: it implies that the Palestinians are not only imitators of Mao and Che, but preceded them.

The allure of activism is presumably very powerful for the Palestinians. The Palestinians suffered not only from the agony of defeat, deprivation, refugee status, living in camps, but from contempt by the other Arabs. Losing their land and property was a blow to their dignity, as traditionally the criterion for position and prestige in Arab society is ownership of real estate. Activism and "revolutionarism" are means of gaining self-respect, especially for the younger generation. This generation is ambivalent towards their parents—they reproach them for their weaknesses and failings, calling them "the generation of defeat," or "the defeated generation" (*Jil al-Hazima, Al-Jil al-Munhar*). Whereas the young generation dubbed itself (already before the six-day war) the "generation of resistance" or "the generation of revenge" (*Jil al-Muqawama, Jil-al-Naqma*). On the other hand, in order to bolster themselves up as Palestinians, they have to praise the Palestinian record and stress the continuity of the struggle.

Activism has the psychological function of atoning for past failings and inadequacies. It symbolizes the Palestinians' regeneration, and a reaction against fatalism, proverbial in Arab society, about which the young generation feels uneasy. Activism is a manly quality, hailed in a masculine society, and a reaction against emotionalism treated derogatorily in Arab political literature, including *Fatah*'s. "Revolutionarism" (*Thauria*) exerts a strong influence in most of the Arab world signifying a radical change, spectacular and forceful, a protest against the past, and a guarantee of success for the future. The adjective "revolutionary" is attached to all kinds of nouns in Arab political literature as a word of approbation and optimism.

Fatah described what this Palestinian revolution will accomplish: "The staging of the revolutionary movement is a conscious transcendence of the circumstances of the Arab Palestinian people, of the traditional leadership, of the stagnated situations, of the opportunism and the self-seeking political arrangements, or those directed from beyond the Palestinian pale, it is a rejection of this fragmented reality. The Palestinian revolutionary movement on this level is a social revolution and a mutation in the social relationship of the Palestinian Arab people."

Adulation of Violence

It is not by sheer accident that the third *Fatah* pamphlet entitled *The Revolution and Violence, the Road to Victory* is a selective précis of Frantz Fanon's book *The Wretched of the Earth*. Fanon's influence is manifested in other *Fatah* writings, especially on the psychological impact of Israel on the Arabs and on the transformations that their armed struggle will produce in the Palestinians. "Violence," "Violent Struggle" and "Vengeance" are expressions of great frequency in *Fatah* literature. The reader of these texts is introduced to a world of simmering frustrated hatred and a drive for unquenchable vengeance.

Violence is described as imperative in wiping out colonialism, for between the colonialist and the colonized there is such a contradiction that no coexistence is possible. One of the two has to be liquidated. (Descriptions of the Arab-Israel conflict as both a zero-sum game and a deadly quarrel are frequent in Arab publications.) Such a conflict is "a war of annihilation of one of the rivals, either wiping out the national entity, or wiping out colonialism. . . . The colonized will be liberated from violence by violence. "The 'Palestinian Revolution" is such a cataclysmic event that it can only be achieved by violence.

Violence liberates people from their shortcomings and anxieties. It inculcates in them both courage and fearlessness concerning death. Violence has a therapeutic effect, purifying society of its diseases. "Violence will purify the individuals from venom, it will redeem the colonized from inferiority complex, it will return courage to the countryman." In a memorandum to Arab journalists, *Fatah* stated: "Blazing our armed revolution inside the occupied territory [i.e. Israel, it was written before the six-day war] is a healing medicine for all our people's diseases."

The praising of violence as purgative, may imply also an element of self-indictment for flaws which will now be rectified, and a desire to exorcize the record of failings. The praising of violence may have as well the function of giving cathartic satisfaction as a substitute for operational action.

Violence, *Fatah* asserts, will have a unifying influence on people, forging one nation from them. It will draw the individuals from the pettiness of their ego, and imbue them with the effusiveness of collective endeavour, as bloodshed will produce a common experience binding them together. Thus, "the territoriality, [i.e. the fragmentation into different Arab states] which was imposed by Imperialism and Arab leaderships and which was sustained by traditional circumstances in the societies, will end."

The struggle, besides its political goals, will have as a by-product an important impact on those who participate in it. It is "a creative struggling" (*Nidalia khallaqa*). Violence, Revolutionarism, Activism, "the battle of vengeance," "armed struggle," all coalesce in an apocalyptic vision of heroic and just aggression, meting out revenge on Israel.

Engineering a Revolution

Fatah ideologists have been inclined to deal with general ideas of guerrilla warfare, rather than specifying in detail how their objectives will be accomplished through it. Like the other exponents of guerrilla warfare *Fatah* deals with the more practical problems, by means of tracing the phases by which the war or the revolution will evolve. It is called "revolution" in which warfare proper is only a part of a larger complex of activities, mobilizing the support and the participation in the struggle of the masses, and their own transformation through it.

The Pamphlet entitled *How Will the Armed Popular Revolution Explode?* dwells on the mechanism and process of this "revolution." It explains that a revolution originates when the oppressed people become aware of the evils of the present reality, and as a result of the growth of an urge to avenge themselves upon it. Needless to say, the reality here is Israel. Though the feelings of revolt against the oppressive reality are spontaneous, they have to be assisted and to be organized. The revolution has to be orchestrated by stages, by its leaders, the "Revolutionary Vanguard."

In *Fatah*'s descriptions of the stages and their names there are some inconsistencies. They may originate either from different authorship, reflecting diverse influences, or be caused by simple imprecision and vagueness. This vagueness is even more accentuated by the lack of differentiation between the organizational and the operational aspects of the stages, and the relationship between the two.

The parts of *Fatah*'s writings which deal with the phases of war make uneasy reading. *Fatah*'s terminology and formulation may seem both esoteric and highfalutin'. However, what may be more wearisome for the reader who is not versed in such parlance is the generality and abstraction of the discussion. It contains a mixture of a terminology influenced by Marxist literature, attempting to interpret developments in a rational way, with mythical overtones expressed in figures of speech like the "ignition" or "detonation" or a revolution, and leaves the reader wondering how it is to be done.

The organizational stages symbolize the expansion of the circles of those involved in the revolution or war. Stage one is the *Formation of the Revolutionary Vanguard.* This is achieved by "the movement of revolutionary gathering of the revengeful conscious wills." "The individual of the Revolutionary Vanguard is distinguished by his revolutionary intuition." His task is "to discover the vital tide in his society, for its own sake and for its usefulness for action and movement, and then to realize what obstacles hamper his movement in accordance with history's logic." Thus, "the Revolutionary Vanguard signifies the type of human who interacts positively with the reality [of his predicament], and so elevates himself by his consciousness until he releases himself from reality's grip, in order to pursue the superseding of this reality by another, which differs basically in its values and traits. To take a concrete example, the reality of Arab Palestinian people is fragmented, disfigured and corrupted, and shows signs of stagnation. However, despite this stagnation and immobility, the historical direction imposes the existence of a current of vitality among the Palestinian people, so long as the Palestinian man treasures vengeance on this reality. As this wish for vengeance grows, the current of vitality congeals in the form of a Revolutionary Vanguard.''

The second stage is the *Formation of the Revolutionary Organization.* In it the Revolutionary Vanguard achieves a psychological mobilization of the Palestinian masses by stimulating their urge for revenge, until ''the constructive revolutionary anxiety embraces all the Palestinian Arabs.'' It is thus called the stage of *Revolutionary Embracing* (*Al-Shumul al-Thauri*). Indoctrination of the masses will not precede the staging of the armed struggle but will be achieved by it. ''Mistaken are those who advocate the need for rousing a national consciousness before the armed struggle assumes a concrete form. . . . Ineluctably the armed struggle and mass consciousness will go side by side, because the armed struggle will make the masses feel their active personality and restore their self-confidence.'' The Vanguard will galvanize the masses by means of its example and sacrifice in guerrilla activities.

Fatah's publications state that irresistible might is stored in the Arab masses. They are ''latent volcanoes,'' they are the main ''instrument'' of the struggle. This explosive capacity has to be activated and this task is allotted to the Vanguard.

The revolution's success is dependent on co-operation between the Vanguard and the masses. ''The Revolution in its composition has a leadership and a basis, necessitates the accomplishment of a conscious interaction between the basis, which is the masses, and the leadership, in order to ensure the revolution's success and continuation.''

The third stage is the *Formation of the Supporting Arab Front.* Popular support for the ''Palestinian Revolution'' is to be secured in all Arab countries in order to safeguard rear bases in Arab countries for the war, and as a means of putting pressure on the Arab governments not to slacken or deviate from aiding the Palestinian Revolution by pursuit of their local interests. The Supporting Arab Front is thus expressed on two levels, the popular and the governmental. The popular support is used as an instrument of pressure against the Arab governments.

In the same publications the overall development of the revolution is divided into two major stages: one, *Organization and Mobilization*, called elsewhere the *Phases of Revolutionary Maturing*, comprises the organizational stages already enumerated. The second stage is called that of the *Revolutionary Explosion* (*Marhal atal-Tafjir al-Thauri*). The stage of the Revolutionary Explosion is described in colourful language: ''The hating revengeful masses plunge into the road of revolution in a pressing and vehement fashion as pouring forces that burn everything that stands in their way.'' In this stage ''tempests of revenge'' will be let loose. However, the Vanguard should ensure mass discipline to prevent violence going berserk. ''The Revolution's Will should obey its regulating brain.''

While the first stage is preparatory, the second is the main interesting stage. Unfortunately, *Fatah*'s description of it is rather rudimentary. Even the question of the timing of its beginning is not clear. *Fatah* specified: ''Our operations in the occupied territory can never reach the stage of the aspired revolution unless all Palestinian groups are polarized around the revolution.'' *Fatah* does have an ambition to become the central leader of all the Palestinians, proving that the other movements, which have not matured round what has been described as a Revolutionary Vanguard like itself, are artificial and ''counterfeited.'' Thus the stage of revolution will arrive only when *Fatah* has mobilized *all* the Palestinians.

Nevertheless, *Fatah*'s small action at the beginning of January 1965 is frequently hailed as the ''detonation of the revolution,'' implying that the revolution started then. By the same token, at the beginning of 1968, *Fatah*'s official journal celebrated the fourth anniversary ''of our Palestinian people's revolution in the occupied territory.'' Perhaps this ambiguity as to the timing of the revolutionary stage stems from *Fatah*'s emphasis of the need to precipitate action. Once action is launched the development proceeds spontaneously.

Influences

The theories of guerrilla warfare have been developed in the twentieth century several times over. They have been popularized and romanticized to the extent of becoming almost part of this generation's culture. No wonder that *Fatah* repeats ideas expounded elsewhere. It would be excessive to expect its approach to be completely original, nor does it pretend to be all original. Actually, the temptation to pose as original is less than the confidence Fatah can draw from the success of these theories in China, Algeria, Cuba or Vietnam. These successes are presented as precedents guaranteeing *Fatah*'s success as well. The feeling of kinship of sorts in a family of successful revolutionaries and guerrilla fighters inspires optimism and pride. Thus, *Fatah* makes no bones about its indebtedness to the exponents of guerrilla warfare. Its spokesmen are fond of explaining that, although they have learnt from others, they rely only on their own specific experience. No doubt the singularity of the Palestinian case limits the possibility of benefiting from lessons from elsewhere.

The main guerrilla treatises of Mao Tse-tung, Giap, Che Guevara and Régis Debray, have been translated into Arabic in several editions, and serialized in the press. In its main series of ''Revolutionary Lessons and Trials,''

Fatah published pamphlets bearing the titles *The Chinese Experience*, *The Vietnamese Experience*, and *The Cuban Experience*.

In their books on guerrilla warfare, General Talas and Colonel Sha'ir too give long and detailed accounts of the doctrines of guerrilla warfare as developed by its major exponents.

Though Algeria, as an Arab case, should have served as the main source of inspiration, it seems that the greatest influence was exerted by Cuba. (Algeria has not codified her guerrilla experience in the same way as the other guerrilla practitioners. At least such a publication, if it does exist, has not come to the general notice. Perhaps the reason is that Boumedienne was more of a commander of the regular forces outside Algeria in Tunisia than a guerrilla leader.)

The reasons for *Fatah*'s seeing Cuba as the main source of inspiration seem obvious: Mao has stressed that guerrilla warfare can succeed only in a large country like China where the guerrillas can establish a base out of the reach of enemy forces. Mao has specified that guerrilla warfare cannot succeed in a country the size of Belgium. Mao's words thus disprove *Fatah*, whereas Cuba is a success story of guerrilla warfare in a small country.

Che Guevara radiates optimism. He lightheartedly urged taking the plunge before conditions matured, while Mao is both more cautious and sombre. The first sentence of the *Fatah* pamphlet on Cuba reads: "The Cuban experience has proved the error of those who see a need for waiting until the maturing of the objective and the subjective circumstances for the revolution, instead of the continuous effort to accelerate the formation of these circumstances."

In China and Vietnam the bearers of the revolution were the Communist Party. *Fatah* disapproves of the need to set out as a party. In Cuba it all started from the wanderings of the first twelve people in the Sierra Maestra. Thus the Cuban model suits *Fatah* better, precisely because it was not a popular movement.

General Talas, who dedicated his book to Guevara, and praises him to the skies as the "guide of War of National Liberation," explains in the introduction that his main contribution was the idea of the "revolutionary focus," the nucleus of the revolt which, though numerically small, can start the movement off and win.

Representatives of *Fatah* and the other organizations established relations with China, Vietnam and Cuba, and were given help and advice. Some of *Fatah*'s leaders were sent to Algeria and China for training.

During the years 1963 to 1967 there was a spate of articles in the Arab press on the different aspects of Arab strategy against Israel. A wide range of problems was discussed, such as the kind of war the Arabs should wage, how it should be initiated, analyses of strategic strengths and weaknesses of the two sides, the impact of nuclear weapons—should Israel acquire them, problems arising from Western intervention, the influence of Egyptian missiles, the timing of war, the possibilities of a preventive war by Israel, and the whole field of guerrilla warfare.

To the strategic analyst part of this material may seem amateur—an exercise in imitation of the style of strategic discussions in the West. However, these publications are interesting, as they throw light on the mood and thinking of some important Arab circles. It would be tedious to try fully to report on the views expressed. My purpose is to isolate some of the strands of thought on guerrilla warfare, and Arab strategy in general, not in a micro-historic way—tracing chronologically the details of the debate in Arab countries, identifying the people who took part in it, and the circles they represented—but rather in a conceptual way, reconstructing the possible different positions on the problem of the Arab programme of action against Israel.

Fedayeen not the Solution

The basic suitability of guerrilla warfare as advocated by *Fatah* was questioned. Naji Alush writing his book in 1963–64 directed his criticism against articles published in 1962 in *Our Palestine*, the journal in which *Fatah* made its ideological debut. Alush asked, "Why should we suppose that the Israeli Army will stand with its hands tied in the face of *Fedayeen*'s attacks? The Israeli Army will destroy Arab villages and cities, and even may take a decisive step, and, for example, occupy the whole West Bank. . . .

"The Journal considered that in the present circumstances the Arab armies are incapable of wiping out Israel, whereas it sees that the Palestinian entity is capable of accomplishing this miracle. How will it be? With the help of the Arab states and the non-Arab states?

"Naturally we see the Revolutionary Road, which *Our Palestine* has chosen, as an unwarranted one, because it is built on improvisation, excitement and spontaneity. It will restore the issue to 1947 [i.e. to another defeat]. . . .

"Smashing Israel cannot be done by *Fedayeen*'s attacks because of the completeness of her preparations and arms."

The relevance of the Algerian case to the Palestinian condition came under criticism from several quarters. Naji Alush admonished, "The legend of the liberation of Algeria may push the liberation of Palestine into an abyss. The heroic triumph of the Algerian revolt made some Palestinians and some progressive Arabs fancy that following the same road will bring the same result."

Alush spelled out the differences between Algeria and Palestine, invoking the authority of an analysis by Professor Walid Al-Khalidi:

1. *The Combat Area.* Algeria was a colony with a small French

minority and ten million Algerians. Palestine is divided into three: a small Arab minority in Israel concentrated in a few zones, and limited in its possibilities of action; the West Bank has become a Jordanian colony occupied by the "Forces of the Desert and mercenaries," where the Palestinians are prohibited from organizing themselves; the Gaza Strip is administered as occupied territory by an Arab government, withholding from its inhabitants self-government which might have transformed them into a nucleus from which serious action for the liberation of Palestine could have been developed. The Palestinians in Gaza and the West Bank have first to overcome Arab government domination, before they can organize themselves for war.

2. *The Nature of the Battle.* In Algeria it was a battle for independence . . . which is not the case in Palestine. There is a battle for the uprooting of a state recognized by the United Nations, supported by world public opinion and the principal capitalist states. . . . Britain and the United States were ready to accept the independence of Algeria, but they are not ready to accept the liquidation of the Zionists' state. The Algerian struggle for independence could be compared to the Palestinians' struggle before 1948 . . . after 1948 the nature of the situation changed in Palestine.

3. Algerians could have bases in Tunisia and Morocco. However, no Arab government will tolerate the organization of the Palestinians on its territory, unless they constitute a part of its forces and are subservient to its policy.

4. *The Problem of Power.* The Algerian people could paralyze, by employing guerrilla warfare, a large French army, owing to the vastness of Algeria which is 852,600 square miles, in which there were many mountains, thick bushes and roadless regions, which rendered movement of the army difficult and made way for successful guerrilla warfare. As regards Palestine, most of the occupied territory is a plain, settled with fortified settlements, connected by an extensive network of roads, which facilitates army movements and renders the task of *Fedayeen* difficult.

5. When the revolution erupted in Algeria, its active organizations were in Algeria. As regards the Palestinians, the organization of a revolution must grow outside of the occupied territory. . . . Since the revolutionary organizations are outside the boundaries of the Zionists' state, any action by them necessitates an armed invasion against which the usurping state will launch a military operation directed against the Arab neighboring countries.

6. In Algeria, the fighters were men attached to their people who left the towns and their sham for the bosom of the masses. The propagandists of revolution in Palestine are chatterboxes of the bourgeoisie who prefer coffee houses in Beirut, Damascus, or Gaza to the sands of the occupied territory and the mountains of what was left in Palestine west of the Jordan. They organize themselves in Gaza, Lebanon, and Kuwait issuing

thousands of proclamations without remembering once where the battlefield is, or discovering its boundaries and purpose.

7. Arab states' aid to Algeria was very small, yet, despite its smallness, Algeria achieved victory because her conditions made that meagre aid sufficient. However, in the battle for Palestine, the aid will not be adequate even if it is large. This is because the aim is to uproot the usurping state and not to spread fear and ruin inside its borders. The Palestinian people, divided and oppressed, cannot mobilize the necessary power to squash the Zionists' state which is defended by 300,000 well-trained and well-armed soldiers.

8. The Algerian campaign took a territorial shape [i.e. pertaining to one Arab people or state] . . . the struggle stopped at the traditional borders of Algeria, and it recognized the borders drawn by colonialism. This nature of territoriality made the Palestinians demand a territorial struggle [i.e. by the "Palestinian entity" as distinct from the rest of the Arabs], but that is impossible in Palestine. Algeria could be liberated without a clash with Tunisia or Morocco and their reactionary governments, while the revolutionary operation for the liberation of Palestine must collide with the Government of Jordan.

No doubt this is sound criticism. It spares the need for a military evaluation of guerrilla prospects in the area, which, coming from an Israeli, might be suspected as partisan.

"The Struggle Continues"

**President Nasser's Speech at the Opening of the
Second Session of the Arab Socialist Union
National Congress at
Cairo University, March 27, 1969**

In the name of God the All-Merciful, we open the Arab Socialist Union National Congress.

Brothers, before beginning with the proceedings of the session I ask you to observe one minute's silence in memory of General Abd al-Mun'im Riyad—the brave soldier who offered his life on the battlefield and who gave a high example of Egyptian military honour, and in memory of all our heroic martyrs on the Egyptian front, and the martyrs of the Palestine resistance and the martyrs of the Palestine masses confidently and faithfully struggling on their soil.

Compatriots, members of the ASU National Congress, your Congress is now holding its second session in accordance with the 30th March statement—that the elected ASU National Congress should exist until the effects of the aggression were overcome and should hold a plenary session every three months to follow up and guide the stages of the struggle and adopt whatever it deemed appropriate in this respect.

Although the agenda of this session includes many questions, the foremost question under the 30th March statement—and the primary question of concern to the masses—is one before any other: this is the question of the comprehensive struggle of our people and nation to restore and establish their rights and to liberate and honour the land. There is no other issue before this question, under the 30th March statement and by virtue of our masses' concern. There is no other issue above this question by virtue of the current phase of the foremost issue of comprehensive Arab struggle, which is the centre of attention and the sphere of every sacrifice and hope we offer or expect.

This session of the National Congress begins when our struggle is in a very important and at the same time very dangerous phase. This phase is reflected in particular in both the military and political sides of the Middle East crisis.

On the military side, the phase is apparent in the continued escalation of military operations along the Egyptian front, the escalation of the Palestine resistance organisations, and the escalation of the Palestine people's steadfastness, which is openly and fully challenging the Israeli occupation. At the same time, the enemy's wrath has escalated. We see the effects of this in the repeated raids on Jordanian towns and cities on the pretext of deterring the Palestine resistance.

Brothers, this means that with this escalation we are entering a stage which is inevitable, with the continuation of Israeli aggression on one side, and on the other with our increased capacity for steadfastness and daily support for our comprehensive force in defending our sacred rights. We are now entering a stage in which we should expect strikes by the enemy and in which we should return the enemy's strikes more heavily. We will discuss this in detail later.

On the political side, the phase is apparent in the collaboration of international political activity surrounding the Middle East crisis, which is crystallising in the forthcoming meeting of the four big-power permanent member States of the Security Council, which issued the 22nd November 1967 resolution on the Middle East crisis. The meeting, coming about eighteen months after adoption of the resolution, is to discuss that resolution and what has been done to implement it, in the midst of pressures affirming to every fair observer and every individual sincerely concerned about peace that the Middle East crisis cannot possibly wait any longer.

It is a miracle that the crisis has lasted so long without exploding—an explosion which would have far-reaching and unlimited effects. This means that politically and militarily we are entering a very critical and sensitive stage. Representatives of the four big powers will meet in New York. These powers will study and debate various possibilities. The importance of the subject is that the attitude of these four powers will be a new measurement that will help us clearly and beyond doubt to determine the attitudes of enemies and friends. Perhaps I should sincerely say that the attitudes of the various States in this connection will determine for each the extent of their relations with our Arab nation for years to come, whatever the consequences.

In this connection, and without awaiting other details on the political side, which I will deal with later, I wish to explain to you that the destiny of the Middle East will be determined in the Middle East itself and that nobody can dictate to the Arab nation what this nation regards as against justice or its lawful, historical rights. Peace cannot be imposed, but peace can come by itself if justice forms the basis. We should always remember that the balance of power may change but the foundations of justice are always firmly rooted and perpetual.

Brother compatriots, members of the Congress, the current session of your Congress begins with a new military and political phase—a phase in which events are moving faster and taking a serious turn. Therefore we must be extremely alert, cautious and fully prepared. . . .

Brothers, we will now take a look at some of our fronts near the enemy lines.

First, the Egyptian front. When we refer to the Egyptian front, we begin with the issue of the reconstruction of the armed forces. We all know the situation of our armed forces after the aggression and the cease-fire decision. The reconstruction of our armed forces was a difficult operation. It was not at all an easy operation. First of all we were in need of arms, then we needed reorganisation, then we needed hard training. All this requires the exertion of great efforts and means that our officers and soldiers must accustom themselves to leading a hard—a very hard—life. Naturally, the formation, organisation, and training of our armed forces is not enough. We must also train the brains that command these forces and units. This too has not been an easy task. The formation, training and command of all levels of our leadership has not been easy. When we speak about the reconstruction of the armed forces, we mean that we are reconstructing an army in whose arming, organisation, training and command we have confidence. The armed forces command is the brain that directs the battle and fighting. We also refer to the standard and efficiency of the men in our armed forces.

All these operations were delicate operations that require planning. What was wanted was fighting spirit, a spirit of sacrifice, and the restoration of confidence in our armed forces after the defamatory campaign to which our armed forces had been exposed in the world.

In reality we lost the battle in 1967 without coming face-to-face with the enemy. We lost the war without entering into it. We lost the battle without fighting. Despite this, our armed forces were exposed to many defamatory campaigns. The only confrontation in 1967 took place on 5th

June. On that day, our armed forces fought well. However, in view of what happened to our air force on 5th June, instructions to withdraw were issued on 6th June. So, since we did not have the opportunity to enter the war we cannot say that we lost. We did not have the opportunity to confront the enemy. What happened was that an attempt was made to defame our armed forces so that the people would lose their confidence in the armed forces and so that the armed forces would lose confidence in themselves.

Therefore, after the organisation and arming of our armed forces and after the creation of a command, we had to examine the standard of our men and the spirit of confidence which was restored. We had to see that the fighting spirit was spread among all members of our armed forces. We had to feel the spirit of sacrifice return among the members of our armed forces and to see that cohesion was present between officers and men. We had to see that everyone was sacrificing his time and that we worked day and night.

Brothers, I saw all this during my visits to the armed forces. The people gave a good example of their feelings when they attended the funeral of the martyr Abd al-Mun'im Riyad. Abd al-Mun'im Riyad worked till midnight every day. All members of the armed forces knew this. He used to pay constant visits to army units. He had constant discussions with everyone. The members of our armed forces were used to sudden visits by Abd al-Mun'im Riyad at any post.

During my recent visits to the armed forces at the time of the feast [Id al-Adha], a soldier spoke to me about a certain issue. When the soldier approached me I thought that he was going to complain to me or that he was going to refer to a private issue. However, he did not speak to me about a private issue. He spoke about an issue concerning the use of the arms in his unit. In fact, when he said what he wanted, I asked him: Do you not want anything? He said: No, I do not want anything. I asked him: Have you no complaints? He said: No, I have no complaints. I asked him: From what college did you graduate? He said: I graduated from the Faculty of Arts of Cairo University. We discussed the subject he brought up. Abd al-Mun'im Riyad also spoke to him on the same subject. At the end of our visit that night we went to rest. After dinner I noticed that Abd al-Mun'im Riyad had asked for the soldier who spoke to us earlier. Riyad sat down with him and asked him about the details of the subject for which he had had no time during the visit. He sat with him and talked about all issues.

This is the spirit of our men in the armed forces. This is the spirit of the Chief of Staff of our armed forces and the spirit of a soldier of the Egyptian armed forces which are now in position on the battlefield.

Brothers, the efforts to train our armed forces are great. We know that the enemy had been preparing for this battle since 1956. This fact appeared in books written by the enemy. They said they were mobilising themselves until they saw that we were about to become stronger than they. They launched their aggression against us at that time so that they could prevent us from becoming their superiors.

We have learned many lessons from what happened in 1967. We are now working hard day and night to make good our losses. With regard to training, training means one is deprived of leave for a long period, for there is training day and night. We feel that the officers and men of the armed forces are doing difficult work and are assuming heavy responsibilities. They work for long periods without leave, but every one of them knows that we want to make good our losses in the shortest period possible. We also want to use the weapons we have received with full competence. This is as far as training is concerned.

As far as science and technology is concerned, we are endeavouring to catch up with what we have missed in all types. We are developing and expanding our war industry. When I speak in this way some people may think that I am divulging secrets. Well, I am not divulging secrets. How can we enter the war if we are not trained and if we do not have a command, arms and armed forces in which we have complete confidence?

With regard to arms, the subject of the supply of arms demands our careful consideration. By such consideration we learn a few lessons, and also we can be more sure of the correctness of the course we have maintained. Several points have to be considered in this matter.

(i) The Soviet Union is supplying us with the weapons we need. Immediately after the setback and the aggression the Soviet Union began supplying us with arms, with aircraft. We were able in a short period to obtain enough arms to help us meet any Israeli aggression. Had it not been for these arms we could not have succeeded in attaining a position from which we could answer or repel the enemy.

(ii) The United States and its allies are supplying arms to our enemy. There is a distinction between the US supply of arms to Israel and the Soviet supply of arms to us. After the June 1967 aggression Israel had more arms than it needed, while we hardly had enough. Moreover, we needed the arms to defend our homelands and to liberate our occupied territories. The supply of arms to Israel—which was the aggressor—could only mean that Israel was being encouraged to continue the aggression and to insist on achieving gains from this aggression.

(iii) The Soviet Union is supplying us with the arms we need without exerting pressure on our current financial resources, which are bearing the heavy burden of the war. It is enough to tell you that we have not yet paid a single penny for all the arms we have received so far from the Soviet Union. The first consignment of arms we received from the Soviet Union was free. After that, all other arms consignments were paid for with long-term loans.

I want you to know that the United States gives arms to Israel practically free of charge. The US Export-Import Bank offers Israel long-term loans with which it purchases arms for nominal sums, while generous American donations to Israel take care of these loans when the time for payment comes.

(iv) When arms are obtained from States and not by smuggling, the matter is no longer a commercial deal but is firmly linked with the countries exporting the arms. A country cannot possibly give arms to a country contrary to its own policy. This means quite frankly that the imperialist powers cannot give arms to countries which openly oppose and challenge imperialism, even if these countries are ready to pay for the arms in hard currency. They cannot get the arms until they succumb to imperialism, or if there is hope of making them succumb to imperialism. We tried this with Britain in 1953 and with the United States in 1954. I want to say quite clearly that supposing we did have the foreign hard currency to purchase the arms, if we could manage that—and I say that we could manage—if we had the currency and went to Washington or London to purchase the arms, we would not get anything. Proof of this is clearly before our eyes.

(v) From the point of view of our national independence, in particular from the point of view of our main and basic existence, our supply of arms from the Soviet Union is a firm guarantee and the only door open to us. This makes us always feel most grateful for the Soviet Union's attitude to us, to our questions of destiny and to our legitimate struggle for our cause.

We have obtained arms from the Soviet Union since 1955. From 1955 to this date, the Soviet Union has neither dictated any political restriction nor made a single condition. It has not made any request which could affect our national prestige. Relations are based mainly on the belief in the popular liberation movement, hostility to imperialism, and resistance to imperialist influence and plans.

After obtaining arms, we must grasp arms. The armed forces are now day and night doing so, grasping and training so that the arms may have full weight on the battlefield. After obtaining the arms, we asked the Soviet Union to provide us with Soviet military technicians—who are at present with our armed forces in their various units and corps. We asked the Soviet Union for technicians and have insisted on our request. Why? To compensate for shortcomings. These shortcomings appeared in various fields in June 1967—in the use of arms, in the command and in various aspects. We also asked the Russians to assist us in training, in grasping arms, and in modernising the various commands—from the supreme to the subordinate commands. I insisted on requesting Soviet experts for deployment with the armed forces because of my conviction that to confront the Israeli enemy we needed the full assistance of Soviet arms and also of those who could instruct us on the use of the arms and who could help us in command training.

In fact, we have benefited a great deal in the recent months from the Soviet experts and advisers who are with our units. They have left their families behind and are earnestly working with us day and night so that we may benefit from their experience and so that our armed forces may attain full proficiency to enable them to stage the battle to liberate the land. . . .

Brother citizens, members of the National Congress. Before leaving the subject of the Egyptian front to view the remaining Arab fronts surrounding the enemy, we must stop carefully to consider the excellent activities that the Arab Sinai Organisation has begun to carry out. The activities of this organisation, which was founded by the young people of Sinai and by other groups of young people from the whole of the homeland who have voluntarily joined its ranks—who defied danger and found their way to this dear part of our nation—began to be felt a few months ago.

During the past few weeks the organisation began to expand its activities in extremely dangerous circumstances, and to fight the enemy in unsuitable natural conditions. Despite all this, the young people of this organisation carried out their great and extremely dangerous tasks in solemn silence. Their attacks were direct. They came face-to-face with the enemy's military forces concentrated in the desert. Our young people formed fighting patrols and clashed with the enemy. They raided enemy headquarters and laid mines. Not a single day passed without the sound of the explosion of these mines reaching the enemy's ears. These explosions inflicted personal and material losses on the enemy.

Regardless of the enemy's repeated threats of revenge against the activities of this organisation, no one is now able to prevent these national young people from carrying out their role in the battle. The Arab fida'iyin action is linked with the Israeli occupation of Arab soil. Therefore, as long as this occupation continues, the people's resistance against it cannot be stopped. This resistance is manifested in all possible ways, both in a negative way and in a popular or military way. This resistance will continue until the end of the occupation.

Brothers, we shall now move on to consider the other fronts of Arab military action. The matters I shall discuss are not secret, because some of Israel's leaders have discussed them and the facts may have also been published by newspapers in Israel or in some Arab newspapers.

The second point I want to discuss is the eastern command. Actually, ever since June 1967 we have been thinking of co-ordinating the joint Arab fronts. Meetings and other long secret meetings actually took place, until it was eventually possible to establish the eastern front and form a command for this eastern front. This command is actually of great importance. Therefore it is necessary that there should be an eastern front and a western front. It is also necessary that there should be complete co-ordination between the eastern and western fronts. The enemy is aware of this importance and of what can possibly result from the formation of strong eastern and western fronts.

The importance of the eastern front was stressed in one of the books of the Strategic Studies Institute. The book points out that Israel's principal target these days is to break up this eastern front. I can say that the establishment of the eastern front has succeeded to a great extent. What has been achieved?

The eastern front has been formed, composed of Syria, Iraq and Jordan. A command for this eastern command has been formed and complete coordination has been achieved between the forces of Syria, Iraq and Jordan. What I am now saying is not a secret, because the Israeli Defence Minister discussed it in the Israeli newspapers. Contacts are now taking place between the eastern front and Kuwait and Saudi Arabia.

After this short discussion of the eastern front, I will now speak about the resistance forces. We have spoken about the resistance forces before and revealed our view on them. We have also spoken of our policy. Our policy towards the resistance forces is summed up in consolidation of the resistance forces by every material and military means. We have also said that it is the right of the Palestine people to resist occupation, to fight and to demand their full rights.

We will now speak about the Palestine popular resistance. As we speak about the Palestine popular resistance, which has broken out everywhere in the territory the enemy occupied after June 1967, we must mention the resistance being carried out in valiant Gaza—the Palestine Arab people in valiant Gaza, these people who refuse to surrender. We are aware of the difficult circumstances the people of Gaza are facing in economic and other ways. Despite these circumstances, however, Gaza refuses in every way—through its young men, its sons, its daughters, its men and its old people—refuses to surrender or to keep silent.

We must also mention the Palestine popular resistance in the West Bank. We must mention the Palestine popular resistance in Jerusalem and the reaction by Israel, seeking to turn Jerusalem into a Jewish city. I tell our brothers, the people of Jerusalem, that we, the people of the UAR, give our pledge that we shall in no circumstances accept the fait accompli Israel seeks to impose in Jerusalem. Arab Jerusalem is a part of the Arab nation and no one can abandon Arab Jerusalem. . . .

Brother citizens, I am aware that there is a big question in your mind and in the mind of our people and nation. The question is: When will the battle be? I should like to tell you—out of a sense of responsibility—that I cannot answer this question. I can only say that everything physically possible is being mobilised for the day of the battle. In fact, superhuman efforts are being made for the battle. This is being done with the work, knowledge, faith and resolve of our men in all fields of national struggle, both at the front and on the home front immediately behind it.

Therefore I hope that you will see eye to eye with me that we should not accelerate the battle to make it take place before its due time, not even by one day. However, I promise you in the meantime that we shall not delay the battle, not even by one day, from the date it is due.

Brother citizens, members of the National Congress, before leaving military matters to discuss political matters, I must remind you that the War Minister will be here with you tomorrow at a closed session to give you further details which you would like to know and on which you may ask for explanations. The same thing will apply to the Foreign Minister, who will also attend the closed session with you tomorrow. He will talk to you about things that you would like to know within his field.

For this reason, I shall make my talk about political matters as brief as possible so as not to place obstacles before the contacts among the four big Powers which will begin in the next few days. However, it might be appropriate to review certain general topics so that we may not expect more than the circumstances allow.

1. No one can ask us to do more than we committed ourselves to do when we accepted the 22nd November 1967 Security Council resolution. Despite our absolute belief in a principle which we have declared and which we shall untiringly repeat—that what has been taken by force can be regained only by force—we have presented everything possible, within the principles in which we believe, to the UN Middle East envoy Gunnar Jarring, who is to supervise the implementation of the Security Council resolution.

2. We have realised from the beginning that any hope in Ambassador Jarring's mission is difficult to realise because Israel rejects the Security Council resolution. It rejects the resolution because it provides for two things of great importance. These are: (i) the need for withdrawal from Arab territories occupied after 5th June, and (ii) that no territory can be annexed by aggression. Israel wants to expand and is seeking land. We have brought to the attention of the world statements by Israeli leaders and officials sufficient to condemn them and to expose their intentions and plans.

3. Towards the end of last year the problem was again taken to the Security Council in an indirect manner. It was evident then that Ambassador Jarring was unable to proceed with his mission and that the authority issuing the resolution should express another view on it before it was too late.

4. Since that time three new attempts have emerged. The first was a timetable presented by the Soviet Union for the implementation of the resolution. The second was a set of ideas contributing to the implementation of the resolution. These ideas have been presented by France for discussion at a four-power meeting, proposed by her, to include the four big powers which are permanent Security Council members, in their capacity as the effective force in the Council. Finally, a few days ago, there was the US working document.

5. I do not want to express an opinion after which it might be said that we are making difficulties before the meeting of the big four powers. However, I cannot conceal from you that the USA bears a great responsibility for the dangerous road on which the Middle East crisis is proceeding. From the beginning of the crisis, the US attitude has been identical to that of Israel all along the line and without reservations, despite its alleged friendships with the Arab world—which are a subject of great doubt—and despite its enormous interests in the Arab world—about which there is no doubt. Following the recent US Presidential elections, which brought in a new government, we tried—and I add further that we are still trying—but I am bound in honesty to say immediately that so far I do not see any indications of a change in the US attitude, which supports Israel all the way.

Brothers, after perusing the recent US working document, I can assert that the US attitude is one of complete support for the Israeli point of view. I have only one answer to this US support for Israel—the constant support before and after June 1967—I have only one answer. It is that we Arabs will in no circumstances surrender or accept any pressure.

Brothers, the Israeli newspapers reported that the USA had accepted Israel's point of view, during Eban's visit, on the subject of negotiations between the Arabs and Israel and on the subject of refugees. The Israeli newspapers said that the USA had adopted Israel's point of view on these subjects.

Brothers, the serious situation that may arise if the big four countries, in their capacity as the principal powers in the Security Council, are unable to find a means of implementing the Council's resolution—this situation we and everybody are aware of.

Brother compatriots, members of the National Congress, whatever the case may be, before and after all this, one fact above all remains. Our Arab nation will always have the last word concerning the most important issues of its struggle. Our nation will not give up any of its principles, rights or territory. It will work, struggle, resist and fight so that its destiny will always be guarded by its will. God is its supporter. Peace be with you.

Syrian Ba'th Party Congress Resolutions

Text of statement by Ba'th Regional Command on the Party's Extraordinary Fourth Regional Congress, April, 1969.

Brother citizens, the Extraordinary Fourth Regional Congress was convened at a time when the Arab nation stands, with all its present and future aspirations and hopes, at a cross roads. It will either assert itself, its freedom and its rights in life and determine its future, or slip again into a lost road to live deprived and powerless. This national situation imposed itself on the conference throughout. In a responsible spirit the past stage, including both its achievements and its gaps, was reviewed. In the light of this, the Congress was able to arrive at a unified view of the future, avoiding the gaps and enabling the achievements to take effect. It was also able to surmount the crisis and begin a new stage which it is hoped will be filled with action and achievement.

The recent crisis tackled by the Congress is not the first of its type in the history of the Party. Throughout its march, the Party, like any other revolutionary party, has faced bitter strife from within and acute domestic struggles, but has always emerged strong and more capable of confronting future events however hard these may be. Nevertheless, in view of the present circumstances of the Arab homeland, the recent crisis was the most dangerous and sensitive crisis for the future of the current stage of our people. The Syrian Region, in the light of its doctrinal line which it raised through the Party's leadership, has become one of the main guarantees for continuing the line opposing colonialism, imperialism and Zionism in a constructive way. Prompted by our national and domestic responsibility, it behooves us to defend the Party leading the revolution in this Region.

There were various past and recent causes for the difficult, hard conditions which the Arab homeland has experienced since the setback, and the Party's own conditions have played a major role in these causes. In the light of the situation imposed by the setback, liberation has become the noblest and principal aim of this stage, and the armed struggle has become the axis of the Party's policy in all fields. It was natural that views should differ on the means and methods to guarantee the best possible situation for confronting the occupation and aggression in our land. This has led to attitudes which differ in certain aspects from the attitudes of the political Command.

Those resolutions adopted by Congresses convened after 23rd February [1966] on building up the Party and developing sound Party relations have not been fully implemented. Furthermore, there has been a co-ordination between the implementation of the Congresses' resolutions on domestic policy and the realisation of the slogan "Every citizen has his role in the battle" on the one hand, and major advances in building the material base of the revolution on the other. There has also been no coordination between the will of the revolution to build the ideological army and the provision of the means and the adoption of the practical steps necessary to achieve this.

In addition to a number of other factors, these circumstances have led to the appearance of the signs of a crisis which continued to develop to the point when some measures were adopted that led to a collision course. The crisis thus extended beyond the Party framework to become a domestic and national crisis which affected both the Arab masses and leaders. Action to end this crisis in a manner ensuring Party unity and the preservation of the revolution became a general domestic and national demand.

The Party's bases, represented by the Regional Congress members, called for an extraordinary Congress in accordance with the Party's statutes. The Command agreed to call the Congress for an extraordinary session which was attended by the representatives of the various popular organisations and some Party organisations abroad. The meetings continued from 20th March to 31st March 1969. The reports submitted to the Congress regarding the crisis and its causes, as well as ways of tackling it, were discussed. The congress discussions were comprehensive, objective, and within the framework of the domestic and national responsibility demanded by the present fateful stage.

Brother citizens, on the basis of the fateful circumstances facing the Arab nation, which dictate that the main aim of the Arab people in this stage should be the liberation of the land from the colonialist Zionist occupation and working for the unification of all the human, military, political and economic efforts and resources and placing them in the service of the armed struggle to achieve the aim of liberation; and out of the Party's obligation to face its historic responsibilities towards the Arab revolution; the Congress has adopted the following resolutions and recommendations: . . .

In connection with the battle. Everything we say, build and plan is in accordance with the logic of the current fateful battle in all its dimensions and requirements. This Region has had a clear policy towards the battle based on principle. The policy was drawn up by the former Party Congresses on the basis of the slogan "Everything for the battle." In addition to affirming the resolutions of the former Congresses in this connection, the Congress has decided: (a) To complete popular mobilisation in keeping with the new stage. (b) To stress the achievement of effective coordination between the Arab fronts.

In the field of Arab policy. The Party has always believed that Arab unity and the battle in which the Arab nation is now engaged are two faces of the same fact, namely the Arab nation's awareness of its nationhood. Both are a living and practical expression of this awareness. Any step on the path to comprehensive unity gives support to the battle and is a step towards victory. Any victory we win in the battle will undoubtedly strengthen the Arab people's self-confidence and self-knowledge, and their ability to apply this knowledge in establishing unity.

In view of the fateful circumstances of the Arab homeland and the hostile plot against the Arab land and national existence, and on the strength of its absolute faith in the sound character of the Arab nation, the Congress has recommended the following: (a) That all initiatives be taken to achieve any possible step towards unity with the progressive Arab States, to work in all circumstances to create an atmosphere for unity, and to produce with these States a unified policy for the present stage. (b) To continue the work to bring all Arab resources into the battle and to achieve a unified Arab military stand and provide the necessary atmosphere for this stand.

In the field of foreign policy. The Congress views with satisfaction the fact that this Region has done everything necessary to strengthen relations with our friends, especially the Soviet Union and the States of the socialist camp, and to develop these relations to serve the battle of freedom and existence in which the Arab nation is engaged. Also, the Congress expresses satisfaction that this Region has responded to France's ban on arms for Israel, and that the Region is willing to develop friendly relations with France and do everything necessary to encourage the just French policy concerning the aggression. The Congress is gratified at this Region's firm stand towards all those States whose attitudes have proved them to be enemies of the Arab people and this people's legitimate aspirations to a free dignified life. These States include particularly the USA, Britain and Western Germany.

The Congress has also viewed with satisfaction the great efforts by this Region in political struggle on the international level, including influencing world opinion—a political struggle which supports the armed struggle. The Congress has decided to continue to work for implementation of the Party Congresses' resolutions on foreign affairs, stressing especially the Party's strategy of faith in armed struggle, rejection of so-called peaceful solutions, and the determination of our attitude towards other States in the light of their policies on the Palestine issue.

In the Party field. (a) All measures adopted because of the crisis shall be abolished and the Command shall restore the situation to normality immediately. (b) The Regional Congress denounces the exchanges of uncorroborated accusations which accompanied the crisis and enhanced it, and asks the Command to pay special attention to dealing with such a phenomenon, which threatens proper moral practices within the Party. (c) The Party bases called for a Regional Congress and the Command's response to this call has strengthened the Party's organisational principles and confirmed that the solution to any crisis within the Party can only be achieved through its institutions.

Brother citizens, the concern for the forward march of the Party and the revolution shown by friends throughout the world, many Arab brothers and honourable progressive and mass organisations in this country, and the responsible, mature attitude shown by all citizens throughout the crisis, have greatly impressed the Party's bases and Congress members. The Party Command praises these friendly and fraternal attitudes and renews its pledge to perform all its commitments of struggle in domestic, Arab and international policies. The Command underlines the importance of complete expression, in both policies and actions, of the Arab people's historic determination to retrieve the usurped land and restore the disgraced dignity.

Long live the struggle of the Arab people against imperialism and Zionism! Long live the struggle of the Palestinian Arab people for the liberation of their usurped land! Glory and immortality to the martyrs of the resistance and fida'iyin movements throughout the battlefields!

(Signed) The Regional Command of the Ba'th Party.

The Strategy of the War of Attrition

By Hassanain Haykal*

The coming stage of the struggle will be full of great and precious sacrifices. No matter how saddening or painful this may be, it is a destiny from which there can be no escape in view of several considerations arising from the battle fronts in the Arab-Israeli conflict:

1. . . . In the Israeli view, supported so far by Britain and the USA the present cease-fire lines provide an opportunity for forcing the Arab nation to submit completely to a plan for domination of which Israel is only the spearhead. This view assumes that, placed as they are along the cease-fire lines, the Arabs are in no position to reject anything.

In the Arab view, supported by the USSR and understood by France, the present cease-fire lines are new burdens in an old crisis, a new more serious complication in an already dangerous situation, and such a complication twice compounded would be the last foundation on which any long- or short-term solution can be based.

2. Israel believes that the present cease-fire lines will enable it to exert a dual-purpose pressure on Egypt, Syria and Jordan to secure the following:

(a) Recognition of the 1948 armistice lines as the international boundaries of Israel; (b) annexation of new areas, on the West Bank, the Golan Heights, and perhaps in the Egyptian Sinai desert as well where claims might exist but have not been made public yet.

In the face of this dual-purpose pressure, however, none of the three Arab States directly concerned can either: (a) make any bargains over its national territory under any pressure; . . . once a State concedes part of its territory, it collapses and loses any justification for its continued existence; or (b) decide on anything inside the Palestinian territory, because the Palestinian people now speak for themselves and nobody has the right to speak on their behalf, particularly in matters affecting their land. . . .

3. There is a time bomb in the shape of the cease-fire lines. This is a

* Excerpts from articles published in *Al Ahram*, March 27, April 11, April 25, 1969.

dangerous situation for which the influence of the USA and of pro-Israeli world opinion are to blame more than anybody else. . . . It was inevitable that the cease-fire lines turned into a time bomb, for the Arab States which accepted the cease-fire did so because they had no alternative and because they wanted to wait for the results of the efforts that might be made by the forces concerned with the peace of the area and the world. But the state of no alternative is liable to change and waiting has a limit.

The enemy has poured fuel on the fire. When the enemy felt the Arab impatience growing at the cease-fire lines, he tried to prolong the situation by the only means he has: violence. . . .

It is only natural for us to become impatient at the cease-fire lines. Likewise, the enemy's violence will increase, for this is his nature. Accordingly, we must expect that the enemy will increase his violence, extending it to the entire cease-fire lines and beyond them to any spot he can.

All this means that a different stage of confrontation will develop and will be full of great and precious sacrifices, as I have already said. We shall lose heroes. . . . We shall lose installations built with much sweat. . . .

I was one of those who after the battles of 1967 wrote frankly that one of the advantages achieved by the enemy was his occupation of Sinai which had brought the Canal area within range of his guns. No matter how hard or painful this may be, the area installations must be considered exposed to danger. Undoubtedly, it is one of our prime duties to defend every wall against the enemy guns as long as this is possible. But the vulnerability of the areas to the enemy guns must not for one single moment prevent us from acting. Otherwise, the enemy would be successful in using the hostage as he had calculated from the start. In fact, this area has been in danger since the day it came within range of the enemy guns in June 1967. Whatever solution is achieved for the Middle East crisis— even if it is a peaceful or diplomatic solution—the enemy will most likely vent his wrath by pouring fire into this area before withdrawing from it.

The phase which prevailed for almost a year after the June battles could be described as the phase of calm along the cease-fire lines. It was a phase in which calm was the rule and impatience was the exception, expressing signs of the Arab rejection that has been suppressed by the state of waiting without alternative.

But for some months, the features of a new phase have been developing and have not taken clear shape. It is the phase of impatience along the cease-fire lines. It is a phase in which impatience is the rule and calm is the exception. This phase will grow every day because the enemy has only violence, and human experience has shown that violence does not extinguish fires but fans them, turning impatience into indignation, indigation into wrath, and wrath into an explosion. The enemy's losses during the growing phase of impatience will be great no matter how hard he tries to conceal or deny them. We shall benefit from this phase no matter how many heroes we lose in the battlefield, no matter how valuable the installations exposed to enemy fire on and away from the battlefield. I will only speak of some of the benefits and completely ignore the rest.

1. The enemy has exploited the shock the Arabs suffered following their defeat in the battles of June 1967 and the period of calm that followed, to unburden himself of the commitments of general mobilisation which he could not endure for long because of his limited manpower resources. . . .

2. When the Arab resistance operations rose in intensity inside the occupied territory, the enemy employed a brigade of paratroopers to help the Nahal, police and intelligence forces. He also employed a squadron of helicopters, learning from the US experiences in Vietnam. Thus the enemy's burden was increased.

3. When the civil disobedience waves began against the enemy authority and later turned into bloody clashes in Gaza, Nablus, Hebron and Jerusalem, the enemy rushed to set up an electronic defence line to prevent the resistance men from entering the occupied territory. Thus, he was able to divert some of his forces to deal with the Palestinian cities which rose with pride and dignity against the enemy's authority and presence. The line, however, failed to achieve the desired aim and the enemy had to deploy part of his force in the occupied area surrounding Jerusalem.

4. When the artillery exchanges along the Suez Canal increased and Egyptian armed resistance patrols entered Sinai, as the Israeli delegate to the Security Council said, and fought battles near the Mitlah pass, the enemy immediately thought of setting up a defence line of steel installations along the East Bank of the Canal. This led to more clashes and the Egyptian artillery fire was so strong that it destroyed a large part of these installations and prevented the setting up of others. Israel then rushed to declare partial mobilisation to reinforce its troops in Sinai. Thus, the size of the Israeli forces almost doubled, from one and a half divisions to almost three divisions.

5. With the continuation of the artillery operations along the Egyptian front and the pouring of troops into Sinai, Israel resorted to another method for dealing with the resistance organisations. It is called "active pursuit" by aircraft. . . .

6. The use of Israeli aircraft in such battles is likely to have several effects: (a) the aircraft will be in constant need of maintenance due to extensive use. (b) The aircraft will be continuously exposed to being shot down . . . (c) The Arab fighters will become accustomed to living under the threat of air strikes and to fighting this threat. This in itself will help to dispel the state of unjustified panic that had developed after the six-day

battles. Furthermore, aircraft may be effective in strategic operations but in tactical operations, without the conditions of a comprehensive war, the effect will be limited, particularly on fighters who are helped by the nature of the ground on which they are fighting and by their training to protect themselves against air attacks.

7. When Israel increased its troop concentrations in Sinai, the Arab Sinai organisation began to play its most serious part, for this increase has provided it with more targets for more effective blows. . . .

The new phase along the battle fronts has meant the following to us: (1) Loss of more heroes; (2) further exposure of our installations to danger; (3) the cease-fire line is proving to the world every day that it is a time bomb; (4) the growing belief of our masses in their right to self-defence and their power to practise it, despite the shackles imposed by the stage of waiting without alternative; and (5) preparation of our fighters for the battle so that they will not be taken by surprise as in June 1967.

To the enemy, the new phase has meant: (1) Increase in the occupation costs; (2) loss of more blood; (3) exhaustion of more equipment; and (4) increase of economic burdens because of the confrontation.

The difference between us and the enemy is that whatever losses we suffer will not be high compared with our losses in June 1967, while anything the enemy loses will be great after its cheaply won victory in 1967. . . .

The Israeli enemy does not appear to be at his best these days. Usually our enemy is orderly and organised, but these days he appears confused and contradictory. There is a great deal of evidence of this. . . . Perhaps the most striking evidence of apparent confusion and contradiction can be summed up as follows:

1. So far the enemy has not taken an appropriate decision on the defence of his positions in Sinai. Will he adopt a static or mobile defence? Both methods have advantages and contain dangers. Static defence from reinforced positions would save him men and would not require him to increase his concentrations in the open desert. It would at the same time rob him of his best advantage: the capability of rapid movement. . . .

2. When the recent fierce artillery battles began, the Israeli Defence Minister Gen. Moshe Dayan described them "as a kind of fireworks—neither harmful nor beneficial." Nevertheless, a few days later the Israeli Army began constructing what they later called the Bar Lev Line, after the Israeli Army Chief of Staff. It seems Bar Lev was once one of the leading proponents of the static defence method. The Bar Lev Line is composed of more than 100 reinforced concrete positions. . . . When the Egyptian artillery destroyed more than half of these fortified positions, the enemy rapidly increased his concentrations in the desert.

3. When the Egyptian forces advanced one step in their strategy of

positive defence and launched combat patrol operations across the Canal to attack the Israeli positions and engage in face-to-face combat with the men and officers in those positions, the enemy's behaviour was a vivid example of his state of confusion and contradiction. The first operation was carried out last Sunday night. The enemy kept it secret despite his losses. He did not expect Egypt to say anything about it because any such statement would be tantamount to an admission of violating the cease-fire line by crossing the Suez Canal. When the Egyptian military spokesman mentioned the operation in his daily statement about incidents on the fighting front, the enemy appeared surprised. The enemy restrained himself, and eighteen hours after the operation and three hours after the statement by the Egyptian military spokesman, he hastened to issue an admission of the operation. He tried however to minimise its significance. . . .

When Monday night's operation followed, Israel was the first to issue a statement on it. Again Israel's statement was an attempt to minimise the significance of the operation. This attempt was reinforced by the statement of the UN Israeli Delegate that instructions had been issued to him to lodge a complaint against Jordan to the President of the Security Council on operations of the "saboteurs"—meaning the Palestine resistance organisations—but that Israel did not intend to lodge any complaint about operations by the Egyptian combat patrols, because those operations were so insignificant as to deserve no attention.

Nevertheless, at dawn on Tuesday the Israeli Air Force retaliated against an Egyptian radar unit which is on Jordanian territory in accordance with the requirements of the direct military co-ordination between the two countries and within the framework of the activities of the Eastern Command. . . . Even the Israeli retaliatory operation was not as well planned as usual. The Israeli raid on the Egyptian radar position near the town of Mazar in the Karak district did not take the Egyptian anti-aircraft artillery responsible for protecting the position by surprise, even though the attack took place at dawn. Radar equipment worth not more than 10,000 dollars was destroyed, but Israel lost a Vautour and a Mirage worth not less than 10,000,000 dollars. . . .

My purpose in this article is not merely to cite the evidence of the enemy's current state of confusion and contradiction. This is only an introduction to my purpose. But there is one question that must be answered in connection with this introduction before arriving at my main purpose. The question is: What is the explanation of this current state of the enemy?

The only explanation is that on most of the Arab fronts the enemy is facing something for which he is not prepared. . . .

On the Egyptian front, to be specific, the Israeli enemy imagined that any bullet fired on the Egyptian front would be "a political bullet" intended either to bring pressure to bear on the great Powers to convince them that the Middle East situation was about to explode, or to influence the Arab masses and convince them of the earnest intention to fight. Conceived in this frame of mind, Israel's assessments overlook the most important factor in the Arab stand on all the fighting fronts: the incentive of liberation. The enemy forgets that the picture changed fundamentally after 1967. Before then, the enemy claimed the Arabs were working to bring about his defeat. . . . Since 1967, the enemy no longer accuses the Arabs of working to defeat him, although in fact their sole aim in life is now to bring about his defeat by any means. The enemy acquits the Arabs now not because he feels reassured about their intentions, but because he feels reassured about their present capabilities. Yet, the enemy forgets the incentive of liberation, which was not as strong before 1967. . . . In view of this powerful incentive, the enemy should not make his calculations according to the traditional criteria, but on the basis of different factors that will definitely prove their effectiveness. . . . After the introduction and the related question, the purpose of this article is to draw attention to a number of vital points at the present stage of the Arab-Israeli struggle.

1. The Israeli enemy will soon wake up from the confusion and contradiction that now afflict him. This is because he has many means, above all his military strength, which will enable him to recover his balance quickly. Military force will be the first means the enemy will use intensively to rid himself of the state of confusion and contradiction now afflicting him. This means that the enemy will strike violent blows so as at least to regain the initiative and, if he can, to reduce the pent-up power of the Arab incentive of liberation which has gathered force since the setback. . . .

The Israelis planned their war with us in a modern, logical way which involved no miracles or near-miracles. But when they arrived to fight us, we were not really there. This was due to many factors—previously discussed by me—which imposed defeat without a fight on the Arab force. Acute anxiety prevailed in Israel before the decision was taken to enter the war on 5th June 1967. Israel's Grand Old Man Ben Gurion was against the risk. The former Premier Levi Eshkol was hesitant. Israel entered a war which the Arabs entered not with their strength but with their shortcomings. In fairness, and according to all sources of reference, it must be said that the units that had the opportunity to fight acquitted themselves well. The reasons for the Arab shortcomings were at a higher level than the sacrifices of those who fought. It will suffice to say that four-fifths of the Egyptian force in Sinai did not have an opportunity to engage the enemy. . . .

The first thing, then, the enemy will use to recover his balance and rid himself of the state of confusion and contradiction that now afflicts him is his military strength. He will strike with it because it is the only weapon he has, and because the legend of its victory is the most precious thing he possesses. All this means that the enemy will strike and strike violently. He cannot recover his balance and regain the initiative unless he drives the Arabs back, at least psychologically, to their position at the end of the battles of June 1967.

2. No one should exaggerate in presenting the evidence of Israel's confusion and contradiction. This is not yet the end, nor even the beginning of the end. What is now taking place on the Arab fronts is closer to being the beginning of the beginning. The next part of the road will be rough beyond imagination. I can even say that the famous saying that we will wrest our territory from the enemy's occupation inch by inch is not a mere slogan but it is most probably what will actually happen, because we will fight on every inch of this land.

We must face the rough road with steady hearts and not be swayed by joy one day because the enemy lost two or three aircraft, or because dozens of his soldiers fell to our guns, or because our fighting patrols hit his positions. We must, in return, expect unlimited losses in men and equipment on our side. If one day we give ourselves to tumultuous rejoicing, we may find ourselves in the grip of gloomy grief the next day. We must not let the days pass in this way—one very cold and another very hot. . . .

What I said about the need to put the brakes on feelings now may appear to be a call for people to become computers, devoid of sentiment. This is impossible, because it is inhuman. This is not exactly what I am asking. I am trying to avoid further human misfortune. . . . It is usual for many to resort to hope to bridge the wide gap between reality and their desires. The danger is that such hopes may become day-dreams. Daydreams may exceed capability and disable it. This will double the strength of any enemy strikes. . . .

Someone might contradict by asking: Why do I say this when we are moving along a road which we must follow to the end? The answer is: This is what should really be said at this time and in these circumstances. It is the nature of war to strike, to be prepared to be struck by the enemy without letting this be a surprise, and to be prepared at all times to give death to the enemy, and to take death from him. Such is the nature of war. . . .

To my mind there is one chief method which cannot be ignored or avoided in tipping the balance of fear and assurance in the Arab-Israeli conflict in favour of the Arabs. This course, which meets all the requirements and necessities and is in harmony with logic and nature—this main course to tip the balance in our favour, or merely precisely to adjust it, is: to inflict a clear defeat on the Israeli Army in battle, in one military battle.

I should like to be more specific because there is no room under present conditions for irresponsible talk. I would make the following points: (1) I am not speaking about the enemy's defeat in the war, but his defeat in a battle. There is still a long way to go before the enemy can be defeated in the war. The possibilities for this are still not within sight. But the enemy's defeat in one battle presupposes capabilities which could be available at an early stage in the long period before the end of the war. (2) I am not speaking of a battle on the scale of that of 5th June 1967—a 5th June in reverse, with the Arabs taking the initiative and Israel taken by surprise. Most likely 5th June will not be repeated either in form or in effect. In the coming battle neither we nor the enemy will be taken by surprise.... I am speaking about a limited battle which would result in a clear victory for the Arabs and a clear defeat for Israel—naturally within the limits of that battle. (3) The requirements and necessities I am speaking about, and which will impose the military battle, do not include any marked consideration for the so-called revenge for injured Arab dignity....

To these three reservations regarding the battle, which I consider necessary and vital, I should like to add more, in the hope that they will give a clearer picture of what I am saying. (1) The current artillery exchanges along the Egyptian front are not the battle I am thinking of—the battle that I feel the requirements and necessities are imposing. What I am envisaging is far greater and broader. The artillery exchanges are important, indeed very important, but they are not the battle which can achieve the aim of inflicting a clear defeat on the Israeli Army. (2) Neither are the activities of the resistance organisations at their present level the battle I am thinking of or the battle imposed by the requirements and possibilities. . . . (3) In simple and general terms the battle I am speaking about . . . is one in which the Arab forces might, for example, destroy two or three Israeli Army divisions, annihilate between 10,000 and 20,000 Israeli soldiers, and force the Israeli Army to retreat from the positions it occupies to other positions, even if only a few kilometres back.

I am speaking, then, about a battle and not the war; about a battle that is limited as battles naturally are; about a real battle, however, resulting in a clear defeat for the Israeli Army. Such a limited battle would have unlimited effects on the war. . . .

1. It would destroy a myth which Israel is trying to implant in the minds—the myth that the Israeli Army is invincible. Myths have great psychological effect. . . .

2. The Israeli Army is the backbone of Israeli society. We can say that the greatest achievement placed on record by the Arab resistance against Zionism—an achievement resulting from the simple act of refusal—has been to dispel the Zionist dreams. Because of the Arab refusal, Israel has become a military stronghold and Israeli society has become the society of a besieged stronghold—a military garrison society. . . .

3. Such a battle would reveal to the Israeli citizens a truth which would destroy the effects of the battles of June 1967. In the aftermath of these

battles, Israeli society began to believe in the Israeli Army's ability to protect it. Once this belief is destroyed or shaken, once Israeli society begins to doubt its Army's ability to protect it, a series of reactions may set in with unpredictable consequences.

4. Furthermore, such a battle would shake the influence of the ruling military establishment. The establishment has the whip hand in directing and implementing Israeli policy on the excuse of acting as Israel's sole protector and guardian of Zionist plans.

5. Such a battle would destroy the philosophy of Israeli strategy, which affirms the possibility of "imposing peace" on the Arabs. Imposing peace is in fact, a false expression which actually means "waging war."

6. Such a battle and its consequences would cause the USA to change its policy towards the Middle East crisis in particular, and towards the Middle East after the crisis in general.

There are two clear features of US policy. One which concerns the Middle East crisis, is that the USA is not in a hurry to help in finding a solution to the crisis. No matter how serious or complicated the situation may become, the USA will continue to move slowly as long as Israel is militarily in a stronger position. This situation would surely change once the Israel position of strength was shaken.

The other phenomenon concerns the Middle East after its present crisis. It is that the USA sees in Israel an instrument for attaining its aims in the area. No matter how far the Arabs go in their revolt against the US influence and how much they defy this influence, the US aims are guaranteed as long as Israel remains capable of intimidating the Arabs. If Israel's ability to intimidate becomes doubtful, US policy will have to seek another course. Israel has proved to the USA that for the time being it is more useful to it than the Arabs. Although all the US interests in the Middle East lie with the Arabs, the USA continues to support Israel. The strange contradiction in the Middle East at present is that the USA is protecting its interests in the Arab world by supporting Israel. Israel is thus the gun pointed at the Arabs, the gun which the USA is brandishing to attain its aims and protect its interests. . . .

After all this, the question remains: is such a battle possible?

The answer is: I do not claim military experience, yet I say that there is no doubt or suspicion as to the possibilities of such a battle which could inflict defeat on the Israeli Army. My belief is based on the following considerations:

1. The only myths in the Israeli system are those fabricated by bold and daring propaganda or by great imagination. Israeli society is not a straw as some believe, nor a rock as others imagine. . . . Israeli society cannot live independently. It is a society which cannot produce any genuine economic or political force. What matters most is the intrinsic force

and not the apparent force, which is deceptive in most cases. Myths that are based on apparent force are bound to be dispelled by experience, especially if met by a capable force.

2. Israel has lost its once-in-a-lifetime opportunity. After 5th June 1967 its myth acquired all the elements it needed. Yet Israel could not attain its goal of turning the end of the battle into the end of the war. Arab steadfastness proved that the battle has ended but the war will continue. Thus Israel has lost its opportunity.

3. In any future battle, the Israeli Army would fight under conditions different from those in all previous battles. The Israeli Army would not be able to advance easily from its present positions along the Jordan river, the Suez Canal and the Golan Heights without finding itself passing through densely populated Arab areas, with the danger that these would absorb all its striking forces, exhaust it and make it easy to pounce on the Israeli Army's scattered remains one by one. With the exception of the Air Force effort, the Israeli Army would have to fight a sustained battle or a defensive battle, whereas it is accustomed to fighting offensive battles with its characteristic tactics of indirect approach and fast outflanking movements. The Israeli lines of communication between the bases and the fronts have become long and arduous, especially in times of operations. As a result of the long lines of communication it would be impossible for the Israeli Army to move quickly on the Arab fronts as it did in the past when it was able to strike on one front and then switch its forces by its short lines of communication to strike at another Arab front. . . .

4. In any future battle the Israeli Army would face Arab armies with different standards of fire power and its use, different command structures benefiting from past experience, and a higher morale, as the Arab forces would be aware of fighting for the heart of their homeland and not only for its borders.

At the beginning of my article I said that a battle ending in a clear defeat for the Israeli Army should be the chief method of tipping the balance of fear and assurance. . . . I did not say it is the only method because there are other secondary methods. . . . I will give the following examples in this respect.

1. Our acceptance of the Security Council resolution on the Middle East—the resolution which international society has endorsed—is a valuable step, particularly since Israel has rejected the resolution and thereby defied the whole of international society. Despite Israel's daily proclaimed disrespect for the international organisation, the question is not so simple. I mean that the Israeli citizens' awareness of being at odds with the entire world will undoubtedly influence their mood, and so affect the balance of fear and assurance in the Arab-Israeli conflict.

2. The Soviet Union's support for the Arabs and its continued help to them in rebuilding their military forces after the tragedy of June 1967 will

undoubtedly affect the feelings of the Israeli people in the balance of fear and assurance.

3. France's stand cannot fail to affect the balance of fear and assurance for the Israeli inhabitants who realise that the greater part of their military power in 1967 came from France and that—from 1954 to 1964 at least —France was an ally of Israel joined by special ties.

4. The current four-power talks in New York arouse Israel's suspicions, to say the least, because they indicate clearly that the Middle East crisis cannot for long remain confined to the Middle East and that it might lead to a nuclear confrontation between the great Powers. The talks may produce a solution to the problem which—to put it at its lowest—will fail to give Israel everything it feels to be within its reach. Irrespective of their results and what the Arabs think of these results, the talks will play their part in affecting the balance of fear and assurance in the Israeli people's feelings.

I expect Israel will take this article and submit a copy of it to the Security Council, as it has done in the past, saying: Look, they admit that the battle is the only course and that the political attempts are only secondary courses paving the way for the chief method. Taking all the Israeli attempts into consideration, and we must admit its tireless activities, I should like to say: Our aim is to eliminate the aggression. How we wish that all the secondary methods might lead to the attaining of that aim! Facts and evidence keep reminding us that what has to be done must be done.

Returning to Palestine

By Ahmed Baha Ed-Dine

The withdrawal of the forces of aggression behind the frontiers of June 5, 1967 is undoubtedly the logical slogan, conforming with the phase through which we are passing at this time. It denotes the scope of the "first indispensable step" which has to be taken before we can even contemplate going on to the next stages. *Nevertheless, it would be an error to imagine that "the elimination of the consequences of aggression" implies the restoration of the exact same situation in the Arab world as existed prior to the aggression.*

Many situations will change and many ideas and methods will be modified.

We should also now be thinking of what ought to change—in particular with regard to the Palestinian problem itself.

The most elementary lesson we can draw from the defeat is to ask ourselves the following question: Have the ways we have been following up to now in order to try to solve the Palestinian problem been adequate or should we be thinking of other means and new methods . . . with a view to fully restoring the rights of the Arabs?

The conditions which existed in the Arab world from 1948 to 1967 fossilized the Arab position towards the Palestinian problem. For close to twenty years, the Arabs have obtained no other result than a verbal "rejection" of the state of affairs created in 1948. Now that this "frozen" situation has been thawed by Israeli aggression, we find ourselves facing a new situation that can be molded anew.

At this time, news is reaching us concerning the heroic Palestinian resistance put up in the occupied territory—a resistance which is the only serious step imaginable prior to realizing and consolidating our aims. Consequently we must draw the most important lesson of our defeat from that reality.

Before we envisage the possibility of different circumstances, of leaving the defense trenches in order to tackle the Palestine problem anew, we must admit that the simplest and most important "line of defense" against Israel would be, in the first place, for *Palestine to become a reality*.

The Zionist invasion of 1948 succeeded in tearing away one part of Palestine while we Arabs, instead of preserving what was left to us of that country, and seeing to it that it was made monolithic, firm and able to demand its rights, set about dismembering that part of the territory of Palestine which we controlled.

The Zionist invasion of 1948 set out to gather together Jewish immigrants and refugees from all over the world and to transform them into active citizens—farmers, artisans and fighters; while the Arabs reconciled themselves to the Palestinian citizens of being transformed into emigrants and refugees.

In the course of the years, the idea of creating a Palestinian entity and a Palestinian organization took form and began to develop. It is thus that the Palestinian (Liberation) Organization came into being, although it lacked one of the most important conditions enabling it to speak on behalf of the people and the homeland; namely, the territory. Yet, this territory, though reduced, did exist. The Palestinian "struggle" was consequently directed from Cairo, Beirut and every other Arab country—but not Palestine.

This state of affairs gave the world the feeling that Palestine no longer existed; that there was no real Palestinian people laying claim to its own territory; that it was merely a case of the neighboring Arab states putting up a resistance to another state named Israel.

Somewhat similar situations—but with innumerable variants and nuances—have been imposed on some other countries by international and colonialist circumstances. In this way Korea was divided into two sides, each side claiming to represent the country's only authentic state; but neither did away with itself because the colonialists were occupying the other state. In Vietnam, foreign forces imposed divisions upon the country, recognizing the victory of the national revolution in North Vietnam and preserving a colonialist base in the South. But the amputated nation which did not succeed in having its own right triumph fully—instead of knuckling under, mustered its strength and turned itself into a base for the liberation of its usurped, colonized nation.

What should we do, as a result?

Restore the Name of Palestine

It is clear that the indispensable point of departure, which must be examined and organized immediately, is the re-establishment of a state called Palestine. This state would include Jordan—consisting of the West and the East Bank of the Jordan—and the Gaza sector. In other words, it would comprise the remaining parts of Palestine, to which would be added the area which was Transjordan and which has become integrated with Palestine in the course of the years. It might be argued that this proposal would change nothing and simply suggest a change of name. Our reply to this is that any political initiative may confine itself to titles and be void of substance, but may equally, by persevering action, bring about a radical change and assume a new substance.

Only the restoration of the name, "Palestine," could have a major psychological—and subsequently political—influence on the world, and affect the future of this problem. The authentic name of the country would be reborn; the Palestinian state, of which one part was usurped, would rise up solidly along the front line against the usurper and claim its legitimate rights.

The re-establishment of the name of Palestine on Palestinian soil should be accompanied by the return of the Palestinian people to the soil of Palestine.

What actually has happened during the past nineteen years to the Palestinian people, with the exception of those who stayed in their own homes on the West Bank of the Jordan?

The Palestinian faced the following dilemma: either to become a powerless refugee living in tents, or to become an ex-Palestinian emigrant in some other part of the world—Canada, Latin America or one of the Arab countries from Algeria to the West to Kuwait in the East.

Who emigrated? The most capable, competent and gifted of Palestine's sons. Those who had succeeded in their careers as businessmen, engineers, doctors, economists and journalists. The elite among these competent and intelligent people had no other path open before them than emigration, than working outside Palestine and choosing some other nationality than the Palestinian. Only those who had left families in their country of origin kept up any ties with Palestine, while the others detached themselves from it completely. Thus, at the very same time that Israel was knocking at every door to attract Jews from Yemen, from Europe and the Maghreb in order to transform them into citizens and thereby enhance the density of her own population and her demographic and social solidity, the Arabs, for their part, were allowing the Palestinian entity, as a demographic reality and as a civilization, to disintegrate, to disperse, and gradually to lose its most precious asset: its human resources.

Build a New Life

The restoration of the name of the Palestinian state would of course be of no value as long as it was not accompanied by real action aimed at turning the tide of emigration and dispersion into one of return and regrouping. Before talking of "returning" to occupied Palestinian territory, we must achieve the return to the territory where Palestinians are still living. The Arab bulwark deployed to face Israel cannot be composed of a desert zone of refugee camps and of a society becoming more depleted from day to day. On the contrary, it should be supported by a society that is economically, socially, politically and therefore militarily, powerful.

A different kind of life must be launched in Palestine—a life that could absorb the capacities of its people, that would not encourage them to emigrate but instead would attract former emigrants to return to their country. Though it is true that such a new life is an expression of the duty of patriotism and the wish to solve the Palestine problem, it is no less true that Palestine must make it possible for all to work there, to live, to advance and to develop in that country.

Our call for a return to Palestine is not a marginal or secondary problem. Despite the current international and political interest surrounding the Palestinian problem it is indispensible that a Palestine exist. Palestine, which is the principal party to this problem must affirm its presence, demonstrate that it exists, and prove that its existence is real and meaningful. It must express its claims and exert continuing pressure. It was precisely the feeling of the importance of this factor that undoubtedly prompted the Summit Conferences to create a Palestinian entity represented by the Palestine Liberation Organization. What was it, however, that caused that organization to fail and what was its weak point? The factor which proved fatal to the organization was the lack of a territory, and of a people attached to that territory. Its existence was more fragile than that of the Jewish Agency before the creation of the State of Israel. In fact, the Jewish Agency and even the Zionist Movement itself only owe their effectiveness to the fact that they were attached to a territory, to their concentration on Palestinian territory, through the agricultural settlements, the towns and the population centers which they controlled.

The call for a return is not a subsidiary problem. The human factor is the decisive one in this national struggle, the bitter struggle which sets noble national destinies against those of an invading people that is seeking to create a new nationalism. In the final instance, it is the human factor which will prove decisive, and above all, it will be the Palestinian human factor, aided and supported by the Arab human factor as its strategic extension. The Palestinian human factor does not depend only on quantity but also on quality; as much in the sphere of education as of skills, productivity and the country's economic, political, social and military institutions.

It is of little importance, after all, what the regime of the country will be: whether it will be a monarchy or something else. The homeland is greater than the regime in power. People may disagree regarding the regime, with all that this implies, but there can be no disagreement concerning the national homeland itself. No one makes it a pre-condition that the regime of his country be according to his own tastes before thinking of living, working and fighting there. The Palestinian's feelings concerning the return to the country and the Palestinian cause, his struggle and activities, should be no less strong than that of the Jew who emigrates from the other end of the earth to a country he has never seen, which he does not know and whose language he does not even speak. Undoubtedly, the Palestinian attachment is no less powerful than that attraction.

Let the Palestinian of today—of Lebanese, Kuwaiti or Argentinian nationality be able to benefit solely from his Palestinian nationality. The Palestinians must be in Palestine if Palestine is to belong to the Palestinians.

Those who are ready to sacrifice their lives today fighting in the occupied territories under extremely difficult conditions show that they are tackling the problem in a sound manner and that their way is perfectly feasible.

Should the Refugees Live in Tents?

The proposal, however, raises a delicate and sensitive point—of the Palestinian refugees. And here I refer to those living in the camps situated around Israel's frontiers in Gaza, Syria, Lebanon and Jordan. Since 1948, that is, for the past 20 years, approximately one million Palestinians have been living in tents in the refugee camps supported by international welfare organizations. Their circumstances are such that they cannot lead any sort of civilized lives; they are not cultivating the land, they are not working and they are not learning properly.

They are living in tents because they constitute the main contingent of those who were literally driven off their land and out of their dwellings. Their kind of life symbolizes to them the determination of the Palestinian people to reoccupy their homes, or at least to apply the resolutions successively adopted by the United Nations in their favor. No one wants to eliminate the refugee problem either by abandoning their right to return or by diverting them from claiming that right. The following question arises, however: should this large mass of Palestinian people, after 20 years of living in tents, continue to live in these same tents for a further period, whose duration no one knows?

I believe that to be impossible, unjust to the refugees and without any purpose.

In this comprehensive proposal I have put forward for the renaissance of "the Palestinian state," I don't have any precise answers to this question. But, nevertheless, I can define the objective and refer it to the writers, the experts, the thinkers and the politicians to discuss the ways it could be fulfilled. The aim is a double one:

1. to reform the life of that dispersed mass of human beings on the land of Palestine which we control. These people should, upon Palestinian soil, transform themselves into a powerful, enlightened, advanced and productive society, that will promote its agriculture and arm itself. A kind of "powerful climate" along the front line with Israel could be created. Finally, this human mass will no longer find itself behind barriers of infirmity, illiteracy, incapacity and stunted development;

2. to prevent any action liable to put an end to their right to return or in any way to undermine their cause.

I do not believe that this is impossible to achieve.

It is exceedingly important not to liquidate their problem since it is the spearhead of the entire Palestinian affair as a whole. But it is equally important for the refugees to become an efficient and influential force so that they may become a Palestinian Arab power. Let us recall once more that the Jews also constructed camps for the refugees they took in, but in these camps they worked, they trained for jobs, they lived and produced.

This is the proposal I am putting forward.

I will allow myself to return to one point. The problem of settling the land, of forming an attachment to it and of turning it into a powerful base, may appear to be of secondary importance, not pointing to a clear and rapid solution. But then, there are no easy, decisive, and rapid solutions for any of the world's really great problems. Nevertheless, in the course of time a new influential and unalterable situation can be created through initiatives, decisions and actions.

Israel is keenly aware of this problem; that is why she has always based her actions accordingly. Therefore, right after seizing any parcel of land she sets out to establish a settlement there. That is—a populated, productive fighting unit organically attached to the soil; in other words, it sets out rapidly to create a new demographic, geographic and political reality.

This is how the Israelis have been acting for almost a century, ever since the first Jewish immigrants began to arrive in Palestine. And that is how they acted only a few days ago when they began to set up new settlements near Jerusalem.

A Soldier Reflects on Peace Hopes

By Moshe Dayan*

At this course, people learn how to make war. But on this occasion, if I may, I should like to discuss the other side of the picture—the question of peace between us and the Arabs, or, more precisely, the problematics of peace. In a brief address, obviously, it is impossible to treat the subject exhaustively, and I, at all events, am not capable of doing so. I shall therefore merely try to cast some light on the subject.

I have chosen Dr. Arthur Ruppin as one personality who casts light on the subject. He came to Israel for the first time in 1907, was expelled "forever" by the Turkish Governor Jemal Pasha, and came back to the country after the English conquest, this time really forever.

Two unique elements are involved, if we wish to present the problem through the eyes of Dr. Ruppin. The first is the period in which he lived. From 1920 to 1942, Dr. Ruppin was one of the architects of the Zionist venture, the "father of Zionist settlement." This was the inter-war era, a concentrated period of 20 successive years, whose distance from us lends itself to evaluation and review. At the same time, the period is not quite so distant that its links with the present day are severed. From this stand-point of distance on the one hand, and links on the other, it might perhaps be proper to pinpoint 1936 as the focal year of the period. This was the year of the riots, which raged 30 years before the Six Day War.

Not only was the period unique, but perhaps the man himself more so. Not the man as a typical representative of the period, but Dr. Ruppin with his special qualities, which permitted him to see things with greater clarity, depth and honesty than many other men of his day.

Dr. Ruppin was a humanist by nature, a man of conscience, and when he encountered the "Arab question," he wanted to be persuaded that Zionism could be fulfilled without detriment to the Arabs of Palestine. In his education and schooling alike, he was a scientist, and he studied things not only through their concrete expression, but also through the forecast of their future development and transformation. Above all, Ruppin was a man of action: "For the Jews of Europe," he wrote in his diary, "Zionism is a religion, but for me, it means action." And in the "Arab question," he did not look for appropriate formulas but for practical solutions. More-over, since his life was utterly dedicated to Jewish settlement in Israel, he inevitably saw the "Arab question" as it was reflected through settlement.

* Text of an address by General M. Dayan to a graduating class at the Israel Army Staff and Command College (*Jerusalem Post*, September 27, 1968).

The ground he had his feet on was Zionist fulfillment, and he was only prepared to turn his gaze towards what was capable of achievement, without quitting this basic posture.

I cannot conclude my remarks about Ruppin the man, without including a paragraph from Berl Katznelson's eulogy of him:

> From generation to generation we see the 36 righteous men, whom we depict in the form of drawers of water, foresters or peasants. It would never occur to us to seek one of these 36 righteous men on some congress platform, in an office, in a university chair, or among public figures. I would not have used this figure of speech, had I considered it an exaggeration. Ruppin embodied unique characteristics which we associate solely with the 36 righteous men. He was modest without being self-effacing. He was not infected by the taint of power. Even the great publicity which he enjoyed from time to time in the course of his functions left him unspoiled.

I do not think it would be too outrageous of me to assume that most of the people here have not read the three volumes of Dr. Arthur Ruppin's autobiography. I shall therefore permit myself, in the following, to quote relevant extracts from this diary of his.

Ruppin was put in charge of Zionist settlement in Israel in 1920, after the First World War. He obviously anticipated that with the collapse of the Ottoman Empire, the wave of national liberation would also reach the Arab countries, and the Palestine Arabs as well. In the first days of his work he may perhaps have not realized the implications of this development for Zionism. But in 1923, three years after taking over his functions, not only did the "Arab question" reveal itself to him, but he also discovered that his predecessors had overlooked it.

At this period, in 1923, Ruppin underwent the first phase in his approach to the "Arab question." He not only recognized the existence of the problem but even diagnosed a solution, namely the merging and integration of the Jews among the peoples of the Middle East. Although he was already nearing his fifties, his criticism of others, and his confidence in himself, are steeped in the spirit of youth. In 1923 he wrote in his diary:

> Herzl's conception was naive, and can be explained by the fact that he failed utterly to understand the conditions among the peoples of the Orient, and create, along with our brethren of the same race—the Arabs (and the Armenians)—a new Near East cultural community. More than ever before, it appears to me, Zionism can only find its justification in the racial association of the Jews with the peoples of the Near East. I am currently gathering material for a book about the Jews, whose basic premise will be the racial issue. I propose to include pictures of the

ancient Oriental peoples, and of the modern populations, and to portray types which were to be found in the past, as well as in the present, among the group of nations of Syria and Asia Minor. I intend to show that those very same types are still to be found among present-day Jewry.

Ruppin understood that this approach implied a fundamental change in the Zionist concept, but he was not deterred by this fact. "Zionism will last," he wrote, "only if it is given a radically different scientific basis." The need to set Zionist fulfillment on a scientific foundation, the aspiration to find in Zionism some justification vis-à-vis the Palestine Arabs, and the need to lay down realistic answers based on a knowledge of local conditions—these principles are an integral part of Ruppin's nature. He clung to them later too, even when he discovered that the question was more complicated than it appeared at first, and required other solutions.

Ruppin did not hold on for very long to this idea of integration among the Arab peoples. As soon as he got to know realities better, he sensed that the common racial origins of Israelis and Arabs, and the resemblance between the Jewish nose and the Armenian nose, did not constitute an adequate basis on which to construct a "new Near East cultural community." In 1925, Ruppin arrived at the second phase of the "Arab question"—the bi-national phase.

During his bi-national state phase, which coincided with his adherence to the Brit Shalom Movement, which he founded in 1926 and left after differences with his fellow-members in 1929, Ruppin believed that Eretz Israel ought to be a common state for two nations. The Jews and the Arabs, in other words, should continue their existence as different and separate peoples, and not merge into a "new cultural community"—but at the same time they should maintain one single state, a bi-national state.

At this point, two things should be stressed. First, as Ruppin grew more and more immersed in his Zionist work and increased in stature, his awareness of the need to ensure the further independent continuation of the profound. He believed that this could be attained, if the aims of Zionism were realized. "World history knows no laws, not even the laws of reasonableness. There is therefore no sense in predicting the future. This is also the answer to those who claim to 'prove' that Zionism has no future." (1932) The second thing is that he saw the essence of Zionism as persistent and expanding immigration and settlement. He regarded these as "essential conditions," and did not diverge from them even when he feared there might be a contradiction between Zionism and the "Arab question."

As early as 1928, in fact, inner doubts of this sort troubled him. "In that conversation it became clear how difficult it is to realize Zionism and still bring it continually into line with the demands of general ethics. I was well and truly depressed. Will Zionism indeed deteriorate into a pointless chauvinism? Is there in fact no way of assigning, in Israel, a sphere of activity to a growing number of Jews, without oppressing the Arabs? I see a special difficulty in the restricted land area. Surely the day is not far off, when no more unoccupied land will be available and the settlement of a Jew will automatically lead to the dispossession of an Arab *fellah*? What will happen then?''

The idea of the bi-national state was supposed to reply to three problems. The first problem was that of nationality. Each people would preserve its own nationality. The second problem was to prevent the Jews dominating the Arabs, and vice-versa. ''Under the aegis of the League of Nations, Eretz Israel must become a state in which Jews and Arabs live side by side, as two nations with equal rights. Neither shall be dominant, and neither shall be enslaved.'' On the third problem, that of Jewish immigration and the dispossession of the Arabs, Ruppin wrote: ''Just as it is the right of the Arabs to remain in the country, so is it the right of the Jews to immigrate thereto.'' (1929)

This phase, like its predecessor, was a revolutionary one. Here again, as before, Ruppin believed that points of difference could be ironed out objectively speaking but in order to achieve this, other mistakes must not be repeated. ''We want to extricate ourselves from the error which was prevalent in Europe for 100 years, and which caused the World War— namely that only one nation can rule in one state.''

As regards the abstract formulation, the bi-national state may have provided the answer for Ruppin to the question of how Arabs and Jews would live in common. But as he came to know realities better, he discovered more and more difficulties, and Ruppin, with his intellectual integrity, did not allow generalizations to obscure factual truth. ''I am therefore convinced that a number of serious conflicts of interest exist between the Jews and the Arabs. For the time being I do not see how these conflicts can be resolved in such a way as to allow the Jews the possibility of free immigration, and free cultural and economic development—things which are essential conditions for Zionism and in such a way that the interests of the Arabs should not be impaired, on the other hand.'' (1928)

Ruppin knew, moreover, that the idea of the bi-national state was merely an ideological point of departure, an indication of framework within whose bounds he hoped it would be possible to solve the problem. ''In the course of debates within the Brit Shalom Movement, we formulated the concept that the solution must necessarily lie within a bi-national state . . . even the bi-national state, obviously, gave a general reply to the problem, and it was my intention to make use of the Brit Shalom further, as a means of clarifying decisive questions, which would emerge from this general answer.'' (1936)

And the questions, in fact, still remain: ''The 'conflicts of interest' were of a substantive nature.'' There was the question of land. ''On every site where we purchase land and where we settle people, the present cultivators will inevitably be dispossessed." Thus he wrote about immigration: "Since our immigrants, for the vast majority, are people without means, the possibility should not be ruled out that these immigrants would take away the livelihood of the Arabs." Then there was the different standard of living and other factors.

But the main difficulty stemmed from the fact that the Arabs simply did not want the Jews to come to Eretz Israel. Every solution—including the establishing of a bi-national state—faced the alternative of either making allowances for the views and desires of the Arabs, and putting an end to Zionism, or carrying on with immigration, land purchase and settlement, while denying the right of the Arabs of Palestine to determine the future of the country. Any solution, or arrangement, which would be contingent on the agreement of the Arabs, or on the introduction of a democratic constitution whereby decisions on questions at issue would be taken by a majority (an Arab majority naturally)—this implied the cessation of immigration, and of Jewish economic development.

Ruppin understood this, and in his letter to Hans John (May 30, 1928) he wrote: "During our last conversation, you pointed out quite rightly that all the Arabs of Eretz Israel oppose the Zionist Movement, and until we are capable of suggesting a satisfactory solution to the conflict of interests they will carry on being our antagonists. If, under these circumstances, a constitution worthy of the name were granted, it would stand to reason that the Arabs would make use of all the rights assured them by the constitution, to prevent, as a majority, all economic progress on the part of the Jewish minority. The meaning of this would be, quite simply, the end of the Zionist movement."

The crux of the problem, therefore, lies in the impossibility of arriving at agreement and cooperation with the Arabs. But, at this stage, Ruppin still believed that it was possible to find the "redeeming formula," which would serve as a bridge for understanding between Arabs and Jews. And so he founded the Brit Shalom Movement.

As time went on, the "Arab question" did not become any less grave, but in fact worsened. In 1936, Ruppin needed to find a solution for it, no less than he did in 1923, and in fact more. He saw this as a vital necessity, not just to resolve the conflict with the Arabs, but also in order to put relations with himself and with his conscience into proper order. But was there a way of squaring the circle? Did the magic formula exist, to reach agreement with the Arabs, "without thereby ceding the fundamentals of Zionism"?

I was at odds with the other members of the Brit Shalom, in my appraisal of the prospects of reaching an agreement with the Arabs. In this respect, the Brit Members displayed great optimism. They thought that economic advantages, and certain political guarantees, would in themselves be calculated to persuade the Arabs to accept the Jewish national home. There was nothing new in this concept. It was, in fact, just a continuation of the false approach towards the Arabs, which had prevailed in the Zionist movement from its beginning. Nobody ever imagined, beforehand, that those very same Arabs who during the days of Turkish oppression were prepared with equanimity to accept year by year a few hundred meek Jews who lived on *halluka* charity, would struggle by force against tens or hundreds of thousands of strong, straight-backed Zionists at a time when the country was under a free British administration. The "peaceful infiltration," which they hoped for so much, proved in reality to be a deceptive illusion. If we could learn any lesson from the history of the world in recent decades, this lesson would be that the political posture of nations is not dependent on considerations of good sense, but on instincts. All the economic advantages, and all the logical considerations, will not move the Arabs to give up the control of Eretz Israel in favour of the Jews, after they consider it was handed to them, or to share this control with the Jews, as long as the Arabs constitute the decisive majority in Eretz Israel. I gave expression to these ideas in a letter to Dr. Jacobson, December 3, 1931, when I wrote: What we can get today from the Arabs—we don't need. What we need—we can't get.

The year 1936 brought Ruppin to the third phase of his approach to the "Arab question." He ceased believing in the possibility of persuading the Arabs to agree to cooperate. No "legal formula," no "political guarantees," no "economic advantages," and no "negotiations" would bring the Arabs to consent to the Jews' return to Zion. This was undoubtedly due not only to the cumulative failures of attempts at dialogues with the Arab leaders, but also to the fact that the Arabs' anti-Zionist political stand grew a great deal more outspoken, and found expression in bloody outbreaks of violence, especially during the 1936 riots.

What next? What are the conclusions? After 16 years of trial and inner doubts, Ruppin demolished his own entire ideological structure. He had long since abandoned the Brit Shalom Movement. He was perhaps disappointed, he was certainly wiser, but he did not despair, on any account:

Nowadays, I personally am in a mood of calm and dispassion. I have formulated the following theory for myself: It is only natural and inevitable, that Arab opposition to Jewish immigration should find an outlet from time to time in outbreaks of this sort. It is our destiny to be in a state of continual warfare with the Arabs, and there is no other alternative but that lives should be lost. This situation may well be undesirable, but such is the reality. If we want to continue our work in Eretz Israel, against the desires of the Arabs—then we shall be compelled to take such loss of life into consideration!

As regards his own conscience, and as regards his self-recounting, Ruppin was calm and dispassionate. He had formulated a theory for himself, and it satisfied him. But what of the practical aspect? "And what ought to be done in order to reduce or remove tensions between the two peoples, since after all, this tension cannot continue interminably? To my mind, no negotiations with the Arabs today can help us move forward, since the Arabs still hope to be able to get rid of us, over our heads . . . not negotiations, but the development of Eretz Israel, as we increase our ratio of the population, and strengthen our economic power, can lead to a lessening of tension. When the time comes, and the Arabs realize that it is not a question of negotiations, in which they are asked to grant us something which we do not yet have, but of conceding the existence of a reality, then the weight of facts will lead to a lessening of tension."

To create the facts: immigration, settlement, economic development and so forth. In these activities, Ruppin sees not only the fulfillment of Jewish longings. Once translated into facts, they will also convince the Arabs to stop fighting against us. "We must increase our strength and our numbers, until we reach parity with the Arabs. The life or death of the Zionist movement will depend on this. . . . Perhaps a bitter truth, but it is the truth with a capital T." (1936) "The weight of facts—the increase of our strength and numbers will lead to a lessening of tension with the Arabs. When will we reach that stage? Within five to ten years." (1936) In this time-table, things like the policy of Hitler, the World War and the end of the Mandate, were not taken into account.

Ruppin's heart-searching over the path to agreement with the Arabs had thus come full circle. The fulfillment of Zionism embodied the solution to the "Arab question." Does this mean that Ruppin realized he was wrong, while his colleagues in the leadership, whom he called "naive" and "ignorant of the Arab problem," were correct? Not at all. The prevalent point of view held that the "Arab question" should be left alone, and it would find its own solution thanks to the prosperity, the development, the progress and the culture which the Jews would bring to the Arabs of the country. Ruppin, on the other hand, stopped dealing with the "Arab question," because he realized that the Arabs would not agree to Zionism, *in spite* of all these things.

In the years that followed, developments were determined as a result of factors unconnected with the pattern of relationships between the "Arab question" and Zionist fulfillment. Nevertheless, I should like to quote Ruppin's point of view on two more issues: the Peel Commission's partition proposal, and the White Paper. They are of interest for the subject of this lecture—if not directly, then indirectly.

Apart from Ruppin, the British Empire too was in a quandary in those years, over the question of Arabs and Jews in Eretz Israel. The solution it proposed (the Peel Commission, 1939) was partition—not integration, not a bi-national state, and not cooperation. This means the establishment of separate states for Jews and Arabs. The Jewish State was assigned an area of some 5,000 sq.km. To give some idea of the proportion, the State of Israel, today, has an area of 20,250 sq.km., in other words four times as large, while the area within the present cease-fire lines is 88,000 sq.km., 18 times larger than the area of the "Jewish State" in the Peel Commission's proposals.

On August 1, 1937, Ruppin wrote:

> After studying the partition proposal, I have come to the conclusion that we shall not be able to absorb the 300,000 Arabs in it. Since it will be impossible to get them to leave of their own accord, it is essential that the Jewish State should have other boundaries, inside of which not 300,000 but at the most 100,000 Arabs, would remain. I have put my "personal" plan for the new Jewish State in writing. According to this plan, the area will be reduced from 5m to 1.5m. dunams.

It should be recalled that in those days there were 363,000 Jews in Eretz Israel, and the 100,000 Arabs whom Ruppin was ready to absorb in the Jewish State would have been equivalent to 750,000 Arabs, absorbed by the Jewish State we have today.

During the Zionist Congress in Zurich, Ruppin brought to the Zionist Executive his proposal to give up two-thirds of the area proposed by the Royal Commission, and to establish a midget Jewish State on an area of 1.5 million dunams. After the Executive meeting he wrote in his diary: "I explained my ideas to him [Weizmann]. I did not feel they made a great impression . . ." (1937) We may disagree with Ruppin's conclusion, but we cannot accuse him of not having learnt the bitter lesson of life side-by-side with the Arabs.

And finally—the White Paper:

> The White Paper was eventually published yesterday. It contains no surprise. . . . I do not know why, but this document irritates me far less than it irritates all the other Jews. Is it because I have grown old, and my senses are dulled? Or perhaps it is because I no longer believe in policies on paper? This White Paper is a direct function of a specific political setup (a united Arab front, England's fear of the Arabs) and it will be just as short-lived as this political setup. (1939)

Chief of staff, officers and guests: I trust you will forgive me for having spoken at length. In other circumstances, I would have been able to end at this point. But in the present forum and in these days, in surveying the development of Ruppin's ideas on the Arab question, I do not want to avoid making a number of concrete observations.

Firstly about what Ruppin called "political setup." When he said that the White Paper was the product of a political setup, and that this would leave nothing of the White Paper when it vanished, he was perfectly correct. Ruppin understood this, not because old age had dulled his senses, but because he had amassed wisdom during his years of work. His view of the White Paper was the result of his understanding, and not of dull senses.

Between then and now, the political setup has in fact changed entirely. A Jewish State has been established, with close to three million inhabitants. We have been victorious in three wars. We have an army whose strength should not be underestimated, and a people standing behind it, investing huge sums of money to aid our economy. Second, the dimensions have changed. When Ruppin thought in terms of Arabs, he meant the Palestine Arabs. When we talk about Arabs nowadays, we mean the Arab states. Not only that, but these states are also supported by the world's second greatest power—the Soviet Union.

Dimensions have changed in the "demographic question" in terms of the size of our own population as well as that of the Palestine Arabs. Geographically, too, there have been changes in the areas settled by us, as well as the areas occupied by our forces today.

Third, the facts are no longer the same. Ruppin was wrong to hope that by creating facts, tensions between us and the Arabs would be lessened. What greater "creation of facts" could there be than the establishment of the State, the concentration of 2.5m. Jews there, and the victories in three wars? But despite this, do the Arabs today agree to sign a peace agreement with us? The facts have been created, but the tension is no less than it was before.

Here I shall permit myself to add one observation. We see the facts which we ourselves create, but everybody who believes that facts are decisive in this issue, must remember that the Arabs, too, could well point to facts—their large and steadily increasing numbers, their influence in the world, the oil resources at their disposal, and so forth. In other words, everybody who adheres to the formula whereby the facts we create will bring the other side to accept us, can just as well point to significant facts on the Arab side the moment he steps into the Arabs' shoes.

At any rate, if we return to Ruppin's forecasts, the facts he hoped for, as regards the increase in strength and numbers, did come to pass. But I fear that they have not yet convinced the Arabs to accept us, or our political existence, to regard us as an acceptable neighbour state with equal rights. Perhaps Ruppin's error on this point stemmed from the fact that he thought in rational categories, whereas Arab opposition stems from emotions.

Fourth, there is his letter to Jacobson of April 12, 1931—about the prospects of an agreement with the Arabs, in which he said: "What we can get today from the Arabs, we don't need. What we need—we can't get.'' This definition sounds to me very up-to-date, when I sometimes read that today the Arabs are offering us the 1947 partition plans.

And finally, today too, unfortunately, a year after the war, and despite the fact that we are standing on the Suez Canal and on the River Jordan, in Gaza and in Nablus; despite all our efforts—including a willingness for far-reaching concessions—to bring the Arabs to the peace table—the things which Ruppin said 32 years ago still seem sound. It was during the 1936 riots that he wrote:

> The Arabs do not agree to our venture. If we want to continue our work in Eretz Israel against their desires, there is no alternative but that lives should be lost. It is our destiny to be in a state of continual warfare with the Arabs. This situation may well be undesirable, but such is the reality.

Annexation and Democracy

By Yehoshua Arieli*

My subject today is democracy and the problem of the occupied territories. I will commence by saying that more than one year and a half has elapsed since the war; the peace that was expected at the close of the war hasn't come and the prospects of obtaining it seem to be decreasing. This change in the prospects of peace and of the perspective in general has also led to changes in attitudes towards the occupied territories. It actually seemed at one time that the policies conducted particularly in Samaria and Judea held hopes of creating some kind of normalization. Today, things look different, but then it appeared as if the policy of open bridges would help maintain the status quo without harming too much the national sentiments of the population of these territories.

The same thing happened as far as Sinai is concerned. It can be said that the Sinai Peninsula has become a permanent element in not only military, but also, to some extent, economic planning. As far as the Sinai Peninsula is concerned, here too there seems to be a growing impression that occupation will be maintained for a long time. The formula which the National Unity Government adopted a year and a half ago of holding on to the territories until a negotiated peace has been achieved, has for all practical purposes turned into an excuse not to state the terms and aims of the peace and at the same time not to define clearly the aims and methods in the occupied territories, in the fear that any definition con-

* Reprinted by special permission from *New Outlook*, July, 1969.

cerning either peace or the territories would lead to breaking up the coalition and the beginning of a domestic struggle that all sides, of course, want to avoid.

It is therefore not surprising that in this present, what seems to be interim and undefined period, there is a growing tendency, of indeterminate strength, to believe that it is to Israel's advantage to hold on as long as possible, or forever, to the status quo. This view has been explicitly formulated by the group that has made it its ideology: the Movement for a Greater Israel. I am convinced that if the views of this group, or of those knowingly or not close to it, were adopted as policy by the Government, they would have led us to the edge of the abyss and threatened the very existence of the State of Israel. They would destroy our democracy, damage our souls and create a fanatic and retrogressive society in Israel, culturally and morally. Indeed, you have to be either a demagogue or very naive to say that the path to peace is a short one and that we are sure to find it. There is, however, a tremendous difference between policies that are imposed upon us by the force of reality and those we choose for ourselves as desirable. The partisans of annexation and of including the territories within the State of Israel as an aim and goal of policy, bar the way to any other solution and are prepared to endanger both peace and security for an aim which may have various justifications, into which I won't go here.

The question that arises is, therefore, what would happen—and I shall speak only of the domestic aspects—if we really carried out the policy of permanently including the territories formally, or even informally, within the borders of the State of Israel.

I see the danger in three fields: in that of the political regime, of society, and of personal and collective attitudes. The famous Spanish-American philosopher, George Santayana, once said that anyone who isn't prepared to learn from history will have to repeat it. Those who love their country and are concerned over its fate must look at the problems not from the aspect of the present situation or of our desires, but historically, and ask, what will happen, how will our society develop in the supposed new situation of annexing the territories. Implementing a program of that kind would lead to immediate changes in two fields: in our international status and in the composition of the society that for practical purposes would be under the jurisdiction of the State of Israel; in other words, the national composition of our population. As I have already pointed out, the State of Israel has so far defined its position in keeping with international practice, that is that a settlement reached with the signing of a peace treaty would include the return of the occupied territories to a full or at least great extent.

However, if, in one way or another, we were to begin actually to annex the territories and to ignore the fact that we were only in an interim situation, our international situation would change radically. It could be assumed—and today after the illusions that certain circles cultivated concerning America have proven false—it is even clearer that theoretical or practical policies of annexation would have left us in a situation of international isolation, and facing not only a U.N. condemnation but the danger of perhaps being expelled from the U.N. or of the application of sanctions. If we assume that for domestic reasons the United States would not have wanted to participate, these sanctions would be made the responsibility of other countries who were ready to apply them, and we would thereby become a country under siege.

The Siege Situation

I do not want to prophecy whether the State of Israel would be ready to enter into that situation or could hold out in such a situation. For the sake of argument I will assume that we could hold out in a situation of siege and total isolation, the way Rhodesia is actually doing. In many ways, though, of course, the situation isn't the same. Our geopolitical environment is unlike that of Rhodesia. We don't have the tremendous support of a great and rich country like South Africa, nor do the new nations of Africa resemble the Arab world. But let us assume for a moment that we could succeed in holding out in such a situation. There is no doubt that for a state under siege the permanent condition of life is one of war as a natural state of affairs, of being permanently preoccupied with fighting for its very existence. Both society and government would have to reorganize themselves on the basis of a permanent state of emergency. All the economic and human resources would be permanently mobilized to maintain the state's existence and security; the planning and control of manpower resources and economic factors would be concentrated in the hands of an emergency authority. In such conditions no country can allow itself the luxury of party politics or of using the country's resources for the wasteful ways of a working democracy. Actually a kind of unity would have to be established that would not permit any deviations or outlays that were not related to the emergency situation. In this situation, the State cannot be dependent upon a public opinion which may not always support it and will have to guide public opinion and impose on it those views that fit in with what the government thinks necessary for the emergency.

In such a situation the society would also adopt the hierarchical structure of the army command in which the borders between civil and military fields would tend to disappear and in which a new ruling bureaucratic, technological, military and managerial elite would be formed, no longer dependent upon institutions and processes based on the democratic procedure of elections, representation and public control. A state of emergency demands internal cohesion and cannot afford freedom of expression.

Censorship and public indoctrination would become necessary to maintain the state of emergency.

We can also assume that the Arab population of the territories would intensify its resistance and terror if this situation became a permanent one for it. The authorities would therefore have to apply increasingly harsh measures of repression, leading to a further vicious circle of terror and repression. Concomitantly with the society's adaption to the state of emergency politically and socially, a process of psychological adaptation would also have to take place. It is impossible to maintain a situation of war under conditions of emergency and fear for an extended time, without the individual's developing defense mechanisms making it possible to withstand the tension of continuing danger and strain.

This last need creates a tendency to reject any criticism coming from the outside and to develop a fanatic nationalism and selfrighteousness refusing to consider any alternatives or to listen to the voice of doubt. A value system will come into being centered completely around the values and norms of national cohesion and national identification. There would also come into being a strange combination of narrow-minded tribalism and fanatic, historic nationalism. That is the kind of combination that exists today in South Africa and which, to some extent, has always been present in situations like those described above.

Ultimately we would be driven into a situation that the American sociologist, Harold Lasswell, has called the "garrison state." This is not a new phenomenon; it has appeared in history at various times and in similar situations. The Spartan community was like that, as were the states established by the feudal warrior-classes in the Middle Ages, the Turkish Mongols at certain times, Sweden at the beginning of the 18th and France in the 19th centuries. As for the 20th century, I shall only recall Japan and South Africa, and, to a certain degree, Soviet Russia.

I have just spoken of the problems implied by international isolation which could be a result of adopting decisions in keeping with the views of our maximalist movement. However, even if we assume, for the sake of argument, that we won't have to face that kind of situation, that we won't be isolated, that we will find persons or groups or countries to help us out of the siege, the question still remains: What will our situation be like politically and socially from the standpoint of the relations between the Arab minority and ourselves if we absorb the large Arab minority of the occupied territories into our midst.

Arabs in a Jewish State

There is no doubt that if we add the Arabs of the West Bank and Gaza to our present Arab citizens, we are talking about one and a quarter million inhabitants today. If we assume that the Arab natural increase and our natural increase plus immigration remain more or less stable, it is not hard to see that within a short time the Arab minority will grow to about 40 per cent. How will a state with a 40 per cent Arab minority be able to maintain and develop its institutions and unique democratic character?

Among the members of the Greater Israel Movement, and its knowing and unknowing supporters, there are some who argue that it would be possible to grant immediate civil rights to the large minority on condition that the State forego its national and Zionist character. I have no debate with these people since it is clear that giving up the State's mission puts the situation of the Arabs in a new light, though I doubt whether the Arab side, for its part, would be prepared to give up its own national character. My argument, however, is with those circles who, in the name of Jewish history, of the historic rights of the Jewish people, of Israel's security as a Jewish State, want to annex this minority and thereby, with their own hands, destroy the character of our society as both a Jewish society and a democratic one.

We, therefore, have to ask what would happen if, as we would be obliged to do, we granted equal civil rights to this large Arab minority. From this standpoint, the State of Israel is undoubtedly not like other countries. There are countries, especially in the West, and my example is the United States, where both nationality and citizenship are defined in general and universal terms. That is—both citizens and the state are defined in inclusive terms permitting any person to become a citizen and identify himself with the state. The definition of citizens may either be historical or universal as in the United States and to some lesser extent in the enlightened democracies of Europe.

The situation in Israel is different. Without going into evaluations or into details, Israel is the national state *par excellence*. It is the classic antithesis to American democracy from the viewpoint of national character. The State of Israel's uniqueness lies first and foremost in the simple fact that it was formed and exists in order to solve the problem of the Jewish people as a whole, which is dispersed the world over and which can return to its land if it wants. What is more, this state's function is not limited, as in most of the countries existing today, to those problems deriving from the existing population within its borders. The state's functions are transcendental—that is, go beyond the borders of the State and beyond the given present to the future and to the people as a whole, in order to solve its problem.

It is clear now that for this kind of state and nationalism the possibilities of non-Jewish identification are limited. Even when the non-Jew has full rights, can identify with the society as one maintaining law and security, supplying services and the possibilities of livelihood and personal development, he can only if he is a Zionist at heart identify himself with the transcendental aims of the state. This is true too for the Arab community living in the country who are citizens of Israel and whom we considered full citizens. Though this minority never fled or was caused to flee from the country, has lived and chosen to live with us from the very beginning, has developed with the State of Israel itself, improved its situation and found many common points of contact with the state, there is still no doubt that this minority has been torn in its hearts and in its loyalties.

However, there is a considerable difference between the situation of the Arab citizens of Israel and the large minority we are adding to them, on whom we are imposing citizenship against its will, which has been educated in blind hatred for 20 years, has gone through the suffering of the refugee camps and therefore justly or unjustly looked upon this country as an expropriator. In practice, we can assume that this minority would never be ready to accept citizenship, and if it accepted it with its 40 per cent minority, would form an irredentist movement destroying the democratic structure of the country and compelling us against our will to move from a situation of equality and equal citizenship to increasing repression and all that involved.

Dangers of Discrimination

I therefore, don't assume that that would be the path we would take. It is much more reasonable to assume that those supporting this aim are actually talking of what they call encouraging emigration of a transition period without civil rights. It is clear that as long as this encouragement of emigration is left to natural trends, it will not succeed. The Arabs have learnt the lesson that it doesn't pay to leave this country if there is no need. This encouragement would, therefore, have to adopt other methods, which would only intensify the hatred of the refugees and worsen their situation immeasurably, or compel us to go over to a situation of open discrimination.

It is clear that a situation of complete discrimination would bring us back to the same situation that I spoke of when I spoke of the results of international isolation. It would put us into a situation where the state would have to deny to one part of its population its essential rights. It would have to differentiate between the one community and the other, and here I would like to quote Abraham Lincoln, changing only one word, that: a democratic government cannot remain for a long time half democratic and half oppressive. It must change and become either the one or the other. I have no doubt what would happen to us. We would have to adapt ourselves to a state that was unwillingly turning into a police state, to a government whose need to maintain a special class with the responsibility for repression would affect its own mentality. We would have lost our souls for some additional territory.

I have drawn for you here the two results that seem to me to be inevitable if we make the inclusion of the Arab community and the annexation of territory an end in itself rather than a temporary problem which we have to solve. Finally I would like to point out that in these circles—which to my sorrow include persons who grew up in the labor movement and were educated to socialism—we find developing a kind of nationalist and mythological mentality which prepare them psychologically and intellectually for a situation in which one part of the State would become a ruling people and the other part a people without rights and without self-determination.

I don't say that these attitudes are held today by a large part of the Jewish community. On the contrary, I am sure that their part is small, though it is very influential and vocal especially in the mass media. But I would like to warn ourselves not to allow ourselves to drift against our will and by endless improvisations, into a position and situation that will force us into roles and activities we would abhor and avoid by all means if we had a choice.

Speech (October 15, 1973)

By Hafiz al-Asad*

Brother compatriots, brother military men, sons of our Arab people, with great pride in you and your great steadfastness I address you today from the bastion of steadfastness, the immortal Damascus whose great steadfastness against the enemy's barbarous raids has become the symbol of the steadfastness of our entire Arab homeland and a cause for pride of all our Arab nation. This city will remain as towering as [Mount] Qasyun in the protection of its sons who are meeting the challenges with strong resolve and who are facing difficulties, no matter how big, with more resolve and iron will and increased determination to achieve victory.

The steadfastness of Damascus stems from the steadfastness of its sister towns of this struggling country; from the steadfastness of Homs, Latakia, Tartus and Baniyas, and also from the steadfastness of Cairo and every capital, town and village in the Arab homeland. This is because, basically, this steadfastness is the practical expression of the will of our people and their determination to live the life of dignity to which they aspire and to make bright the future that they wish for themselves and for all the peoples of the world.

Ten days ago I addressed you on the day which marked the end of a stage during which the enemy had wanted his repeated aggressions to consolidate occupation and expansion and pave the way for imposing his will on our nation. Today I address you as the battle takes its real shape

* President and Supreme Commander of the Armed Forces, Syria. Radio and television broadcast (Damascus).

as a full war of liberation. Its first achievement has been the liberation of the Arab will from the elements of pressure. God willing, it will end with the liberation of the land which its sons have long desired.

In those 10 glorious days of ferocious battles waged by our armed forces with all their arms and with extreme manhood, bravery and unshakable faith in victory—in those days of magnificent, heroic steadfastness of our people we corrected many erroneous ideas which had almost become established abroad about our nation. We have restored self-confidence to the Arab individual after dressing his wounded dignity and proving to the enemy and all the world that our people are not an easy prey that the enemy thought it could easily swallow. We have proved that certain death awaits anyone who tries to humiliate our people or debase an inch of our land.

You have revived the traditions of our glorious nation, of the fathers and the forefathers. You have pleased God, the homeland and the sense of moral goodness. With chaste blood you have charted on the map of Arab struggle a road which will never change after today. It is a road to victory.

You have been supporting the cause of your nation and therefore your nation rose to support your steadfastness. You have been with the cause of freedom and therefore the free men in the world rushed to express their support for your giant stand. They have expressed it in various ways.

You have won the respect, appreciation and admiration of everyone. The reason for all this was our steadfastness, both by civilians and military, in our readiness to meet hardship with selflessness and in our insistence on proceeding steadily towards the goal, regardless of how costly the sacrifice or however long the road.

During these critical days I was, through my senses and feelings, with every individual. I was with the soldier, the NCO and officer while smashing the enemy tanks with his tank, shelling the concentrations of aggressors with his gun and directing precise fire at the enemy planes which fell in wreckage on the ground; I was with the pilot while defending the homeland's sky with his plane, chasing the enemy planes and smashing the legend of the invincible Israeli air force; I was with the sailor while protecting our coasts with his naval unit and gun and writing new chapters of Arab glory on the seas; I was with every citizen of our noble people; with the worker in his factory while operating the machine with one hand and carrying arms with the other; with the peasant while tilling the land and carrying his rifle; with the employee in his office while doing his duty towards his compatriots in the best manner and with a sense of responsibility; with the man responsible for security and civil defence while carrying out his duties with loyalty and devotion; with the doctor and the nurse as they stood in complete readiness and preparedness to fulfill humane and national duties; with the merchant in his shop as he met the needs of citizens with high patriotic spirit; with the housewives as they cared for the families and children; and with the army of loyal and sincere citizens in their various jobs as they managed the homeland's daily life.

Brothers, you may have questions on your mind which you would probably expect me to answer. Or perhaps you wish me to talk about national and international activities related to the battle, whether these were of a positive or negative nature. But you realize that war has its conditions and requirements which make it incumbent upon us to avoid discussing any matter that would not benefit the war effort.

Nevertheless, in this regard I am anxious to point out that our steadfastness in the war of liberation has begun to give the slogan, "pan-Arabism of the battle", a practical and real meaning. In this regard I would like to express, on your behalf, the greatest appreciation for the role of the sisterly Iraqi forces whose men fought heroically against the enemy and whose blood was mixed with that of their brothers in the Syrian forces. Their participation in the battle has been a true expression of the pan-Arabism of the battle. Greetings to the Iraqi Army and to our people in sisterly Iraq.

The day will come when the Saudi forces and the Jordanian forces will also take part in the battle and play their role in the national battle. Also, the two sisterly states Algeria and Libya, from the first moment [of the battle] took the initiative to give practical backing and actual support with various forms. The United Arab Amirates and the state of Qatar also extended a helping hand.

The support that was given to the northern front was matched by support to the western front where the valiant Egyptian forces are fighting major battles against the enemy after they humiliated him and defeated him. This defeat made the enemy resort to contradictions and exposed him to the entire world. This happened when the Egyptians crossed the Suez Canal, destroyed the enemy fortified positions and continued their advance into Sinai steadily and with strength.

If this indicates anything, it indicates Arab unity. It also indicates that our nation is alive. Our unity and vitality appear most gloriously during crises and hardships. We should not forget that our steadfastness is the fundamental and basic factor in every stand. On this rock all the enemy's attempts will be crushed. Continuous steadfastness increases the rally of the Arab nation around us and their support for us will double.

Our heroes have transformed Israel's aggression, since 6th October, to a retreat of the enemy forces. As I told you on that day, our forces rushed to repulse the aggression, forcing the occupation forces to withdraw before them. They continued their advance and expelled the enemy forces from Mount Hermon, Qunaytirah, Jibbin, Khushniyah, Jukhadar, Awl Al, Tall al-Faras and Rafid and other villages and positions in the Golan. They inflicted on the enemy losses which deeply shook the Zionist entity. At that time, while the enemy was hiding his losses and defeats from the people of Israel and from the outside world—a method which he is still following—we in turn kept quiet about the victories of our forces and postponed announcing them.

While the enemy's reports and statements exposed themselves day after day and uncovered more contradictions, we preferred to wait before announcing what we had achieved and until the repelling of the enemy forces is final and the liberation of the land is complete.

We could have announced the liberation of the greater part of the Golan on the fourth day of the battle. The faith of our armed forces in God—praise be to Him—as well as our armed forces' confidence in our people, their proper use of the good weapons in their possession, and their faith in the cause they are fighting for have all reflected on the course of fighting through the victories that our forces have achieved and are still achieving in every field and on every level. The heroic acts of our army have compelled the enemy to admit that the battle is tough and that the fighting is intense.

On our part, we have not anticipated an easy victory or that the enemy would accept his expulsion from our land without ferocious resistance. We know the enemy's expansionist ambitions and know that there are forces encouraging these ambitions and supporting the attempts to achieve these ambitions. In the aftermath of his losses and defeats in the first days of fighting, the enemy hastened to enlist the help of these forces, asking them for assistance and large numbers of foreigners to offset his losses in men in the various corps, particularly the air force as well as new weapons to offset his losses in weapons. With the quick supplies he received and which were added to the calculated reserve forces, the enemy heavily concentrated on one sector of our front and began to exert pressure with the larger part of his forces, tanks and planes and was able to achieve a limited penetration of our lines. Nevertheless, our forces initiated a quick reply and waged, from new positions, fierce fighting in which every member of our forces fought most valiantly and repulsed the enemy counter-offensive and inflicted heavy losses on his tanks and planes and forced him to retreat.

Our forces continue to pursue the enemy and strike at him and will continue to strike at enemy forces until we regain our positions in our occupied land and continue then until we liberate the whole land.

We know that our enemy has a source to supply him and offset his losses in men and weapons. However, we are confident of the resources of our people and nation and the sources of our support. I say to those who are supporting the falsehood and aggression of Israel that they should consider and think of the consequences that their hostile aggressive attitudes will have on their many interests in the Arab homeland. By gaining the animosity of the masses of our nation, they are arousing the anger of these masses. And when peoples become angry, no force can stand in their way.

Brother compatriots, brother soldiers, freedom and dignity have a price and the price is no doubt costly. However, we are ready to pay this price in order to preserve honour, to defend freedom, to liberate the land and to regain the rights so that we can give the coming Arab generations their right to an affluent life and a shining, smiling future in which they can enjoy freedom, security, reassurance and peace.

We are knocking at the door of freedom with our hands and with all our strength, realizing that the enemies of peoples do not voluntarily recognize the freedom of these peoples. We are determined that the liberation of the land and the achievement of victory in this war be the great goal from which we shall not budge, God willing. For the sake of the great goal, every sacrifice and effort will be cheap. As long as our goal is great and as long as we believe in this goal, our effort and struggle will be commensurate with our goal. As long as we believe in the goal, all enemy efforts and psychological warfare tactics will be defeated and fail and will definitely not affect the morale of our people and their ability to hold out and resist.

We are a people who, in the hour of decisiveness, are capable of creating miracles. The hour of decisiveness has come. Let us adapt ourselves to continue the war of liberation to its victorious end. Let us continue the war of liberation with a deep breath, believing in God, confident in ourselves and of our ability to make victory with our own hands.

Finally, on your behalf, I convey a greeting—coming from a heart full of love and appreciation—to all the men of our armed forces. I hail their courage, valour, high efficiency, firm faith in the cause of their homeland and their certain capability to wrest the right. Greetings from the heart to every Arab soldier who is helping to make victory in the battle of liberation certain. Greetings to every one of you. Let us all reiterate at all times: either martyrdom or victory.

Message to Hawari Boumedien
(October 9, 1973)

By Leonid I. Brezhnev*

President Hawari Boumedien [of Algeria] late last night received the USSR Ambassador, who handed him an important message from the CPSU Central Committee General Secretary on the Middle East situation. The message said:

The responsibility for the new military flare-up in the Middle East lies wholly and completely with the Tel Aviv leaders. While enjoying the support and protection of imperialist circles, Israel continues its aggression started in 1967 against the Arab countries, and foils every effort to establish a just peace in the Middle East and deliberately carries out provoca-

---

* As broadcast at Algiers.

tions, including armed provocations, against Syria, Egypt and Lebanon, thus aggravating to the extreme the situation in this region.

I believe, dear comrade President, you agree that [in] the struggle at present being waged against Israeli aggression, for the liberation of Arab territories occupied in 1967 and the safeguarding of the legitimate rights of the Arab people of Palestine, Arab fraternal solidarity must, more than ever before, play a decisive role. Syria and Egypt must not be alone in their struggle against a treacherous enemy. There is an urgent need for the widest aid and support of the progressive regimes in these countries who, like Algeria, are the hope for progress and freedom in the Arab world.

The Central Committee of the CPSU and the Soviet Government are firmly convinced that the Algerian leaders, who are widely experienced in the anti-imperialist struggle, understand full well all the peculiarities of the present situation and that, guided by the ideals of fraternal solidarity, will use every means and take every step required to give their support to Syria and Egypt in the tough struggle imposed by the Israeli aggressor.

Dear comrade President, your high personal prestige in the Third World countries which in particular contributed to the great success of the fourth non-aligned conference, clearly gives you the indisputable means to act with the Arab states with a view to bringing about a united stand in the face of the common danger.

As for the Soviet Union, it gives to the friendly Arab states multilateral aid and support in their just struggle against the imperialist Israeli aggression.

Speech (October 16, 1973)

By Anwar Sadat*

In the name of God, brothers and sisters, I would have liked to have come to you before today and meet you and the masses of our people and nation, but I was preoccupied with what you know about and in the way you want. I am confident that you will understand and excuse me.

However, I felt your presence and that of our people and nation with me in every opinion. I felt your presence and that of our people and nation with me in every decision. You were all with me in the matter that I have shouldered as an expression of the will of the nation and of the destiny of a people.

Then I found it suitable to come to you today to speak to you and to the masses of our people and the peoples of our nation as well as to a world that is interested in what is happening in our land because it is

* Address to the People's Assembly (Cairo).

closely related to humanity's gravest issues, the issue of war and peace. This is because we do not consider our patriotic and national struggle as a local or regional phenomenon, since the area in which we live has its strategic and cultural role at the heart of the world and the centre of its movement. And since the events are important and the developments were successive and the decisions were decisions of destiny, I would like to begin straight away with what I would like to talk to you about. I shall concentrate on two points: war and peace.

First, war. I do not think you expect me to stand before you so that we can together boast about what we have achieved in 11 days of the most important and gravest—in fact the greatest and most glorious—days in our history.

Perhaps the day may come when we shall sit together, not to boast, but to remember and to study and also to teach our children and grand-children generation after generation the story and hardships of struggle, the bitterness and sufferings of defeat and the sweetness and hopes of victory. Yes, the day will come when we shall sit and relate what everyone of us has done in his own position and how everyone of us shouldered his trust and carried out his role. We shall tell how the heroes of this people and this nation came out in pitch black days to carry the lighted torches to lighten the path so that their nation can cross the bridge between despair and hope. The time will come for all that.

I think you will agree with me that we have problems and tasks to which we must devote all our time and efforts. If I may pause a little— although I know that you are craving to hear more—then I say the following:

(1) Regarding myself I have tried to fulfil my pledges to God and to you exactly three years ago today. I pledged to God and to you that the question of liberating the patriotic and national soil was the first respon- sibility I assumed in loyalty to our people and to everyone. I pledged to God and to you that I would spare no efforts or sacrifices, regardless of their costs to me, for the sake of enabling the nation to reach a situation where it can raise its will to the level of its aspirations. For I have always believed and still do that a wish not backed by will is like daydreaming. My love for and loyalty to this homeland refused to fall prey to the mirage or fog of daydreaming. . . .

I say without pretence that history will record for this nation that its setback was not a downfall but a passing stumble, and that its movement was not an outburst but a lofty rise. Our people have exerted unlimited efforts, made unlimited sacrifices and shown unlimited maturity. More important than all that—the efforts, sacrifices and maturity—the people have maintained unlimited faith. This was the dividing line between the setback and failure.

I have felt that from the first day I assumed responsibility and willingly accepted the burdens God placed on my shoulders, I knew that the people's faith was the foundation. If the foundation were sound, then we could regain everything that we lost and once again return to the place we retreated from. Despite many manifestations, some of which were natural and others fabricated owing to the psychological warfare waged against us, the question facing me and others every succeeding day was: is the foundation sound? I was confident that no psychological warfare, no matter how fierce, could affect the firmness of this foundation. So long as the foundation was all right, then everything else should be all right. The rest was nothing but a storm in a teacup, as they say.

I (? admit) we faced many real problems, problems in the services, supply, and production and also in political work. I knew the truth, but I was not in a position to explain it. I knew that we had to make life bearable for the people and at the same time take precautions for what was expected. I was certain that the day would come when the truth would be known to others as it was clear to me. When the truth is known, the people will know and appreciate it. I thank God.

(3) There were clear indications that the entire Arab nation was in a state of rupture. I thought this was natural because of social and cultural reasons that were aggravated by the bitterness of the setback. Some asked me and asked themselves as well: Will the nation be able to face its terrible trial while in this state of rupture? I used to say: In addition to its natural causes, this rupture reflects the contrast between reality and hope. There is no advantage in this. I even believed that there would be no cure or rest from what the nation's conscience was suffering from, except when the nation would face the moment of challenge. At certain times I was not prepared to enter into futile discussions: Should we deal with the rupture before facing the challenge, or accept the challenge despite the presence of indications of rupture? My opinion has been that nations can discover themselves or their mettle only through engaging in struggle. The greater the challenge is, the greater will be the awakening of the nation and its discovery of its capabilities.

I do not deny the existence of social and cultural differences, for this is the course of history. But at the same time I realize that great nations, when faced with great challenges, are capable of clearly determining the priorities for themselves in a way that leaves no room for doubt. I have believed in the soundness and firmness of the call of Arab nationalism. I have been aware of the various interactions which motivate the progress of the one nation. But I have also been confident that unity of action would impose itself on all the powers, quarters and currents because they would all realize that the present condition is not one for competition between various interpretations, but one of struggle involving the life or death of an entire nation, thank God.

(4) I have been aware of the quality of our armed force. When I spoke about them I was not predicting the future or speculating. I have come up

from the ranks of these armed forces and personally lived according to their traditions. I had the honour of serving in their ranks and under their banners. The record of these forces is bright, but our enemies—old and new imperialism and world Zionism—concentrated against this record in a terrible manner because they wanted to make the nation doubt its shield and its sword. I had no doubt whatsoever that these armed forces were the victim but never the cause of the 1967 setback.

In 1967 these forces would have been able to fight with the same valour and courage with which they are fighting today had their military command not lost its nerve after the strike against which Abd an-Nasir [Nasser] had warned, or had the command not issued an order at that time for a general retreat from Sinai without Abd an-Nasir's knowledge as well. These forces were not given the chance to fight in defence of the nation, its honour and its soil. They were not defeated by the enemy but were exhausted by the conditions, which did not give them a chance to fight. I participated with Jamal Abd an-Nasir in the rebuilding of the armed forces. Then destiny decreed that I should bear the responsibility of completing the rebuilding operation as well as of being their supreme commander.

The Egyptian armed forces have achieved a miracle by any military standard. They have fully devoted themselves to their duty. They have efficiently absorbed all the weapons and methods of training of the modern age, as well as its sciences.

When I gave them the order to reply to the enemy's provocation and to check his deceit, they proved themselves. After the orders were given them, these forces took the initiative, surprised the enemy and threw him off balance with their quick movement. I shall not be exaggerating to say that military history will make a long pause to study and examine the operation carried out on 6th October 1973 when the Egyptian armed forces were able to storm the difficult barrier of the Suez Canal which was armed with the fortified Bar Lev Line to establish bridgeheads on the east bank of the Canal after they had, as I said, thrown the enemy off balance in six hours.

The risk was great and the sacrifices were big. However, the results achieved in the first six hours of the battle in our war were huge. The arrogant enemy lost its equilibrium at this moment. The wounded nation restored its honour.

The Middle East political map has changed. While we say so out of pride, as some of the pride is faith, we are duty bound to record here, on behalf of the people and this nation, our absolute confidence in our armed forces; our confidence in their command, which drew up the plan; our confidence in the officers and men who have implemented the plan with fire and blood. We record our confidence in the armed forces' faith and knowledge, our confidence in the armed forces' arms and in their capability of absorbing the arms. I say in brief that this homeland can be assured and feel secure, after fear, that it now has a shield and a sword.

From here I want to draw your attention with me to the northern front, where the great Syrian army is fighting one of the most glorious battles of the Arab nation under the loyal and resolute command of brother President Hafiz al-Asad.

I want to tell our brothers on the northern front: You made a promise and you were faithful to the promise. You made a friendship and you have turned out to be the most honest friends. You have fought and you have proved to be the most courageous fighters. You have fought like men and stood fast like heroes. We could not have found more reassuring and praiseworthy men in this comradeship in which we had to fight together against a common enemy, the enemy of the whole Arab nation.

We have been the vanguards of the battle. Together we have borne its brunt and paid most dearly with our blood and resources. We shall continue the fighting and defy danger. We shall continue, backed by our brothers who have sincerely and faithfully joined the battle, to pay the price in sweat and blood until we reach an objective acceptable to us and to our nation in this serious stage of its continuous struggle.

That was about war—and now that about peace. When we speak about peace we must remember and not forget—just as others also must not pretend to forget—the real reasons for our war. You will allow me specifically and categorically to put some of these reasons to you.

(1) We have fought for the sake of peace, the only peace that really deserves to be called peace—peace based on justice. Our enemy sometimes speaks about peace. But there is a vast difference between the peace of aggression and the peace of justice. David Ben Gurion was the one who formulated for Israel the theory of imposing peace. Peace cannot be imposed. The talk about imposing peace means a threat to wage war or actually waging it.

The great mistake our enemy has made is that he thought the force of terror could guarantee security. But the futility of this theory has been proved in practice on the battlefield. It has been proved that if this theory did work at one time, due to the weakness of the opposite side, it does not work if these people rally their forces every day. I do not know what David Ben Gurion would think if he were in command in Israel today. Would he have been able to understand the nature of history or would he be like the Israeli command today—in opposition to history?

Peace cannot be imposed. The peace of a fait accompli cannot exist and cannot last. There can only be peace through justice alone. Peace cannot be established through terror however oppressive and whatever illusions the arrogance of power or the stupidity of power might give. Our enemy has persisted in this arrogance and stupidity not only over the past six years, but throughout the past 25 years—that is, since the Zionist state usurped Palestine.

We might ask the Israeli leaders today: Where has the theory of Israeli security gone? They have tried to establish this theory once by violence and once by force in 25 years. It has been broken and destroyed. Our military power today challenges their military power. They are now in a long protracted war. They are facing a war of attrition which we can tolerate more and better than they can. Their hinterland is exposed if they think they can frighten us by threatening the Arab hinterland. I add, so they may hear in Israel: We are not advocators of annihilation, as they claim.

Our Zafir-type trans-Sinai Egyptian Arab rockets are now in their bases ready to be launched at the first signal to the deepest depth in Israel.

We could have given the signal and the order from the very first moment of the battle, particularly as the Israelis' haughtiness and vicious pride gave them the illusion that they could bear greater consequences than they really could sustain. But we are aware of the responsibility of using certain types of arms, and we ourselves restrain ourselves from using them. The Israelis should remember what I once said and still say: an eye for an eye, a tooth for a tooth and death for death.

(2) We do not fight to attack the territory of others, but we fought and will continue to fight for two objectives: (a) to restore our territory which was occupied in 1967; and (b) to find ways and means to restore and obtain respect for the legitimate rights of the people of Palestine.

These are our objectives in accepting the risks of the fighting. We have accepted them in reply to unbearable provocations. We were not the first to begin these, but we acted in self-defence to defend our land and our right to freedom and life.

Our war was not for aggression, but against aggression. In our war we did not depart from the values and laws of international society as stipulated in the UN Charter, which the free nations have written with their blood after their victory over Fascism and Nazism.

We may say that our war is a continuation of humanity's war against Fascism and Nazism; for, by its racist claims and its reasoning of expansion through brute force, Zionism is nothing but a feeble replica of Fascism and Nazism which is contemptible rather than frightening and calls for disdain more than for hatred.

In our war we have behaved in accordance with the provisions and spirit of the UN Charter, and not vice versa. In addition, we have behaved out of respect for the UN resolutions, both those of the General Assembly and of the Security Council.

Brothers and sisters, the entire world has supported our rights and praised our courage in defending these rights. The world has realized that we were not the first to attack, but that we immediately responded to the duty of self-defence. We are not against but are for the values and laws of the international community. We are not warmongers but seekers of peace. The world has realized all this, and in the light of it sympathizes with our cause.

Today, the world sympathizes with us more out of its respect for our determination to defend this cause. We were sure of world sympathy, and now we are proud of its respect for us. I tell you in all sincerity and honesty that I prefer world respect, even without sympathy, to world sympathy that is without respect. I thank God.

Brothers and sisters, a single state has differed from the whole world —not just from us, but from the whole world, as I said. This state is the United States. The United States claims it was shocked because we tried to repulse the aggression. We do not understand how or why the United States was shocked. This state, it said, was not only shocked but has recovered from the shock without coming to its senses.

It is regrettable and sad that this should be the attitude of one of the two superpowers in this age. We were expecting; or perhaps wishing, despite all the indications and experiences, that the United States would recover from the surprise and come to its senses. But this did not happen. We have seen the United States recovering from the surprise and turning towards manoeuvres. Its first objective is to stop the fighting and bring a return to the lines that existed before 6th October. We could have been angered by this inverse logic, but we were not. This is because, on the one hand, we are confident of ourselves, and, on the other, we really do want to contribute to world peace.

The world is entering an era of detente between the two superpowers. Now we oppose the policy of detente. We had one reservation about this policy and this reservation still exists. If we want the world, after a world war has become impossible, to enter an era of peace, then peace is not an abstract or absolute meaning. Peace has one single meaning: that all the peoples of the world should feel that it is peace for them and not peace imposed on them.

I would like to say before you and to all the world that we want the policy of detente to succeed and to be consolidated. We are prepared to contribute to the success of this consolidation. But we rightly believe that this cannot happen while aggression is being committed against an entire Arab nation, which lies strategically in the heart of the world and possesses its most important economic resources. Any disregard of this logical fact is not only disregard but also an insult, which we do not accept, either for ourselves or for the world, which is aware of the importance and value of this area in which we live. Therefore, the world must realize now that this area can give and can withhold.

Brothers and sisters, the United States, after a manoeuvre we refused even to discuss—especially after we had forged the path of right with the force of arms—has resorted to a policy that neither we nor our Arab nation can keep silent about. It has established a quick bridge to transport military aid to Israel. The United States was not content with the fact that it was its arms that enabled Israel to obstruct all attempts for a peaceful solution of the Middle East question. It has now involved itself in something with more serious and more dangerous consequences.

While we are fighting aggression and are trying to remove its nightmare from over our occupied territories, the United States rushes to the aid of the aggressor to compensate him for his losses and to supply him with what he did not have before.

The United States has established a sea and air bridge along which new tanks, new aircraft, new guns, new rockets and new electronics [equipment] pour into Israel. We tell them: This will not frighten us. But before matters reach the point of no return, you and we must understand: What is this leading to, and for how long? Where [are you going] to, when we and not Israel shape the map of the Middle East? Where to, when your entire interests are with us and not with Israel? Where to and for how long?

Brothers and sisters, I have thought of sending President Richard Nixon a letter in which I would clearly define our position. But I hesitated lest this might be misinterpreted. For this reason, I have decided instead to address an open message to him from here. This is a message dictated not by fear but by confidence. It is a message that emanates not from weakness but from a genuine desire to protect peace and bolster detente. I wish to tell him clearly that our aim in the war is well known and there is no need for us to explain it again. If you want to know our terms for peace, then here is our peace plan:

(1) We have fought and will fight to liberate our territories which the Israeli occupation seized in 1967 and to find a means to retrieve and secure respect for the legitimate rights of the Palestinian people. In this respect, we uphold our commitment to the UN resolutions, [those of] the General Assembly and the Security Council.

(2) We are prepared to accept a cease-fire on the basis of the immediate withdrawal of the Israeli forces from all the occupied territories, under international supervision, to the pre-5th June 1967 lines.

(3) We are prepared, as soon as the withdrawal from all these territories has been completed, to attend an international peace conference at the United Nations, which I will try my best to persuade my comrades, the Arab leaders directly responsible for running our conflict with the enemy [to accept]. I will also do my best to convince the Palestine people's representatives about this so that they may participate with us and with the assembled states in laying down rules and regulations for a peace in the area based on the respect of the legitimate rights of all the peoples of the area.

(4) We are ready at this hour—indeed at this very moment—to begin clearing the Suez Canal and to open it for world navigation so that it may resume its role in serving world prosperity and welfare. I have actually issued an order to the head of the Suez Canal Authority to begin this operation on the day following the liberation of the eastern bank of the Canal. Preliminary preparations for this operation have already begun.

(5) In all this, we are not prepared to accept any ambiguous promises or loose words which can be given all sorts of interpretations and only

waste time in useless things and put our cause back to the state of inaction, which we no longer accept whatever reasons the others may have or whatever sacrifices we have to make. What we want now is clarity: clarity of aims and clarity of means.

Brothers and sisters, we have said our word. I pray to God Almighty that all will understand it within its true framework and will see it squarely and will assess matters rightly. The present hours demand the courage and the minds of men.

For our part, we are facing these hours with the humility of those who are true to God, to themselves, to their nation and to mankind. The biggest battles ever fought with conventional weapons, even in the wars between the giants, are taking place during these hours. Destinies are being shaped and relations are being determined during these hours. The relations that are being determined will impose themselves on the future and are asserting themselves even now.

During these hours heroes are marching forward. During these hours martyrs are falling or, rather, rising up. Conflicting feelings are felt during these hours, hours during which the feelings of happiness are mixed with other deep feelings. This is because we wanted and still want right and not war. But we wanted and still want right even if war was imposed on us. When the elation of victory filled all hearts, I— between myself and my God—was aware of all the sufferings we are undergoing for the sake of victory. I have been following the news of our victory with humility because I know the truth. The dear Almighty has taught us: You have been destined to fight although it is hateful to you [Koranic verse].

Brothers and sisters, these are the moments in which we know ourselves and know our friends and our foes. We have known ourselves; we have known our friends. They have been the most sincere and loyal friends that we could ask for. We have always known our enemy. We do not wish to increase the number of our enemies. On the contrary, we have given one message after another, one notification after another and one warning after another so as to give everyone an opportunity to make revisions [of their attitudes], hoping they would retreat. However, we are, God willing, capable, after saying the word and giving notification and warning, of dealing one blow after another. We shall know when, where and how to do so if they want to escalate what they are doing now.

The entire Arab nation, on whose behalf I take the liberty to speak, has not forgotten the positions taken up during these hours. The Arab nation will not forget the friends of these hours who stand with it. It will not forget the enemies of these hours who stand with its enemy.

God, be our support and guide. God, bless our people and our nation. God, you have promised and your promise is truth. If you support God He will support you and guide your steps. Peace be upon you.

Press Conference (October 31, 1973)

By Anwar Sadat*

. . . The second reason for accepting the cease-fire, in addition to the two superpowers' guarantees of this cease-fire and the immediate implementation of the resolution, is that frankly I do not fight against America. I fought Israel for 11 days. As the Israeli Defence Minister said yesterday, his ammunition would have run out in three days. This was also my assessment. But I am not prepared to fight America.

There was reaction to the cease-fire in this country, in the Arab nation and within our armed forces. But these are the reasons just as I am giving them. It is for these two reasons that I accepted the cease-fire.

In the military situation, there was this question of the wedge in the Deversoir area. In those 11 days everything was taking place in the east, then the new weapons arrived.

This operation reminds me of a similar one which took place about the end of the second world war. The attack was called the two-lands attack. The Allies had closed in on Germany. Then one day the weather forecast said the weather would not be good for flying. The Germans launched a suicidal operation and drove a huge wedge between the allied forces. It was a huge, suicidal operation. Acting on that famous Goebbels formula, the Germans wove a big story. Actually, Germany's fate was decided before that attack. Germany was finished, but it still carried out that desperate attack.

This was what happened. The Deversoir operation was exactly the same operation. It was a desperate operation. They came to the west bank for the purpose of causing confusion in the German fashion, as I told you. We noticed that Israel had adopted the Nazi mentality in all its actions, even in regard to the Bar Lev line they had set up to face us and the other lines behind it. It was exactly like the so-called Atlantic Wall. The Bar Lev line was the first wall followed by three other lines behind it. It was exactly like the situation in Normandy. They borrowed German methods and Goebbels's propaganda methods as well.

They created the Deversoir gap. It was a suicidal operation like that of the two-lands attack. It was, in fact, a small affair. We do not deny that there were errors on our part. The main purpose and aim of all this was for it to be a psychological and political operation rather than a military operation so that they could weave the big story that they have been weaving in the past five or six days. They created a major uproar in Europe

* Excerpt from a press conference at Cairo.

saying that they were about 50 kilometres or miles from Cairo, that they were on the west side and so forth. It was a huge psychological warfare operation to draw the attention of the whole world to the Israeli military.

The Israeli militarists themselves know better than anyone else that the wedge existing today, the pocket existing today on the west bank, is no more than a pocket. As a result the Israeli militarists exploited the cease-fire. They violated the cease-fire after we had accepted it and advanced so that they could say: We are about 50 miles from Cairo. We are on the west bank and are occupying so many square miles. We have seized a town, etc., etc., so we can make up for the Egyptian crossing and the storming of the Bar Lev line.

Our Egyptian young soldiers in the east, whether in the Second or Third Armies, are standing firm. The Israeli operation was no more than a psychological warfare operation. They tried to create a military victory out of it. It was a desperate operation, the aims of the operation are no more than psychological and political ones.

Now they say that they have cut off the Third Army's lines of communication and that they have encircled the Third Army. Just for your information, the Third Army is not only on the east [bank]. The Third Army holds a sector in the east and a larger sector in the west. They know what part of the Third Army is facing them in the west. The positions are intermingled. In the east there is the Third Army. So they came behind in the west. Behind them directly is the rest of the Third Army, or the major part of it. The positions are intermingled, but they wanted to claim: We have taken the west bank and encircled the Third Army.

The story of the Third Army has been exploited in the Goebbels manner. As I have told you, the Third Army has occupied positions and stands as firm as a rock on the east bank, that is, a part of the Third Army. The major part is in the west behind the Israelis. They know this, but they carried out the operation after the cease-fire and put me in a dilemma. Because, with the major part of the Third Army behind them in the west, I could storm my way through and finish off all these people between the east and the west, between the two flanks of the army, but we had committed ourselves to the cease-fire and were embarking on a new affair.

If peace is what is required, then we want peace. I am putting pressure on and restraining my military personnel with great difficulty, because they want to settle this matter and this entire problem. Settling it is easy and the Israelis know this. They know that settling it is easy. I reveal what the Israelis said. This is exposed and verbatim so that I will tell them, and they hear me now [as heard]. They told each other that their position, verbatim, is fragile. They hear me now.

My military personnel are asking me [to continue to fight] but I say let us not break the cease-fire. Let us not have more war. We want to proceed towards solving [the issue]. This is the reason for Isma'il Fahmi's visit to Washington. Presidents Brezhnev and Nixon are aware of all the details of this, minute by minute.

This is the military situation. There is one more point about the military situation. They went to Suez. The Goebbels of Tel Aviv announced that they had occupied Suez. They also took a picture of Mrs. Meir near one of the oil tanks in Suez. For three days they tried to occupy Suez but could not.

The UNEF commander entered Suez. He announced that there was nobody at all in Suez, that it has not been occupied, and that Suez is Egyptian. They wanted to occupy one of the canal towns, particularly Suez because the Canal is named after it. [They tried] for three days. Suez town's resistance and the number of tanks it destroyed merits great praise. The resistance prevented the Israelis from occupying an inch of Suez town.

The Israelis stayed out near Zaytiyah. They brought Mrs. Meir and took her picture near one of the Zaytiyah oil tanks. This was a psychological operation aimed at shaking us. This would enable them to claim that Suez is finished and that they are marching towards Cairo. This is Goebbels's method of propaganda. This is psychological warfare. No, we will not be affected. Our nerves are very strong.

Speech (April 3, 1974)

By Anwar Sadat*

I want to digress here a while to talk about the war decision. You recall that in 1971, I announced that this year must be the year of decision. You also recall that during the same year, 1971, only a few months had passed since I assumed my office. I made an initiative on 4th February 1971 after the termination of the second cease-fire, which was due to be ended on 5th February 1971, for the sake of peace.

The US Secretary of State, Mr. Rogers, came in May 1971. You will also recall that he announced he had nothing to request from Egypt— nothing. After the announcement of the initiative in February, he announced in May that he had nothing to request from Egypt and that Egypt had fully done its part. At that time, we also answered Jarring's memorandum of 8th February 1971.

We waited. May and June passed. On 6th July 1971, I received notification from the US Secretary of State that the United States would intervene to achieve a peaceful solution in accordance with the initiative I had submitted. They asked some questions, including a question about the Egyptian-Soviet treaty which was concluded at that time, May 1971.

* Students' conference (Alexandria). Excerpts.

After the US Secretary of State had visited here, President Podgornyy came. We concluded the treaty in late May. They [the Americans] put questions, and I answered them. My answer has always been that all our decisions express our free will. Since 23rd July 1952, our will has been free to take whatever decision we see fit to take.

July passed without anything happening. August and September passed. On 11th October 1971 I went to the USSR. I had a long session with the three Soviet leaders. As I have told you before, and as you heard at the [ASU] Central Committee, we reached agreement. We removed the clouds that existed in our relations with the USSR. We agreed in October 1971 on specific deals, and the arms were to arrive before the end of 1971. They asked about the year of decision, why I held to this and why I insisted that the situation be reactivated militarily—because there was no other way.

I explained the matter to them very clearly and frankly and in a friendly manner. As I have said, we agreed on arms deals, and the arms were to arrive before the end of 1971.

Relations between ourselves and the United States at that time were not progressing well. On the contrary, their promises in May and July and their failure to fulfil all these promises prompted me to reveal the true American attitude to the people. I attacked them most violently.

This is because the attitude of the US Secretary of State at that time was indeed regrettable. He had reason to feel ashamed and I did shame him before our people, the Arab nation and the whole world.

In 1971, when the first shipments began to arrive, we were supposed to be able to make a decision on the battle on 8th December. I was in the Soviet Union in October. October passed and so did November. And then December came, but there was absolutely no information about the arrival of any shipments or anything. On 8th December the battle between India and Pakistan began. As we all know, the Soviet Union had commitments towards India. We entered December and then more than half of December had gone by—nothing had arrived. The understanding was that these shipments would arrive in October, November and December so that before the end of 1971 we could make a decision and begin operations.

At that time I notified the Soviet Union. About the middle of December I told them that there were only 15 days left before the end of the year and we did not yet even have the dates for the arrival of shipments or vessels. We had no information about them and they had not appeared. I had fixed the year as the year of decision, and therefore I asked if I could visit them in order to avert this situation and that we might solve it together. They fixed a date for my visit—not in January 1972 but in February 1972. This was so that the whole of December and January might have passed, and so would February. As a matter of fact, I almost rejected this date. However, I always place the sublime interest of the cause and the country above personal considerations.

As you have seen, in the past three years, I have experienced and suffered a great deal. I learned [something about the background] afterwards. I went [to the Soviet Union] in February and, as I understood it, their purpose in delaying the date was to let me calm down or cool off a little. This was because I had fixed 1971 as the year of decision and they did not approve of it. Actually they did not approve of any action other than political or diplomatic action.

I went in February, and two months after February in the same year —that is in April. This time they had asked that I visit them and insisted on it because Nixon was going to visit them in May. The first summit conference in Moscow was in May 1972. I visited the Soviet Union again late in April. It was the fourth time. The first was in March 1971. The second was in October 1971. The third in February 1972, and the fourth in April 1972.

The core of the discussion between us was—and I always said it— that the issue would not be activated or solved without military action. The Soviet Union's view was against military action. The discussions used to finish up with the view that even in order to reach a peaceful solution, Israel must be made to feel that we are in a position to talk about a peaceful solution from a position of strength, not weakness. This was the result that we used to end up with, and they used to promise to supply us with arms, etc. etc.

I am not saying this to belittle the arms that we have received. I am continuing the explanation. The April 1972 meeting was held, as I told you, and we agreed at that meeting that after the summit meeting between President Nixon and Secretary Brezhnev in May, [the process of] consolidating Egypt's capability would begin quickly because we agreed that there would be nothing new in the US position in 1972 since it was an election year in the United States. We also agreed that after the elections, that is immediately after November, we had to be prepared. They agreed to this.

I returned from this visit, and in May the summit conference was held in Moscow. I waited for a notification, and after 14 days, I received a notification, including an analysis by the Soviet Union similar to what we had predicted, that is, that there was nothing new in the US position because the US position viewed Egypt and the Arabs as a motionless corpse and they only respect force. So if Egypt and the Arabs were a motionless corpse, why should they [the Americans] act or change their position? The Soviet analysis was the same as our predictions before the April visit, and it came after 14 days. I replied and said: All right, now that the analysis is the same as the one we agreed upon, the questions, as agreed upon with you, are the following:

There were seven clauses—this, that and the other thing. Therefore, as we agreed, these clauses were to have reached me by November. We would then be standing on solid ground after the US elections in November. If they spoke about a peaceful solution, we would be standing on solid ground and in a position to speak and say yes or no—we reject or we agree. Why should a solution be proposed to us when we are weak? The solution proposed would exactly reflect the extent of our strength.

My reply was sent to them and I said simply that my reply was on its way. A whole month passed during which I received no answer. We calculated in days the period between the Moscow visit, that is the meeting, and November so as not to lose a single day for the seven clauses that I had requested and that we had agreed upon. A whole month passed. The first 15 days passed before I received the analysis and one month before I received an answer. I was surprised by the answer I received. There was absolutely no mention of anything about the battle except in the last three lines of the answer.

Before that, there was the statement about the Moscow summit meeting between the two giants. The statement included the phrase military relaxation—military relaxation while Israel had complete superiority and we were short of several things. However, we were asked to embark on military relaxation. What did this mean? It meant that if such military relaxation took place in the area at a time when Israel was superior and we were at the level of our position at that time, the question would not be solved. It would be a case of the stronger side dictating conditions to us. We would either accept or reject. Whether we accepted or not, they would say: We are staying where we are and that is all.

When I received the answer a month later and it included absolutely no mention of what we had agreed upon in April, I made my decisions regarding the Soviet experts, a decision that you learned about in the summer. As I said afterwards, the real aim of these decisions was also strategic; analysts should have been more aware than they were—because anyone who had studied my decisions even a little would have understood that I intended to enter a battle when I ousted the Soviet experts. The Soviet experts were not fighters. They would not enter the battle with me. In fact, they were banned from going near the Canal. All of them were here in the interior as experts on arms and other types of training. Some were manning SAM-3 missiles after the Abu Za'bal raid.

Our sons were already trained and ready to take over everything. In fact, when the Soviet experts left, our sons took over the SAM-3 emplacements in a matter of seconds. There was no vacuum at all that would have left a gap in our air defences. This never happened because our sons took over immediately.

Actually, my purpose, as I have said, was a pause with the friend on the one hand and, on the other, to tell everyone that I was entering the battle—a 100 per cent Egyptian battle. No one at all can claim that anyone has fought it for me. I do not even have experts for weapons training. That was among the reasons for my decision at that time.

The situation continued. Our brothers in the Soviet Union took a long time despite the fact that I sent the Prime Minister, who was Dr. Aziz Sidqi at that time. I sent him because before we proclaimed the decision [on the Soviet experts] we had to agree on a joint declaration in order to cover anything that the West might exploit. They refused and we declared it unilaterally. The issue was settled and the decision was implemented.

Relations remained frozen between us and the Soviet Union all during the summer. The decisions were taken in July. Relations remained frozen all during the summer until October came, when our brother, President Hafiz al-Asad, went to Moscow and intervened in the matter. Dr. Aziz Sidqi left on 16th October and then returned. It was clearly apparent that relations had begun to move again. However, this was on the surface only. In fact and in essence, relations did not move at all.

It was necessary for the Soviet Union to take time to find out that I did not carry out the operation in agreement with the United States behind their backs. I allowed them to take enough time to find out that the matter was not a dagger in their back in agreement with the United States or others. Not at all. It was a national decision. It was a pause to tell them this procedure was unacceptable—a procedure which amounts to a kind of "wait a little, cool off a little, you cannot move until we want you to move". We do not accept this. We do not accept this procedure. It is not according to our will, which has been free since 23rd July 1952. No one at all can direct us or impose any trusteeship on us.

In December 1972 three months were left before the expiration of an agreement between us and them over facilities in the Mediterranean. We gave them facilities in the Mediterranean, not bases. We do not give bases to anyone. Since 23rd July no one has had bases here with us. We are nonaligned. However, we have extended facilities to them. The agreement was to end in March 1973. Five years would have passed of the agreement, for it was concluded in 1968. The agreement stipulates that three months before its expiry the two sides will agree either to terminate or renew it. At that time, relations were disrupted—exactly as I have told you, and everything was at a standstill.

I asked Field Marshal Isma'il to call the Russian General at the Embassy here and tell him that we had decided for our part, to extend the facilities for another period. This happened three months before the expiration of the agreement.

Nevertheless, I still say that the USSR stood by us in the dark moments of 1967. We are a grateful people. We do not forget past favours.

The Field Marshal called the General and told him about this. The facilities have remained ever since. Early in 1973, Field Marshal Isma'il and Hafiz Isma'il left for the USSR. The two of them concluded a deal. After February 1973 our relations began to be, or to become, normal. Some of [the arms included in] this deal began reaching us after Field Marshal Isma'il's return from the USSR.

As I have told you and as you have already heard from me, the decision on the battle was made last April, April 1973. As I have told you, some of the deal began reaching us after the Field Marshal's return in February. We were happy that our relations would return to normal. But the USSR persisted in the view that a military battle must be ruled out and that the question must await a peaceful solution.

The month of June came and with it the second summit conference between President Nixon and Brezhnev. The first meeting was held in Moscow in May 1972. As I have told you, that meeting resulted in military relaxation. This meant that everything must stop and that Israel would remain superior and that we would remain in our position. It was clear from the statement issued in June 1973 that the two super powers had taken another leap forward. They agreed that nothing should happen anywhere in the world. They agreed to abide by this. The only [trouble] spot left in the world was the Middle East. The Vietnam issue was decided. Nothing would happen there. So the Middle East was the only spot left. Nothing should happen here and everyone should await a peaceful solution. On reading the statement, we found that our issue had been put into cold storage pending a peaceful solution.

Security Council Resolution 338
(October 22, 1973)

THE SECURITY COUNCIL

1. Calls upon all parties to the present fighting to cease all firing and terminate all military activity immediately, no later than 12 hours after the moment of the adoption of this decision, in the positions they now occupy;

2. Calls upon the parties concerned to start immediately after the cease-fire the implementation of Security Council Resolution 242 (1967), in all of its parts;

3. Decides that immediately and concurrently with the cease-fire, negotiations start between the parties concerned under appropriate auspices aimed at establishing a just and durable peace in the Middle East.

Statement in the Knesset
(October 23, 1973)

By Golda Meir

Members of the Knesset:

On 22 October the Government of Israel unanimously decided to respond to the approach of the U.S. Government and President Nixon and announce its readiness to agree to a cease-fire according to the resolution of the Security Council following the joint American-Soviet proposal.

According to this proposal, the military forces will remain in the positions they hold at the time when the cease-fire goes into effect.

The implementation of the cease-fire is conditional on reciprocity. Our decision has been brought to the notice of the Foreign Affairs and Security committee, and now to the notice of the Knesset.

As regards the second paragraph of the Security Council resolution, the Government decided to instruct Israel's representative at the United Nations to include in his address to the Security Council a passage clarifying that our agreement to this paragraph is given in the sense in which it was defined by Israel when it decided in August 1970 to respond positively to the United States Government's initiative for a cease-fire, as stated in the United Nations on 4 August, 1970, and by the Prime Minister in the Knesset on the same day. This was also made clear to the U.S. Government. Israel's acceptance of a cease-fire with Egypt is conditional upon Egypt's agreement, but is not conditional upon Syria's agreement to a cease-fire, and vice-versa.

The Government also decided to clarify with the U.S. Government a series of paragraphs intimately connected with the content of the Security Council resolution and the procedure required by it. It is our intention to clarify and ensure, inter alia, that:

The cease-fire shall be binding upon all the regular forces stationed in the territory of a State accepting the cease-fire including the forces of foreign States, such as the armies of Iraq and Jordan in Syria and also forces sent by other Arab States which took part in the hostilities.

The cease-fire shall also be binding upon irregular forces acting against Israel from the area of the States accepting the cease-fire.

The cease-fire shall assure the prevention of a blockade or interference with free navigation, including oil tankers in the Bab-el-Mandeb straits on their way to Eilat.

It shall ensure that the interpretation of the term referring to "negotiations between the parties" is direct negotiations—and, naturally, it must be assured that the procedures, the drawing up of maps and the subject of cease-fire supervision shall be determined by agreement.

A subject of great importance, one dear to our hearts, is the release of prisoners. The Government of Israel has decided to demand an immediate exchange of prisoners. We have discussed this with the Government of the United States, which was one of the initiators of the cease-fire.

I spoke about this with the Secretary of State, Dr. Kissinger. We will insist on an immediate exchange of prisoners. When Dr. Kissinger's plane arrived at Andrews Air Base, the State Department spokesman, Mr. Mc-Closkey, made the following statement to newsmen:

"We believe one of the early priorities should be a release of prisoners on both sides, and we and the Soviet Union have pledged our efforts to obtain assurances that this will be done as a priority matter."

I stress again that this subject is one of the principal tests of the cease-fire, and that there will be no relaxation of our demand that the obligations undertaken by the initiators of the cease-fire be indeed carried out.

I will say several things about our military situation on the Syrian and Egyptian fronts before the cease-fire:

On the Syrian Front

The lines we are holding today on the Syrian front are better than those we held on the 6th of October.

Not only do we now hold all the territory which was under our control before, but our situation has been considerably improved by the holding of positions on the Hermon ridge and also on the front line in the east, which has shifted the previous cease-fire line to a better line supported by a strong flank in the north, on the Hermon ridge.

On the Egyptian Front

The Egyptians did indeed gain a military achievement in crossing the Canal, but in a daring counter-offensive by the Israel Defense Forces, our forces succeeded in regaining control of part of the Eastern Canal line, and to gain control of a large area west of the Canal, an area which opens before us both defensive and offensive possibilities:

(a) This deployment deprives the Egyptian army of its capacity to constitute an offensive threat in the direction of Sinai and Israel, and also prevents them from being able to attack essential installations or areas in our territory.

(b) The forces of the I.D.F. west of the Suez Canal constitute a strong military base for the development of operations initiated by us if required.

In connection with the cease-fire issue, the U.S. Secretary of State, Dr. Henry Kissinger, and his aides called here on their way from Moscow to Washington. The visit was an appropriate opportunity for a thoroughgoing discussion of questions arising from the cease-fire, as well as for an exchange of views, in a friendly spirit, on what was about to happen and what was called for as a result of Israel's response to the U.S. Government's request for agreement to a cease-fire. During this visit, we continued and strengthened the contacts which preceded the Security Council resolution.

In all our contacts with the United States, I learnt that not only does the U.S. have no plan for the borders and other components of peace, but that it is its view that those who offer their "good services" should see to it that the parties themselves—and they alone—should make proposals, plans, for the future.

Furthermore, I must emphasize that, in accordance with authoritative information to hand, the Moscow talks contained nothing more than is contained in the Security Council resolution. I have to inform you that the Syrian Government has so far not responded to the cease-fire resolution. The fighting on that front continues, and the I.D.F. will operate there in accordance with its plans.

As for the Egyptian front—firing against our forces has not yet ceased, and the I.D.F. is obliged to operate as required as long as the firing continues.

At this stage, I will state only that we are examining the conduct of the Egyptians with close military and political attention. Should Egypt persist in belligerent activity, we shall deem ourselves free to take any action and move called for by the situation.

I shall not go into elaborate evaluations of the political activity which preceded the cease-fire. In any event, it was not we who made approaches concerning a cease-fire. As far as the situation on the fronts was concerned, there was no reason for such an approach on our part. It was not we who initiated the timing and clauses of the Security Council's resolution. On the fronts, our forces were not in an inferior battle position. As aforesaid, we deemed it right to respond to the call of the United States and its President, since:

(a) The State of Israel, by its nature, has no wish for war, does not desire loss of life. All Governments of Israel have been convinced that war would not promote peace.

(b) The cease-fire proposal has come when our position is firm on both fronts, when the achievements we hold are of great value and justify agreement to a cease-fire, despite the enemy's achievement east of the Suez Canal.

(c) We responded to the call by the United States and its President out of appreciation and esteem for its positive policy in the Middle East at this time.

Great importance attaches to our response insofar as concerns the continued strengthening of Israel, with particular reference to the continued military and political aid in the war that has been forced upon us . . .

The Egyptian rulers' attitude to war and to loss of life is different from ours. On record is the statement by the Egyptian President concerning his readiness to sacrifice millions of his people. On 16 October, after the I.D.F. had succeeded in establishing a bridgehead west of the Canal, the Egyptian President delivered a boastful address, mocked at a cease-fire and said inter alia:

"We are prepared to agree to a cease-fire on the basis of withdrawal of the Israeli forces from all the occupied territories forthwith—under international supervision—to the pre 5 June 1967 lines."

Only a few days passed and Egypt agreed to a cease-fire. Not one of the conditions raised by Sadat in his speech was included in the Security Council resolution.

Paragraph 3 of the Security Council resolution says:

The Security Council decides that immediately and concurrently with the cease-fire, negotiations start between the parties concerned under appropriate auspices aimed at establishing a just and durable peace in the Middle East.

According to the agreed version of representatives of the U.S.A., the meaning of negotiations between the parties is direct negotiations between Israel and her neighbors on the subject of a just and enduring peace. No such explicit statement was included in Resolution 242 of the Security Council. Moreover, the present resolution also specifies the timing of the beginning of these negotiations—immediately and concurrently with the cease-fire. And there is no need to stress that we attribute great importance to paragraph 3 of the Security Council resolution, if our neighbors will indeed carry it out . . .

On various occasions the Government of Israel has officially defined its attitude towards Security Council Resolution 242. These statements were made from international platforms and at diplomatic meetings, and we have brought them to the knowledge of the Knesset, its Defense and Foreign Affairs Committee and the public at large.

At this time I shall refer to one statement made on 4 August, 1970, to the U.S. Government, to the United Nations and to the Knesset. This statement too, is connected with a cease-fire, and I shall not tire the Knesset by quoting it in full. However, I consider it necessary to quote from my statement in the Knesset on 5 August. This statement was made on the eve of possible talks with the Arab States, and it is still completely valid.

Israel has publicly declared that, by virtue of her right to secure borders, defensible borders, she will not return to the frontiers of 4 June 1967, which make the country a temptation to aggression and which, on various fronts, give decisive advantages to an aggressor. Our position was and still remains that, in the absence of peace, we will continue to maintain the situation as determined at the cease-fire. The cease-fire lines can be replaced only by secure, recognized and agreed boundaries demarcated in a peace treaty.

In accepting the American Government's peace initiative, Israel was not asked to, and did not, undertake any territorial commitments. On the contrary, the Government of Israel received support for its position that not a single Israeli soldier will be withdrawn from the cease-fire lines until a binding contractual peace agreement is reached.

This terrible war that was forced upon us reinforces our awareness of the vital need for defensible borders, for which we shall struggle with all our vigor.

It is worth noting that, since the outbreak of the war on Yom Kippur, the terrorists have also resumed activities from Lebanese territory. Up to this morning, during this period of 17 days, 116 acts of aggression have been perpetrated, 44 civilian settlements on the northern border have been attacked and shelled, and some 20 civilians and 6 soldiers were killed or wounded in these actions. Our people living in the border settlements may be confident that Israel's Defense Forces are fully alert to this situation. Despite the defensive dispositions operative on this front, it has been proved once again that defensive action alone is not sufficient to put an end to acts of terror.

The war in which we are engaged began with a concerted attack on two fronts. The aggressive initiative afforded our enemies preliminary achievements—but, thanks to the spirit and strength of Israel's Defense Army, which is backed by the entire nation, this attack was broken. The aggressors were thrown back. Considerable portions of their forces were destroyed, and the I.D.F. broke through and crossed the cease-fire lines. From holding battles our forces went over to the offensive and gained brilliant achievements.

On both fronts our forces are now holding strong positions beyond the cease-fire lines, unbroken in spirit. The people is united in support of our army.

Israel wants a cease-fire. Israel will observe the cease-fire on a reciprocal basis, and only on that basis. With all her heart Israel wants peace negotiation to start immediately and concurrently with the cease-fire. Israel is capable of evincing the inner strength necessary for the promotion of an honorable peace within secure borders.

We shall be happy if such readiness is also shown by the people and Government of Egypt. However, if the rulers of Egypt propose to renew the war, they shall find Israel prepared, armed and steadfast in spirit . . .

The Agranat Commission Report

On the Public Atmosphere

This report, which is the third—and last—report of the Commission, deals with the subject of the Israel Defence Forces' preparation for the Yom Kippur War in general and with the subject of the operations it conducted in order to contain the enemy. These are the last remaining subjects which the Commission was empowered to investigate, by its terms of reference. With the submission of this report, we reconfirm our conclusions in the first partial report of April 1, 1974, which dealt with the subject of information and its evaluation and the IDF's preparedness in the days before the war, and our reasons for these conclusions, contained in the second partial report of July 10, 1974, which may now be regarded as final conclusions. Accordingly, all three reports must be deemed to be "the Commission's report," within the meaning of section 19(a) of the Inquiry Commissions Law, 1968.*

Before discussing the contents of this report we wish to say a few words about the public atmosphere in which most of our report was prepared. Even before the appointment of this Commission there was a deeply-rooted feeling amongst many citizens that grave blunders had been committed by both the military and civilian authorities. This feeling undoubtedly contributed to the tension even before the Commission began its work and led to the expectation that the Commission would complete its work and publish a report exposing the blunders and errors and naming those responsible therefor with the utmost expedition.

However, the immense scope and breadth of the inquiry made it impossible for the Commission to meet these expectations. This was not appreciated by all sections of the public, particularly since the Commission's work was conducted in camera and in the strictest secrecy. The members of the Commission could well appreciate this and were not unduly hampered by the atmosphere of tension referred to above, while remaining alive to the necessity of taking considerable care to refrain from allowing themselves to be influenced by any preconceived opinions.

However, when the first partial report of the Commission was published in April 1974, on the assumption that the public was entitled to know as soon as possible what conclusion had been reached by the members of the Commission with respect to those subjects whose investigation they had completed, there were certain members of the public, including public figures and journalists, who did not agree with these conclusions and recommendations and who did not confine their criticism to the merits of these conclusions—fair and substantive criticism being of course both permissible and desirable in a democratic regime—but resorted to allegations of "favouritism" and "discrimination" on the part of members of the Commission.

It should be noted that just as the law makes it a criminal offence to defame a judge within the framework of his judicial duties, so does it

---

* One matter, which was garbled in the first partial report, must be rectified: Where it is stated that the Prime Minister decided in favour of "total mobilization of the reserves," the words in quotation marks should be replaced by the following: "mobilization as recommended by the Chief of Staff and later approved by the Cabinet."

prohibit the publication of insulting and defamatory matter against members of inquiry commissions. But even apart from these provisions it is obvious that there is nothing more likely to poison the atmosphere than allegations of this nature against judges or members of inquiry commissions.

Furthermore, section 41(a) of the Judges Law prohibits the publication of anything likely to influence the course of a court action and this applies equally to the proceedings of inquiry commissions. The purpose of this provision is to prevent the conclusions of a court (or inquiry commission) or tribunal from being influenced by anything save the evidence before it and at the same time to prevent creating, by means of "trial by the press" any preconceived ideas in the minds of the public as to what conclusions and decisions a tribunal should draw.

During the course of our inquiry, however, articles and comments on the subject matter pending before us appeared which were in blatant contravention of these provisions with respect to sub justice. Furthermore, some of the matter published was as irresponsible as to constitute an infringement of the vital demands of security, besides being inaccurate and false. This manifestation provided not only a general cause for alarm but it hindered the Commission from proceeding quietly with its work, particularly since the Commission was unable to reveal the real truth to the public.

This tense—and even ugly—atmosphere made our mission, which was sufficiently difficult as it was, almost impossible, and this raises the question of the future of inquiry commissions, in general, within the framework of the present law. If despite the fact that we were exposed to the barbs of insulting and non-substantive criticism, without being able to react to and refute it publicly we should still have decided to continue with our mission, this was only because we regarded its completion as of the greatest importance and likely to contribute towards enabling the Government to face the test confronting it: that of strengthening and improving the organism on which the safety of the State depends—the IDF.

We wish to make a further general remark at this stage: we do not see any cause for apologising for the fact that it took us 14 months of almost continuous sessions to complete our inquiry, in the light of the number of involved and complicated subjects included in our terms of reference and of the fact that we studied each of them thoroughly and in the greatest detail.

Blocking Actions

In connection with this subject it is important to note the following:

The wealth of documentation, together with the detailed testimony of most ranking officers, permitted us to examine the blocking actions in detail.

The documentation includes discussions and decisions at the government general staff and area command level; orders and reports made at the various military levels; conversations between senior officers before and during the battles; battlefield developments from the point of view of the divisions, brigades and battalions, etc.

We strove mainly to elicit from the mass of material the decisive questions, to pinpoint basic faults and to point to the lessons to be learned from them in order that these might be implemented in the future.

We did not find it to be our task to analyse the political-strategic decisions, the goals of the war or the principles of one war plan or another. These were for us background for examination of the conduct of the battles (in order to examine, for example, if this conduct involved substantial deviations from the principles fixed for the execution of counterattacks or if some of the steps taken to stop the enemy went counter to IDF battle doctrine).

As for the conduct of battle commanders, evaluation in certain instances involved purely professional judgements and we have recommended that these be investigated by the IDF.

We have decided to concentrate our investigation of the blocking actions in the events of October 8 on the southern front and the events of October 6–7 (till the afternoon) on the northern front. The reasons, in brief, follow:

We had two alternatives—either to examine in a general way all the battles involved in the blocking stage or to analyse in depth the battle that was decisive. We chose the second. Our job was not to write the history of the blocking actions—that would have involved years of work—but to pinpoint the main defects uncovered in this stage.

Many of the defects in this stage derive from the element of surprise. A distinction must be made between the southern and the northern fronts. In the south, the surprise was complete both in time and method of attack so that no effective steps were taken beforehand. In the north, on the other hand, the surprise mainly involved the objectives of the enemy and his method, not so much the attack itself. We chose to examine the battle of October 8 in the south because these were to be the first time that the IDF took the initiative.

What caused this battle to go wrong, among other things, was the deviation from the objectives defined by the Chief of Staff as well as lack of control on the part of the command and its inability to correctly read the progress of the battle. Furthermore, some of the steps taken that day by various command echelons stemmed consciously or unconsciously from opinions formed by commanders a long time before the Yom Kippur War and not from an analysis of the current situation. It is not our purpose to contradict or endorse these assumptions but only to examine to what extent it was appropriate to apply them given the circumstances.

From this, it is clear that a detailed study should be of the lessons and implications of this battle. It had a far-reaching effect on the entire strategy adopted thereafter by the IDF in the war and it also had potential or actual political implications.

In the South

The exhaustive consideration, running to 746 pages, which we have devoted to these battles, is divided into four parts: the build-up of the forces, the plan, the fighting (the political level, the General Staff and the Command), and the divisions in the battle.

In summing up the results of the battles of October 8, we note the following:

Although the battles failed inasmuch as they did not attain the objectives set by the Southern Command, they were of great significance in the progress of the war. They contained the enemy's bridgeheads, preventing him from completely achieving the first stage of his plan. Although one reserve division was unsuccessful in its attempt to wipe out the bridgeheads, its hard fight contributed to the containment of the enemy's advance and prepared the ground for counterattack. Although another reserve division did not fight for most of that same day due to reasons beyond its control and although it sustained heavy losses on the evening of October 8 and the morning of October 9, these battles opened the way for further moves.

On Tuesday afternoon, October 9, the division deployed for a westward advance. The attempt did not succeed. But when the battle ended towards evening, a battalion reached the vicinity of the canal and thereby exposed the weak spot in the Egyptian alignment through which the IDF would subsequently cross the canal.

Finally, it must again be stressed that on the battlefields where these fights were waged, there were unsurpassed manifestations of sacrifice and bravery on the part of officers and men alike.

At the conclusion of discussions of the October 8 battles, the Commission adds some reservations and remarks about the evidence submitted on this subject.

In the North

These battles were analysed in a special section covering 311 pages. At the outbreak of the war, and in its early stages, certain basic facts characterized the situation of the Northern Command.

The Command was aware that hostilities might break out and took appropriate measures. Reinforcements were sent in and although the number of units was fewer than considered necessary for the defence of the Golan Heights in the event of an overall war, the imbalance was not intolerable. Units on the Golan were on a relatively high state of alert, although they too were taken aback by the scope and timing of enemy operations when war broke out.

The regulars who fought on the Golan in the initial stages distinguished themselves generally by their stubborn fight and their perseverance, like the reserves who joined them later. Supreme courage was manifest at all levels. At the front itself, units led by junior officers showed great resource. Their sometimes independent and even lone operations influenced the tide of battle in certain cases.

After the Syrian attack had been stemmed, the Northern Command switched from a situation in which the enemy had penetrated to the vicinity of the River Jordan and endangered Eastern Galilee, over to a counter-offensive which left the troops close to the enemy capital and in control of the Hermon crest.

The interim reports issued last year covered the intelligence aspect in the days before the fighting began. The probe of the intelligence aspect after the fighting began, covered the quality and organization of intelligence work, which preceded and accompanied the October 8 offensive on the southern front, as well as the intelligence reaching the units which took part in the fighting itself.

Some of the lessons emerging from what the Intelligence Corps did on the eve of the war and how it functioned hold true for the course of the fighting as well. In the initial stages, field intelligence as such scarcely existed. The Intelligence Corps, moreover was shackled by preconceived patterns of thought.

On the Southern Front, faulty intelligence had a considerable influence on the battles to stem the Egyptian advance.

Officers' Control

The degree of control of the situation, exercised by officers at various levels and their control of the units at their command, constituted a central problem in the battles to stem the Egyptian advance, and to a lesser degree the Syrian advance.

When the war broke out, this problem largely stemmed from the difficulties of applying the theory of control and reporting, in the sudden sharp transition, with only the slightest warning, from a state of lull, to a state of overall war.

Difficulties of control continued to exist after the initial stages as well. Accordingly, the probe also covered the various elements involved in control by officers, in time of war, as applied during the battles to stem the enemy advance. This showed up a series of faulty procedures and erroneous concepts.

Future of the Defence Forces

This, as our previous reports, is of a sharply critical nature. Clearly this is the result of the investigative function we were called upon to carry out. At the same time it is important to emphasize that our eyes were upon the future of the Israel Defence Forces and of the State—so that that which should be corrected will in fact be so.

The true test of any army is not only in its being able to win when it has the initiative, but precisely when it starts from difficult circumstances and goes ahead to victory. However, having been witnesses to the brilliance with which the army of the people stood up to its difficult test, it is essential to ensure that it will not have to meet a similar test in the future and it was this that we bore in mind in drawing up the three reports. It is to be hoped that the lessons to which we have pointed will be assimilated and that our recommendations will be implemented.

And finally, on the long road of this investigation, we could live—insofar as this is possible through hearing of testimony—the experiences of our soldiers, their sacrifice and their heroism. And this only strengthened our recognition that the task entrusted to us was not only a heavy public responsibility but a great privilege.

Discipline Indivisible

The Commission paid special attention to the question of discipline in the army, which it considered of great importance. For this reason it weighed publishing this section of the report in full, but finally decided that security considerations would not permit it.

The subject of discipline has been on the army's agenda all along, the Commission noted. How strict discipline should be, the unfavourable influence at times of civilian society, the kind of means to be used to impose discipline—these and other questions have always been discussed by the General Staff.

Army discipline expresses itself in the fact that the individual soldier accepts the authority of his superiors, which is itself based upon army regulations for the purpose of carrying out a military task, whether routine or operational.

This discipline can be administrative, that is, concerned with the daily behaviour of the soldier, or technical, concerned with care of equipment, or operational, concerned with soldier's behaviour in carrying out his duty in an operation against the enemy.

Army drill aims to make it "second nature" for the soldier to carry out his special duties in battle despite the external and subjective pressures upon him.

Discipline, command and obedience characterize the military profession. Without discipline an army is transformed into an armed mass unable to perform correctly. Administrative shortcomings can exist in any army, but without good discipline they cannot be corrected.

The more complex the means of warfare, the larger the size of the forces, the longer the chain of command, and the greater the deployment and dispersal of forces and the speed of battle, the greater becomes the need for discipline and proper administration.

Discipline is indivisible. For example, a soldier who becomes accustomed in time of peace not to observe the minor rules, such as in matters of personal appearance, without being alerted to this failure by his superior officer, will in the end be negligent in carrying out operational orders.

Moreover, the soldier cannot be expected to carry out his orders scrupulously, if he sees that his commanding officer does not demand the same of himself.

A soldier who is not scrupulous in matters of personal cleanliness will in the end also not be scrupulous about the cleanliness and fitness of his personal weaponry. A soldier who becomes used to violating traffic laws in peace-time, and sees his commanding officer doing the same, won't observe the rules of moving traffic in war and will thus impede the flow of forces to the front.

The conclusion is that good habits of discipline in small matters as in large add up to fatefully affect the preservation of life and equipment.

Captivity

While the Commission was collecting general testimony, it heard about various situations in which soldiers were taken prisoner. This material was referred to the Chief of Staff, for his study, so that he could take the appropriate decisions.

Training

The Commission considered it important to conduct an additional study of the Army's preparedness and deployment before the war, and its manner of fighting during the battles to stem the enemy advance, from the standpoint of officers' and soldiers' training before the war. The aim of this additional study was to point up what was wrong institutionally in the system of training, its aims and its content. Lessons could thus be drawn, and improvements made.

The Commission therefore asked R/A Haim Laskov (Res.), a former head of IDF training, to prepare a special chapter as a supplement to this report. Submitted as R/A Laskov's separate opinion, it nevertheless largely fits in with the rest of this report. It expands on the training aspect, where it concerns battle intelligence regimen and discipline, emergency depot units, and the battles of October 8.

Sharon Supported

We wish to dwell on a particular question on the subject of discipline, which gave rise to public debate in the wake of a press interview ("Ma' ariv" of January 25, 1974) granted by Major-General (Res.) Ariel Sharon, and from which it would appear that in his opinion, there are certain circumstances in which a commander may refrain from carrying out an operational order addressed to him.

When General Sharon appeared before us as a witness we examined him on this question, in order to set the record straight. General Sharon testified to having been disturbed by a question of conscience in the wake of something which happened on one of the final days of the Yom Kippur War. On that day, he had been ordered to lead the division under his command to attack a certain target. He had believed that implementation of the order would result in many casualties and that if the commander who had issued the order had been fully aware of the situation on the battlefield—knowledge which he lacked in General Sharon's opinion— he would not have issued the order. He, General Sharon, therefore opposed the order for hours, but finally, the order not having been rescinded, he obeyed it and carried out the attack. Discovering no achievements thereafter to induce him to change the opinion he held before the operation, he cites this instance as an example of an order which it would have been justified not to carry out, answering for it thereafter. In his testimony, he stressed that such cases are very rare.

We believe that Major-General Sharon's outlook, as he described it to us, is consistent with military discipline. At a time of battle—and we are not of course dealing here with an order which has to be carried out forthwith—very rare instances may occur in which the commander who receives an order is convinced that if his commander was fully aware of the facts in the field he would not insist on its being carried out. Thus he who receives the order is caught on the horns of a dilemma, between his obligation to carry out any order, unless it is clearly illegal, and his conviction that on the basis of the facts of the situation, such an order is out of the question.

When a commander finds himself in such a situation, and he has exhausted all the accepted means, insofar as these are at his disposal in the circumstances, to have the order changed: informing the commander who gave the order of the facts of the situation, and trying to persuade him to change the order, appealing against the order to a higher echelon—and all to no avail, the commander is then obliged by military law to carry out the order to the best of his ability, and afterwards demand the establishment of a committee of inquiry to investigate the circumstances under which the order was given and carried out.

If he does not carry out the order, his superior officer may remove him from his command forthwith, and he is then liable for court-martial for deliberate refusal to obey an order, and all that remains is for him to inform the court-martial of his grounds for not carrying out the order, as an extenuating circumstance.

Final Remarks

It is generally accepted by the IDF that there were serious disciplinary faults. A minority of the commanders believed these did not adversely affect the IDF's fighting conduct during the Yom Kippur War. Our opinion on the basis of the evidence before us is different. We explained above that there is a strong link between the level of everyday discipline in the army and the quality of performance during the supreme test of war. The readiness to sacrifice and the ability to improvise as they were revealed during the Yom Kippur War—and these are not substitutes for discipline—to a large extent extricated the army from its straits. But who knows what hitches might have been prevented had a greater degree of discipline been added to the readiness to fight.

One cannot promote trust in the IDF, insofar as it has been impaired, by banal declarations and demands for an attitude of civilian trust in respect to the army. Our public is linked by a thousand threads to the army, and reserve soldiers know very well what is going on within it. If the soldier and the junior officer work in a climate in which there is proper discipline, fulfilment of standing army orders and proper administration based on fixed rules, there is a corresponding increase in mutual trust within the ranks, in willingness to join the permanent army and in devotion of soldiers at all levels. And there will disappear of its own accord the regrettable occurrence of reserve soldiers speaking badly of the army, and the army will gain the full public trust it enjoyed in the past.

There can be no postponing the effort to remedy things that are wrong; this must be integrated with the difficult task of broadening the forces and physically strengthening them, because between these two there is a strong reciprocal link. The IDF and Israel's people are indeed one. Thus it is precisely for the IDF, and primarily for its senior command, to pave the way for the elimination of faults which began to penetrate into its ranks from the civilian sector—and thus to make a decisive contribution to the improvement of society generally. The IDF is capable of meeting this difficult task for which it was given instruments and sanctions that are not at the disposal of civilian society.

Interview (August 3, 1974)

By George Habash*

Q. What is your analysis of the Palestinian and Arab political situations after the October War?

A. Almost nine months have elapsed since the cease-fire; during this time, some Arab and some international powers have worked from the principle of political struggle based on Security Council Resolutions 242 and 338 to insure the Israeli withdrawal from the Arab territories, on the

---

* General Secretary of the Popular Front for the Liberation of Palestine. Excerpts from *Al-Hadaf* (Beirut).

one hand, and to achieve what was called giving the Palestinian people their full right to self-determination.

What are the results of this policy? Part of the Arab land was regained—on the Syrian and Egyptian fronts—but in lieu of what? What exactly is the price?

On the imperialistic level: the prominent achievement of American imperialism as a result of this policy is the return of American influence to the area, and the continuous expansion of this influence politically, economically and morally. This truth reaffirms the enemy's nature and its aggressive identity, in spite of all attempts by the subservient systems and reactionary forces to decorate imperialism's ugly face. The results of the return of imperialism's influence to the area affected the close relations between the USSR and the Arab people. These are the most important concrete truths that surfaced during the recent nine months.

On the Arab level: in return for the disengagement steps on the Egyptian and Syrian fronts, those systems sacrificed their power of military confrontation which enables them to continue the struggle and secures for them the complete extraction of their rights. Additionally, there was the step of lifting the oil embargo from the imperialistic countries which supported Zionism in its war against the Arab people.

Here, it must be indicated that the proposed plans of "settlement" might be affected by the internal developments in America (for example, the Watergate scandal) or any developments that may occur in the world. But what must be clear is that America will remain eager and will push in the direction of settlement as long as this "settlement" guarantees the return of its interests and their continuity for the longest possible interval. Therefore, efforts will continue in the direction of more steps towards "settlement." Based on this obvious principle, in return for every piece of land recovered by the Arab side, the Arabs are required to pay the price to the imperialistic powers and Israel—part of this price paid to imperialism and part to Israel.

Q. What is the position of the Front toward the official visit of the PLO delegation, headed by Yasser Arafat, to the USSR in August of this year?

A. The Front decided not to join the delegation. This position is not against the USSR despite our disagreements on many issues. Rather, we consider the USSR a power that is supporting our people's struggle. We also consider the Soviets friends of the Arab and Palestinian struggle. It is a mistaken position to put the Soviets and the Americans in one basket for only their general convergence of opinion concerning Resolution 242 and their agreement on the general lines of a political settlement. We consider the USSR a friend of the Palestinian struggle. We are convinced that the continuity of the Palestinian political and military struggle and our success in guaranteeing this continuity, eventually to the level that will mobilize the Arab masses according to a well-rooted revolutionary political line, will definitely lead to a reconsideration by the USSR of the nature of the existing struggle in the area, and the truths about the presence of the Zionist state which means no more than the existence of a racist, fascist and aggressive state. No peace will materialize as long as the Zionist state exists. This is the only conclusion that can be drawn by our masses based on this fact. The day will come when the Communist and leftist powers will uncover the true core and substance of the Zionist system.

We should not misinterpret international contradictions. The Front's decision not to participate in the PLO's delegation to Moscow does not express a position estranged from the Soviets, for whom we possess every appreciation, but it is a position against the PLO's leadership who wished the delegation travelling to Moscow to be "homogeneous." In our opinion, homogeneity means the common representation of a political line, which is the line leading towards political settlement. But we must keep in mind that within the Palestinian circle there exist two completely contradictory political lines, one on either end. One line wants the PLO to be a part of the political settlement and the other line considers this a dangerous national divergence, and considers the present mission of the struggle to keep the PLO outside the boundaries of the settlement. Based on this came our demand that the delegation be composed of all the member organizations of the Executive Council so that the delegation fairly represents the coexisting and contradictory political lines within the Liberation Organization.

There is another reason for our nonparticipation in the organization's delegation to Moscow: the delegation which was appointed to travel left without the Executive Council of the organization discussing the specific missions to be deliberated with our Soviet comrades, and without specifying a position on all the subjects proposed. The unilateral decision-making of the PLO must not continue. Our position is an expression of our rejection of the sense of unilateral decision-making that is predominant in the leadership of the PLO.

Q. What practical steps will the "rejection front" take at the Palestinian and Arab levels?

A. In fact what is called the rejection forces is nothing but an expression of Palestinian and Arab forces that emerged from an analysis, summarized as follows: the Palestinian revolution is strained and ends when it becomes a part of the political settlement presently proposed, and the continuity of the revolution is only ensured by resisting and fighting the proposed political settlement plans. These forces now work as though they are one front. But such a front did not arise until now. It is the duty of these forces to organize one front that has its own political programme, a list of specified organizational interrelationships and consolidated struggle programmes. Presently it is the duty of this front to work within the framework of the Liberation Organization to prevent its complete deviation, so that the Liberation Organization does not become part of the settlement.

But, in the event that the PLO goes to Geneva, the rejection front becomes the sole representative of the continuity of the revolution.

The subject that should be given chief priority is the necessity for the transformation of these Palestinian and Arab forces from the state of reflexive cooperation to the state of a clear frontal format according to a precise political programme.

Q. What is the PFLP's understanding of the relationship between the resistance and the Arab masses for the near future?

A. We believe that the Palestinian resistance will not be able to get out of the dilemma it is living in if it remains dependent on the masses of the Palestinian people, even if the revolutionary Palestinian party existed and the united Palestinian front existed. Even though important, it is not sufficient to defeat the plans of imperialism since the subject is really the balance of power. Because of this, the only true way out from the resistance's dilemma is for the Palestinian revolution to become an integral part of the Arab revolution, fused with it in all sections of the Arab nation. It is the Palestinian, Jordanian, Syrian, Egyptian, Iraqi and Lebanese masses who are able to guarantee the victory of our Palestinian people's struggle. When the Palestinian military struggle movement becomes able to move from a geographical and human depth that is not confined by the boundaries of the land of Palestine or the west and east banks, but extends to include all the lands surrounding Palestine, then the military struggle feature will rely upon such a human and geographical depth. At that time, it will be an impossibility for the oppressing forces to hit the Palestinian revolution.

Q. What is the explanation of the Front's acceptance of the ten points during the recent Palestinian National Council?

A. It is important for me to clarify what I heard and what reverberated during and after the convention—that I had personally, and in my own hand-writing, initiated these ten points. All what was said are lies and it is sad that attempts to slander our position as a popular front in front of the Palestinian masses occurred, whether premeditatedly or not. I put together some points as a basis for a political programme that might be agreed upon by the National Council during its twelfth convention. These points cumulatively put the resistance movement outside the framework of the settlement by opposing it in a way that cannot be disputed. Among those points is the definitive rejection of Resolution 242 and the Geneva Conference. The points which I wrote in the name of the Popular Front are in line with the political line represented by the Popular Front. But the ten points which the Palestinian National Council adopted are a compromise position attempting to prevent the explosion within the Palestinian circle. There have been several attempts aimed at concealing the contradictions within the Palestinian circle. But I take this opportunity to declare at the top of my voice that two contradictory political lines exist within the PLO, and the necessity of maintaining the struggle against any attempt to cover or weaken this contradiction is imperative.

One political line says that the only way open for the resistance movement is to enter into the framework of the political solution and to struggle within this framework to achieve whatever is possible. On the other hand, there is another line that believes in the continuity of the revolution and in staying away from political settlements in spite of the imperialistic powers' proposed dissolution attempts and plots.

There can be no real and strong national unity, in the long run, based upon the ten points . . . National unity cannot exist except upon a unified political stand: the Liberation Organization must reject in a clear and firm way, free from ambiguity or misunderstanding, all the forms of the proposed settlements.

In this respect, I announce in the name of the PFLP that it is important for us to remain within the PLO inasmuch as the Liberation Organization remains outside the framework of the Geneva Conference. Participation in the Geneva Conference means to us a dangerous national deviation which we will fight with all our power, based on the strength of the masses. When the Organization is in Geneva, the subject becomes black and white . . .

The attempts to dissolve the contradictions in the Palestinian circle must not continue. It is incorrect to state that disagreements do not exist. We must not bury our heads in the sand. There is a line that is devoted to the subservient Arab bourgeois system's policy of trying to dampen and cover the Palestinian and Arab proletariat's line in its struggle against the subservient bourgeois policy, on the Arab and Palestinian levels . . .

Q. What are the PFLP's expectations on the Lebanese front for the next phase?

A. Of course, it is necessary to expect attacks on the resistance and especially in Lebanon. This is a scientific deduction. Why? Because the proposed settlement aims at containing the Palestinian resistance. This is a fact. And it is natural for the resistance movement to hesitate in front of the humiliating format that American imperialism will propose to contain the revolution. At the same time, there will be a plan drawn to direct political and military attacks on the Palestinian resistance movement so that the resistance is compelled at the end to enter into the framework of the settlement from a position of weakness, permitting the plan to achieve its aims. This point must be engrained in our minds because the resistance in Lebanon still constitutes a revolutionary feature. The Palestinian gun is still held up in this area. Through the ability of the resistance movement to express its political line to the Palestinian and Arab masses through its overt existence in this and other circles, it is natural for the enemy to work against the existence of this revolutionary feature until he reaches the position that enables him to contain the resistance movement within a format that does not conflict with the basic benefits of his imperialistic appendages and his long-range benefits . . .

What do I mean exactly?

Any Israeli imperialistic reactionary plan against the resistance as a whole will face opposition from all the resistance movement. We will find ourselves in front of the picture of May again. In other words, all the resistance movement will have a united stand. Will the enemy be able to come and isolate and attack the Popular Front in Shatila? No. Because that will result in a confrontation with all the Palestinian guns, whether carried by a Popular Front or Fateh member. All will face this attempt. By this we see the difficulty of directing a military blow to the resistance movement. But what may happen is that some Palestinian forces, for some excuse or another, based upon the claim of enforcing discipline in the camps, will hit another Palestinian group with the blessing of the reactionary forces. Here occurs intact the painful blow to the resistance movement as a whole.

The area in this case will be full of action. Thus, we must keep our eyes open in order to prevent the enemy from achieving its objectives. Of course, the principal dependence or main line in facing any plots of any kind aiming to hit the Palestinian resistance in any form is that of complete fusion between the resistance and the Lebanese mass movement. It is only this format of fusion that can crush all the plots.

Address to the UN General Assembly (November 13, 1974)

By Yasir Arafat*

Mr. President, I thank you for having invited the Palestine Liberation Organization to participate in this plenary session of the United Nations General Assembly. I am grateful to all those representatives of States of the United Nations who contributed to the decision to introduce the question of Palestine as a separate item of the agenda of this Assembly. That decision made possible the Assembly's resolution inviting us to address it on the question of Palestine.

The roots of the Palestinian question reach back into the closing years of the 19th century, in other words, to that period which we call the era of colonialism and settlement as we know it today. This is precisely the

* Excerpts (29th Session).

period during which Zionism as a scheme was born; its aim was the conquest of Palestine by European immigrants, just as settlers colonized, and indeed raided, most of Africa. This is the period during which, pouring forth out of the west, colonialism spread into the further reaches of Africa, Asia, and Latin America, building colonies everywhere, cruelly exploiting, oppressing, plundering the people of those three continents. This period persists into the present. Marked evidence of its totally reprehensible presence can be readily perceived in the racism practised both in South Africa and in Palestine.

Just as colonialism and its demagogues dignified their conquests, their plunder and limitless attacks upon the natives of Africa with appeals to a "civilizing and modernizing" mission, so too did waves of Zionist immigrants disguise their purposes as they conquered Palestine. Just as colonialism as a system and colonialists as its instrument used religion, color, race and language to justify the African's exploitation and his cruel subjugation by terror and discrimination, so too were these methods employed as Palestine was usurped and its people hounded from their national homeland.

Just as colonialism heedlessly used the wretched, the poor, the exploited as mere inert matter with which to build and to carry out settler colonialism, so too were destitute, oppressed European Jews employed on behalf of world imperialism and of the Zionist leadership. European Jews were transformed into the instruments of aggression; they became the elements of settler colonialism intimately allied to racial discrimination.

Zionist theology was utilized against our Palestinian people: the purpose was not only the establishment of Western-style settler colonialism but also the severing of Jews from their various homelands and subsequently their estrangement from their nations. Zionism is an ideology that is imperialist, colonialist, racist; it is profoundly reactionary and discriminatory; it is united with anti-Semitism in its retrograde tenets and is, when all is said and done, another side of the same base coin. For when what is proposed is that adherents of the Jewish faith, regardless of their national residence, should neither owe allegiance to their national residence nor live on equal footing with its other, non-Jewish citizens—when that is proposed we hear anti-Semitism being proposed. When it is proposed that the only solution for the Jewish problem is that Jews must alienate themselves from communities or nations of which they have been a historical part, when it is proposed that Jews solve the Jewish problem by immigrating to and forcibly settling the land of another people—when this occurs exactly the same position is being advocated as the one urged by anti-Semites against Jews.

Thus, for instance, we can understand the close connection between Rhodes, who promoted settler colonialism in southeast Africa, and Herzl, who had settler colonialist designs upon Palestine. Having received a certificate of good settler colonialist conduct from Rhodes, Herzl then turned around and presented this certificate to the British Government, hoping thus to secure a formal resolution supporting Zionist policy. In exchange, the Zionists promised Britain an imperialist base on Palestine soil so that imperial interests could be safeguarded at one of their chief strategic points.

The Jewish invasion of Palestine began in 1881. Before the first large wave of immigrants started arriving, Palestine had a population of half a million; most of the population was either Moslem or Christian, and only 20,000 were Jewish. Every segment of the population enjoyed the religious tolerance characteristic of our civilization.

Palestine was then a verdant land, inhabited mainly by an Arab people in the course of building its life and dynamically enriching its indigenous culture.

Between 1882 and 1917 the Zionist Movement settled approximately 50,000 European Jews in our homeland. To do that it resorted to trickery and deceit in order to implant them in our midst. Its success in getting Britain to issue the Balfour Declaration once again demonstrated the alliance between Zionism and imperialism. Furthermore, by promising to the Zionist movement what was not hers to give, Britain showed how oppressive the rule of imperialism was. As it was constituted then, the League of Nations abandoned our Arab people, and Wilson's pledges and promises came to nought. In the guise of a mandate, British imperialism was cruelly and directly imposed upon us. The mandate document issued by the League of Nations was to enable the Zionist invaders to consolidate their gains in our homeland.

In the wake of the Balfour Declaration and over a period of 30 years, the Zionist movement succeeded, in collaboration with its imperialist ally, in settling more European Jews on the land, thus usurping the properties of Palestine Arabs.

By 1947 the number of Jews had reached 600,000: they owned about 6 percent of Palestinian arable land. The figure should be compared with the population of Palestine which at that time was 1,250,000.

As a result of the collusion between the mandatory Power and the Zionist movement and with the support of some countries, this General Assembly early in its history approved a recommendation to partition our Palestinian homeland. This took place in an atmosphere poisoned with questionable actions and strong pressure. The General Assembly partitioned what it had no right to divide—an indivisible homeland. When we rejected that decision, our position corresponded to that of the natural mother who refused to permit King Solomon to cut her son in two when the unnatural mother claimed the child for herself and agreed to his dismemberment. Furthermore, even though the partition resolution granted the colonialist settlers 54 percent of the land of Palestine, their dissatisfaction with the decision prompted them to wage a war of terror against the civilian Arab population. They occupied 81 percent of the total area of Palestine, uprooting a million Arabs. Thus, they occupied 524 Arab towns and villages, of which they destroyed 385, completely obliterating them in the process. Having done so, they built their own settlements and colonies on the ruins of our farms and our groves. The roots of the Palestine question lie here. Its causes do not stem from any conflict between two religions or two nationalisms. Neither is it a border conflict between neighboring states. It is the cause of a people deprived of its homeland, dispersed and uprooted, and living mostly in exile and in refugee camps.

With support from imperialist and colonialist Powers, it managed to get itself accepted as a United Nations Member. It further succeeded in getting the Palestine Question deleted from the agenda of the United Nations and in deceiving world public opinion by presenting our cause as a problem of refugees in need either of charity from do-gooders, or settlement in a land not theirs.

Not satisfied with all this, the racist entity, founded on the imperialist-colonialist concept, turned itself into a base of imperialism and into an arsenal of weapons. This enabled it to assume its role of subjugating the Arab people and of committing aggression against them, in order to satisfy its ambitions for further expansion on Palestinian and other Arab lands. In addition to the many instances of aggression committed by this entity against the Arab States, it has launched two large-scale wars, in 1956 and 1967, thus endangering world peace and security.

As a result of Zionist aggression in June 1967, the enemy occupied Egyptian Sinai as far as the Suez Canal. The enemy occupied Syria's Golan Heights, in addition to all Palestinian land west of the Jordan. All these developments have led to the creation in our area of what has come to be known as the ''Middle East problem.'' The situation has been rendered more serious by the enemy's persistence in maintaining its unlawful occupation and in further consolidating it, thus establishing a beachhead for world imperialism's thrust against our Arab nation. All Security Council decisions and appeals to world public opinion for withdrawal from the lands occupied in June 1967 have been ignored. Despite all the peaceful efforts on the international level, the enemy has not been deterred from its expansionist policy. The only alternative open before our Arab nations, chiefly Egypt and Syria, was to expend exhaustive efforts in preparing forcefully to resist that barbarous armed invasion—and this in order to liberate Arab lands and to restore the rights of the Palestinian people, after all other peaceful means had failed.

Under these circumstances, the fourth war broke out in October 1973, bringing home to the Zionist enemy the bankruptcy of its policy of occupation, expansion and its reliance on the concept of military might. Despite all this, the leaders of the Zionist entity are far from having learned any lesson from their experience. They are making preparations for the fifth war, resorting once more to the language of military superiority, aggression, terrorism, subjugation and, finally, always to war in their dealings with the Arabs.

It pains our people greatly to witness the propagation of the myth that its homeland was a desert until it was made to bloom by the toil of foreign settlers, that it was a land without a people, and that the colonialist entity caused no harm to any human being. No: such lies must be exposed from this rostrum, for the world must know that Palestine was the cradle of the most ancient cultures and civilizations. Its Arab people were engaged in farming and building, spreading culture throughout the land for thousands of years, setting an example in the practice of freedom of worship, acting as faithful guardians of the holy places of all religions. As a son of Jerusalem, I treasure for myself and my people beautiful memories and vivid images of the religious brotherhood that was the hallmark of our Holy City before it succumbed to catastrophe. Our people continued to pursue this enlightened policy until the establishment of the State of Israel and their dispersion. This did not deter our people from pursuing their humanitarian role on Palestinian soil. Nor will they permit their land to become a launching pad for aggression or a racist camp predicated on the destruction of civilization, cultures, progress and peace. Our people cannot but maintain the heritage of their ancestors in resisting the invaders, in assuming the privileged task of defending their native land, their Arab nationhood, their culture and civilization, and in safeguarding the cradle of monotheistic religion.

By contrast, we need only mention briefly some Israeli stands: its support of the Secret Organization in Algeria, its bolstering of the settler-colonialists in Africa—whether in the Congo, Angola, Mozambique, Zimbabwe, Azania or South Africa—and its backing of South Vietnam against the Vietnamese revolution. In addition, one can mention Israel's continuing support of imperialists and racists everywhere, its obstructionist stand in the Committee of Twenty-Four, its refusal to cast its vote in support of independence for the African States, and its opposition to the demands of many Asian, African and Latin American nations, and several other States in the Conferences on raw materials, population, the Law of the Sea, and food. All these facts offer further proof of the character of the enemy which has usurped our land. They justify the honorable struggle which we are waging against it. As we defend a vision of the future, our enemy upholds the myths of the past.

The enemy we face has a long record of hostility even towards the Jews themselves, for there is within the Zionist entity a built-in racism against Oriental Jews. While we were vociferously condemning the massacres of Jews under Nazi rule, Zionist leadership appeared more interested at that time in exploiting them as best it could in order to realize its goal of immigration into Palestine.

If the immigration of Jews to Palestine had had as its objective the goal of enabling them to live side by side with us, enjoying the same rights and assuming the same duties, we would have opened our doors to them, as far as our homeland's capacity for absorption permitted. Such was the case with the thousands of Armenians and Circassians who still live among us in equality as brethren and citizens. But that the goal of this immigration should be to usurp our homeland, disperse our people, and turn us into second-class citizens—this is what no one can conceivably demand that we acquiesce in or submit to. Therefore, since its inception, our revolution has not been motivated by racial or religious factors. Its target has never been the Jew, as a person, but racist Zionism and undisguised aggression. In this sense, ours is also a revolution for the Jew, as a human being, as well. We are struggling so that Jews, Christians and Moslems may live in equality enjoying the same rights and assuming the same duties, free from racial or religious discrimination.

We do distinguish between Judaism and Zionism. While we maintain our opposition to the colonialist Zionist movement, we respect the Jewish faith. Today, almost one century after the rise of the Zionist movement, we wish to warn of its increasing danger to the Jews of the world, to our Arab people and to world peace and security. For Zionism encourages the Jew to emigrate out of his homeland and grants him an artificially-created nationality. The Zionists proceed with their terrorist activities even though these have proved ineffective. The phenomenon of constant emigration from Israel, which is bound to grow as the bastions of colonialism and racism in the world fall, is an example of the inevitability of the failure of such activities.

We urge the people and governments of the world to stand firm against Zionist attempts at encouraging world Jewry to emigrate from their countries and to usurp our land. We urge them as well firmly to oppose any discrimination against any human being, as to religion, race, or color.

Why should our Arab Palestinian people pay the price of such discrimination in the world? Why should our people be responsible for the problems of Jewish immigration, if such problems exist in the minds of some people? Why do not the supporters of these problems open their own countries, which can absorb and help these immigrants?

Those who call us terrorists wish to prevent world public opinion from discovering the truth about us and from seeing the justice on our faces. They seek to hide the terrorism and tyranny of their acts, and our own posture of self-defense.

The difference between the revolutionary and the terrorist lies in the reason for which each fights. For whoever stands by a just cause and fights for the freedom and liberation of his land from the invaders, the settlers and the colonialists, cannot possibly be called terrorist; otherwise the American people in their struggle for liberation from the British colonialists would have been terrorists, the European resistance against the Nazis would be terrorism, the struggle of the Asian, African and Latin American peoples would also be terrorism, and many of you who are in this Assembly Hall were considered terrorists. This is actually a just and proper struggle consecrated by the United Nations Charter and by the Universal Declaration of Human Rights. As to those who fight against the just causes, those who wage war to occupy, colonize and oppress other people—those are the terrorists, those are the people whose actions should be condemned, who should be called war criminals: for the justice of the cause determines the right to struggle.

Zionist terrorism which was waged against the Palestinian people to evict it from its country and usurp its land is registered in our official documents. Thousands of our people were assassinated in their villages and towns, tens of thousands of others were forced at gun-point to leave their homes and the lands of their fathers. Time and time again our children, women and aged were evicted and had to wander in the deserts and climb mountains without any food or water. No one who in 1948 witnessed the catastrophe that befell the inhabitants of hundreds of villages and towns—in Jaffa, Lydda, Ramle and Galilee—no one who has been a witness to that catastrophe will ever forget the experience, even though the mass blackout has succeeded in hiding these horrors as it had hidden the traces of 385 Palestinian villages and towns destroyed at the time and erased from the map. The destruction of 19,000 houses during the past seven years, which is equivalent to the complete destruction of 200 more Palestinian villages, and the great number of maimed as a result of the treatment they were subjected to in Israeli prisons, cannot be hidden by any blackout.

Their terrorism fed on hatred and this hatred was even directed against the olive tree in my country, which has been a proud symbol and which reminded them of the indigenous inhabitants of the land, a living reminder that the land is Palestinian. Thus they sought to destroy it. How can one describe the statement by Golda Meir which expressed her disquiet about "the Palestinian children born every day"? They see in the Palestinian child, in the Palestinian tree, an enemy that should be exterminated. For tens of years Zionists have been harassing our people's cultural, political, social and artistic leaders, terrorizing them and assassinating them. They have stolen our cultural heritage, our popular folklore and have claimed it as theirs. Their terrorism even reached our sacred places in our beloved and peaceful Jerusalem. They have endeavoured to de-Arabize it and make it lose its Moslem and Christian character by evicting its inhabitants and annexing it.

I must mention the fire of the Aksa Mosque and the disfiguration of many of the monuments, which are both historic and religious in character. Jerusalem, with its religious history and its spiritual values, bears witness to the future. It is proof of our eternal presence, of our civilization, of our human values. It is therefore not surprising that under its skies the three religions were born and that under that sky these three religions shine in order to enlighten mankind so that it might express the tribulations and hopes of humanity, and that it might mark out the road of the future with its hopes.

The small number of Palestinian Arabs who were not uprooted by the Zionists in 1948 are at present refugees in their own homeland. Israeli law treats them as second-class citizens—and even as third-class citizens since Oriental Jews are second-class citizens and they have been subject to all forms of racial discrimination and terrorism after confiscation of their land and property. They have been victims to bloody massacres such as that of Kfar Kassim; they have been expelled from their villages and denied the right to return, as in the case of the inhabitants of Ikrit and Kfar-Birim. For 26 years, our population has been living under martial law and has been denied the freedom of movement without prior permission from the Israeli military governor—this at a time when an Israeli law was promulgated granting citizenship to any Jew anywhere who wanted to emigrate to our homeland. Moreover, another Israeli law stipulated that Palestinians who were not present in their villages or towns at the time of the occupation were not entitled to Israeli citizenship.

The record of Israeli rulers is replete with acts of terror perpetrated on those of our people who remained under occupation in Sinai and the Golan Heights. The criminal bombardment of the Bahr-al-Bakar School and the Abou Zaabal factory are but two such unforgettable acts of terrorism. The total destruction of the Syrian city of Kuneitra is yet another tangible instance of systematic terrorism. If a record of Zionist terrorism in South Lebanon were to be compiled, the enormity of its acts would shock even the most hardened: piracy, bombardments, scorched earth, destruction of hundreds of homes, eviction of civilians and the kidnapping of Lebanese citizens. This clearly constitutes a violation of Lebanese sovereignty and is in preparation for the diversion of the Litani River waters.

Need one remind this Assembly of the numerous resolutions adopted by it condemning Israeli aggressions committed against Arab countries, Israeli violations of human rights and the articles of the Geneva Conventions, as well as the resolutions pertaining to the annexation of the city of Jerusalem and its restoration to its former status?

The only description for these acts is that they are acts of barbarism and terrorism. And yet, the Zionist racists and colonialists have the temerity to describe the just struggle of our people as terror. Could there be a more flagrant distortion of truth than this? We ask those who usurped our land, who are committing murderous acts of terrorism against our people and are practising racial discrimination more extensively than the racists of South Africa, we ask them to keep in mind the United Nations General Assembly resolution that called for the one-year suspension of the membership of the Government of South Africa from the United

Nations. Such is the inevitable fate of every racist country that adopts the law of the jungle, usurps the homeland of others and persists in oppression.

For the past 30 years, our people have had to struggle against British occupation and Zionist invasion, both of which had one intention, namely the usurpation of our land. Six major revolts and tens of popular uprisings were staged to foil these attempts, so that our homeland might remain ours. Over 30,000 martyrs, the equivalent in comparative terms of 6 million Americans, died in the process.

When the majority of the Palestinian people was uprooted from its homeland in 1948, the Palestinian struggle for self-determination continued under the most difficult conditions. We tried every possible means to continue our political struggle to attain our national rights, but to no avail. Meanwhile, we had to struggle for sheer existence. Even in exile we educated our children. This was all a part of trying to survive.

The Palestinian people produced thousands of physicians, lawyers, teachers and scientists who actively participated in the development of the Arab countries bordering on their usurped homeland. They utilized their income to assist the young and aged amongst their people who remained in the refugee camps. They educated their younger sisters and brothers, supported their parents and cared for their children. All along the Palestinian dreamed of return. Neither the Palestinian's allegiance to Palestine nor his determination to return waned; nothing could persuade him to relinquish his Palestinian identity or to forsake his homeland. The passage of time did not make him forget, as some hoped he would. When our people lost faith in the international community which persisted in ignoring its rights and when it became obvious that the Palestinians would not recuperate one inch of Palestine through exclusively political means, our people had no choice but to resort to armed struggle. Into that struggle it poured its material and human resources. We bravely faced the most vicious acts of Israeli terrorism which were aimed at diverting our struggle and arresting it.

In the past 10 years of our struggle, thousands of martyrs and twice as many wounded, maimed and imprisoned were offered in sacrifice, all in an effort to resist the imminent threat of liquidation, to regain our right to self-determination and our undisputed right to return to our homeland. With the utmost dignity and the most admirable revolutionary spirit, our Palestinian people has not lost its spirit in Israeli prisons and concentration camps or when faced with all forms of harassment and intimidation. It struggles for sheer existence and it continues to strive to preserve the Arab character of its land. Thus it resists oppression, tyranny and terrorism in their ugliest forms.

It is through our popular armed struggle that our political leadership and our national institutions finally crystalized and a national liberation movement, comprising all the Palestinian factions, organizations, and capabilities, materialized in the Palestine Liberation Organization.

Through our militant Palestine national liberation movement, our people's struggle matured and grew enough to accommodate political and social struggle in addition to armed struggle. The Palestine Liberation Organization was a major factor in creating a new Palestinian individual, qualified to shape the future of our Palestine, not merely content with mobilizing the Palestinians for the challenges of the present.

The Palestine Liberation Organization can be proud of having a large number of cultural and educational activities, even while engaged in armed struggle, and at a time when it faced the increasingly vicious blows of Zionist terrorism. We established institutes for scientific research, agricultural development and social welfare, as well as centers for the revival of our cultural heritage and the preservation of our folklore. Many Palestinian poets, artists and writers have enriched Arab culture in particular, and world culture generally. Their profoundly humane works have won the admiration of all those familiar with them. In contrast to that, our enemy has been systematically destroying our culture and disseminating racist, imperialist ideologies; in short, everything that impedes progress, justice, democracy and peace.

The Palestine Liberation Organization has earned its legitimacy because of the sacrifice inherent in its pioneering role, and also because of its dedicated leadership of the struggle. It has also been granted this legitimacy by the Palestinian masses, which in harmony with it have chosen it to lead the struggle according to its directives. The Palestine Liberation Organization has also gained its legitimacy by representing every faction, union or group as well as every Palestinian talent, either in the National Council or in people's institutions. This legitimacy was further strengthened by the support of the entire Arab nation, and it was consecrated during the last Arab Summit Conference which reiterated the right of the Palestine Liberation Organization, in its capacity as the sole representative of the Palestinian people, to establish an independent national State on all liberated Palestinian territory.

Moreover, the Palestine Liberation Organization's legitimacy was intensified as a result of fraternal support given by other liberation movements and by friendly, like-minded nations that stood by our side, encouraging and aiding us in our struggle to secure our national rights.

Here I must also warmly convey the gratitude of our revolutionary fighters and that of our people to the nonaligned countries, the socialist countries, the Islamic countries, the African countries and friendly European countries, as well as all our other friends in Asia, Africa and Latin America.

The Palestine Liberation Organization represents the Palestinian people, legitimately and uniquely. Because of this, the Palestine Liberation Organization expresses the wishes and hopes of its people. Because of this, too, it brings these very wishes and hopes before you, urging you not to shirk a momentous historic responsibility towards our just cause.

For many years now, our people has been exposed to the ravages of war, destruction and dispersion. It has paid in the blood of its sons that which cannot ever be compensated. It has borne the burdens of occupation, dispersion, eviction and terror more uninterruptedly than any other people. And yet all this has made our people neither vindictive nor vengeful. Nor has it caused us to resort to the racism of our enemies. Nor have we lost the true method by which friend and foe are distinguished.

For we deplore all those crimes committed against the Jews, we also deplore all the real discrimination suffered by them because of their faith.

I am a rebel and freedom is my cause. I know well that many of you present here today once stood in exactly the same resistance position as I now occupy and from which I must fight. You once had to convert dreams into reality by your struggle. Therefore you must now share my dream. I think this is exactly why I can ask you now to help, as together we bring out our dream into a bright reality, our common dream for a peaceful future in Palestine's sacred land.

As he stood in an Israeli military court, the Jewish revolutionary, Ahud Adif, said: "I am no terrorist; I believe that a democratic State should exist on this land." Adif now languishes in a Zionist prison among his co-believers. To him and his colleagues I send my heartfelt good wishes.

And before those same courts there stands today a brave prince of the church. Bishop Capucci. Lifting his fingers to form the same victory sign used by our freedom-fighters, he said: "What I have done, I have done that all men may live on this land of peace in peace." This princely priest will doubtless share Adif's grim fate. To him we send our salutations and greetings.

Why therefore should I not dream and hope? For is not revolution the making real of dreams and hopes? So let us work together that my dream may be fulfilled, that I may return with my people out of exile, there in Palestine to live with this Jewish freedom-fighter and his partners, with this Arab priest and his brothers, in one democratic State where Christian, Jew and Moslem live in justice, equality, fraternity and progress.

Is this not a noble dream worthy of my struggle alongside all lovers of freedom everywhere? For the most admirable dimension of this dream is that it is Palestinian, a dream from out of the land of peace, the land of martyrdom and heroism, and the land of history, too.

Let us remember that the Jews of Europe and the United States have been known to lead the struggles for secularism and the separation of Church and State. They have also been known to fight against discrimination on religious grounds. How can they continue to support the most fanatic, discriminatory and closed of nations in its policy?

In my formal capacity as Chairman of the Palestine Liberation Organization and leader of the Palestinian revolution I proclaim before you that when we speak of our common hopes for the Palestine of tomorrow we include in our perspective all Jews now living in Palestine who choose to live with us there in peace and without discrimination.

In my formal capacity as Chairman of the Palestine Liberation Organization and leader of the Palestinian revolution I call upon Jews to turn away one by one from the illusory promises made to them by Zionist ideology and Israeli leadership. They are offering Jews perpetual bloodshed, endless war and continuous thraldom.

We invite them to emerge from their moral isolation into a more open realm of free choice, far from their present leadership's efforts to implant in them a Masada complex.

We offer them the most generous solution, that we might live together in a framework of just peace in our democratic Palestine.

In my formal capacity as Chairman of the Palestine Liberation Organization, I announce here that we do not wish one drop of either Arab or Jewish blood to be shed; neither do we delight in the continuation of killing, which would end once a just peace, based on our people's rights, hopes and aspirations had been finally established.

In my formal capacity as Chairman of the Palestine Liberation Organization and leader of the Palestinian revolution I appeal to you to accompany our people in its struggle to attain its right to self-determination. This right is consecrated in the United Nations Charter and has been repeatedly confirmed in resolutions adopted by this august body since the drafting of the Charter. I appeal to you, further; to aid our people's return to its homeland from an involuntary exile imposed upon it by force of arms, by tyranny, by oppression, so that we may regain our property, our land, and thereafter live in our national homeland, free and sovereign, enjoying all the privileges of nationhood. Only then can Palestinian creativity be concentrated on the service of humanity. Only then will our Jerusalem resume its historic role as a peaceful shrine for all religions.

I appeal to you to enable our people to establish national independent sovereignty over its own land.

The Meaning of
"A Democratic Palestinian State"*

By Y. Harkabi

1. The Internal Debate

The crux of the Arab conflict with Israel has been the problem of safeguarding the country's Arab character. Arab demands during the Mandate

* Excerpts from an article originally published in 1970, with a postscript of 1974. From Y. Harkabi: *Palestinians and Israel*, Jerusalem, 1974.

for the prohibition of the sale of land to Jews and curtailment of Jewish immigration served the same purpose: that of keeping the ownership of land and Palestine's ethnic character inviolate. The difficulties confronting the Arabs in their attempt to halt Judaization were aggravated with the end of the Mandate and the foundation of the State of Israel: from then on it was a question of turning back the wheel of history and erasing the Jewish state.

The problem of eliminating the Jewish state is heightened by the presence of a considerable Jewish population. For a Jewish state depends upon the existence of Jewish citizens, and therefore elimination of the state requires in principle a "reduction" in their number. Hence the frequency and dominance of the motif of killing the Jews and throwing them into the sea in Arab pronouncements. Their position, insofar as it was *politicidal* (i.e., calling for annihilation of a state), was bound to have *genocidal* implications, even had the Arabs not been bent upon revenge.

When, after the Six-Day War, the Arabs realized that their wild statements had harmed their international reputation, they moderated their shrill demands for the annihilation of Israel. Arab propagandists denied that they had ever advocated the slaughter of the Jewish population, asserting that, at most, "Jewish provocations" had aroused their anger and wild statements which, they alleged, were not meant to be taken literally. Ahmed Shukeiry insisted that he never advocated throwing the Jews into the sea, that the whole thing was merely a Zionist libel. What he meant, he explained, was that the Jews would return to their countries of origin by way of the sea: "They came by the sea and will return by the sea" (*Palestine Documents for 1967*, p. 1084).

After the Six-Day War, Arab spokesmen put forward the concept of "a Democratic Palestinian State in which Arabs and Jews will live in peace." This slogan was well received and regarded by the world at large as evidence of a new Arab moderation. Many people overlooked the ambiguity of the pronouncement and disregarded the fact that it did not contradict basic Arab contentions: for the wording might well imply the reduction of Jews to an insignificant minority, which would then be permitted to live in peace. Once this line was adopted, its meaning was keenly debated among the Palestinian Arabs.

An indication of the slogan's true significance, as understood by the Palestinian organizations, is found in a circular to its members sent by the Popular Democratic Front for the Liberation of Palestine, reporting on the deliberations of the sixth session of the Palestinian National Assembly. This fedayeen organization, headed by Na'if Hawatmeh, broke away from George Habash's Popular Front for the Liberation of Palestine in February 1969. A delegation of the Popular Democratic Front proposed to the Assembly that the slogan "Democratic State" should be given "a progressive content." The Assembly rejected their proposal suggesting that the main purpose of the "Democratic State" concept was to improve the Arab image. Moreover, the inclusion of this slogan in the national program would, it was stressed, impair the Arab character of Palestine. Nevertheless, since it had been well received abroad, the Assembly considered it worth retaining.

The relevant passage in the Popular Democratic Front's report entitled "Internal Circular concerning Debates and Results of the Sixth National Assembly" reads:

> The slogan "The Democratic Palestinian State" has been raised for some time within the Palestinian context. Fatah was the first to adopt it. Since it was raised, this slogan has met with remarkable world response. Our delegation presented the Congress [i.e., the Assembly] with a resolution designed to elucidate its meaning from a progressive aspect, opposing in principle the slogan of throwing the Jews into the sea, which has in the past seriously harmed the Arab position.
>
> When the subject was first debated, it was thought that there was general agreement on it. But as the debate developed, considerable opposition showed itself. In the course of the discussion the following views came to light.
>
> 1. One which maintains that the slogan of "The Democratic Palestinian State" is a tactical one which we propagate because it has been well received internationally.
>
> 2. Another suggests that we consider this slogan to be strategic rather than tactical, but that it should be retained even though it is not a basic principle. This position, but for a mere play of words, corresponds to the previous one.
>
> 3. The third view was more straightforward in rejecting the slogan and its progressive content as proposed by our delegation. The position of this faction was based on the assertion that the slogan contradicts the Arab character of Palestine and the principle of self-determination enshrined in the National Covenant of the [Palestine] Liberation Organization, and that it also advocates a peaceful settlement with the Jews of Palestine. . . .

In this way the "democratic solution" is presented as a compromise between two chauvinistic alternatives—a Jewish state, and driving the Jews into the sea—as if these were comparable propositions. By this supposedly fair solution, the Arabs renounce the extermination of Jews, and the Jews renounce their state. Although the Palestinian state will become a popular democracy, its Arab character will be preserved by being part of a larger "democratic" Arab federation. The final paragraph is meant to repudiate objections that a democratic Palestine would remain, owing to its mixed population, an anomaly among the Arab states and difficult to digest within the framework of Arab unity.

The Democratic Front's pronouncement may be mistakenly interpreted as favoring a binational state: "The Palestinian state will eliminate racial discrimination and national persecution and will be based on a democratic solution to the conflict brought about by the coexistence (*ta'āyush*) of the two peoples, Arabs and Jews" (*The Present Situation . . .* , p. 136). The recognition of "a Jewish people" is a significant innovation. Hitherto Arabs have mostly held that Jews constitute only a religion and do not therefore deserve a national state. However, this admission of a Jewish nationhood is qualified, for Jews as a people are not entitled to a state of their own but must settle for incorporation in a state of Palestinian nationality. Their nationhood, therefore, has only cultural and not national-political dimensions. Thus, Hawatmeh tells Lutfi al-Khuli, editor of *at-Tali'a*:

> We urged initiation of a dialogue with the Israeli socialist organization Matzpen, which advocates an Arab-Jewish binational state. But we have not been able to convince Matzpen to adopt a thoroughly progressive, democratic position on the Palestine question which would mean liquidation (*tasfiaya*) of the Zionist entity and establishment of a democratic Palestinian state opposed to all kinds of class and national suppression (*at-Tali'a*, November, 1969, p. 106).

The proposal for a binational state, as advocated by Matzpen, is not sufficiently progressive for Hawatmeh. In his view, Jewish nationhood implies only cultural autonomy for a religious community. But this is no innovation; Mr. Shukeiry was prepared to grant the same.

2. Bafflements and Contradictions

In Arab journalism, particularly in periodicals, interesting articles and symposia are often published concerning social problems, self-criticism and the Arab-Israel conflict. Israeli newspaper reporting usually skips over these articles because it is by its nature more concerned with political events, more with Arabs' actions and less with their ideas. Such journalistic portrayal of the Arab world becomes pallid because of the absence of the human-ideological dimension of events. Human beings not only operate, they also think about their actions. Furthermore, our concern for the opponent's reflections tends to humanize him by viewing him along with all his human problems. The Six-Day War and its aftermath raised questions for the Arabs and stimulated them to reassess their procedure in the conflict. They began to grapple with the question of their *objective* in the conflict. This wrestling is primarily concerned now with the slogan "Democratic Palestinian State."

In the weekly supplement of the Beirut newspaper *al-Anwar* (March 8,

1970), a long symposium was published concerning the meaning of the slogan "The Democratic State," in which the views of most of the prominent fedayeen organizations were represented. A translation of extracts (italicized text) from this symposium is here presented, along with comments by the author and a summary concerning its significance.

Representative of the Democratic Front: . . . The adoption of a particular slogan, in our estimation, does not stem from a subjective position or a subjective desire but from a study and analysis of the evolution of the objective situation, the objective possibilities present in society and within history—moving forces, as well as the nature of the potential evolution of these forces in the future. . . .

Coexistence (ta'āyush) *with this entity (Israel) is impossible, not because of a national aim or national aspiration of the Arabs, but because the presence of this entity will determine this region's development in connection with world imperialism, which follows from the objective link between it and Zionism. Thus, eradicating imperialist influence in the Middle East means eradicating the Israeli entity. This is something indispensable, not only from the aspect of the Palestinian people's right of self-determination, and in its homeland, but also from the aspect of protecting the Arab national liberation movement, and this objective also can only be achieved by means of armed struggle. . . .*

The representative of the Arab Liberation Front (a fedayeen organization under Iraqi influence): *There is no special [separate] solution for the Palestine issue. The solution must be within the framework of the Arab revolution, because the Palestine issue is not merely the paramount Arab issue but the substance and basic motivation of the Arab struggle. If the Arab nation suffers from backwardness, exploitation and disunity, these afflictions are much more severe in Palestine. That is, the Arab cause in the present historical stage is epitomized in the Palestine issue. . . .*

The liberation of Palestine will be the way for the Arabs to realize unity, not to set up regional State No. 15, which will only deepen disunity. The unified State will be the alternative to the Zionist entity, and it will be of necessity democratic, as long as we understand beforehand the dialectical connection between unity and Socialism. In the united Arab State all the minorities—denominational and others—will have equal rights . . .

The intention is not to set up a Palestinian State as an independent unit, but to incorporate it within a unified Arab State which will be democratic because it is progressive, and which will grant the Israeli Jews minority rights.

Shafiq al-Hut (a leader of the PLO and head of its Beirut office): . . . *The Palestinian problem is that of a Zionist-colonialist invasion at the expense of a land and a people known for thirteen centuries as the Palestinian Arab people. . . . I side with Farid al-Khatib in holding that there is no benefit in expatiating upon the slogan "Democratic Palestinian State." I hope the fedayeen organizations will not do so, although I would encourage discussion of it by those who are not in responsible positions. Whatever discussion of it there is on the part of the fighting groups may cause a sense of helplessness, despair or weakness. . . .*

As far as it concerns the human situation of the Jews, which Farid al-Khatib mentioned, we should expose the Zionist movement and say to the Jew: The Zionist movement which brought you to Palestine did not supply a solution to your problem as a Jew; therefore you must return whence you came to seek another way of striving for a solution for what is called "the problem of the persecuted Jew in the world." As Marx has said, he (the Jew) has no alternative but to be assimilated into his society. . . .

Even if we wished, by force of circumstances, a Democratic Palestinian State "period," this would mean its being non-Arab. Let us face matters honestly. When we speak simply of a Democratic Palestinian State, this means we discard its Arab identity. I say that on this subject we cannot negotiate, even if we possess the political power to authorize this kind of decision, because we thereby disregard an historical truth, namely, that this land and those who dwell upon it belong to a certain environment and a certain region, to which we are linked as one nation, one heritage and one hope—Unity, Freedom and Socialism. . . .

The implication that the Israeli Jews would be allowed to stay in the Democratic State raises difficulties concerning its Arab character.

If the slogan of the Democratic State was intended only to counter the claim that we wish to throw the Jews into the sea, this is indeed an apt slogan and an effective political and propaganda blow. But if we wish to regard it as the ultimate strategy of the Palestinian and Arab liberation movement, then I believe it requires a long pause for reflection, for it bears upon our history, just as our present and certainly our future.

Representative of as-Sa'iqa (a Syrian fedayeen organization): *I was among those who thought five years ago that we must slaughter the Jews. But now I cannot imagine that, if we win one night, it will be possible for us to slaughter them, or even one tenth of them. I cannot conceive of it, neither as a man, nor as an Arab.*

If so, what do we wish to do with these Jews? This is a problem for which I do not claim to have a ready answer. It is a problem which every Arab and Palestinian citizen has an obligation to express his opinion about, because it is yet early for a final, ripe formulation to offer the world and those living in Palestine.

Thus, I think that among many Jews, those living in Palestine, espe-

cially the Arab Jews, there is a great desire to return to their countries of origin, since the Zionist efforts to transform them into a homogeneous, cohesive nation have failed. There is a well-known human feeling—yearning for one's homeland, one's birthplace. There are a number of known facts concerning the Jews living in Palestine today which clearly point to this feeling among them. They desire to return to their countries of origin, especially Jews from the Arab region. . . .

Moderator: . . . *Can we consider the Kurdish problem and the manner of its solution as similar to the Jewish problem and its solution under the heading of the slogan of one Democratic State? . . .*

Representative of the Liberation Front: *Our view of the subject of Kurdish national rights follows from objective and historical considerations which substantially contradict the nature and objectives of the Zionist movement. The Kurds comprise a nationality having a distinct, well-known historical, geographical and human dimension. . . .*

Farid al-Khatib: *As far as the Arab character of the Democratic State is concerned, the Jews in Palestine have the right to express their view concerning the Arab character of the Democratic State in a democratic manner. And although it is possible to say that the Democratic State is Arab, and to say furthermore that it is a union, it is advisable to hold back additional information until the appropriate stages in the evolution of the resistance are reached. When the Zionist movement came to Palestine, it first sought a refuge, afterward a homeland, and then a State; and now it is striving to build an empire within and outside Palestine.*

Zionism also disclosed its objectives in stages.

There is nothing to be gained by summoning the Jews in the Zionist State to join the national liberation movement, as Shafiq al-Hut proposed, when he advocated convening the unified State at once. This will not convince the Jews of the world and world public opinion.

As far as it concerns the number of Palestinians, all those who emigrated to Latin America in the nineteenth century, and those who live in the desert, in exile, under conquest, or in prison, all are citizens in the State. For example: the number of Bethlehemite residents living in South America exceeds the number of those Bethlehemites living in occupied Palestine, and the combined total [of all Palestinians] is not less than that of the Jews now living in the Zionist State. . . .

The Palestinians are more numerous than the Israeli Jews and will determine the character of the State.

Shafiq al-Hut: *First, how can Farid (al-Khatib) think that the Jews and Zionists who came to set up an empire in our country have the privilege to express their democratic right in the Palestinian State? Second, how can he claim that it is difficult to convince Jewish citizens to join the liberation movement?*

Farid al-Khatib: *I think that most of the Jews living in Palestine are groups of people who were deceived by the Zionist movement and the world imperialist movement. And the Jew, as a man, has the right to express his opinion in a democratic manner regarding his future life after the collapse of the Zionist State, which is opposed to the Democratic State insofar as it discriminates between the Eastern Jew and the Western Jew and the Circassian Jew.*

The second point: The greatest ambition of the revolution is to draw the Jews of the Zionist State into the ranks of the resistance movement. . . . But what I wanted to say is that it is difficult to persuade the Jews to join the resistance movement because its immediate objective is to dissolve the Zionist contradiction within the Zionist State. . . .

Representative of the Democratic Front: *It seems to me that many of the disagreements that exist concerning this idea can be traced to some manner of misunderstanding or lack of communication. . . . This State is not bi-national in the sense that there would be two national States joined together in one form or another. This solution must be rejected, not only because it is inconsistent with our own desire, but also because it is not a true democratic solution. It is rather a solution that will represent the continuation of the national conflict which exists between the Jews and Arabs, not a solution of this conflict. It is impossible to speak of a democratic solution if it is powerless to eliminate the conflict between the different denominations and peoples within the Democratic State. When we speak of democracy it must be clear that we do not mean liberal democracy in the manner of "one man, one vote."*

OLD ILLUSIONS AND NEW AWARENESS

If the number of Jews living in Israel is not reduced, then, on a national level their quantitative and qualitative weight will dilute the Arab character of the liberated state, and on a personal level there will not be sufficient room for these Jews as well as for the Palestinians who supposedly *all* desire to return. In order to evade these difficulties, the spokesmen in the symposium try to breathe life into old ideas: that the Jews brought to the country were misguided by Zionist deceit (Zionism therefore not being a vital need), and that they remain by coercion (criticism by Israelis of themselves and their state, in a manner unknown in Arab countries, is interpreted as a sign of hatred for the state and a desire to emigrate). On these grounds it is believed that the Jews would rejoice at the opportunity to leave. An interesting element of self-deception is added, that the Jews from Arab countries wish to return to their countries of origin. One may suspect that this illusion contains the psychological dimension of *amour-*

propre and self-adulation: the Arabs are so good and were so kind to the Jews that it is inconceivable for the Jews not to desire ardently to return to live under their protection. However, along with these notions, there are signs of recognition that this is a false hope, and that the Jews have nowhere to return to, especially those born in the country, who will soon become the majority of the Jewish community. An attempt to grapple with these contradictory notions is most evident in the words of the as-Sa'iqa representative, who maintains at one and the same time that most Israeli Jews have nowhere to go, and yet that many will emigrate.

The spokesmen also try to evade this problem by claiming that the Israeli Jews are not a people. Their attachment to the country is therefore weak, and the hope that they will emigrate is reinforced. Moreover, in the clash between the Jewish group, whose cohesion is supposedly religious and not national, and the group whose cohesion is national, the latter will prevail, thereby determining the character of the country. Therefore, even if a considerable Jewish community remains there will be no such thing as a partnership between two homogeneous groups, creating a bi-national state. The Democratic Front, which stresses the Palestinianism of the Democratic State more than its Arab character, also regards membership in an Arab unity as inherent in the very idea of the Democratic State, while the Iraqi organization rejects the notion of the Palestinian State and regards it at best as a district within a unified state. (For this organization, the struggle in Palestine has the value of a catalyst for the rest of the changes in Arab countries, or a spark that will ignite a revolution that will spread to all of them.) Along with these hopes of reducing the number of Jews in the Democratic State there is the notion of tipping the population scales in the Arabs' favor by considering all Palestine Arabs, whereever they may live, as prospective citizens of the state according to an Arab Law of Return of sorts.

All the participants in the symposium agree that the Jews do not presently constitute a people. However, the recognition gnaws at some of them that nationalism is not something static but an evolution, and as time goes on, the Jews in Israel will become consolidated into a people and a nation. Hence the conclusion that this process must be forestalled by the founding of a Palestinian State. The temporal factor thus works against the idea that the Israelis are not a people, and against the possibility of founding a Palestinian State. It is no accident that Shafiq al-Hut vigorously maintains the essential and permanent nature of the Jewish status as non-people and non-nation. According to the view presented by Arabs, only a people has the right of political self-determination and deserves a state of its own. If the Jews are indeed becoming a people, this means that they are in the process of acquiring these rights.

AN ARAB PANDORA'S BOX

For most of the participants, the slogan "Democratic State" is merely tactical, the aim being to give the outside world a positive impression and to enchant the Israelis who, as the speaker who describes Fatah's views says, will only eventually discover its full meaning. For the Democratic Front this is presumably not merely a slogan, but a *principle* they sincerely hold as an implication of the progressivism they profess. However, even they wrestle with the slogan; they safeguard themselves by various qualifications or *hedges*: the state will be a member within an Arab federation, and the democracy will not be formal, nor expressed in a numerical representation, but a "true" democracy of "the contents"—that is, its policy will represent progressiveness as expressed by "the Palestinian revolution." The final qualification is their insistence upon the precondition for establishing the Democratic State, that Israel be destroyed.

For those who regard the slogan "Democratic State" as merely a tactic, the problem arises that it is impossible to lead the public only by tactical slogans; one must present the objectives of a national vision. While the slogan "Democratic State" may be helpful externally, it is quite destructive internally, impairs the state's Arabism and undermines confidence in the feasibility of "returning" to the country, if it would not be evacuated. Shafiq al-Hut states bluntly that acceptance of this slogan means abandoning the idea of Arabism. From the Arab viewpoint another two-fold question arises: 1) if the Jews are a people, it is doubtful whether they will consent to live in a non-Jewish state, and hence the expressed hope that they will emigrate; 2) since the Palestinians are a people, they will certainly be opposed to returning to a state which is not Arab.

It appears that the Palestinians and Arabs are beginning to sense the difficulty of their ideological position. In the past they could be content with the formulations "restoration of rights" and "restoration of the homeland," which were restricted to the meaning of the objective as bearing upon what would be given to the Arabs, and the implication concerning what would be taken away from the Jews was overlooked. Arab spokesmen in foreign countries are still striving to focus on the need to rectify the injustice inflicted on the Palestinians, while evading the implication of this rectification for the Jews. The necessity of defining the position in all its aspects and the debate concerning the Democratic Palestinian State undermine the Arab position. The slogan of a "Democratic State" seemed to be an escape from a genocidal position, but it was revealed as the first step of retreat, and the source of problems and bewilderment. I think it is no exaggeration to say that this slogan opened a Pandora's box for the Arab position in the conflict. Hence the deep apprehensions of all the participants in the discussion concerning this slogan, and the dramatic agreement of everyone at the end of it that the slogan

"Democratic State" is premature, even though this contradicted the previous insistence by some on the need for a clear definition of the objective.

It appears that those who formulated the Palestinian Covenant of 1968 sensed the difficulties inherent in the Arab position and wished to anticipate them by nailing down the qualification that only a small Jewish minority (the descendants of those who came to the country before 1917) would be given citizenship in "the liberated state," thus assuring the Arab character of the country. If this stipulation manifests radicalization of the position, the reason was probably the apprehension that otherwise the ground would begin sliding beneath the Arab position.

The slogan of the "Democratic State" was offered as an escape from the odium that Article 6 of the 1968 Covenant brought upon the PLO stand, and as if the former superseded the latter, even without the formal act of amending the Covenant. It seems that the difficulties in which the idea of the Democratic State is enmeshed and the internal controversies it aroused, as expressed in this symposium, explain why Article 6 has not been amended, despite the fact that it damaged the Palestinian cause.

3. Postscript

The slogan of the "Democratic State" was hailed by Arab spokesmen as an all-important innovation demonstrating the liberal humanitarian nature of the Palestine movement. Yasser Arafat, to strengthen this impression, even said that its president can be Jewish. However, scrutiny shows that it is neither so liberal nor new.

The objective of setting up a Democratic Palestine was enshrined in the resolutions of the Eighth Palestinian National Assembly (March 1–5, 1971). The resolution was carefully formulated and it does not say, as Palestinian spokesmen purport to interpret the slogan, that *all* Israelis will be allowed to stay, but that the state will be based on equality of rights for all its citizens: "The future state in Palestine . . . will be Democratic, in which all will enjoy the same rights and obligations." This is quite compatible with the quantitative limitation included in the infamous Article 6 of the 1968 Covenant.

It is not new. All along the Palestinians have repeatedly declared that their state will be democratic. That is part of the spirit of the age, when even autocratic regimes call themselves democratic. For instance, the Congress, which set up the "All-Palestine Government" in Gaza and which unanimously elected the former Mufti of Jerusalem, Hajj Amin al-Husaini, as its president, proclaimed on October 1, 1948 "the establishment of a free and democratic sovereign state. In it the citizens will enjoy their liberties and their rights. . . ."

Even if the slogan of the "Democratic State" were free of inconsistency and insincerity it is not acceptable to the Israelis. The Israelis have no less a right to national self-determination than the Palestinian Arabs. They do not want to become Palestinians of Jewish faith; they intend to remain Israelis.

The difficulties for the Arabs inherent in the slogan of the "Democratic State" caused a decline in its discussion at subsequent Palestinian Congresses. This does not mean that it was discarded, as the alternative is to fall back on the brutality of the former, blatant, politicidal-genocidal position.

No Need To Worry Now

Perhaps the most common attitude is to concentrate at this stage on the demand for "self-determination for the Palestinians in their homeland" and leave the rest. This demand is an objective that can be easily justified. Defining the final objective now, it is argued, is a waste of time, and only a source of bafflement. Political objectives should be set in a time sequence. The problem of reconciling the existence of a large Jewish community with the conversion of the country into a Palestinian state is one for the distant future and should not bother the Arabs and Palestinians now. Now they should exert all their efforts in the struggle against Israel and in attaining of their national and social objectives. The achievement of these and the return of the Palestinians will produce new conditions which may solve the entire problem.

This approach was already alluded to in the Symposium. It has been expressed with greater clarity by Alias Murqus in his book criticizing the platform of the Lebanese Communist Party (LCP) at its Second Congress in the summer of 1968. Murqus commends the LCP stand in defining that the "final solution to the Palestinian problem should be based on positions of principle, stemming from the inalienable right of the Palestinian Arabs in their land and homeland and hence their right to return there and achieve their self-determination . . . as the existence of the Jews in Palestine cannot impair the Palestinian natural and historical right in their homeland." He stresses that "the final solution to the Palestinian problem is Palestine as an Arab homeland," and as regards the future it calls for "the complete eradication of the State of Israel." He goes on:

How shall we reconcile the existence of two million Jews and two million Palestinian Arabs? This is not our task or yours now. Let us define our objective in principle and nothing more. Let us define the present way to the goal: The fighting and the falling of hundreds of thousands from the Arabs and the Jews (from the Arab more than from the Jews). With the victory of the Algerian revolution the majority of the French, young and old, went, returned to France. With Arab victory in the Near East (the battle will be longer, fiercer and with heavier casualties), it is possible that the Jews in great numbers will return whence they came—Baghdad, Aleppo, Yemen, Morocco, Tunisia, Algeria, Egypt, Poland and other places, to France, or they will settle in Canada, the USA and Australia. This problem should not worry us, as its solution is by the struggle (*Marxism, Leninism and the World and Arab Development in the Platform of the Lebanese Communist Party*, (Arabic) Dar al-Haqiqa, Beirut, 1970, pp. 362–363).

Peace with Egypt?

By Walter Laqueur*

Any discussion of the current prospects for peace between Israel and the Arab countries has to begin by rehearsing the history of the Middle East between the Six-Day War of June 1967 and the Yom Kippur War of October 1973. Efforts to reach a peace settlement in those seven years were protracted, highly complicated, and ultimately futile. All the many plans that were proposed—the Rogers plan, the Jarring plan, and the nameless others—seem now of merely academic interest (although it is entirely possible that one or another of them will be disinterred for future use). The story of these negotiations is a melancholy one, not least for the question it raises of possible opportunities missed by the various parties to the conflict, especially Israel. Not that Israel ignored any genuine peace overture from the Arabs; there was none. But it is another matter whether an interim accommodation might not have been reached with Egypt alone, based on a demilitarization of the Sinai, and whether such an arrangement would not have lessened the likelihood of a new round of fighting.

After the Arab attack of October 1973 it was noted in Israel that the strategic depth offered by the Sinai was in fact a lifesaver; had the attack been launched from the pre-June 1967 lines it would have threatened Israel's very existence. This is very true. But the argument assumes that the 1967 borders were the only feasible alternative to the Bar Lev line, when in fact a demilitarized Sinai might have functioned as a more effective warning zone than did the Suez Canal. Nor can it be taken for granted that the attack itself was inevitable, since Egypt faced a great many problems at home and abroad, and had some sort of interim agreement been reached on the Sinai, the Egyptians might not have felt such an overriding urgency to recover all the lost territories.

Similarly, a settlement might have been made with Jordan; although not with Syria. Yet Syria in isolation could not have caused a great deal of damage. The same goes for Al-Fatah and its rival groups, who would anyway have kept up their sporadic attacks from across the border and

* Reprinted with kind permission from *Commentary* (March, 1974).

the hijacking of airplanes. In the course of time, however, the Palestinians might have come to see that they could not longer rely on the Arab governments in their struggle and they too might have come to accept the existence of the state of Israel.

This particular line of thinking was dismissed in the late 60's as a dangerous delusion by those who claimed to know Arab political psychology. Yet it later appeared that the terrorist organizations were actually afraid of a more flexible Israeli policy, lest it put them out of business. "Thank God for Dayan," wrote Yasir Arafat in retrospect:

> After the 1967 defeat, Arab opinion, broken and dispirited, was ready to conclude peace at any price. If Israel, after its lightning victory, had proclaimed that it had no expansionist aims and withdrawn its troops from the conquered territories, while continuing to occupy certain strategic points necessary to its security, the affair would have been easily settled. . . .*

Arafat exaggerates: the affair would not have been easily settled. Still, there was a chance that de-escalation might have worked, and the truth is that those opportunities which did exist were not explored.

The reasons for this were manifold. Deep down the Israelis have always inclined toward a "worst-case" analysis of their situation, arising perhaps from a determination (which is hardly difficult to understand in the light of recent history) not to take any risks with Jewish lives. Arab leaders had threatened Israel with extinction for many years prior to 1967, and these threats could not easily be dismissed as idle. When in the wake of the 1967 war the Arabs officially opted at the Khartoum conference for a policy of immobility ("No peace, no recognition, no negotiation") it was only natural for Israel to react accordingly. Any other course would have been interpreted as evidence of weakness, and it was well known that Arabs respected strength alone. From a military point of view the 1967 armistice lines seemed ideal. Before the war, Jordanian territory extended to within 30 km. of Tel Aviv, Egyptian territory to within 80; now the Egyptians were many hundreds of kilometers away, and the Jordanians were beyond the Jordan River. Israeli planes could reach Cairo in a few minutes' time. A good case could be, and was, made for not withdrawing from these lines—quite apart from the biblical prophecies and other divine injunctions invoked by the few Israeli annexationists.

No one in Israel expected all the territories taken in the Six-Day War to be retained, at least at first. Immediately after the war Moshe Dayan came out against an Israeli presence at the Suez Canal, Abba Eban warned against an "intoxication with victory," David Ben-Gurion on more than

---

* Quoted in John K. Cooley, *Green March, Black September* (New York, 1973), p. 99.

one occasion reiterated that a strong army, although vital, was no substitute for a political solution which in his view should include a return of the West Bank under agreed terms and a satisfactory settlement of the Sinai issue. Differences of opinion within the ranks of the Israeli government itself manifested themselves in such proposals as the Allon plan, recognizing the Palestinian Arabs' right to self-determination. But as time went on, Dayan, Golda Meir, Israel Galili, and other Israeli leaders became increasingly pessimistic about the prospects of a peace settlement. As long as the Arabs were unwilling to talk, Israel had to stand fast. A growing reluctance was felt even to discuss the possible terms of a settlement. The general attitude became that the Arab-Israeli confrontation, like every other conflict in history, had to run its full course. At some date in the future, when the Arabs were psychologically ready to accept the existence of Israel, it would be possible to find mutually acceptable solutions to all the outstanding questions—but for the time being Israel had to stand firm.

This policy had much to recommend it, but it also had several major flaws. It ignored the fact that the Arab-Israeli conflict was not purely regional in character, and that with regard to the two superpowers involved, an asymmetry existed between American support for Israel and Soviet support for the Arabs: America had to consider its other interests in the Middle East whereas the Soviet Union could give all-out assistance to its clients. It underrated the effective force of the Arab armies built up by the Russians since 1967. It overrated détente. And, above all, it did not take into consideration the growing importance of the oil weapon as a means of isolating Israel on the international scene: as far as Western Europe and Japan were concerned, Israel was expendable but Arab oil was not. The international constellation, in brief, was changing, and not in Israel's favor. A major power might have stood by and watched these changes with some degree of equanimity; a small country did so at its peril.

With the end of the 1973 war came a new willingness in Israel to rethink the Arab-Israeli dispute, and to consider new ways of settling it. A spate of articles and speeches, symptomatic of the confusion caused by war, suggested all kinds of panaceas: a National Security Council, a mutual-defense pact with the U.S., a "charismatic minister of information." Only after an interval of several weeks were serious attempts undertaken to analyze the lessons of the October war in broader perspective and greater depth. This soul-searching coincided with the electoral campaign in which the parties had to clarify their policies for the future. The right-wing Herut claimed in its election propaganda that the people of Israel had won a magnificent victory on the battlefield and should not have to pay for the defeat of the Western world on the oilfields of Arabia; but Herut also denied that it was a "war party" and asserted that it was much better equipped than the Labor coalition to lead Israel toward peace.

The Liberals, Herut's partners in the Likud coalition, advocated a more moderate line, suggesting Israeli concessions in return for peace; the debate among Liberals was whether these concessions should be spelled out or not.

As for the Labor alignment, it had to accommodate conflicting trends in its declared policy. The preamble of the 14-point program accepted last November stated that "Our platform must reflect the lessons of the Yom Kippur War." But what were these lessons, apart from the need (on which everyone agreed) to maintain the strength of the defense forces? The platform insisted on defensible borders based on a territorial compromise. There would be no return to the June 1967 boundaries; a peace agreement with Jordan would be based on the existence of two independent states— Israel, with Jerusalem as its capital, and an Arab state to the east; efforts would be made to continue settling Israelis in the occupied areas "in keeping with cabinet decisions giving priority to national security considerations." The last point was a concession to the "hawks" in the Labor alignment, but as a whole the Labor platform constituted a decisive victory for the doves and a retreat from the maximalist demands voiced before the war.

By sheer coincidence, the Labor platform was published on the same day the demands of the Arabs were made known at the Algiers meeting of Arab heads of state. These stated that the struggle against the Zionist "invasion" was a long-term historic responsibility which would call for many more trials and sacrifices. A cease-fire was not peace, which would come only when a number of conditions had been met, two among them paramount and unequivocal: first, the evacuation by Israel of all occupied Arab territories and above all Jerusalem; second, the re-establishment of full national rights for the Palestinian people. Yet inasmuch as no objections were voiced to negotiations with Israel, something which the Khartoum conference in 1967 had expressly rejected, it appeared to many observers that the "moderate" line of President Sadat had won out in Algiers. The final communiqué stated that the meeting had been a great success, but since Iraq and Libya boycotted the conference, and Syria subsequently decided not to participate in the Geneva conference at all, Arab unity could by no means be said to be complete. As the weeks passed the Algiers resolution was shrilly rejected by Arab extremists. A broadcast emanating from Baghdad on December 21, 1973 (the day the Geneva talks opened) announced: "The masses will not be bound by the regimes of treason and defeatism at the Geneva conference." Radio Tripoli asked: "Has our Arab nation become so servile in the eyes of those leaders [i.e., Sadat] that they belittle its dignity and injure its pride without fearing its wrath?"

Israel's "khaki elections" took place on the last day of the old year. If public-opinion polls published last September are to be trusted, the results would have been similar even if the war had not taken place. The Labor alignment, deeply split and under fire from within not only because of the military handling of the war but for the lack of flexibility shown by Mrs. Meir's inner circle in recent years, lost ground. Were it not for the obvious necessity to preserve the unity of the alignment in view of the international situation, it is quite possible that both Mrs. Meir and General Dayan might have had to resign under pressure from large sections of their party. But Likud had no cause to be overjoyed by the results of the elections either; if the party of Menahem Begin could not overtake its rivals in such nearly ideal conditions, it never would—unless, of course, the Labor alignment should disintegrate entirely.

The campaign was confused because the Israeli voter was not given a clear choice. As one Israeli commentator wrote, "Those who want to purchase Dayan must buy Allon. Those who want the Liberals must buy Begin." In the absence of a clear choice, the outcome of the elections was bound to be inconclusive: no clear mandate emerged for any one course of action. Menahem Begin may have been relieved not to receive more votes than he did; victory would have almost certainly compelled him to make concessions in Geneva contrary to what he promised during the campaign. Yet the absence of consensus—more accurately, the sharp polarization of public opinion—will make the task of the Israeli negotiators beyond the first stage of the talks very difficult. The effect of the vote, the London *Economist* wrote, was to block any government from making the vital decisions that the Geneva talks demand. Since such a state of affairs cannot continue for very long, the deadlock will probably be broken either by new fighting or by a new election, or perhaps both.

II

Throughout history there has been one kind of war notoriously difficult to conclude: the war of faith, the holy war, the crusade. In these conflicts it is not the leader or the government of the other side that is the enemy, but every individual in the enemy camp.

To what extent do the Arabs regard their conflict with Israel as a religious war, or a war of national liberation, to use the modern parlance? The recent Algiers summit conference proclaimed that the war aim of the Arab states was the restoration of the national rights of the Palestinian Arabs, that the Palestine Liberation Organization was the only legal representative of the Palestinians, and that its interpretation of the "national rights" was binding. The PLO interpretation was in turn laid down in the Palestinian National Covenant of July 1968, which says that the establishment of Israel is "null and void." The Algiers resolution, in other words, as much as stated that the purpose of any peace conference would be to discuss the liquidation of Israel.

In the eyes of some, this means that it is pointless for Israel to attend the Geneva conference. Fortunately, however, even in the war aims of religious or quasi-religious movements a discrepancy often exists between the desirable and the possible. In theory Catholics and Protestants should not coexist to this day, nor should Muslims and Christians, or Communists and non-Communists. All such movements have come at one stage or another to the realization that with an enemy who cannot be defeated, temporary compromises have to be made. The old enmity, the *odium theologicum*, is itself subject to gradual erosion as such compromises become permanent; the formulas of hatred may linger on but they no longer carry the same conviction.

At the Geneva peace conference Israel will establish in due course whether, at this stage in the conflict, a readiness to compromise has been reached by the Arab states. With regard to Egypt in particular a peace conference may have been long overdue. So far as the psychological readiness of other Arabs to accept the existence of Israel is concerned, the conference may turn out to be premature. Geneva may be just the beginning of a long process, perhaps the first in a series of conferences that will be interrupted by crises, pressure, threats, breakdown, new fighting, new negotiations.

The Geneva peace conference opened on December 21 in an atmosphere of cautious optimism. President Nixon had said soon after the alert in October that the prospects for peace had never before been so good. Dr. Kissinger, in his opening speech at the conference, spoke of a "historic chance for peace"; there were promising noises from Jerusalem, Moscow, and even Cairo. All this optimism was based, no doubt, on the undisputed fact that immediately after a war the prospects almost always seem brightest and formerly unacceptable conditions suddenly seem acceptable after all.

It was not by chance that the conference concentrated in its first phase on Israel and Egypt; and certainly the issue of troop disengagement, an issue speedily settled in the agreement signed on January 17, was not the only motivating factor. The Israel-Egypt "problem" does not at first glance seem insurmountable. If Egyptian sovereignty over Sinai were recognized and Egypt were to accept an effective system of demilitarization, there would then remain only the matter of a token Israeli demilitarized zone and the question of the Gaza Strip and Sharm el-Sheikh. Neither side is particularly eager to accept responsibility for Gaza (though neither will admit it) and the importance of Sharm el-Sheikh to Israel has been somewhat exaggerated (the recent Egyptian blockade at Bab el-Mandeb almost nullified the strategic usefulness of an Israeli presence at Sharm el-Sheikh). Assuming that Israel were to withdraw gradually from Sinai and the Egyptians were to accept the principle of demilitarization, a settlement between the two countries could be envisaged—following hard bargaining, of course.

Israel, however, would hardly agree to withdraw in return for a mere armistice, and it is here that the real difficulties may set in. Egypt has assured its Arab allies that it will under no circumstances make peace with Israel unless Israel withdraws from all occupied Arab territories and unless the national rights of the Palestinians are restored. The official interpretation of this formula, as I have noted, means the liquidation of the state of Israel. There are, however, several other interpretations possible and there are, in addition, legitimate grounds for doubting the strength of Egypt's commitment to the cause of its allies.

For twenty-five years Egypt has borne the brunt of the struggle against Israel, yet pan-Arab feeling is less deeply rooted in Cairo than elsewhere in the Arab world. Even the late Gamal Abdel Nasser, the champion of pan-Arabism, recognized toward the end of his life that he had taken upon himself an impossible and thankless task. In the struggle against Israel Egypt has received a great deal of verbal aid and unsolicited advice, but when the hour of truth comes, as it did in October 1973, little more than token support is ever forthcoming from its Arab friends. Syria and Iraq harbor strong feelings of resentment toward Egypt; leadership in the Arab world, they maintain, should rightfully be theirs. Colonel Qaddafi of Libya has on many occasions decried Egypt's "decadence" and "corruption," and there is not much love lost between Egypt and Algeria either. The Egyptians for their part regard Syria and Iraq as semi-barbaric lands and they have contempt for the Palestinians.

All in all, there is a strong inclination inside Egypt today to put Egyptian interests first, pan-Arab interests second. The Six-Day War came as a great shock to Egypt, and there was universal agreement that the shame of 1967 had to be expiated on the field of battle and Sinai regained. But with these aims achieved, Egypt may no longer feel an overriding obligation to champion the further struggle against Israel. To be sure, one can find hundreds of articles and dozens of books published in Egypt all proclaiming the inadmissibility of a Jewish state in the Middle East. But these declarations should not necessarily be taken at face value. If Israel could be made to disappear overnight, no Egyptian leader would object, but the prospect of many more years of hard fighting and severe damage to the country has little appeal. The Egyptian army was eager to fight for Ismailia; it is not so eager to fight (much less to die) for Nablus and Tulkarm. When addressing their more radical Arab brethren, Egyptians will stress that the final goal is the total liberation of the whole of Palestine, but this, they are apt to add quickly, will happen only in a generation or two or perhaps three. In the meantime much water will have flowed down the Nile and the Jordan.

It should have been Israeli policy after 1967—and especially after Nasser's death in 1970—to concentrate on a separate deal with Egypt, and this should be its foremost objective now. I do not wish to discount the difficulty of accomplishing this objective. Egypt is desperately poor, and financially dependent on Saudi Arabia and the Persian Gulf states. These countries for a variety of reasons, have a vested interest in the prolongation of the struggle against Israel, which for them is tantamount to an insurance policy against the radical forces in the Arab world that threaten their own existence. Sadat's position is stronger now than before the war, but this is not saying much. Nor would an Egyptian-Israeli deal mark the end of the Arab-Israeli conflict, and in the event of a new flare-up the danger would always exist that Egypt might be drawn into the campaign. Finally, an opening to Egypt on Israel's part would involve a basic psychological reorientation: since 1948 Egypt has been *the* enemy for Israel. Nevertheless, despite all these considerations, the fact remains that the interests of the two countries are not necessarily incompatible, and normal, if not friendly, relations between them should not be ruled out as a future possibility. There will be many realignments in the Arab world in the years to come and, unlikely as this may appear now, it is by no means unthinkable that one day Israel will break out of its present isolation and align itself with one or more of the Arab countries against one or more of the others.

For if a settlement with Egypt entails grave risks, the two other alternatives are even more dangerous. One is not to give up anything, the other to tackle the problem at its core and strive for a settlement which would satisfy the Palestinian Arabs. As for the first, if one assumes (as some do) that any Israeli withdrawal is bound to be just the first step in the gradual dismemberment of the country as a whole by its Arab neighbors, it would of course be preferable in every respect to make a stand now, rather than later when the boundaries will be harder to defend. Israel is already isolated, according to this view, and there is no further point in trying to appease world opinion by capitulation. The U.S. in the last resort can be counted on to remain steadfast, for its prestige is deeply involved and Israel is by now a cornerstone of its foreign policy. This line of thought, if put into action, would almost certainly bring about a new war in the Middle East, perhaps within a few months, for Sadat is under considerable domestic pressure to show results or to renew the fighting. But the prospect does not deter the advocates of such a policy. A new war, they argue, might be a protracted and hard struggle, but in the end Israel would win and this time the victory would be decisive.

A more sophisticated version of the hard-line argument maintains that since the deck has been stacked in advance, it would be fatal for Israel to act "reasonably" and "responsibly" in the present situation, as it is being urged to do on all sides. A superpower like the Soviet Union can swallow whole countries and go uncriticized, while Israel is denied the right to defensible borders and is expected to conform to the wishes of the great powers. Since the game is fixed, why not behave "irrationally"—like the

Arab oil producers, say, or the Arab terrorists? There would be much general indignation, the Russians would issue threats, a few more countries would break off relations, pressure would be exerted by Washington, but nothing much worse would be likely to happen. The coming years will in any case see far-reaching changes in world politics—perhaps the total collapse of Europe, or, less likely, the reassertion of Europe's power. War might break out between the Soviet Union and China. International relations are increasingly being dictated by the law of the jungle, and unless Israel adapts itself to these conditions, the argument concludes, its chances of survival will be slim. Israel should be tough, unpredictable, and to a certain degree irresponsible.

This reasoning cannot be dismissed out of hand (for the simple fact that anything is possible in politics) but the chances of such a policy in the real world cannot be rated high. It underestimates the extent of Israel's military and economic dependence on the United States, and exaggerates American readiness to help Israel in the future. But even more decisively, it is not a policy that the government of a democratic country can easily pursue.

Then there is the alternative of an accommodation with the Palestinians—in every way the ideal solution. If Palestinians and Israelis could reach agreement on the basis of the establishment of a Palestinian state on the West Bank, Israeli willingness to take back some refugees, and the resettlement elsewhere of those for whom a home could not be found, an end would be put to the conflict once and for all. For the fate of the Palestinian Arabs is the heart of the matter; without a solution of this issue, the wider conflict will not be solved.

Unfortunately, however, the Palestinian issue is also the least tractable by far of all the issues of contention between Israel and the Arab world. A Palestinian Arab state would not be economically viable, and would be heavily dependent on the other Arab countries and the Soviet Union. Moreover, the policy of such a state would most likely be dictated not by the forces of peace but by the radical elements, which would consider the West Bank merely a base for the continuation of the armed struggle against Israel. Nor does the domestication of the terrorists seem a likely prospect for the near future. The main Palestinian organizations, Fatah and PLO, deny the Israelis' right to national self-determination, and their aim is the destruction of the "Zionist state." When they speak of the "democratic secular Palestinian state" that will replace Israel, they mean an Arab state in which Jews would have the right to be buried in their own cemeteries.

Thus, whatever the Geneva conference may achieve, it will almost certainly not bring an overall peace to the area. But if the chances for overall peace are remote, there does exist now (as after 1967) an opportunity for defusing the conflict, for rendering unlikely the renewal of fighting on a large scale. This can be done principally by Israel's meeting the basic demands of the Egyptians—gradual withdrawal of Israeli foreigners from large parts of the Sinai and the recognition in principle of Egyptian sovereignty there, in exchange for demilitarization. Unless this demand is met, a new outbreak of hostilities seems likely, with the almost certain outcome a peace settlement dictated by the superpowers and even more detrimental to Israel's interests.

III

The prospect of an imposed settlement by the superpowers to the detriment of Israel raises the specter of the infamous Munich conference of 1938. And, in fact, Czechoslovakia in the late 1930's has been invoked rather frequently in the last few months as offering an instructive analogy to the situation in which Israel now finds itself. A small democratic country in the center of Europe, Czechoslovakia was dismembered in two stages following a decision dictated by the powers. "Munich" and "appeasement" have become part of our political vocabulary, shorthand words connoting a sellout à la 1938. There are those who see such a sellout— of Israel—shaping up in today's Middle East.

Drawing historical parallels is always dangerous and sometimes downright misleading, but there is no denying that a comparison with Czechoslovakia is of some help in understanding the present situation. Though democratic in character, Czechoslovakia contained a substantial minority —3,500,000 Germans—which, from the very beginning, did not want to be part of the Czechoslovak state formed after World War I, gravitating rather toward Germany; the stronger Germany became, the stronger the pull toward Berlin. Hitler demanded the "return" of the Sudeten regions, where the German minority was concentrated; the Czechs maintained that these regions were economically and militarily vital to Czechoslovakia.

All through 1938, while the Nazis were stepping up the pressure on Prague, a great deal of sharp criticism was being voiced in the West about the state of affairs inside Czechoslovakia. The British and French press published scathing condemnations of the Czechs for their treatment of the German minority. The Czech state, it was claimed, was an artificial creation, founded a mere twenty years before in what was now seen to have been a regrettable error. The idea that France should "commit suicide," or that a "single Frenchman should die for this misbegotten state" was grotesque. Not surprisingly, the Jews too were brought in; Léon Daudet, son of a famous father, wrote in 1938 in *L'Action Française*: "Peasant or worker, the average Frenchman is expected to commit suicide at the merest nod of a Jew who detests him, in some obscure and faraway village of which he hasn't the vaguest idea." Later that same year, Neville Chamberlain echoed these sentiments in similar terms: the Paris treaty-makers had committed an error, he declared, and the treaty should have been revised long ago; it was unthinkable to Chamberlain that Britons should go to war for a faraway land about which they knew nothing.

The anti-Czech comment of 1938, which bears an uncanny resemblance to remarks in the Western press, particularly the British and French, during the recent Middle East crisis and after, was by no means limited to the Right or to proponents of *Realpolitik.* The Left too castigated Czechoslovakia for not being a genuinely neutral country like Switzerland; France and Britain after all could not play the role of international policeman forever. Czech policy was called a danger to world peace; although the term "détente" had not yet been invented, the phrase used at the time was just as expressive: *"Conciliation entre les états democratiques."* The only alternative to such concilation was the unleashing of war. What the world needed was disarmament, and in the long run Czechoslovakia too was assured it would find security in a disarmed world.*

The status of Czechoslovakia was supposed to be settled by the agreements reached in Munich. The Sudeten regions were returned to Germany in exchange for an international guarantee of the new boundaries of Czechoslovakia against unprovoked aggression. Yet when, six months later, German troops invaded what remained of Czechoslovakia after Munich, no one came to the rescue.

Munich provides some highly instructive lessons about the psychology of appeasement and the value of international guarantees, and as such it is useful as a warning in the present negotiations. But there is a danger in pushing the analogy too far. Not every peace treaty in world history has been violated, after all, nor every international guarantee ignored. The lessons of Munich, that is to say, are of limited value as a guide for the future and cannot in my view be used as an alibi by those who oppose any concessions whatsoever on Israel's part.

The international constellation and the balance of power in the Middle East do not resemble Europe in 1938. Czechoslovakia faced a relentless enemy who could not possibly be deflected from his course. Israel, on the other hand, confronts a coalition of states that have neither the cohesion nor the power of Nazi Germany. That this coalition should have come into being at all was unusual—to a certain extent it may have come into being as a result of Israeli diplomatic inflexibility—and it will last only by a miracle. Hitler was reasonably certain that Czechoslovakia, facing the overwhelming power of the Reich, would not fight. And as for the Czechs, surrender meant the loss of independence, in itself a national disaster but not the end of the Czech people. For many centuries the Czechs had survived under foreign rule, and the conviction was strong that sooner or later Hitler's policy would lead to a war in which the

---

* Michael Harrington in a recent article has offered the current version of this argument. See his "Israel, the War, and American Politics," *Midstream*, December 1973.

Germans would be defeated, and then an independent Czechoslovakia would rise again—as indeed it did seven years later. No such hope exists for Israel, and this in itself precludes an Israeli surrender. But Israel is not only more resolute than Czechoslovakia, it is also infinitely stronger. Even Hitler would not have attacked Czechoslovakia if, for argument's sake, it had meant risking the destruction of Berlin, Munich, and other German centers.

For Israel, the years to come, fraught as they will be with danger, will require not only constant military preparedness, a high degree of flexibility, and economic sacrifice, but also, very likely, political concessions. Nevertheless, and despite the efficaciousness of the oil weapon in Arab hands, the outlook is not all that unpromising. As long as the "Zionist menace" overshadowed all other factors in the Arab political consciousness, a certain degree of unity prevailed in the Arab world. But as the "enemy" assumes a lower profile, all the suppressed dissensions among Arab nations and Arab ideologies are bound to reassert themselves. The fact that some Arab countries will earn fabulous riches during the years to come while others will not is going to exacerbate existing divisions; sooner or later, there will be a free-for-all for the spoils. The oil-producing countries are already becoming increasingly unpopular all over the world because of their extortionist policies, and they are going to have to defend themselves and their riches against more immediate dangers than Israel. Assuming that the global balance of power does not radically change in the next decade, that America does not become substantially weaker, and that some sort of détente continues to hold between the two superpowers, the risk will be reduced of an all-out Arab attack.

But in the final analysis, Israel's fate will depend on its own policies and on its own inner character. It certainly cannot afford the luxury of an internal factional war such as once before in history caused the destruction of a Jewish commonwealth. Israel in the days to come will need unity, strong nerves, and a readiness to compromise combined with a firm resolve to repel any new threat to its existence.

The Arab-Israeli Conflict

By Elie Kedourie*

At its beginnings just over half a century ago, what is now known as the Arab-Israeli conflict was relatively simple and limited, but since then—and this is perhaps its most important and ominous characteristic—it has become progressively more complicated and envenomed.

* From *Arab Political Memoirs and Other Studies* (London: Frank Cass, 1974).

The Zionists in whose favour the Balfour declaration was issued in November 1917 had been neither numerically important nor politically significant before the world war in the territory which shortly afterwards came to be officially called Palestine. They were known to the original inhabitants as immigrant foreigners upon whom the Ottoman authorities —whether at the time of Abd al-Hamid or later—did not look with much favour and whose ingress they tried to restrict as much as possible; and known also for their agricultural settlements which were occasionally involved in friction and dispute with their rural and nomadic neighbours.

The Balfour declaration, therefore, could not but come as a shock to a population which, being overwhelmingly Muslim, was already disoriented by the collapse of a Muslim authority which had lasted for four centuries, and its replacement by Christian European conquerors. And these conquerors were proposing to bestow privileges, the extent of which was uncertain, on this handful of foreigners, privileges which in the end might even lead Jews to exercise power over the Muslims who had hitherto believed in their divinely ordained right to rule over Christians and Jews. This feeling of Muslim superiority which a century of reverses at the hands of Europe had shaken but also exacerbated, goes far to make intelligible the uncompromising opposition which from the very beginning the Palestinians offered to Zionism. Also the very vagueness of the Balfour declaration, while arousing the worst fears of the Palestinians, encouraged them to hope that unyielding and strenuous opposition might lead to the declaration being interpreted restrictively, or even actually disowned.

But, when all is said and done, the conflict between the Zionists and their opponents all through the 1920s and the first half of the '30s, remained confined to Palestine. Opposition to Zionism erupted in riots and violence in 1920, 1921 and 1929. The first two incidents may be seen as unsuccessful attempts by the Palestinians to overawe and intimidate a new government and compel it to bow to their wishes. Whilst the third—and most serious—outbreak, that of 1929, coming as it did after a period of actual Jewish emigration from Palestine, may be interpreted as a bid by the mufti of Jerusalem at once to demonstrate his supremacy in Palestinian Arab politics, and to hurry the Jews on their way out. But such incidents, serious as they were, involved only the Mandatory, the Zionists and the Arabs of Palestine, and hardly involved other governments or groups. Indeed, it may be argued that the mufti may have been right in 1929 when he reckoned that Zionism was a declining force.

The advent of Hitler in 1933 introduced an entirely new and unforeseen element in the Palestinian problem. It increased, beyond any previous expectation, the demand for immigration into Palestine; imbued the Zionist leaders with a new sense of urgency and imposed new pressures on them; and by upsetting the European balance, indirectly weakened the British position in the Mediterranean and encouraged those who wanted to challenge it. Nazism, in short, seriously complicated the Palestine problem, made it perhaps well-nigh intractable. The British, we may note in passing, have been repeatedly blamed for encouraging Zionist settlement in a country occupied by a large group of people naturally unwilling to be swamped and dominated by another, aggressive and enterprising, group. This, however, is to condemn *ex post facto*, for no one in 1917 could have reasonably foretold the rise and triumph of Nazism which, by confronting European Jewry with sudden ruin and destruction, overturned the assumptions and expectations on which the Balfour declaration policy implicitly rested.

The next complication which befell Palestine dates from 1938–9. In 1936 strikes organized by the Arab higher committee degenerated into serious disorders. This compelled the British government to look anew at the problem. A Royal Commission was appointed which recommended in 1937 partition of the country into Arab and Jewish areas as the measure most likely to issue in appeasement and to produce a settlement. The government first accepted this line of policy, but soon afterwards it began to have second thoughts. It appointed in 1938 a technical commission ostensibly to examine further the detailed scheme of partition proposed by the Royal Commission, the chairman of this commission, however, being given secretly to understand that partition was no longer the policy which the government favoured. A new departure was clearly being envisaged.

The new policy was unveiled at the end of 1938, when the government announced the convening of a conference on Palestine, to which were to be invited not only the Jewish Agency and representatives of the Palestinian Arabs, but also, on the one hand, representatives of Arab states—even of a state as far away as Yemen—and on the other, of world Jewry, the latter being, in point of political importance or sovereign attributes, by no means the equal or the equivalent of the Arab states. This was a fateful and perhaps fatal move, the consequences of which even now are far from being exhausted. For this move recognized and sanctioned the intervention of a number of sovereign states in the affairs of a territory under British control. For the administration of Palestine, Great Britain was indeed responsible to the League of Nations, but it had certainly hitherto not acknowledged responsibility to a collection of states who shared more or less vaguely the epithet 'Arab.' Indeed, up to the middle of 1937, we find the British government firmly resisting Egyptian and Iraqi attempts to intervene officially in Palestinian affairs.

Whatever the various reasons and justifications for this new policy, it was one which appreciably limited British freedom of action, since the right to intervene, once conceded to outsiders, would be difficult if not impossible again to withdraw. This was to burden future British policy, as well as Palestine and the Palestinians with—to use a legal metaphor—a heavy servitude. There is no evidence that the British government was disquietened by this prospect. When an annex to the Charter of the Arab League in 1945 officially stated that the signatories had a collective right of intervention, the British government never protested at a claim now all the more enhanced for being enshrined in a formal instrument.

This development exacerbated the conflict in Palestine by introducing a large number of sovereign states, each with their particular, and conflicting, interests into what had been a relatively limited dispute between two groups in a mandated territory. The consequence of such a step appeared clearly in the Palestine war of 1948–9. After the U.N. vote, in November 1947, to partition Palestine—the very solution proposed by the Royal Commission ten years before—and the British decision to lay down the mandate which followed, King Abdullah decided that here at last was an opportunity to enhance a position which he had ever regarded as beneath his abilities and deserts. First he hoped that, supported by Iraq, he would compel the Zionists to accept his overlordship without a fight. When this failed, he embarked on war. Up to the end of April 1948, Egypt was not contemplating military intervention, but she could not allow the Hashemites to aggrandize themselves by annexing Palestine. At the last minute, therefore, an Egyptian army, by all accounts unprepared for battle, was ordered to march into Palestine. Syria, fearful of Abdullah's ambitions, likewise intervened. The conflict between Palestinians and Zionists thus became embroiled with the discordant ambitions of Egypt and Syria, Jordan and Iraq, all the more intransigent for being proclaimed in the ideological vocabulary of pan-Arabism, rather than expressed in the more modest language of interests.

The next complication in the Palestine problem first appeared in 1955–6, and became manifest in all its danger during the Six-Day war and since. The conflict, which initially was local to Palestine, and then was transformed into a regional conflict, now became inextricably involved in the rivalries of the great powers. This happened because the Soviet Union began to exert the power and influence which Tsarist Russia used traditionally to have in the region and which, so to speak, unnaturally disappeared between 1917 and 1955. In the Suez affair, the Israeli government deliberately took advantage of the British and French quarrel with Egypt in order to defeat and neutralize the most important of its enemies. An American-Soviet 'collusion'—an appropriate term to use in this context —prevented it from gaining its object. This American-Soviet collusion ruined British and French power and influence in the Mediterranean and the middle east, thus destroying the possibility of the rivalry between the two super-powers being effectively mediated or moderated by the action of other powers as used to happen in the classical eastern question before 1914. As became clear during and after the Six-Day war, the U.S.A. and the Soviet Union now stand face to face in the middle east, and their conflict is linked precisely with the Arab-Israeli conflict. This is an inherently unstable and dangerous position, made even more dangerous by the fact that neither super-power is fully in control of the actions of its clients, and is thus liable to get drawn into quarrels neither sought nor foreseen.

These then are the parties involved in this conflict: the Zionists, who have succeeded in creating and maintaining the State of Israel; the native

Palestinians; the Arab States; and the U.S.A. and the U.S.S.R. Each of these parties will influence, more or less as the case may be, the further course of the conflict and any possible settlement. There is a great deal of variety in the aims and purposes of these parties, as well as in the price which they are prepared to pay for attaining them. But for all of them the conflict may be said to be primarily political (and therefore, at times, military). Political in the sense that two groups (the Israelis and the Palestinians) dispute sovereign control over a territory; political also in the sense that this original dispute has become for other local states a means for attaining regional primacy or increasing their territory; political lastly in the sense that each of the super-powers sees in this dispute a way of increasing its power and influence in the Mediterranean and middle east, and of diminishing that of its rival.

But the political conflict between Israel and its neighbours is further complicated by what might be called a cultural conflict, or perhaps misunderstanding. A clue to its nature may be gathered from the frequency with which the dispute between Israel and her neighbours is described as a conflict between 'Jews' and 'Arabs'. Are these two groups actually in conflict? Jews as a group certainly have an identity supplied by a religion which has kept them together. So far as 'culture' goes—if by culture we mean broadly a way of life—the Jews have experienced huge variations of culture throughout their history. Some of them, in particular, have shared, or still share, the culture of those called 'Arabs'. To the extent that there is cultural conflict, it must be between the 'Arabs' and those Jews who have not shared in their outlook, values and way of life.

But who are the 'Arabs'? Some sixty years ago, the term 'Arab' generally meant Bedouin. Since then this term has undergone a great change. It has ceased primarily to designate a group of nomads; it has rather become an ideological term indicating an aspiration to create a new political order, in which all 'Arabs' would be members of an autonomous, sovereign entity. In this new usage, who the 'Arabs' are has changed from time to time, and even now the notion is not yet quite stable. But one thing at least can be affirmed, namely, that they are, in an overwhelming majority, Muslim, that they are, and have been part of the Muslim world and of an Islamic culture. Islam has generally looked upon Jews as a subject community docile and unwarlike, to be treated with contemptuous tolerance, and whom it is quite unthinkable to consider as political equals. This surely accounts for a great deal of intransigence with which the Palestinians and the Arab states have refused sometimes in clear disregard of their interests to negotiate directly or to sit at the same table with Zionists or Israelis. But the Jews with whom they had to deal in Palestine were, in fact, the antithesis of the Jews to whom the Muslims were accustomed. They were politically activist, aggressive and by no means deferential towards Muslims.

On the contrary, the Jews who invented Zionism and worked for the establishment of the State of Israel, coming from eastern Europe, and imbued with European notions and prejudices, were wholly pre-occupied with European issues and European problems. They knew little about the indigenous inhabitants of Palestine, and looked down upon them as backward, primitive and incompetent. The history of the Palestine problem from the Balfour declaration to the Six-Day war must have served to confirm them in this view. The political conflict over Palestine has thus been further complicated by mutual incomprehension, to which have contributed, on the one hand, the European prejudices of the Zionists, and, on the other, the Muslim prejudices of the Arabs. Misunderstanding, it has been said, makes the world go round. Mutual contempt is another story.

To review this conflict and its progressive exacerbation is thus to admit the unlikelihood of a speedy settlement. What must increase pessimism is that a state of war between Israel and its neighbours has now lasted for almost a quarter of a century and that, as we may suspect, it has become for various governments a cosy habit and a convenient state of affairs. It is said, no doubt with a great deal of truth, that a state of war enables the Israeli government to transform a heterogeneous collection of immigrants into a homogeneous nation-state, and to mobilize the sympathies and resources of world Jewry. It is probably just as true that military régimes, such as those of Egypt, of Syria and of Iraq, apprehend in a state of peace a serious threat to their stability, or even to their very existence.

But let us review in turn the various parties to the conflict, their ability to make peace, and the inducements and pressures which may incline them thereto. On the Arab side, it seems to be the case that ability to influence the course of the quarrel is almost in inverse proportion to a party's vital interest in it. This is, and has been, most true of the Palestinians. For some twenty years, from the British occupation until the end of 1938, the Palestinian leaders attempted by continuous pressure and protest, as well as by occasional violence, to resist the establishment and extension of the National Home to which the mandatory was committed. This campaign almost from the beginning went hand in hand with the campaign of Hajj Amin al-Husayni, whom Sir Herbert Samuel had tacitly allowed to become mufti of Jerusalem in 1921, to establish his dominance over the Palestinians. In declaring his uncompromising hostility to Zionism the mufti indeed faithfully expressed the sentiments of those whom he claimed to lead; but it remains true that he was leader not because he was elected or appointed by the Palestinians, but only owing to the initial support of the mandatory, to his subsequent use of the *Waqf* resources which the government allowed him to control without any supervision, and in the later stages to a campaign of murder and terrorism. He was thus practically free to pursue whatever policy he liked, and in the end was tempted by armed rebellion, intrigues with Italy and Germany, and with elements in Syria and Iraq who wanted to use the Palestine issue as a weapon in their own struggle for power. His policies failed, and he may fairly be said to have served his people ill.

The period 1937–9 may be considered a watershed in the sombre, disaster-strewn history of the Palestinians. It was then that the mufti fled to the Lebanon, an action which, in retrospect, marks the failure of his policies. Self-appointed and self-seeking as he was, yet his policies, however unwise or undesirable, in their fashion were primarily concerned with the interests of the Palestinians. When the Arab states were invited at the end of 1938 to intervene in the Palestine problem, Palestinian interests necessarily became a pawn or a weapon in the hands of these states in their pursuit of power and primacy. Between 1939 and the Six-Day war the Palestinians had no say or no control over their affairs. Such leadership as Hajj Amin and his lieutenants had provided was dispersed and destroyed, and the Arab states and the Arab League undertook to defend the Palestinians' interests. During this period, successive catastrophes befell the Palestinians which they have been utterly powerless to avert.

Since the Six-Day war the Palestinians have once again come to the fore. Once again leaders claim to speak in their name and to defend their particular interests. The character and the tactics of these leaders bear a disturbing resemblance to those of the 1930s. In so far as they are not promoted or supported for its purposes by one or other of the Arab states, they too are self-appointed. Undoubtedly in their utter hostility to Israel, they speak for all the Palestinians, but these have no say whatever over policies or tactics, which are decided by small groups in secret. Again like Hajj Amin, the new leaders have a partiality for guerrilla warfare. This partiality has indeed been reinforced by the great popularity which the doctrine of Mao, Guevara and the Vietcong have found in Asia and Africa. Quite recently, Yassir Arafat, the leader of the Palestine Liberation Organization, declared in an interview (*Le Monde*, 12 November 1970): 'I will tell you why the Americans, in spite of their undoubted power, do not have, and will never have the upper hand over the Vietcong: a guerrilla movement which has popular support is invincible. No electronic machine is able to measure the will of our people to conquer their right to life and freedom. Their ability to resist is practically infinite'.

The words were uttered after three years of fruitless guerrilla action against Israel—fruitless itself, and fruitless in that guerrilla warfare has not been changed (as the theory requires) into a 'people's war'. These words also followed the clash with King Husayn's army which has decisively shown that, in middle eastern conditions at any rate, a resolute government disposing of planes, tanks and artillery, is more than a match for guerrillas who wish to take it over. Even if Husayn were killed or deposed, it is by no means clear that the guerrillas would be able to take over Jordan. If this is so, then the future for Palestinian resistance is not bright. At best, the guerrillas may become a kind of IMRO (Internal Macedonian

Revolutionary Organization), able to use spasmodic terror, but quite unable to effect a substantial change. There is another reason for pessimism: if as has been here argued, it was a misfortune for the Palestinian cause to be, so to speak, pan-Arabized, then the guerrilla organizations in relying, as they must, on this or that Arab state, are doing nothing to save the Palestinians from the ruinous attentions of their protectors.

The guerrillas then are unlikely to achieve military victory over Israel, or to force it to give in to their demands. The clash with the Jordanians indicates that they are also unlikely to be able to force an Arab state to wage war on their behalf. It follows that they are not in a position, should they want it, on their own to negotiate or conclude a compromise peace with Israel. A peace of this kind which did not suit Jordan or Syria or Egypt can easily be upset by them. Jordan which, after the Palestinians, is the party most vitally interested in the conflict, is in scarcely a better position.

To Abdullah's ambitions, as has been seen, must be attributed in large part the outbreak of war in 1948. But bold and ambitious as he was, yet he was not a man to persist in a manifestly unprofitable enterprise. Having emerged from the war of 1948 as the only beneficiary on the Arab side, he was quite willing to attempt a settlement with his fellow-beneficiary Israel. But Jordan was no longer the pastoral emirate over which he had ruled for a quarter of a century. It now included a large and turbulent population of Palestinians, many of them refugees: it was he who had made this bed and he must now lie on it. He had to reckon with these Palestinians in his attempts at a settlement, and with the trouble which a defeated and embittered Egypt would make for him among the Palestinians. His room for manoeuvre became very exiguous, and the final reckoning came when they assassinated him in that Jerusalem which he had wanted so much to possess. His grandson was at no time in a better position to negotiate. Much as he wanted a settlement, particularly after the Six-Day war, he too has never been in a position to conclude it on his own. A satisfactory peace for him must include the return of the west bank, if not of east Jerusalem. A Jordan permanently confined within the frontiers of the old emirate would destroy his prestige and put his throne at risk. But even if he could make a satisfactory deal with the Israelis, he would not be in a position to go through with it in the face of opposition from other members of the Arab League, and particularly Egypt.

Let us consider the character of this opposition, leaving aside Egypt for the moment. The opposition is likely to come from countries like Syria, Iraq, Libya or Algeria—none of them as intimately touched by the conflict as Jordan, the two latter being indeed very far from the scene. This opposition would be expressed in activist and doctrinaire terms, in the style customary to a party like the Ba'th in Syria or Iraq, or the FLN in Algeria. A passage in a recent article by the Algerian minister of information and culture, Ahmed Taleb-Ibrahimi, provides an excellent specimen of this style and outlook. He wrote (*Le Monde*, 12 September 1970):

No smoke-screen and no inspired article will make us forget the decisive importance of the potential power of the Arab masses who are already impressing on those who were meditating a treacherous blow, that the Palestinian cause cannot be betrayed with impunity.

Today's struggle [referring to Husayn's recent attack on the guerrillas] must not be taken for a classic battle, as was the case in the Spanish civil war, where some parties try out their weapons. It is not a matter of tanks or rockets. The resistance must be organized and must spread to all the Arab countries. For those who think to justify their defeatism (which, of course they call realism) by declaring that the struggle in the East takes place under peculiar conditions, is different from the struggle of the Vietminh or of the FLN, examples are not lacking which prove that resistance can develop in mountains as well as in cities, in the steppes as well as in deserts of sand or ice. The problem is not one of terrain, but of will: what in the end is victorious is not war material, however perfected, but rather the man who operates the weapon, and the faith which moves the man.

To take another point, how can Algeria advise the Palestinian resistance to accept that which it had refused to accept for itself twelve years ago? A cease-fire in present-day conditions reminds us too much of that *'paix des braves'* by means of which it was hoped to undermine the morale of the Algerians.

Rhetoric of this style invites, and sometimes compels, political activity of a similar style. But even if it did not, even if those who use it have no intention of themselves being carried away by it, they may yet consider that their interest requires the encouragement of intransigence. Algeria is a rival of Egypt in north Africa, and one way by which to assert her claim is to adopt an uncompromising stand over Palestine. Again, Syria and Iraq, both governed by Ba'hist officers consumed with mutual dislike, confronting each other in a gladiatorial posture, and in any case looking on King Husayn as fair game for revolutionaries, would also have good reason to encourage, singly or in unison, an uncompromising stand.

But by themselves, neither Iraq nor Syria nor Algeria are decisive, just as the Palestinian guerrillas and Jordan can effect nothing on their own. For all these parties are dwarfed and overshadowed by Egypt which, it is no exaggeration to say, holds, among Israel's enemies, the key to a settlement. Egypt's involvement in the Palestine conflict was a deliberate step by Faruq to secure primacy in the middle east. The adventure, in a sense, cost him his throne. But his ambition was taken over by those who overthrew him, and from beginning to end Nasser sought, by means of a victory over Israel, to crush his opponents in the Arab world and establish Egypt as *the* middle-eastern great power. Egypt's resources and military capacity did not prove equal to such an aim, the pursuit of which has brought so far nothing but loss and catastrophe. But Nasser's régime and his prestige had become intimately bound up with this policy. As is known, so long as he was unwilling to consider a settlement which might advertise and consecrate the failure of this policy, no other Arab state or group would have dared even enter into negotiations. This was because Nasser's prestige and Egypt's power were too great to be challenged by the other Arab states. Whether Nasser himself would have been prepared to abandon the policy he took over from Faruq, and to work for a purely Egyptian-Israeli settlement will never now be known.

His successors do not enjoy his prestige either inside or outside Egypt, and this may in fact be one potent reason why they dare not abandon a policy associated with one who, because of his death in office, has so to speak become the tutelary deity of the régime. What is clear at any rate is that they persist in using the rhetoric of pan-Arabism and in proclaiming themselves the champions of all the Arabs against Israel. Thus, in a declaration in the National Assembly, Anwar al-Sadat said that the struggle was for them 'the priority of all priorities'. By struggle he meant 'the total liberation of all occupied Arab territories, with no exception whatever. To give up anything whatever means giving up everything'. Again: 'To give up the total liberation of these territories is tantamount to submitting to the Israeli imperialist aggressor and those who give him support. No one in the Arab world will agree to the liberation of one portion of the territory, and the abandonment of another. Let the world understand that we are against all half-solutions, all bargaining and all auctions.' The U.A.R. he stated, 'is unshakeably convinced that the Arab nation is one, that its progress is one and that its aspirations are the same for all the Arabs.' (*Le Monde*, 21 November 1970). This is the language of Nasserism. But Sadat has also introduced a new, Islamic, accent which must greatly appeal to, and move, his audience. In an eloquent address delivered in April 1972 on the anniversary of the Prophet's birthday he compared the struggle on which his people were engaged to the trials which faced Muhammad at the beginning of his apostolate. We are fated, he said, to fight the battle to liberate our land and, with our land, Jerusalem, the first *qibla* and third *haram.* 'We will, with God's help' he affirmed, 'take it back from those of whom our Book says that lowliness and submissiveness is their lot.' Sadat also declared that he refused to negotiate directly with people whom the Prophet had found, in his dealings with them, to be vile, treacherous and faithless. (Text of Sadat's address reproduced in an appendix in Fu'ad Matar, *Russya alnasiriyya wa Misr al-misriyya* (Nasserite Russia and Egyptian Egypt), Beirut, 1972, pp. 202–5). Whether these words represent an extension of Nasserism, or are used to cover a retreat from it, time will tell.

Egypt has never been powerful enough to win, or even to maintain its position—witness the occupation of Sinai and the closure of the canal, but has been powerful enough to prevent a settlement. Israel, contrariwise, has been powerful enough to win many campaigns and improve its positions, but not powerful enough to impose a settlement. Hence the deadlock, and the mutual and cumulative mistrust. But as between Israel and its neighbours the position is asymmetrical in one respect which is crucial. The Israelis are convinced that the conflict is for them a life-and-death issue, that a defeat or a retreat for them will end not merely in a humiliating peace but in the destruction of their state. Hence another element of intransigence. But what kind of a settlement, one may ask, does Israel envisage? The answer is by no means clear, and this very lack of clarity is in itself yet one more obstacle to a settlement. Israel's objective has always been twofold: recognition and secure frontiers. The Six-Day war put it at least in the short term in a better bargaining position, but did not bring the attainment of these aims nearer. It may have even perhaps made this more difficult, since the conquest of so much territory in 1967 has tempted some Israeli politicians to believe that they could attain both recognition and a larger Israeli territory, or else that Israel, secure behind the shield of its new conquests, need not sacrifice anything for recognition by its neighbours. Since Israel's is a parliamentary régime in which government has been carried on from the start by means of coalitions, it has always been easier to register disagreement over policies, than to resolve on a particular policy. Moreover, disagreement about policy is accompanied by confusion about the character of the conflict in which Israel is engaged.

The conflict at the outset was one with the indigenous population of Palestine. During the 1920s and '30s the belief widely prevailed among Zionist leaders that this local conflict could somehow be dissolved if the Palestinians could be submerged in a wider Arab entity. The Zionists, in other words, were themselves pan-Arabs. Events have shown this line of reasoning to be quite fallacious, but many Israeli leaders still hanker after it. They now do so in the belief that to admit the existence of Palestinians as Palestinians is somehow to throw doubt on the legitimacy of Israel and its right to the territory it occupies. Hence the curious immobility of Israeli policy after 1967. Internal deadlock—political and intellectual—in Israel reinforces the external deadlock.

But Israel and its enemies, checkmated by one another, find themselves further constrained by their dependence on the super-powers who, of course, are primarily concerned with the safeguard and advancement of their own interests, and for whom the middle east is merely one element in a world-wide rivalry and the Arab-Israeli conflict by no means the most important issue in the middle east. It was to outflank and neutralize the American and, generally, the western positions in the middle east that the U.S.S.R. began an active policy in Egypt in 1955. In the decade which followed the Soviet stake in the middle east and in the Mediterranean increased enormously. Its naval contingent in the Mediterranean, its liberal supply of arms to Egypt, Syria, Iraq and other Arab states, its financing of the high dam: all these meant that Soviet prestige became bound up with the survival and success of those Arab states which had become its clients. It is the logic of this situation, rather than deliberate choice, which has made the U.S.A. the patron and protector of Israel. For it has been a constant theme of Soviet propaganda that just as the Soviets were committed to the protection of the Arab states, so the United States was committed to the protection of Israel. The Six-Day war and the events which followed somehow seemed to give body and reality to this propaganda. By espousing so unconditionally the cause of the defeated Arab states, the U.S.S.R. forced the U.S.A. to link its prestige to the survival of Israel and to its protection against defeat. Such a position is necessarily irksome to the U.S.A. which, by reason of its interests elsewhere in the middle east, cannot afford to seem unconditionally to support Israel. Hence the continuous ambiguity and tension in the relations between these two states. One reason, presumably, for American initiatives to break the deadlock between Israel and its neighbours is eagerness to escape from the position into which the Soviets have cornered them.

The American position, seemingly weak, is not, however, without its strength. Its protégé, Israel, has a stranglehold over the Suez Canal, to open which is a more pressing Soviet than American interest. Israel, again, is militarily superior to its neighbours and does not need the kind of direct support which the U.S.S.R. has had to give Egypt. Lastly, so long as the protégés of the Soviets are involved with Israel, they cannot busy themselves very much with subverting states such as Saudi Arabia or the Lebanon to protect which is an American interest. Whether the U.S.A. considers these as strong cards, and whether it would consider them nonetheless worth sacrificing for the sake of a local settlement with the Soviets, we do not yet know. If the former is the case then the deadlock is likely to last for some time, if the latter then a new situation will emerge about which it is fruitless to speculate. For in such a situation what will be important will be not the exact territorial character of an Arab-Israeli settlement, but rather the stance in which the superpowers and their protégés will find themselves for prosecuting their ambitions in an area which seems doomed to turbulence and disorder for a long time to come.

The Egyptian-Israeli Accord on Sinai (September 1, 1975)

The Government of the Arab Republic of Egypt and the Government of Israel have agreed that:

ARTICLE I

The conflict between them and in the Middle East shall not be resolved by military force but by peaceful means.

The agreement concluded by the parties Jan. 18, 1974, within the framework of the Geneva peace conference constituted a first step towards a just and durable peace according to the provisions of Security Council Resolution 338 of Oct. 22, 1973; and they are determined to reach a final and just peace settlement by means of negotiations called for by Security Council Resolution 338, this agreement being a significant step towards that end.

ARTICLE II

The parties hereby undertake not to resort to the threat or use of force or military blockade against each other.

ARTICLE III

(1) The parties shall continue scrupulously to observe the cease-fire on land, sea and air and to refrain from all military or para-military actions against each other.

(2) The parties also confirm that the obligations contained in the annex and, when concluded, the protocol shall be an integral part of this agreement.

ARTICLE IV

A. The military forces of the parties shall be deployed in accordance with the following principles:

(1) All Israeli forces shall be deployed east of the lines designated as lines J and M on the attached map.

(2) All Egyptian forces shall be deployed west of the line designated as line E on the attached map.

(3) The area between the lines designated on the attached map as lines E and F and the area between the lines designated on the attached map as lines J and K shall be limited in armament and forces.

(4) The limitations on armament and forces in the areas described by paragraph (3) above shall be agreed as described in the attached annex.

(5) The zone between the lines designated on the attached map as lines E and J will be a buffer zone. On this zone the United Nations Emergency Force will continue to perform its functions as under the Egyptian-Israeli agreement of Jan. 18, 1974.

(6) In the area south from line E and west from line M, as defined in the attached map, there will be no military forces, as specified in the attached annex.

B. The details concerning the new lines, the redeployment of the forces and its timing, the limitation of armaments and forces, aerial reconnaissance, the operation of the early warning and surveillance installations and the use of the roads, the U.N. functions and other arrangements will all be in accordance with the provisions of the annex and map which are an integral part of this agreement and of the protocol which is to result from negotiations pursuant to the annex and which, when concluded, shall become an integral part of this agreement.

ARTICLE V

The United Nations Emergency Force is essential and shall continue its functions, and its mandate shall be extended annually.

ARTICLE VI

The parties hereby establish a joint commission for the duration of this agreement. It will function under the aegis of the chief coordinator of the United Nations peace-keeping missions in the Middle East in order to consider any problem arising from this agreement and to assist the United Nations Emergency Force in the execution of its mandate. The joint commission shall function in accordance with procedures established in the protocol.

ARTICLE VII

Nonmilitary cargoes destined for or coming from Israel shall be permitted through the Suez Canal.

ARTICLE VIII

(1) This agreement is regarded by the parties as a significant step toward a just and lasting peace. It is not a final peace agreement.

(2) The parties shall continue their efforts to negotiate a final peace agreement within the framework of the Geneva peace conference in accordance with Security Council Resolution 338.

ARTICLE IX

This agreement shall enter into force upon signature of the protocol and remain in force until superseded by a new agreement.

The U.S. Proposal for Early-Warning System in Sinai

In connection with the early-warning system referred to in Article IV of the agreement between Egypt and Israel concluded on this date and as an integral part of that agreement (hereafter referred to as the basic agreement), the United States proposes the following:

[1]

The early-warning system to be established in accordance with Article IV in the area shown on the attached map will be entrusted to the United States. It shall have the following elements:

A. There shall be two surveillance stations to provide strategic early warning, one operated by Egyptian and one operated by Israeli personnel. Their locations are shown on the map attached to the basic agreement. Each station shall be manned by not more than 250 technical and administrative personnel. They shall perform the functions of visual and electronic surveillance only within their stations.

B. In support of these stations, to provide tactical early warning and to verify access to them, three watch stations shall be established by the United States in the Mitla and Gidi Passes as will be shown on the agreed map.

These stations shall be operated by United States civilian personnel. In support of these stations, there shall be established three unmanned electronic-sensor fields at both ends of each pass and in the general vicinity of each station and the roads leading to and from those stations.

[2]

The United States civilian personnel shall perform the following duties in connection with the operation and maintenance of these stations:

A. At the two surveillance stations described in paragraph 1A, above, United States personnel will verify the nature of the operations of the stations and all movement into and out of each station and will immediately report any detected divergency from its authorized role of visual and electronic surveillance to the parties to the basic agreement and the UNEF.

B. At each watch station described in paragraph 1B above, the United States personnel will immediately report to the parties to the basic agreement and to UNEF any movement of armed forces, other than the UNEF, into either pass and any observed preparations for such movement.

C. The total number of United States civilian personnel assigned to functions under these proposals shall not exceed 200. Only civilian personnel shall be assigned to functions under these proposals.

[3]

No arms shall be maintained at the stations and other facilities covered by these proposals, except for small arms required for their protection.

[4]

The United States personnel serving the early-warning system shall be allowed to move freely within the area of the system.

[5]

The United States and its personnel shall be entitled to have such support facilities as are reasonably necessary to perform their functions.

[6]

The United States personnel shall be immune from local criminal, civil, tax and customs jurisdiction and may be accorded any other specific privileges and immunities provided for in the UNEF agreement of Feb. 13, 1957.

[7]

The United States affirms that it will continue to perform the functions described above for the duration of the basic agreement.

[8]

Notwithstanding any other provision of these proposals, the United States may withdraw its personnel only if it concludes that their safety is jeopardized or that continuation of their role is no longer necessary. In the latter case the parties to the basic agreement will be informed in advance in order to give them the opportunity to make alternative arrangements. If both parties to the basic agreement request the United States to conclude its role under this proposal, the United States will consider such requests conclusive.

[9]

Technical problems including the location of the watch stations will be worked out through consultation with the United States.

Annex to the Sinai Agreement

Within five days after the signature of the Egypt-Israel agreement, representatives of the two parties shall meet in the military working group of the Middle East peace conference at Geneva to begin preparation of a detailed protocol for the implementation of the agreement. In order to facilitate preparation of the protocol and implementation of the agreement, and to assist in maintaining the scrupulous observance of the cease-fire and other elements of the agreement, the two parties have agreed on the following principles, which are an integral part of the agreement, as guidelines for the working group.

1. DEFINITIONS OF LINES AND AREAS

The deployment lines, areas of limited forces and armaments, buffer zones, the area south from line E and west from line M, other designated areas, road sections for common use and other features referred to in Article IV of the agreement shall be as indicated on the attached map (1:100,000— U.S. edition).

2. Buffer Zones

(a) Access to the buffer zones shall be controlled by the UNEF, according to procedures to be worked out by the working group and UNEF.

(b) Aircraft of either party will be permitted to fly freely up to the forward line of that party. Reconnaissance aircraft of either party may fly up to the middle line of the buffer zone between E and J on an agreed schedule.

(c) In the buffer zone, between line E and J, there will be established under Article IV of the agreement an early-warning system entrusted to United States civilian personnel as detailed in a separate proposal, which is a part of this agreement.

(d) Authorized personnel shall have access to the buffer zone for transit to and from the early-warning system; the manner in which this is carried out shall be worked out by the working group and UNEF.

3. Area South of Line E and West of Line M

(a) In this area, the United Nations Emergency Force will assure that there are no military or paramilitary forces of any kind, military fortifications and military installations; it will establish checkpoints and have the freedom of movement necessary to perform this function.

(b) Egyptian civilians and third-country civilian oil-field personnel shall have the right to enter, exit from, work and live in the above-indicated area, except for buffer zones 2A, 2B and the U.N. posts. Egyptian civilian police shall be allowed in the area to perform normal civil police functions among the civilian population in such numbers and with such weapons and equipment as shall be provided for in the protocol.

(c) Entry to and exit from the area, by land, by air or by sea, shall be only through UNEF checkpoints. UNEF shall also establish checkpoints along the road, the dividing line and at other points, with the precise locations and number to be included in the protocol.

(d) Access to the airspace and the coastal area shall be limited to unarmed Egyptian civilian vessels and unarmed civilian helicopters and transport planes involved in the civilian activities of the area, as agreed by the working group.

(e) Israel undertakes to leave intact all currently existing civilian installations and infrastructures.

(f) Procedures for use of the common sections of the coastal road along the Gulf of Suez shall be determined by the working group and detailed in the protocol.

4. Aerial Surveillance

There shall be a continuation of aerial reconnaissance missions by the U.S. over the areas covered by the agreement following the same procedures already in practice. The missions will ordinarily be carried out at a frequency of one mission every seven to 10 days, with either party or UNEF empowered to request an earlier mission. The U.S. will make the mission results available expeditiously to Israel, Egypt and the chief co-ordinator of the U.N. peace-keeping mission in the Middle East.

5. LIMITATION OF FORCES AND ARMAMENTS

(a) Within the areas of limited forces and armaments the major limitations shall be as follows:

(1) Eight (8) standard infantry battalions.

(2) Seventy-five (75) tanks.

(3) Sixty (60) artillery pieces, including heavy mortars (i.e., with caliber larger than 120 mm.), whose range shall not exceed 12 km.

(4) The total number of personnel shall not exceed eight thousand (8,000).

(5) Both parties agree not to station or locate in the area weapons which can reach the line of the other side.

(6) Both parties agree that in the areas between lines J and K, and between line A (of the disengagement agreement of Jan. 18, 1974) and line E, they will construct no new fortifications or installations for forces of a size greater than that agreed herein.

(b) The major limitations beyond the areas of limited forces and armament will be:

(1) Neither side will station nor locate any weapon in areas from which they can reach the other line.

(2) The parties will not place anti-aircraft missiles within an area of 10 kilometers east of line K and west of line F, respectively.

(c) The U.N. Force will conduct inspections in order to insure the maintenance of the agreed limitations within these areas.

6. PROCESS OF IMPLEMENTATION

The detailed implementation and timing of the redeployment of forces, turnover of oil fields and other arrangements called for by the agreement, annex and protocol shall be determined by the working group, which will agree on the stages of this process, including the phased movement of Egyptian troops to line E and Israeli troops to line J. The first phase will be the transfer of the oil fields and installations to Egypt. This process will begin within two weeks from the signature of the protocol with the introduction of the necessary technicians, and it will be completed no later than eight weeks after it begins. The details of the phasing will be worked out in the military working group.

Implementation of the redeployment shall be completed within five months after signature of the protocol.

1974 Accord

Mediterranean Sea

Port Said

Suez Canal

E G Y P T

U.N. ZONE

EGYPTIAN LIMITED-FORCE ZONE

Suez

Bir Gafgafa

GIDI PASS

MITLA PASS

ISRAELI LIMITED-FORCE ZONE

SINAI PENINSULA

ISRAEL

Abu Aweigila

Gulf of Suez

Abu Rudeis

0 MILES 25

Copyright © 1975 by The New York Times Company. Reprinted by permission.

381

Present Accord

Mediterranean Sea

Port Said

Suez Canal

ISRAEL

E G Y P T

U.N. ZONE

Abu Aweigila

Bir Gafgafa

UMM KHISHEIB

EGYPTIAN LIMITED-FORCE ZONE

GIDI PASS

Suez

MITLA PASS

SINAI PENINSULA

ISRAELI LIMITED-FORCE ZONE

Sudr

Gulf of Suez

Abu Rudeis

0 MILES 25

Copyright © 1975 by The New York Times Company.
Reprinted by permission.

382

Part V

Camp David
and War in Lebanon

The years following the 1973 war were filled with dramatic events. President Anwar Sadat's visit to Jerusalem began a round of new peace plans and culminated in the Camp David accords, an Egypt-Israel peace treaty, and proposals for West Bank autonomy. Other Arab states and the Palestinians rejected this framework. The Israeli governments of Prime Minister Menachem Begin and his successor, Yitzhak Shamir, continued settlement activities on the West Bank. Saudi Crown Prince Fahd suggested a new Arab position, hinting at acceptance of Israel, but this was watered down by the 1982 Arab summit. The Israeli invasion of Lebanon set off a new chain of events. Secretary of State George Shultz indicated heightened U.S. concern over the issues involved, a massacre of Palestinians by Lebanese Christians provoked further feelings of urgency, and the Reagan Plan proposed a future peace arrangement involving Arab recognition of Israel and a Jordan–West Bank federation. This, too, was rejected by Israel, the PLO, and Jordan and was followed by an internal revolt, led by Said Musa under Syrian sponsorship, in the largest PLO group, Al Fatah.

Harold H. Saunders: U.S. Foreign Policy and Peace in the Middle East (November 12, 1975)*

Mr. Chairman, a just and durable peace in the Middle East is a central objective of the United States. Both President Ford and Secretary Kissinger have stated firmly on numerous occasions that the United States is determined to make every feasible effort to maintain the momentum of practical progress toward a peaceful settlement of the Arab-Israeli conflict.

We have also repeatedly stated that the legitimate interests of the Palestinian Arabs must be taken into account in the negotiation of an Arab-Israeli peace. In many ways, the Palestinian dimension of the Arab-Israeli conflict is the heart of that conflict. Final resolution of the problems arising from the partition of Palestine, the establishment of the State of Israel, and Arab opposition to those events will not be possible until agreement is reached defining a just and permanent status for the Arab peoples who consider themselves Palestinians. . . . The U.S. has provided some $620 million in assistance—about sixty-two percent of the total international support ($1 billion) for the Palestinian refugees over the past quarter of a century.

Today, however, we recognize that, in addition to meeting the human needs and responding to legitimate personal claims of the refugees, there is another interest that must be taken into account. It is a fact that many of the three million or so people who call themselves Palestinians today increasingly regard themselves as having their own identity as a people and desire a voice in determining their political status. As with any people in this situation, there are differences among themselves, but the Palestinians collectively are a political factor which must be dealt with if there is to be a peace between Israel and its neighbors.

The statement is often made in the Arab world that there will not be

* Prepared statement of Harold H. Saunders, Deputy Assistant Secretary for Near Eastern and South Asian affairs, before the House Foreign Affairs Subcommittee on the Middle East.

peace until the "rights of the Palestinians" are fulfilled, but there is no agreed definition of what is meant and a variety of viewpoints have been expressed on what the legitimate objectives of the Palestinians are:

Some Palestinian elements hold to the objective of a binational secular state in the area of the former mandate of Palestine. Realization of this objective would mean the end of the present state of Israel, a member of the United Nations, and its submergence in some larger entity. Some would be willing to accept merely as a first step toward this goal the establishment of a Palestinian state comprising the West Bank of the Jordan River and Gaza.

Other elements of Palestinian opinion appear willing to accept an independent Palestinian state comprising the West Bank and Gaza, based on acceptance of Israel's right to exist as an independent state within roughly its pre-1967 borders.

Some Palestinians and other Arabs envisage as a possible solution a unification of the West Bank and Gaza with Jordan. A variation of this which has been suggested would be the reconstitution of the country as a federated state, with the West Bank becoming an autonomous Palestinian province.

Still others, including many Israelis, feel that with the West Bank returned to Jordan, and with the resulting existence of two communities—Palestinian and Jordanian—within Jordan, opportunities would be created thereby for the Palestinians to find self-expression.

In the case of a solution which would rejoin the West Bank to Jordan or a solution involving a West Bank/Gaza state, there would still arise the property claims of those Palestinians who before 1948 resided in areas that became the State of Israel. These claims have been acknowledged as a serious problem by the international community ever since the adoption by the United Nations of Resolution 194 on this subject in 1948, a resolution which the United Nations has repeatedly reaffirmed and which the United States has supported. A solution will be further complicated by the property claims against Arab states of the many Jews from those states who moved to Israel in its early years after achieving statehood.

In addition to property claims, some believe they should have the option of returning to their original homes under any settlement.

Other Arab leaders, while pressing the importance of Palestinian involvement in a settlement, have taken the position that the definition of Palestinian interests is something for the Palestinian people themselves to sort out, and the view has been expressed by responsible Arab leaders that realization of Palestinian rights need not be inconsistent with the existence of Israel.

No one, therefore, seems in a position today to say exactly what Palestinian objectives are. . . . What is needed as a first step is a diplomatic process which will help bring forth a reasonable definition of Palestinian interests—a position from which negotiations on a solution of the Palestinian aspects of the problem might begin. The issue is not whether Palestinian interests should be expressed in a final settlement, but how. There will be no peace unless an answer is found.

Another requirement is the development of a framework for negotiations—a statement of the objectives and the terms of reference. The framework for the negotiations that have taken place thus far and the agreements they have produced involving Israel, Syria, and Egypt, has been provided by United Nations Security Council Resolutions 242 and 338. In accepting that framework, all of the parties to the negotiation have accepted that the objective of the negotiations is peace between them based on mutual recognition, territorial integrity, political independence, the right to live in peace within secure and recognized borders, and the resolution of the specific issues which comprise the Arab-Israeli conflict.

The major problem that must be resolved in establishing a framework for bringing issues of concern to the Palestinians into negotiation, therefore, is to find a common basis for the negotiation that Palestinians and Israelis can both accept. This could be achieved by common acceptance of the above-mentioned Security Council resolutions, although they do not deal with the political aspect of the Palestinian problem.

A particularly difficult aspect of the problem is the question of who negotiates for the Palestinians. It has been our belief that Jordan would be a logical negotiator for the Palestinian-related issues. The Rabat Summit, however, recognized the Palestinian Liberation Organization as the "sole legitimate representative of the Palestinian people." . . .

However, the PLO does not accept the United Nations Security Council resolutions, does not recognize the existence of Israel, and has not stated its readiness to negotiate peace with Israel; Israel does not recognize the PLO or the idea of a separate Palestinian entity. Thus we do not at this point have the framework for a negotiation involving the PLO. We cannot envision or urge a negotiation between two parties as long as one professes to hold the objective of eliminating the other—rather than the objective of negotiating peace with it.

There is one other aspect to this problem. Elements of the PLO have used terrorism to gain attention for their cause. Some Americans as well as many Israelis and others have been killed by Palestinian terrorists. The international community cannot condone such practices, and it seems to us that there must be some assurance if Palestinians are drawn into the negotiating process that these practices will be curbed.

This is the problem which we now face. If the progress toward peace which has now begun is to continue, a solution to this question must be found. We have not devised an American solution, nor would it be appropriate for us to do so. This is the responsibility of the parties and the purpose of the negotiating process. But we have not closed our minds to any reasonable solution which can contribute to progress toward our overriding objective in the Middle East—an Arab-Israeli peace. The step-by-step approach to negotiations which we have pursued has been based partly on the understanding that issues in the Arab-Israeli conflict take time to mature. It is obvious that thinking on the Palestinian aspects of the problem must evolve on all sides. As it does, what is not possible today may become possible.

Our consultations on how to move the peace negotiations forward will recognize the need to deal with this subject. As Secretary Kissinger has said, "We are prepared to work with all the parties toward a solution of all the issues yet remaining—including the issue of the future of the Palestinians." We will do so because the issues of concern to the Palestinians are important in themselves and because the Arab governments participating in the negotiations have made clear that progress in the overall negotiations will depend in part on progress on issues of concern to the Palestinians. We are prepared to consider any reasonable proposal from any quarter, and we will expect other parties to the negotiation to be equally open-minded.

Platform of the Likud Coalition (March 1977)*

The Right of the Jewish People to the Land of Israel (Eretz Israel)

a. The right of the Jewish people to the land of Israel is eternal and indisputable and is linked with the right to security and peace; therefore, Judaea and Samaria will not be handed to any foreign administration; between the sea and Jordan there will only be Israeli sovereignty.

b. A plan which relinquishes parts of western Eretz Israel, undermines our right to the country, unavoidably leads to the establishment of a "Palestinian State," jeopardizes the security of the Jewish population, endangers the existence of the State of Israel, and frustrates any prospect of peace.

Genuine Peace—Our Central Objective

a. The Likud government will place its aspirations for peace at the top of its priorities and will spare no effort to promote peace. The Likud will act as a genuine partner at peace treaty negotiations with our neighbors, as is

---

* Excerpts from Prime Minister Begin's election platform.

customary among the nations. The Likud government will attend the Geneva Conference. . . .

d. The Likud government's peace initiative will be positive. Directly or through a friendly state, Israel will invite her neighbors to hold direct negotiations, in order to sign peace agreements without pre-conditions on either side and without any solution formula invented by outsiders ("invented outside").

At the negotiations each party will be free to make any proposals it deems fit.

Settlement

Settlement, both urban and rural, in all parts of the Land of Israel is the focal point of the Zionist effort to redeem the country, to maintain vital security areas and serves as a reservoir of strength and inspiration for the renewal of the pioneering spirit. The Likud government will call the younger generation in Israel and the dispersions to settle and help every group and individual in the task of inhabiting and cultivating the wasteland, while taking care not to dispossess anyone.

Arab Terror Organizations

The PLO is no national liberation organization but an organization of assassins, which the Arab countries use as a political and military tool, while also serving the interests of Soviet imperialism, to stir up the area. Its aim is to liquidate the State of Israel, set up an Arab country instead and make the Land of Israel part of the Arab world. The Likud government will strive to eliminate these murderous organizations in order to prevent them from carrying out their bloody deeds.

President Anwar Sadat: Peace with Justice (November 20, 1977)*

. . . I come to you today on solid ground to shape a new life and to establish peace. We all love this land, the land of God, we all, Moslems, Christians and Jews, all worship God.

Under God, God's teachings and commandments are: love, sincerity, security and peace.

I do not blame all those who received my decision when I announced

---

* Excerpts from speech delivered by the Egyptian President before the Israeli Parliament.

it to the entire world before the Egyptian People's Assembly . . . with surprise and even with amazement. . . .

Many months in which peace could have been brought about have been wasted over differences and fruitless discussions on the procedure of convening the Geneva conference. All have shared suspicion and absolute lack of confidence.

But to be absolutely frank with you, I took this decision after long thought, knowing that it constitutes a great risk, for God Almighty has made it my fate to assume responsibility on behalf of the Egyptian people, to share in the responsibility of the Arab nation, the main duty of which, dictated by responsibility, is to exploit all and every means in a bid to save my Egyptian Arab people and the pan-Arab nation from the horrors of new suffering and destructive wars, the dimensions of which are foreseen only by God Himself. . . .

Those who like us are shouldering the same responsibilities entrusted to us are the first who should have the courage to make determining decisions that are consonant with the magnitude of the circumstances. We must all rise above all forms of obsolete theories of superiority, and the most important thing is never to forget that infallibility is the prerogative of God alone.

If I said that I wanted to avert from all the Arab people the horrors of shocking and destructive wars I must sincerely declare before you that I have the same feelings and bear the same responsibility toward all and every man on earth, and certainly toward the Israeli people.

Any life that is lost in war is a human life, be it that of an Arab or an Israeli. A wife who becomes a widow is a human being entitled to a happy family life, whether she be an Arab or an Israeli.

Innocent children who are deprived of the care and compassion of their parents are ours. They are ours, be they living on Arab or Israeli land.

They command our full responsibility to afford them a comfortable life today and tomorrow.

For the sake of them all, for the sake of the lives of all our sons and brothers, for the sake of affording our communities the opportunity to work for the progress and happiness of man, feeling secure and with the right to a dignified life, for the generations to come, for a smile on the face of every child born in our land—for all that I have taken my decision to come to you, despite all the hazards, to deliver my address.

I have shouldered the prerequisites of the historic responsibility and therefore I declared on Feb. 4, 1971, that I was willing to sign a peace agreement with Israel. This was the first declaration made by a responsible Arab official since the outbreak of the Arab-Israeli conflict. Motivated by all these factors dictated by the responsibilities of leadership on Oct. 16, 1973, before the Egyptian People's Assembly, I called for an international conference to establish permanent peace based on justice. I was not heard.

I was in the position of man pleading for peace or asking for a cease-fire, motivated by the duties of history and leadership, I signed the first disengagement agreement, followed by the second disengagement agreement in Sinai.

Then we proceeded, trying both open and closed doors in a bid to find a certain road leading to a durable and just peace. . . .

How can we achieve permanent peace based on justice? Well, I have come to you carrying my clear and frank answer to this big question, so that the people in Israel as well as the entire world may hear it. All those devoted prayers ring in my ears, pleading to God Almighty that this historic meeting may eventually lead to the result aspired to by millions.

Before I proclaim my answer, I wish to assure you that in my clear and frank answer I am availing myself of a number of facts which no one can deny.

The first fact is that no one can build his happiness at the expense of the misery of others.

The second fact: never have I spoken, nor will I ever speak, with two tongues; never have I adopted, nor will I ever adopt, two policies. I never deal with anyone except in one tongue, one policy and with one face.

The third fact: direct confrontation is the nearest and most successful method to reach a clear objective.

The fourth fact: the call for permanent and just peace based on respect for United Nations resolutions has now become the call of the entire world. It has become the expression of the will of the international community, whether in official capitals where policies are made and decisions taken, or at the level of world public opinion, which influences policymaking and decision-taking.

The fifth fact, and this is probably the clearest and most prominent, is that the Arab nation, in its drive for permanent peace based on justice, does not proceed from a position of weakness. On the contrary, it has the power and stability for a sincere will for peace.

The Arab declared intention stems from an awareness prompted by a heritage of civilization, that to avoid an inevitable disaster that will befall us, you and the whole world, there is no alternative to the establishment of permanent peace based on justice, peace that is not swayed by suspicion or jeopardized by ill intentions.

In the light of these facts which I meant to place before you the way I see them, I would also wish to warn you, in all sincerity I warn you, against some thoughts that could cross your minds. . . .

First, I have not come here for a separate agreement between Egypt and Israel. This is not part of the policy of Egypt. The problem is not that of Egypt and Israel.

An interim peace between Egypt and Israel, or between any Arab confrontation state and Israel, will not bring permanent peace based on justice in the entire region.

Rather, even if peace between all the confrontation states and Israel were achieved in the absence of a just solution of the Palestinian problem, never will there be that durable and just peace upon which the entire world insists.

Second, I have not come to you to seek a partial peace, namely to terminate the state of belligerency at this stage and put off the entire problem to a subsequent stage. This is not the radical solution that would steer us to permanent peace.

Equally, I have not come to you for a third disengagement agreement in Sinai or in Golan or the West Bank.

For this would mean that we are merely delaying the ignition of the fuse. It would also mean that we are lacking the courage to face peace, that we are too weak to shoulder the burdens and responsibilities of a durable peace based upon justice.

I have come to you so that together we should build a durable peace based on justice to avoid the shedding of one single drop of blood by both sides. It is for this reason that I have proclaimed my readiness to go to the farthest corner of the earth.

Here I would go back to the big question:

How can we achieve a durable peace based on justice? In my opinion, and I declare it to the whole world, from this forum, the answer is neither difficult nor is it impossible despite long years of feuds, blood, faction, strife, hatreds and deep-rooted animosity.

The answer is not difficult, nor is it impossible, if we sincerely and faithfully follow a straight line.

You want to live with us, part of the world.

In all sincerity I tell you we welcome you among us with full security and safety. This in itself is a tremendous turning point, one of the land-marks of a decisive historical change. We used to reject you. We had our reasons and our fears, yes.

We refused to meet with you, anywhere, yes.

We were together in international conferences and organizations and our representatives did not, and still do not, exchange greetings with you. Yes. This has happened and is still happening.

It is also true that we used to set as a precondition for any negotiations with you a mediator who would meet separately with each party.

Yes. Through this procedure, the talks of the first and second disen-gagement agreements took place.

Our delegates met in the first Geneva conference without exchanging direct word, yes, this has happened.

Yet today I tell you, and I declare it to the whole world, that we accept to live with you in permanent peace based on justice. We do not want to encircle you or be encircled ourselves by destructive missiles ready for launching, nor by the shells of grudges and hatreds.

I have announced on more than one occasion that Israel has become a fait accompli, recognized by the world, and that the two superpowers have undertaken the responsibility for its security and the defense of its existence. As we really and truly seek peace we really and truly welcome you to live among us in peace and security.

There was a huge wall between us which you tried to build up over a quarter of a century, but it was destroyed in 1973. It was the wall of an implacable and escalating psychological warfare.

It was a wall of the fear of the force that could sweep the entire Arab nation. It was a wall of propaganda that we were a nation reduced to immobility. Some of you had gone as far as to say that even for 50 years to come, the Arabs would not regain their strength. It was a wall that always threatened with a long arm that could reach and strike anywhere. It was a wall that warned us of extermination and annihilation if we tried to use our legitimate rights to liberate the occupied territories.

Together we have to admit that that wall fell and collapsed in 1973. Yet, there remains another wall. This wall constitutes a psychological barrier between us, a barrier of suspicion, a barrier of rejection; a barrier of fear, of deception, a barrier of hallucination without any action, deed or decision.

A barrier of distorted and eroded interpretation of every event and statement. It is this psychological barrier which I described in official statements as constituting 70 percent of the whole problem.

Today, through my visit to you, I ask you why don't we stretch out our hands with faith and sincerity so that together we might destroy this barrier? Why shouldn't our and your will meet with faith and sincerity so that together we might remove all suspicion of fear, betrayal and bad intentions? . . .

Ladies and gentlemen, to tell you the truth, peace cannot be worth its name unless it is based on justice and not on the occupation of the land of others. It would not be right for you to demand for yourselves what you deny to others. With all frankness and in the spirit that has prompted me to come to you today, I tell you you have to give up once and for all the dreams of conquest and give up the belief that force is the best method for dealing with the Arabs.

You should clearly understand the lesson of confrontation between you and us. Expansion does not pay. To speak frankly, our land does not yield itself to bargaining, it is not even open to argument. To us, the nation's soil is equal to the holy valley where God Almighty spoke to Moses. Peace be upon him.

We cannot accept any attempt to take away or accept to seek one inch of it nor can we accept the principle of debating or bargaining over it.

I sincerely tell you also that before us today lies the appropriate chance for peace. If we are really serious in our endeavor for peace, it is a chance that that may never come again. It is a chance that if lost or wasted, the resulting slaughter would bear the curse of humanity and of history.

What is peace for Israel? It means that Israel lives in the region with her Arab neighbors in security and safety. Is that logical? I say yes. It means that Israel lives within its borders, secure against any aggression. Is that logical? And I say yes. It means that Israel obtains all kinds of guarantees that will ensure these two factors. To this demand, I say yes.

Beyond that we declare that we accept all the international guarantees you envisage and accept. We declare that we accept all the guarantees you want from the two superpowers or from either of them or from the Big Five or from some of them. Once again, I declare clearly and unequivocally that we agree to any guarantees you accept, because in return we shall receive the same guarantees.

In short then, when we ask what is peace for Israel, the answer would be that Israel lives within her borders, among her Arab neighbors in safety and security, within the framework of all the guarantees she accepts and which are offered to her.

But, how can this be achieved? How can we reach this conclusion which would lead us to permanent peace based on justice? There are facts that should be faced with courage and clarity. There are Arab territories which Israel has occupied and still occupies by force. We insist on complete withdrawal from these territories, including Arab Jerusalem.

I have come to Jerusalem, the city of peace, which will always remain as a living embodiment of coexistence among believers of the three religions. It is inadmissible that anyone should conceive the special status of the city of Jerusalem within the framework of annexation or expansionism. It should be a free and open city for all believers.

Above all, this city should not be severed from those who have made it their abode for centuries. Instead of reviving the precedent of the Crusades, we should revive the spirit of Omar Emil Khtab and Saladin, namely the spirit of tolerance and respect for right.

The holy shrines of Islam and Christianity are not only places of worship but a living testimony of our interrupted presence here. Politically, spiritually and intellectually, here let us make no mistake about the importance and reverence we Christians and Moslems attach to Jerusalem.

Let me tell you without the slightest hesitation that I have not come to you under this roof to make a request that your troops evacuate the occupied territories. Complete withdrawal from the Arab territories occupied after 1967 is a logical and undisputed fact. Nobody should plead for that. Any talk about permanent peace based on justice and any move to ensure our coexistence in peace and security in this part of the world would become meaningless while you occupy Arab territories by force of arms.

For there is no peace that could be built on the occupation of the land of others, otherwise it would not be a serious peace. Yet this is a foregone conclusion which is not open to the passion of debate if intentions are sincere or if endeavors to establish a just and durable peace for our and for generations to come are genuine.

As for the Palestine cause—nobody could deny that it is the crux of the entire problem. Nobody in the world could accept today slogans propagated here in Israel, ignoring the existence of a Palestinian people and questioning even their whereabouts. Because the Palestine people and their legitimate rights are no longer denied today by anybody; that is nobody who has the ability of judgment, can deny or ignore it.

It is an acknowledged fact, perceived by the world community, both in the East and in the West, with support and recognition in international documents and official statements. It is of no use to anybody to turn deaf ears to its resounding voice, which is being heard day and night, or to overlook its historical reality.

Even the United States of America, your first ally, which is absolutely committed to safeguard Israel's security and existence and which offered and still offers Israel every moral, material and military support—I say, even the United States has opted to face up to reality and admit that the Palestinian people are entitled to legitimate rights and that the Palestine problem is the cause and essence of the conflict and that so long as it continues to be unresolved, the conflict will continue to aggravate, reaching new dimension.

In all sincerity I tell you that there can be no peace without the Palestinians. It is a grave error of unpredictable consequences to overlook or brush aside this cause.

I shall not indulge in past events such as the Balfour Declaration 60 years ago. You are well acquainted with the relevant text. If you have found the moral and legal justification to set up a national home on a land that did not all belong to you, it is incumbent upon you to show understanding of the insistence of the people of Palestine for establishment once again of a state on their land. When some extremists ask the Palestinians to give up this sublime objective, this in fact means asking them to renounce their identity and every hope for the future.

I hail the Israeli voices that called for the recognition of the Palestinian people's right to achieve and safeguard peace.

Here I tell you, ladies and gentlemen, that it is no use to refrain from recognizing the Palestinian people and their right to statehood as their right of return. We, the Arabs, have faced this experience before, with you. And with the reality of the Israeli existence, the struggle which took us from war to war, from victims to more victims, until you and we have today reached the edge of a horrible abyss and a terrifying disaster unless, together, we seize this opportunity today of a durable peace based on justice.

You have to face reality bravely, as I have done. There can never be any solution to a problem by evading it or turning a deaf ear to it. Peace cannot last if attempts are made to impose fantasy concepts on which the world has turned its back and announced its unanimous call for the respect of rights and facts.

There is no need to enter a vicious circle as to Palestinian rights. It is useless to create obstacles, otherwise the march of peace will be impeded or peace will be blown up. As I have told you, there is no happiness [based on] the detriment of others.

Direct confrontation and straightforwardness are the shortcuts and the most successful way to reach a clear objective. Direct confrontation concerning the Palestinian problem and tackling it in one single language with a view to achieving a durable and just peace lie in the establishment of that peace. With all the guarantees you demand, there should be no fear of a newly born state that needs the assistance of all countries of the world.

When the bells of peace ring there will be no hands to beat the drums of war. Even if they existed, they would be stilled.

Conceive with me a peace agreement in Geneva that we would herald to a world thirsting for peace. A peace agreement based on the following points:

Ending the occupation of the Arab territories occupied in 1967.

Achievement of the fundamental rights of the Palestinian people and their right to self-determination, including their right to establish their own state.

The right of all states in the area to live in peace within their boundaries, their secure boundaries, which will be secured and guaranteed through procedures to be agreed upon, which will provide appropriate security to international boundaries in addition to appropriate international guarantees.

Commitment of all states in the region to administer the relations among them in accordance with the objectives and principles of the United Nations Charter. Particularly the principles concerning the nonuse of force and a solution of differences among them by peaceful means.

Ending the state of belligerence in the region.

Ladies and gentlemen, peace is not a mere endorsement of written lines. Rather it is a rewriting of history. Peace is not a game of calling for peace to defend certain whims or hide certain admissions. Peace in its essence is a dire struggle against all and every ambition and whim.

Perhaps the example taken and experienced, taken from ancient and modern history, teaches that missiles, warships and nuclear weapons cannot establish security. Instead they destroy what peace and security build.

For the sake of our peoples and for the sake of the civilization made by man, we have to defend man everywhere against rule by the force of arms so that we may endow the rule of humanity with all the power of the values and principles that further the sublime position of mankind.

Allow me to address my call from this rostrum to the people of Israel. I pledge myself with true and sincere words to every man, woman and child in Israel. I tell them, from the Egyptian people who bless this sacred mission of peace, I convey to you the message of peace of the Egyptian people, who do not harbor fanaticism and whose sons, Moslems, Christians and Jews, live together in a state of cordiality, love and tolerance.

This is Egypt, whose people have entrusted me with their sacred message. A message of security, safety and peace to every man, woman and child in Israel. I say, encourage your leadership to struggle for peace. Let all endeavors be channeled toward building a huge stronghold for peace instead of building destructive rockets.

Introduce to the entire world the image of the new man in this area so that he might set an example to the man of our age, the man of peace everywhere. Ring the bells for your sons. Tell them that those wars were the last of wars and the end of sorrows. Tell them that we are entering upon a new beginning, a new life, a life of love, prosperity, freedom and peace.

You, sorrowing mother, you, widowed wife, you, the son who lost a brother or a father, all the victims of wars, fill the air and space with recitals of peace, fill bosoms and hearts with the aspirations of peace. Make a reality that blossoms and lives. Make hope a code of conduct and endeavor. . . .

PLO: Six-Point Program
(December 4, 1977)*

In the wake of Sadat's treasonous visit to the Zionist entity, all factions of the Palestinian Resistance Movement have decided to make a practical answer to this step. On this basis, they met and issued the following document:

We, all factions of the PLO, announce the following:

FIRST: We call for the formation of a "Steadfastness and Confrontation Front" composed of Libya, Algeria, Iraq, Democratic Yemen, Syria and the PLO, to oppose all capitulationist solutions planned by imperialism, Zionism and their Arab tools.

SECOND: We fully condemn any Arab party in the Tripoli Summit which rejects the formation of this Front, and we announce this.

THIRD: We reaffirm our rejection of Security Council resolutions 242 and 338.

FOURTH: We reaffirm our rejection of all international conferences based on these two resolutions, including the Geneva Conference.

FIFTH: To strive for the realization of the Palestinian people's rights to return and self-determination within the context of an independent Palestinian national state on any part of Palestinian land, without reconciliation,

---

* Signed by leaders of the PLO's constituent organizations in Tripoli, Libya.

recognition or negotiations, as an interim aim of the Palestinian Revolution.

SIXTH: To apply the measures related to the political boycott of the Sadat regime.

In the name of all the factions, we ratify this unificatory document.

Arab League Summit Conference Declaration (December 5, 1977)*

With a sense of complete pan-Arab responsibility, the conference discussed the dimensions of the current phase through which the Arab cause in general and the Palestinian question in particular are passing and the American-Zionist plans aimed at imposing capitulatory settlements on the Arab nation, prejudicing the established national rights of the Palestinian people, liquidating the national Arab accomplishments and striking at the Arab liberation movement as a prelude to subduing the Arab area and controlling its destiny and tying it to the bandwagon of world imperialism.

The conference also discussed the visit made by President Sadat to the Zionist entity as being a link in the framework of the implementation of the hostile schemes. . . .

Those attending the conference studied the current situation with all of its dimensions and concluded that the objectives of the plot are as follows:

To undermine the possibility of the establishment of a just and honorable peace which would safeguard the national rights of the Arab nation and guarantee for it the liberation of its occupied territories, the foremost of which is Jerusalem, and for the Palestinian people their established national rights.

. . . To enable the forces hostile to the Arab nation, headed by the United States, to realize gains that will upset the international balance in favor of the Zionist-imperialist forces and Zionism and undermine the national independence of the Afro-Asian and Latin American countries.

To establish an alliance between the Zionist enemy and the current Egyptian regime aimed at liquidating the Arab issue and the issue of Palestine, split the Arab nation and forfeit its national interests.

Out of its belief in the nature of the Zionist and imperialist challenges aimed at weakening the Arab will for liberation and harming the firm national rights of the Palestinian people which have been confirmed by international legitimacy—the foremost of which is their right to return and decide their own destiny and build their independent state on the soil of

* Excerpts. The Arab League Summit Conference was held in Tripoli, Libya, December 2–5, 1977.

their homeland under the leadership of the PLO, which is the sole legitimate representative of the Palestinian people—and proceeding from the reality of pan-Arab and historic responsibility, the summit conference decided the following:

1. To condemn President al-Sadat's visit to the Zionist entity since it constitutes a great betrayal of the sacrifices and struggle of our Arab people in Egypt and their armed forces and of the struggle, sacrifices and principles of the Arab nation. While appreciating the role of the great Egyptian people in the national struggle of the Arab nation, the conference stresses that Egypt is not the beginning or the end and that if the Arab nation is great with Egypt, the latter's greatness is only possible within the Arab nation, without which it can only diminish in importance.

2. To work for the frustration of the results of President al-Sadat's visit to the Zionist entity and his talks with the leaders of the Zionist enemy and the subsequent measures including the proposed Cairo meeting. The conference warns that anyone who tries to pursue a similar line or to have any dealings with the said results shall be held responsible for his deed nationally and on the pan-Arab level.

3. To freeze political and diplomatic relations with the Egyptian Government, to suspend dealings with it on the Arab and international levels and to apply the regulations, provisions and decisions of the Arab Boycott against Egyptian individuals, companies and firms which deal with the Zionist enemy.

4. To decide not to take part in Arab League meetings which are held in Egypt and to undertake contacts with the Arab League member states to study the question of its headquarters and organs and the membership of the Egyptian regime.

5. The conference salutes the Palestinian Arab people, who are standing fast in the occupied homeland, including all of their national and other popular organizations which are struggling against the occupation and which reject the visit of al-Sadat to occupied Palestine. The conference also warns against any attempt to prejudice the legitimacy of the PLO representation of the Palestinian people.

6. The conference takes satisfaction in recording the preliminary positions taken by the Arab states which have denounced the visit and rejected its consequences. Out of its responsibility and in compliance with its commitment and collective resolutions, the conference calls on these states to adopt practical measures to face the serious character of this capitulatory policy, including the suspension of political and military support. The conference also condemns the disgraceful stands adopted by those who praise this visit or support it and warn them of the consequences of their despondent and defeatist policies.

7. The conference appeals to the Arab nation on the official and popular levels to provide economic, financial, political and military aid and

support to the Syrian region, now that it has become the principal confrontation state and the base of steadfastness for dealing with the Zionist enemy and also to the Palestinian people represented by the PLO.

8. The conference greets our Arab people in sisterly Egypt and particularly their national and progressive forces, which have rejected the capitulatory policy being pursued by the Egyptian regime as being a betrayal of the sacrifices of the people and their martyrs and an insult to the dignity of their armed forces.

9. In asserting the importance of the relationship of struggle and nationalism between Syria and the Palestinians, the Syrian Arab Republic and the PLO announce the formation of a unified front to face the Zionist enemy and combat the imperialist plot with all its parties and to thwart all attempts at capitulation. The Democratic and Popular Republic of Algeria, the Socialist People's Libyan Arab Jamahiriyah and the PDRY [People's Democratic Republic of Yemen—South Yemen] have decided to join this front, making it the nucleus of a pan-Arab front for steadfastness and combat which will be open to other Arab countries to join.

10. Members of the pan-Arab front consider any aggression against any one member as an aggression against all members.

The conference pledges to the Arab nation that it will continue the march of struggle, steadfastness, combat and adherence to the objectives of the Arab struggle. The conference also expresses its deep faith and absolute confidence that the Arab nation, which has staged revolutions, overcome difficulties and defeated plots during its long history of struggle—a struggle which abounds with heroism—is today capable of replying with force to those who have harmed its dignity, squandered its rights, split its solidarity and departed from the principles of its struggle. It is confident of its own capabilities in liberation, progress and victory, thanks to God.

The conference records with satisfaction the national Palestinian unity within the framework of the PLO.

Prime Minister Menachem Begin: Autonomy Plan for the Occupied Territories (December 28, 1977)*

. . . With the establishment of peace we shall propose the introduction of an administrative autonomy for the Arab residents of Judea, Samaria and the Gaza Strip on the basis of the following principles:

The administration of the military rule in Judea, Samaria and the Gaza

* Excerpts from the Prime Minister's speech to the Israeli Parliament.

Strip will be abolished. In Judea, Samaria and the Gaza Strip an administrative autonomy of, by and for the Arab residents will be established. The residents of Judea, Samaria and the Gaza Strip will elect an administrative council which will be composed of 11 members. The administrative council will act according to the principles postulated in this document. Every resident 18 years old or older, regardless of his citizenship or the lack of it, will be entitled to vote for the administrative council. Every resident who is 25 years old or older the day the list of candidates for the administrative council is presented will be entitled to be elected to the administrative council. The administrative council will be elected in general, direct, personal, equal and secret elections. . . .

The administrative council will establish the following departments: department of education; department of transportation; department of construction and housing; department of industry, commerce and tourism; department of agriculture; department of health; department of labor and social betterment; department for the rehabilitation of refugees; department of legal administration and supervision of the local police force. The administrative council will issue regulations pertaining to the activities of those departments.

Security and public order in the areas of Judea, Samaria and Gaza will be entrusted to the Israeli authorities. . . .

Residents of Judea, Samaria and Gaza, regardless of their citizenship or lack of it, will have the free option to receive either Israeli or Jordanian citizenship. . . . A committee of representatives of Israel, Jordan and the administrative council will be established to examine the law in Judea, Samaria and the Gaza district and to determine which laws will remain valid, which will be abolished and what the authority of the administrative council will be to issue regulations. The decisions of this committee will be adopted unanimously.

Israeli residents will be entitled to purchase land and settle in the areas of Judea, Samaria and Gaza. Arab residents of Judea, Samaria and the Gaza district who become, in accordance with the free option granted them, Israeli citizens will be entitled to purchase land and settle in Israel. A committee of representatives of Israel, Jordan and of the administrative council will be established to determine immigration rules for the areas of Judea, Samaria and Gaza. The committee will postulate those rules which will permit Palestinian refugees outside Judea, Samaria and Gaza immigration in a reasonable volume into these areas. The decision of the committee will be adopted unanimously.

Israeli residents and the residents of Judea, Samaria and the Gaza district will be assured free movement and free economic activity in Israel, in Judea, in Samaria and in the Gaza district.

The administrative council will name one of its members to represent it before the Government of Israel for the purpose of discussing common issues, and one of its members will represent it before the Government of Jordan for the discussion of common issues.

Israel insists on its rights and demand for its sovereignty over Judea, Samaria and the Gaza Strip. Knowing that other demands exist, it proposes, for the sake of the agreement and of peace, to leave the question of sovereignty in those areas open.

Regarding the administration of the places holy to the three religions in Jerusalem, a special proposal will be prepared and presented, insuring free admission for all believers to the places sacred to them.

These principles will lend themselves to reexamination after a period of five years. . . .

We do not even dream of the possibility—if we are given the chance to withdraw our military forces from Judea, Samaria and Gaza—of abandoning those areas to the control of the murderous organization that is called the PLO. . . . This is history's meanest murder organization, except for the armed Nazi organizations. It also bragged two days ago about the murder of Hamdi al-Qadi, deputy director of the Education Bureau in Ramallah.

It is a frightening proposition that someone's solution to the problems in the Middle East might be a single bullet dispatched to the heart of Egyptian President as-Sadat as the PLO's predecessors did at Al-Aqsa Mosque to King Abdallah. One single bullet. No wonder that the Egyptian Government has declared that should such a single shot be fired, Egypt would retaliate with a million shots. We wish to say that under no condition will that organization be allowed to take control over Judea, Samaria and Gaza. If we withdraw our army, this is exactly what would happen. Hence, let it be known that whoever desires an agreement with us should please accept our announcement that the IDF will be deployed in Judea, Samaria and Gaza. And there will also be other security arrangements, so that we can give to all the residents, Jews and Arabs alike, in Eretz Yisrael a secure life—that is to say, security for all. . . .

. . . We have a right and a demand for sovereignty over these areas of Eretz Yisrael. This is our land and it belongs to the Jewish nation rightfully. We desire an agreement and peace. We know that there are at least two other demands for sovereignty over these areas. If there is a mutual desire to reach an agreement and to promote peace—what is the way?

Should these contradictory demands remain, and should there be no answer to the collision course between them, an agreement between the parties would be impossible. And for this reason, in order to facilitate an agreement and make peace, there is only one possible way. One way and no other: to agree to decide that the question of sovereignty remain open and to deal with people, with nations. That is to say, administrative autonomy for the Arabs of Eretz Yisrael; and for the Jews of Eretz Yisrael— genuine security. This is the fairness that is inherent in the content of the proposal. And in that spirit the proposal was also accepted abroad. . . .

President Jimmy Carter: Statement on Palestinian Rights (January 4, 1978)*

It is an honor and a pleasure for us to be in this great country, led by such a strong and courageous man.

Mr. President, your bold initiative in seeking peace has aroused the admiration of the entire world. One of my most valued possessions is the warm, personal relationship which binds me and President Sadat together and which exemplifies the friendship and the common purpose of the people of Egypt and the people of the United States of America.

The Egyptian-Israeli peace initiative must succeed, while still guarding the sacred and historic principles held by the nations who have suffered so much in this region. There is no good reason why accommodation cannot be reached.

In my own private discussions with both Arab and Israeli leaders, I have been deeply impressed by the unanimous desire for peace. My presence here today is a direct result of the courageous initiative which President Sadat undertook in his recent trip to Jerusalem.

The negotiating process will continue in the near future. We fully support this effort, and we intend to play an active role in the work of the Political Committee of Cairo, which will soon reconvene in Jerusalem.

We believe that there are certain principles, fundamentally, which must be observed before a just and a comprehensive peace can be achieved.

• First, true peace must be based on normal relations among the parties to the peace. Peace means more than just an end to belligerency.
• Second, there must be withdrawal by Israel from territories occupied in 1967 and agreement on secure and recognized borders for all parties in the context of normal and peaceful relations in accordance with U.N. Resolutions 242 and 338.
• Third, there must be a resolution of the Palestinian problem in all its aspects. The problem must recognize the legitimate rights of the Palestinian people and enable the Palestinians to participate in the determination of their own future.

Some flexibility is always needed to insure successful negotiations and the resolution of conflicting views. We know that the mark of greatness among leaders is to consider carefully the views of others and the greater

* Delivered in Aswan, Egypt.

benefits that can result among the people of all nations which can come from a successful search for peace.

Mr. President, our consultations this morning have reconfirmed our common commitment to the fundamentals which will, with God's help, make 1978 the year for permanent peace in the Middle East.

Camp David Frameworks for Peace (September 17, 1978)*

Preamble

The search for peace in the Middle East must be guided by the following:

—The agreed basis for a peaceful settlement of the conflict between Israel and its neighbors is United Nations Security Council Resolution 242, in all its parts.

—After four wars during thirty years, despite intensive human efforts, the Middle East, which is the cradle of civilization and the birthplace of three great religions, does not yet enjoy the blessings of peace. The people of the Middle East yearn for peace so that the vast human and natural resources of the region can be turned to the pursuits of peace and so that this area can become a model for coexistence and cooperation among nations.

—The historic initiative of President Sadat in visiting Jerusalem and the reception accorded to him by the Parliament, government and people of Israel, and the reciprocal visit of Prime Minister Begin to Ismailia, the peace proposals made by both leaders, as well as the warm reception of these missions by the people of both countries, have created an unprecedented opportunity for peace which must not be lost if this generation and future generations are to be spared the tragedies of war.

—The provisions of the Charter of the United Nations and the other accepted norms of international law and legitimacy now provide accepted standards for the conduct of relations among the states.

—To achieve a relationship of peace, in the spirit of Article 2 of the United Nations Charter, future negotiations between Israel and any neighbor prepared to negotiate peace and security with it, are necessary for the purpose of carrying out all the provisions and principles of Resolutions 242 and 338.

* Excerpts. This document was signed by Egyptian President Anwar Sadat and Israeli Prime Minister Menachem Begin and witnessed by President Jimmy Carter at Camp David, in Thurmont, Maryland.

—Peace requires respect for the sovereignty, territorial integrity and political independence of every state in the area and their right to live in peace within secure and recognized boundaries free from threats or acts of force. Progress toward that goal can accelerate movement toward a new era of reconciliation in the Middle East marked by cooperation in promoting economic development, in maintaining stability, and in assuring security.

—Security is enhanced by a relationship of peace and by cooperation between nations which enjoy normal relations. In addition, under the terms of peace treaties, the parties can, on the basis of reciprocity, agree to special security arrangements such as demilitarized zones, limited armaments areas, early warning stations, the presence of international forces, liaison, agreed measures for monitoring, and other arrangements that they agree are useful.

Framework

Taking these factors into account, the parties are determined to reach a just, comprehensive, and durable settlement of the Middle East conflict through the conclusion of peace treaties based on Security Council Resolutions 242 and 338 in all their parts. Their purpose is to achieve peace and good neighborly relations. They recognize that, for peace to endure, it must involve all those who have been most deeply affected by the conflict. They therefore agree that this framework as appropriate is intended by them to constitute a basis for peace not only between Egypt and Israel, but also between Israel and each of its other neighbors which is prepared to negotiate peace with Israel on this basis. With that objective in mind, they have agreed to proceed as follows:

A. West Bank and Gaza

1. Egypt, Israel, Jordan and the representatives of the Palestinian people should participate in negotiations on the resolution of the Palestinian problem in all its aspects. To achieve that objective, negotiations relating to the West Bank and Gaza should proceed in three stages:

(a) Egypt and Israel agree that, in order to ensure a peaceful and orderly transfer of authority, and taking into account the security concerns of all the parties, there should be transitional arrangements for the West Bank and Gaza for a period not exceeding five years. In order to provide full autonomy to the inhabitants, under these arrangements the Israeli military government and its civilian administration will be withdrawn as soon as a self-governing authority has been freely elected by the inhabitants of these areas to replace the existing military government. To negotiate the details of a transitional arrangement, the Government of Jordan will be invited to join the negotiations on the basis of this framework. These new arrangements should give due consideration both to the principle of self-government by the inhabitants of these territories and to the legitimate security concerns of the parties involved.

(b) Egypt, Israel, and Jordan will agree on the modalities for establishing the elected self-governing authority in the West Bank and Gaza. The delegations of Egypt and Jordan may include Palestinians from the West Bank and Gaza or other Palestinians as mutually agreed. The parties will negotiate an agreement which will define the powers and responsibilities of the self-governing authority to be exercised in the West Bank and Gaza. A withdrawal of Israeli armed forces will take place and there will be a redeployment of the remaining Israeli forces into specified security locations. The agreement will also include arrangements for assuring internal and external security and public order. A strong local police force will be established, which may include Jordanian citizens. In addition, Israeli and Jordanian forces will participate in joint patrols and in the manning of control posts to assure the security of the borders.

(c) When the self-governing authority (administrative council) in the West Bank and Gaza is established and inaugurated, the transitional period of five years will begin. As soon as possible, but not later than the third year after the beginning of the transitional period, negotiations will take place to determine the final status of the West Bank and Gaza and its relationship with its neighbors, and to conclude a peace treaty between Israel and Jordan by the end of the transitional period. These negotiations will be conducted among Egypt, Israel, Jordan, and the elected representatives of the inhabitants of the West Bank and Gaza. Two separate but related committees will be convened, one committee, consisting of representatives of the four parties which will negotiate and agree on the final status of the West Bank and Gaza, and its relationship with its neighbors, and the second committee, consisting of representatives of Israel and representatives of Jordan to be joined by the elected representatives of the inhabitants of the West Bank and Gaza, to negotiate the peace treaty between Israel and Jordan, taking into account the agreement reached on the final status of the West Bank and Gaza. The negotiations shall be based on all the provisions and principles of UN Security Council Resolution 242. The negotiations will resolve, among other matters, the location of the boundaries and the nature of the security arrangements. The solution from the negotiations must also recognize the legitimate rights of the Palestinian people and their just requirements. In this way, the Palestinians will participate in the determination of their own future through:

1) The negotiations among Egypt, Israel, Jordan and the representatives of the inhabitants of the West Bank and Gaza to agree on the final status of the West Bank and Gaza and other outstanding issues by the end of the transitional period.

2) Submitting their agreement to a vote by the elected representatives of the inhabitants of the West Bank and Gaza.

3) Providing for the elected representatives of the inhabitants of the West Bank and Gaza to decide how they shall govern themselves consistent with the provisions of their agreement.

4) Participating as stated above in the work of the committee negotiating the peace treaty between Israel and Jordan.

All necessary measures will be taken and provisions made to assure the security of Israel and its neighbors during the transitional period and beyond. To assist in providing such security, a strong local police force will be constituted by the self-governing authority. It will be composed of inhabitants of the West Bank and Gaza. The police will maintain continuing liaison on internal security matters with the designated Israeli, Jordanian, and Egyptian officers.

During the transitional period, representatives of Egypt, Israel, Jordan, and the self-governing authority will constitute a continuing committee to decide by agreement on the modalities of admission of persons displaced from the West Bank and Gaza in 1967, together with necessary measures to prevent disruption and disorder. Other matters of common concern may also be dealt with by this committee.

Egypt and Israel will work with each other and with other interested parties to establish agreed procedures for a prompt, just and permanent implementation of the resolution of the refugee problem.

B. Egypt-Israel

1. Egypt and Israel undertake not to resort to the threat or the use of force to settle disputes. Any disputes shall be settled by peaceful means in accordance with the provisions of Article 33 of the Charter of the United Nations.

2. In order to achieve peace between them, the parties agree to negotiate in good faith with a goal of concluding within three months from the signing of this Framework a peace treaty between them, while inviting the other parties to the conflict to proceed simultaneously to negotiate and conclude similar peace treaties with a view to achieving a comprehensive peace in the area. The Framework for the Conclusion of a Peace Treaty between Egypt and Israel will govern the peace negotiations between them. The parties will agree on the modalities and the timetable for the implementation of their obligations under the treaty.

C. Associated Principles

1. Egypt and Israel state that the principles and provisions described below should apply to peace treaties between Israel and each of its neighbors—Egypt, Jordan, Syria and Lebanon.

2. Signatories shall establish among themselves relationships normal to states at peace with one another. To this end, they should undertake to abide by all the provisions of the Charter of the United Nations. Steps to be taken in this respect include:

(a) full recognition;

(b) abolishing economic boycotts;

(c) guaranteeing that under their jurisdiction the citizens of the other parties shall enjoy the protection of the due process of the law.

3. Signatories should explore possibilities for economic development in the context of final peace treaties, with the objective of contributing to the atmosphere of peace, cooperation and friendship which is their common goal.

4. Claims Commissions may be established for the mutual settlement of all financial claims.

5. The United States shall be invited to participate in the talks on matters related to the modalities of the implementation of the agreements and working out the timetable for the carrying out of the obligations of the parties.

6. The United Nations Security Council shall be requested to endorse the peace treaties and ensure that their provisions shall not be violated. The permanent members of the Security Council shall be requested to underwrite the peace treaties and ensure respect for their provisions. They shall also be requested to conform their policies and actions with the undertakings contained in this Framework.

. . . The following matters are agreed between the parties:

(a) the full exercise of Egyptian sovereignty up to the internationally recognized border between Egypt and mandated Palestine;

(b) the withdrawal of Israeli armed forces from the Sinai;

(c) the use of airfields left by the Israelis near El Arish, Rafah, Ras en Naqb, and Sharm el Sheikh for civilian purposes only, including possible commercial use by all nations;

(d) the right of free passage by ships of Israel through the Gulf of Suez and the Suez Canal on the basis of the Constantinople Convention of 1888 applying to all nations; the Strait of Tiran and the Gulf of Aqaba are international waterways to be open to all nations for unimpeded and non-suspendable freedom of navigation and overflight;

(e) the construction of a highway between the Sinai and Jordan near Elat with guaranteed free and peaceful passage by Egypt and Jordan; and

(f) the stationing of military forces listed below.

Stationing of Forces

A. No more than one division (mechanized or infantry) of Egyptian armed forces will be stationed within an area lying approximately 50 kilometers (km) east of the Gulf of Suez and the Suez Canal.

B. Only United Nations forces and civil police equipped with light weapons to perform normal police functions will be stationed within an area lying west of the international border and the Gulf of Aqaba, varying in width from 20 km to 40 km.

C. In the area within 3 km east of the international border there will be Israeli limited military forces not to exceed four infantry battalions and United Nations observers.

D. Border patrol units, not to exceed three battalions, will supplement the civil police in maintaining order in the area not included above.

The exact demarcation of the above areas will be as decided during the peace negotiations.

Early warning stations may exist to ensure compliance with the terms of the agreement.

United Nations forces will be stationed: (a) in part of the area in the Sinai lying within about 20 km of the Mediterranean Sea and adjacent to the international border, and (b) in the Sharm el Sheikh area to ensure freedom of passage through the Strait of Tiran; and these forces will not be removed unless such removal is approved by the Security Council of the United Nations with a unanimous vote of the five permanent members.

After a peace treaty is signed, and after the interim withdrawal is complete, normal relations will be established between Egypt and Israel, including: full recognition, including diplomatic, economic and cultural relations; termination of economic boycotts and barriers to the free movement of goods and people; and mutual protection of citizens by the due process of law.

Egypt-Israel Peace Treaty (March 26, 1979)*

ARTICLE I

1. The state of war between the Parties will be terminated and peace will be established between them upon the exchange of instruments of ratification of this Treaty.

2. Israel will withdraw all its armed forces and civilians from the Sinai behind the international boundary between Egypt and mandated Palestine, as provided in the annexed protocol . . . and Egypt will resume the exercise of its full sovereignty over the Sinai. . . .

ARTICLE II

The permanent boundary between Egypt and Israel is the recognized international boundary between Egypt and the former mandated territory of

* Excerpts from peace treaty drawn up at Camp David meetings.

Palestine . . . without prejudice to the issue of the status of the Gaza Strip. The Parties recognize this boundary as inviolable. Each will respect the territorial integrity of the other, including their territorial waters and airspace.

ARTICLE III

. . . Each Party undertakes to ensure that acts or threats of belligerency, hostility, or violence do not originate from and are not committed from within its territory, or by any forces subject to its control or by any other forces stationed on its territory, against the population, citizens or property of the other Party. Each Party also undertakes to refrain from organizing, instigating, inciting, assisting or participating in acts or threats of belligerency, hostility, subversion or violence against the other Party, anywhere, and undertakes to ensure that perpetrators of such acts are brought to justice.

The Parties agree that the normal relationship established between them will include full recognition, diplomatic, economic and cultural relations, termination of economic boycotts and discriminatory barriers to the free movement of people and goods, and will guarantee the mutual enjoyment by citizens of the due process of law.

Arab League Summit Communiqué (March 31, 1979)*

As the Government of the Arab Republic of Egypt has ignored the Arab summit conferences' resolutions, especially those of the sixth and seventh conferences held in Algiers and Rabat; as it has at the same time ignored the ninth Arab summit conference resolutions—especially the call made by the Arab kings, presidents and princes to avoid signing the peace treaty with the Zionist enemy—and signed the peace treaty on 26 March 1979;

It has thus deviated from the Arab ranks and has chosen, in collusion with the United States, to stand by the side of the Zionist enemy in one trench; has behaved unilaterally in the Arab-Zionist struggle affairs; has violated the Arab nation's rights; has exposed the nation's destiny, its struggle and aims to dangers and challenges; has relinquished its pan-Arab duty of liberating the occupied Arab territories, particularly Jerusalem, and of restoring the Palestinian Arab people's inalienable national rights, including their right to repatriation, self-determination and establishment of the independent Palestinian state on their national soil.

---

* Excerpts. The communiqué was issued in Baghdad, Iraq.

. . . The Arab League Council, on the level of Arab foreign ministers, has decided the following:

1. A. To withdraw the ambassadors of the Arab states from Egypt immediately.

B. To recommend the severance of political and diplomatic relations with the Egyptian Government. The Arab governments will adopt the necessary measures to apply this recommendation within a maximum period of one month from the date of issuance of this decision, in accordance with the constitutional measures in force in each country.

2. To consider the suspension of the Egyptian Government's membership in the Arab League as operative from the date of the Egyptian Government's signing of the peace treaty with the Zionist enemy. This means depriving it of all rights resulting from this membership.

3. To make the city of Tunis, capital of the Tunisian Republic, the temporary headquarters of the Arab League. . . .

Foreign Minister Andrei Gromyko: On the Camp David Agreement (September 25, 1979)*

The Middle East problem, if divested of the immaterial, boils down to the following—either the consequences of the aggression against the Arab states and peoples are eliminated or the invaders get a reward by appropriating lands that belong to others.

A just settlement and the establishment of durable peace in the Middle East require that Israel should end its occupation of all the Arab lands it seized in 1967, that the legitimate rights of the Arab people of Palestine including the right to create their own state be safeguarded and that the right of all states in the Middle East, including Israel, to independent existence under conditions of peace be effectively guaranteed.

The separate deal between Egypt and Israel resolves nothing. It is a means designed to lull the vigilance of peoples. It is a way of piling up on a still greater scale explosive material capable of producing a new conflagration in the Middle East. Moreover, added to the tense political atmosphere in this and the adjacent areas is the heavy smell of oil.

It is high time that all states represented in the United Nations realized how vast is the tragedy of the Arab peoples of Palestine. What is the worth of declarations in defence of humanism and human rights—whether for refugees or not—if before the eyes of the entire world the inalienable

---

* From a speech delivered to the UN General Assembly by the Soviet Foreign Minister.

rights of an entire people driven from its land and deprived of a livelihood are grossly trampled upon?

The Soviet policy with respect to the Middle East problem is one of principle. We are in favour of a comprehensive and just settlement, of the establishment of durable peace in the Middle East, a region not far from our borders. The Soviet Union sides firmly with Arab peoples who resolutely reject deals at the expense of their legitimate interests.

Yasir Arafat: Interview on Camp David (November 19, 1979)*

First, we must consider the events in the occupied land, since it is one of the main fronts on which we are fighting the Camp David plot. At the same time, it is a front against which the tripartite alliance—Carter, Begin, al-Sadat—launched their counterattack in retaliation for the resolutions of the Front of Steadfastness and Confrontation and those of the Baghdad summit and the Arab foreign and economy ministers' conference, which implemented all resolutions that were agreed upon.

This attack centered on our people in the occupied land by means of fascist, mean and oppressive measures in addition to the confiscation of land, building of settlements and terrorism such as deportation of the population, arrest and mass punishment against towns and villages as well as confiscation of springs. Our kinfolk's reply was magnificent and is now crowned by this splendid popular uprising against the Zionist authorities, protesting against the Zionist authorities' decision to deport one of our cadres and leaders in the occupied land: Bassam ash-Shak'ah, the Nablus mayor.

The other face of the battle is the mounting war of attrition against the Lebanese and Palestinian peoples. The most modern weapons, even the internationally banned ones, are being used in this war. This is resulting in the destruction of many Lebanese towns and villages and Palestinian camps and in the eviction of hundreds of thousands of Lebanese and Palestinian people. Actually, this terrorist and hellish plan is still continuing, and the Zionist enemy leaders continue to implement it. This, however, will neither intimidate us nor make us hesitate to reply to the enemy actions, both in the occupied land and in southern Lebanon, and with all forms of the military and political struggle. We have practiced this and we will never retreat. We have all the Arabs on our side. Our steadfastness has proved that the Arab nation does not lack will and steadfastness. . . .

* Interview in the Algerian newspaper *Al-Sha'b*.

President Hafiz al-Asad: Speech
(March 8, 1980)*

To us, to the whole world and as outlined in the UN resolutions, peace means Israel's complete withdrawal from the occupied Arab territories and the acknowledgement of the Palestinians' inalienable rights, including their right to determine their own destiny and set up their independent state. Peace under the Camp David accords means Israel's false withdrawal from Sinai—and it has not yet withdrawn—so that eventually it would be in a position to take all Egypt.

To us, peace means that Arab flags should fly over the liberated territories. Under the Camp David accords, peace means that the Israeli flag should be hoisted in an official ceremony in Cairo, while Israel is still occupying Egyptian, Syrian and Palestinian territory and is still adamantly denying Palestinian rights.

To us, peace means we should exercise our free will. Under the Camp David accords, peace means that the al-Sadat regime should keep Egypt's doors wide open to a Zionist economic, cultural and psychological invasion. It also means that Israel should continue to expand settlements.

To us, peace means a step further toward Arab unity. Under the Camp David accords, peace means Egypt should disengage from the Arab nation and move closer to usurper and aggressor Israel.

We do not make any distinction between one Arab territory and another, while the Camp David partners insist on making a distinction between Egyptian territory and other Arab territories.

The whole world calls for the establishment of a Palestinian state, while al-Sadat and his two allies talk about autonomy. The whole world knows, and the Israeli opposition leaders confirm, that the autonomy farce is a figment of Begin's imagination which he presented during his visit to Ismailia. On the other hand, al-Sadat presents autonomy as the distillation of his genius and most ideal solution.

Israel stresses daily that it will not withdraw from the West Bank and Gaza at any time in the future, and al-Sadat does not stop speaking about great hopes for the success of the autonomy farce. Despite their meager means, our heroic people in the occupied territory are resisting and waging a mighty struggle against the plot. But al-Sadat is using every material and psychological pressure on these people to force them to surrender to the plot.

The world condemns Israel's policy and aggression and supports the

* Excerpts from a speech delivered in Damascus by the Syrian President.

just Arab cause. But al-Sadat considers his close friend Begin as the messenger of peace, and his own Arab nation as the enemy of peace. Al-Sadat makes peace with the Israeli leaders and slanders the Arab nation, to which he has turned his back, forgetting that Egypt is part of this nation.

As for the third party, or the full partner as they like to call it, or the honest broker as it likes to call itself, it is determined not to annoy the Israeli leaders even in words. It is not prepared to draw a line between U.S. and Israeli interests in this region. To the United States, therefore, Israeli interests must come first, before anything else.

The Palestine question is the central issue of our struggle and the substance of our cause. We consider the PLO the sole legitimate representative of the Palestinian people. We will continue to support and strengthen the Palestinian revolution against all potential dangers. Syria and the Palestinian revolution are in one trench, something which must be understood by both friend and foe.

I frankly and truly say that the Soviet Union is the real friend of all peoples fighting for their freedom and independence. In my opinion, the imperialists have discovered from experience that they cannot weaken this friendship. But this does not mean that they will stop their attempts to destroy this friendship if they can. We know that we need the assistance of this big friend in our current battle. We must not miscalculate. This is a big battle. Israel is backed by the United States with large quantities of sophisticated weapons. Therefore, how can we possibly shut our eyes to a maneuver aimed at dragging us into a conflict with this big friend and closing the door through which we obtain assistance in the fiercest confrontation that we and all Arabs have in this age?

European Council: Venice Declaration (June 13, 1980)*

The heads of state and government and the ministers of foreign affairs . . . agreed that growing tensions affecting this region constitute a serious danger and render a comprehensive solution to the Israeli-Arab conflict more necessary and pressing than ever.

. . . The time has come to promote the recognition and implementation of the two principles universally accepted by the international community: the right to existence and to security of all the states in the region, including Israel, and justice for all the peoples, which implies the recognition of the legitimate rights of the Palestinian people.

* Excerpts from a declaration by the European Council issued at the conclusion of a two-day conference in Venice.

All of the countries in the area are entitled to live in peace within secure, recognized and guaranteed borders. The necessary guarantees for a peace settlement should be provided by the United Nations by a decision of the Security Council and, if necessary, on the basis of other mutually agreed procedures. The Nine declare that they are prepared to participate within the framework of a comprehensive settlement in a system of concrete and binding international guarantees, including guarantees on the ground.

A just solution must finally be found to the Palestinian problem, which is not simply one of refugees. The Palestinian people, which is conscious of existing as such, must be placed in a position, by an appropriate process defined within the framework of the comprehensive peace settlement, to exercise fully its right to self-determination.

. . . These principles apply to all the parties concerned, and thus the Palestinian people, and to the Palestine Liberation Organization, which will have to be associated with the negotiations.

. . . The Nine stress that they will not accept any unilateral initiative designed to change the status of Jerusalem and that any agreement on the city's status should guarantee freedom of access of everyone to the holy places.

The Nine stress the need for Israel to put an end to the territorial occupation which it has maintained since the conflict of 1967, as it has done for part of Sinai. They are deeply convinced that the Israeli settlements constitute a serious obstacle to the peace process in the Middle East. The Nine consider that these settlements, as well as modifications in population and property in the occupied Arab territories, are illegal under international law.

Concerned as they are to put an end to violence, the Nine consider that only the reunification of force or the threatened use of force by all the parties can create a climate of confidence in the area, and constitute a basic element for a comprehensive settlement of the conflict in the Middle East. . . .

Israel Government: Fundamental Policy Guidelines (August 5, 1981)*

The right of the Jewish people to the land of Israel is an eternal right that cannot be called into question, and which is intertwined with the right to security and peace.

The Government will continue to place its aspirations for peace at the

* Excerpts from Begin Government's Second Coalition agreement.

head of its concerns, and no effort will be spared in order to further peace. The peace treaty between Israel and Egypt is a historic turning point in Israel's status in the Middle East.

The Government will continue to use all means to prevent war.

The Government will diligently observe the Camp David agreements.

The Government will work for the renewal of negotiations on the implementation of the agreement on full autonomy for the Arab residents of Judea, Samaria and the Gaza Strip.

The autonomy agreed upon at Camp David means neither sovereignty nor self-determination. The autonomy agreements set down at Camp David are guarantees that under no conditions will a Palestinian state emerge in the territory of western "Eretz Yisrael."

At the end of the transition period, set down in the Camp David agreements, Israel will raise its claim, and act to realize its right of sovereignty over Judea, Samaria and the Gaza Strip.

Settlement in the land of Israel is a right and an integral part of the nation's security. The Government will act to strengthen, expand and develop settlement. The Government will continue to honor the principle that Jewish settlement will not cause the eviction of any person from his land, his village or his city.

Equality of rights for all residents will continue to exist in the land of Israel, with no distinctions [on the basis] of religion, race, nationality, sex, or ethnic community.

Israel will not descend from the Golan Heights, nor will it remove any settlement established there. It is the Government that will decide on the appropriate timing for the imposition of Israeli law, jurisdiction and administration on the Golan Heights.

Prince Fahd ibn Abd al-Aziz: The Fahd Plan (August 7, 1981)*

. . . There are a number of principles which may be taken as guidelines toward a just settlement; they are principles which the United Nations has taken and reiterated many times in the last few years. They are:

First, that Israel should withdraw from all Arab territory occupied in 1967, including Arab Jerusalem.

Second, that Israeli settlements built on Arab land after 1967 should be dismantled.

---

* Excerpts from an interview in Jidda with Saudi Arabian Crown Prince Fahd, now King of Saudi Arabia.

Third, a guarantee of freedom of worship for all religions in the holy places.

Fourth, an affirmation of the right of the Palestinian people to return to their homes and to compensate those who do not wish to return.

Fifth, that the West Bank and the Gaza Strip should have a transitional period, under the auspices of the United Nations, for a period not exceeding several months.

Sixth, that an independent Palestinian state should be set up with Jerusalem as its capital.

Seven, that all states in the region should be able to live in peace.

Eight, that the United Nations or member states of the United Nations should guarantee to execute these principles. . . .

I wish to reaffirm that the principles of a just comprehensive solution have become familiar and do not require great effort:

1. An end to unlimited American support for Israel.

2. An end to Israeli arrogance, whose ugliest facet is embodied in Begin's government. This condition will be automatically fulfilled if the first condition is fulfilled.

3. A recognition that, as Yasir Arafat says, the Palestinian figure is the basic figure in the Middle Eastern equation.

West Bank Palestinians: Reactions to Camp David (August 30, 1981)*

The Palestinian masses in the occupied West Bank and Gaza Strip continue to reject the declaration made by Sadat and Begin . . . that they had agreed to resume talks concerning so-called "autonomy" for the inhabitants of the West Bank and the Gaza Strip. A large number of Palestinian figures and personalities have commented . . . that the autonomy plan does not concern them in any respect, and that they consider the autonomy plan to be a conspiracy directed against the hopes and aspirations of the Palestinian people who are striving to attain their legitimate rights—which have been established by the international community, as represented by the UN. . . .

Dr. Amin al-Khatib, head of the Federation of Charity Associations in Jerusalem, said: "I do not believe that any plan for a solution to the Palestine problem which does not include the establishment of an independent Palestinian state in the territory of Palestine will be successful, no matter how skillfully its sponsors choose names for it and think up methods of attempting to convince us to accept it. We are quite confident

* Excerpts from an article in the Algerian newspaper *Al-Sha'b.*

that a people such as the Palestinian people, who have gone through great hardships and have become seasoned concerning all different types of plans and half-solutions, will not be able to accept or be content with any solution other than a Palestinian state. . . .

"We have the following to say to Sadat: 'The Palestinian people, inside the occupied territories, do not wish to have you speak or negotiate in their behalf. Give both yourself and us some peace and do not bother us with this whirlpool which is called "autonomy." ' "

Zalikhah Shihabi, the head of the Jerusalem Women's Federation, said: "Everything concerning autonomy—whether it be the autonomy talks, resumption of such talks, their cessation, or the breaking off of such talks altogether—does not concern us. The reason for this is that we know that it is merely a waste of time, and the objective of those who are calling for autonomy is to decrease the resentment of world public opinion against them, to attempt to outflank and encircle the PLO, and to flee from the truth which is shining as brightly as the sun. This truth is that the PLO is the only body authorized to discuss all matters which concern the Palestine question. All of us here agree that there should be an independent Palestinian state. Anything other than that will only meet with rejection and indifference on the part of the Palestinian people."

Mustafa 'Abd al-Nabi al-Natshah, deputy mayor of Hebron: "Autonomy is a continuation of military occupation, only with a mask over it. Autonomy, which is tantamount to local rule, does not contain any of the elements of establishing an independent state. It is a deception utilized in order to impose permanent occupation and would confer permanent legitimacy upon the military occupation. This is something which we totally reject."

Ibrahim al-Tawil, mayor of al-Birah, said: "Our people have not rejected autonomy for no reason. The rejection is based on the convictions of Palestinians living both inside and outside the occupied territories. What is called 'autonomy' is nothing more than a creation of the occupation and a part of it. Agreeing to this autonomy means conferring legitimacy upon the occupation."

Mr. al-Tawil then asked: "What kind of autonomy is it that does not grant our Palestinian people their legitimate rights—people who, like any other people, are demanding to live in peace and tranquility?"

He added: "Autonomy, as the Israelis understand it, means withdrawing army patrols and leaving [military] camps and settlements all over the West Bank. Furthermore, Begin has threatened to open the doors of his jails if any of the autonomy officials think about establishing their own state. So what is this autonomy which is nothing more than another version of the occupation? What it is is the deception and misleading of world public opinion and the other people of the world."

Mr. al-Tawil asserted that there are no people—and that there never will be people—who will participate in carrying out this step. He said that if there were any such mercenaries, they would not represent anybody and would not number even 1 person out of 10,000. He said that all [Palestinian] citizens reject this plan.

President Hosni Mubarak: Egypt and Israel (October 14, 1981)*

Egypt, the state and the people, is continuing along the road to a lasting and comprehensive peace based upon the framework that has been agreed upon at Camp David and that is based on the peace treaty between Egypt and Israel in letter and in spirit. Egypt, the state and the people, will spare no effort or time in continuing the autonomy talks until we put the Palestinian people along the beginning of the correct course for achieving their legitimate rights.

We, as the late leader repeatedly declared, do not speak on behalf of the Palestinian people. We do not claim that we are achieving the final solution of the question. The Palestinian people are the owners of the right and owners of the first and last responsibility for solving their problem. However, we are continuing in our role, dictated by our historical responsibility. We will make all efforts and pave the way for a transitional period during which the Palestinian people will determine their fate.

Egypt, the state and the people, is implementing the peace treaty. Egypt's position before the complete Israeli withdrawal in April 1982 is the same as Egypt's position after the complete withdrawal.

It pleases me to announce to you that we have received categorical assurances that the final Israeli withdrawal will take place on schedule, without delay and without slowing down. This coming 25th of April will, God willing, not pass without Egypt's flag waving high over Rafah, Sharm ash-Shaykh and every foot of the sacred land of the Sinai. The martyr of justice will have thus given his country and nation the greatest fulfillment by liberating the territory, restoring dignity and opening the road to a great future. With this historic event, the glorious Egyptian people and their valiant armed forces will have completed their most tremendous achievement in their contemporary history, lighting an eternal flame on the sands of Sinai that time cannot extinguish. Brothers, the historic peace initiative undertaken by our departed leader was the initiative of 42 million Egyptians. In fact, today that initiative does not belong only to the Egyptian people but also to all the peoples of the world.

Since President Reagan assumed power, the United States has an-

* Excerpts from the Egyptian President's inaugural address.

nounced the continuation of the U.S. commitment as a full partner in all the peace steps that are now taking their normal course.

I take this opportunity to declare to all the peoples of the world that the Egyptian people, who have faith in the peace miracle achieved by the hero of peace, today believe even more strongly in the continuation of the peace process, today they are more determined to protect all the fruits of peace.

The result of the referendum on my assumption of the responsibility on Sadat's road is the best evidence of the will and decision of the Egyptian people. It is a will for peace and it is a decision for peace.

U.S.–Israel Memorandum of Understanding (November 30, 1981)*

PREAMBLE

This Memorandum of Understanding reaffirms the common bonds of friendship between the United States and Israel and builds on the mutual security relationship that exists between the two nations. The Parties recognize the need to enhance strategic cooperation to deter all threats from the Soviet Union in the region. Noting the long-standing and fruitful cooperation for mutual security that has developed between the two countries, the Parties have decided to establish a framework for continued consultation and cooperation to enhance their national security by deterring such threats in the whole region.

The Parties have reached the following agreements in order to achieve the above aims:

ARTICLE I

United States-Israeli strategic cooperation, as set forth in this Memorandum, is designed against the threat to peace and security of the region caused by the Soviet Union or Soviet-controlled forces from outside the region introduced into the region. It has the following broad purposes:

A. To enable the Parties to act cooperatively and in a timely manner to deal with the above mentioned threat;

B. To provide each other with military assistance for operations of their forces in the area that may be required to cope with this threat;

C. The strategic cooperation between the Parties is not directed at any State or group of States within the region. It is intended solely for defensive purposes against the above mentioned threat.

* Excerpts. Memorandum announced simultaneously in Washington and Jerusalem.

ARTICLE II

1. The fields in which strategic cooperation will be carried out to prevent the above mentioned threat from endangering the security of the region include:

A. Military cooperation between the Parties, as may be agreed by the Parties;

B. Joint military exercises, including naval and air exercises in the eastern Mediterranean Sea, as agreed upon by the Parties;

C. Cooperation for the establishment and maintenance of joint readiness activities, as agreed upon by the Parties;

D. Other areas within the basic scope and purpose of this agreement, as may be jointly agreed.

Israeli Law on the Golan Heights (December 14, 1981)*

1. The law, jurisdiction and administration of the State shall apply to the Golan Heights. . . .

2. This law shall become valid on the day of its passage in the Knesset.

3. The Minister of the Interior shall be charged with the implementation of this law, and he is entitled, in consultation with the Minister of Justice, to enact regulations for its implementation and to formulate in regulations transitional provisions and provisions concerning the continued application of regulations, orders, administrative orders, rights and duties which were in force on the Golan Heights prior to the application of this law.

Defense Minister Ariel Sharon: Israel's Security (December 15, 1981)†

As I see them, our main security problems during the 1980's will stem from external threats to Israel, her integrity and her sovereign rights . . .

One—The Arab confrontation.

Second—The Soviet expansion which both builds on the Arab confrontation and at the same time provides it with its main political and military tools.

Later on, I will comment on the implications in terms of political and military requirements in order to cope with the threat and to ensure Israel's national security in the 1980's.

* Source: Israel Press Office.

† Excerpts from a speech by Defense Minister Ariel Sharon at the Center for Strategic Studies, Tel Aviv University.

Starting with the Arab challenge, I must touch upon the three major factors which, in my mind, contribute the most to sustain Arab enmity and confrontation at a level that presents an actual danger to our security and which, I believe, will continue to sustain it in the foreseeable future —at a level which might confront us with a potential threat to the existence and integrity of Israel.

Those factors are:

A. First, the national ideology of radical Arab regimes (such as in Syria, Libya, Iraq and South Yemen) and their political and strategic ambitions which motivate them to invest, on a first-priority basis, in the creation of a political-military setting designed to serve a strategy of political and military stages for the liquidation of the State of Israel.

The main elements of this strategy of stages can be summed up as follows:

1) A combined effort of sustained political pressure and, when needed, limited military action aimed at the harassment and weakening of Israel.

2) The build-up of a military power, conventional and eventually nonconventional, to be used in appropriate conditions in the future, for a decisive onslaught against Israel.

3) The third element of the strategy is the political and military reliance on the Soviet Union, to ensure the Arab capability to initiate and carry out the confrontation.

4) The fourth element is to maximize the political strategic impact of the oil weapon.

5) And the fifth is the political and military backing to the PLO as an instrument to carry out terrorist activities. This constitutes a central element in the strategy of stages, so long as Israel's deterrent posture and other political considerations prevent the formation of an Arab coalition, ready to wage war.

That brings me to the second major factor, which is the PLO. On the challenge presented by the PLO, I will say only this: The PLO poses a political threat to the very existence of the State of Israel and remains one of the main obstacles to the resolution of the Palestinian problem on the basis of the Camp David accords.

It constitutes a framework for terrorist organizations operating against Israel, in its territory or in the world at large, with the following purposes:

—To undermine the domestic stability in Israel and its security.

—To generate international pressure on Israel.

—To drag the confrontation states to war against Israel.

—To deter Arab countries and moderate Palestinian elements from negotiations with Israel on the basis of Camp David.

The third factor is one of growing concern to us and to the Western world, and might well develop as the main challenge of the 1980's. It has to do with the Soviet strategy of expansion in the Middle East and Africa. The Soviet strategy is under no pressure of time, but its achievements since the middle of the 1950's are really impressive. . . . It is a strategy of expansion which, if not checked, could eventually enable the Soviet Union:

—To ensure a sea-control capability in the Mediterranean, the Indian Ocean, the Red Sea and the Persian Gulf.

—To establish the military infrastructure for direct or indirect operations.

—To expand and penetrate other key countries in the Middle East and the Persian Gulf, from the direction of Afghanistan, Iraq, South Yemen and Syria.

—To outflank NATO's eastern tier (Turkey) through Iran, Iraq, Syria and Lebanon.

—To outflank NATO's southern tier in the Mediterranean, through Libya, Syria and Algeria.

—To gain control over other key countries in Africa, from the direction of Libya, Algeria, South Yemen, Ethiopia, Mozambique, Angola and Congo-Brazzaville. . . .

Today, as in the past two decades, the Soviet strategy of expansion in the area continues to build on:

—Arab regimes which Soviet political and military support enables to survive, to carry out their own ambitions and to maintain military confrontations—including the confrontation with Israel.

—Radical elements and terrorist organizations, which Soviet political and military support enables to create upheavals threatening to shift the region towards Soviet political-strategic patronage.

The shadow of Soviet presence in the Middle East and Africa endangers the stability of the region and vital interests of the free world. I want to stress this point with all possible emphasis. The greatest danger to the free world in the 1980's would be to continue to indulge in the wishful thinking and the inaction which have characterized Western attitudes to Soviet gradual expansion during the last two decades. . . .

Obviously, in order to be able to protect our national security interests, we will have to ensure our ability to maintain a balance of forces and a qualitative and technological edge over any combination of Arab war coalition; in other words:

—To prevent war by maintaining a deterrent posture against the threats to the existence of Israel.

—Should deterrence break down and war erupt, to ensure a military capability to preserve the integrity of Israel's territory, in any war-opening situation including a sudden Arab attack, and to disrupt the war coalition by damaging the core of its offensive capability.

To achieve these goals, we will have to structure our military strength on new approaches, taking into account:

—The lack of territorial depth and therefore the necessity to establish a strong territorial defense system, based on populous and high quality settlement of key border areas in Judaea, Samaria, the Gaza district, the Golan Heights, the Galilee and the Negev.

—The need to provide maximum protection to human life.

—The need to develop and produce weapon systems and equipment which should enable us to maintain a permanent qualitative advantage over Arab confrontation states—including with regard to advanced and sophisticated equipment they might get from Eastern and Western sources.

As a rule, while striving to establish ties of strategic cooperation with the United States to enhance stability and security in the region as a whole, we will continue to ensure our own independent ability to cope with the Arab military threats to our existence and security.

In order to cope with the threat, Israel cannot build on a balance of power based on a simple quantitative ratio of military forces. We cannot hope to match Arab numbers. Therefore, Israel's defense policy will have to ensure our ability to maintain a military balance based, beyond the quantitative ratio, on a clear qualitative and technological superiority. Israel is confronted by the challenge of maintaining a balance in peace of countries which have practically no limitations in funds to finance their military effort and furthermore in the . . . military technology and sophisticated weaponry they receive from all three sources—the Soviet, the American and the West-European supply sources, which are all competing by the same means for influence and economic advantages. Among the three sources of supply the United States remains sensitive to the need of maintaining a balance in the Arab-Israeli confrontation. But there is no control on the influx of armament from Soviet and European sources. Therefore, Israel has to build on her independent capability to develop and produce systems which are vital to ensure our qualitative advantage and our security. This puts a tremendous burden on our defense budget and on Israel's national economy. . . . The second "safety valve" if I can use that concept, in our defense policy, is our resolve and our ability to prevent the disruption of the territorial military status in neighboring countries. That includes our resolve.

—One—To prevent the violation of security arrangements laid down in political agreements such as in the Sinai with Egypt, and the Golan with Syria. It must be crystal clear: We did sign the peace treaty with Egypt and we faithfully carry out its provisions of withdrawal to the international border, but we have no intention to accept any violation of the status and of the security arrangements in the Sinai as agreed between us.

—Two—We will prevent any violation of the status quo ante in south Lebanon.

—Three—We will prevent any change in the geographical-military status of the confrontation area which might present unacceptable threat such as the massive introduction of Iraqi forces into Jordan or southern Syria or Syrian forces into Jordan. Such an accumulation of forces in the confrontation area would endanger our very existence and is therefore unacceptable to Israel. . . .

The third element in our defense policy for the 1980's is our determination to prevent confrontation states or potentially confrontation states from gaining access to nuclear weapons. Israel cannot afford the introduction of the nuclear weapon. For us it is not a question of a balance of terror but a question of survival. We shall therefore have to prevent such a threat at its inception.

There are three major elements in our defense policy for the 1980's. We shall, of course, also maintain our freedom of action and our ability to act in order to overcome the terrorist threat. To sum up—in order to strengthen the foundation of its national security, in face of the direct Arab threat as well as in face of the challenge from outside the region, Israel will make special efforts:

—One—To ensure our qualitative advantage and maintain the required balance of forces.

—Two—To expand and consolidate our economic, industrial, scientific, demographic and physical infrastructure, so as to carry the burden of our national security.

—Three—To hold political negotiations from a position of security for the purpose of continuing the peace process between Israel and her neighbors.

—Four—To consolidate and nurture national unity in Israel, as well as the ties between Israel and the Jewish people in the Diaspora.

—Five—To enhance strategic cooperation with the United States and to develop security relationships with Middle-Eastern and African countries and with other countries in the world. In that respect, I want to stress that Israel is not a liability but an asset, as the United States has gradually come to realize. For the common defense of the Free World, beyond our military capabilities, Israel has to offer an example of true democracy and stability in the midst of regional uncertainties and upheavals, and moreover the capability to contribute to the well-being of developed and less-developed nations, in many important fields such as science, medicine, food production and sophisticated agricultural technology in general.

Yitzhak Shamir: Israel's Role in a Changing Middle East (Spring 1982)*

Traditionally, the twin goals of Israel's foreign policy have always been peace and security—two concepts that are closely interrelated: Where there is strength, there is peace—at least, shall we say, peace has a chance. Peace will be unattainable if Israel is weak or perceived to be so. This,

* Excerpts from an article in *Foreign Affairs*, Spring 1982. Yitzhak Shamir became Israel's Foreign Minister in March 1980 and its Prime Minister in October 1983.

indeed, is one of the most crucial lessons to be learned from the history of the Middle East since the end of the Second World War—in terms not only of the Arab-Israel conflict, but of the area as a whole.

The Middle East is a mosaic of peoples, religions, languages and cultures. Although the Muslim-Arab culture is predominant, it has not produced any homogeneity. A vast number of currents—religious and political—are vying with each other, cutting across political borders. The region is permanently in ferment, and frequently unrest flares up in violence, terror, insurrection, civil strife and open and sometimes prolonged warfare. . . .

The most remarkable feature, in our context, of these chronic manifestations of unrest and belligerence is the fact that the great majority of them have nothing to do with Israel or with the Arab-Israel conflict. There were some outsiders, 20 and 30 years ago, who sincerely, but out of ignorance, believed that a solution of the Arab-Israel conflict would lead to regional stability and open a new era of progress. Nothing could be further from the truth. There have, it is true, been four major wars between Israel and its Arab neighbors. However, a full count of the instances of trouble and strife, both domestic and international, in North Africa and Western Asia, would show that the overwhelming majority have no connection whatsoever with the Arab relationship to Israel. . . .

Reduced to its true proportions, the problem is clearly *not* the lack of a homeland for the Palestinian Arabs. That homeland is Trans-Jordan, or eastern Palestine. There are, however, 1.2 million Palestinian Arabs living in the territories which have been administered by Israel since 1967 in Judea, Samaria and Gaza. Their status and problems were discussed at great length at Camp David. The granting of sovereignty to those areas was ruled out by Israel. A second Palestinian Arab state to the west of the River Jordan is a prescription for anarchy, a threat to both Israel and Jordan, and a likely base for terrorist and Soviet penetration. Hence, it was finally resolved at Camp David to implement an Autonomy Plan for the inhabitants of those areas, on a five-year interim basis. The proposal was made by Israel and accepted by the other partners of the Camp David accords, Egypt and the United States. It is not intended as the ultimate solution of the problem represented by these areas and their inhabitants, but as an interim arrangement designed to achieve two objectives: (a) to allow the Arab inhabitants of these areas the fullest feasible freedom in running their own lives, and (b) to create optimal conditions of peaceful coexistence between Arab and Jew.

Israel has made it clear, at Camp David and since, that it has a claim to sovereignty over Judea, Samaria and Gaza. In order, however, to keep the door open to a solution that will be acceptable to the parties, as envisaged at Camp David, Israel has deliberately refrained from exercising its rights under this claim. The claim will undoubtedly be presented at the end of the five-year interim period, and, while it is realized that there will be a similar claim on the Arab side, by that time one would hope that the kind of atmosphere will have been created that will make it possible to reach an agreement involving a solution acceptable to both sides. It should be clearly understood, therefore, that just as Israel is refraining from pushing its own solution at this time, by the same token the Arab side must refrain from pushing now for measures or the adoption of principles (such as self-determination, an embryo parliament in the autonomous territories, and the like) that would clearly fall beyond the parameters of Camp David and that would tend to prejudge the ultimate outcome of the negotiations on the final status of these areas. Autonomy, in other words, must be allowed to perform the function it was intended to perform—namely, to serve as an interim arrangement, pending the ultimate solution that is to be addressed at a later stage.

Meanwhile, Israelis and Arabs are learning to coexist in Judea, Samaria and Gaza—ultimately the best way to reconciliation and peace. Israelis will continue to reside in those areas. As in the past, this will not be done, of course, at the expense of the Arab inhabitants and their property. But, as Judea and Samaria constitute the heartland of the Jewish people's birth and development as a nation, Israel will not be party to a design that would deny Jews residence in those areas.

No less important, the Israeli presence in these areas, both civilian and military, is vital to Israel's defense—as should be abundantly clear against the background of the recent history of the region and of Israel's patent inability to maintain a large standing army on its borders. The defunct pre-1967 armistice lines—which for nearly 20 years proved to be a prescription for chronic instability and warfare—have long since ceased to have any relevance in the context of the search for a viable Middle East peace. Certainly, Israel will not entertain any notion of a return to those lines or anything approximating them. On this point there is, in Israel, virtually universal agreement.

A final word on the Palestinian subject. There are some, no doubt well-intentioned but largely unaware of some very important facts, who have proposed that Israel negotiate with the PLO. They point to the absence of any organized voice, other than the PLO, representing "the Palestinians" and to the existence of ostensibly moderate elements in that organization that may be encouraged to seek a political solution that would include recognition of Israel.

The real problem is not whether to deal with the PLO or not, but whether it would serve any useful purpose whatsoever. Even if one were to overlook their bloodthirsty modus operandi, their subservience to Soviet aims and their key role in international terror, the PLO's very raison d'être is the denial of Israel's right to exist, thinly veiled behind the cover of an ostensibly legitimate call for Palestinian statehood. The very act of granting the PLO a status—any status—in the political negotiations would be self-defeating. It would elevate its standing from that of a terrorist organization to that of a recognized aspirant to a totally superfluous political entity. Hence, association of the PLO with any aspect whatsoever of the political process and the prospects of peace are mutually exclusive.

On its part, Israel will do everything it can to ensure that the peace treaty with Egypt will serve as a solid base from which to expand the peace process toward a wider circle of participants. This can be achieved only by means of an Israel-Egypt partnership that is encouraged by active U.S. participation. It has a chance of success, provided that no alternative proposals and plans other than the Camp David accords are introduced into the process. No one is so naïve as to believe that this is a goal which will be easily attained. But this combination of states, working together toward a worthy and vital objective, has already proved its capacity to overcome obstacles and make progress. Together, they are a formidable force for stability that cannot be bypassed by any factor in the Middle East. In order for this policy to bear fruit, much patience and persistent effort are required. . . .

The magnitude of Israel's sacrifice for the achievement of the peace treaty has not been given proper recognition by the international community. From 1968 onward, Israel invested $17 billion in the Sinai Peninsula—in airfields, military installations, development of oilfields, infrastructure, towns and farm villages. The cost of the military redeployment to the Negev is estimated at $4.4 billion. Beyond the financial burden, and the strategic significance of the withdrawal from Sinai, the uprooting of several thousand Israelis who built their homes in the townships and villages along the eastern edge of Sinai is a traumatic event that has made a deep imprint on the entire nation.

With the transfer of the Sinai Peninsula to Egyptian sovereignty and the normalization of relations with Egypt under the peace treaty, Israel has gone a long way toward implementing the provisions of the 1967 U.N. Security Council Resolution 242. The Sinai Peninsula, it should be remembered, covers more than 90 percent of the territory that came into Israel's possession in the Six-Day War. Thus Israel has demonstrated, through concrete action and considerable risk and sacrifice, that it seeks peace and coexistence with its neighbors. It is now up to its neighbors to come forth with a similar demonstration of peaceful intent and readiness. . . .

Thus, within the context of a powerful, basically unchanging ideological rejection of Israel, there are two conflicting currents coursing through the Arab world. One—which is, as of now, the prevailing current—rejects the Jewish State wholly and without reservation, in theory and in practice. The other—only just beginning to crack the surface of developments in the Middle East—accepts the fact of Israel's existence and is ready, in some sort of pragmatic fashion, to come to terms with that existence. Israel is learning to live with this reality, and to try to build on the hope that, in the course of time, this pragmatism can be developed into something more permanent and more meaningful.

A crucial role in determining the future direction of events in the region can be played by forces and influences outside the region.

The history of the involvement of foreign governments in Middle Eastern politics is not a happy one. Attracted by the strategic importance of the region and, more recently, by its immense natural resources and bank deposits, most governments have sought to apply a political gloss to their perceived economic interests by making political statements on the Arab-Israel issue in response to Arab pressures.

. . . Arab hopes of exercising the military option against Israel would not have been sustained as they are if not for the immense supplies of sophisticated offensive military supplies from Russia. The Soviet Government has steadily increased its political and military support of the PLO in spite of, or perhaps because of, this organization's central role in international terror and its declared aim of destroying Israel and its population. This totally one-sided stand by the Soviet Union is compounded by its policy of boycotting Israel, and of persisting in its non-relations with Israel since 1967.

Soviet actions demonstrate clearly that the Soviet Union is opposed to peace in the Middle East, is bent on expanding its presence and influence in the region at the expense of regional stability, and has no problem in the choice of means to achieve its objective. Public opinion is far from being a factor in Soviet decisionmaking. . . .

Peace is fundamental to Israel's way of life, and Israel's determination to achieve it is permanent. Security is a vital guarantee of the viability and maintenance of peace. Together these two objectives provided the conceptual framework that produced the Camp David accords, and the march along this road must continue unabated.

A program for continued action to secure regional stability and peace must originate from the countries and governments that will have to implement the peace and live by it. Israel believes that it should include the following elements:

1. Negotiations between Israel and each of its neighbors, aimed at agreement on a just and lasting peace, laid out in formal peace treaties, that would provide for the establishment of normal diplomatic, economic and good-neighborly relations.

2. Recognition of the sovereignty and political independence of all existing states in the region, and of their right to live in peace within secure and recognized boundaries, free from threats or acts of force, including terrorist activity of any kind.

3. Autonomy for the Arab inhabitants of Judea, Samaria and the Gaza

district for a five-year interim period, as set forth in the Camp David accords, and deferment of the final determination of the status of these areas until the end of this transitional period.

4. Restoration of the full independence of Lebanon, through the withdrawal of Syrian and PLO forces from Lebanese territory.

5. Negotiations, among all the states of the Middle East, aimed at declaring the region a nuclear-weapons-free zone, for the security and well-being of all its inhabitants.

Boutros Boutros-Ghali: The Foreign Policy of Egypt in the Post-Sadat Era (Spring 1982)*

. . . Broadly speaking, Egyptian foreign policy in the last three decades has been directed toward two main challenges: how to contain Israeli ambitions and how to solve the Palestinian problem, the core of the Middle East crisis. This task, difficult in itself and rendered more complex by virtue of the multifaceted nature of the conflict, has been further complicated by the differences among Arabs, and the inability of some to adopt a rational attitude or to discard shortsighted policies toward the problem.

Thus, Egypt's efforts to resolve the contradictions between Palestinian national rights and Israeli national aims had to take place in the framework of an equation that would strike a balance between Egypt's conviction that Arab initiative is an important factor in any peace process and the necessity for her to exercise her traditional leadership in order to break the deadlock that has existed for well over 30 years. . . .

President Sadat presented the elements of Egypt's peace plan before the Knesset, as follows:

—the termination of the Israeli occupation of all the Arab territories occupied since 1967, including East Jerusalem;

—the realization of the inalienable rights of the Palestinian people and their rights to self-determination including the right to establish their own state;

—the right of all states in the area to live in peace within secure boundaries, based on the recognition that the security of international borders can be established through agreed-upon arrangements and international guarantees;

—the commitment by all states in the region to conduct relations among themselves according to the purposes and principles of the U.N.

* Excerpts from an article in *Foreign Affairs*, Spring 1982. Boutros Boutros-Ghali is Minister of State for Foreign Affairs of the Arab Republic of Egypt.

Charter, in particular the peaceful settlements of disputes and the absten-
tion from the threat or use of force; and
—the termination of the state of belligerency in the area.

Thus it was abundantly clear that Egypt viewed the Palestinian problem
as being at the very heart of the Middle East conflict and that an unjust
peace that would not guarantee the rights of the Palestinian people would
have no future. Indeed, Egypt is seeking a comprehensive peace and not
a separate or bilateral agreement with Israel. And during long hours of
negotiations with the Israelis, Egyptians have sought to link the withdrawal
of Israeli forces from Egyptian territory to the withdrawal of Israeli forces
from Palestinian territory. Every effort was exerted by Egypt to associate
the solution of the Egyptian question with that of the Palestinian question,
in order to lay special emphasis on her comprehensive approach to the
peace process. . . .

What Egypt has in mind is that the Palestinians and other Arab parties
concerned join these negotiations. It is obvious, however, that only tangible and positive results would induce them to do so. Hence the emphasis
laid by Egypt on the necessity for the Israelis to adopt a number of confidence-building measures, to discard the policies of economic sabotage,
psychological warfare and cultural frustration being conducted against the
Palestinians in the occupied lands. . . .

Occupation by Israel of the West Bank and Gaza will have to end, for
three million Israelis cannot go on forever governing one-and-a-half million Palestinians and ignoring their national rights and aspirations.

Needless to say, Egypt feels as strongly about ending the occupation
of the Golan Heights as she does about ending the occupation of Gaza
and the West Bank, including East Jerusalem. Egypt rejects totally both
the annexation of East Jerusalem and that of the Golan, as illegal, unacceptable and obnoxious measures that are not conducive to the atmosphere
that is necessary to reach a peaceful comprehensive solution. Such unilateral measures contradict the letter and the spirit of the Camp David
accords. Egypt in an official statement on December 15, 1981, strongly
condemned the Israeli decision to extend Israeli law, jurisdiction and administration to the occupied Syrian territory of the Golan Heights and
termed it an illegal measure and a violation of international law and the
Charter of the United Nations. In U.N. Security Council Resolution 242,
which is the basis of the Camp David accords, it is stipulated that the
acquisition of territory by war is inadmissible and that it is essential to
respect the sovereignty and territorial integrity of every state in the area,
including Syria.

When Saudi Arabia took the bold step of putting forward what has
become known as the "Fahd Peace Plan," Egypt could only welcome the
fact that a major Arab state would opt for a constructive approach that
could end the indecisiveness that has plagued the Arab scene. The Saudi

proposals are a set of principles derived from Security Council Resolution 242 and other U.N. resolutions. But to translate these principles into practical realities, one would still need a framework and a negotiating process, which Camp David has provided. In other words, the Saudi proposals are not an alternative to Camp David, but they need a "Camp David" to be implemented satisfactorily.

Thus, Egypt does not consider that peace in the Middle East is her own exclusive concern. Any proposals are welcomed by Egypt provided that they build upon what has already been achieved through Camp David, take into account what has already been acquired through the present negotiations, and meet with the approval of all the parties concerned. Until such a formula is proposed and accepted by these parties, Egypt under President Mubarak is intent on pursuing the negotiations and efforts to reach a comprehensive, peaceful solution that would bring justice and security for all. Egypt is equally intent on continuing to play her historical role in the peace process and in the negotiations that may take place between the Arabs and Israel to achieve that goal.

The diplomatic relations established between Egypt and Israel will, needless to say, continue at the same level. As stipulated in the peace treaty, relations between the two countries are "normal" relations, the word normal meaning exactly what it says and not implying in any way a concept of special relations, alliance or strategic cooperation. This kind of cooperation might be envisaged the day a comprehensive and just peace is achieved, but nothing in the peace treaty commits Egypt to anything that goes further than normal relations between any two given countries.

The role of the United States in establishing a just, comprehensive peace cannot be overemphasized. The full partnership role played by the United States in the negotiations between Egypt and Israel has borne fruit in the form of the peace treaty. It is expected that the United States would continue to play the same positive role in order to achieve a just and lasting solution to the Palestinian problem, the crux of the Middle East problem.

Egypt's conviction is that American participation in the peace negotiations is an essential element. This participation has been instrumental in reaching the Camp David accords and the peace treaty. But there is an even more vital role for U.S. diplomacy to play in helping to define the terms of full Palestinian autonomy and to convince the Israelis that only a self-governing Palestinian body with wide-ranging jurisdiction in all fields would have a chance to be accepted by the Palestinians. The United States can also play a part in convincing the Palestinians and the Palestine Liberation Organization (PLO) that their legitimate rights can be obtained by negotiation and that they can find their place in the family of nations through a peaceful and legitimate process. But to be able to do that, the United States would have to start talking to the Palestinians, to the organization that is accepted by the majority of them as representative of their aspirations, to the organization that is recognized by the majority of nations—namely the PLO. Contacts have to be established between the U.S. government and the PLO and not only through impromptu meetings in the corridors of the United Nations or at diplomatic parties. This was the gist of the message carried by President Sadat on his last trip to Washington in August 1981. This remains a strong belief of Egyptian diplomacy. . . .

Certain Arab governments criticize the peace process but have been unable to unite not only behind an alternative process but even behind the goals to be attained by such a process. This failure on the part of the Arab governments emphasizes the importance of Egypt's leadership. In playing a leading role in the search for a peaceful and just solution to the Arab-Israeli conflict, Egypt maintains a balance between her own national interests and the wider interests of the Arab nations. . . .

Sooner or later, Egypt's actions will make the other Arab governments grasp that the withdrawal of Israeli forces and the return of Sinai to full Egyptian sovereignty constitute a valuable precedent, in accordance with the text of the Egyptian-Israeli Treaty of Peace, which states in its preamble that: "The (Camp David) Framework is intended to constitute a basis for peace not only between Egypt and Israel, but also between Israel and each of its Arab neighbors. . . ." The success of the Camp David accords is bound to have a "snowball" effect and give the peace process more strength, more dynamism and more credibility in Arab eyes. Sooner or later, Arab governments are bound to join the peace process and Egypt's efforts to induce them to do so will be successful.

This is because the present disagreement between Egypt and a number of Arab countries is not in any way the first inter-Arab dispute and will not be the last.

In spite of the severance of diplomatic relations between Cairo and those Arab capitals, transnational relations have continued and even increased: more than two million Egyptian workers, technicians and experts, teachers, doctors and judges are performing a well-appreciated mission in these Arab countries; private Arab investment continues to flow into Egypt; and Cairo remains the favorite destination of Arab tourists. Thousands of Arabs of every nationality are learning in schools and colleges in Egypt, and Arab military and police officers are still being trained in Egyptian academies.

Reconciliation at the official level between Egypt and the governments of the other Arab states is bound to come and President Mubarak has made it quite clear that Egypt does not object to such a reconciliation. Ever since his accession to the presidency, he has underlined the futility of press campaigns among Arabs that can only exacerbate the differences, and he has urged Egyptian journalists and editors to refrain from attacking or abusing Arab governments.

There is hardly any doubt, however, that a rapprochement between Cairo and the dissenting Arab capitals will have to take into account the reality of the relations existing between Egypt and Israel. Egypt would not be the only country able to maintain relations both with Israel and the Arab states. A number of countries in the area itself manage to do that quite successfully, namely Turkey, a Muslim country, and Cyprus which has diplomatic representatives from both Israel and the PLO. Besides, the European and the Latin American countries and the United States all have excellent relations with both the Arab states and Israel. So why should the same thing be impossible to realize in Egypt's case? Certainly the fact that Egypt is an Arab country might seem to complicate the issue, but should not the Arabs accept from a sister state what they readily accept from others? . . .

Secretary of State George P. Shultz: Congressional Testimony (July 12, 1982)*

In late 1974 I visited Beirut, at the time a beautiful and thriving city, even then marked by the presence of Palestinian refugees. But since then Lebanon has been racked by destruction, enduring the presence of armed and assertive PLO and other forces.

Coherent life and government are impossible under those conditions and inevitably Lebanon became a state in disrepair. The Lebanese deserve a chance to govern themselves, free from the presence of the armed forces of any other country or group. The authority of the Government of Lebanon must extend to all its territory.

The agony of Lebanon is on the minds and in the hearts of us all. But in a larger sense Lebanon is but the latest chapter in a history of accumulated grief stretching back through decades of conflict. We are talking here about a part of the globe that has had little genuine peace for generations. A region with thousands of victims—Arab, Israeli and other families torn apart as a consequence of war and terror. What is going on now in Lebanon must mark the end of this cycle of terror rather than simply the latest in a continuing series of senseless and violent acts.

We cannot accept the loss of life brought home to us every day even at this great distance on our television screens; but at the same time we can, as Americans, be proud that once again it is the United States, working most prominently through President Reagan's emissary, Ambassador

---

* Excerpts from confirmation hearing for the Secretary of State–designate before the Senate Foreign Relations Committee.

Philip Habib, that is attempting to still the guns, achieve an equitable outcome and alleviate the suffering.

Mr. Chairman, the crisis in Lebanon makes painfully and totally clear a central reality of the Middle East: The legitimate needs and problems of the Palestinian people must be addressed and resolved—urgently and in all their dimensions. Beyond the suffering of the Palestinian people lies a complex of political problems which must be addressed if the Middle East is to know peace. The Camp David framework calls as a first step for temporary arrangements which will provide full autonomy for the Palestinians of the West Bank and Gaza. That same framework then speaks eloquently and significantly of a solution that "must also recognize the legitimate rights of the Palestinian people."

The challenge of the negotiations in which the United States is, and during my tenure will remain, a full partner, is to transform that hope into reality. For these talks to succeed, representatives of the Palestinians themselves must participate in the negotiating process. The basis must also be found for other countries in the region, in addition to Israel and Egypt, to join in the peace process.

Our determined effort to stop the killing in Lebanon, resolve the conflict, and make the Government of Lebanon once again sovereign throughout its territory underscores the degree to which our nation has vital interests throughout the Arab world. Our friendly relations with the great majority of Arab states have served those interests and, I believe, assisted our efforts to deal with the current Lebanon crisis.

But beyond the issues of the moment, the importance to our own security of wide and ever-strengthening ties with the Arabs is manifest. It is from them that the West gets much of its oil; it is with them that we share an interest and must cooperate in resisting Soviet imperialism; it is with them, as well as Israel, that we will be able to bring peace to the Middle East.

Finally, and most important, Mr. Chairman, the Lebanese situation is intimately linked to the vital question of Israel's security. Israel, our closest friend in the Middle East, still harbors a deep feeling of insecurity. In a region where hostility is endemic, and where so much of it is directed against Israel, the rightness of her preoccupation with matters of security cannot be disputed. Nor should anyone dispute the depth and durability of America's commitment to the security of Israel or our readiness to assure that Israel has the necessary means to defend herself. I share in this deep and enduring commitment. And more, I recognize that democratic Israel shares with us a deep commitment to the security of the West.

Beyond that, however, we owe it to Israel, in the context of our special relationship, to work with her to bring about a comprehensive peace— acceptable to all the parties involved—which is the only sure guarantee of true and durable security.

Prime Minister Menachem Begin:
The Wars of No Alternative
and Operation Peace for Galilee
(August 8, 1982)*

Let us turn from the international example to ourselves. Operation Peace for Galilee is not a military operation resulting from the lack of an alternative. The terrorists did not threaten the existence of the State of Israel; they "only" threatened the lives of Israel's citizens and members of the Jewish people. There are those who find fault with the second part of that sentence. If there was no danger to the existence of the state, why did you go to war?

I will explain why. We had three wars which we fought without an alternative. The first was the War of Independence, which began on November 30, 1947, and lasted until January 1949. . . . We carried on our lives then by a miracle, with a clear recognition of life's imperative: to win, to establish a state, a government, a parliament, a democracy, an army—a force to defend Israel and the entire Jewish people.

The second war of no alternative was the Yom Kippur War and the War of Attrition that preceded it. What was the situation on that Yom Kippur day [October 6, 1973]? We had 177 tanks deployed on the Golan Heights against 1,400 Soviet-Syrian tanks; and fewer than 500 of our soldiers manned positions along the Suez Canal against five divisions sent to the front by the Egyptians.

It is any wonder that the first days of that war were hard to bear? I remember Gen. Avraham Yaffe came to us, to the Knesset Foreign Affairs and Defence Committee, and said: "Oy, it's so hard! Our boys, 18- and 19-year-olds, are falling like flies and are defending our nation with their very bodies."

In the Golan Heights there was a moment when the O/C Northern Command—today our chief of staff—heard his deputy say, "This is it." What that meant was: "We've lost: we have to come down off the Golan Heights." And the then O/C said, "Give me another five minutes."

Sometimes five minutes can decide a nation's fate. During those five minutes, several dozen tanks arrived, which changed the entire situation on the Golan Heights.

If this had not happened, if the Syrian enemy had come down from the heights to the valley, he would have reached Haifa—for there was not

* Excerpts from a speech delivered at the National Defence College in Israel.

a single tank to obstruct his armoured column's route to Haifa. Yes, we would even have fought with knives—as one of our esteemed wives has said—with knives against tanks. Many more would have fallen, and in every settlement there would have been the kind of slaughter at which the Syrians are experts.

In the south, our boys in the outposts were taken prisoner, and we know what happened to them afterwards. Dozens of tanks were destroyed, because tanks were sent in piecemeal, since we could not organize them in a large formation. And dozens of planes were shot down by missiles which were not destroyed in time, so that we had to submit to their advances.

Woe to the ears that still ring with the words of one of the nation's heroes, the then defence minister, in whose veins flowed the blood of the Maccabees: "We are losing the Third Commonwealth."

Our total casualties in that war of no alternative were 2,297 killed, 6,067 wounded. Together with the War of Attrition—which was also a war of no alternative—2,659 killed, 7,251 wounded. The terrible total: almost 10,000 casualties.

Our other wars were not without an alternative. In November 1956 we had a choice. The reason for going to war then was the need to destroy the *fedayeen*, who did not represent a danger to the existence of the state.

However, the political leadership of the time thought it was necessary to do this. As one who served in the parliamentary opposition, I was summoned to David Ben-Gurion before the cabinet received information of the plan, and he found it necessary to give my colleagues and myself these details: We are going to meet the enemy before it absorbs the Soviet weapons which began to flow to it from Czechoslovakia in 1955.

In June 1967 we again had a choice. The Egyptian army concentrations in the Sinai approaches did not prove that Nasser was really about to attack us. We must be honest with ourselves. We decided to attack him.

This was a war of self-defence in the noblest sense of the term. The government of national unity then established decided unanimously: We will take the initiative and attack the enemy, drive him back, and thus assure the security of Israel and the future of the nation.

As for Operation Peace for Galilee, it does not really belong to the category of wars of no alternative. We could have gone on seeing our civilians injured in Metulla or Kiryat Shmona or Nahariya. We could have gone on counting those killed by explosive charges left in a Jerusalem supermarket, or a Petah Tikva bus stop.

All the orders to carry out these acts of murder and sabotage came from Beirut. Should we have reconciled ourselves to the ceaseless killing of civilians, even after the agreement ending hostilities reached last summer, which the terrorists interpreted as an agreement permitting them to strike at us from every side, besides Southern Lebanon? They tried to infiltrate gangs of murderers via Syria and Jordan, and by a miracle we captured them. We might also not have captured them. There was a gang of four terrorists which infiltrated from Jordan, whose members admitted they had been about to commandeer a bus (and we remember the bus on the coastal road).

And in the Diaspora? Even Philip Habib interpreted the agreement ending acts of hostility as giving them freedom to attack targets beyond Israel's borders. We have never accepted this interpretation. Shall we permit Jewish blood to be spilled in the Diaspora? Shall we permit bombs to be planted against Jews in Paris, Rome, Athens or London? Shall we permit our ambassadors to be attacked?

There are slanderers who say that a full year of quiet has passed between us and the terrorists. Nonsense. There was not even one month of quiet. The newspapers and communications media, including *The New York Times* and *The Washington Post*, did not publish even one line about our capturing the gang of murderers that crossed the Jordan in order to commandeer a bus and murder its passengers.

True, such actions were not a threat to the existence of the state. But they did threaten the lives of civilians whose number we cannot estimate, day after day, week after week, month after month.

During the past nine weeks, we have, in effect, destroyed the combat potential of 20,000 terrorists. We hold 9,000 in a prison camp. Between 2,000 and 3,000 were killed and between 7,000 and 9,000 have been captured and cut off in Beirut. They have decided to leave there only because they have no possibility of remaining there. The problem will be solved.

We have destroyed the best tanks and planes the Syrians had. We have destroyed 24 of their ground-to-air missile batteries. After everything that happened, Syria did not go to war against us, not in Lebanon and not in the Golan Heights.

For our part, we will not initiate any attack against any Arab country. We have proved that we do not want wars. We made many painful sacrifices for a peace treaty with Egypt. That treaty stood the test of the fighting in Lebanon; in other words, it *stood the test*.

The demilitarized zone of 150 kilometres in Sinai exists, and no Egyptian soldier has been placed there. From the experience of the 1930s, I have to say that if ever the other side violated the agreement about the demilitarized zone, Israel would be obliged to introduce, without delay, a force stronger than that violating the international commitment: not in order to wage war, but to achieve one of two results: restoration of the previous situation, i.e., resumed demilitarization, and the removal of both armies from the demilitarized zone; or attainment of strategic depth, in case the other side has taken the first step towards a war of aggression, as happened in Europe only three years after the abrogation of the demilitarized zone in the Rhineland.

Because the other Arab countries are completely incapable of attacking the State of Israel, there is reason to expect that we are facing a historic period of peace. It is obviously impossible to set a date.

It may well be that "The land shall be still for 40 years." Perhaps less: perhaps more. But from the facts before us, it is clear that, with the end of the fighting in Lebanon, we have ahead of us many years of establishing peace treaties and peaceful relations with the various Arab countries.

The conclusion—both on the basis of the relations between states and on the basis of our national experience—is that there is no divine mandate to go to war only if there is no alternative. There is no moral imperative that a nation must, or is entitled to, fight only when its back is to the sea, or to the abyss. Such a war may avert tragedy, if not a Holocaust, for any nation; but it causes it terrible loss of life.

Quite the opposite. A free, sovereign nation, which hates war and loves peace, and which is concerned about its security, must create the conditions under which war, if there is a need for it, *will not be* for lack of alternative. The conditions must be such—and their creation depends upon man's reason and his actions—that the price of victory will be few casualties, not many.

President Ronald Reagan: The Reagan Plan (September 1, 1982)*

My fellow Americans, today has been a day that should make us proud. It marked the end of the successful evacuation of the Palestine Liberation Organization (PLO) from Beirut, Lebanon. This peaceful step could never have been taken without the good offices of the United States and, especially, the truly heroic work of a great American diplomat, Ambassador Philip Habib [President's special emissary to the Middle East]. Thanks to his efforts, I am happy to announce that the U.S. Marine contingent helping to supervise the evacuation has accomplished its mission. Our young men should be out of Lebanon within 2 weeks. They, too, have served the cause of peace with distinction, and we can all be very proud of them.

But the situation in Lebanon is only part of the overall problem of conflict in the Middle East. So, over the past 2 weeks, while events in Beirut dominated the front page, America was engaged in a quiet, behind-

---

* Speech to the nation by President Reagan from Burbank, California.

the-scenes effort to lay the groundwork for a broader peace in the region. For once, there were no premature leaks as U.S. diplomatic missions traveled to Mid-East capitals, and I met here at home with a wide range of experts to map out an American peace initiative for the long-suffering peoples of the Middle East, Arab and Israeli alike.

It seemed to me that, with the agreement in Lebanon, we had an opportunity for a more far-reaching peace effort in the region, and I was determined to seize that moment. In the words of the scripture, the time had come to "follow after the things which make for peace."

Tonight, I want to report to you on the steps we have taken and the prospects they can open up for a just and lasting peace in the Middle East. America has long been committed to bringing peace to this troubled region. For more than a generation, successive U.S. administrations have endeavored to develop a fair and workable process that could lead to a true and lasting Arab-Israeli peace. Our involvement in the search for Mid-East peace is not a matter of preference, it is a moral imperative. The strategic importance of the region to the United States is well known.

But our policy is motivated by more than strategic interests. We also have an irreversible commitment to the survival and territorial integrity of friendly states. Nor can we ignore the fact that the well-being of much of the world's economy is tied to stability in the strife-torn Middle East. Finally, our traditional humanitarian concerns dictate a continuing effort to peacefully resolve conflicts.

When our Administration assumed office in January 1981, I decided that the general framework for our Middle East policy should follow the broad guidelines laid down by my predecessors. There were two basic issues we had to address. First, there was the strategic threat to the region posed by the Soviet Union and its surrogates, best demonstrated by the brutal war in Afghanistan; and, second, the peace process between Israel and its Arab neighbors. With regard to the Soviet threat, we have strengthened our efforts to develop with our friends and allies a joint policy to deter the Soviets and their surrogates from further expansion in the region and, if necessary, to defend against it. With respect to the Arab-Israeli conflict, we have embraced the Camp David framework as the only way to proceed. We have also recognized, however, that solving the Arab-Israeli conflict, in and of itself, cannot assure peace throughout a region as vast and troubled as the Middle East.

Our first objective under the Camp David process was to insure the successful fulfillment of the Egyptian-Israeli Peace Treaty. This was achieved with the peaceful return of the Sinai to Egypt in April 1982. To accomplish this, we worked hard with our Egyptian and Israeli friends, and eventually with other friendly countries, to create the multinational force which now operates in the Sinai.

Throughout this period of difficult and time-consuming negotiations, we never lost sight of the next step of Camp David: autonomy talks to pave the way for permitting the Palestinian people to exercise their legitimate rights. However, owing to the tragic assassination of President Sadat and other crises in the area, it was not until January 1982 that we were able to make a major effort to renew these talks. Secretary of State Haig and Ambassador Fairbanks [Richard Fairbanks, Special Negotiator for the Middle East Peace Process] made three visits to Israel and Egypt early this year to pursue the autonomy talks. Considerable progress was made in developing the basic outline of an American approach which was to be presented to Egypt and Israel after April.

The successful completion of Israel's withdrawal from Sinai and the courage shown on this occasion by Prime Minister Begin and President Mubarak in living up to their agreements convinced me the time had come for a new American policy to try to bridge the remaining differences between Egypt and Israel on the autonomy process. So, in May, I called for specific measures and a timetable for consultations with the Governments of Egypt and Israel on the next steps in the peace process. However, before this effort could be launched, the conflict in Lebanon preempted our efforts. The autonomy talks were basically put on hold while we sought to untangle the parties in Lebanon and still the guns of war.

The Lebanon war, tragic as it was, has left us with a new opportunity for Middle East peace. We must seize it now and bring peace to this troubled area so vital to world stability while there is still time. It was with this strong conviction that over a month ago, before the present negotiations in Beirut had been completed, I directed Secretary of State Shultz to again review our policy and to consult a wide range of outstanding Americans on the best ways to strengthen chances for peace in the Middle East. We have consulted with many of the officials who were historically involved in the process, with Members of the Congress, and with individuals from the private sector; and I have held extensive consultations with my own advisers on the principles I will outline to you tonight.

The evacuation of the PLO from Beirut is now complete. And we can now help the Lebanese to rebuild their war-torn country. We owe it to ourselves, and to posterity, to move quickly to build upon this achievement. A stable and revived Lebanon is essential to all our hopes for peace in the region. The people of Lebanon deserve the best efforts of the international community to turn the nightmares of the past several years into a new dawn of hope.

But the opportunities for peace in the Middle East do not begin and end in Lebanon. As we help Lebanon rebuild, we must also move to resolve the root causes of conflict between Arabs and Israelis. The war in Lebanon has demonstrated many things, but two consequences are key to the peace process:

First, the military losses of the PLO have not diminished the yearning of the Palestinian people for a just solution of their claims; and

Second, while Israel's military successes in Lebanon have demonstrated that its armed forces are second to none in the region, they alone cannot bring just and lasting peace to Israel and her neighbors.

The question now is how to reconcile Israel's legitimate security concerns with the legitimate rights of the Palestinians. And that answer can only come at the negotiating table. Each party must recognize that the outcome must be acceptable to all and that true peace will require compromises by all.

So, tonight I am calling for a fresh start. This is the moment for all those directly concerned to get involved—or lend their support—to a workable basis for peace. The Camp David agreement remains the foundation of our policy. Its language provides all parties with the leeway they need for successful negotiations.

• I call on Israel to make clear that the security for which she yearns can only be achieved through genuine peace, a peace requiring magnanimity, vision, and courage.
• I call on the Palestinian people to recognize that their own political aspirations are inextricably bound to recognition of Israel's right to a secure future.
• And I call on the Arab states to accept the reality of Israel and the reality that peace and justice are to be gained only through hard, fair, direct negotiation.

In making these calls upon others, I recognize that the United States has a special responsibility. No other nation is in a position to deal with the key parties to the conflict on the basis of trust and reliability.

The time has come for a new realism on the part of all the peoples of the Middle East. The State of Israel is an accomplished fact; it deserves unchallenged legitimacy within the community of nations. But Israel's legitimacy has thus far been recognized by too few countries and has been denied by every Arab state except Egypt. Israel exists; it has a right to exist in peace behind secure and defensible borders; and it has a right to demand of its neighbors that they recognize those facts.

I have personally followed and supported Israel's heroic struggle for survival ever since the founding of the State of Israel 34 years ago. In the pre-1967 borders, Israel was barely 10 miles wide at its narrowest point. The bulk of Israel's population lived within artillery range of hostile Arab armies. I am not about to ask Israel to live that way again.

The war in Lebanon has demonstrated another reality in the region. The departure of the Palestinians from Beirut dramatizes more than ever the homelessness of the Palestinian people. Palestinians feel strongly that their cause is more than a question of refugees. I agree. The Camp David agreement recognized that fact when it spoke of the legitimate rights of the Palestinian people and their just requirements. For peace to endure, it must involve all those who have been most deeply affected by the conflict. Only through broader participation in the peace process—most immediately by Jordan and by the Palestinians—will Israel be able to rest confident in the knowledge that its security and integrity will be respected by its neighbors. Only through the process of negotiation can all the nations of the Middle East achieve a secure peace.

These then are our general goals. What are the specific new American positions, and why are we taking them?

In the Camp David talks thus far, both Israel and Egypt have felt free to express openly their views as to what the outcome should be. Understandably, their views have differed on many points.

The United States has thus far sought to play the role of mediator; we have avoided public comment on the key issues. We have always recognized—and continue to recognize—that only the voluntary agreement of those parties most directly involved in the conflict can provide an enduring solution. But it has become evident to me that some clearer sense of America's position on the key issues is necessary to encourage wider support for the peace process.

First, as outlined in the Camp David accords, there must be a period of time during which the Palestinian inhabitants of the West Bank and Gaza will have full autonomy over their own affairs. Due consideration must be given to the principle of self-government by the inhabitants of the territories and to the legitimate security concerns of the parties involved.

The purpose of the 5-year period of transition, which would begin after free elections for a self-governing Palestinian authority, is to prove to the Palestinians that they can run their own affairs and that such Palestinian autonomy poses no threat to Israel's security.

The United States will not support the use of any additional land for the purpose of settlements during the transition period. Indeed, the immediate adoption of a settlement freeze by Israel, more than any other action, could create the confidence needed for wider participation in these talks. Further settlement activity is in no way necessary for the security of Israel and only diminishes the confidence of the Arabs that a final outcome can be freely and fairly negotiated.

I want to make the American position well understood: The purpose of this transition period is the peaceful and orderly transfer of authority from Israel to the Palestinian inhabitants of the West Bank and Gaza. At the same time, such a transfer must not interfere with Israel's security requirements.

Beyond the transition period, as we look to the future of the West Bank and Gaza, it is clear to me that peace cannot be achieved by the formation of an independent Palestinian state in those territories. Nor is it achievable on the basis of Israeli sovereignty or permanent control over the West Bank and Gaza.

So the United States will not support the establishment of an independent Palestinian state in the West Bank and Gaza, and we will not support annexation or permanent control by Israel.

There is, however, another way to peace. The final status of these lands must, of course, be reached through the give-and-take of negotiations. But it is the firm view of the United States that self-government by the Palestinians of the West Bank and Gaza in association with Jordan offers the best chance for a durable, just and lasting peace.

We base our approach squarely on the principle that the Arab-Israeli conflict should be resolved through negotiations involving an exchange of territory for peace. This exchange is enshrined in U.N. Security Council Resolution 242, which is, in turn, incorporated in all its parts in the Camp David agreements. U.N. Resolution 242 remains wholly valid as the foundation stone of America's Middle East peace effort.

It is the United States' position that—in return for peace—the withdrawal provision of Resolution 242 applies to all fronts, including the West Bank and Gaza.

When the border is negotiated between Jordan and Israel, our view on the extent to which Israel should be asked to give up territory will be heavily affected by the extent of true peace and normalization and the security arrangements offered in return.

Finally, we remain convinced that Jerusalem must remain undivided, but its final status should be decided through negotiations.

In the course of the negotiations to come, the United States will support positions that seem to us fair and reasonable compromises and likely to promote a sound agreement. We will also put forward our own detailed proposals when we believe they can be helpful. And, make no mistake, the United States will oppose any proposal—from any party and at any point in the negotiating process—that threatens the security of Israel. America's commitment to the security of Israel is ironclad. And, I might add, so is mine.

During the past few days, our ambassadors in Israel, Egypt, Jordan, and Saudi Arabia have presented to their host governments the proposals in full detail that I have outlined here today. Now I am convinced that these proposals can bring justice, bring security, and bring durability to an Arab-Israeli peace. The United States will stand by these principles with total dedication. They are fully consistent with Israel's security requirements and the aspirations of the Palestinians. We will work hard to broaden participation at the peace table as envisaged by the Camp David accords. And I fervently hope that the Palestinians and Jordan, with the support of their Arab colleagues, will accept this opportunity.

Tragic turmoil in the Middle East runs back to the dawn of history. In our modern day, conflict after conflict has taken its brutal toll there. In an age of nuclear challenge and economic interdependence, such conflicts are a threat to all the people of the world, not just the Middle East itself. It is time for us all—in the Middle East and around the world—to call a halt to conflict, hatred, and prejudice; it is time for us all to launch a common effort for reconstruction, peace, and progress.

It has often been said—and regrettably too often been true—that the story of the search for peace and justice in the Middle East is a tragedy of opportunities missed. In the aftermath of the settlement in Lebanon we now face an opportunity for a broader peace. This time we must not let it slip from our grasp. We must look beyond the difficulties and obstacles of the present and move with fairness and resolve toward a brighter future. We owe it to ourselves—and to posterity—to do no less. For if we miss this chance to make a fresh start, we may look back on this moment from some later vantage point and realize how much that failure cost us all.

These, then, are the principles upon which American policy toward the Arab-Israeli conflict will be based. I have made a personal commitment to see that they endure and, God willing, that they will come to be seen by all reasonable, compassionate people as fair, achievable, and in the interests of all who wish to see peace in the Middle East.

Tonight, on the eve of what can be a dawning of new hope for the people of the troubled Middle East—and for all the world's people who dream of a just and peaceful future—I ask you, my fellow Americans, for your support, and your prayers in this great undertaking.

Twelfth Arab Summit Conference: Final Statement (September 9, 1982)*

. . . In view of the grave conditions through which the Arab nation is passing and out of a sense of historical and pan-Arab responsibility, their majesties and excellencies and highnesses the kings, presidents and emirs of the Arab nation discussed the important issues submitted to their conference and adopted the following resolution in regard to them.

I. The Arab-Israeli Conflict

The conference greeted the steadfastness of the Palestine revolutionary forces, the Lebanese and Palestinian peoples and the Syrian Arab Armed

---

* The Twelfth Arab Summit Conference convened in Fez, Morocco, on November 25, 1981, was adjourned, and resumed again on September 6, 1982.

Forces and declared its support for the Palestinian people in their struggle for the retrieval of their established national rights.

Out of the conference's belief in the ability of the Arab nation to achieve its legitimate objectives and eliminate the aggression, and out of the principles and basis laid down by the Arab summit conferences, and out of the Arab countries' determination to continue to work by all means for the establishment of peace based on justice in the Middle East and using the plan of President Habib Bourguiba, which is based on international legitimacy, as the foundation for solving the Palestinian question and the plan of His Majesty King Fahd ibn 'Abd al-'Aziz which deals with peace in the Middle East, and in the light of the discussions and notes made by their majesties, excellencies and highnesses the kings, presidents and emirs, the conference has decided to adopt the following principles:

1. Israel's withdrawal from all Arab territories occupied in 1967, including Arab Jerusalem.

2. The removal of settlements set up by Israel in the Arab territories after 1967.

3. Guarantees of the freedom of worship and the performance of religious rites for all religions at the holy places.

4. Confirmation of the right of the Palestinian people to self-determination and to exercise their firm and inalienable national rights, under the leadership of the PLO, its sole legitimate representative, and compensation for those who do not wish to return.

5. The placing of the West Bank and Gaza Strip under UN supervision for a transitional period, not longer than several months.

6. The creation of an independent Palestinian state with Jerusalem as its capital.

7. Security Council guarantees for the implementation of those principles.

8. The drawing up by the Security Council of guarantees for peace for all the states of the region, including the independent Palestinian state.

9. Security Council guarantees for the implementation of these principles.

II. The Israeli Aggression Against Lebanon

The conference declares its strong condemnation of the Israeli aggression against the Palestinian people, and draws the attention of international public opinion to the gravity of this aggression and its consequences on stability and security in the region.

The conference has decided to back Lebanon in everything that will lead to the implementation of the Security Council resolutions, particularly Resolutions 508 and 509 calling for the withdrawal of Israel from Lebanese territory up to the recognized international borders.

The conference affirms the solidarity of the Arab states with Lebanon in its tragedy, and its readiness to render any assistance it demands to remedy and put an end to this tragedy. The conference has been notified of the decision of the Lebanese Government to end the task of the Arab Deterrent Forces in Lebanon provided that negotiations be conducted between the Lebanese and Syrian Governments to make the arrangements in the light of the Israeli withdrawal from Lebanon.

El-Hassan Bin Talal: Jordan's Quest for Peace (Fall 1982)*

. . . Because Jordan is a small country, we are often discounted as a major factor in what is clearly the greatest threat to international security. We do not have a large population like Egypt or Syria. We do not have a position of military superiority like Israel. We do not have oil like Saudi Arabia or Iraq. So, then, why is Jordan important? Do we assert its centrality because we are Jordanian?

No, Jordan's views are important. Apart from the Sinai, which is in the process of being returned to Egypt, most of the territory Israel occupied in 1967, and therefore which is referred to in U.N. Security Council Resolution 242, was Jordanian. East Jerusalem was Jordanian. There are more Palestinians in Jordan than in any other state, most of them refugees from the wars of 1948 and 1967. Jordan and Israel have outstanding territorial conflicts dating from 1948. Although it is our position and belief that the Palestine Liberation Organization is and can only be the sole representative of the Palestinian people, still it is incontestable that large numbers of Arabs in the West Bank continue to attend closely to Jordan's actions and policies.

It is clear today that the sine qua non of any general and effective settlement of the Arab-Israeli conflict must address and resolve the Palestinian issue. It is not our purpose here to posit the requirements for such a resolution; indeed, the requirements are part of the dispute. What is clear, however, is that all parties today recognize that, to use the words of former U.S. Assistant Secretary of State Harold Saunders, "The Palestinians collectively are a political factor which must be dealt with if there is to be a peace between Israel and its neighbors." Even a cursory review of Israeli statements demonstrates conclusively that there too is a recognition of the crucial nature of the Palestinian problem. Whether in terms of "autonomy" proposals or hints that the Palestinians already have their state in

---

* Excerpts from an article in *Foreign Affairs*, Fall 1982. El-Hassan Bin Talal is the Crown Prince of Jordan.

Jordan, it is evident that Israeli leaders, too, have come to accept, implicitly or explicitly, the unavoidable fact that no settlement is possible without dealing with the Palestinian problem.

We Jordanians must add that, practically speaking, a settlement must also take into account our perceptions. Small as Jordan is, our country is politically, socially, economically, militarily and historically inseparable from the Palestinian issue. Not that we can speak in place of the Palestinians; we cannot. As His Majesty King Hussein has said recently, "Palestinians alone have the right to determine their future. There are no other options acceptable to Jordan nor is there any substitute for the Palestine Liberation Organization, the sole legitimate representative of the people of Palestine. . . ." We cannot speak in place of the Palestinians. At the same time, however, as a leading Jordanian social scientist has written, "The Jordanians and Palestinians are now one people, and no political loyalty, however strong, will separate them permanently."

Consider for a moment the following:

—Half Jordan's population is Palestinian.

—The West Bank and East Jerusalem, both captured by Israel in 1967, were part of Jordan.

—If there is large-scale Palestinian migration as a result of any regional settlement, Jordan will necessarily be greatly affected.

—Virtually all Palestinians currently resident in Jordan are Jordanian nationals.

—Israel and Jordan have vital interests in development of regional water resources in the Jordan River. Israel has already illegally diverted much of the Jordan River, but the importance of cooperation in the future cannot be overestimated. In other areas such as tourism, there is also substantial need for cooperation.

—After any settlement as before it, Jordan will share a long border with Israel. For us, development is not just an abstract goal, but a pressing need. We do not wish to continue to divert so much of Jordan's small resource base to a costly armaments program to defend our overexposed position or in order to reduce the risks along this extended border.

—Pending the creation of a Palestinian state, it is still Jordan which pays the salaries and pensions of West Bank officials; it is Jordan that bears some development costs of the territory and whose approval is necessary for such projects; it is in the Jordanian parliament that the inhabitants of the West Bank are represented; it is Jordanian law that has effect in the West Bank. This is not to deny that Israel is also involved in these activities, for that is true, albeit a clear violation of international law. Rather, we intend only to show how concrete and contemporary are Jordan's interests. . . .

. . . Yet lately we in Jordan have begun to hear and read that "Jordan opposes an Arab-Israeli settlement." Let us be clear on this point: no one, no country, no people wants a settlement more than we do. Certainly, no one pays a heavier price for the continuation of the conflict than do we here in Jordan.

After the 1967 War, other Arab governments learned—and what a costly lesson—what we had known for almost two decades: Israel was to be an enduring reality of the Middle East, and the issue was not to undo the 1947 injustice to Palestinians and all Arabs but rather to constrain an Israel hungry for territorial expansion and powerful enough to obtain it.

Perhaps it is germane to say at this point that we Jordanians do not have a precise blueprint of a settlement in mind. Indeed, I believe I can speak for all the Arab countries, and probably for Israel too, in saying that the range of ideas or alternatives or minimums or maximums that is advanced in any of our countries is appallingly varied. For us Jordanians, there are a few clear-cut requirements. Certainly, the same can be said for Egyptians, Israelis, Iraqis, Palestinians, Saudis and Syrians. We have learned through successive tragedies to keep our requirements few, to question them, to be sure they are truly vital. This is true also of other Arab parties. Sadly, it is not true for Israel, whose list of requirements has grown with each passing year. . . .

In spite of Israel's intransigence, which is growing apace with her appetite, the Arab governments including Jordan still seek a settlement. We have to, for let us be candid: Israel has designs on the West Bank, East Jerusalem, the Golan Heights, and southern Lebanon—whose territories are these? Arab territories. We do not want to provide a pretext for further Israeli expansion. So, yes Jordan, and, yes, the other Arab states near Israel favor a settlement.

Yet it is true that we do not favor *any* settlement. Neither Jordan, nor Syria nor Lebanon nor Saudi Arabia nor Egypt nor Israel—none of the Middle East countries—is prepared to accept, or should be prepared to accept, "peace at any price." Again, let us all be honest. A "settlement" that did not resolve the Palestinian problem, or the question of the Golan, or Israel's or Jordan's or Lebanon's or Syria's rights to exist with reasonable security within a recognized territory—such an outcome would be no settlement at all, for natural forces would be at work to overturn it before it was signed. We understand Israel's needs, and believe Israel's truly vital requirements can be met, but we too have a few vital requirements. Each nation must enjoy some security as a result of a settlement, and none of us can have perfect security, for as has often been shown, one nation's perfect security is another's perfect insecurity.

It is true that agreement on what a settlement should look like is lacking both within and among Arab states, as it is lacking in fact within Israel and between Israel and other states. But a resolution to the conflict is much less likely to be found

—if Israel continues to expand what are clearly illegal settlements in the occupied territories;

—if Israel continues to decide unilaterally to annex Arab land;

—if private land is confiscated to be handed out to Israeli settlers;
—if peace agreements are made in the name of rather than with other parties;
—if Israel continues to play with internal vulnerabilities of Arab states, increasing instability and distrust;
—if Israel continues to play with internal vulnerabilities of seeing her role as a regional policeman.

Let there be no mistake. I am not holding the Arabs blameless for the depth and duration of the Arab-Israeli conflict. For too long Arab states thought the monumental injustice perpetrated against the Palestinian people in 1948 was the only reality. For too long many Arabs held that justice would be served in the end, that justice would triumph, and could see only a return to their lands by the refugees as just. After all, we knew the Palestinian Arabs, native to the land, as our Arab brothers. We did not know the Jews who had suddenly seized it. What was to happen to them? Arabs didn't care; they cared deeply, though, about the Palestinians. This was unrealistic. Today, we understand that the Palestinian problem must be dealt with *in the context* of the existence of Israel. Nevertheless, that problem *must* be resolved. We Arabs too have some requirements, but there is no question that we seek, favor, and deeply desire a resolution to this disastrous conflict.

It must be noted that the Israeli annexation of Arab Jerusalem and the Golan have both taken place in the aftermath of the Egyptian-Israeli peace treaty. Even Israelis never claimed historic rights to the Golan. Now that they have purported to annex the Golan Heights, can anyone doubt that the next step will be the West Bank? Never mind the concept of autonomy. Never mind the ideas of Palestinian self-rule. It is clear that Israel is intent upon adding this Arab territory to Greater Israel.

It was the inevitability of this result to the Camp David separate peace that led us to remain outside the discussions. We ask for a process of peace, not a process of annexation. Jordan and other Arab governments want a true peace, a peace of compromise, a peace that will allow Arab and Jew and Christian to live side by side in this region so important to all three faiths and the many peoples who embrace them. We seek a peace that will not force us to divert our meager resources to a constant cycle of arming to deter others and defend ourselves, a peace that will allow us to develop our land, our people, and our society both economically and spiritually, not bury the people in the land with continuing bitterness and hatred.

And what are the essentials of such a peace? Clearly, the modalities must be negotiated, but several prerequisites are manifestly central to bring about a peace that can endure. Happily, the prerequisites are few. Sadly, they are more elusive today than they were when President Sadat traveled to Jerusalem.

First, it is clear that the Palestinians must be allowed to freely exercise their national right of self-determination. The whole world, including the United States, and implicitly even Israel, has recognized that the Palestinian problem is at the core of the continuing Middle East tragedy. Put another way, there will never be a true peace in the region until this first requirement is met.

The second requirement is Israeli withdrawal from territories occupied in the 1967 War. Indeed, these two requirements may be viewed as related. We understand that timing can be important, that security measures (such as arms or forces limitations, observers, and the like) may be an integral part of any agreement. Issues such as security measures, juridical status, corridors of transit and communication, representation, foreign nationals, and so forth are important and are proper subjects of negotiation. Moreover, it is clear that in some cases security requirements may dictate minor modifications to specific lines previously disputed. Yet, such exchanges must result from negotiations aimed at *mutual* security and based on the two principles we have identified, not as a result of force or threat. . . .

The United States has important—some would say, vital—interests in the Middle East. It is also true that we have critical interests in the West, not least with the United States. Much in our tradition is shared, from our great monotheistic traditions to our prolonged and close association with Western Europe. We have resources of faith as well as of minerals; America has resources of science and technology as well as capital. The world is interdependent, and those Arabs who ignore or castigate our interdependence with the West, like their counterparts here, are out of step with more than their compatriots—they are out of step with reality itself.

Thus, when some Arabs say that American or Western interests are at risk in the continued failure to achieve a settlement, what they are really saying is that world interests, our interests as well as yours, are at stake. A future that condemns us to pervert the nature and value of our relationship into that of a gunrunner's, that forces America's friends to confront and even do violence to other friends, that perpetuates poverty and ignorance and narrowly limits the resources to overcome these common enemies—this is not a hopeful destiny, this is not a humane destiny, this is not an acceptable destiny. . . .

The Kahan Commission Report (February 7, 1983)*

Before we discuss the essence of the problem of the indirect responsibility of Israel, or of those who operated at its behest, we perceive it to be

---

* Excerpts from the report of the Kahan Commission to investigate the massacre at the Sabra and Shatilla refugee camps, which was signed by Chairman Yitzhak Kahan and members Aharon Barak and Yona Efrat.

necessary to deal with objections that have been voiced on various occasions, according to which if Israel's direct responsibility for the atrocities is negated—i.e., if it is determined that the blood of those killed was not shed by I.D.F. [Israel Defence Force] soldiers and forces, or that others operating at the behest of the state were not parties to the atrocities—then there is no place for further discussion of the problem of indirect responsibility. The argument is that no responsibility should be laid on Israel for deeds perpetrated outside of its borders by members of the Christian community against Palestinians in that same country, or against Muslims located within the area of the camps. A certain echo of this approach may be found in statements made in the Cabinet meeting of 9.19.82, and in statements released to the public by various sources.

We cannot accept this position. If it indeed becomes clear that those who decided on the entry of the Phalangists into the camps should have foreseen—from the information at their disposal and from things which were common knowledge—that there was danger of a massacre, and no steps were taken which might have prevented this danger or at least greatly reduced the possibility that deeds of this type might be done, then those who made the decisions and those who implemented them are indirectly responsible for what ultimately occurred, even if they did not intend this to happen and merely disregarded the anticipated danger. A similar indirect responsibility also falls on those who knew of the decision: it was their duty, by virtue of their position and their office, to warn of the danger, and they did not fulfill this duty. It is also not possible to absolve of such indirect responsibility those persons who, when they received the first reports of what was happening in the camps, did not rush to prevent the continuation of the Phalangists' actions and did not do everything within their power to stop them.

. . . We would like to note here that we will not enter at all into the question of indirect responsibility of other elements besides the State of Israel. One might argue that such indirect responsibility falls, inter alia, on the Lebanese Army, or on the Lebanese government to whose orders this army was subject, since despite Major General Drori's urgings in his talks with the heads of the Lebanese Army, they did not grant Israel's request to enter the camps before the Phalangists or instead of the Phalangists, until 9.19.82. It should also be noted that in meetings with U.S. representatives during the critical days, Israel's spokesmen repeatedly requested that the U.S. use its influence to get the Lebanese Army to fulfill the function of maintaining public peace and order in West Beirut, but it does not seem that these requests had any result. One might also make charges concerning the hasty evacuation of the multi-national force by the countries whose troops were in place until after the evacuation of the terrorists.

. . . As has already been said above, the decision to enter West Beirut was adopted in conversations held between the Prime Minister and the

Defense Minister on the night between 14–15 September 1982. No charge may be made against this decision for having been adopted by these two alone without convening a Cabinet session. On that same night, an extraordinary emergency situation was created which justified immediate and concerted action to prevent a situation which appeared undesirable and even dangerous from Israel's perspective. There is great sense in the supposition that had I.D.F. troops not entered West Beirut, a situation of total chaos and battles between various combat forces would have developed, and the number of victims among the civilian population would have been far greater than it ultimately was. The Israeli military force was the only real force nearby which could take control over West Beirut so as to maintain the peace and prevent a resumption of hostile actions between various militias and communities. The Lebanese Army could have performed a function in the refugee camps, but it did not then have the power to enforce order in all of West Beirut. Under these circumstances it could be assumed that were I.D.F. forces not to enter West Beirut, various atrocities would be perpetrated there in the absence of any real authority; and it may be that world public opinion might then have placed responsibility on Israel for having refrained from action.

The demand made in Israel to have the Phalangists take part in the fighting was a general and understandable one; and political, and to some extent military, reasons existed for such participation. The general question of relations with the Phalangists and cooperation with them is a saliently political one, regarding which there may be legitimate differences of opinion and outlook. We do not find it justified to assert that the decision on this participation was unwarranted or that it should not have been made.

It is a different question whether the decision to have the Phalangists enter the camps was justified in the circumstances that were created.

In our view, everyone who had anything to do with events in Lebanon should have felt apprehension about a massacre in the camps, if armed Phalangist forces were to be moved into them without the I.D.F. exercising concrete and effective supervision and scrutiny of them. All those concerned were well aware that combat morality among the various combatant groups in Lebanon differs from the norm in the I.D.F., that the combatants in Lebanon belittle the value of human life far beyond what is necessary and accepted in wars between civilized peoples, and that various atrocities against the noncombatant population had been widespread in Lebanon since 1975. It was well known that the Phalangists harbor deep enmity for the Palestinians, viewing them as the source of all the troubles that afflicted Lebanon during the years of the civil war.

The decision on the entry of the Phalangists into the refugee camps was taken on Wednesday (9.15.82) in the morning. The Prime Minister was not then informed of the decision. The Prime Minister heard about the decision, together with all the other ministers, in the course of a report made by the Chief of Staff at the Cabinet session on Thursday (9.16.82) when the Phalangists were already in the camps. Thereafter, no report was made to the Prime Minister regarding the excesses of the Phalangists in the camps, and the Prime Minister learned about the events in the camps from a BBC broadcast on Saturday (9.18.82). With regard to the following recommendations concerning a group of men who hold senior positions in the Government and the Israel Defense Forces, we have taken into account [the fact] that each one of these men has to his credit [the performance of] many public or military services rendered with sacrifice and devotion on behalf of the State of Israel. If nevertheless we have reached the conclusion that it is incumbent upon us to recommend certain measures against some of these men, it is out of the recognition that the gravity of the matter and its implications for the underpinnings of public morality in the State of Israel call for such measures.

The Prime Minister, the Foreign Minister, and the Head of the Mossad

We have heretofore established the facts and conclusions with regard to the responsibility of the Prime Minister, the Foreign Minister, and the head of the Mossad. In view of what we have determined with regard to the extent of the responsibility of each of them, we are of the opinion that it is sufficient to determine responsibility and there is no need for any further recommendations.

The Minister of Defense, Mr. Ariel Sharon

We have found, as has been detailed in this report, that the Minister of Defense bears personal responsibility. In our opinion, it is fitting that the Minister of Defense draw the appropriate personal conclusions arising out of the defects revealed with regard to the manner in which he discharged the duties of his office—and if necessary, that the Prime Minister consider whether he should exercise his authority under Section 21-A(a) of the Basic Law of the Government, according to which "the Prime Minister may, after informing the Cabinet of his intention to do so, remove a minister from office."

The Chief of Staff, Lt.-Gen. Rafael Eitan

We have arrived at grave conclusions with regard to the acts and omissions of the Chief of Staff, Lt.-Gen. Rafael Eitan. The Chief of Staff is about to complete his term of service in April, 1983. Taking into account the fact that an extension of his term is not under consideration, there is no [practical] significance to a recommendation with regard to his continuing in office as Chief of Staff, and therefore we have resolved that it is sufficient to determine responsibility without making any further recommendation.

Closing Remarks

In the witnesses' testimony and in various documents, stress is laid on the difference between the usual battle ethics of the I.D.F. and the battle ethics of the bloody clashes and combat actions among the various ethnic groups, militias, and fighting forces in Lebanon. The difference is considerable. In the war the I.D.F. waged in Lebanon, many civilians were injured and much loss of life was caused, despite the effort the I.D.F. and its soldiers made not to harm civilians. On more than one occasion, this effort caused I.D.F. troops additional casualties. During the months of the war, I.D.F. soldiers witnessed many sights of killing, destruction, and ruin. From their reactions (about which we have heard) to acts of brutality against civilians, it would appear that despite the terrible sights and experiences of the war and despite the soldier's obligation to behave as a fighter with a certain degree of callousness, I.D.F. soldiers did not lose their sensitivity to atrocities that were perpetrated on noncombatants either out of cruelty or to give vent to vengeful feelings. It is regrettable that the reaction by I.D.F. soldiers to such deeds was not always forceful enough to bring a halt to the despicable acts. It seems to us that the I.D.F. should continue to foster the [consciousness of] basic moral obligations which must be kept even in war conditions, without prejudicing the I.D.F.'s combat ability. The circumstances of combat require the combatants to be tough—which means to give priority to sticking to the objective and being willing to make sacrifices—in order to attain the objectives assigned to them, even under the most difficult conditions. But the end never justifies the means, and basic ethical and human values must be maintained in the use of arms.

Among the responses to the commission from the public, there were those who expressed dissatisfaction with the holding of an inquiry on a subject not directly related to Israel's responsibility. The argument was advanced that in previous instances of massacre in Lebanon, when the lives of many more people were taken than those of the victims who fell in Sabra and Shatilla, world opinion was not shocked and no inquiry commissions were established. We cannot justify this approach to the issue of holding an inquiry, and not only for the formal reason that it was not we who decided to hold the inquiry, but rather the Israeli Government resolved thereon. The main purpose of the inquiry was to bring to light all the important facts relating to the perpetration of the atrocities; it therefore has importance from the perspective of Israel's moral fortitude and its functioning as a democratic state that scrupulously maintains the fundamental principles of the civilized world.

We do not deceive ourselves that the results of this inquiry will convince or satisfy those who have prejudices or selective consciences, but this inquiry was not intended for such people. We have striven and have spared no effort to arrive at the truth, and we hope that all persons of good will who will examine the issue without prejudice will be convinced that the inquiry was conducted without any bias.

Yasir Arafat: Speech to Palestine National Council (February 14, 1983)*

To those against whom war is made, permission is given to fight because they have been wronged; and truly God is most powerful for their aid. They are those who have been expelled from their homes in defiance of right, for no cause except that they say, our Lord is God.

. . . The struggle will continue until the aims of our Arab nation are achieved. It will continue so that its domain is protected. . . . This commitment is based on deep conviction and pan-Arab nobility and the revolutionary re-union which has driven and still drives our revolution in strength and gallantry to continue our militant road and our armed revolution until we achieve our firm national rights which are not open to disposal, including our right to return, self-determination, and the establishment of our independent Palestinian state on our national Palestinian soil and until our fluttering banners are raised over holy Jerusalem, capital of our independent Palestine, and over its minarets and over its churches and over its walls. . . .

. . . Our Palestine National Council is convened in these difficult and grave times through which our Arab nation is passing in the shadow of the fateful challenges to our civilization as an Arab nation, and not only as a Palestinian revolution and not as joint Lebanese-Palestinian forces, but as an Arab nation. It is a question of to be or not to be, in the shadow of the U.S. imperialist-Zionist onslaught whose nails and daggers pierce the body of our Arab nation. It tries to spread its domination over our entire Arab nation; it tries to control our resources and tries to annex us to its sphere of influence.

Here is the importance of the posture, the mighty posture displayed by the joint Lebanese-Palestinian forces, and the steadfastness which they continue to display in their confrontation of this all-embracing American onslaught. In the same vein is the unequalled steadfastness of our joint forces and our militant masses in face of the Israeli military operation, fully paid for by the United States, by the racist military clique in the Zionist invasion army, in order to commit these barbarous crimes against the Lebanese and Palestinian people. These crimes reached the summit of barbarism and savagery as is clear from the massacres and butchery in the Sabra and Shatila camps after the gallant fighters of the joint forces had destroyed the arrogance and pomposity of the enemy and turned him back.

Your fighters stood fast in Beirut. Your masses stood fast in Beirut. Your nation stood fast by you in Beirut in the face of untiring attempts by the United States to exhaust the entire Arab nation and kneel before the aggressors, the Zionist invaders and the U.S. imperialists. In 88 days the pride of our contem-

* Excerpts from a speech in Algiers.

porary Arab history . . . stood fast in the face of technological supremacy and challenged the superior and sophisticated U.S. military machine. . . .

Brother President, friends, brothers, by standing fast in Beirut a new phase began in our Arab history. Israel's blitzkrieg wars and its imaginary blitzkrieg victories have ended forever in the face of your mujahidin brothers who have died as martyrs for the existence and dignity of our entire Arab nation. Yes, brother, this is a new phase of our history which we enter with strength and belief after the volcano which erupted in Beirut. It is a phase of Arab transformation with all its values and concepts and with all that surrounds it. Imperialist balances and everything based upon them will not live long after the eruption of this volcano in Beirut.

Beirut has exposed everything. It has exposed everything and nothing is left to our Arab nation except the deep roots produced by the free and noble people and the mujahidin.

. . . For 18 years we have been fighting for our homeland through our Palestinian revolution. Through this last stage of our people's long march, that hard and difficult march, we have learned from our own experiences and those of revolutionaries all over the world that national unity is the guarantee for victory and that the independence of national decision away from all pressures and negative influences is the basis for crystallizing the national personality of our Palestinian people. We have learned that armed struggle complements political struggle in all fields. Despite all obstacles and hurdles and mines—and they are many—we have been guided by these bases. . . .

The rallying of our Palestinian people, internally and externally, around their armed revolution is the protective shield on which the arrows of the aggressors and the plotters always fall. Whatever the disguises and however hard the parties to the plot hide or try to hide themselves, and whatever forms the plot takes, after the Beirut events, they cannot deceive our people and our masses. No force, however great and however much acclaimed, can transform the giant who stood fast in Beirut and Lebanon into a dwarf. . . . Our decision comes from our people and from the barrel of a gun. . . . These firm national objectives, which are not open to modification, are that our people shall live in their homeland, free and as masters.

I beg our Arab nation, and after the Arab summit in Fez approved the Arab peace plan and after the visit paid by the Arab seven-member committee to world capitals, I say to every Arab that peace is the peace of the strong. I say peace is the peace of the strong and there is no peace for the weak or for those who bend. Therefore, our Arab nation is called upon to mobilize all its energies and all its military and political and mass capabilities to confront the challenges of destiny imposed on us at this critical stage which our Arab nation is now experiencing. . . .

We do not fight for the sake of fighting and do not reject for the sake of rejection. We fight for the freedom of our homeland and people and for the sake of our dignity. We reject anything—far or near—that harms our firm national rights. On this basis, the PLO asks all countries in the world to stand beside it in the face of the Israeli aggression, stressing that there is no solution to the Middle East crisis, no peace, no stability, and no security in this region, without the firm national rights of the Palestinian people.

While clinging to the rifle and shouldering it in the face of aggression in order to defend our people and land and for the sake of our freedom, we are advocates of peace based on meeting our people's firm national rights, including the right to return, the right to self-determination, and the right to establish an independent Palestinian state on their natural soil with holy Jerusalem as the capital. Our choice to establish a confederation with our people in fraternal Jordan is a genuine expression of our conviction in comprehensive Arab unity. . . .

Our national unity is the basis of our action and movement, our independent national decision is our guide, which cannot be faulted in defining the target. It is inevitable that our National Council should lay down political programs which fulfill the requirements and reply to the challenges. Ultimately, it is inevitable that we should have absolute unity founded on a democratic and creative basis. Let thousands of flowers blossom but in the gardens of the revolution! . . .

The PLO, entering its new revolutionary stage with firm and strong steps, turns to all those who are free and honorable in the world to stand beside our people's just struggle. At the same time, when the revolution starts this new and regenerated uprising, it reaches out—as it has always done—to all the world's liberation movements. It clasps their hands and stands beside them with all our capabilities.

We turn, with greetings and appreciation, to our friends in the socialist bloc led by the friendly Soviet Union, to the nonaligned countries, to the Islamic countries, to the African countries, and to the friendly countries for their support and their stand beside the just and legitimate struggle of our people. We greet and stand beside the free and revolutionary people in South Africa and Namibia and warmly greet all the free and revolutionary people in America, Latin America, and Asia. We are with every struggler against imperialism, Zionism, and colonialism. We are with every struggler against oppression and racial discrimination and for a better life and future.

Palestine National Council: Political Statement (February 22, 1983)*

On the Palestinian Level:

1. Palestinian National Unity:

The battle of steadfastness of heroism in Lebanon and Beirut epitomizes Palestinian national unity in its best form. The PNC affirms continued adherence to independent Palestinian decisionmaking, its protection, and

* Excerpts from the PNC Political Statement issued in Algiers at the concluding session.

the resisting of all pressures from whatever source to detract from this independence.

Palestinian Armed Struggle:

The PNC affirms the need to develop and escalate the armed struggle against the Zionist enemy. It affirms the right of the Palestine revolution forces to carry out military action against the Zionist enemy from all Arab fronts. . . .

2. The Occupied Homeland:

The PNC salutes our steadfast masses in the occupied territory in the face of the occupation, colonization, and uprooting. It also salutes their comprehensive national unity and their complete rallying around the PLO, the sole legitimate representative of the Palestinian people, both internally and externally. The PNC condemns and denounces all the suspect Israeli and American attempts to strike at Palestinian national unanimity and calls on the masses of our people to resist them. . . .

The National Council salutes the steadfastness of its people living in the areas occupied in 1948 and is proud of their struggle, in the face of racist Zionism, to assert their national identity, it being an indivisible part of the Palestinian people. The council asserts the need to provide all the means of backing for them so as to consolidate their unity and that of their national forces.

Our Dispersed People:

The PNC asserts the need to mobilize the resources of our people wherever they reside outside our occupied land and to consolidate their rallying around the PLO as the sole legitimate representative of our people. It recommends to the Executive Committee to work to preserve the social and economic interests of Palestinians and to defend their gained rights and their basic liberties and security.

Contacts with Jewish Forces:

. . . The PNC calls on the Executive Committee to study movement within this framework in line with the interest of the cause of Palestine and the Palestinian national interest.

On the Arab Level:

Deepening cohesion between the Palestinian revolution and the Arab national liberation movement throughout the Arab homeland so as to effectively stand up to the imperialist and Zionist plots and liquidation plans, particularly the Camp David accords and the Reagan plan, and also ending the Zionist occupation of the occupied Arab land, relations between the PLO and the Arab states shall be based on the following:

A. Commitment to the causes of the Arab struggle, first and foremost the cause of and struggle for Palestine.

B. Adherence to the rights of the Palestinian people, including their right to return, self-determination, and the establishment of their own independent state under the leadership of the PLO—rights that were confirmed by the resolutions of the Arab summit conferences.

C. Adherence to the question of sole representation and national unity and respect for national and independent Palestinian decisionmaking.

D. Rejection of all schemes aimed at harming the right of the PLO to be the sole representative of the Palestinian people through any formula such as assigning powers, acting on its behalf, or sharing its right to representation.

The Arab Peace Plan:

The PNC considers the Fez summit resolutions as the minimum for political moves by the Arab states, moves which must complement military action with all its requirements for adjusting the balance of forces in favor of the struggle and Palestinian and Arab rights. The council, in understanding these resolutions, affirms it is not in conflict with the commitment to the political program and the resolutions of the National Council.

Jordan:

Emphasizing the special and distinctive relations linking the Jordanian and Palestinian peoples and the need for action to develop them in harmony with the national interest of the two peoples and the Arab nation, and in order to realize the rights [as] the sole legitimate representative of the Palestinian people, both inside and outside the occupied land, the PNC deems that future relations with Jordan should be founded on the basis of a confederation between two independent states.

Lebanon:

1. Deepening relations with the Lebanese people and their National Forces and extending support and backing to them in their valiant struggle to resist the Zionist occupation and its instruments.

2. At the forefront of the current missions of the Palestinian revolution will be participation with the Lebanese masses and their National and democratic forces in the fight against and the ending of Zionist occupation.

Relations With Syria:

Relations with sister Syria are based on the resolutions of successive PNC sessions which confirm the importance of the strategic relationship between the PLO and Syria in the service of the nationalist and pan-Arab interests of struggle and in order to confront the imperialist and the Zionist enemy, in light of the PLO's and Syria's constituting the vanguard in the face of the common danger.

The Steadfastness and Confrontation Front:

The PNC entrusts the PLO Executive Committee to have talks with the sides of the pan-Arab Steadfastness and Confrontation Front to discuss how it should be revived anew on sound, clear, and effective foundations, working from the premise that the front was not at the level of the tasks requested of it during the Zionist invasion of Lebanon.

Egypt:

The PNC confirms its rejection of the Camp David accords and the autonomy and civil administrations plans linked to them. The council calls on the Executive Committee to develop PLO relations with Egyptian nationalist, democratic, and popular forces struggling against moves to normalize relations with the Zionist enemy in all their forms.

Reagan's Plan:

Reagan's plan, in style and content, does not respect the established national rights of the Palestinian people since it denies the right of return and self-determination and the setting up of the independent Palestinian state and also the PLO—the sole legitimate representative of the Palestinian people—and since it contradicts international legality. Therefore, the PNC rejects the considering of this plan as a sound basis for the just and lasting solution of the cause of the Palestine and the Arab-Zionist conflict.

Barry Rubin: United It Stalls: The PLO (March 21, 1983)*

Can the Palestine Liberation Organization develop a pragmatic diplomatic policy following its crushing military defeat in Lebanon? The sixteenth Palestine National Council meeting in Algiers last month disappointed those who had hoped so. Although the PLO may be adapting to the new situation, its pace is so slow and hesitant as to throw into doubt its ability or desire to negotiate before it is too late. With Israel daily tightening its hold on the West Bank, and Jordan considering initiatives in its own right,

* Barry Rubin is a professor at Hebrew University's Rothberg School. The article was published in *The New Republic*, March 21, 1983, reprinted by permission of *The New Republic*, © 1983, The New Republic, Inc.

the Palestinian leadership seems again to have thrown away opportunities, and to be further than ever from its goals.

In recent years the PLO has gradually shifted away from its old, unattainable objective of destroying Israel and replacing it with an Arab state. The PLO now proposes a Palestinian state in the West Bank and Gaza, though it persists in refusing to recognize Israel. Last September President Reagan suggested a plan for a Jordanian-Palestinian federation with a large measure of Palestinian self-rule. Since then the Administration has hoped—and a large segment of the media has grasped at straws to imply—that the PLO might accept this proposal. The current government of Israel opposes all these ideas, but President Reagan hopes to induce Prime Minister Begin to change his policy.

The result of the convention of the PNC, the PLO's parliamentary body, was both a clear-cut political victory for Yasir Arafat and a reminder of just how narrow is his room for maneuvering. The Reagan plan was rejected, and resolutions discouraged a proposed negotiating tactic to circumvent PLO-Israel mutual nonrecognition—the creation of a joint Jordanian-Palestinian delegation in which West Bank independents would represent the Palestinians, but take orders from PLO headquarters.

Observers have often overestimated Arafat's courage or ability to change PLO policy, given the caution bred by his constant struggle to mollify PLO factions and Arab regimes that use money, competing militancy, and even assassination in attempts to control the organization. Arafat's own weapons include cagey ambiguity in political positions and consensus above all. These tools have served him well, but also block any moving away of the PLO from a maximalist and rejectionist stance.

There are thus two ironies in the PLO's politics. First, the very policies that preserve the organization also freeze it into self-defeating negativism. Second, Arafat's strong position as leader is best protected by minimum use of his potential leverage. With time no longer on its side and deprived of its base in Lebanon, the PLO may well find such flaws fatal.

PNC Chairman Khalid Fahum and Arafat themselves sketched out, in milder but equally determined language, the reasons why the Reagan plan was unacceptable to the PLO. They scorned it for disregarding refugees' "right to return" to what is now Israel, self-determination, establishment of an independent Palestinian state with East Jerusalem as its capital, and recognition of the PLO as its sole legitimate representative. These four points all concern major issues; the Reagan plan cannot be adjusted to meet them.

Thus the PNC political resolution rejected the U.S. proposal in fairly clear language: "Reagan's plan, in style and content, does not respect the established national rights of the Palestinian people. . . . Therefore, the PNC rejects the considering of this plan as a sound basis for the just and lasting solution of the cause of the Palestine and the Arab-Zionist conflict.'' Fatah leader Salah Khalif said in his speech—not quoted in the U.S. press—''I have not heard a single Palestinian say that he accepted Reagan's plan.''

The PNC took a more favorable position on a confederation with Jordan, which Arafat even defended as an expression of Arab unity. But there was no question of accepting domination from Amman. The resolution called for ''a confederation between two independent states.'' Our people shall live in their homeland, free and as masters,'' said Arafat. The PNC was suspicious about allowing the Jordanians or West Bank mayors to negotiate with the Americans or Israelis. The PNC final resolution called for: ''Rejection of all schemes aimed at harming the right of the PLO to be the sole representative of the Palestinian people through any formula such as assigning powers, acting on its behalf, or sharing its right of representation.''

If the PLO does change course, the Arab regimes will have a great deal to do with it. Despite Syria's negativism, the majority of involved Arab governments favor some accommodation with Israel for the first time in history. Egypt, Jordan, Saudi Arabia, and even Iraq take this ''moderate'' position. The Saudis, however, have been quite timid, even by their standards, in trying to influence the PLO. Their Fez summit resolution, endorsed by the PNC meeting, called for an independent Palestinian state in all the occupied territories with only the vaguest offer of recognition for Israel. So far they have not offered much encouragement to Reagan's efforts.

The PLO's anti-Americanism remains particularly strident. As PLO spokesmen repeatedly stress, the United States is Israel's main supplier of arms and aid, while U.S. guarantees to protect Palestinians in West Beirut proved worthless in the Sabra and Shatila massacres. Arafat's closing oration portrayed Lebanon as a PLO victory, and blamed setbacks on United States involvement. Washington received no thanks for saving the PLO leadership and troops in West Beirut from complete destruction. In Arafat's words, Ambassador Philip Habib and President Reagan decided ''to destroy the foundation of the PLO.'' He even claimed, ''The U.S. 6th fleet . . . was the one that carried out the Israeli military landings. . . .'' But things in Lebanon were not really so bad: ''They speak of this invincible [Israeli] army. But, brothers, by God I have not found it invincible. . . . I wish all my nation was with me to see the feebleness of this army.''

Such rhetoric is aimed at building morale, but it also shapes thinking. PLO strategy is still tied to positions based on illusion or internal politics. Reporters and commentators like to suggest that the failure of the PLO or of Jordan to accept the Reagan plan results from a lack of U.S. credibility and an inability to bring rapid Israeli withdrawal from Lebanon or a settlement freeze on the West Bank. But aside from the misdeeds of the Begin government, the fact is that the PLO has principled differences with American objectives and the Jordanians are hard put to join in without an Arab mandate or PLO acquiescence. The PLO only offers Hussein the unattractive option of risking a great deal to establish a PLO-led state. Unless the Arab side can produce a better offer, Washington will have no incentive to put pressure on Israel, and the creeping annexation of the West Bank will continue. . . .

Jordan's Refusal to Join the Reagan Peace Initiative (April 10, 1983)*

Since the Israeli aggression of June 1967, and through our awareness of the dangers and repercussions of the occupation, Jordan has accepted the political option as one of the basic options that may lead to the recovery of Arab territories occupied through military aggression. Consequently, Jordan accepted Security Council Resolution 242 of November 22, 1967. When the October 1973 war happened, it underlined the importance of continuing work on the political option while in the same time building our intrinsic strength. This war brought about Security Council Resolution 338, which put a stop to military operations and implicitly re-emphasized Security Council Resolution 242.

Based on Security Council Resolution 338, disengagement agreements were concluded between Israel on the one hand and Egypt and Syria on the other. This process completed the Arab circle immediately concerned with the recovery of the occupied lands through political means.

On this basis, Jordan, in cooperation with the Arab states, developed and adopted the concept of forming a unified Arab delegation that would attend an international conference for the purpose of achieving a just and comprehensive peace settlement to the Middle East problem.

In 1974, the Rabat Arab summit conference designated the Palestine Liberation Organization as the sole legitimate representative of the Palestinian people. Jordan went along with the Arab consensus and has been committed to that decision ever since.

The ensuing period saw the disjointment of Arab unity as evidenced by the Camp David accords. Further disintegration in the overall Arab position followed even between those directly affected by the Israeli occupation. All the while, Jordan kept sounding the alarm on the one hand and persevering in its course of action on the other.

* Jordanian Cabinet statement.

Jordan warned repeatedly of the dangers inherent in the continuation of the no-war, no-peace situation, and of the exploitation by Israel of this situation to perpetuate the status quo by creating new facts in the occupied Arab territories, to realize its declared ambitions, aided by Arab disunity and by its military superiority.

Jordan has also cautioned against letting time pass by without concluding a just and comprehensive peace settlement because time was, and still is, essential to Israel's aim of creating new facts and bringing about a fait accompli.

Sixteen years have passed since the occupation, during which Israel established 146 colonies in the West Bank alone and has illegally expropriated more than 50 percent of that land.

Even today, Israel forges ahead in defiance of all international conventions and of the United Nations resolutions with a systematic policy of evacuating the inhabitants of the West Bank to change the demographic composition of the occupied Arab territories, thus realizing its designs to establish the Zionist state on the whole of Palestine.

From the early days of the occupation, and through awareness of the Zionist aims, Jordan made all these warnings and undertook the task of implementing all policies that may support the steadfastness of the Palestinian people and help them stay in their national soil.

With this objective in mind, we worked incessantly on all levels. Domestically, Jordan provides markets for the industrial and agricultural products of the West Bank and Gaza, and continues to extend support to the existing institutions in the West Bank. Also, we continue to attach great importance to building our intrinsic defense capability in cooperation with other Arab states, through the conviction held by all our nation of the great danger posed by Zionist ambitions, which threaten the Arab world and its future generations.

Within this context Jordan paid particular attention to building its armed forces, looked for new sources of arms within the available financial means and enacted the military service law to mobilize all its national resources for self-defense and for the defense of the Arab world because Jordan remains, by virtue of its geographic location, a constant target for Israeli aggression and the first line of defense on the east flank of the Arab world.

On the Arab level, Jordan sought to provide financial support for the steadfastness of the Palestinian people and formed a joint Jordanian-Palestinian committee, which continues to implement the policy of supporting our people in the occupied lands.

On the international level, Jordan worked to mobilize world opinion to bring pressure to bear on Israel, and in the United Nations, through cooperation with Arab and friendly countries, Jordan succeeded in passing resolutions condemning, isolating and putting pressure on Israel.

All the while, Israel continued with its expansionist colonization program, evicting the Arab inhabitants of Palestine and replacing them by Jewish immigrants. We strive to confront this program, which stands to affect Jordan more than any other country and which threatens Jordan's identity and national security.

In June 1982, Israel launched its aggression on Lebanon, which resulted in that country joining the list of occupied Arab territories. Lebanon was not excluded from the ambitions of Israel, which had already annexed Jerusalem and the Golan Heights, and which works for the de facto annexation of the West Bank and Gaza.

Last September, the United States President Ronald Reagan declared his peace initiative to solve the Middle East crisis, and shortly after, the Fez Arab summit conference resumed its proceedings where the Arab peace plan was formulated. It is evident that both peace proposals were inspired by the provisions of Security Council Resolution 242 and by the United Nations resolutions that followed.

Jordan, as well as other Arab and friendly countries, found that the Reagan plan lacked some principles of the Fez peace plan, but in the same time it contained a number of positive elements. Given the realities of the international situation, on the other hand, the Arab peace plan lacked the mechanism that would enable it to make effective progress. The Reagan plan presented the vehicle that could propel the Fez peace plan forward, and Jordan proceeded to explore this possibility.

We believe, and continue to believe, that this aim can be achieved through an agreement between Jordan and the Palestine Liberation Organization on the establishment of a confederal relationship that would govern and regulate the future of the Jordanian and Palestinian peoples. This relationship would express itself, from the moment of its inception, through joint Jordanian-Palestinian action based on the Fez peace plan, Security Council Resolution 242 and the principles of the Reagan initiative. In addition, such a confederal relationship would be sought if only through the faith Arabs have in their joint destiny and in recognition of the bonds that have linked the people of Jordan and Palestine throughout history.

These concepts, and the ideas and assessments that follow from them, formed the subject of intensive discussions held over several meetings between His Majesty King Hussein and PLO chairman Yasir Arafat, as well as between the Government of Jordan and a number of senior members of the PLO, within the framework of a higher committee which was formed for this purpose and which held its deliberations over the five months between October 1982 and the recent convention of the Palestinian National Council in 1982. In addition, a number of prominent Palestinians inside and outside the occupied territories took part in the discussions.

These deliberations resulted in the irrefutable conclusion that Jordan and Palestine are joined by undeniable objective considerations reflected by the common threat against them which united their interests and their goals. There also resulted a joint conviction in the soundness of our approach, and we agreed to form a joint stand capable of pursuing political action, which, with Arab support, can take advantage of the available opportunity to liberate our people, land and, foremost of which, Arab Jerusalem.

Then, upon the request of Mr. Yasir Arafat, we waited to see the results of the Palestinian National Council meeting, where Mr. Arafat assured us he would act to secure the support of the council for the envisaged joint political action, on whose basic elements we agreed, pending their developments in the Palestinian National Council by declaring confederate-union relationship between Jordan and Palestine.

In our latest meeting with Mr. Arafat, held in Amman between March 31 and April 5, we conducted a joint assessment of the realities of the Palestine problem in general, and in particular of the dilemma facing the Palestinian people under occupation.

We also discussed political action in accordance with the Arab and international peace plans, including President Reagan's peace initiative, bearing in mind the resolutions of the PNC. We held intensive talks on the principles and methods, and we reemphasized the importance of a confederal relationship between Jordan and Palestine as being a practical conceptualization from which to work for the implementation of this initiative. We agreed to work together in this delicate and crucial time to form a united Arab stand that would enable us to deal with the practical aspects of these initiatives, in the hope of achieving a just, permanent and comprehensive solution to the Middle East problem, especially the Palestinian problem.

We also agreed to start immediately joint political action on the Arab level to secure Arab support that would contribute enormously to the realization of the common goal of liberating the lands and people under occupation, thus fulfilling our duty to work in all possible ways and to take advantage of every possible opportunity to achieve our aims.

Together with PLO chairman Yasir Arafat, we laid the final draft of our agreement, which required us and Mr. Arafat to make immediate contacts with Arab leaders to inform them of its contents, seeking their blessing and support for the agreement.

The PLO executive committee deliberated on this issue in the course of several meetings, and finally Mr. Arafat decided to discuss the agreement with other PLO leaders outside Jordan and return to Amman after two days to conclude the joint steps necessary for the implementation of the agreement.

Five days later, a delegate was sent by the PLO executive committee chairman to Amman, to convey to us new ideas and to propose a new course of action that differed from our agreement and that did not give priority to saving the land, thus sending us back to where we were in October 1982.

In the light of this, it became evident that we cannot proceed with the course of political action which we had planned together and to which we had agreed in principle and in details, in answer to our historic responsibility to take the opportunities made available by Arab and international initiatives and save our land and people.

In view of the results of the efforts we made with the PLO, and in compliance with the 1974 Rabat summit resolution, and through the strict observance of the independence of the Palestinian decision, we respect the decision of the PLO, it being the sole legitimate representative of the Palestinian people. Accordingly, we leave it to the PLO and the Palestinian people to choose the ways and means for the salvation of themselves and their land, and for the realization of their declared aims in the manner they see fit.

We in Jordan, having refused from the beginning to negotiate on behalf of the Palestinians, will neither act separately nor in lieu of anybody in Middle East peace negotiations.

Jordan will work as a member of the Arab League, in compliance with its resolutions to support the PLO within our capabilities, and in compliance with the requirements of our national security.

Being consistent with ourselves, and faithful to our principles, Arab Jerusalem and holy shrines, we shall continue to provide support for our brothers in the occupied Palestinian territories and make our pledge to them before the Almighty that we shall remain their faithful brothers and side with them in their ordeal.

As for us in Jordan, we are directly affected by the results of the continued occupation of the West Bank and the Gaza Strip through the accelerating colonization program and through the economic pressures systematically being brought on the Palestinian people to force them out of their land.

In the light of these facts, and in the no-war and no-peace situation that prevails, we find ourselves more concerned than anybody else to confront the de facto annexation of the West Bank and Gaza Strip, which forces us to take all steps necessary to safeguard our national security in all its dimensions. Both Jordanians and Palestinians shall remain one family that cares for its national unity to the same extent that it cares to stay on this beloved Arab land.

May God assist us in our aspirations.

The Lebanon-Israel Truce Agreement (May 17, 1983)*

The government of the Republic of Lebanon and the government of the State of Israel, . . .

Having agreed to declare the termination of the state of war between them,

Desiring to ensure lasting security for both their states and to avoid threats and the use of force between them,

Desiring to establish their mutual relations in the manner provided for in this agreement, . . .

Have agreed to the following provisions:

ARTICLE I

1. The parties agree and undertake to respect the sovereignty, political independence and territorial integrity of each other. They consider the existing international boundary between Lebanon and Israel inviolable.

2. The parties confirm that the state of war between Lebanon and Israel has been terminated and no longer exists.

3. Taking into account the provisions of paragraphs 1 and 2, Israel undertakes to withdraw all its armed forces from Lebanon in accordance with the annex of the present agreement.

ARTICLE 2

The parties, being guided by the principles of the Charter of the United Nations and of international law, undertake to settle their disputes by peaceful means in such a manner as to promote international peace and security and justice.

ARTICLE 3

In order to provide maximum security for Lebanon and Israel, the parties agree to establish and implement security arrangements, including the creation of a security region, as provided for in the annex of the present agreement.

ARTICLE 4

1. The territory of each party will not be used as a base for hostile or terrorist activity against the other party, its territory, or its people.

* Excerpts.

2. Each party will prevent the existence or organization of irregular forces, armed bands, organizations, bases, offices or infrastructure, the aims and purposes of which include incursions or any act of terrorism into the territory of the other party, or any other activity aimed at threatening or endangering the security of the other party and safety of its people. To this end, all agreements and arrangements enabling the presence and functioning on the territory of either party of elements hostile to the other party are null and void.

3. Without prejudice to the inherent right of self-defense in accordance with international law, each party will refrain:

A. From organizing, instigating, assisting, or participating in threats or acts of belligerency, subversion, or incitement or any aggression directed against the other party, its population or property, both within its territory and originating therefrom, or in the territory of the other party.

B. From using the territory of the other party for conducting a military attack against the territory of a third state.

C. From intervening in the internal or external affairs of the other party.

4. Each party undertakes to ensure that preventive action and due proceedings will be taken against persons or organizations perpetrating acts in violation of this article.

ARTICLE 5

Consistent with the termination of the state of war and within the framework of their constitutional provisions, the parties will abstain from any form of hostile propaganda against each other.

ARTICLE 6

Each party will prevent entry into, deployment in, or passage through its territory, its air space and, subject to the right of innocent passage in accordance with international law, its territorial sea, by military forces, armament, or military equipment of any state hostile to the other party.

ARTICLE 7

Except as provided in the present agreement, nothing will preclude the deployment on Lebanese territory of international forces requested and accepted by the government of Lebanon to assist in maintaining its authority. New contributors to such forces shall be selected from among states having diplomatic relations with both parties to the present agreement.

ARTICLE 8

1. A. Upon entry into force of the present agreement, a Joint Liaison Committee will be established by the parties, in which the United States

of America will be a participant, and will commence its functions. . . .

B. The Joint Liaison Committee will address itself on a continuing basis to the development of mutual relations between Lebanon and Israel, *inter alia* the regulation of the movement of goods, products and persons, communications, etc. . . .

2. During the six-month period after the withdrawal of all Israeli armed forces from Lebanon in accordance with Article 1 of the present agreement and the simultaneous restoration of Lebanese government authority along the international boundary between Lebanon and Israel, and in the light of the termination of the state of war, the parties shall initiate, within the Joint Liaison Committee, *bona fide* negotiations in order to conclude agreements on the movement of goods, products and persons and their implementation on a nondiscriminatory basis. . . .

ANNEX
SECURITY ARRANGEMENTS

A. A security region [in southern Lebanon] in which the government of Lebanon undertakes to implement the security arrangements agreed upon in this annex is hereby established. . . .

The Lebanese authorities will enforce special security measures aimed at detecting and preventing hostile activities as well as the introduction into or movement through the security region of unauthorized armed men or military equipment. . . .

B. Lebanese Police . . . may be stationed in the security region without restrictions as to their numbers. These forces and elements will be equipped only with personal and light automatic weapons. . . .

C. Two Lebanese Army brigades may be stationed in the security region. One will be the Lebanese Army territorial brigade. . . .* The other will be a regular Lebanese Army brigade. . . .

D. The existing local units will be integrated as such into the Lebanese Army, in conformity with Lebanese Army regulations. . . .

Said Musa: Interview on Internal Dissent (May 26, 1983)†

. . . Fatah's leadership knows that the Palestinian cause is not an issue of an officer or a group of officers, or an issue of a military group of elements in the arena of conflict in Al-Biqa' rebelling against military orders. Ours

---

* Composed of the breakaway force of Major Saad Haddad.
† Excerpts from an interview by *Al-Watan* (Kuwait) with Said Musa (Abu Musa), of the anti-Arafat revolt in the PLO.

is a cry for correcting a mistaken political action that had begun to develop and emerge more clearly following our departure from Beirut. Frankly, there is a political conflict within Fatah that has been going on for years. This conflict has developed into a broad current that believes in political concepts that are committed to Fatah's statutes and political program. . . .

. . . Following our freeze in Beirut, several positive questions evolved. And these should have given us the incentive to stiffen our political stands in order to confront the U.S. imperialist plan and in order for this steadfastness not to become a catalyst for implementing the U.S. plot and program. Following the battle of Beirut, we should have also submitted a struggle plan that commits the Palestinian revolution to confront the U.S. plan on Lebanon's territory by virtue of the fact of the existing occupation and as a field of struggle through alliance with the nationalist movement and the honorable forces who are determined to continue the fight. However, this leadership went to Fez, and we consider that the Fez plan is actually Fahd's plan which stems from Camp David and from UN Resolution 242 despite the inclusion of certain points which at first glance appear positive, such as demanding the establishment of a Palestinian state, the return of refugees, regaining Jerusalem, and eliminating the settlements. But we wonder who is capable of translating this program or that plan. Are Arab summits capable of doing such a thing?

And I answer: No, because from our experience in Lebanon no one moved to provide Beirut's children with a single drink of water. We realize that the establishment of the Palestinian state and the return of the refugees is an issue that requires several wars. When the United States and Israel feel that their interests in the region are threatened, it is only at that moment that our voice as a Palestinian revolution will be heard. Then, the Arab countries can impose their plans, although they are supposed to be on the line of confrontation and in the middle of the conflict and not in a position to make deficient plans. Had these plans been offered by friends or allies or other parties, they could have been accepted, but not from the Arab countries because this is not what is expected of them. However, despite all this we say that whatever the matters may be, there is supposed to be a Palestinian option when there is a state of inability to implement these plans. Our Palestinian option since 1965 has been the option of armed struggle. However, the Palestinian leadership accepted the Arab option and dropped the option of armed struggle. . . .

And as for the Reagan plan, it was proposed on the day on which the last batch left Beirut. We heard the clauses of the plan when we were at sea. Its discussion in the Fatah movement began; we discussed its positive and negative sides. Through a simple political reading of the plan we find that it denies the existence of the Palestinian people and not only the Palestinian question. It also says no to the Palestinian state, no to the PLO, no to Jerusalem and its return, and yes to the settlements and to changing the borders. Despite all this, some voices within Fatah said there were positive points in the plan—that it recognized for the first time that the West Bank and Gaza Strip were under occupation. Is there anything new in this? Is there any justice in this? . . .

After the Reagan plan we plunged into a new whirlpool, the plan for a confederation with Jordan. We began to discuss the details before the state had been established—instead of first establishing the state and then discussing the confederation, which would be a direct result of establishing the state. Without going into all the details of this matter, I say that so far no clear decision has been made on this matter. We have not closed the door on it; it remains unresolved. There should be clear agreement that talks on a confederation are to be held after the establishment of an independent state. . . .

It is not a question of numbers. If it had been so I would have addressed an appeal to all our fedayeen and they would all have joined us. We are an indivisible part of Fatah. We are the conscience of Fatah who have raised their voice and thought aloud, and express the broad faithful base. . . . Therefore, it is necessary to stop and examine what we have achieved. What has this revolution achieved? Is it capable of shouldering the responsibility in confronting these big plans in light of its current reality or should it rearrange itself in a proper manner so that it can confront the coming stage? We say that the . . . National Council when it said yes to many of the political issues is neither a revolutionary nor a clear act. Political clarity is the major base. We understand that in the stages of retreat revolutionary movements adhere more closely to principles and bases.

What should I say to my father who fought in 1936 before the occupation of Palestine and the establishment of the Israeli state? What should I say to those who fought during these years to prevent the establishment of such a state? Are we fighting in order to recognize Israel? This is not reasonable, not reasonable and strange. These issues should be reexplained and corrected. Lastly, is it fair that the Central Committee issues decisions to put us under the command of the commander in chief together with Abu Hajim and Al-Haj Isma'il? Is it fair that it issues decisions to freeze our activity? . . .

Khalid al-Hasan: On the Dissident Rebellion (May 27, 1983)*

. . . Frankly and without exaggerating or underestimating what has been described as a rebellion, mutiny, or split within the Fatah movement, we

* Excerpts from an interview with Fatah Central Committee member Khalid al-Hasan in *Al-Hawadith* (London).

ask: What did really happen, what were its causes, and what repercussions is it likely to have?

Answer: The group involved, including Abu Musa, Qadri, Abu Salih, and others, originally held political views characterized by rejection of the Fez resolutions and other policies. . . . This group, even before Fez, adopted certain political attitudes based on an idealistic rejection of everything or on conditional approval of many things. For example, Brother Abu Salih said that he would support the Fez summit [plan] if it included setting up a Palestinian state and would oppose it if it did not. So, fundamentally, this group has been adopting a certain political attitude for years. We could say that this attitude began to crystallize after the September events, and it has been applied to Jordan and to the recent Fez resolutions. The group included Naji 'Allush, Abu Nidal, and many others. Some of them left the movement and some continued to work within its framework. Even at the recent PNC meetings in Algiers, Abu Musa adopted certain attitudes which stemmed from a comprehensive theory which everyone wished it was possible to implement, even partially. The reason behind the declarations made in Al-Biqa' was certain military organizational decisions made with the approval of the Military Council. They believe that some of these decisions should not have been made, especially the appointment of Abu Hajim as officer in charge of the Al-Biqa' area and Al-Haj Isma'il as officer in charge of the north. Their position developed into a mutiny in the sense that they rejected the new military organizational steps. It was not made on political grounds, although the political aspect later came into it.

As far as discipline is concerned, this matter is serious. Democracy may be required on such matters, but at the level of the Central Committee, not the level of military officers. . . . That is the declared principle of the matter. The other fact is that, very regrettably, Brother Abu Salih overstepped the mark in Fatah's democracy when he extended a hand for funds from a source outside Fatah and cooperated with two Arab states. . . . That money was paid before the PNC conference and it was agreed that five issues would be used to cause a split. They included rejection of the Fez summit, rejection of agreement with Jordan, and rejection of the Reagan initiative. There was no problem there, but to give the dissension a national character they were to use these points and, in the event of failure, they were to raise the issue of the dialogue with Israeli democratic forces. . . .

Another issue had also been raised to cause disunity. That issue was the differences with Syria. . . . I believe that national unity is not unity of the organizations but rather unity of the people behind the leadership and the goals. This does in fact exist because the Palestinian people are united regardless of whether there is a leadership or not. It was the Palestinian people, not an organization or a leadership, who foiled the settlement plots in the fifties. This matter is too great to be undermined. The people are much more united than the organizations. The organizational numbers do not broadly and accurately reflect the real attitudes of the people. One organization or another may have some support here or there, but Abu 'Ammar's leadership is unquestionable and Fatah's political line represents the mainstream. That is why I consider agreement among the organizations to be agreement among the instruments of work—and not national unity because unity is there. Our problem with the unity of the instruments is that some of them are not Palestinian, even though they are identified as such, because they do not take Palestinian orders. National unity or front relations under the National Charter, and in fact under any front regulations anywhere in the world, means agreement on a minimum plan of action with the minority accepting the views of the majority. It is very regrettable that the minority does not accept the opinion of the majority. . . .

Part VI

The Approach of Peace

Several factors contributed to the breakthrough to Arab-Israeli peace in the 1990s. These included the long-term evolution of Arab politics toward concluding that war was futile, compromise was inevitable, Israel was not going to be destroyed, and that continuing the conflict damaged both Arab state and Palestinian interests. The perception of these new conditions permitted a shift in Israeli policies as well. Global changes—including the USSR's collapse, the Cold War's end, and the United States' emergence as the world's sole superpower—made vital contributions to the altered situation.

In this period, the Arab-Israeli peace process went through three stages. First, between 1982 and 1987 came a series of efforts to have Jordan take the lead in negotiating with Israel as the PLO's senior partner under various arrangements. These bids failed and conditions were further altered by the Palestinian uprising in the West Bank and Gaza, the intifada, beginning in December 1987.

This rebellion put pressure on both Israel and the PLO toward new ways to find a negotiated solution. The results included revisions in PLO policy, a U.S.–PLO dialogue, and a series of peace and procedural plans put forward by all sides. By early 1990, however, it was clear that the gaps were still too wide to bridge.

The Iraqi invasion of Kuwait in August 1990 created a

new regional crisis pushing aside the Arab-Israeli conflict. But Iraq's defeat by a U.S.–led coalition in 1991 and concurrent global shifts ended by enhancing chances for progress. The PLO's backing for Iraq weakened that organization and cost it Arab state support, while the intifada by itself was unable to force Israel's capitulation. Arab governments saw that continued conflict with Israel was increasingly irrelevant and even dangerous to themselves. Israel's 1992 elections produced a new government favoring territorial concessions in exchange for peace.

These developments set the scene for the third period, opened by the 1991 Madrid conference, of direct negotiations between Israel and both the Arab states and the Palestinians. Secret contacts between Israel and the PLO led to their Declaration of Principles accord, signed in September 1993, which provided a detailed framework for new arrangements—a PLO-led governing authority was established in the West Bank and Gaza Strip—and the conclusion of peace between them.

This was followed by additional implementing agreements: the March 1994 Cairo agreement laying the basis for implementing the Israel-PLO Declaration of Principles, a July 1994 Israel-Jordan accord (the Washington agreement) ending their state of belligerency and an October 1994 peace treaty. Israel-Syria negotiations continued while a number of moderate Arab states moved toward normalizing relations with Israel. The awarding of the Nobel Peace Prize jointly to PLO and Palestinian Authority Chairman Yasir Arafat, Israeli Prime Minister Yitzhak Rabin, and Foreign Minister Shimon Peres symbolized that the peace process which—while still incomplete—had made much progress toward ending the Arab-Israeli conflict.

King Hussein: Speech to the Palestine National Council (November 22, 1984)

Brothers and sisters, the convocation of your council in Amman represents the unity of your will and the will of your people in the occupied homeland and elsewhere. It also represents the cohesion of the efforts and wills of two fraternal peoples, which have been demonstrated by their confrontation of the common challenge and danger. It is a natural return to what should and would continue to be. The Jordanian people have, more than and before anyone else, shared with the Palestinian people their sorrows, sufferings, and sacrifices and also carried with them their hope, determination, and resolution to regain their legitimate national rights on the land of Palestine. Jordan, and with it my family, have more than and before anyone else stood by the Palestinian people in confronting the Zionist danger in the early days just as we are confronting it today while it is at its peak. We are not saying this in order to outbid, maneuver, or seek praise, but to affirm an objective fact that has been made evident by actual participation in facing the common danger. . . .

I personally opened the first session of the PNC on May 28, 1964 in Jerusalem. I told your brother representatives of the Palestinian people in that meeting, among other things, that your convention represented a unique, historic event in the entire history of the disaster. I said that it was the first meeting of the heroic struggler Palestinian people despite all the designs to scatter them to all the four corners of the globe. So you can see from the historical facts that we—as a Hashemite family and a country—have never disavowed, God forbid, the Palestinian identity and aspirations or tried to dominate Palestine and its people.

Brothers and sisters: Following Israel's occupation of the West Bank in 1967, we in Jordan and our brothers in Egypt devoted our efforts to achieving two objectives: first, rebuilding our Armed Forces which were destroyed by the war; and second, working politically for the sake of regaining the territory that was occupied by force. We cooperated with sister Egypt in issuing UN Security Council Resolution 242 which formed the basis of our political actions. The late leader President Jamal 'Abd al-Nasir urged me during our first meeting after the June war to do anything and exert every effort to regain the occupied territory. I did not need anyone to tell me to do that. By God, I have never showed cowardice and will not show cowardice when it comes to defending Jerusalem and Palestine. I have done all I could with God's help. I have spared no effort and pursued every course.

In the meantime, however, the PLO emerged as an effective party in the Palestinian arena. Its growth produced a natural tendency among the Palestinian people to manifest their national identity on their land. Their effort to regain the occupied territory was marred by doubts about the possibility of establishing their national authority on the land of Palestine once Jordan had regained the West Bank. A clear Palestinian trend evolved to relieve Jordan of this responsibility. This trend was nourished by an illusion that the restoration of the territory was around the corner. It was also nourished by all those who considered the Jordanian-Palestinian relationship as committing all Arabs equally to the fate of the Palestine question and to the duty of saving it, and, consequently, everyone who preferred to place the direct and primary responsibility on the Palestinian people, thereby placing the Arabs in the second rank. [sentence as heard] This was what we resisted as much as we could and considered as a relinquishment of a sacred duty at a time which did not permit such a thing. One could have imagined such a trend, if it had come before the entry of the Arab armies into the land of Palestine in 1984. But for this trend to come after all of the Palestinian territory had fallen to Israel, then it cannot but be construed as an attempt to let down the Palestinian people.

As a result of this, a secret conflict began between Jordan and the PLO. Because of the confused vision, this conflict led to a collision that resulted in regrettable incidents. We in Jordan faced a dilemma. If we capitulated to this approach, we would have improved the position of the enemy, who employed any pretext, however flimsy, in order to deceive world public opinion, strengthen its false claims, and annex the occupied territory. If we had continued our political work as we began it following the 1967 war, without paying attention to our Palestinian brothers' fear, our brothers' doubts concerning our aims would have increased. . . .

Brother and sister PNC members, the years go by, more than 17 years have passed, and the West Bank and Gaza Strip are still under occupation. The enemy continues to plan and implement. Jerusalem remains steadfast, patiently moaning whenever a Jewish castle is built upon it. The Al-Aqsa Mosque and the Dome of the Rock are being threatened with demolition and destruction and declared open to everyone by the delusions and thoughts of the fanatic. The holy and cherished land is being swallowed up every day through confiscation and appropriation or on the pretext of security and planning. The national character of the Palestinian economy is obliterated after becoming part of Israel's economy.

The future is just like the present, shrouded with doubt, anxiety, and uncertainty. As for the kinfolk, may God help them; despite every form of institutionalized pressure against them they remain steadfast. How long will we watch as the enemy exploits the time by greedily swallowing up another part of the remaining land every day while we wildly and thoughtlessly waste the time in arguments and vituperation. How long shall we heed those among us who say: Leave it for future generations. Is this not a clear abdication of responsibility? Is each generation not responsible for the era in which it lives? What makes them believe that the circumstances of future generations will be more conducive to achieving what they are avoiding to achieve? Can they stop time and progress for the enemy, and keep time and progress moving for themselves? What wisdom or morality is there in leaving future generations a heavy legacy more likely to grow than recede? Will the Palestinians, who are lost and suffering in the occupied land, accept such arguments when they know better than anyone else the meaning of giving the enemy more time and the impact of this on their existence and future?

The least that can be said of this argument is that it is escape from responsibility. The least that can be said of the advocates of this argument is that they are those who believe that the world is synonymous with their own existence. This is not the way the world works. Each generation has its own responsibilities. The justifications of the existence of any ruler depends on the wise and courageous fulfillment of his responsibilities and the sincere and vigorous implementation of his duties. If time has any meaning it is in properly using it and not in suspending it. . . .

Perhaps you share with me the view that the picture is bleak, and, consequently, requires a new outlook and course. The new outlook must necessarily start with defining future action. Perhaps the natural starting point is to emphasize the special relationship between Jordan and Palestine—a relationship forged by the purely objective factors of history, geography, and demography which have placed the two fraternal countries and peoples since the turn of the century in the same boat of suffering, hope, interest, harm, history, and destiny.

The special quality of our relationship is not a whimsical description that we have given to ourselves, but is a scientific fact which has made the Palestine question a central daily concern in our life and the pivot of our defense, foreign, and development policies. If the Palestine question is one of the first priorities of our brothers' foreign and defense policies, to us and to you the Palestine question is our top priority. Therefore, Palestine was never a political tool which we used to achieve our national or selfish aims. Palestine embraces Jerusalem, the cradle of Jesus, may peace be upon him; the place from which Muhammad, may peace be upon him, ascended to the heavens; the playground of Al-Shafi'i [founder of one of the 4 orthodox Islamic schools]; the battlefield of Salah al-Din; the resting place of Husayn ibn 'Ali; and the martyrs' ladder to glory. It is also the invaders' threshold to Jordan, just as Jordan is the conquest [fath] gateway to Palestine. Defending Palestine means defending Jordan and vice versa. This is the special relationship which has governed and will continue to govern our Jordanian policy. This is the distinguished policy which the enemy has tried to break up in order to achieve his designs. Some people tried to distort this relationship by giving it attributions it does not possess and that serve the tendency of one wing to dominate another.

This is the relationship within whose framework the first Palestinian conference was held 20 years ago and under whose canopy your council's 17th session is held in Amman today. This special relationship, brothers and sisters, encourages me to speak to you frankly. In order to eliminate any doubts about what I am going to say, I would like to affirm right from the beginning that nothing has been proposed to us in the efforts for a political settlement of the Palestine question. What I will say represents our opinion on the basis of our experience and analysis of the reality, possibilities, and circumstances. I am encouraged in this by the fact that you, too, are experienced people.

I hope that my speech will not be understood to mean that I, God forbid, will interfere in your affairs. The decision is yours. Jordan will not speak on your behalf, although it will remain fully ready to face its fate with you, because our fate is interconnected with yours. If the future seems too dark, as I have said, it is because one of the causes that made it so is that the special relationship binding Jordan with Palestine was eliminated from the Arab and Palestinian action. This has diverted the general effort from its correct course and has expended it in the wrong field.

If matters seem difficult now, it is because of the time we have wasted in differences, disputes, and vituperation. Although we have exerted sincere efforts to rectify matters, the Arab reality prevented us from achieving our aims. We thus enabled the enemy to exploit time in order to change reality on the land of Palestine in its favor. We failed to combine the justice of our cause with our financial and strategic resources in order to curtail the effect of the absolute U.S. support for Israel. We made our regional concerns dominate our pan-Arab responsibilities. All this has led to our present disunity and squandering of our resources.

Brothers and sisters, because we will be harmed the most as a result of the continuation of the present state of affairs, we shoulder the greatest responsibility for rectifying this situation. So far, we have succeeded in foiling attempts to paralyze our role and yours. Experience taught us to renounce immobility, which is no less harmful to your role than the attempts to undermine your legitimacy. Dealing with an issue like the Palestinian issue demands a great amount of flexibility and dynamism that is capable of adapting to circumstances and facing the challenges with the aim of reaching a clear aim—namely, liberating the land and freeing our kinfolk and sacred places. It is stagnation to be satisfied with saying: I want this or nothing. Even adopted positions need revision from time to time and a new look in light of changes and developments.

Dealing with the world necessitates permanent flexibility and dynamism. Let us remember that slogans will not be raised if they become chains which tie those who raise them and prevent them from moving and maneuvering. Principles would not have been embraced had they not been beacons of light to lead the way during work.

Let us be frank with you, brothers, about your sacred cause, which concerns us as much as it concerns you, and the ramifications of which affect us as much as they affect you. In general, the international stand believes that it is possible to regain the occupied territory through a Jordanian-Palestinian formula which gives both sides certain commitments the world considers essential for achieving a just and balanced peaceful settlement. If you are convinced of this option, notwithstanding our bonds as to families as well as the common destiny and common cause that unite us, we are ready to proceed together on this path and to present the world with a joint initiative for which we will rally backing and support.

However, if you believe that the PLO can proceed alone, we will tell you to go ahead, with God's blessing. And we will give you our backing and support. The decision will be first and last yours. And we will respect it, whatever the case. This is because it stems from your esteemed council, which represents the Palestinian people. [applause]

Brothers, if you decide to take the first option—the Jordanian-Palestinian option—then allow me to present to you our idea of how to get out of the present situation and into the arena of effective, rejuvenating action. The existing conditions in the Palestinian, Arab, and international arenas prompt us to adhere to Security Council Resolution 242 as a basis for a just, peaceful settlement. The principle of territory in exchange for peace is our guideline for any initiative we may present to the world. This principle is not a precondition, but the framework through which the negotiations would be held. Therefore, it is not negotiable.

The negotiations which we consider essential within the framework of an international conference for peace would revolve around the ways and means and the adquate guarantees for achieving the principle of territory in exchange for peace. As for the international conference, it shall be held under the supervision of the United Nations with the participation of the permanent member states of the UN Security Council and all the parties to the dispute. The PLO shall attend it on an equal basis with the other parties, because it is the party authorized to speak about the most serious and important dimension in the Middle East crisis—namely, the Palestinian dimension.

As for the question of regulating the Jordanian-Palestinian relationship, it is the primary responsibility of the Jordanian and Palestinian peoples.

No one has the right to determine this relationship on their behalf or to interfere in it, be he enemy, brother, or friend. This is because this would be a detraction from Jordan's sovereignty and open interference in the Palestinian people's right to determine their own destiny. Furthermore, involving this issue in the efforts to regain the territory would enable the enemy to obstruct any serious effort to save this territory from the existing occupation and gradual annexation.

In our opinion, these general outlines can form the overall framework for a Jordanian-Palestinian initiative which we can present to the Arabs so that they can support it under the Fes summit resolutions. Then, we and our Arab brothers would present it to the world, giving it all our support. This would continue until the circle of support for this initiative expands to include the entire influential world. This is our own idea. We do not oblige you to accept it, and we do not impose it on you. The decision is yours, and the responsibility is yours. We are only presenting it to you for the viewpoint of our participation with you in the two states of security and danger, and benefit and harm. We are ready to do anything for the sake of your cause—which is our cause—except concluding a unilateral peace. . . .

Jordan–PLO: Joint Communiqué (February 11, 1985)

Emanating from the spirit of the Fez summit resolution, approved by Arab states, and from United Nations resolutions relating to the Palestinian question,

In Accordance with international legitimacy, and

Deriving from a common understanding on the establishment of a special relations between the Jordan and Palestinian peoples,

The Government of the Hashemite Kingdom of Jordan and the Palestine Liberation Organization have agreed to move together toward the achievement of a peaceful and just settlement of the Middle East crisis and the termination of Israeli occupation of the Occupied Arab Territories, including Jerusalem, on the basis of the following principles:

1. Total withdrawal from the territories occupied in 1967 for comprehensive peace as established in United Nations and Security Council resolutions.

2. Right of self-determination for the Palestinian people:

Palestinians will exercise their inalienable right of self-determination when Jordaninans and Palestinians will be able to do so within the context of the formation of the proposed confederated Arab States of Jordan and Palestine.

3. Resolution of the problem of the Palestinian refugees in accordance with United Nations resolutions.

4. Resolution of the Palestinian question in all its aspects.

5. And on these bases, peace negotiations will be conducted under the auspices of an International Conference in which the five permanent members of the Security Council and all the parties to the conflict will participate, including the Palestine Liberation Organization, the sole legitimate representative of the Palestinian people, within a joint delegation (joint Jordanian-Palestinian delegation).

King Hussein: Ending the Jordan–PLO Initiative (February 19, 1986)

In the past few days, Amman has been the center of attention for much of the world, drawing media people and journalists from all quarters. News coming out of Amman was reported on the front pages of world newspapers and occupied a prominent place in agency reports and news bulletins. But the content of these reports reflected mere speculation or expectations on the possible outcome of discussions held with us and with leading officials of our government by the Palestinian leadership while in Amman. Amman, along with concerned world circles, went through a period of expectation, but we preferred not to issue any declarations or communiques until matters under intensive discussion, whether between us and the Palestinian leadership or among its own members, became clearer.

Now that a measure of clarity has become apparent, I consider it my duty as well as my responsibility towards you, being in the thick of events and in the eye of the hurricane, to appraise you of the most recent phase of political endeavor with regard to our foremost cause: Palestine, its land, its holy places, its people, and their identity. . . .

For a variety of reasons, there is a need for a thorough airing of this question. The shared destiny of Jordan and Palestine requires it. So does the time factor, in view of the fact that the West Bank, the Gaza Strip, and the Golan Heights have been occupied for close to 19 years. The situation is further aggravated by prolonged failure to find a solution and by the growing threat to the Palestinians' true identity resulting from the gradual displacement of the Palestinian people. One also has to consider ramifications with regard to Jordan, the region, and the world. In the final analysis, a people without its land is nothing more than a disjointed community.

Identity without a homeland is but a reservoir of sad memories. Our aim should be the land itself. Now, as at the turn of the century, the

Palestinian cause is inseparable from the Palestinian land, which today is the occupied West Bank and Gaza Strip. This being the case, the Palestinian people, steadfast on Palestinian territory, are our primary concern. For a different reason, they are also the primary concern of the enemy. They are the major obstacle to the advancement of expansionist Zionist programs. Their legitimate resistance poses an overt challenge to claims by Israel and its friends and supporters, be they states or communities, that Israel is a free and democratic society, and places it as an open test within the sight and hearing of the world.

Brothers and sisters, if most of us have so far failed to grasp these rudimentary facts, the enemy has not. It is on the basis of these facts that Israel's aims and policies were formulated from the very beginning: to occupy the land of Palestine and expand the territory of Israel. The Israeli leadership's motives were two-fold. Expanding Israeli territory, through occupation of Palestinian and other neighboring Arab lands, would fulfill one of Zionism's cherished aims while at the same time achieving, from their point of view, a security need arising more from psychological considerations than from those of space, distance, and topography, which Israel attempts to highlight whenever the security issue is raised. . . .

While it is true that Lebanon, Syria, Jordan, and Egypt share a geographical contiguity with Israel, Jordan is the prime target of Israel's step-by-step policy. Thus, the distinctive relationship between Jordan and Palestine is not a question we take lightly. We bring it up in order to draw attention to objective facts and conditions which the enemy attempts to exploit for the purpose of implementing its expansionist policy at the expense of the Jordanian and Palestinian peoples. The common links between the two peoples are not only a matter of shared history, experience, culture, economy, and social structure, but also a question of destiny. They represent a confluence of interest as well as of harm. . . .

The Palestinian people in the occupied territories are weak without the PLO. By the same token, the Palestinian people and the PLO, which represents its aspirations, hopes and interests, are weaker without Jordan, and all three are weaker without the Arab nation as a whole. This has been our vision in all our endeavors. The components are as clear as the sun; and the position we occupy vis-à-vis the Palestinian issue on the one hand, and the Arab world on the other, provides us with no alternative vision. In Jordan we stand in two circles at once: one representing the Palestine tragedy and the other residing in national commitment. This has dictated our position on direct confrontation with Israel on military and political levels.

One facet of our conflict with Israel perhaps lies in the fact that Israel is attempting to dislodge us from the circle of national commitment into the sphere of tragedy. On our part, we are resisting this with all our might, attempting in the process to endow the circle of commitment with content which is both practical and effective. National commitment is not a one-way street, nor is it a passive or negative stance. Armed with true content, it leads to proper preparation and action. If national commitment is taken to mean a state of inaction in regard to declared positions and is characterized by fatalism, dependence, or expectancy of what lies in store, this would mean only one thing to us; acquiescence in the fait accompli as well as a willing acceptance of the loss of what remains of Palestinian land and of the resulting destructive consequences allowing greater room for expansionist Zionist designs.

It is for this reason, dear brothers, that Jordan had to act and must continue to act. We cannot possibly close down borders and deal with the issue as separate from us. Experience has shown that inaction leads to erosion in positions, as well as on the ground. The state of no war–no peace which has been imposed on us is a salient manifestation of this inaction. We must break out of its grasp. We must absolutely assert that the suffocation resulting from giving in to the state of no war–no peace is as reprehensible as the suicide arising from action leading to the relinquishing of rights. As we move towards peace, we reject the latter proposition as strongly as we do the former. . . .

The significance of setting up the PLO as a way station was that the Arab governments at the time wished to reaffirm that the Palestinian issue was an Arab issue while the Palestinian people had a say and a role to play in the struggle for liberation.

This decision represented the first turning point in the Arab position between 1947 and 1964. In other words, the PLO was established not with the purpose of giving the Palestinians an exclusive say, but to include the PLO, in its capacity as a representative of the Palestinian people, in Arab positions and action vis-à-vis the Palestine issue—as a means of keeping it alive. This was confirmed in the years immediately following the establishment of the PLO, when it had no significant weight in matters pertaining to the Palestine issue, since the Arab states continued to hold the reins and make decisions at will. The PLO itself was a tool used by this or that Arab state on the basis of its political positions, whether at the Arab or international levels. When the June war erupted, the PLO was still a form almost devoid of any real content.

But in the wake of the June war, Palestinian resistance to Israeli occupation experienced rapid growth, with the result that form and content became one and the PLO came to embody the resistance to occupation and the struggle for the rights of the Palestinian Arabs. Thus, the PLO rejected Security Council Resolution 242 because it dealt only with occupied Palestinian territory and not with the legitimate national rights of the Palestinian people. Because of our keen awareness of Israel's expansionist aims, it was natural that we should accord priority to restoring the territories occupied by Israel through war. Likewise, because of our sincere commitment to the restoration of the legitimate national rights of the Palestinians, we tried, along with Egypt, to persuade the PLO to separate the two objectives of our political action in the international arena. This separation would call for an attempt by the Arab states, whose territories had been occupied through war and were the subject of Resolution 242, to ensure Israeli withdrawal from these territories, while the PLO would continue to fulfill its role of representing the Palestinian people in their struggle for legitimate national rights above and beyond the mere withdrawal of Israel from the occupied territories.

The PLO, however, rejected this line of thinking, as it had rejected Resolution 242, and proceeded to make this dual rejection a basis for its political stand on the Arab and world scenes. It also became the basis of its dealings with Jordan in particular, on the grounds of the following suspicions. First: There was the probability that Jordan might succeed in restoring the West Bank by virtue of its good relations with the West, which had influence over Israel. Second: Jordan had territorial ambitions in the West Bank. Third: As long as the possibility of Jordan's restoration of the West Bank existed, who would guarantee that Jordan would relinquish the territory thus restored to the PLO?

It is to be noted from this position, which is based on suspicion, that, at the time, the PLO was not fully aware of a basic fact emphasized by us and borne out by events, namely that Israel gave the utmost priority to territorial gain. It was also evident that the PLO based its dealings with Jordan on suspicion rather than trust. . . .

On November 22, 1984, I opened the 17th session of the PNC by delivering a speech which contained our assessment of prevailing Palestinian conditions and our conclusion that we needed to move politically outside the status quo of no peace-no war, which only helped to advance expansionist Zionist designs and posed serious dangers to the Palestinian issue, the Palestinian people, and Palestinian land, as well as a consequent threat to Jordan's national security. We proposed to the PNC members our view of future cooperation, should the PLO decide to work with Jordan to reach a joint Jordanian-Palestinian formula. . . .

In January 1985, we received the reply that the PLO Executive Committee had chosen to work with us on our proposal for joint political action. We started our consultations with 'Arafat's envoys on the third general outline—the Jordanian-Palestinian formula—since this formula constituted the base from which we were to move on the Arab and international arenas to convene an international peace conference.

In February 1985, 'Arafat, accompanied by other members of the Palestinian leadership, arrived in Amman. An expanded meeting was held in Al-Nadwah Palace which was concluded by the signing of the Jordanian-Palestinian agreement, known as the 11 February Accord. This accord incorporated the following principles:

1. Territory in return for peace as established in UN and Security Council resolutions.

2. The right of self-determination for the Palestinian people:
Palestinians will exercise their inalienable right of self-determination when it becomes possible to do so within the context of the formation of the proposed confederated Arab states of Jordan and Palestine.

3. Resolution of the problem of Palestinian refugees in accordance with UN resolutions.

4. Resolution of all aspects of the Palestine question.

5. On this basis, peace negotiations will be conducted under the auspices of an international conference in which the five permanent members of the Security Council and all parties involved in the conflict will participate, including the PLO, the sole legitimate representative of the Palestinian people, within a joint delegation—a joint Jordanian-Palestinian delegation. . . .

The accord became a mover for the peace process because of the principles it contained. These were:

1. The accord's affirmation of a peaceful resolution to the conflict in accordance with the UN Charter.

2. The accord's conformity with the principles of the Arab Peace Plan, derived from United Nations resolutions concerning the Arab-Israeli conflict in general and the Palestinian problem in particular.

3. The agreement between Jordan and the PLO, the sole legitimate representative of the Palestinian people, to form a confederation between Jordan and Palestine.

This last item, while it reflects the objective considerations which require close institutional links between Jordan and a free Palestine to the mutual benefit of their peoples and the Arab nation at large, provides the key, or mechanism, to the peace process for two main reasons:

First, it justifies PLO participation in the proposed international conference within a joint Jordanian-Palestinian delegation. Since confederation is the ultimate objective, why not have the two parties concerned assume one of the confederation's functions before it is established as a reality on the ground, particularly since this function allows for the participation of the PLO in the international conference which in the past decade has posed one of the most difficult obstacles in convening an international peace conference?

Second, it lays the foundations for a responsible role for the PLO in realizing and safeguarding a just settlement through its links with Jordan, the sovereign state which enjoys credible international standing due to its serious and sincere efforts to achieve peace. . . .

Dear brethren, after signing the 11 February accord and the agreement of the PLO Executive Committee, which was empowered by the PNC to arrive at a joint formula with Jordan, we embarked with the Palestinian leadership upon drawing up a plan for our proposed action. Two objectives were defined for this purpose:

1. To rally international support for the convening of an international peace conference, to be attended by the five permanent members of the Security Council and all parties involved in the conflict. This conference would be convened under the auspices of the United Nations and called for by the UN secretary general.

2. To ensure that an invitation will be extended to the PLO, representing the Palestinian people, to attend the conference within a joint Jordanian-Palestinian delegation. . . .

We agree with the Palestinian leadership on the following procedures for joint action:

1. We asked the U.S. Administration to start a dialogue with a joint Jordanian-Palestinian delegation composed of Jordanian Government officials and members chosen by the PLO.

2. After this dialogue, the PLO would declare its acceptance of UN Security Council Resolutions 242 and 338.

3. If this took place, the United States would no longer be bound by its previous position not to conduct any talks with the PLO before the latter's acceptance of the two pertinent Security Council resolutions. Thus, the United States would recognize the PLO and a meeting between U.S. officials and members of the PLO could be held in Washington to discuss the issue of a peaceful settlement and relations between them would be normalized.

4. As a result of the normalization of U.S.-Palestinian relations a major political obstacle blocking the Arab Peace Plan, which gave an important role to the PLO, would have been removed. Arab efforts could then be channeled to pursue the efforts with the United States and other countries to convene an international peace conference.

After agreeing on this procedure with the Palestinian leadership, we accordingly contacted the officials in the U.S. Administration at the end of March 1985 and presented them with the idea of meeting a joint delegation in preparation for the next two steps which would follow as a result of the meeting.

In early April 1985, we received the U.S. reply which, in principle, accepted this proposal provided that the Palestinian members of the joint delegation were not leading members of the PLO or any fedayeen organization.

We consulted with the Palestinian leadership, which provided us with the names of three candidates. The Americans refused them because they did not meet their criteria and asked that we provide them with the names of others who did.

In May 1985, we met with the U.S. secretary of state in Qaba, who reiterated the administration's position regarding the subject of the names. However, he did not exclude those who were members of the PNC.

The U.S. side expressed its government's doubts about the PLO's intentions and its government's fears that if the suggested meeting were to take place between a U.S. official and a joint Jordanian-Palestinian delegation—a meeting after that would not be followed by PLO's acceptance of Security Council Resolutions 242 and 338—the PLO would obtain a political weapon as a result of its member's meeting with an American official. The U.S. Government would then be left to face criticism and political troubles resulting from this in the U.S. arena. Thus, the serious political efforts would end at that point.

Our prime minister conveyed this recent U.S. stand to Yasir 'Arafat in a meeting held at the Prime Ministry on 18 May 1985. At that time, we were preparing for a visit to Washington. In order to remove the U.S. fears, the prime minister agreed with Yasir 'Arafat on the text of a press statement which we would make at the end of our talks with the U.S. President.

The statement which I made at the White House garden on 29 May 1985 says: I also asserted to President Reagan that, on the basis of the Jordanian agreement with the PLO signed on 11 February, as a result of the talks which I recently held with the PLO, and in view of our sincere desire to achieve peace, we are determined to negotiate to achieve a peaceful settlement within the framework of an international conference on the basis of the related UN resolutions, including Security Council Resolutions 242 and 338.

The U.S. officials affirmed, during my talks in Washington, their position regarding Palestinian participation in the joint delegation. They limited the number to four, two from the occupied territories and two from the outside. They requested that we provide them with these names in advance and as soon as possible so that the U.S. Administration could make its decision at the appropriate time.

Upon our return to Amman in June 1985, we conveyed to the Palestinian leadership our discussions in Washington. They in turn accepted this proposal and promised to provide us with the names of the candidates as soon as possible. We waited until 11 July 1985, when some names were provided to us. We were then told that a meeting of the PLO Executive Committee and the Fatah Central Committee had discussed this subject and had agreed upon the names of the candidates.

On 12 July 1985, we relayed a list of seven names to the U.S. Administration and waited for the administration to inform us of its approval of four of the names on that list. We agreed that no public announcement should be made on this issue. But a few days later, we were surprised when the world press began to discuss those names. Suddenly the issue turned into a U.S. political issue. The press began to discuss it and the Zionist lobby activated influential political institutions in opposition to it, culminating in pressure on the U.S. Administration to justify, defend, and finally retract its position. As a result, we received American approval of only two names from the list, instead of four: one from the West Bank and the other from the Gaza Strip. After inquiries we were told by U.S. officials that the administration was still not sure that the PLO would fulfill the second phase of the agreed scenario, namely, to accept Security Council Resolutions 242 and 338.

On 15 August 1985, a meeting was held at our prime minister's residence in Amman attended by the prime minister, the chief of the Royal Hashemite Court, the minister of the court and the foreign minister from the Jordanian side, and Yasir 'Arafat, accompanied by Khalil al-Wazir, Abd al-Razzaq al-Yahya and Muhammad Milhim from the Palestinian side. During that meeting, the prime minister again asked 'Arafat whether he was clear on the method of proceeding, particularly with regard to the second phase—PLO readiness to accept Security Council Resolutions 242 and 338. 'Arafat reaffirmed his acceptance of all steps and arrangements agreed upon between us, including the PLO's readiness to accept the abovementioned resolutions.

In light of 'Arafat's reply, we informed the U.S. Administration that the suspicions it had on this subject were not justified and that we were awaiting their positive reply concerning the date of the meeting between U.S. officials and a joint Jordanian-Palestinian delegation.

On 7 September 1985, we received the U.S. reply, which said that it was not possible to hold the meeting, thus terminating this scenario before the first step, originally expected in June, was taken. This came at the time we were preparing for a visit to New York to celebrate the 40th anniversary of the United Nations, and to Washington to discuss bilateral issues and the peace process with the U.S. Administration.

Assessment of the situation, prior to the visit, led us to believe that we could pursue our dialogue with the United States by concentrating this time on the second phase of the process, the international conference, since not much progress had been achieved on the issue of Palestinian representation. Our reading of the U.S. position led us to believe that further discussions could take place on that other issue, which was last discussed in May 1985. I mentioned earlier that from the beginning our dialogue with the Americans had dealt with two issues seperately: Palestinian representation and the international conference, with emphasis on the subject of Palestinian representation.

I will now turn to our efforts on the second issue, the convening of an international conference.

In May 1985, in our discussions with the U.S. Administration in Washington, we raised the issue of convening such a conference because we considered it to be the venue for all parties concerned to meet, including the PLO. The U.S. position was a flat rejection of an international conference. Instead, the United States proposed that, after the PLO was brought into the peace talks, a meeting should be set up between Israel and a joint Jordanian-Palestinian delegation, under the auspices of the United States, to be held in a U.S. city. Upon learning this, we decided to cut our visit short and reaffirmed to them our definite and unequivocal rejection of seeking a unilateral approach similar to that of Camp David in the negotiations.

The U.S. Administration then changed its position and proposed that the talks could be held at the United Nations in Geneva. Once again, we informed the U.S. Administration that we rejected this proposal, like the one before it, as we did not see that the problem was one of where the talks should be held. We reiterated that Jordan's unwavering position was that it sought to reach a comprehensive settlement through the convening of an international conference attended by all the parties to the conflict, including the permanent members of the Security Council. As a result, the U.S. Administration reconsidered its proposal and promised to seriously ponder the issue of convening an international conference. We accepted this and continued our discussions concerning the issue of Palestinian representation.

During talks in Washington in October 1985, we again raised the issue of an international conference after having proposed it to the administration prior to our departure for the United States. Meetings were held between Jordanian and U.S. officials in Washington. The United States submitted a proposal concerning the international conference, which, after careful examination, seemed to suggest a conference in name only. We on the other hand insisted that the conference should have clear powers.

Among the various U.S. suggestions was the inclusion of the Soviet Union in the conference only after it restored diplomatic relations with Israel, because this was an Israeli condition. We argued for the rejection of this approach for the following reasons:

1. An international conference without the participation of the Soviet Union would be a flawed conference.

2. If the reason to exclude the Soviet Union from the conference was that it had no diplomatic relations with Israel, which is a party to the conflict, the United States on its part does not recognize the PLO, which is equally a party to the conflict. Thus, in this regard, the Soviet Union and the United States were in the same position.

3. It would be futile to plan seriously to convene an international peace conference if any party had the right to place conditions on who could attend. This applies to the five permanent members of the Security Council as well as the parties involved in the conflict. Therefore, it was imperative that an invitation be extended to Syria, the PLO, and the Soviet Union to attend the conference if the peace process was to continue and the efforts for a just and comprehensive peace were to produce fruitful results.

After extensive discussions lasting 3 days, the United States accepted the following points which we proposed:

1. The UN secretary general would issue invitations to an international conference under UN auspices.

2. Invitations to attend the conference would be issued to the permanent members of the Security Council, including the Soviet Union, in addition to the parties involved in the conflict.

3. Security Council Resolutions 242 and 338 would form the basis for the international conference.

4. The Americans held to their position of requiring acceptance by the PLO of Security Council Resolutions 242 and 338, since these formed the basis for the convening of the international conference. We agreed to this understanding on the basis that 'Arafat had himself agreed to this last August.

We continued our intensive discussions with the U.S. Administration concerning the powers of the conference and we insisted that it should not be a conference in name only, but rather that it should be one that was effective and had a clear mandate. Despite prolonged discussions, we did not reach a final understanding with the U.S. Administration regarding this issue. We agreed to continue our discussions on this central point, and considered that what we had agreed upon constituted a basis from which to proceed. While we were still in Washington, the cycle of terrorism and counterterrorism began with the Larnaca incident, followed by the Israeli raid on the PLO headquarters in Tunis. This had a negative effect on the peace process and our efforts were once again jeopardized by fears and suspicions.

Upon our return to Amman in October 1985 we informed the Palestinian leadership of what we had accomplished during our talks in Washington. We informed them that the PLO would be required to accept Security Council Resolutions 242 and 338 in order to be invited to the international conference, to accept the principle of participating in negotiations with the Government of Israel as part of a joint Jordanian-Palestinian delegation within the context of the international conference, which would be convened to establish a comprehensive settlement, and to renounce terrorism. We also informed the Palestinian leadership that our discussions with the U.S. Administration regarding the question of the mandate of the conference were still inconclusive, and that further discussions would follow. We made it clear to the Palestinian leadership that a written statement of acceptance was needed from them, while leaving them to choose the appropriate time to announce that approval. The written acceptance was needed so that we could encourage the U.S. Administration to proceed earnestly to convene an international conference and to reassure them that the PLO was anxious to participate in the peace process. We had already made clear to the U.S. Administration that Jordan would not attend the conference unless invitations were extended to the PLO, sister Syria, and all other parties involved in the conflict, because we are after a comprehensive peace.

We also promised the Palestinian leadership that their acceptance would be kept confidential and shown only to the concerned U.S. officials until they themselves decided to announce it.

On 7 November 1985, after talks with President Husni Mubarak, Yasir 'Arafat issued a statement in Cairo denouncing terrorism in all its forms, irrespective of its source. The PLO Executive Committee then held a meeting in Baghdad, and as we were not officially notified of its decisions, we awaited 'Arafat's visit to Amman to hear from him, once again, the final position of the PLO on Security Council Resolution 242.

Meanwhile, I made a private visit to London on 7 January 1986 for medical reasons. While I was there, the assistant secretary of state for Near Eastern affairs [Richard Murphy] arrived in London with a U.S. delegation. He requested to see me to continue our discussions regarding the issue of the international conference. We held two rounds of talks in London, the first attended by the prime minister and the chief of the Royal Court on 18 January, and the second, on 20 January, attended by the chief of the Royal Court. Throughout both meetings the discussions focused on defining the mandate of the international conference and the participation of the PLO, as both issues had become interwoven as a result of progress achieved in the peace process. The American position had developed to the extent of agreeing to the right of the concerned parties to submit any disagreements between them to the conference. However, we could not reach full agreement regarding the role of the conference in settling disputes among the negotiating parties.

Concerning the issue of PLO participation in the conference, the American delegation reiterated its previous position requiring that the PLO should first accept Security Council Resolution 242 in order for the United States to start a dialogue with it. The United States did not commit itself to accepting the inviting of the PLO to the conference. Our reply was that we wanted the United States to agree to have the PLO invited to participate in the conference if it accepted Security Council Resolution 242. This point became the subject of extensive discussions, during which I asked for a clear American position to relay to the PLO. The American delegation agreed to take this up at the highest level on its return to Washington.

On 21 January 1986, I returned to Amman having achieved these results on the issues of an international conference and PLO participation. On 25 January 1986, our efforts bore fruit when I received a final reply from the U.S. Administration concerning PLO participation in the international conference. Their reply came in a written commitment which said:

When it is clearly on the public record that the PLO has accepted

Resolutions 242 and 338, is prepared to negotiate peace with Israel, and has renounced terrorism, the United States accepts the fact that an invitation will be issued to the PLO to attend an international conference.

The United States would then start contacts with the Soviet Union with the purpose of having them participate, together with the other permanent members of the Security Council, in the international conference, which would be convened by the secretary general of the United Nations.

On that same day, 'Arafat arrived in Amman with a Palestinian leadership delegation. We held 4 extensive meetings in 4 days. I presided over three of these meetings. The discussion concentrated on the subject of American assurances and the PLO's position regarding those assurances. We assumed that the PLO would accept these since:

1. The assurances met the PLO's requirements.

2. They reflected a significant change in the U.S. position in favor of the PLO. The U.S. position regarding the PLO when we first started our intensive year-long dialogue had been that the United States would only enter into talks with the PLO after the latter's acceptance of Security Council Resolution 242. Now, by comparison, the present U.S. position was that it was willing to go one step beyond talking to the PLO by agreeing to have the PLO invited to the international conference.

But our brothers in the Palestinian leadership surprised us by refusing to accept Security Council Resolution 242 within this context, while acknowledging what they described as our "extraordinary effort," which had caused a significant change in the U.S. position, and which would not have been possible had it not been for the respect, credibility and trust which our country, Jordan, enjoyed in this world.

In spite of this, we continued our discussions with the PLO leadership in the hope of convincing them that their acceptance would cement a very important link in peace efforts leading to an international conference, which in the unanimous view of the Arabs and all peace-loving peoples constitutes the major venue for the establishment of a comprehensive, permanent, and just peace. It is towards the objective of convening such a conference that we have worked tirelessly for the past 9 years, but to no avail. Now that the opportunity presented itself, we hoped that it would not be wasted like other missed opportunities if we were to remain faithful to our goals of saving our people and liberating our land and Holy Places.

The answer of the brothers in the Palestinian leadership was that they wanted an amendment to the proposed text in return for acceptance of Resolution 242. The amendment would require the addition of a statement indicating the agreement of the United States to the legitimate rights of the Palestinian people, including their right to self-determination within the context of a confederation between Jordan and Palestine, as stated in the February 11 accord. We reminded the Palestinian leadership that the subject of self-determination within the context of a confederation was a matter for Jordanians and Palestinians and that no other party had anything to do with it. Nothing was to be gained from the support of this or that state as long as we ourselves were committed to this text. The important thing was to achieve withdrawal first, then to proceed with what we had agreed upon. We reminded them that this had always been our position and that it had been clear all along, starting from my opening address in Amman at the 17th PNC session, in which I referred to the proposed Jordanian-Palestinian relationship, and continuing through all our discussions to date.

We also said to them that involving the United States, or others, in this matter meant that we were voluntarily opening the door to others to interfere in our common concerns and those of a people who had a sovereign right to their land and their own decisionmaking—unless they were dealing with us on a basis of lack of confidence. But despite this, our brothers in the Palestinian leadership insisted on their position. And despite the fact that the most recent American position had satisfied PLO demands, we agreed to resume contacts with officials in Washington through the American Embassy in Amman on the evening of 27 January 1986.

The American response was as follows:

1. The February 11 accord is a Jordanian-Palestinian accord which does not involve the United States.

2. The United States supports the legitimate rights of the Palestinian people as stated in the Reagan peace initiative.

3. The PLO, like any other party, has the right to propose anything it wishes, including the right of self-determination, at the international conference.

4. For all these reasons, the United States adheres to its position.

We relayed the American response to Yasir 'Arafat during an enlarged meeting at Al-Nawdah Palace on 28 January 1986, but he insisted that we try again. We indicated to him that we had gone as far as we could with the U.S. Administration at that stage, but he insisted. Thus, we got in touch once again and the reply was still that the United States adhered to its position.

On the morning of 29 January 1986, an enlarged meeting was held at the Prime Ministry and I headed the Jordanian side. I informed Yasir 'Arafat and his party of the American position as reaffirmed to us once again. The meeting ended with a statement by Yasir 'Arafat saying that he needed to consult the Palestinian leadership. We asked him to give us the final answer on the PLO position with regard to Resolution 242 while he was still in Amman, although we had ascertained, only then, that the PLO's decision to reject Resolution 242 had been made during the meeting of the PLO leadership in Baghdad on 24 Novemebr 1985. We had not, however, officially been notified of that.

On the same evening, 29 January 1986, we received a suggestion from the U.S. Administration to the effect that the United States felt that since the PLO could not presently decide to accept Resolution 242, the PLO could wait until a time it considered appropriate. The United States felt that the peace process could still proceed with Palestinian participation from the occupied territories. The opportunity would remain available for the PLO to take part in the international conference the moment it accepted Resolution 242.

In our reply to the United States, we rejected this suggestion, indicating that this time the suggestion concerned not only the PLO but Jordan as well, since our unwavering position was: no separate settlement.

President Reagan wrote to me on 31 January 1986 explaining his inability to proceed in his efforts with Congress for the sale of sophisticated U.S. arms to Jordan. We had sought to acquire the arms since 1979 in the face of fierce Zionist opposition. I had received assurances from the President that our requirements would be met.

On the evening of the same day, the minister of the court informed Yasir 'Arafat of the latest American suggestion to proceed with the peace process without the PLO until it met the set conditions. He also informed him of our categorical refusal of this suggestion and apprised him of President Reagan's letter explaining his inability to meet Jordan's requirements.

On 5 February 1986, the American side presented a new text containing the approval by the United States to convene an international conference on the basis of Security Council Resolutions 242 and 338, including the realization of the legitimate rights of the Palestinian people. We met with Yasir 'Arafat on the same evening at Al-Nadwah Palace and we handed him the new American text. He promised to study it and at the same time gave us three differently worded texts which were the same in substance, reaffirming the same PLO position which we had heard from the start of this round of meetings.

On 6 February, Yasir 'Arafat had a meeting with our prime minister at his residence. The meeting was attended by the chief of the Royal Court and by 'Abd al-Razzaq al-Yahya and Hani al-Hasan from the Palestinian side. 'Arafat informed the prime minister that despite the positive development of the American position, recognition of the legitimate rights of the Palestinian people did not encompass the right to self-determination to which, the PLO insisted, the United States ought to give its prior approval.

On 7 February, Yasir 'Arafat left Amman still insisting on his position and on the reasons why the PLO was unable to accept Resolution 242. Hinging on this agreement, of course, was an immediate opening of a U.S.-Palestinian dialogue on the basis of which we would have continued our efforts to convene an international peace conference to which the PLO would be invited to participate as a representative of the Palestinian people.

Thus, another chapter came to an end in the search for peace. Another extremely important and significant round of Jordanian-Palestinian action was terminated—after a full year of serious and persistant efforts to transform the PLO role, referred to in the Arab Peace Plan, into a significant reality that would go beyond a mere statement of positions. It would have led to the presence and participation by the PLO in an international conference at the invitation of the UN secretary general, to represent its people and speak on their behalf with their adversary under the eyes of the world, side by side with the other parties concerned and the five permanent members of the Security Council. . . .

But if this phase of political action with the PLO has ended differently from what we had hoped for, the principles and tenets of the Jordanian-Palestinian accord will continue to embody the foundations governing relations between the Jordanian and Palestinian peoples with regard to equality of rights and obligations in facing our joint destiny.

Brothers, it has been my destiny to experience the various phases of the Palestine tragedy, as well as the results of the implementation of Zionist plans drawn up by forces which know what they want and carry out what they have planned, stage by stage. I have not seen or observed any emergence of the long-awaited Arab plan which would be capable of defending the most just cause of a brotherly and dear people who surely deserve better than their continued plight currently holds for them.

Israel-Jordan: The "London Document" (April 11, 1987)

Invitation by the UN secretary general:

The UN secretary general will send invitations to the five permanent members of the Security Council and to the parties involved in the Israeli-Arab conflict to negotiate an agreement by peaceful means based on UN resolutions 242 and 338 with the purpose of attaining comprehensive peace in the region and security for the countries in the area, and granting the Palestinian people their legitimate rights.

Decisions of the international conference:

The participants in the conference agree that the purpose of the negotiations is to attain by peaceful means an agreement about all aspects of the Palestinian problem. The conference invites the sides to set up regional bilateral committees to negotiate bilateral issues.

Nature of the agreement between Jordan and Israel: Israel and Jordan agree that:

1) the international conference will not impose a solution and will not veto any agreement reached by the sides;

2) the negotiations will be conducted in bilateral committees in a direct manner;

3) the Palestinian issue will be discussed in a meeting of the Jordanian, Palestinian, and Israeli delegations;

4) the representatives of the Palestinians will be included in the Jordanian-Palestinian delegation;

5) participation in the conference will be based on acceptance of UN resolutions 242 and 338 by the sides and the renunciation of violence and terror;

6) each committee will conduct negotiations independently;

7) other issues will be resolved through mutual agreement between Jordan and Israel.

This document of understanding is pending approval of the incumbent governments of Israel and Jordan. The content of this document will be presented and proposed to the United States.

PLO Executive Committee on the Intifada (December 1987)

The PLO Executive Committee held a joint meeting with the Higher Committee for Occupied Homeland Affairs this morning to continue discussing the current giant uprising of our people in the occupied territory—the uprising which has entered its 2d week. The conferees expressed great pride in the struggle being waged by the Palestinian masses in the cities, villages, and camps of Gaza, the West Bank, and Jerusalem. The conferees also expressed their appreciation for the militant united stand exhibited by our masses in the Galilee, the Galilee Triangle, and the Negev.

This heroic steadfastness continues in the face of the Zionist and racist fascism and the tools of repression, killing, and crime used against our Palestinian people. This continuation proves that the iron will of the people to resist and confront occupation cannot soften or retreat until we extract our national inalienable rights, particularly our right to repatriation, self-determination, and an independent state under the leadership of the PLO, the sole, legitimate representative.

Our great masses in the occupied homeland today express, through their historical uprising, through the blood of the hundreds of martyrs and wounded, through their bravery, through the vigor of our prisoners, and through the struggle of all Palestinians—men, women, youths, and children—their determination to defeat the occupation forces and to expel them from the homeland regardless of the dear sacrifice and high price.

The entire world today looks with high appreciation and respect at this second uprising of all our people in our occupied territory for the sake of freedom, dignity, and independence. This uprising affirms that all fascist Zionist crimes, terrorism, and repression cannot save the criminal occupation from its inevitable crisis and fate; that is, their defeat and removal from the sacred Palestinian land, the land of fathers and grandfathers.

The names of our cities, villages, and camps have attracted the attention of all those who love and defend freedom in our Arab homeland and the entire world. These names have become symbols and titles of bravery and heroism to the entire world. Fascist crimes are perpetrated today by the Zionist occupation forces against women and children and against our defenseless people. The hospitals and places of worship are stormed. The camps and peaceful houses are treated as a battlefield. Thousands are arrested and put into mass detention camps. Children, old men, and women are killed. Tanks, planes, and combat units attack camp streets and homes. Herds of settlers are sent to practice bloody terrorism against our people. All these are crimes perpetrated by Zionist forces. These crimes disclose to human conscience and world public opinion the reality of this racist occupation and its objectives to annihilate our people, expel them from their homeland, and destroy all aspects of their existence.

The Zionist rulers today appear before the world as the inheritors of Nazism and fascism. However, crimes and terrorism cannot defeat our people's determination and steadfastness. Such crimes and terrorism will increase the Zionists' impasse and isolation and expose the collusion of their protectors in the U.S. Administration who have always mourned in defense of human rights. The Palestinian people are killed, tortured, and arrested. Their houses, hospitals, places of worship, and holy places are destroyed. Palestinian lands are seized. Palestinian water and food are stolen. Palestinian children are assassinated. While all this happens, those who claim to defend human rights do not even move to curb their tools and small agents, the Zionist rulers of Israel.

The powerful uprising has affirmed the strength and unity of all the factions of our people inside and outside occupied Palestine. It has also affirmed the people's rallying around the PLO and their strong rejection of all suspect calls and projects aimed at dominating our people, forging our people's will, and peddling the Zionist-U.S. plot to deprive them of their inalienable national rights. In their brave uprising, our people reject distributing roles, as well as any bribery for the so-called improvement of living, instead of ending the nightmare of the occupation and liberating the Al-Aqsa Mosque, from which the prophet descended and in which Christ was born.

By their brave uprising, our masses are defending the unity of all the Palestinian people inside and outside the homeland. They also defend the Palestinian people's unity of cause and rights and voice their adherence to every inch of their soil. They reject any attempt to divide the cause of the homeland, any encroachment on our established national rights, and adhere to the PLO's program for struggle to liberate the holy land. Our people also call for holding an international conference as urged by UN resolutions, the Arab summit, nonaligned countries, and socialist and friendly countries.

At these historical and fateful moments in our people's struggle, the PLO appeals to our Arab brothers—governments, parties, forces, institutions, and popular bodies—to increase their solidarity with and support for the uprising of our people. The pan-Arab responsibility and ties of brotherhood and solidarity are being shown today through support for our people by our brothers in our glorious Arab nation. This support asserts the unity of fate, struggle, and pan-Arab goals.

The PLO expresses its appreciation for the brotherly positions declared by many leaders, parties, and organizations. It also voices its pride in our nation's solidarity with and unity of position toward their brothers, the sons of the Palestinian people. The PLO also expresses its appreciation for the positions of friendly countries, forces, allies, all African countries, nonaligned countries, Islamic countries, socialist countries, friendly countries, and many friendly parties and forces. These groups hastened to announce their solidarity with the uprising of our people, their condemnation of the crimes of the Zionist occupiers, and their call for ending the Zionists' crimes against our people and terminating the nightmare of the Palestinian people's homeland.

Our people appreciate this support for their struggle against occupation. It encourages their struggle and reinforces their confidence in victory. The Security Council discussions express the depth and comprehensiveness of this support for our people's struggle, as well as the isolation, the disappointment, and the condemnation of the Zionist occupiers and their supporters. The PLO also voices appreciation for the positions of the democratic forces in Israel who voiced support for our people's uprising, condemned the crimes of the Zionist rulers and their fascist army, and called for ending the occupation of our homeland. The PLO calls on those who are concerned about just peace to take a responsible position required by these historic moments against the fascist military ruling clique whose hands are stained with the blood of our people and who ignore the facts of the age and the clear Palestinian reality.

O our glorious people inside and outside the occupied homeland. O you who continue steadfastness in Gaza, the West Bank, the Triangle, Galilee, and the Negev. O you who continue struggle in Lebanon's camps and in all areas of diaspora. Our people reiterate that the way of struggle and unity is the only way to victory, to regain their firm national rights, and to establish an independent state with Jerusalem as its capital. Your uprising in the occupied homeland enters human history because it expresses adherence to life, peace, freedom, honor, independence, the liberation of the homeland, and victory. Defenders of the Lebanon camps also support their brothers in the occupied homeland. They will retaliate for any Zionist aggression against southern Lebanon and the Palestinian camps side by side with the Lebanese national forces. They will stress with blood and martyrdom the people's unity, struggle, and steadfastness.

In light of this, the PLO Executive Committee has passed a series of resolutions and made arrangements to continue a large-scale movement in Arab and international arenas to provide all the requirements of steadfastness and resistance for our people in the occupied homeland. It has decided that the employees of the PLO and the revolution's institutions will donate a 7-day salary to the uprising. It also thanks President Saddam Husayn for his noble and brotherly initiative to support the families of the martyrs of the popular uprising and for calling on Palestinian and Arab masses to set up support committees. Glory to our people's struggle and righteous martyrs. Greetings to our imprisoned heroes. Victory for our great people's struggle. Revolution until victory.

West Bank–Gaza Palestinian Leaders: The Fourteen Points (January 14, 1988)

During the past few weeks the Occupied Territories have witnessed a popular uprising against Israel's occupation and its oppressive measures. This uprising has so far resulted in the martyrdom of tens of our people, the wounding of hundreds more, and the imprisonment of thousands of unarmed civilians.

This uprising has come to further affirm our people's unbreakable commitment to its national aspirations. These aspirations include our people's firm national rights of self-determination and of the establishment of an independent state on our national soil under the leadership of the PLO, as our sole legitimate representative. The uprising also comes as further proof of our indefatigable spirit and our rejection of the sense of despair which has begun to creep to the minds of some Arab leaders who claim that the uprising is the result of despair.

The conclusion to be drawn from this uprising is that the present state of affairs in the Palestinian Occupied Territories is unnatural and that Israeli occupation cannot continue forever. Real peace cannot be achieved except through the recognition of Palestinian national rights, including the right of self-determination and the establishment of an independent Palestinian State on Palestinian national soil. Should these rights not be recognized, then the continuation of Israeli occupation will lead to further violence and bloodshed, and the further deepening of hatred. The opportunity for peace will also move farther away.

The only way to extricate ourselves from this scenario is through the convening of an international conference with the participation of all concerned parties including the PLO, the sole legitimate representative of the Palestinian people, as an equal partner, as well as the five permanent members of the Security Council, under the supervision of the two superpowers.

On this basis we call upon the Israeli authorities to comply with the following list of demands as a means to prepare the atmosphere for the convening of the suggested international peace conference, which conference will ensure a just and lasting settlement of the Palestinian problem in all its aspects, bringing about the realization of the inalienable national rights of the Palestinian people, peace and stability for the peoples of the region, and an end to violence and bloodshed:

1. To abide by the 4th Geneva Convention and all other international agreements pertaining to the protection of civilians, their properties and rights under a state of military occupation; to declare the Emergency Regulations of the British Mandate null and void, and to stop applying the iron fist policy;

2. The immediate compliance with Security Council Resolutions 605 and 607, which call upon Israel to abide by the Geneva Convention of 1949 and the Declaration of Human Rights; and which further call for the achievement of a just and lasting settlement of the Arab-Israeli conflict;

3. The release of all prisoners who were arrested during the recent uprising, and foremost among them our children. Also the rescinding of all proceedings and indictments against them;

4. The cancellation of the policy of expulsion, allowing all exiled Palestinians, including the four sent yesterday into exile, to return to their homes and families; also the release of all administrative detainees and the cancellation of the hundreds of house arrest orders. In this connection, special mention must be made of the several hundreds of applications for family reunions, which we call upon the authorities to accept forthwith;

5. The immediate lifting of the siege of all Palestinian refugee camps in the West Bank and Gaza, and the withdrawal of the Israeli army from all population centres;

6. Carrying out a formal inquiry into the behaviour of the soldiers and settlers in the West Bank and Gaza, as well as inside jails and detention camps, and taking due punitive measures against all those convicted of having caused death or bodily harm to unarmed civilians;

7. A cessation of all settlement activity and land confiscation and the release of lands already confiscated, especially in the Gaza Strip, and an end to the harassments and provocations of the Arab population by settlers in the West Bank and Gaza as well as in the Old City of Jerusalem. In particular, the curtailment of the provocative activities in the old city of Jerusalem by Sharon and the ultra-religious settlers of Shuvu Banim and Ateret Cohanim;

8. Refraining from any act which might impinge on the Muslim and Christian holy sites or which might introduce change to the status quo in the city of Jerusalem;

9. The cancellation of the VAT and all other Israeli taxes which are imposed on Palestinian residents in Jerusalem, the rest of the West Bank, and in Gaza; and the putting to an end of the harassments caused to Palestinian business and tradesmen;

10. The cancellation of all restrictions on political freedoms, including the restrictions on meetings and conventions; also making provisions for free municipal elections under the supervision of a neutral authority;

11. The immediate release of monies deducted from the wages of labourers from the Occupied Territories who worked and still work inside the green line, which amount to several hundreds of millions of dollars. These accumulated deductions, with interest, must be returned to their rightful owners through the agency of the nationalist institutions headed by the worker's unions;

12. The removal of all restrictions on building permits and licences for industrial projects and artesian wells as well as agricultural development programs in the Occupied Territories, and the rescinding of all measures taken to deprive the Occupied Territories of their water resources;

13. The termination of the policy of discrimination being practised against industrial and agricultural produce from the Occupied Territories either by removing the restrictions on the transfer of goods to within the green line, or by placing comparable trade restrictions on the transfer of Israeli goods into the Occupied Territories.

14. The removal of the restrictions on political contacts between inhabitants of the Occupied Territories and the PLO, in such a way as to allow for the participation of Palestinians from the Occupied Territories in the proceedings of the Palestinian National Council, in order to ensure a direct input into the decision-making processes of the Palestinian Nation by the Palestinians under occupation.

Unified National Command of the Intifada: Call No. 6 (February 4, 1988)

Masses of our people, uprising multitudes in the camps, rural areas, and cities; you who by your will and determination have triumphed over the policy of entrenching the Zionist occupation and made your resounding voice heard throughout the world; creators of the mounting struggle action, which has snatched the initiative from the hands of the Tel Aviv rulers and put them under siege and in a position of international condemnation; you who by your struggle are paving every day and every hour the road to victory, the defeat of occupation, and the establishment of an independent national state under the leadership of the PLO, our sole, legitimate representative; our masses: In order to save the Zionist occupation from certain defeat, as well as to save Israel from a strangulating crisis and isolation on an international level, U.S. imperialism at this time is continuing to hatch plots in the region with the support of its collaborators. It is attempting to undermine the gains of the uprising by proposing plans for capitulatory solutions. Foremost among these plans are those related to the United States, such as the U.S. State Department's attempts to suggest that certain people produce an alternative to the PLO's leadership, our sole, legitimate leadership.

Our masses, in the name of our Palestinian people in the interior, who have made precious sacrifices represented by the martyrdom of scores of their most beloved sons and daughters, the thousands of detainees, the hundreds of injured, and the attacks on many of our camps, villages, and cities by the Zionists, we say in the name of our people, who have endured and are still enduring such sacrifices with courage and pride, that we affirm our rejection of all plots and all attempts by imperialism's envoys, including Philip Habib, to circumvent our legitimate leadership and to dictate surrender conditions such as recognition of Resolution 242. We affirm the determination of the people and the masses of the glorious uprising to foil all plots regardless of the different masks used by those behind them.

The PLO is our sole, legitimate representative. Therefore, whoever tries to represent the masses of the uprising from outside the PLO and to appoint a suspect leadership to make concessions and to surrender will be confronted by the Palestinian people. He will only face disappointment and miserable defeat.

Sons of our people, let us concert all efforts. Let all national key figures, organizations, and popular committees be united by a common will to escalate the uprising. Let all suitable organizations such as committees and units be formed in every area, on every street, and in every city, village, and camp in order to pave the road toward general civil disobedience as a more advanced struggle action. Disobedience means boycotting all enemy organs. It means boycotting the enemy economically and not paying taxes.

Therefore, let us climb another rung of the ladder by declaring this disobedience. Let us reinforce the spirit of sacrifice and common action following the war of molotov cocktails, stones, and the raising of flags. The disobedience will be a strong blow to the enemy, its economy, and its plunder of our people's wealth and resources. This lifeline must be cut off.

To pave the way for the implementation of this organized process, the Unified National Leadership of the Uprising calls on our workers to stop work immediately in the Israeli settlements of the Palestinian West Bank and Gaza Strip. It calls on our workers in institutions and factories to abide by the days of the general strike and to be prepared to declare a go-slow strike for a few days in all Israeli places and institutions.

O our heroic people, the Unified National Leadership of the Uprising, while greeting your heroism, sacrifices, and the epics of struggle being recorded by our people in Nabulus and in all parts of the homeland, and while emphasizing that struggle will continue, calls for the following:

The immediate resignation of the appointed municipal councils as a prelude to holding democratic elections at the appropriate time;

The [words indistinct] and abstain from paying taxes as a prelude to force the Zionist occupation authorities to cancel their [word indistinct] taxes; abstain from paying exorbitant and unfair fines imposed by the Zionist courts against the uprising detainees . . . the owners of real estate not to demand rents from shopowners due to the current circumstances;

Abidance by the boycott of the agent AL-NAHAR newspaper as mentioned in the previous call; and

Urging our masses to encourage the national economy and to boycott the Israeli goods and markets and use national goods instead.

O masses of the glorious uprising, let the confrontation escalate, let demonstrations and marches be staged next week, let the popular sit-in strikes and the burning of tires continue on every street, let the stones of the uprising and the molotov cocktails pour down on the heads of the Israeli occupation soldiers, let all the lines of settlements be cut off, let crowded prayers be performed in mosques and churches as a prelude to declaring a comprehensive strike on Sunday and Monday, 7 and 8 February 1988, to mark the elapse of 2 months of the successful uprising and commemorate the fall of the first group of uprising martyrs. . . .

Secretary of State George Shultz: Plan (March 6, 1988)

The agreed objective is a comprehensive peace providing for the security of all the States in the region and for the legitimate rights of the Palestinian people.

Negotiations will start on an early date certain between Israel and each of its neighbors which is willing to do so. Those negotiations could begin by May 1, 1988. Each of these negotiations will be based on United Nations Security Council Resolutions 242 and 338, in all their parts. The parties to each bilateral negotiation will determine the procedure and agenda of their negotiation. All participants in the negotiations must state their willingness to negotiate with one another.

As concerns negotiations between the Israeli delegation and Jordanian-

Palestinian delegation, negotiations will begin on arrangements for a transitional period, with the objective of completing them within six months. Seven months after transitional negotiations begin, final status negotiations will begin, with the objective of completing them within one year. These negotiations will be based on all the provisions and principles of the United Nations Security Council Resolution 242. Final status talks will start before the transitional period begins. The transitional period will begin three months after the conclusion of the transitional agreement and will last for three years. The United States will participate in both negotiations and will promote their rapid conclusion. In particular, the United States will submit a draft agreement for the parties' consideration at the outset of the negotiations on transitional arrangements.

Two weeks before the opening of negotiations, an international conference will be held. The Secretary-General of the United Nations will be asked to issue invitations to the parties involved in the Arab-Israeli conflict and the five permanent members of the United Nations Security Council. All participants in the conference must accept United Nations Security Council Resolutions 242 and 338, and renounce violence and terrorism. The parties to each bilateral negotiations may refer reports on the status of their negotiations to the conference, in a manner to be agreed. The conference will not be able to impose solutions or veto agreements reached.

Palestinian representation will be within the Jordanian-Palestinian delegation. The Palestinian issue will be addressed in the negotiations between the Jordanian-Palestinian and Israeli delegations. Negotiations between the Israeli delegation and the Jordanian-Palestinian delegation will proceed independently of any other negotiations.

This statement of understandings is an integral whole. The United States understands that your acceptance is dependent on the implementation of each element in good faith.

PLO Executive Committee: Statement on the Intifada (April 1988)

O masses of our great people, our people, through their continuous struggle and their blessed revolutionary uprising that is entering its (?5th month), have scored additional achievements and victories. This has led to a deepening of the crisis of the Zionist occupation and its protectors in Washington. The entire world is now certain that this great people are determined to continue the way of jihad and struggle until, with the help of God, they achieve full victory and establish an independent Palestinian state on our sacred national soil.

The glorious Land Day, on which a total strike was observed throughout our occupied homeland, has proven that the solid and firm unity of our nation, the cohesion and solidarity of our ranks, and the firm insistence on the singleness of representation [wihdaniyat al-tamthil] are the strongest factors in confronting all Zionist-U.S. plots and all forms of oppression, slaughter, and destruction perpetrated by the Zionist occupation troops and the herds of the armed fascist settlers. Land Day was a day of cohesion and national solidarity among all the masses of our Palestinian people in the steadfast Galilee, the Triangle, and the Negev and in a position of clash and struggle in Lebanon and its south and in all areas of the diaspora.

It was another day of glory and confrontation in the steadfast West Bank and Gaza against all methods of fascist terrorism invented by Israel's rulers and generals including the war of starvation, the economic and media blockade, the perpetration of crimes and acts of slaughter against women, children, and defenseless citizens, and the demolishing of houses and communal arrests. Our heroic and faithful people have shown that these crimes can never weaken their escalating resistance or extinguish the flame of the uprising which is shaking the earth under the feet of the occupants and invaders.

The PLO Executive Committee, having discussed in detail all developments, tasks, and ways to escalate and develop the sturggle of our people and their great uprising, stresses the following:

1. Extending a salutation of pride and appreciation to the struggling masses of the Palestinian people in the Galilee, the Triangle, and the Negev for their great actions on Land Day and throughout all of the days of the blessed uprising as they firmly and faithfully joined the masses of the West Bank and Gaza and their escalating continuous revolution which constitutes, through our nation inside and outside the occupied homeland, this unified innovative revolutionary fabric. The Executive Committee calls for further consolidation, entrenchment, and adherence to national unity and to further cohesion of the ranks of our peoples masses—children, men, and women; cadres, heroes, and revolutionaries—on the path of liberation, return, and victory.

2. Emphasizing great appreciation for the role of the democratic forces which support the mammoth uprising of our people and firmly condemn the Nazi terrorism of Israel's rulers against our uprising masses who demand freedom and independence, the PLO Executive Committee calls for deepening and developing this role in all fields—political and media—to break the blockade that the Israeli rulers impose with the aim of concealing their barbaric crimes from the eyes of the world.

3. The PLO Executive Committee expresses, in the name of our entire people in all locations, the highest pride in the legendary steadfastness embodied by the blessed popular uprising through its daily epics in all sites. Every village, camp, neighborhood, and city in our occupied territory

has provided its share of martyrdom, heroism, and sacrifice. They stood as a strong barrier before the enemy forces at a time when our masses in Lebanon and its south continue to pay the price of the confrontation and the clashes with more martyrs and sacrifices. All of our people proved that the banner of jihad will continue to fly high [words indistinct] with our blood, the souls of our martyrs, our captives, wounded, and detainees until the establishment of our independent state and the liberation of the precious soil of our homeland from the aggression and occupation of the Zionists.

4. The PLO Executive Committee emphasizes the need to continue to develop all forms of revolutionary cohesion, empathy, and support by the groupings of our Palestinian people outside the homeland for the blessed popular uprising and harness all struggle, political, media, and material capabilities and resources for that purpose on the Palestinian, Arab, and international levels.

5. The PLO Executive Committee emphasizes the need to adopt all measures and means to develop all forms of mass organization and action to maintain and escalate the uprising and to develop the role of the popular national committees in all positions under the banner of the PLO, the Unified National Command of the Uprising, until the uprising achieves its objectives of shattering the fascist racist terrorism inflicted upon the masses of our people and eliminating the abhorrent Zionist occupation and until the inalienable national rights of our struggling and persevering people are achieved.

6. The PLO Executive Committee emphasizes the stand on which our people are unanimous in confronting the serious U.S. plans: that a just and comprehensive solution must be based on the achievement of the national rights of our people and their right to national independence under the leadership of the PLO, their sole and legitimate representative.

The PLO reaffirms its complete rejection of all liquidatory plans and all forms of autonomy and the sharing of roles whatever their color and under whatever name. The PLO believes that the appropriate framework for a just solution is a UN-sponsored international conference with effective powers attended by the five permanent members of the Security Council and all the parties to the conflict in the region including the PLO, on an equal footing with the other parties and on the basis of international legality and UN resolutions on the Palestine question and the Middle East.

We are confident that U.S. imperialism and its ally the Zionist enemy, which is squatting on our land and sanctities, will not be able to bring our people to their knees or deprive them of their legitimate right to self-determination. Our people will wrest their inalienable national rights through blood and enormous sacrifices. Foremost among these rights are their right to repatriation, to self-determination, and to establish a free and independent state with Jerusalem as its capital.

7. The PLO Executive Committee, while it salutes the masses of our Arab nation, all of its forces, parties, institutions, and national bodies for their sincere stands in support of our people and their struggle, calls on the Arab masses to develop their support for our people's uprising and to stand firmly in opposing liquidatory U.S.-Israeli plans which they are trying to impose on our Arab nation and the entire region. The PLO Executive Committee appeals with confidence and faith to the entire Arab nation to achieve effective Arab solidarity based on implementing the resolutions that reject separate solutions and deals. The PLO Executive Committee calls for the consolidation of the inalienable national rights of the Palestinian people on the basis of Arab commitment and Arab resolutions.

8. The PLO Executive Committee affirms its great appreciation for the extensive solidarity with our people's valiant and just struggle which has embarrassed and isolated the rulers of Israel and exposed official U.S. collusion with the crimes of the racist Zionists and their savage terrorism against our people, children, and women.

In this regard the PLO Executive Committee salutes all friends and honorable people in the world who support our people and just cause, particularly in the African, nonaligned, and Muslim states as well as the socialist states, led by the Soviet Union and the PRC, and the friendly European countries.

9. In accordance with its responsibilities, the PLO Executive Committee will continue its efforts through all means, forms, and capabilities to maintain the continuity of our revolutionary march and to escalate our people's valiant uprising. The PLO Executive Committee calls upon international and friendly bodies to provide more support and backing for our struggling masses and our just cause, particularly in confronting the organized and official war of terrorism and the crimes perpetrated against our people by the fascist and racist Zionist occupation authorities.

O masses of our proud people, thanks to your enormous sacrifices the day of victory is approaching. With your great unity we face the enemy and his bloody terrorism. More struggle, more unity, and more organization. Dawn is definitely coming. Our independent state is definitely coming. Our victory will be achieved with God's blessing. In the name of God, the merciful, the compassionate. Say work, for God, His messenger, and the believers will see your work. [Koranic verse]

Long live our people's great uprising. Glory and immortality to the martyrs. Greetings to our detainees, prisoners, and wounded. Greetings to our valiant children, our struggling women, and our heroic men. Revolution until victory!

[Signed] The PLO Executive Committee

United National Leadership of the Intifada Issues Calls No. 12, 16, and 18 (April–May 1988)

Call No. 12

In the name of God, the merciful, the compassionate. Call, call, call. No voice can rise above the voice of the uprising; no voice can rise above the voice of the Palestinian people, the voice of the PLO. Call No 12, [word indistinct] issued by the PLO—the Unified National Leadership. We will die standing, we will not submit. They will not pass, and the uprising will triumph. O masses of our heroic people; O people of stones and Molotov cocktails; you are recording in blood and light the history of your Arab nation. You are making light with your blood to brighten the long darkness of the Arabs. O children of the triumphant uprising, our uprising is continuing, baptized in chaste blood day after day, watering the beloved soil of the homeland, realizing important achievements, and strengthened by the little triumphs which are accumulating one above the other to make great victories and establish the independent Palestinian state.

Despite the harshness of the Zionist enemy and its machine of repression and tyranny, the strong arms are challenging all military orders. The Zionist arrogance, which boasts of repressing the uprising, is being defied by our children, women, youths, and old men whose sacred stones and generous wrath are burning the occupation and its henchmen. . . .

Our triumphant uprising and popular revolution is in its 5th month. Our Palestinian masses are facing more than two-thirds of the Israeli Army and all the herds of the Zionist settlers whom the enemy sent to the streets of our camps, villages, and towns to confront our unarmed people. This overwhelming revolution cannot be ended or liquidated by the breaking of bones, fascist killing and terrorism, mass arrests, or economic harassment. Hundreds of thousands of Palestinians across our beloved homeland declare today there is no going back, that the stone revolution will not stop before the establishment of our independent state. This was demonstrated in the immortal Land Day when 2 million Palestinians identified themselves with the united people. Now they are rising united behind the banner which will never fall, the banner of the PLO, the banner of the unified national leadership, the banner of liberation and and the independent homeland. To raise this banner over the hills of Jerusalem, the Palestinians in all towns, villages, camps, and streets are rising as one man.

O people of Palestine, O people of the PLO, O people of the unified national leadership. After its failure to put out the fires of the revolution through repression and terror, the occupation today is resorting to rumors and to spreading lies and forged statements allegedly signed by the Unified National Leadership in an attempt to cast doubt over our people—individuals and groups. The occupation is trying to sow the seeds of factionalism and sectarianism. It is spreading rumors about arresting the editors of the calls of the Unified National Leadership. All this is aimed at weakening the front of the burning uprising. The Unified National Leadership is certain that our people will be able to confront all the false rumors of the occupation. It affirms that the Unified National Leadership is the people of the uprising, represented by all its strata, groups, and sectors.

The Unified National Leadership includes the great martyrs whose blood is daily watering the soil of the homeland. This leadership consists of the children and youths of the stones and Molotov cocktails, the women who miscarried from the gas bombs and posion gas, the women whose husbands and sons are languishing in the Nazi prisons. The leadership consists of thousands of peasants and workers who stopped work in the Zionist settlements and who are protecting their villages, camps, and towns day and night against the tyranny and repression of the settlers and occupation soldiers.

O masses of our generous people, O mothers of martyrs, detainees, and wounded, O all mothers of Palestine, the rulers of the Zionist entity believe that by mass arrests and night stormings they can break our back and weaken our faith. But they do not know that our people are an inexhaustible store of generosity and are accustomed to making sacrifices for the sake of the homeland. So no matter how harsh Zionist repression and fascist measures are and no matter how many heroes and men of the uprising are detained, the Zionist enemy will not be able to put an end to this sweeping revolution—the revolution of the holy stones. Our people today are unified like a mighty giant destroying all the theories of the Zionist entity, intensifying the tribulation and dilemma of the Zionists, and increasing the confusion of their soldiers. More generosity means the breaking of the dawn of freedom forging its way in the darkness of coercion and heralding the independent Palestinian state.

While we are on the threshold of the 5th month of our glorious uprising and while we are hailing these days the 40th anniversary of the battle of heroism and sacrifice—the Battle Of Al-Qastal and the commemoration of the martyrdom of hero commander 'Abd al-Qadir al-Husayni—the Unified National Leadership affirms the following:

1. Denouncing attempts to disrupt the convocation of the Arab summit in the first half of April. The summit should be held as soon as possible to back the struggle of the people of the uprising on the land of Palestine. We assure the Arab kings and presidents that we do not want funds. We would rather starve and remain destitute than bow down. We would rather

die martyrs than concede our rights before final victory. However, we want the summit to abide in practice by its previous resolutions by asserting our people's inalienable rights to establish our independent state under the flag of the PLO, the leader of our struggle and our sole, legitimate representative, and abide by an international conference with full powers with the participation of all parties, including the PLO in an equal and independent manner. We also call on the summit to close all Arab doors to the Shultz plot, which seeks to liquidate the uprising, by categorically rejecting it and closing Arab airports before his shuttle tours as well as to all other U.S. envoys. Shultz and all those Arab regimes colluding with him should know that his only address is the PLO. It is the party concerned and the sole, legitimate representative.

2. The Unified National Leadership and the masses of the uprising denounce the oppressive authorities' recent measures represented by isolating the West Bank and Gaza, imposing a curfew on Gaza for 3 days, and considering the West Bank a closed area to the movement of citizens and journalists in a desperate attempt to prevent the people of the uprising from commemorating immortal Land Day. We tell them that all these desperate attempts are doomed to miserable failure. The will of the revolution of the stones and the uprising shall triumph over all their fascist and Nazi methods.

3. Denouncing the occupation authorities' decision to consider the youth movement [harakat al-shabibah] illegal and to close a number of trade union complexes and establishments and considering these measures as contrary to the most fundamental human rights and all international pacts and norms. The Unified National Leadership affirms that these measures will only make us more determined to continue the struggle.

4. The Unified National leadership and the masses of the uprising evaluate the unified collective stand taken by merchants of the Ramallah area who pledged at a public meeting attended by 30 merchants not to pay taxes and who adhered to their pledge in practice. We consider this experiment an example that should be emulated by all merchants in all parts of the West Bank and Gaza.

5. The Unified National Leadership greets the stand taken by the members of the municipal and village committees who responded to the call for resignation by the Unified National Leadership and the masses of the uprising. The leadership announces the squandering of the blood and property of the chairmen and members of the committees who have not resigned. We tell them that the masses of the uprising will trample upon whoever deviates from the stands of national unanimity and does not respond to the call and voice of the uprising.

6. The Unified National Leadership and the masses of the uprising evaluate the mass resignation of the tax and customs departments employees in Gaza and calls on the employees of these departments in the

West Bank to follow their example. The leadership also evaluates the mass resignation of the policemen who responded to the call of the uprising and calls on municipality members to immediately resign from their posts. The Unified National Leadership urges all national popular committees to continue the work of setting up and generalizing cultivation, protection, and public order committees to prevent enemy authorities' attempts at sabotage and confusion. The Unified National leadership also appeals to all our industrial firms to cooperation with the national popular committees in employing [resigning] policemen and tax and customs departments employees.

7. The Unified National Leadership urges agricultural engineers, owners of plant nurseries, and those with experience and capabilities to give every support and guidance to the masses of peasants, farmers, and striking workers to achieve maximum levels of self-sufficiency and to confront the measures of economic restriction used by the occupation authorities. Let us continue to reclaim and cultivate lands to meet our needs and support besieged areas. We should all realize the task of all the masses of the uprising is to intensify their work and to increase their production during our long struggle. We must realize that strike does not mean not working. The Unified National Leadership, while continuing on the long and difficult road of defeating the occupation and establishing our independent state, calls on the masses of the uprising to entrench the following struggle activities:

a. Declaring Monday, 4 April, a general strike day as an expression of the uprising masses' rejection of the plot by George Shultz, the secretary of U.S. imperialism. We reaffirm the PLO's stand and our determination to use the uprising to boycott any meetings with Shultz or any other U.S. envoy.

b. Declaring Monday, Tuesday, and Wednesday, 4, 5, and 6 April, days of various struggle activities by the uprising, masses, committees, striking groups, and various national frameworks against Shultz' visit and in solidarity with the uprising and detainees and wounded, including sit-ins and various public and women's demonstrations.

c. Considering Tuesday, 5 April, a day of national action in which all national establishments and factories shall operate at full capacity in the interests of those affected by the uprising, such as the families of martyrs, wounded, detainees, besieged areas, and workers who lost their jobs for ceasing to work in Zionist settlements and projects and also those who resigned in response to the call of the uprising. The national committees in every city, village, camp, and quarter shall distribute the revenues of this day.

d. On the occasion of World Health Day on 7 April, the Unified National Leadership greets all doctors, pharmacists, and nurses who have performed the duty of providing health care and relief work to the wounded of the uprising by returning to work in the camps, villages, and cities. The leadership calls on all those employed in the health care field to receive more patients and provide more medical treatment.

e. Declaring Thursday, 7 April, the anniversary of the Battle of Al-Qastal and the martyrdom of Palestinian commander 'Abd al-Qadir a day of violent clashes with the occupation forces and the cowardly settlers. Tumultuous demonstrations must come out in the streets and all our camps, villages, and cities must turn into fortresses of confrontation and fortification for the uprising.

f. Declaring Saturday, 9 April, which is the anniversary of the martyrdom of the first group of martyrs in the uprising as well as the martyrs of the Dayr Yasin massacre, and the beginning of the 5th month of our uprising, a day of people's authority in which processions shall proceed to the graves of the martyrs, sit-ins shall be organized in municipalities and establishments, and demonstrations shall be staged everywhere. It should be declared a day of sweeping indignation against the occupation authorities and their oppressive measures. Let the ground erupt like a volcano under the feet of the invader occupiers.

g. Considering Friday and Sunday, 8 and 10 April, days of prayer for the repose of the souls of the uprising's martyrs. Processions and demonstrations shall be staged and sit-ins shall be organized in mosques and churches.

8. Monday, 11 April, shall be a day of of general strike and of guiding the masses of our people on volunteer work for cultivating lands, developing Palestinian rural areas, and promoting environmental economy. O people of the uprising continue to move forward. O cubs of the stones march ahead. They will not pass. The uprising shall triumph, shall triumph.

[Signed] The PLO, the Unified National Leadership of the Uprising in the occupied areas.

Call No. 16

In the name of God, the merciful, the compassionate. Call, call, call. No voice can rise above the voice of the uprising; no voice can rise above the voice of the Palestinian people, the people of the PLO.

Call No 16, Palestine call, issued by the PLO, the Unified National Leadership of the Uprising in the occupied territory.

O masses of our great people: Your triumphant uprising is now beginning its 6th month, defying the wounds; embracing the Palestinian sky through martyrdom and victory; challenging all kinds of oppression, tyranny, and killing which our enemy is pursuing; opening the door to our triumphant revolution and the originator of our struggle, the PLO; exposing our enemies' ugly faces before the whole world; foiling all the conspiratorial projects against our steadfast people; strengthening our people's unity around the PLO, the sole legitimate representative; and protecting our independent national decisionmaking. There will be no trusteeship or alternative except Palestine, the alternative which is baptized with the blood of our righteous martyrs.

O masses of our people, we are living the 40th anniversary of the Palestine disaster of 1948, the infamous day when tens of thousands of our people were expelled from their homeland and dispersed in all countries of the world, entrenching the presence of the colonialist Zionist occupation on our chaste soil under the shadow of Arab trusteeship over our people and through the defeated Arab regimes, which were under the influence of colonialist powers, especially Britain. Palestine was a victim of this trusteeship and weakness. From the bleeding wound emerged the Palestinian revolution, which declared at its birth in 1965 that there is no alternative to struggle against the usurping enemy through the methods of prolonged people's war and armed struggle until liberation and victory.

With the presence of the PLO and the continuation of the Palestinian struggle within its framework, and with the increasing number of martyrs, our triumphant revolution and our heroic masses were able to wrest their independent national decisionmaking at the 1974 Rabat summit conference. Our people won their independent decisionmaking, represented by declaring the PLO as the sole legitimate representative of the Palestinian people everywhere. And despite all the desperate attempts to strike at our triumphant revolution and our enemies' efforts to circumvent this representation, the Palestinian giant was able to confront all its enemies and to turn our Palestinian cause into a central cause for the whole world despite the wounds, the rivers of blood, the large number of martyrs, and our people's immense suffering.

Then came our sacred uprising to renew our people's resolve to attain their legitimate rights no matter what the sacrifices or how long the wait. It has grown into a giant, striking terror in the hearts of all enemies. Your glorious uprising is delivering painful blows to the Nazi occupation, foiling its measures against our struggling masses. Despite the fascist oppression, our masses are ever rallying around the uprising and its sacred slogans through a commitment to the PLO and the unified leadership of the uprising, withholding taxes, boycotting occupation goods, resigning en masse from the Zionist administration, economizing on expenses, intensifying local agriculture, land reclamation, and education, and building alternative bodies via popular committees, neighborhoods, education, and health as a key prelude to civil disobedience.

Having despaired of squelching and aborting the uprising, the rulers of Tel Aviv committed the crime of murdering the leader, the symbol Abu Jihad [Khalil al-Wazir], in Tunis in an attempt to end it. O our heroic masses, comrades, and brothers of the martyr hero Abu Jihad [words indistinct]. Abu Jihad's blood will not have been wasted. All our people are

Abu Jihad. We will continue the march along the path of struggle until victory. This escalation has been crowned by the international consensus on denouncing the Zionist entity and its fascist policies, the Palestinian-Soviet agreement, reconciliation with Syria, and reopening the intra-Palestinian dialogue toward developing the unity of the PLO.

Then came the Algerian and Libyan efforts and Arab meetings to convene an Arab summit—the uprising summit to promote common Arab action in support of the uprising and build a wide Arab front in the face of conspiratorial plots led by the Shultz project, which our people have turned down. In the shadow of these great achievements, the Zionist enemy mounted an attack against Lebanon, laid a siege to some villages, and used repression and oppression against the innocent in renewed attempts to divert international attention from the uprising and in a desperate attempt to undo the militant, harmonious, integral relationship between the popular uprising in the occupied land and the Palestinian revolution on one hand and the Lebanese nationalist movement on the other.

At a time when the need to close ranks and train guns on the usurper enemy has never been greater, a handful of aberrant dissidents in Lebanon who have broken away from the will of our people made a wretched attempt to split and undermine the various efforts seeking to realize a national consensus within the PLO and direct the guns at the usurper enemy to consolidate the triumphant uprising of our people.

O our heroic Palestinian people, while marking these days—the 22d anniversary of the Arab regimes' defeat and of the occupation of the remainder of our dear homeland, amid the convening of the Moscow summit and the Arab summit and also in view of George Shultz' attempts to resume the conspiracy aimed at aborting the uprising—our people's masses are daily escalating their victorious uprising. There will be no return nor will there be any retreat until occupation is removed and an independent Palestinian state is established under the PLO's leadership.

Our masses know their path through revolution to obtain their rights. It is the path of persistent struggle. More than 20 years of coercion, persecution, oppression, and attempts to liquidate our identity and our people's national cause have created the generation of the uprising—the generation of freedom, independence, and of building an independent national state on its sacred national soil. This generation is determined to make occupation pay a dear price for desecrating our land and holy places. It is also determined to turn occupation into a hell that will burn the occupying soldiers and settlers.

The Unified National Leadership of the Uprising calls on our masses to further escalate the delivery of painful blows to the new Nazis and to further entrench and organize the generation of the uprising and its specialized committees and strike teams along the path of carrying out a comprehensive civil disobedience and fulfilling the slogans and just demands of the uprising as a basic introduction to wrest our people's national legitimate rights to repatriation, self-determination, and the establishment of an independent state.

These slogans and demands include the need to implement the four Geneva Conventions; dispatch international observers to provide the necessary protection for the sons of our people; withdraw the army from the cities, villages, and camps; lift the siege clamped on them; release the detainees; return deportees to their homeland; cancel the taxes and other laws and legislations enacted by the occupation authorities; hold democratic elections for the municipal and village councils; and remove restrictions imposed on our national production to allow for the building and developing of the industrial, agricultural, and services sectors.

The PLO, the Unified National Leadership, along with our people's masses, while waging a tough struggle within a firmly established national unity, calls on the Arab summit leaders to shoulder their responsibilities before their peoples and history by supporting this Palestinian struggle not through denunciation, condemnation, and verbal backing, but by:

1. Adopting a clear and unified political stand before the whole world in support of the PLO and the soleness and legitimacy of its representation of our people and providing all means of support enabling our people to continue their struggle.

2. Rejecting all liquidationist solutions, headed by the Shultz initiative, and insisting on the need to hold a fully empowered international conference with the participation of the PLO in an independent delegation just like the other parties.

3. Releasing political prisoners from Arab prisons, giving democratic freedoms to the Arab masses so they can act in solidarity and cohesion with our people's triumphant uprising, and allowing for fedayeen action across Arab borders in the direction of occupied Palestine.

Along the path of implementing a comprehensive civil disobedience, the Unified National Leadership of the Uprising, the PLO, emphasizes the following:

—The need for the immediate resignation of workers in traffic and licensing departments, organization and housing departments, and identity cards and people's registration offices. After the occupation authorities have been forced to reopen schools, it is essential to reprogram the curriculum to compensate the students for what they missed, especially secondary school students in their final year. We trust that schools will continue to be the strong citadels of the uprising. Popular education should play a complementary role in raising our students' efficiency.

—Total withholding of cooperation with the institutions through which the occupation seeks to restrict the movement of the population by boycotting certifications of good conduct and relevant official documents and refusing to have dealings with defeatists and appointed agent municipal committees. Here, it should be emphasized that the popular committees in every location are called upon to mobilize the population for a commitment to this patriotic stand.

—Banning the payment of all kinds of taxes, boycotting Zionist goods—industrial or agricultural—and completely withholding labor from Zionist settlements.

—Refusal by our sons in the [Gaza] Strip to receive the new identity cards. The popular committees are called upon to play a mobilizing role toward that end to consolidate the boycott and in compliance with PLO resolutions—the Unified Leadership of the Uprising.

—An intensification of the formation and organization of popular committees, neighborhood committees, health committees, sentry committees, security committees, agricultural committees, mobilization guidance committees, information committees, and strike forces—the militant arm of the Unified National Leadership of the Uprising—as well as the economic committees, and encouraging, developing, and entrenching household agriculture and rationalized consumption and spending.

—Directing and intensifying blows to dissenters from the will of our people in the appointed village and city council committees, customs offices, and police and intensifying the use of the means of popular struggle beginning with the stone and ending with the gasoline bomb against all the enemies.

O masses of our struggling people, the PLO—the Unified National Leadership—calls on all segments of our people to mark the following days with sweeping mass anger coinciding with forthcoming political events by executing and implementing the following militant activities:

First, dedicating 28 and 29 May to massive marches and rallies involving all national cadres, organizations, and personalities so our voice —the voice of the uprising—may be heard loud and clear by the superpower leaders in Moscow.

Second, dedicating 30 May to an all-out strike and raising the pitch of the militant struggle to mark the Gorbachev-Reagan summit and increasing the writing of nationalist slogans and raising flags in all villages, cities and camps.

Third, dedicating 1 June—International Children's Day—to children's demonstrations raising Palestinian slogans and flags. In the meantime, various committees, especially committees of solidarity with victims of our people, will distribute gifts to the children of the martyrs, the wounded, detainees, and deportees.

Fourth, dedicating 3, 4, 5, and 6 June to full-scale strikes to mark the [Mideast] visit of Shultz, the Lebanese invasion, and the 22d [as heard] anniversary of the Zionist occupation. In the meantime, our masses and strike forces will stage demonstrations and confrontations with occupiers and their agents. May the land scorch the feet of the usurping occupiers and their agents.

Fifth, dedicating 7 June to Arab solidarity with the glorious uprising of our people, holding massive demonstrations, and urging Arab masses to stage rallies of sympathy with our victorious uprising.

[Signed] The PLO—the Unified National Leadership of the Uprising, 28 May 1988

Call No. 18

O masses of our heroic people, who have destroyed the illusions of occupation in more than 20 years, who have refuted the claims about our people's coexistence with occupation, and who have destroyed all attempts to create feeble alternatives to our people's sole legitimate representative, the PLO, through destroying alternatives to the right to repatriation, to self-determination, and to an independent national state: You continue to proceed on the road through your suffering, through the huge sacrifices, and through the constant flow of blood on the road to achieving freedom and independence for our militant people.

Here is the victorious uprising destroying the apparatus and tools of the fascist occupation, which were established to serve the occupation's interests and to link the interests of our people's masses with the occupation. On the ruins of these tools you are building the apparatus of the heroic people's authority through the popular committees with their various tasks.

Here is the uprising restoring to our national cause its natural size as the cause of a people who are struggling for the sake of their legitimate national rights. This cause has thus become an important topic on the agenda of the Moscow summit as well as the major topic at the summit of the uprising in Algiers.

While saluting the combatants who returned to the ranks of the mother revolution, thereby rejecting the spilling of blood for the sake of achieving the objectives of those who reneged on our people's will, as well as those of Abu Musa [Sa'id Musa Muraghah], the one who reneged on this will, and his clique, the uprising masses appeal to the Lebanese nationalist movement to unify its ranks to confront the Zionist enemy and end their narrow differences, thus unifying the militant endeavors of the militant and pan-Arab Lebanese-Palestinian parties to make them serve as a significant factor and a principal pillar conducive to the achievement of victory.

At the same time, these masses appeal to all those exerting sincere efforts to accelerate the process of inter-Palestinian dialogue, to bolster the militant relationship with Syria, and to build an Arab base of steadfastness capable of achieving our nation's pan-Arab objectives. O you, masses of the valiant uprising. O you, people of martyrs. With steady and confident strides, we, along with you, are going through one phase after another in our popular uprising and revolt, strengthening the people's rules and authority on the road to general and comprehensive civil disobedience, which will take the form of securing a complete boycott between our people and the institutions of the occupying authority in all spheres.

This requires that we display further observance of the program of the phase and of that of the phases of the popular uprising, as well as of the decisions made by the Unified National Leadership, the PLO leadership.

We call upon our masses to remain alert and display serious and studied readiness to meet the requirements of civil disobedience. This readiness can materialize through providing the necessary supplies which can provide citizens' needs for at least 1 month. It includes enhancing self-sufficiency, displaying an eagerness to provide adequate quantities of water by preserving water wells, making available first aid, and enhancing the program of various committees—the popular, guard, information, and labor committees. Furthermore, this readiness can also materialize when emphasis is laid on the formation of further strike groups, the militant arm of our blessed popular revolution.

The PLO leadership, the Unified National Leadership of the Uprising, treading on the path of realizing comprehensive civil disobedience, emphasizes the following:

1. All sectors and walks of life are to enhance the complete boycott [of Israeli authorities] through their failure to pay all forms of taxes to the suckers of our people's blood.

2. The comprehensive boycott is to be enhanced and continued by our workers through their failure to head for their worksites inside the institutions of the Zionist entity and its crumbling organizations.

3. The Unified National Leadership calls upon our heroic masses in the proud Gaza Strip to boycott the receipt of identity cards, which the enemy authorities seek to force upon them with the objective of restricting the movement of citizens and forcing them to pay taxes. This hateful method seeks to weaken the growing flame of the uprising. Hence, we call upon you, our masses, to boycott completely this measure.

4. The Unified National Leadership of the Uprising calls upon the general directors working in the departments of the Civil Administration in the Gaza Strip to respond favorably to the call voiced by the uprising masses by tendering their resignations. We call upon the strike forces, the knights of the great clashes, and the faithful masses of our people to strike with an iron fist all those who refuse to carry out this decision. We also call upon the guard and security committees to maintain surveillance over these directors and to carry out their program in this regard.

5. The Unified National Leadership salutes the uprising masses and our valiant kinfolk in the camps of the Gaza Strip for their steadfastness and their legendary challenge, which took the form of breaking the curfews imposed on Palestinian camps and also the form of staging tumul-

tuous demonstrations and violent clashes against the Nazi occupation troops.

6. The Unified Leadership of the Uprising calls upon our people's masses to form solidarity committees inside the occupied homeland to bolster the ties of social solidarity, cooperation, and mutual aid among our well-off families and our families that have been harmed.

7. The Unified National Leadership of the Uprising calls upon the lawyers' sector to form information and legal committees to work intensively to expose the Nazi methods being perpetrated by the occupation authorities against our masses, our prisoners, and our deportees—methods that contravene all international and human laws and norms. Special emphasis is to be laid on the methods being used by the occupation authorities in the new Nazi detention camps; namely, Ansar, the Negev desert prison, the Al-Zahiriyah prison, the Al-Fari'ah prison, and the remaining prisons.

8. The Unified National Leadership stresses the need to remain alert and to beware of forged statements which are being distributed by the well-known agent Hamadi al-Rishq by orders of Yitzhaq Rabin.

On the occasion of the blessed 'Id al-Fitr, the PLO leadership, the Unified National Leadership of the popular uprising, greets the masses of our people, detainees, wounded, and the families of our martyrs—the candles. It also greets the harmed families, our merchants, workers, deportees, and the revolution fighters in all arenas. It congratulates them on the blessed feast, which coincides with the escalation of our gigantic popular revolution and the victorious beginning of its 6th month. It greets our sons' heroic stands in their struggle over the recent months and during the blessed Al-Qadr night [the night between the 26th and 27th of Ramadan in which the Koran was revealed].

Naturally, the Unified Leadership calls for concealing all celebrations and to confine them to performing religious rites, prayers, and chants of God is great. It calls for formation of further committees and intensification of the following militant programs and activities on the path to a comprehensive civil disobedience:

1. On 13 May, the masses of our people shall head for mosques, perform prayers over the souls of our righteous martyrs, and take to the streets in massive demonstrations against the occupation and the herds of its armed settlers.

2. The 15th of May, the ill-omened day of the catastrophe, shall be considered a day for a comprehensive strike, a day of distinctive anger, and a new beginning in which Palestinian flags shall be hoisted over houses, poles, village council buildings, appointed municipalities, and everywhere. On this day the heroic strike groups shall confront the occupiers and all those departing from the will of our people, including the members of the appointed municipal councils, taxes, police, and misled criminal agents.

3. The 1st day of the blessed 'Id al-Fitr shall be announced as a day for national mourning in protest of Arab and Islamic silence and impotence and to honor and glorify the blood of our revolutionary martyr and symbol, Brother Abu Jihad, and all the righteous uprising martyrs. On this day, our masses shall head [for mosques] to perform prayers and visit the tombs of martyrs and cemeteries and shall stage popular processions and massive, mammoth demonstrations in defiance of the Zionist means of repression and torture.

4. The Unified National Leadership calls on the masses of our people and various committees to pay solidarity visits to the families of our heroic martyrs, prisoners, wounded, and deportees on the 2d and 3d days of the blessed 'Id.

5. The 21st of May shall be declared a day of comprehensive strike and a day for enhancing popular teaching in all our cities, villages, and camps in protest of the inhuman arbitrary decisions of closing down various centers of learning. The teachers sector is called upon to organize protest processions.

6. The rest of the days and Fridays and Sundays shall be considered days for enhancing and intensifying the work of various militant activities, especially the strike forces, and for dealing painful blows to the flabby bodies of occupiers and their agents and setting ablaze the ground under the feet of the Zionist occupiers with fire and anger.

7. With the exception of what has been mentioned, our masses shall be committed to all the decisions declared in previous calls, especially regarding the hours of partial trade strike, which will be as usual.

O valiant sons of our people and makers of Palestinian glory. We will continue to resist with a strong will, profound belief, great sacrifices, and innovative and creative revolutionary action on the path of martyrs. We will continue to challenge all forms and means of systematic Zionist repression. O our heroic masses and strike forces, hurl more stones and flaming Molotov cocktails on all enemies and the forces of wickedness, injustice, and aggression. Continue using bows and arrows, poisoned nails, and all means of popular struggle.

Carry out further committee militant activities toward a stage of comprehensive civil disobedience on the path of an independent Palestinian state under the leadership of the PLO. Victory is undoubtedly imminent. Together, we will achieve our liberation and certain national independence on the soil of Palestine with Jerusalem as our everlasting capital. We will triumph.

[Signed] The PLO, the Unified National Leadership of the Uprising in the occupied territories, 12 May 1988

King Hussein: Disengagement from the West Bank (July 31, 1988)

Our decision as you know, comes after thirty-eight years of the unity of the two banks, and fourteen years after the Rabat summit resolution, designating the Palestine Liberation Organisation (PLO) as the sole legitimate representative of the Palestinian people. It also comes six years after the Fez summit resolution that agreed unanimously on the establishment of an independent Palestinian state in the occupied West Bank and the Gaza Strip, as one of the bases, and results of the peaceful settlement. . . .

We had never imagined that the preservation of the legal and administrative links between the two banks could constitute an obstacle to the liberation of the occupied Palestinian land. Consequently, during the period before adopting these measures we did not see a reason to do so, particularly since our position which calls for, and supports, the Palestinian people's rights to self determination was clear beyond equivocation.

Lately, it has transpired that there is a general Palestinian and Arab orientation towards highlighting the Palestinian identity in a complete manner, in every effort or activity related to the Palestinian question and its developments. It has also become clear that there is a general conviction, that maintaining the legal and administrative links with the West Bank, and the ensuing Jordanian interaction with our Palestinian brothers under occupation, through Jordanian institutions in the occupied territories, contradicts this orientation. It is also viewed that these links hamper the Palestinian struggle to gain international support for the Palestinian cause, as the national cause of a people struggling against foreign occupation.

In view of this line of thought, which is certainly inspired by genuine Palestinian will, and Arab determination to support the Palestinian cause, it becomes our duty to be part of this direction, and to respond to its requirements. After all, we are a part of our nation, supportive of its causes, foremost among which is the Palestinian cause. Since there is a general conviction that the struggle to liberate the occupied Palestinian land could be enhanced by dismantling the legal and administrative links between the two banks, we have to fulfill our duty, and do what is required of us. At the Rabat summit of 1974 we responded to the Arab leaders appeal to us to continue our interaction with the occupied West Bank through the Jordanian institutions, to support the steadfastness of our brothers there. Today we respond to the wish of the Palestine Liberation Organisation, the sole legitimate representative of the Palestinian people, and to the Arab orientation to affirm the Palestinian identity in all its aspects. We pray God that this step be a substantive addition to the intensifying Palestinian struggle for freedom and independence. . . .

At the same time it has to be understood in all clarity and without any ambiguity or equivocation, that our measures regarding the West Bank, concern only the occupied Palestinian land and its people. They naturally do not relate in any way to the Jordanian citizens of Palestinian origin in the Hashemite Kingdom of Jordan. They all have the full rights of citizenship and all its obligations, the same as any other citizen irrespective of his origin. They are an integral part of the Jordanian state. They belong to it, they live on its land and they participate in its life and all its activities. Jordan is not Palestine; and the independent Palestinian state will be established on the occupied Palestinian land after its liberation, God willing. There the Palestinian identity will be embodied, and there the Palestinian struggle shall come to fruition, as confirmed by the glorious uprising of the Palestinian people under occupation.

National unity is precious in any country; but in Jordan it is more than that. It is the basis of our stability, and the spring-board of our development and prosperity. It is the foundation of our national security and the source of our faith in the future. It is the living embodiment of the principles of the Great Arab Revolt, which we inherited, and whose banner we proudly bear. It is a living example of constructive plurality, and a sound nucleus for wider Arab unity.

Based on that, safeguarding national unity is a sacred duty that will not be compromised. Any attempt to undermine it, under any pretext, would only help the enemy carry out his policy of expansion at the expense of Palestine and Jordan alike. Consequently, true nationalism lies in bolstering and fortifying national unity. Moreover, the responsibility to safeguard it falls on every one of you, leaving no place in our midst for sedition or treachery. With God's help, we shall be as always, a united cohesive family, whose members are joined by bonds of brotherhood, affection awareness, and common national objectives.

It is most important to remember, as we emphasize the importance of safeguarding national unity, that stable and productive societies, are those where orderliness and discipline prevail. Discipline is the solid fabric that binds all members of a community in a solid, harmonious structure, blocking all avenues before the enemies, and opening horizons of hope for future generations.

The constructive plurality which Jordan has lived since its foundation, and through which it has witnessed progress and prosperity in all aspects of life, emanates not only from our faith in the sanctity of national unity, but also in the importance of Jordan's pan-Arab role. Jordan presents itself as the living example of the merger of various Arab groups on its soil, within the framework of good citizenship, and one Jordanian people. This paradigm that we live on our soil gives us faith in the inevitability of attaining Arab unity, God willing. In surveying contemporary tendencies, it becomes clear that the affirmation of national identity does not contradict the attainment of unitary institutional formats that can enjoin Arabs as a whole. There are living examples within our Arab homeland that attest to this, as there are living examples in foreign regions. Foremost among them is the European Community, which now seeks to realize European political unity, having successfully completed the process of economic complementarity among its members. It is well known that the bonds linking the Arabs are far greater than those linking European nations.

Citizens, Palestinian brothers in the occupied Palestinian lands, to dispel any doubts that may arise out of our measures, we assure you that these measures do not mean the abandonment of our national duty, either towards the Arab-Israeli conflict, or towards the Palestinian cause, nor do they mean relinquishing our faith in Arab unity. As I have stated, those steps were taken only in response to the wish of the Palestine Liberation Organisation, the sole legitimate representative of the Palestinian people, and the prevailing Arab conviction that such measures will contribute to the struggle of the Palestinian people and their glorious uprising. Jordan will continue its support for the steadfastness of the Palestinian people, and their courageous uprising in the occupied Palestinian land, within its capabilities. . . .

Hamas: Charter (August 1988)

ARTICLE SIX

The Islamic Resistance Movement is a distinct Palestinian Movement which owes its loyalty to Allah, derives from Islam its way of life and strives to raise the banner of Allah over every inch of Palestine. Only under the shadow of Islam could the members of all regions coexist in safety and security for their lives, properties and rights. In the absence of Islam, conflict arises, oppression reigns, corruption is rampant and struggles and wars prevail. . . .

ARTICLE NINE

Hamas finds itself at a period of time when Islam has waned away from the reality of life. For this reason, the checks and balances have been upset, concepts have become confused, and values have been transformed; evil has prevailed, oppression and obscurity have reigned; cowards have turned tigers, homelands have been usurped, people have been uprooted and are wandering all over the globe. The state of truth has disappeared and was replaced by the state of evil. Nothing has remained in its right place, for when Islam is removed from the scene, everything changes. These are the motives.

As to the objectives: discarding the evil, crushing it and defeating it, so that truth may prevail, homelands revert [to their owners], calls for prayer be heard from their mosques, announcing the reinstitution of the Muslim state. Thus, people and things will revert to their true place. . . .

ARTICLE ELEVEN

The Islamic Resistance Movement believes that the land of Palestine has been an Islamic Waqf throughout the generations and until the Day of Resurrection, no one can renounce it or part of it, or abandon it or part of it. No Arab country nor the aggregate of all Arab countries, and no Arab King or President nor all of them in the aggregate, have that right, nor has that right any organization or the aggregate of all organizations, be they Palestinian or Arab. . . .

ARTICLE TWELVE

Hamas regards Nationalism (Wataniyya) as part and parcel of the religious faith. Nothing is loftier or deeper in Nationalism than waging Jihad against the enemy and confronting him when he sets foot on the land of the Muslims. And this becomes an individual duty binding on every Muslim man and woman; a woman must go out and fight the enemy even without her husband's authorization, and a slave without his masters' permission.

This [principle] does not exist under any other regime, and it is a truth not to be questioned. While other nationalisms consist of material, human and territorial considerations, the nationality of Hamas also carries, in addition to all those, the all important divine factors which lend to it its spirit and life; so much so that it connects with the origin of the spirit and the source of life and raises in the skies of the Homeland the Banner of the Lord, thus inexorably connecting earth with Heaven. . . .

ARTICLE THIRTEEN

[Peace] initiatives, the so-called peaceful solutions, and the international conferences to resolve the Palestinian problem, are all contrary to the beliefs of the Islamic Resistance Movement. For renouncing any part of Palestine means renouncing part of the religion; the nationalism of the Islamic Resistance Movement is part of its faith, the movement educates its members to adhere to its principles and to raise the banner of Allah over their homeland as they fight their Jihad: ''Allah is the all-powerful, but most people are not aware. . . .''

Those conferences are no more than a means to appoint the nonbelievers as arbitrators in the lands of Islam. Since when did the Unbelievers do justice to the Believers?

''And the Jews will not be pleased with thee, nor will the Christians, till thou follow their creed. Say: Lo! the guidance of Allah [himself] is the Guidance. And if you should follow their desires after the knowledge which has come unto thee, then you would have from Allah no protecting friend nor helper.'' *Sura 2 (the Cow) verse 120.*

There is no solution to the Palestinian problem except by Jihad. The initiatives, proposals and International Conferences are but a waste of time, an exercise in futility. The Palestinian people are too noble to have their future, their right and their destiny submitted to a vain game. . . .

ARTICLE FOURTEEN

The problem of the liberation of Palestine relates to three circles: the Palestinian, the Arab and the Islamic. Each one of these circles has a role to play in the struggle against Zionism and it has duties to fulfill. It would be an enormous mistake and an abysmal act of ignorance to disregard anyone of these circles. For Palestine is an Islamic land where the First Qibla and the third holiest site are located. That is also the place whence the Prophet, be Allah's prayer and peace upon him, ascended to Heavens.

"Glorified be He who carried His servant by night from the Inviolable Place of worship to the Far Distant Place of Worship, the neighborhood whereof we have blessed, that we might show him of our tokens! Lo! He, only He, is the Hearer, the Seer.'' *Sura XVII (al-Isra'), verse 1.*

In consequence of this state of affairs, the liberation of that land is an individual duty binding on all Muslims everywhere. This is the base on which all Muslims have to regard the problem; this has to be understood by all Muslims. When the problem is dealt with on this basis, where the full potential of the three circles is mobilized, then the current circumstances will change and the day of liberation will come closer. . . .

ARTICLE TWENTY

Islamic society is one of solidarity. The Messenger of Allah, be Allah's prayer and peace upon him, said:

What a wonderful tribe were the Ash'aris! When they were overtaxed, either in their location or during their journeys, they would collect all their possessions and then would divide them equally among themselves.

This is the Islamic spirit which ought to prevail in any Muslim society. A society which confronts a vicious, Nazi-like enemy, who does not differentiate between man and women, elder and young ought to be the first to adorn itself with this Islamic spirit. Our enemy pursues the style of collective punishment of usurping people's countries and properties, of pursuing them into their exiles and places of assembly. It has resorted to breaking bones, opening fire on women and children and the old, with or without reason, and to setting up detention camps where thousands upon thousands are interned in inhuman conditions. In addition, it destroys houses, renders children orphans and issues oppressive judgments against thousands of young people who spend the best years of their youth in the darkness of prisons. The Nazism of the Jews does not skip women and children, it scares everyone. They make war against people's livelihood, plunder their moneys and threaten their honour. In their horrible actions they mistreat people like the most horrendous war criminals. Exiling people from their country is another way of killing them. As we face this misconduct, we have no escape from establishing social solidarity among the people, from confronting the enemy as one solid body, so that if one organ is hurt the rest of the body will respond with alertness and fervor. . . .

The Powers Which Support the Enemy

ARTICLE TWENTY-TWO

The enemies have been scheming for a long time, and they have consolidated their schemes, in order to achieve what they they have achieved. They took advantage of key-elements in unfolding events, and accumulated a huge and influential material wealth which they put to the service of implementing their dream. This wealth [permitted them to] take over control of the world media such as news agencies, the press, publication houses, broadcasting and the like [They also used this] wealth to stir revolutions in various parts of the globe in order to fulfill their interests and pick the fruits. They stood behind the French and the Communist Revolutions and behind most of the revolutions we hear about here and there. They also used the money to establish clandestine organizations which are spreading around the world, in order to destroy societies and carry out Zionist interests. Such organizations are: the Free Masons, Rotary Clubs, Lions Clubs, B'nai B'rith and the like. All of them are destructive spying organizations. They also used the money to take over control of the Imperialist states and made them colonize many countries in order to exploit the wealth of those countries and spread their corruption therein.

As regards local and world wars, it has come to pass and no one objected that they stood behind World War I, so as to wipe out the Islamic Caliphate. They collected material gains and took control of many sources of wealth. They obtained the Balfour Declaration and established the League of Nations in order to rule the world by means of that organization. They also stood behind World War II, where they collected immense benefits from trading with war materials, and prepared for the establishment of their state. They inspired the establishment of the United Nations and the Security Council to replace the League of Nations, in order to rule the world by their intermediary. There was no war that broke out anywhere without their fingerprints on it:

". . . As often as they light a fire for war, Allah extinguishes it. Their efforts is for corruption in the land and Allah loves not corrupters." *Sura V (Al-Ma'ida—the Tablespread), verse 64.*

The forces of imperialism in both the Capitalist West and the Communist East support the enemy with all their might, in material and human terms, taking turns between themselves. When Islam appears, all the forces of Unbelief unite to confront it, because the Community of Unbelief is one.

"Oh ye who believe! Take not for intimates others than your own folk, who would spare no pain to ruin you. Hatred is revealed by [the utterance of] their mouth, but that which their breasts hide is greater. We have made plain for you the revelations if you will understand . . .", *Sura III, (Al-Imran), verse 118.*

It is not in vain that the verse ends with God's saying: "If you will understand. . . ."

ARTICLE TWENTY-SIX

The Hamas, while it views positively the Palestinian National Movements which do not owe their loyalty to the East or to the West, does not refrain from debating unfolding events regarding the Palestinian problem, on the local and international scenes. These debates are realistic and expose the extent to which [these developments] go along with, or contradict, national interests as viewed from the Islamic vantage point.

ARTICLE TWENTY-SEVEN

The PLO is among the closest to the Hamas, for its constitutes a father, a brother, a relative, a friend. Can a Muslim turn away from his father, his brother, his relative or his friend? Our homeland is one, our calamity is one, our destiny is one and our enemy is common to both of us. Under the influence of the circumstances which surrounded the founding of the PLO, and the ideological confusion which prevails in the Arab world as a result of the ideological invasion which has swept the Arab world since the rout of the Crusades, and which has been reinforced by Orientalism and the Christian Mission, the PLO has adopted the idea of a Secular State, and so we think of it. Secular thought is diametrically opposed to religious thought. Thought is the basis for positions, for modes of conduct and for resolutions. Therefore, in spite of our appreciation for the PLO and its possible transformation in the future, and despite the fact that we do not denigrate its role in the Arab-Israeli conflict, we cannot substitute it for the Islamic nature of Palestine by adopting secular thought. For the Islamic nature of Palestine is part of our religion, and anyone who neglects his religion is bound to lose.

"And who forsakes the religion of Abraham, save him who befools himself?" *Sura II (Al-Baqra—the Co), verse 130.*

When the PLO adopts Islam as the guideline for life, then we shall become its soldiers, the fuel of its fire which will burn the enemies. And until that happens, and we pray to Allah that it will happen soon, the position of the Hamas towards the PLO is one of a son towards his father, a brother towards his brother, and a relative towards his relative who suffers the other's pain when a thorn hits him, who supports the other in the confrontation with the enemies and who wishes him divine guidance and integrity of conduct. . . .

ARTICLE TWENTY-EIGHT

The Zionist invasion is a mischievous one. It does not hesitate to take any road, or to pursue all despicable and repulsive means to fulfill its desires. It relies to a great extent, for its meddling and spying activities, on the clandestine organizations which it has established, such as the Free Masons, Rotary Clubs, Lions, and other spying associations. All those secret organizations, some which are overt, act for the interests of Zionism and under its directions, strive to demolish societies, to destroy values, to wreck answerableness, to totter virtues and to wipe out Islam. It stands behind the diffusion of drugs and toxics of all kinds in order to facilitate its control and expansion.

The Arab states surrounding Israel are required to open their borders to the Jihad fighters, the sons of the Arab and Islamic peoples, to enable them to play their role and to join their efforts to those of their brothers among the Muslim Brothers in Palestine.

The other Arab and Islamic states are required, at the very least, to facilitate the movement of the Jihad fighters from and to them. We cannot fail to remind every Muslim that when the Jews occupied Holy Jerusalem in 1967 and stood at the doorstep of the Blessed Aqsa Mosque, they shouted with joy:

"Muhammed is dead, he left daughters behind."

Israel, by virtue of its being Jewish and of having a Jewish population, defies Islam and the Muslims. . . .

ARTICLE THIRTY-ONE

Hamas is a humane movement, which cares for human rights and is committed to the tolerance inherent in Islam as regards attitudes towards other religions. It is only hostile to those who are hostile towards it, or stand in its way in order to disturb its moves or to frustrate its efforts.

Under the shadow of Islam it is possible for the members of the three religions: Islam, Christianity and Judaism to coexist in safety and security. Safety and security can only prevail under the shadow of Islam, and recent and ancient history is the best witness to that effect. The members of other religions must desist from struggling against Islam over sovereignty in this region. For if they were to gain the upper hand, fighting, torture and uprooting would follow; they would be fed up with each other, to say nothing of members of other religions. The past and the present are full of evidence to that effect.

"They will not fight you in body safe in fortified villages or from behind wells. Their adversity among themselves is very great. Ye think of them as a whole whereas their hearts are diverse. That is because they are a folk who have no sense." *Sura 59 (al-Hashr, the Exile), verse 14.*

Islam accords his rights to everyone who has rights and averts aggression against the rights of others. The Nazi Zionist practices against our people will not last the lifetime of their invasion, for "States built upon oppression last only one hour, states based upon justice will last until the hour of Resurrection."

"Allah forbids you not those who warred not against you on account of religion and drove you not out from your houses, that you should show them kindness and deal justly with them. Lo! Allah loves the just dealers." *Sura 60 (Al-Mumtahana), verse 8.*

The Attempts to Isolate the Palestinian People

ARTICLE THIRTY-TWO

World Zionism and Imperialist forces have been attempting, with smart moves and considered planning, to push the Arab countries, one after another, out of the circle of conflict with Zionism, in order, ultimately to isolate the Palestinian People. Egypt has already been cast out of the conflict, to a very great extent through the treacherous Camp David Accords, and she has been trying to drag other countries into similar agreements in order to push them out of the circle of conflict.

Hamas is calling upon the Arab and Islamic peoples to act seriously and tirelessly in order to frustrate that dreadful scheme and to make the masses aware of the danger of coping out of the circle of struggle with Zionism. Today it is Palestine and tomorrow it may be another country or other countries. For Zionist scheming has no end, and after Palestine they will covet expansion from the Nile to the Euphrates. Only when they have completed digesting the area on which they will have laid their hand, they will look forward to more expansion, etc. Their scheme has been laid out in the Protocols of the Elders of Zion, and their present [conduct] is the best proof of what is said there.

Leaving the circle of conflict with Israel is a major act of treason and it will bring curse on its perpetrators.

"Who so on that day turns his back to them, unless manoeuvering for battle or intent to join a company, he truly has incurred wrath from Allah, and his habitation will be hell, a hapless journey's end." *Sura 8 (Al-Anfal—spoils of war), verse 16.*

We have no escape from pooling together all the forces and energies to face this despicable Nazi-Tatar invasion. Otherwise we shall witness the loss of [our] countries, the uprooting of their inhabitants, the spreading of corruption on earth and the destruction of all religious values. Let everyone realize that he is accountable to Allah. . . .

"Whoever does a speck of good will [the consequences] and whoever does a speck of evil will see [the consequences]."

Within the circle of the conflict with world Zionism, the Hamas regards itself the spearhead and the avant-garde. It joins its efforts to all those who are active on the Palestinian scene, but more steps need to be taken by the Arab and Islamic peoples and Islamic associations throughout the Arab and Islamic world in order to make possible the next round with the Jews, the merchants of war. . . .

The greedy have coveted Palestine more than once and they raided it with armies in order to fulfill their covetousness. Multitudes of Crusades descended on it, carrying their faith with them and waving their Cross. They were able to defeat the Muslims for a long time, and the Muslims were not able to redeem it until they sought the protection of their religious banner; then, they unified their forces, sang the praise of their God and set out for Jihad under the Command of Saladin al-Ayyubi, for the duration of nearly two decades, and then the obvious conquest took place when the Crusaders were defeated and Palestine was liberated.

"Say (O Muhammed) unto those who disbelieve: ye shall be overcome and gathered unto Hell, an evil resting place." *Sura III (Al-Imran), verse 12.*

This is the only way to liberation, there is no doubt in the testimony of history. That is one of the rules of the universe and one of the laws of existence. Only iron can blunt iron, only the true faith of Islam can vanquish their false and falsified faith. Faith can only be fought by faith. Ultimately, victory is reserved to the truth, and truth is victorious. . . .

Palestine National Council: Political Resolution (November 15, 1988)

The primary features of our great people's *intifada* were obvious from its inception and have become clearer in the twelve months since then during which it has continued unabated: It is a total popular revolution that embodies the consensus of an entire nation—women and men, old and young, in the camps, in the villages, and the cities—on the rejection of the occupation and on the determination to struggle until the occupation is defeated and terminated.

This glorious *intifada* has demonstrated our people's deeply rooted national unity and their full adherence to the Palestine Liberation Organization, the sole, legitimate representative of our people, all our people, wherever they congregate—in our homeland or outside it. This was manifested by the participation of the Palestinian masses—their unions, their vocational organizations, their students, their workers, their farmers, their women, their merchants, their landlords, their artisans, their academics—in the *intifada* through its Unified National Command and the popular committees that were formed in the urban neighborhoods, the villages, and the camps. . . .

In addition to this Arab solidarity, our people's revolution and their blessed *intifada* have attracted widespread worldwide solidarity, as seen in the increased understanding of the Palestinian people's issue, the growing support of our just struggle by the peoples and states of the world, and the corresponding condemnation of Israeli occupation and the crimes it is committing, which has helped to expose Israel and increase its isolation and the isolation of its supporters.

Security Council resolutions 605, 607, and 608 and the resolutions of the General Assembly against the expulsion of the Palestinians from their land and against the repression and terrorism with which Israel is lashing the Palestinian people in the occupied Palestinian territories—these are strong manifestation of the growing support of international opinion, public and official, for our people and their representative, the Palestine Liberation Organization, and of the mounting international rejection of Israeli occupation with all the fascist, racist practices it entails.

The UN General Assembly's Resolution 21L/43/1 of 4/11/1988, which was adopted in the session dedicated to the *intifada,* is another sign of the stand the peoples and states of the world in their majority are taking against the occupation and with the just struggle of the Palestinian people and their firm right to liberation and independence. . . .

In addition to the rejection of the occupation and the condemnation of its repressive measures by the democratic and progressive Israeli forces, Jewish groups all over the world are no longer able to continue their defense of Israel or maintain their silence about its crimes against the Palestinian people. Many voices have risen among those groups to demand an end to these crimes and call for Israel's withdrawal from the occupied territories in order to allow the Palestinian people to exercise their right to self-determination.

The fruits that our people's revolution and their blessed *intifada* have borne on the local, Arab, and international levels have established the soundness and realism of the Palestine Liberation Organization's national program, a program aimed at the termination of the occupation and the achievement of our people's right to return, self-determination, and statehood. Those results have also confirmed that the struggle of our people is the decisive factor in the effort to snatch our national rights from the jaws of the occupation. It is the authority of our people, as represented in the Popular Committees, that controls the situation as we challenge the authority of the occupation's crumbling agencies.

The international community is now more prepared than ever before to strive for a political settlement of the Middle East crisis and its root cause, the question of Palestine. The Israeli occupation authorities, and the American administration that stands behind them, cannot continue to ignore the international will, which is now unanimous on the necessity of holding an international peace conference on the Middle East and enabling the Palestinian people to gain their national rights, foremost among which is their right to self-determination and national independence on their own national soil.

In the light of this, and toward the reinforcement of the steadfastness and blessed *intifada* of our people, and in accordance with the will of our masses in and outside of our homeland, and in fidelity to those of our people that have been martyred, wounded, or taken captive, the Palestine National Council resolves:

First: On the Escalation and Continuity of the Intifada:

A. To provide all the means and capabilities needed to escalate our people's *intifada* in various ways and on various levels to guarantee its continuation and intensification.

B. To support the popular institutions and organizations in the occupied Palestinian territories.

C. To bolster and develop the popular committees and other specialized popular and trade union bodies, including the attack groups and the popular army, with a view to expanding their role and increasing their effectiveness.

D. To consolidate the national unity that emerged and developed during the *intifada*.

E. To intensify efforts on the international level for the release of detainees, the return of those expelled, and the termination of the organized, official acts of repression and terrorism against our children, our women, our men, and our institutions.

F. To call on the United Nations to place the occupied Palestinian land under international supervision for the protection of our people and the termination of the Israeli occupation.

G. To call on the Palestinian people outside our homeland to intensify and increase their support, and to expand the family-assistance program.

H. To call on the Arab nation, its people, forces, institutions, and governments, to increase their political, material, and informational support for the *intifada*.

I. To call on all free and honorable people worldwide to stand by our people, our revolution, our *intifada* against the Israeli occupation, the repression, and the organized, fascist official terrorism to which the occupation forces and the armed fanatic settlers are subjecting our people, our universities, our institutions, our national economy, and our Islamic and Christian holy places.

Second: In the Political Arena:

Proceeding from the above, the Palestine National Council, being responsible to the Palestinian people, their national rights and their desire for peace as expressed in the Declaration of Independence issued on 15 November 1988; and in response to the humanitarian quest for international entente, nuclear disarmament, and the settlement of regional conflict by peaceful means, affirms the determination of the Palestine Liberation Organization to arrive at a comprehensive settlement of the Arab-Israeli conflict and its core, which is the question of Palestine, within the framework of the United Nations Charter, the principles and provisions of international legality, the norms of international law, and the resolutions of the

United Nations, the latest of which are Security Council resolutions 605, 607, and 608, and the resolutions of the Arab summits, in such a manner that safeguards the Palestinian Arab people's rights to return, to self-determination, and the establishment of their independent national state on their national soil, and that institutes arrangements for the security and peace of all states in the region.

Toward the achievement of this, the Palestine National Council affirms:

1.—The necessity of convening the effective international conference on the issue of the Middle East and its core, the question of Palestine, under the auspices of the United Nations and with the participation of the permanent members of the Security Council and all parties to the conflict in the region including the Palestine Liberation Organization, the sole, legitimate representative of the Palestinian people, on an equal footing, and by considering that the international peace conference be convened on the basis of United Nations Security Council resolutions 242 and 338 and the attainment of the legitimate national rights of the Palestinian people, foremost among which is the right to self-determination and in accordance with the principles and provisions of the United Nations Charter concerning the right of peoples to self-determination, and by the inadmissibility of the acquisition of the territory of others by force or military conquest, and in accordance with the relevant United Nations resolutions on the question of Palestine.

2.—The withdrawal of Israel from all the Palestinian and Arab territories it occupied in 1967, including Arab Jerusalem.

3.—The annullment of all measures of annexation and appropriation and the removal of settlements established by Israel in the Palestinian and Arab territories since 1967.

4.—Endeavoring to place the occupied Palestinian territories, including Arab Jerusalem, under the auspices of the United Nations for a limited period in order to protect our people and afford the appropriate atmosphere for the success of the proceeding of the international conference toward the attainment of a comprehensive political settlement and the attainment of peace and security for all on the basis of mutual aquiescence and consent, and to enable the Palestinian state to exercise its effective authority in these territories.

5.—The settlement of the question of the Palestinian refugees in accordance with the relevant United Nations resolutions.

6.—Guaranteeing the freedom of worship and religious practice for all faiths in the holy places in Palestine.

7.—The Security Council is to formulate and guarantee arrangements for security and peace between all the states concerned in the region, including the Palestinian state.

The Palestine National Council affirms its previous resolutions concerning the distinctive relationship between the Jordanian and Palestinian peoples, and affirms that the future relationship between the two states of Palestine and Jordan should be on a confederal basis as a result of the free and voluntary choice of the two fraternal peoples in order to strengthen the historical bonds and the vital interests they hold in common.

The National Council also renews its commitment to the United Nations resolutions that affirm the right of peoples to resist foreign occupation, colonialism, and racial discrimination, and their right to struggle for their independence, and reiterates its rejection of terrorism in all its forms, including state terrorism, affirming its commitment to previous resolutions in this respect and the resolution of the Arab summit in Algiers in 1988, and to UN resolutions 42/195 of 1987, and 40/61 of 1985, and that contained in the Cairo declaration of 1985 in this respect.

Third: in the Arab and International Arenas:

. . . The Palestine National Council, as it hails the Arab states and thanks them for their support of our people's struggle, calls on them to honor the commitments they approved at the summit conference in Algiers in support of the Palestinian people and their blessed *intifada.* The Council, in issuing this appeal, expresses its great confidence that the leaders of the Arab nation will remain, as we have known them, a bulwark of support for Palestine and its people. . . .

The Palestine National Council expresses its deep gratitude to all the states and international forces and organizations that support the national rights of the Palestinians, and affirms its desire to strengthen the bonds of friendship and cooperation with the Soviet Union, the People's Republic of China, the other socialist countries, the nonaligned states, the Latin American states, and the other friendly states, and notes with satisfaction the signs of positive evolution in the position of some West European states and Japan in the direction of support for the rights of the Palestinian people, applauds this development, and urges intensified efforts to increase it. . . .

The Council notes with considerable concern the growth of the Israeli forces of fascism and extremism and the escalation of their open calls for the implementation of their policy of annihilation and individual and mass expulsion of our people from their homeland, and calls for intensified efforts in all arenas to confront this fascist peril. The Council at the same time expresses its appreciation of the role and courage of the Israeli peace forces as they resist and expose the forces of fascism, racism, and aggression; support our people's struggle and their valiant *intifada;* and back our people's right to self-determination and the establishment of an independent state. The Council confirms its past resolutions regarding the reinforcement and development of relations with these democratic forces.

The Palestine National Council also addresses itself to the American people, calling on them all to strive to put an end to the American policy that denies the Palestinian people's national rights, including their sacred right to self-determination, and urging them to work toward the adoption of policies that conform with the human rights character and the international conventions and resolutions and serve the quest for peace in the Middle East and security for all its peoples, including the Palestinian people. . . .

Palestine National Council: Declaration of Independence (November 15, 1988)

In the name of God, the Compassionate, the Merciful

Palestine, the Land of the three monotheistic faiths, is where the Palestinian Arab people was born, on which it grew, developed and excelled. The Palestinian people was never separated from or diminished in its integral bonds with Palestine. Thus the Palestinian Arab people ensured for itself an everlasting union between itself, its land and its history.

Resolute throughout that history, the Palestinian Arab people forged its national identity, rising even to unimagined levels in its defence, as invasion, the design of others, and the appeal special to Palestine's ancient and luminous place on that eminence where powers and civilizations are joined . . . All this intervened thereby to deprive the people of its political independence. Yet the undying connection between Palestine and its people, secured for the Land its character, and for the people its national genius.

Nourished by an unfolding series of civilizations and cultures, inspired by a heritage rich in variety and kind, the Palestinian Arab people added to its stature by consolidating a union between itself and its patrimonial Land. The call went out from Temple, Church and Mosque that to praise the Creator, to celebrate compassion and peace was indeed the message of Palestine. And in generation after generation, the Palestinian Arab people gave of itself unsparingly in the valiant battle for liberation and homeland. For what has been the unbroken chain of our people's rebellions but the heroic embodiment of our will for national independence? And so the people were sustained in the struggle to stay and to prevail.

When in the course of modern times a new order of values was declared with norms and values fair for all, it was the Palestinian Arab people that had been excluded from the destiny of all other peoples by a hostile array of local and foreign powers. Yet again had unaided justice been revealed as insufficient to drive the world's history along its preferred course.

And it was the Palestinian people, already wounded in its body, that was submitted to yet another type of occupation over which floated the falsehood that "Palestine was a land without people." This notion was foisted upon some in the world, whereas in Article 22 of the Covenant of the League of Nations (1919) and in the Treaty of Lausanne (1923), the community of nations had recognized that all the Arab territories, including Palestine, of the formerly Ottoman provinces, were to have granted to them their freedom as provisionally independent nations.

Despite the historical injustice inflicted on the Palestinian Arab people resulting in their dispersion and depriving them of their right to self-determination, following upon UN General Assembly Resolution 181 (1947), which partitioned Palestine into two states, one Arab, one Jewish, yet it is this resolution that still provides those conditions of international legitimacy that ensure the right of the Palestinian Arab people to sovereignty.

By stages, the occupation of Palestine and parts of other Arab territories by Israeli forces, the willed dispossession and expulsion from their ancestral homes of the majority of Palestine's civilian inhabitants was achieved by organized terror; those Palestinians who remained, as a vestige subjugated in its homeland, were persecuted and forced to endure the destruction of their national life.

Thus were principles of international legitimacy violated. Thus were the Charter of the United Nations and its resolutions disfigured, for they had recognized the Palestinian Arab people's national rights, including the right of Return, the right to independence, the right to sovereignty over territory and homeland.

In Palestine and on its perimeters, in exile distant and near, the Palestinian Arab people never faltered and never abandoned its conviction in its right of Return and independence. Occupation, massacres and dispersion achieved no gain in the unabated Palestinian consciousness of self and political identity, as Palestinians went forward with their destiny, undeterred and unbowed. And from out of the long years of trial in ever mounting struggle, the Palestinian political identity emerged further consolidated and confirmed. And the collective Palestinian national will forged for itself a political embodiment, the Palestine Liberation Organization, its sole, legitimate representative recognized by the world community as a whole, as well as by related regional and international institutions. Standing on the very rock of conviction in the Palestinian people's inalienable rights, and on the ground of Arab national consensus, and of international legitimacy, the PLO led the campaigns of its great people, moulded into unity and powerful resolve, one and indivisible in its triumphs, even as it suffered massacres and confinement within and without its home. And so Palestinian resistance was clarified and raised into the forefront of Arab and world awareness, as the struggle of the Palestinian Arab people achieved unique prominence among the world's liberation movements in the modern era.

The massive national uprising, the Intifada, now intensifying in cumulative scope and power on occupied Palestinian territories, as well as the unflinching resistance of the refugee camps outside the homeland, have elevated awareness of the Palestinian truth and right into still higher realms of comprehension and actuality. Now at last the curtain has been dropped around a whole epoch of prevarication and negation. The Intifada has set siege to the mind of official Israel, which has for too long relied exclusively upon myth and terror to deny Palestinian existence altogether. Because of the Intifada and its revolutionary irreversible impulse, the history of Palestine has therefore arrived at a decisive juncture.

Whereas the Palestinian people reaffirms most definitively its inalienable rights in the Land of its patrimony:

Now by virtue of natural, historical and legal rights, and the sacrifices of successive generations who gave of themselves in defence of the freedom and independence of their homeland;

In pursuance of Resolutions adopted by Arab Summit Conferences and relying on the authority bestowed by international legitimacy as embodied in the resolutions of the United Nations Organization since 1947;

And in exercise by the Palestinian Arab people of its rights to self-determination, political independence, and sovereignty over its territory;

The Palestine National Council, in the name of God, and in the name of the Palestinian Arab people; hereby proclaims the establishment of the State of Palestine on our Palestinian territory with its capital Holy Jerusalem (Al-Quds Ash-Sharif).

The State of Palestine is the state of Palestinians wherever they may be. The state is for them to enjoy in it their collective national and cultural identity, theirs to pursue in it a complete equality of rights. In it will be safeguarded their political and religious convictions and their human dignity by means of a parliamentary democratic system of governance, itself based on freedom of expression and the freedom to form parties. The rights of minorities will duly be respected by the majority, as minorities must abide by decisions of the majority. Governance will be based on principles of social justice, equality and non-discrimination in public rights of men or women, on grounds of race, religion, colour or sex under the aegis of a constitution which ensures the rule of law and an independent judiciary. Thus shall these principles allow no departure from Palestine's age-old spiritual and civilizational heritage of tolerance and religious coexistence.

The State of Palestine is an Arab state, an integral and indivisible part of the Arab nation, at one with that nation in heritage and civilization, with it also in its aspiration for liberation, progress, democracy and unity. The State of Palestine affirms its obligation to abide by the Charter of the League of Arab States, whereby the coordination of the Arab states with each other shall be strengthened. It calls upon Arab compatriots to consolidate and enhance the emergence in reality of our state, to mobilize potential, and to intensify efforts whose goal is to end Israeli occupation.

The State of Palestine proclaims its commitment to the principles and purposes of the United Nations, and to the Universal Declaration of Human Rights. It proclaims its commitment as well to the principles and policies of the Non-Aligned Movement.

It further announces itself to be a peace-loving State, in adherence to the principles of peaceful coexistance. It will join with all states and peoples in order to assure a permanent peace based upon justice and the respect of rights so that humanity's potential for well-being may be assured, an earnest competition for excellence may be maintained, and in which confidence in the future will eliminate fear for those who are just and for whom justice is the only recourse.

In the context of its struggle for peace in the Land of Love and Peace, the State of Palestine calls upon the United Nations to bear special responsibility for the Palestinian Arab people and its homeland. It calls upon all peace- and freedom-loving peoples and states to assist it in the attainment of its objectives, to provide it with security, to alleviate the tragedy of its people, and to help it terminate Israel's occupation of the Palestinian territories.

The State of Palestine herewith declares that it believes in the settlement of regional and international disputes by peaceful means, in accordance with the UN Charter and resolutions. Without prejudice to its natural right to defend its territorial integrity and independence, it therefore rejects the threat or use of force, violence and terrorism against its territorial integrity or political independence, as it also rejects their use against the territorial integrity of other states.

Therefore, on this day unlike all others, November 15, 1988, as we stand at the threshold of a new dawn, in all honour and modesty we humbly bow to the sacred spirits of our fallen ones, Palestinian and Arab, by the purity of whose sacrifice for the homeland our sky has been illuminated and our land given life. Our hearts are lifted up and irradiated by the light emanating from the much blessed Intifada, from those who have endured and have fought the fight of the camps, of dispersion, of exile, from those who have borne the standard for freedom, our children, our aged, our youth, our prisoners, detainees and wounded, all those whose ties to our sacred soil are confirmed in camp, village and town. We render special tribute to that brave Palestinian woman, guardian of sustenance and life, keeper of our people's perennial flame. To the souls of our sainted martyrs, to the whole of our Palestinian Arab people, to all free and honorable peoples everywhere, we pledge that our struggle shall be continued until the occupation ends, and the foundation of our sovereignty and independence shall be fortified accordingly.

Therefore, we call upon our great people to rally to the banner of Palestine, to cherish and defend it, so that it may forever be the symbol of our freedom and dignity in that homeland, which is a homeland for the free, now and always. In the name of God, the Compassionate, the Merciful:

"Say:

"O God, Master of the Kingdom,
Thou givest the Kingdom to whom Thou wilt,
and seizest the Kingdom from whom Thou wilt,
Thou exaltest whom Thou wilt,
and Thou abasest whom Thou wilt;
in Thy hand is the good;
Thou art powerful over everything."

President Husni Mubarak:
The Inevitability of Peace
(January 21, 1989)

. . . I hope this year will be a year of peace. In fact, we are exerting the utmost efforts for the sake of peace. All our contacts with the friendly and European states are also channeled in the direction of peace because peace is the only path leading to a real solution to all key issues. I believe that wars have not decisively resolved any issue, as best proved by the war of Vietnam with the United States. That war continued for many years and was settled only through negotiations. We hope that 1989 will be a year of peace, and we, together with our brothers in the Arab countries, are exerting our utmost efforts to promote the Middle East peace process. We are helped in this regard by the European states, the big powers, and the peace-loving forces in Israel itself. As long as we have confidence in peace, the opposing forces will certainly respond because the current of peace is sweeping and nobody can stop it. . . .

Enough of "wars." I once again ask what is wrong with peace? Has it prevented any steps in our or the Arab nation's favor? We are helping the Palestine question more than anyone else. I will speak frankly and without resentment. For example, when I visited the United States last January, I did not forget Syria. Asked about Syria, I said verbatim: We will not forget Syria. During the visit, Richard Murphy and Philip Habib visited Syria and I was told in Dallas about the meeting and what took place during it. We are helping movement toward all the Arab nation's issues.

As for Libya, they say there is nothing called Israel although the world's countries, including the two superpowers and the European, Asian, and African states, recognize Israel. The Soviet Union has recognized it and even helped it join the other members of the United Nations. The colonel [Al-Qadhdhafi] is free not to recognize it, but this does not mean that it is not recognized. He asks the entire Arab world to wage war. God has granted us a mind with which to think. We fought for many years, but where did we get? We also spent 100 billion [currency not specified] on wars, apart from thousands of martyrs, until we reached the present situation from which we are now suffering. I am therefore not ready to take more risks. Moreover, wars have generally not solved any problem. Regardless of the difficulties or obstacles surrounding the present peace process, our real effort focuses on removing these obstacles and bringing viewpoints closer. We are not all all pessimistic. Today's world is one of peace, peaceful negotiations, and fruitful dialogue, which leads to real results away from blood and fire.

[Mubarak] All world public opinion supports the international conference with the exception of Yitzhaq Shamir, who does not agree to it. He should respond to the call of peace because the peace-loving forces in Israel and elsewhere are increasing. War has exhausted the region's forces, including Israel. It has also lowered the people's standard of living in Israel itself and the entire region. Let me ask: Is it possible for this situation to continue? Shamir must respond to the call of peace sooner or later because this is the will of the people. Peace will come even though it seems to be a long way ahead. Israel will sooner or later respond to the international conference, and I am optimistic that peace is coming. . . .

Prime Minister Yitzhak Shamir: Peace Plan (May 14, 1989)

Basic Premises

3.—The initiative is founded upon the assumption that there is a national consensus for it on the basis of the basic guidelines of the Government of Israel, including the following points:

a) Israel yearns for peace and the continuation of the political process by means of direct negotiations based on the principles of the Camp David Accords.

b) Israel opposes the establishment of an additional Palestinian state in the Gaza district and in the area between Israel and Jordan.

c) Israel will not conduct negotiations with the PLO.

d) There will be no change in the status of Judea, Samaria and Gaza other than in accordance with the basic guidelines of the Government.

Subjects to Be Dealt With in the Peace Process

4.—Israel views as important that the peace between Israel and Egypt, based on the Camp David Accords, will serve as a cornerstone for enlarging the circle of peace in the region, and calls for a common endeavour for the strengthening of the peace and its extension, through continued consultation.

b) Israel calls for the establishment of peaceful relations between it and those Arab states which still maintain a state of war with it for the purpose of promoting a comprehensive settlement for the Arab-Israeli conflict, including recognition, direct negotiations, ending the boycott, diplomatic relations, cessation of hostile activity in international institutions or forums and regional and bilateral cooperation.

c) Israel calls for an international endeavour to resolve the problem of the residents of the Arab refugee camps in Judea, Samaria and the Gaza district in order to improve their living conditions and to rehabilitate them. Israel is prepared to be a partner in this endeavour.

d) In order to advance the political negotiation process leading to peace, Israel proposes free and democratic elections among the Palestinian Arab inhabitants of Judea, Samaria and the Gaza district in an atmosphere devoid of violence, threats and terror. In these elections a representation will be chosen to conduct negotiations for a transitional period of self-rule. This period will constitute a test for co-existence and cooperation. At a later stage, negotiations will be conducted for a permanent solution during which all the proposed options for an agreed settlement will be examined, and peace between Israel and Jordan will be achieved.

e) All the above-mentioned steps should be dealt with simultaneously.

f) The details of what has been mentioned in (*d*) above will be given below.

The Principles Constituting the Initiative

Stages

5.—The initiative is based on two stages

a) Stage A—A transitional period for an interim agreement.

b) Stage B—Permanent Solution.

6.—The interlock between the Stages is a timetable on which the Plan is built: the peace process delineated by the initiative is based on Resolutions 242 and 338 upon which the Camp David Accords are founded.

Timetable

7.—The transitional period will continue for 5 years.
8.—As soon as possible, but not later than the third year after the beginning of the transitional period, negotiations for achieving a permanent solution will begin.

Parties Participating in the Negotiations in Both Stages

9.—The parties participating in the negotiations for the First Stage (the interim agreement) shall include Israel and the elected representation of the Palestinian Arab inhabitants of Judea, Samaria and the Gaza district. Jordan and Egypt will be invited to participate in these negotiations if they so desire.
10.—The parties participating in the negotiations for the Second Stage (Permanent Solution) shall include Israel and the elected representation of the Palestinian Arab inhabitants of Judea, Samaria and the Gaza district, as well as Jordan: furthermore, Egypt may participate in these negotiations. In negotiations between Israel and Jordan, in which the elected representation of the Palestinian Arab inhabitants of Judea, Samaria and the Gaza district will participate, the peace treaty between Israel and Jordan will be concluded.

Substance of Transitional Period

11.—During the transitional period the Palestinian Arab inhabitants of Judea, Samaria and the Gaza district will be accorded self-rule by means of which they will, themselves, conduct their affairs of daily life. Israel will continue to be responsible for security, foreign affairs and all matters concerning Israeli citizens in Judea, Samaria and the Gaza district. Topics involving the implementation of the plan for self-rule will be considered and decided within the framework of the negotiations for an interim agreement.

Substance of Permanent Solution

12.—In the negotiations for a permanent solution every party shall be entitled to present for discussion all the subjects it may wish to raise.
13.—The aim of the negotiations should be:

a) The achievement of a permanent solution acceptable to the negotiating parties.

b) The arrangements for peace and borders between Israel and Jordan.

Details of the Process for the Implementation of the Initiative

14.—First and foremost dialogue and basic agreement by the Palestinian Arab inhabitants of Judea, Samaria and the Gaza district, as well as Egypt and Jordan if they wish to take part, as above-mentioned, in the negotiations, on the principles constituting the initiative.

15.—*a*) Immediately afterwards will follow the stage of preparations and implementation of the election process in which a representation of the Palestinian Arab inhabitants of Judea, Samaria and Gaza will be elected. This representation:

I) Shall be a partner to the conduct of negotiations for the transitional period (interim agreement).

II) Shall constitute the self-governing authority in the course of the transitional period.

III) Shall be the central Palestinian component, subject to agreement after three years, in the negotiations for the permanent solution.

b) In the period of the preparation and implementation there shall be a calming of the violence in Judea, Samaria and the Gaza district.

16.—As to the substance of the elections, it is recommended that a proposal of regional elections be adopted, the details of which shall be determined in further discussions.

17.—Every Palestinian Arab residing in Judea, Samaria and the Gaza districts, who shall be elected by the inhabitants to represent them—after having submitted his candidacy in accordance with the detailed document which shall determine the subject of the elections—may be a legitimate participant in the conduct of negotiations with Israel.

18.—The elections shall be free, democratic and secret.

19.—Immediately after the election of the Palestinian representation, negotiations shall be conducted with it on an interim agreement for a transitional period which shall continue for 5 years, as mentioned above. In these negotiations the parties shall determine all the subjects relating to the substance to the self-rule and the arrangements necessary for its implementation.

20.—As soon as possible, but not later than the third year after the establishment of the self-rule, negotiations for a permanent solution shall begin. During the whole period of these negotiations until the signing of the agreement for a permanent solution, the self-rule shall continue in effect as determined in the negotiations for an interim agreement.

President Husni Mubarak: Ten-Point Plan (September 1989)

1.—The necessity for the participation of all citizens of the West Bank and Gaza (including the residents of East Jerusalem) in the elections both in the voting and in the right to stand as a candidate for any person who has not been convicted by a court of committing a crime. This allows for the participation of those under administrative detention.

2.—Freedom to campaign before and during the elections.

3.—Acceptance of international supervision of the election process.

4.—Prior commitment of the government of Israel that it will accept the results of the elections.

5.—Commitment of the government of Israel that the elections will be part of the efforts which will lead not only to an interim phase, but also to a final settlement and that all efforts from beginning to end will be based on the principles of solution according to the US conception, namely resolutions 242 and 338, territory for peace, insuring the security of all the states of the region including Israel, and Palestinian political rights.

6.—Withdrawal of the Israeli army during the election process at least one kilometer outside the perimeters of the polling stations.

7.—Prohibition of Israelis from entering the West Bank and Gaza on election day with permission to enter only for those who work there and the residents of the settlements.

8.—The preparatory period for the elections should not exceed two months. These preparations shall be undertaken by a joint Israeli-Palestinian committee. (The US and Egypt may assist in forming this committee).

9.—Guarantee by the US of all the above points together with a prior declaration to that effect on the part of the government of Israel.

10.—A halt to settlement.

Chairman Yasir Arafat: Speech on the Intifada (September 1989)

In the name of God, the merciful, the compassionate. So lose not heart, nor fall into despair: For ye must gain mastery if ye are true in faith. If a wound hath touched you, be sure a similar wound hath touched the others. Such days (for varying fortunes) we give to men and men by turns: That God may know that those believe, and that He may take to Himself from your ranks martyr-witnesses (to truth). And God loveth not those who do wrong.

O the great masses of our Palestinian people, O the epic of the brave intifadah [uprising] on the soil of the homeland, O steadfast heroes in the camps and on the borders of the homeland, O struggles in every field of struggle inside and outside the beloved homeland, victory is yours, as you are making your dear sacrifices on the path of national independence. Freedom and victory are yours as you daily create events of unique heroism and distinguished experience for your giant intifada, which has occupied its lofty peak since its first waves in the history of mankind as a major landmark and a new contribution to the experience of peoples struggling against the forces of colonialism, Zionism, racism, coercion, and injustice.

O women of my country; O heroes of my country; O brave and heroic youths and men of my country; you continue the march with more resolution and stronger will as you are entering the 22d month of the sacred stones intifada. Despite all repressive and terrorist attempts and despite the great sacrifices, you have continued—with legendary courage—to raise the banner of resistance. And, with your stones, you are pounding the structure of the transient occupation and building our forthcoming Palestinian state, making the certain date of independence and freedom nearer for our people. Who in the world, beloved ones, could have believed or predicted—in those days of January 1987—that the intifada would continue and escalate? Who in the world was ready to admit our people's great ability to continue the march to achieve the goal which we will not relinquish, the goal of independence, freedom, and victory. Many people refused to believe our signs. Many people were not interested in our talk about the escalating volcano inside and outside the homeland. Many people were also not interested in our talk about the gathering storm throughout the region. Then the intifada came, the intifada came so that we could storm the walls of the world's conscience. Its news also reached every house around the world and our people's cause has recorded its shining and prominent regional and international presence. The phoenix has set out each day to occupy new positions, which would not have existed without the great sacrifices and the procession of martyrs who fill the path of heroism and glory—the path of the dear sons and righteous beloved ones. This is in addition to the sacrifices and heroism of our wounded, prisoners, and detainees that emerged through this mammoth popular momentum of the great people of the intifada, through their inspiring legendary steadfastness, and through this firmness and resistance of our heroes in the positions of combat and conflict. . . .

The masses of the blessed intifada were affirming, every moment and in every way before the whole world, that whoever for one moment thinks of the possibility of peddling the settlement project, which does not provide for our people's firm and national rights, is dreaming and cannot read the revolutionary reality or know the revolutionary will of our people. They do not know how to observe the current course of history flowing to the delta of liberty and independence.

They are still haunted by the ghosts and delusions of the old eras of occupation, control, and expansion. These delusions are extinct and the blessed stones of our women, children, and men are now declaring the end of these extinct delusions. Nay, this forces many of these deluded to recognize the impossibility of torpedoing the unity of the Palestinian stand which manifests a unique example of the revolutionary world march through creating splits and divisions in its ranks, casting doubts, or liquidation. This is a great revolutionary example of unity and revolutionary cohesion. . . .

O masses of the blessed intifada; O heroes of the stones and songs; O courageous strike forces; O you steadfast people in every location: The fascist occupation have been trying—since the outbreak of the intifada—to impose a media blackout on the intifada activities to prevent the arrival of your brave voice to world conscience and to prevent the exposure of their racist crimes and crazy terrorism. However, despite all their repressive measures, the Palestinian blood has infiltrated the siege while the Palestinian shout reached the heart and conscience of the world.

You, courageous heroes, knew that confronting the campaigns of siege and news blackout will escalate the defiance and steadfastnes and with more jihad and struggle that are entrenched on the ground in the form of daily effective blows which had their effect in shaking and shattering the authority and might of the enemy. The power of the people, the power of the intifada, and the power of revolution, which has been entrenched by Qawim, will emerge along with our broad, believing masses, the effectiveness of the popular committees, and the activities of the strike forces. This power has also been entrenched by this accurate popular organization that has gathered all factions of our people and forces in the crucible of a firm national unity to entrench the foundations of national independence. In the name of God, the merciful, the compassionate: God truly loves those who fight in his cause in battle array, as if they were a solid cemented structure.

Hence, my brothers, your boycott of Israeli goods has succeeded, and your organized strikes have affected labor in Israeli concerns and the enemy's labor activity and economy. The national agricultural, industrial, and vocational projects have succeeded in supporting the national and local production and in bolstering the home economy. Therefore, we have to work actively and confidently to promote national institutions and all their projects, to support national production, and to boost family economy. We should also work toward expanding the activity of mass institutions, specialized committees, popular education, national media, and others. In addition, we should concentrate on mass education and establishing well-being committees to solve the problems of peoples, and there are many problems.

Revolutionary discipline should also be practiced to prevent the negative aspects and crush deviations, because the enemy will try to push his secret agents among us to intensify these negative points and deviations in order to make people hate the march and to distract them from their blessed intifada. So, you are urged to show more and more revolutionary discipline, more and more fight against anarchy, and more and more serious work to end the negative aspects and increase the positive ones.

No revolution can emerge victorious unless supported by its masses, and no militant march can continue without sound revolutionary discipline. It cannot continue without bolstering the unity of its ranks, commitment to the calls of the Unified National Leadership, supporting the structure of the popular committees, and firmly confronting all attempts to create divisions, especially in the way of dealing with the sons of our people who lost their way and fell in the trap of the enemy. We should push them toward repentance, first, second, and third; "Let he who is without sin cast the first stone." Otherwise we will fall in the trap that our enemy is making for us, as happened to the revolution of 1936. I therefore appeal to you to commit yourselves to this fraternal and revolutionary policy; "Strong against unbelievers, (but) compassionate among each other" [part of Koranic verse]. I also appeal to you to be alert against falsehoods against the march of the intifada and the discipline of the masses, which make a unified whole. Hence came the orientation not to issue statements in the names of the various frameworks of the intifada and its unified strike force. This was a clear reference to the statements issued to disintegrate and undermine the firmness of the intifada and its unified strike forces, which are remote from organizational bragging and nonsense. We all have the heart of one man. In the name of God, the merciful, the compassionate: Our Lord, decide thou between us and our people in truth, for thou art the best to decide.

We realize, my beloved brothers, that this great revolutionary achievement, which is daily being entrenched on the ground, exasperates the facist occupiers, who fully understand its significance and essence. They, therefore, intensify their terrorist campaigns and attempts to infiltrate our ranks, confuse our minds, and undermine our unity. They declare the war of murder in cold blood; they also declare the war of starvation, blockade, and detention in an unsuccessful attempt to crush the blessed intifada. ''Fain would they extinguish God's light with their mouths, but God will not allow but that His light should be perfected, even though the unbelievers may detest (it).''

By this, they prove their failure to learn the lesson and absorb the bright fact. This intifada will continue, continue, with God's help, despite all difficulties, wave after wave, until the hateful Israeli occupation of our land and sacred places is ended. There are endless queues of heroes proceeding one after the other to receive the banner whenever a struggler falls or another is imprisoned in occupation jails.

O courageous people of the intifada, O hero strugglers of the Unified National Leadership, popular committees, and strike force. O strugglers of mass institutions—women, youths, students, workers, peasants, professionals, vocationalists, academicians, landowners, farmers, and, especially, the cubs of the revolution: O captive heroes, makers of the epic of steadfastness in prisons; our valiant wounded, who lift the banners of triumph over your wounds; O steadfast people in all positions of struggle in the homeland and abroad; O masses of the great Arab nation: Our intifada today enters its 22d month with full confidence in the inevitability of victory, God willing. Freedom has never been so near and within reach as it seems to us now. It needs the efforts of friends, support of brothers, and sacrifices of revolutionaries. After we imposed our existence on the political map, it is inevitable that we impose it on the geographical map. Let us boost the unity of our ranks and the cohesion of our front. Unity, unity among all, among our broad masses, all our organizations—Hamas, Fatah, the Popular Front [for the Liberation of Palestine], the Democratic Front [for the Liberation of Palestine], the Jihad, the communists, the [Palestinian Popular] Struggle Front, the Palestinian Front, and all and trade unions, popular forces and the institutions—all united in one framework. Let us affirm strong commitment to the calls of the Unified National Leadership of the intifada, and escalate the war of the sacred stones with utmost vigor and strength, and let the strike forces escalate their struggle with firmness and solidity against the occupiers, all of whose weapons cannot conceal their political and historical crisis. Your intifada is continuing until the state is established, and your steadfastness will continue until victory is achieved. The state is within a stone's throw, the victory is coming, and our Palestinian flag will be raised, God willing, over Jerusalem, the capital of our city, the first of the two qiplas [direction in which Muslims position themselves during prayer—Jerusalem and Mecca] and the third sacred shrines, the birthplace of the Messiah and the city to where Prophet Muhammad made his night journey. In the name of God, the merciful, the compassionate: "And another (favor will He bestow, which ye do love—help from God and a speedy victory. So give the glad tidings to the believers."

Secretary of State James Baker: Five-Point Plan (October 1989)

1.—The United States understands that because Egypt and Israel have been working hard on the peace process, there is agreement that an Israeli delegation should conduct a dialogue with a Palestinian delegation in Cairo.

2.—The United States understands that Egypt cannot substitute itself for the Palestinians and Egypt will consult with Palestinians on all aspects of that dialogue. Egypt will also consult with Israel and the United States.

3.—The United States understands that Israel will attend the dialogue only after a satisfactory list of Palestinians has been worked out.

4.—The United States understands that the Government of Israel will come to the dialogue on the basis of the Israeli Government's May 14 initiative. The United States further understands that Palestinians will come to the dialogue prepared to discuss elections and the negotiating process in accordance with Israel's initiative. The U.S. understands, therefore, that Palestinians would be free to raise issues that relate to their opinions on how to make elections and the negotiating process succeeed.

5.—In order to facilitate this process, the U.S. proposes that the Foreign Ministers of Israel, Egypt, and the U.S. meet in Washington within two weeks.

President Saddam Hussein: Two Speeches to the Arab Cooperation Council (February 1990)

I.

We Arabs, Iraqis included, have a habit of either underrating or overrating our power. I believe that through cooperation among ourselves and the prevalence of a brotherly spirit, we will reach a way of thinking that will prevent us from overestimating ourselves to the point of delirium, or underestimating ourselves to the point of missing our chance to play an influential role.

The Arabs possess an extraordinary ability to accelerate the creation of an international balance because, in addition to the known traditional elements including the known strategic elements involving the region's geography and their influence, there is an additional element: the possession of an energy source unparalleled in the world. All the major influential powers are affected by this, be it the United States, Japan, or Europe, or even the Soviet Union. Consequently, when Arab influence, by virtue of this extra element, reaches this point, then we can speed up the creation of a balance that at least does not make Arab interests vulnerable. . . .

The Arabs should not only settle their differences, but also organize their course of action by adopting positive steps. The more their course is organized through positive action, the more their influence will be. But, if we concern ourselves only with extinguishing fires, we will lose much of our energy inasmuch as we will be handicapped and unable to move forward.

Praise be to God, we hope that the new spirit in the Arab League will bring about leaders' meetings and other meetings and produce fraternal cooperation at the level of the three groupings—the Arab Maghreb Union, the Gulf Cooperation Council, and the ACC. All these are positive signs. At the same time, our enemies will take the positive steps we announce into their calculations of the balances of power. They will take into account that behind every statement we make there is real action they have to deal with. They will assume that we mean what we say. When we do not translate what we say we will be the losers because our enemy will be aware that we are only making statements and not taking action.

What draws attention in the Americans' behavior is the quick appearance of the spirit of unilateralism although the international imbalance is not old. An example of this is encouraging Jewish emigration, particularly Soviet Jewish immigration to the occupied territory, although the declared U.S. position is that it works for peace and that it is in touch with Egypt and the Palestinians on the basis that it wants to establish peace. Would someone who wants to achieve peace act this way? It is a superpower and it has become the first-ranking superpower, while the USSR, as a superpower, is undergoing a series of changes. In addition to this, we have taken note of U.S. statements on the Gulf and the assertions that the Israelis can use weapons stored in Israel. None of these signs is good.

In case of danger, there are always early signs. Israel always takes international changes and their effect into consideration. Israel has never lost an opportunity to take advantage of the atmosphere of change. Since the establishment of Israel—and even before it was established when it opened contacts with the Ottoman Empire and until the Balfour Declaration—the Jews who believe in the establishment of the State of Israel have always exploited opportunities. We must expect Israel to exploit the opportunity resulting from the current changes in the world.

Israel now is facing a clear question; that is, in light of its present situation time is not on its side. Tension in relations among the Arabs has begun to ease; the Arabs want to understand, resolve their problems, and cooperate among themselves. There is a real desire to know about the changes in the world and their effect on their situation; they want to know what they should do to become effective in the world. Arab scientific cadres are being formed and our intrinsic military capabilities are growing. The Israelis say that the news of Arab capabilities have surprised them.

Therefore, all this makes the Israelis realize that time is against them in terms of topography and politics, as well as other factors. Let us not rule out that some Israeli strategists will say that time is against us in this situation. If we can change this situation and change the military geography, time might be on our side.

Therefore, we should be alert over the next five years because when Israel wants to embark on military aggression it will take new land; it might launch a new attack to come out of its deadlock. Who will oppose them internationally?

The answer is no one, even if no one offered direct support to encourage it to launch aggression, no one will stand against Israeli aggression, as happened in the wars of 1967 and 1973 because the United States has remained alone in the arena of the big powers, and the U.S. policy is the policy we are now experiencing. Will the Soviet Union be capable of confronting the aggression if it takes place, or will it be Europe that confronts the aggression? All this makes us wonder what then is the situation?

The most influential stand vis-a-vis such a situation should come from within ourselves and our capabilities. There is no better way than this to remove the minefields that mar Arab relations. The second best way under these circumstances is also to push ahead joint action as expeditiously as possible. Faced with the quick developments, we should have a joint policy as Arabs on the regional level. It is not sufficient that Iraq has a policy, whether this policy is viewed as sound, or wrong in varying degrees, or that Egypt has such a policy, or Kuwait and Saudi Arabia, and Algeria too. We are dutybound as Arabs to have a joint regional policy. The basic pillars of this joint regional policy are to reduce the number of the Arab nation's enemies, or to reduce the frictions that will add further enemies. Our relations with Ethiopia should not be bad. We must try to solve our problems with Iran as Arabs and within boundaries that safeguard our rights and do not encroach on its rights.

All these elements limit the Israeli ability to make inroads during the mentioned five-year period not only in the Arab land but also in terms of influencing the Arabs in the technological, political and military fields with its own efforts or with the help of Jewish influence in the world. If the Arabs take all these elements into consideration, they will find themselves in an excellent position and will prevent the wave from destroying their barriers. The wave will merely move from one place to another because their barriers are high and impregnable. The wave will thus be forced to change direction and to destroy barriers in other places. . . . Moreover, when interest in the Palestine question diminishes, the Arabs will not act either. When a long time passes without effective action, interest in an issue fades away. There is another important issue, which is the situation in the occupied territories and the valiant popular resistance there.

It is not enough to show Arab solidarity with the intifada in a traditional manner that may become ineffective if it remains unchanged. It is necessary to overhaul the means and formulas of attention and support. At the top of the list is extending real financial support to the militant Palestinian people and enhancing organized and meaningful political action in the international arena. . . . the intifada and its actions represent an Arab army corps that is carrying out the task of weakening the Zionists in the occupied territories by using stones. We must provide the intifada with its needs out of pan-Arab principles and regional security considerations. Let us then provide it with what an army corps needs in supplies and ammunition. Then, and only then, will we ensure the strength of the intifada.

What weakens the enemy most is psychological exhaustion. Israel used to say that its soldier was invincible and some of us even believed it. Now, and due to the intifada, that soldier looks weak and undisciplined. He no longer wears his beret or helmet and does not rise to salute his officers when they pass by. This, and other things, show that he lacks discipline. It is well known that the soldier's strength lies in his discipline.

The intifada of the young people and valiant women has shown us the true, pathetic state of the Israeli soldier. They have told us: Here you see the Israeli soldier—a man whom we can defeat if we exhaust him. If we, the little ones and women, have destroyed the Israeli soldiers' morale, then Arabs, united and with greater power, are able to defeat the enemy and regain their rights.

Now we see certain new factors emerging on the ground that affect the residents of the West Bank and Gaza. Immigration to Israel has made some of them leave their lands and go to Jordan. Last year, Mr. President, 55,000 young Palestinians left the West Bank and Gaza and came to Jordan. This should make us think about maintaining, through resistance, what is left of Arab rights on the land until such time as we can use more effective methods to regain more than what we can regain now. We know that 80 percent of Israelis live on the Mediterranean coast and do not care about the intifada. As for us, we are affected by the intifada. The Israeli people have become used to the fact that there are children throwing stones, and the one who is really affected is the Israeli soldier who returns to his home town at the weekend. What I mean, Mr. President, is that without real, constant, and strong support for the intifada, it may become ineffective in the future. Immigration itself and the absorption of thousands of new immigrants into Palestinian territory—whether in Israel or in the occupied territories—aim to end the Arab presence in Palestinian territory.

Palestine was usurped through deliberate planning, and it can only be restored through deliberate planning backed by determination to achieve justice. The struggler sons of Palestine have proved to be an example of determination and readiness for sacrice. The loss of Palestine was not essentially due to the Zionists' faith in the Zionist cause, but due to the Arabs' abandonment of the Arab cause. It was also not essentially due to Zionist strength, but to Arab weakness. Now that the Arabs have realized—through different factors and reasons, including their triumph over their enemies and the enemies of God on the eastern front and the heroic stand of the people of the deadly stones—that they are capable of taking action, then Palestine will return. Light will chase out darkness and the banners of justice shall fly over holy Jerusalem, God willing. . . .

Among the most important developments since the international conflict in World War II has been the fact that some countries which used to enjoy broad international influence, such as France and Britain, have declined, while the influence and impact of two countries expanded until they became the two superpowers among the countries of the world—I mean the United States and the Soviet Union. Of course, with these results, two axis have developed: the Western axis under the leadership of the United States, with its known capitalist approach and its imperialist policy; or the East bloc under the leadership of the Soviet Union and its communist philosophy.

Among the results of World War II: The Zionist state has become a reality, and the original owners of the land, the Palestinians, have become refugees. While the imperialist Western world helped the expansionist scheme and aggression of the Zionist entity in 1967, the communist bloc sided with the Arabs in the concept of balance of interests in the context of the global competition between the two blocs, and sought to secure footholds for the East Bloc against the Western interests in the Arab homeland. The East bloc, led by the USSR, supported the Arabs' basic rights, including their rights in the Arab-Zionist conflict. The global policy continued on the basis of the existence of two poles that were balanced in term of force. They are the two superpowers, the United States and the USSR.

And suddenly, the situation changed in a dramatic way. The USSR turned to tackle its domestic problems after relinquishing the process of continuous conflict and its slogans. The USSR shifted from the balanced position with the United States in a practical manner, although it has not acknowledged this officially so far. The USSR went to nurse the wounds that were inflicted on it as a result of the principles and the mistaken policy it followed for such a long time, and as a result of the wave of change it embarked on, which began to depart from the charted course. It has become clear to everyone that the United States has emerged in a superior position in international politics. This superiority will be demonstrated in the U.S. readiness to play such a role more than in the predicted guarantees for its continuation.

We believe that the world can fill the vacuum resulting from the recent changes and find a new balance in the global arena by developing new perspectives and reducing or adding to this or that force. The forces that laid the ground for filling the vacuum and for the emergence of the two superpowers, the U.S. and the USSR, after World War II at the expense of France, Britain, and Germany can develop new forces, which we expect will be in Europe and Japan. America will lose its power just as quickly as it gained it by frightening Europe, Japan, and other countries through the continuous hinting at the danger of the USSR and communism. The United States will lose its power as the fierce competition for gaining the upper hand between the two superpowers and their allies recedes.

However, we believe that the U.S. will continue to depart from the restrictions that govern the rest of world throughout the next five years until new forces of balance are formed. Moreover, the undisciplined and irresponsible behavior will engender hostility and grudges if it embarks on rejected stupidities.

Given the relative erosion of the role of the Soviet Union as the key champion of the Arabs in the context of the Arab-Zionist conflict and globally, and given that the influence of the Zionist lobby on U.S. policies is as powerful as ever, the Arabs must take into account that there is a real possibility that Israel might embark on new stupidities within the five-year span I have mentioned. This might take place as a result of direct or tacit U.S. encouragement. On the other hand, the Arabs have a plus, and that is Arab solidarity that will be effective if the Arabs work out a well-defined plan of action and devise regional policies vis-à-vis neighboring foreign countries, and if they forge fruitful cooperation based on strong foundations oriented toward clear goals. The cooperation will have to encompass culture, politics, economics, and other areas. Recent American utterances and behavior as far as pan-Arab security and Palestinian Arab rights to their homeland are concerned inevitably cause alarm and warrant Arab vigilance, or are supposed to evoke such a reaction on our part. One may cite recurrent statements by U.S. officials about their intention to keep their fleets in the Gulf for an unlimited period of time, and their support for an unprecedented exodus of Soviet Jews to Palestinian territory, neither of which would have been possible solely under the cover of the human rights slogan had not the Americans put pressure on the Soviets, exploiting the latter's special circumstances so as to incorporate the issue into their bilateral agreements with the Soviets. Add to that the increasing support for the Zionist entity's strategic arms stockpiles and giving it license to deploy them when necessary, the judgment on when to use them being left up to Israel. This is above and beyond U.S. assistance to Israel in other areas.

We all remember, as does the whole world, the circumstances under which the United States deployed and bolstered its fleets in the Gulf. Most important of these circumstances: The war that was raging between Iraq and Iran; Iranian aggression had extended to other Arabian Gulf countries, most notably the sisterly state of Kuwait. At the time, beyond the conflicting views regarding the presence of foreign fleets in Arab territorial waters and foreign bases on their territory and their repercussions for pan-Arab security, that excessive deployment was somehow comprehensible. But now, and against the background of the recent world developments and the cessation of hostilities between Iraq and Iran, and with Kuwait no longer being the target of Iranian aggression, the Arabian Gulf states, including Iraq, and even the entire Arabs would have liked the Americans to state their intention to withdraw their fleets.

Had they said that under the same circumstances and causes they would have returned to the Gulf, it might have been understandable also. But U.S. officials are making such statements as if to show that their immediate and longer-term presence in Gulf waters and, maybe, on some of its territory, is not bound to a time frame. These suspect policies give Arabs reason to feel suspicious of U.S. policies and intentions as to whether it is officially and actually interested in a termination of the Iraq-Iran war and thus contribute to much needed regional stability.

The other side is the immigration of Soviet Jews to the occupied Palestinian land. How can we explain the Americans' support and backing for Jewish immigration to the occupied Arab territories, except that the United States does not want peace as it claims and declares. If it really and actually wants peace, the United States would not have encouraged Israel and the aggressive trends in it to adopt such policies, which enhance Israel's capability to commit aggression and carry out expansion.

We the Arabs, proceeding from a long-standing friendship with the Soviet Union, did not expect that the Soviets would give in to this U.S. pressure in such a way that it would lead to these grave consequences for the Arabs and their pan-Arab security. As we tackle these challenges, it would be just as compromising to the destiny and cause of the Arabs to feel fear as it would be to be lax in our evaluating and working out a reaction to them. Therefore, there is no place among the ranks of good Arabs for the fainthearted who would argue that as a superpower, the United States will be the decisive factor, and others have no choice but to submit. At the same time, there is no place in our midst for those who fail to take note of recent developments that have added to U.S. strength, thus prompting it to the possible commission of follies against the interests and national security of the Arabs—either directly or by fanning and encouraging conflicts detrimental to the Arabs, irrespective of their source.

We are not thus out to antagonize or to incite public opinion against the United States on the strength of mere speculation over potential developments. We are only making the point that the Arabs seek peace and justice throughout the world and want to forge relations of friendship with those who show respect to what friendship is all about—be it the United States or any other nation. It is only natural that the Arabs take a realistic approach to the new posture and power of the United States that has led the Soviet Union to abandon its erstwhile position of influence. However, America must respect the Arabs and respect their rights, and should not interfere in their internal affairs under any cover. The United States must not forget that the Arab nation is a great nation that taught humanity things it had been ignorant of. Otherwise, there is no room for unilateral friendship or unilateral respect, and there will be no consideration for the interests and rights of any party unless it is capable of understanding and respecting the Arabs' rights, interests, dignity, options, and pan-Arab security. Against the backdrop of the vital issues related to the substance of national Arab security, the question arises as to what we the Arabs have to do.

One of certain indisputable things, brothers, is that the correct description for a certain situation is not necessarily the correct solution to that situation, but an inevitable introduction leading to the correct solution. Therefore, in all cases, a solution does not merely consist of defining which issues are rejected, both concerning our behavior or the behavior and thinking of others who harm our pan-Arab security and national and pan-Arab interests. Another thing over which there is no room for dispute is that the policy of the age is not set by concerned foreign parties on any basis other than policies and strategies whose expected final result is to serve the interests of their countries.

Zionism realized these facts and concentrated its international effort here and there in accordance with an accurate perception and longer-lasting knowledge than that of the Arabs. The Zionists were progressive initiators in fields where they would disrupt the calculations and influences of the Arabs. In accordance with this basis, and not only on the basis of developing public opinion, Zionism directed its special concentration on the United States of America to involve it in its strategy, after realizing that the future of its goals and joint action with the Europeans would come up against special obstacles. The United States accepted the concept of joining interests and action with Zionism out of its concept of its own interests, after the United States had taken over the role of the European colonialists following World War II.

Despite all the harm the United States inflicted upon the Arabs due to its alliance with Zionism, there remained the fear of communism, the Soviet Union, and the Arab friends and allies of the Soviet Union in the region, in addition to other factors. This continued to prevent the Arabs from taking influential stands towards U.S. policy, with minor exceptions. Their stands became restricted to a mere ineffective rejection or an ineffective silence and acceptance. The United States began not to take Arab stances seriously. The United States may have the famous red lines beyond which it does not tread concerning the interests of other nations that deal peacefully with it, but its policy so far has no red lines warning the concerned sides in the United States not to tread beyond them where Arab interests are concerned.

Realizing Arab solidarity on the basis of pan-Arab interests, correctly defining Arab interests, clearly and accurately defining everything that threatens their security and stability, and proceeding from this basis of capability, frankness, and solidarity with the United States, or other countries in general, prevents these countries from exceeding the proper bounds with the Arab nation and thus becoming a threat.

This might be a realistic basis for the establishment of Arab relations with the United States and other states, based on the principles I have mentioned. These are mutual respect, noninterference in internal affairs, and respect for the requirements of pan-Arab security and common interests on a legitimate and agreed-upon basis.

Brothers, Zionism and its entity, Israel, have been used to embark upon areas and affairs to which the Arabs do not pay attention. The Arabs have also been used on occasion to rise all together to counter the Zionists' political, informational, or any other offensive for which Zionism has prepared all requirements through effective work over a long period of time. The Arabs would launch a counteroffensive without being fully prepared and soon their rising would dwindle and vanish. Therefore, the Arab reaction is often verbal or ineffective even if part of it takes the form of real action. In politics as well as in war, responsibility and experience have taught us that the counteroffensive should not necessarily be on the same axis that is always chosen by the enemy, especially when the encounter lasts a long time and when it is possible to choose one or more axis or one or more places other than those from which the enemy began its offensive and for which it prepared the requirements of confrontation and took into consideration Arab reaction. In such a case it might be enough to preoccupy the enemy on the axis selected for its offensive against us, and then we would attack it from another axis if the desired results were possible on the other axis. Accordingly, the direct offensive on the harmful plans and means used by the U.S. and Zionism against the Arabs in a certain field might not be always the right solution if we use all of our potential at one time in a manner that takes us away from other fields.

The big does not become big nor does the great earn such a description unless he is in the arena of comparison or fighting with someone else on a different level. The big powers became big only when small and medium-sized countries were found on this earth around these big powers. The big powers do not become big unless they are influential in small and medium-sized countries. Accordingly, among the means to weaken hostile policies and the harmful influence of those who harm us is to weaken the one who harms us inside or outside his national soil. Accordingly, and because interest is the basis of the Soviet Union's new policy, as well as the policy of the East European states, as it has always been the basis of the policy of other states, we are dutybound to ask and answer accurately how we can approach these states in order to weaken our enemies' influence on them or how we can benefit from our common financial, economic, political, informational, and other powers to achieve better results.

It has been proven that Arabs are capable of being influential when they make a decision and set their minds to it for actual application purposes. We have much evidence of how effective they can be; for example, the joint Iraqi-Saudi resolution of 6 August 1980, and the warning the two countries issued together that embassies must not be moved to Jerusalem, one of whose direct results in less than a month—the duration of the warning—was not only that the concerned countries did not transfer their embassies to Jerusalem, but also that embassies that had already long been transferred to the city returned to Tel Aviv.

The reason the United States stays in the Gulf is that the Gulf has become the most important spot in the region and perhaps the whole world due to developments in international policy, the oil market, and increasing demands from the United States, Europe, Japan, Eastern Europe, and perhaps the Soviet Union, for this product. The country that will have the greatest influence in the region through the Arab Gulf and its oil will maintain its superiority as a superpower without an equal to compete with it. This means that if the Gulf people, along with all Arabs, are not careful, the Arab Gulf region will be governed by the U.S. will. If the Arabs are not alerted and the weakness persists, the situation could develop to the extent desired by the United States; that is, it would fix the amount of oil and gas produced in each country and sold to this or that country in the world. Prices would also be fixed in line with a special perspective benefitting U.S. interests and ignoring the interests of others.

If this possibility is there and it is convincing, those who are convinced by it must conclude that peace in the Middle East is remote from the U.S. point of view because U.S. strategy, according to this analysis, needs an aggressive Israel, not a peaceful one. Peace between Iraq and Iran could be far off as long as Iran does not react favorably from an aware and responsible position and with the peace initiatives proposed by Iraq. The region could witness inter-Arab wars or controlled wars between the Arabs and some of their neighbors, if tangible results are not achieved on the basis of the principles of noninterference in others' internal affairs and nonuse of military force in inter-Arab relations.

Agreement should be reached over clear and widespread pan-Arab cooperation programs among Arab countries in the economic, political, and educational fields, as well as other fields. Love and peace of mind will take the place of suspicion, doubt, mistrust, and giving in to information and speculation propagated by rumormongers such as prejudiced Westerners and some rootless Arabs.

Brothers, the weakness of a big body lies in its bulkiness. All strong men have their Achilles' heel. Therefore, irrespective of our known stand on terror and terrorists, we saw that the United States as a superpower departed Lebanon immediately when some Marines were killed, the very men who are considered to be the most prominent symbol of its arrogance. The whole U.S. Administration would have been called into question had the forces that conquered Panama continued to be engaged by the Panamanian Armed Forces. The United States has been defeated in some combat arenas for all the forces it possesses, and it has displayed signs of fatigue, frustration, and hesitation when committing aggression on other peoples' rights and acting from motives of arrogance and hegemony. This is a natural outcome for those who commit aggression on other peoples' rights. Israel, once dubbed the invincible country, has been defeated by some of the Arabs. The resistance put up by Palestinian and Lebanese militia against Israeli invasion forces in 1982 and before that the heroic Egyptian crossing of the Suez Canal in 1973 have had a more telling psychological and actual impact than all Arab threats. Further, the threat to use Arab oil in 1973 during the October war proved more effective than all political attempts to protest or to beg at the gates of American decisionmaking centers. The stones in occupied Palestine now turn into a virtual and potentially fatal bullet if additional requirements are made available. It is the best proof of what is possible and indeed gives us cause to hold our heads high.

Just as Israel controls interests to put pressure on the U.S. Administration, hundreds of billions invested by the Arabs in the United States and the West may be similarly deployed. Indeed, for instance, some of these investments may be diverted to the USSR and East European countries. It may prove even more profitable than investment in the West, which has grown saturated with its national resources. Such a course of action may yield inestimable benefits for the Arabs and their national causes.

Our purported weakness does not lie in our ideological and hereditary characteristics. Contemporary experience has shown our nation to be distinguished and excellent, just as our nation's history over the centuries has shown this to be the case. Our purported weakness lies in a lack of mutual trust among ourselves, our failure to concentrate on the components of our strength, and our failure to focus on our weaknesses with a view to righting them. Let our motto be: All of us are strong as long as we are united, and all of us are weak as long as we are divided. Then we will see how all of us will reach safe shores, God willing, so we can take off together on the road of stability and prosperity, heartening our people and ourselves. We will also see how Satan will grow weaker wherever he may be and the evil will depart our homeland and our nation. We are proceeding with resolve and firmness. God willing, to reach this goal through brotherly cooperation that would serve as a model for common Arab action and developed brotherly cooperation. Let us go forward.

Brother leaders of the ACC countries; brother members of the audience. These are ideas and concepts that we are proposing for brotherly dialogue in the context of an exchange of views and experience among us on all issues of concern to our Arab countries and nation. We ask success from God toward the good. The peace and blessings of God be upon you, brothers.

Chairman Yasir Arafat:
The PLO and the Gulf Crisis
(December 13, 1990)*

Do not forget that I was continually warning about the constant possibility of an escalation in this region. Most specifically, last April I pointed out two possible explosive points: On the one hand this involved increased U.S.–Israeli threats to Iraq and the Palestinians in southern Lebanon, and on the other the mass settlement of Jews into our occupied Palestine—a problem that I was constantly pointing out and to which I was trying to attract the world's attention because it involved a move with unpredictable consequences. I also said that the Arab summit in Baghdad in March this year should be a summit to straighten things out. Anyway, I will give you the letter the Americans sent us at that time through the Arab League. This is the dangerous letter that no one has wanted to talk about. I will give you a copy: go ahead and publish it if you wish. In this letter they openly announce that they will increase their presence in the Gulf and warned the Arabs that they will not tolerate any resistance to their presence. When I spoke about this on 17 May, two lines concerning the U.S. intentions were already apparent among the Arabs. One line approved of their presence and the other did not.

Another issue was the question of Israel and its expansion. The letter itself was a classic ultimatum. They issued a metal coin—here, I will give you one—with a sketch on it of the map of Israel as they see it. This Israel contains half of Iraq, half of Syria, the whole of Lebanon, Jordan, the whole of Palestine, a part of Saudi Arabia, and a good part of Sinai. They have not

* Interview with *Vjesnik* (Zagreb), December 8, 1990.

forsaken this dream. When I left Beirut in 1982, I said that the storm that had overtaken that city would not stop. The storm at that point had one center, one "eye" as we would say: Palestine. Today that storm has two eyes—one in the Gulf and the other in Palestine. . . .

A few days ago, when I was with Saddam Husayn, it seemed to me that the chances of peace were great. What the Americans have prepared through the Security Council, however . . . this is some kind of declaration of war. This is an ultimatum. Really, there is the danger of the Middle East's exploding, not only in the Gulf but on all sides. If Israel is in this war—and it certainly will be—we will fight against it as well as against the Americans. They must know that not one single Arab soldier—neither Egyptian, nor Syrian, nor Saudi—will agree to be in the same trench as Israeli soldiers. This is the reality.

There is no doubt about it. No matter what the outcome of the war, the Arab order as a whole will collapse. . . .

We are the greatest losers even now. Our people in Kuwait were the richest. The total losses of the Palestinian colony in Kuwait amounted to $8.5 billion. Our people had almost $3 billion in the banks there alone. Look what happened. The U.S.-European committee discussed, and to a considerable extent has already paid, compensation to the whole world for the money lost in Kuwait, but the Palestinians did not receive anything. What is this meant to be? A punishment for the Palestinians? Where are the principles here? Are they not ashamed of this? Or do they really only want to ignite a new explosion? Viewed in the long term, perhaps there is cause for optimism. In the shorter term, the situation is exceptionally difficult. It seems that we have definitely come closer to a war which will leave behind nothing but catastrophe. Both Asia and Europe will feel the repercussions. In order for people to come to their senses, it is necessary for a lot of effort to be made throughout the world. But there is no sense. Look at the Security Council—what is its duty? To foment war or to seek peaceful solutions? I cannot accept this. As regards the solution, it is very strange that, for example, it is being demanded of the Palestinians that they talk with the Israelis while they are occupying the Palestinians' country, but at the same time we are not being allowed to ask that Arabs look for a solution among themselves for the new problem in the Gulf. So one can have negotiations among enemies but not among Arabs. What do they want? That I reject one occupation but accept another, or something like this? I cannot accept a foreign presence in this region. I know that they are literally punishing the Palestinians because of this, but I will not sell my opinion for any sum of money. I could easily say that I support the Saudis or the Americans. You know, however, that I have fought for principles, and I will not betray them.

Palestine National Council: Political Communiqué (September 28, 1991)

In the name of God, the merciful, the compassionate. From the date of its beginning in 1965, the Palestinian revolution has embarked on a long, bitter, and strenuous struggle during which our people have made huge sacrifices. This beginning came after years of excluding the Palestinian question and considering it a refugee question.

The long years of struggle in all forms, under the PLO leadership, the sole legitimate representative of our people, have again posed the question of Palestine to the international community on the grounds that it is the national cause of a people entitled to liberation, self-determination, and independence.

The question of Palestine occupied a central position in the Arab-Israeli conflict. Peace, security, and stability in the Middle East cannot be secured unless this conflict is resolved.

Then came the blessed intifada, with its popular and democratic depth, as a creative continuation of the Palestinian national struggle. It has constituted a distinct phase which has left its imprint on the whole world and reverberated around it. It has consolidated international recognition of our people's rights and of the PLO, which has always and immediately put such international support and polarization to use.

Thus, our National Council convened its 19th session and launched the Palestinian peace initiative, and the historic birth of the state of Palestine was proclaimed on 15 November 1988.

The world had welcomed our peace initiative through the resolutions of the UN General Assembly in its 43rd session, which was held in Geneva. Also, most countries recognized the state of Palestine and established diplomatic and political relations with it.

Despite the international welcome with which the Palestinian initiative and the historic speech by the president of the state of Palestine, brother Yasir 'Arafat, who demonstrated to the whole world our wish for a just peace, was met—thus for the first time the United States announced the opening of an official dialogue with the PLO—the Israeli policy of stubbornness and pressure led to the failure of all initiatives and peaceful efforts, bringing them down a dead-end street.

Afterwards, there came regional and international developments, most prominent of which was the Gulf war and the changes that occurred in the socialist bloc. This resulted in a substantial change in the balance of power. Thus, the cold war came to an end, and the features of a new age in international relations began to develop, especially in the field of U.S.-Soviet relations and cooperation between the two nations to resolve regional conflicts and problems peacefully.

The PLO has closely monitored the course of events in the world and their effect on the Palestinian question and the Arab-Israeli conflict. If the Palestinian people have had their homeland usurped as a result of the prejudices of the old world order, it is impermissible, according to any logic, that they be denied these rights in a phase witnessing the emergence of the new world order that raises slogans of democracy, human rights, and the sanctity of peoples' right to self-determination.

The current situation requires us to deal with it in the spirit of political responsibility and national realism and to examine the new regional and international developments. This situation also requires us to learn the lessons and experience from the popular intifada that has turned the aim of Palestinian independence into a feasible program.

In harmony with the Palestinian initiative proposed in 1989 and with international and Arab legitimacy, the PLO has dealt positively and effectively with international and peaceful ideas, proposals, and initiatives that relied on international legality. The PLO also welcomed the positive elements mentioned in the declaration of U.S. President George Bush and the positions of the EEC, the Soviet Union, the Nonaligned Movement states, and other international quarters.

The PLO, which had welcomed the current peaceful efforts and initiatives and dealt with them positively, including the call launched by Presidents Bush and Gorbachev for convening a peace conference related to settling the conflict in the Middle East, believes that the success of the efforts aimed at holding the peace conference requires the continuation of work with the other sides so as to achieve the following foundations:

1. The peace conference should rely on international legitimacy and its resolutions, including UN Security Council Resolutions 242 and 338, and should undertake to implement them. These resolutions secure a full Israeli withdrawal from Arab and Palestinian occupied territories, including sacred Jerusalem; the realization of the land-for-peace exchange principle; and the national and political rights of the Palestinian people.

2. It must be stressed that Jerusalem is an indivisible part of occupied Palestinian territory and that what applies to the rest of the occupied territories applies to it, as stipulated by the resolutions of the Security Council and the United Nations.

3. Halting settlement in the occupied territories, including holy Jerusalem, is an indispensable necessity to start the peace process, and international guarantees must be provided to achieve that.

4. The PLO, as the legitimate and sole representative of the Palestinian people, has the right to form the Palestinian delegation from within and outside the homeland, including Jerusalem, and to define the formula of

their participation in the peace process on an equitable basis and in a way that stresses its authority.

5. Arab positions should be coordinated to ensure the realization of a comprehensive settlement, excluding unilateral solutions, in accordance with the resolutions of Arab summits.

6. The connection between the stages of the settlement toward reaching a comprehensive settlement should be ensured according to the resolutions of international legitimacy.

The PLO, which starts from these bases and premises on the peace efforts, aims to accomplish the following:

1. The right to self-determination must be secured for our Palestinian people in a way that guarantees the right to freedom and national independence.

2. There must be a full Israeli withdrawal from all Palestinian and Arab lands occupied in 1967, including Holy Jerusalem.

3. The problem of Palestinian refugees driven out of their homeland by force and against their will must be resolved, in accordance with UN resolutions, especially Resolution 194, issued by the UN General Assembly.

4. Any provisional arrangements must include the right of our people to sovereignty of land, water, natural resources, and all political and economic affairs.

5. International protection for the Palestinian people, in preparation for the exercise of the right to self-determination, must be provided.

6. Full guarantees must be provided for an effort to remove the existing settlements by declaring them illegal, in accordance with the resolutions of international law, including UN Security Council Resolution No. 465.

The National Council charges the Executive Committee to continue current efforts to provide the best conditions for guaranteeing the success of the peace process in accordance with the resolution of the Palestine National Council [PNC]. However, the committee will submit the results to the Central Council to make a final decision in light of the supreme national interest of our people.

The PLO, which in the previous phase made all possible efforts to propel the peace process, hopes that the other parties, especially the United States and the USSR, will also make efforts to help ease the obstacles placed by Israel before this ongoing political process and to leave the door open for a return to the UN Security Council so as to implement the resolutions of international legitimacy.

Working toward the achievement of our national objectives in the next phase and toward facing up to obstacles marring our struggle requires the consolidation and entrenchment of national unity in various fields. It requires developing the contribution of all national forces, bodies, and personalities inside and outside the occupied homeland—along with the political leadership of the PLO—to all issues related to our people's future and the ongoing political process, and to finding the appropriate formula for achieving this purpose.

In this respect, the PNC calls for increasing the activities and role of the PLO Central Council in monitoring and implementing the resolutions of the National Council as a way of consolidating democracy and its practice. The council considers promoting the intifada and consolidating its popular and democratic character and the participation of our entire people in backing and supporting it to be the real guarantee for securing the political and national objectives in the next phase of our national struggle.

In this respect, the Council addresses its struggle greetings to the masses of the brave intifada and stresses the consolidation of the role and prestige of the Unified National Command of the Intifada, the development of its struggle wings, the continuation of the formation of cadres, and the setting up of supreme sectorial councils.

The Council reaffirms that the protection and support of the intifada and the provision of all requirements for its development are at the forefront of Palestinian national action.

The Council extends greetings to our heroic prisoners in the detention centers of Zionist occupation and to our brave wounded who are watching over the path of the intifada, which was built by our pure martyrs.

The National Council extends its struggle greetings to the masses of our steadfast people in Galilee, the Triangle, Negev, and the coast, and reaffirms its appreciation of their struggle in defense of their rights against the policies of persecution and segregation and their active support for the brave intifada.

The council also affirms that guaranteeing the realization of the objectives of our people and Arab nation, through the peace process, in order to secure a full Israeli withdrawal from Arab and Palestinian lands, and to guarantee the right of return, the self-determination to our people, and the setting up of a Palestinian state with Holy Jerusalem as its capital, require the restoration of inter-Arab solidarity in order to protect the Arab future in light of current international and regional changes.

In this respect, the council invites the five Arab states concerned in the peace process to achieve the highest levels of political and diplomatic coordination between them, in order to face up to the requirements of the coming stage and to reinforce the Arab negotiating position, so as to guarantee the realization of a comprehensive solution at all levels and prevent any separate solutions at the expense of the national rights of our people and the rights of our Arab nation. . . .

The PNC urges the international community to deal with the issue of Jewish colonizing emigration in a way that ensures that Israel does not use it to serve its objectives of expansion, colonization, and depriving our people of the right to decide their destiny in the territory of their homeland.

The Council believes that the continuation of this emigration, in accordance with Israeli plans to intensify settlement in our occupied land, constitutes a direct obstacle, a danger threatening the future of peace in the region, and a violation of the Palestinian people's rights and international conventions.

The PNC draws attention to the attempts and endeavors currently under way in some international circles to repeal the UN General Assembly's resolution on Zionism as a form of racism. The Council urges the Executive Committee to work with the friendly and fraternal states to face up to these attempts and to abort them. . . .

Finally, the PNC addresses greetings, compassion, and love to our steadfast and patient Palestinian people, both inside our occupied land and in the diaspora, and to the masses of our Arab nation and its influential forces for their positions supporting and backing the jihad of our Palestinian people and their national, inalienable rights. The Council urges them to stand firmly in the face of the conspiracies hatched by the enemies of our Arab nation in order to preserve our Arab nation, its existence, pride, dignity, and national security.

U.S. Letter of Assurances
to the Palestinians (October 18, 1991)

The Palestinian decision to attend a peace conference to launch direct negotiations with Israel represents an important step in the search for a comprehensive, just and lasting peace in the region. The United States has long believed that Palestinian participation is critical to the success of our efforts.

In the context of the process on which we are embarking, we want to respond to your requests for certain assurances related to this process. These assurances constitute US understandings and intentions concerning the conference and ensuring negotiations.

These assurances are consistent with United States policy and do not undermine or condradict United Nations Security Council Resolutions 242 and 338. Moreover, there will be no assurances provided to one party that are not known to all the others. By this we can foster a sense of confidence and minimize chances for misunderstandings.

As President Bush stated in his March 6, 1991, address to Congress, the United States continues to believe firmly that a comprehensive peace must be grounded in United Nations Security Council Resolutions 242 and 338 and the principle of territory for peace. Such an outcome must also provide for security and recognition for all states in the region, including Israel, and for the legitimate political rights of the Palestinian people. Anything else, the President noted, would fail the twin tests of fairness and security.

The process we are trying to create offers Palestinians a way to achieve these objectives. The United States believes that there should be an end to the Israeli occupation which can occur only through genuine and meaningful negotiations. The United States also believes that this process should create a new relationship of mutuality where Palestinians and Israelis can respect one another's security, identity, and political rights. We believe Palestinians should gain control over political, economic and other decisions that affect their lives and fate.

Direct bilateral negotiations will begin four days after the opening of the conference; those parties who wish to attend multilateral negotiations will convene two weeks after the opening of the conference to organize those negotiations. In this regard, the United States will support Palestinian involvement in any bilateral or multilateral negotiations on refugees and in all multilateral negotiations. The conference and the negotiations that follow will be based on UN Security Council Resolutions 242 and 338. The process will proceed along tow tracks through direct negotiations between Israel and Arab states and Israel and Palestinians. The United States is determined to achieve a comprehensive settlement of the Arab-Israeli conflict and will do its utmost to ensure that the process moves forward along both tracks toward this end.

In pursuit of a comprehensive settlement, all the negotiations should proceed as quickly as possible toward agreement. For its part, the United States will work for serious negotiations and will also seek to avoid prolongation and stalling by any party.

The conference will be co-sponsored by the United States and the Soviet Union. The European Community will be a participant in the conference alongside the United States and the Soviet Union and be represented by its Presidency. The conference can reconvene only with the consent of all the parties.

With regard to the role of the United Nations, the UN Secretary General will send a representative to the conference as an observer. The co-sponsors will keep the Secretary General apprised of the progress of the negotiations. Agreements reached between the parties will be registered with the UN Secretariat and reported to the Security Council, and the parties will seek the Council's endorsement of such agreements. Since it is in the interest of all parties for this process to succeed, while this process is actively ongoing, the United States will not support a competing or parallel process in the United Nations Security Council.

The United States does not seek to determine who speaks for Palestinians in this process. We are seeking to launch a political negotiation process that directly involves Palestinians and offers a pathway for achieving the legitimate political rights of the Palestinian people and for participation in the determination of their future. We believe that a joint Jordanian-Palestinian delegation offers the most promising pathway toward this end.

Only Palestinians can choose their delegation members, which are not subject to veto from anyone. The United States understands that members of the delegation will be Palestinians from the territories who agree to negotiations on two tracks, in phases, and who are willing to live in peace with Israel. No party can be forced to sit with anyone it does not want to sit with.

Palestinians will be free to announce their component of the joint delegation and to make a statement during the opening of the conference. They may also raise any issue pertaining to the substance of the negotiations during the negotiations.

The United States understands how much importance Palestinians attach to the question of east Jerusalem. Thus, we want to assure you that nothing Palestinians do in choosing their delegation members in this phase of the process will affect their claim to east Jerusalem, or be prejudicial or precedential to the outcome of negotiations. It remains the firm position of the United States that Jerusalem must never again be a divided city and that its final status should be decided by negotiations. Thus, we do not recognize Israel's annexation of east Jerusalem or the extension of its municipal boundaries, and we encourage all sides to avoid unilateral acts that would exacerbate local tensions or make negotiations more difficult or preempt their final outcome. It is also the United States position that a Palestinian resident in Jordan with ties to a prominent Jerusalem family would be eligible to join the Jordanian side of the delegation.

Furthermore, it is also the United States position that Palestnians of east Jerusalem should be able to participate by voting in the elections for an interim self-governing authority. The United States further believes that Palestinians from east Jerusalem and Palestnians outside the occupied territories who meet the three criteria should be able to participate in the negotiations on final status. And, the United States supports the right of Palestinians to bring any issue, including east Jerusalem, to the table.

Because the issues at stake are so complex and the emotions so deep, the United States has long maintained that a transitional period is required to break down the walls of suspicion and mistrust and lay the basis for sustainable negotiations on the final status of the occupied territories. The purpose of negotiations on transitional arrangements is to effect the peaceful and orderly transfer of authority from Israel to Palestinians. Palestinians need to achieve rapid control over political, economic, and other decisions that affect their lives and to adjust to a new situation in which Palestinians exercise authority in the West Bank and Gaza. For its part, the United States will strive from the outset and encourage all parties to adopt steps that can create an environment of confidence and mutual trust, including respect for human rights.

As you are aware with respect to negotiations between Israel and Palestinians, negotiations will be conducted in phases, beginning with talks on interim self-government arrangements. These talks will be conducted with the objective of reaching agreement within one year. Once agreed, the interim self-government arrangements will last for a period of five years. Beginning the third year of the period of interim government arrangements, negotiations will take place on permanent status. It is the aim of the United States that permanent status negotiations will be concluded by the end of the transitional period.

It has long been our position that only direct negotiations based on UN Security Council Relolutions 242 and 338 can produce a real peace. No one can dictate the outcome in advance. The United States understands that Palestinians must be free, in opening statements at the conference and in the negotiations that follow, to raise any issue of importance to them. Thus, Palestinians are free to argue for whatever outcome they believe best meets their requirements. The United States will accept any outcome agreed by the parties. In this regard and consistent with longstanding US policies, confederation is not excluded as a possible outcome of negotiations on final status.

The United States has long believed that no party should take unilateral actions that seek to predetermine issues that can only be resolved through negotiations. In this regard the United States has opposed and will continue to oppose settlement activity in the territories occupied in 1967, which remains an obstacle to peace.

The United States will act as an honest broker in trying to resolve the Arab-Israeli conflict. It is our intention, together with the Soviet Union, to play the role of a driving force in this process to help the parties move forward toward a comprehensive peace. Any party will have access to the co-sponsors at any time. The United States is prepared to participate in all stages of the negotiations, with the consent of the parties to each negotiation.

These are the assurances that the United States is providing concerning the implementation of the initiative we have discussed. We are persuaded that we have a real opportunity to accomplish something very important in the peace process. And we are prepared to work hard together with you in the period ahead to build on the progress we have made. There will be difficult challenges for all parties. But with Palestinians' continues commitment and creativity, we have a real chance of moving to a peace conference and to negotiation and then on toward the broader peace that we all seek.

Prime Minister Yitzhak Shamir and Haydar Abd al-Shafi: Speeches at the Madrid Peace Conference (October 31, 1992)

Prime Minister Yitzhak Shamir

We pray that this meeting will mark the beginning of a new chapter in the history of the Middle East; that it will signal the end of hostility, violence, terror, and war; that it will bring dialogue, accommodation, co-existence, and above all, peace.

Ladies and gentlemen, to appreciate the meaning of peace for the people of Israel, one has to view today's Jewish sovereignty in the Land of Israel against the background of our history. Jews have been persecuted throughout the ages in almost every continent. Some countries barely tolerated us; others oppressed, tortured, slaughtered, and exiled us. This century saw the Nazi regime set out to exterminate us. The Shoah—the Holocaust, the catastrophic genocide of unprecedented proportions which destroyed a third of our people—became possible because no one defended us. Being homeless, we were also defenseless. But it was not the Holocaust which made the world community recognize our rightful claim to the Land of Israel. In fact, the rebirth of the State of Israel so soon after the Holocaust has made the world forget that our claim is immemorial. We are the only people who have lived in the Land of Israel without interruption for nearly 4,000 years. We are the only people, except for a short Crusader kingdom, who have had an independent sovereignty in this land. We are the only people for whom Jerusalem has been a capital. We are the only people whose sacred places are only in the Land of Israel. No nation has expressed its bond with its land with as much intensity and consistency as we have. For millennia, our people repeated at every occasion the cry of the psalmist: If I forget thee, Jerusalem, may my right hand lose its cunning. For millennia, we have encouraged each other with the greeting: Next year in Jerusalem. For millennia, our prayers, literature, and folklore have expressed powerful longing to return to our land. Only Eretz Yisra'el, the Land of Israel, is our true homeland.

Any other country, no matter how hospitable, is still a diaspora, a temporary station on the way home. To others, it was not an attractive land; no one wanted it. Mark Twain described it only 100 years ago as a desolate country which sits in sackcloth and ashes—a silent, mournful expanse which not even imagination can grace with the pomp of life.

The Zionist movement gave political expression to our claim to the

Land of Israel, and in 1922, the League of Nations recognized the justice of this claim. They understood the compelling historic imperative of establishing a Jewish homeland in the Land of Israel. The United Nations organization reaffirmed this recognition after World War II.

Regrettably, the Arab leaders, whose friendship we wanted most, opposed a Jewish state in the region. With a few distinguished exceptions, they claimed that the Land of Israel is part of the Arab domain that stretches from the Atlantic to the Persian Gulf. In defiance of international will and legality, the Arab regimes attempted to overrun and destroy the Jewish state even before it was born. The Arab spokesmen at the United Nations declared that the establishment of a Jewish state would cause a bloodbath which would make the slaughters of Genghis Khan pale into insignificance. In its declaration of independence on May 15, 1948, Israel stretched out its hand in peace to its Arab neighbors, calling for an end to war and bloodshed. In response, seven Arab states invaded Israel. The UN resolution that partitioned the country was thus violated and effectively annulled.

The United Nations did not create Israel. The Jewish state came into being because the tiny Jewish community in what was Mandatory Palestine rebelled against foreign imperialist rule. We did not conquer a foreign land; we repulsed the Arab onslaught, prevented Israel's annihilation, declared its independence, and established a viable state and government institutions within a very short time.

After their attack on Israel failed, the Arab regimes continued their fight against Israel with boycott, blockade, terrorism, and outright war. Soon after the establishment of Israel, they turned against the Jewish communities in Arab countries. A wave of oppression, expropriation, and expulsion caused a mass exodus of some 800,000 Jews from lands they had inhabited from before the rise of the Islam. Most of the Jewish refugees, stripped of their considerable possessions, came to Israel. They were welcomed by the Jewish state, they were given shelter and support, and they were integrated into Israeli society, together with half a million survivors of the European Holocaust.

The Arab regimes' rejection of Israel's existence in the Middle East and the continuous war they have waged against it are part of history. There have been attempts to rewrite this history, which depicts the Arabs as victims and Israel as the aggressor. Like attempts to deny the Holocaust, they will fail. With the demise of totalitarian regimes in most of the world, this perversion of history will disappear.

In their war against Israel's existence, the Arab governments took advantage of the cold war. They enlisted the military, economic, and political support of the communist world against Israel, and they turned a local regional conflict into an international powder keg. This caused the Middle East to be flooded with arms, which fueled wars and turned the area into a dangerous battleground and a testing arena for sophisticated weapons.

At the UN, the Arab states mustered the support of other Muslim countries and the Soviet bloc. Together, they had an automatic majority for countless resolutions that perverted history, paraded fiction as fact, and made a travesty of the UN and its charter.

Arab hostility to Israel has also brought tragic human suffering to the Arab people. Tens of thousands have been killed and wounded; hundreds of thousands of Arabs who lived in Mandatory Palestine were encouraged by their own leaders to flee from their homes. Their suffering is a blot on humanity. No decent person—least of all a Jew of this era—can be oblivious to this suffering. Several hundreds of thousands of Palestinian Arabs live in slums known as refugee camps in Gaza, Judaea, and Samaria. Attempts by Israel to rehabilitate and house them have been defeated by Arab objections. Nor has their fate been any better in Arab states. Unlike the Jewish refugees who came to Israel from Arab countries, most Arab refugees were neither welcomed nor integrated by their hosts. Only the Kingdom of Jordan awarded them citizenship. Their plight has been used as a political weapon against Israel. The Arabs who have chosen to remain in Israel—Christian and Muslim—have become full-fledged citizens, enjoying equal rights and representation in the legislature, in the judiciary, and in all walks of life.

We, who over the centuries were denied access to our holy places, respect the religion of all faiths in our country. Our law guarantees freedom of worship and protects the holy places of every religion.

Distinguished cochairmen, ladies, and gentlemen, I stand before you today in yet another quest for peace—not only on behalf of the State of Israel, but in the name of the entire Jewish people that has maintained an unbreakable bond with the Land of Israel for almost 4,000 years. Our pursuit of accommodation and peace has been relentless. For us, the ingathering of Jews into their ancient homeland, their integration into our society, and the creation of the necessary infrastructure are at the very top of our national agenda.

A nation that faces such a gigantic challenge would most naturally desire peace with all its neighbors. Since the beginning of Zionism, we formulated innumerable peace proposals and plans. All of them were rejected. The first crack in the wall of hostility occurred in 1977, when the late President Anwar al-Sadat of Egypt decided to break the taboo and come to Jerusalem. His gesture was reciprocated with enthusiasm by the people and Government of Israel, headed by Menahem Begin. This development led to the Camp David accords and a treaty of peace between Egypt and Israel. Four years later, in May 1983, an agreement was signed with the lawful government of Lebanon. Unfortunately, this agreement was not fulfilled because of outside intervention. But a precedent was set, and we look forward to courageous steps, similar to those of Anwar al-

Sadat. Regrettably, not one Arab leader has seen fit to come forward and respond to our call for peace.

Today's gathering is a result of a sustained American effort based on our own peace plan of May 1989, which in turn was founded on the Camp David accords. According to the American initiative, the purpose of this meeting is to launch direct peace negotiations between Israel and each of its neighbors and multilateral negotiations on regional issues among all the countries of the region. We have always believed that only direct bilateral talks can bring peace. We have agreed to precede such talks with this ceremonial conference, but we hope that Arab consent to direct bilateral talks indicates an understanding that there is no other way to peace. In the Middle East, this has special meaning, because such talks imply mutual acceptance, and the root cause of the conflict is the Arab refusal to recognize the legitimacy of the State of Israel.

The multilateral talks that would accompany the bilateral negotiations are a vital component in the process. In these talks, the essential ingredients of coexistence and regional cooperation will be discussed. There cannot be genuine peace in our region unless these regional issues are addressed and resolved.

We believe the goal of the bilateral negotiations is to sign peace treaties between Israel and its neighbors and to reach an agreement on interim self-government arrangements with the Palestinian Arabs. But nothing can be achieved without goodwill. I appeal to the Arab leaders—those who are here and those who have not yet joined the process: Show us and the world that you accept Israel's existence. Demonstrate your readiness to accept Israel as a permanent entity in the region. Let the people in our region hear you speak in the language of reconciliation, coexistence, and peace with Israel. In Israel, there is an almost total consensus for the need for peace. We only differ on the best ways to achieve it. In most Arab countries, the opposite seems to be true. The only differences are over the ways to push Israel into a defenseless position and, ultimately, to destruction. We would like to see in your countries an end to poisonous preachings against Israel. We would like to see an indication of the kind of hunger for peace which characterizes Israeli society.

We appeal to you to renounce the jihad against Israel; we appeal to you to denounce the PLO Covenant which calls for Israel's destruction; we appeal to you to condemn declarations that call for Israel's annihilation, like the one issued by the rejectionist conference in Tehran last week; we appeal to you to let Jews who wish to leave your countries go. And we address a call to the Palestinian Arabs: Renounce violence and terrorism. Use the universities in the administered territories, whose existence was made possible only by Israel, for learning and development, not agitation and violence. Stop exposing your children to danger by sending them to throw bombs and stones at soldiers and civilians.

Just two days ago, we were reminded that Palestinian terrorism is still rampant, when the mother of seven children and the father of four were slaughtered in cold blood. We cannot remain indifferent and be expected to talk with people involved in such repulsive activities.

We appeal to you to shun dictators like Saddam Husayn who aim to destroy Israel. Stop the brutal torture and murder of those who do not agree with you. Allow us and the world community to build decent housing for the people who now live in refugee camps. Above all, we hope you finally realize that you could have been at this table long ago, soon after the Camp David accords were first concluded, had you chosen dialogue instead of violence, coexistence instead of terrorism.

Ladies and gentlemen, we come to this process with an open heart, sincere intentions, and great expectations. We are committed to negotiating without interruption, until an agreement is reached. There will be problems, obstacles, crises, and conflicting claims, but it is better to talk than to shed blood. Wars have not solved anything in our region; they have only caused misery, suffering, bereavement, and hatred.

We know our partners to the negotiations will make territorial demands on Israel but, as an examination of the conflict's long history makes clear, its nature is not territorial. It raged well before Israel acquired Judaea, Samaria, Gaza, and the Golan in a defensive war. There was no hint at recognition of Israel before the war in 1967, when the territories in question were not under Israel's control.

We are a nation of 4 million. The Arab nations from the Atlantic to the Gulf number 170 million. We control only 28,000 square km. The Arabs possess a land mass of 14 million square km. The issue is not territory, but our existence. It will be regrettable if the talks focus primarily and exclusively on territory. It is the quickest way to an impasse.

What we need, first and foremost, is the building of confidence, the removal of the danger of confrontation, and the development of relations in as many spheres as possible. The issues are complex, and the negotiations will be lengthy and difficult. We submit that the best venue for the talks is in our region, in close proximity to the decisionmakers, not in a foreign land. We invite our partners to this process to come to Israel for the first round of talks. On our part, we are ready to go to Jordan, to Lebanon, and to Syria for the same purpose. There is no better way to make peace than to talk in each other's home. Avoiding such talks is a denial of the purpose of the negotiations. I would welcome a positive answer from the representatives of these states here and now. We must learn to live together. We must learn to live without war, without hatred.

Judaism has given the world not only the belief in one god, but the idea that all men and women are created in God's image. There is no greater sin than to ravage this image by shedding blood. I am sure that there is no Arab mother who wants her son to die in battle, just as there is no Jewish mother who wants her son to die in war. I believe every mother wants her children to learn the art of living, not the science of war.

For many hundreds of years, wars, deep antagonisms, and terrible suffering cursed this continent on which we meet. The nations of Europe saw the rise of dictators and their defeat after lengthy and painful struggles. Now they are together, former bitter enemies, in a united community. They are discussing the good of the community, cooperating in all matters, acting almost as one unit. I envy them. I would like to see such a community rise in the Middle East, and I believe that despite all differences between us we should be able, gradually, to build a united regional community. Today it is a dream, but we have seen in our own lifetimes some of the most fantastic dreams become reality. Today the gulf separating the two sides is still too wide, the Arab hostility to Israel too deep, the lack of trust too immense to permit a dramatic, quick solution, but we must start on the long road to reconciliation with this first step in the peace process.

We are convinced that human nature prefers peace to war and belligerence. We, who have had to fight seven wars and sacrifice many thousands of lives, glorify neither death nor war. The Jewish faith exalts peace, even to the extent that it considers it a synonym for the Creator himself. We yearn for peace; we pray for peace.

We believe the blessing of peace can turn the Middle East into a paradise, a center of cultural, scientific, medical, technological creativity. We can foresee a period of great economic progress that would put an end to misery, hunger, and illiteracy. It could put the Middle East, the cradle of civilization, on the road to a new era. Such a goal merits our devotion and dedication for as long as it is necessary, until, in the words of the prophet Isaiah, we shall be able to turn swords into plowshares and bring the blessings of peace to all the peoples of our region. . . .

Haydar Abd al-Shafi

. . . We, the people of Palestine, stand before you in the fullness of our pain, our pride, and our anticipation, for we long harbored a yearning for peace and a dream of justice and freedom. For too long, the Palestinian people have gone unheeded, silenced and denied. Our identity negated by political expediency; our right for struggle against injustice maligned; and our present existence subdued by the past tragedy of another people. For the greater part of this century we have been victimized by the myth of a land without a people and described with impunity as the invisible Palestinians. Before such willful blindness, we refused to disappear or to accept a distorted identity. Our intifada is a testimony to our perseverance and resilience waged in a just struggle to regain our rights. It is time for us to narrate our own story, to stand witness as advocates of truth which has long lain buried in the consciousness and conscience of the world. We do not stand before you as supplicants, but rather as the torch-bearers who know that, in our world of today, ignorance can never be an excuse. We seek neither an admission of guilt after the fact, nor vengeance for past inequities, but rather an act of will that would make a just peace a reality.

We speak out, ladies and gentlemen, from the full conviction of the rightness of our cause, the verity of our history, and the depth of our commitment. Therein lies the strength of the Palestinian people today, for we have scaled walls of fear and reticence, and we wish to speak out with the courage and integrity that our narrative and history deserve. The co-sponsors have invited us here today to present our case and to reach out to the other with whom we have had to face a mutually exclusive reality on the land of Palestine. But even in the invitation to this peace conference, our narrative was distorted and our truth only partially acknowledged.

The Palestinian people are one, fused by centuries of history in Palestine, bound together by a collective memory of shared sorrows and joys, and sharing a unity of purpose and vision. Our songs and ballads are full of tales and children's stories, the dialect of our jokes, the image of our poems, that hint of melancholy which colors even our happiest moments, are as important to us as the blood ties which link our families and clans. Yet, an invitation to discuss peace, the peace we all desire and need, comes to only a portion of our people. It ignores our national, historical, and organic unity. We come here wrenched from our sisters and brothers in exile to stand before you as the Palestinians under occupation, although we maintain that each of us represents the rights and interests of the whole.

We have been denied the right to publicly acknowledge our loyalty to our leadership and system of government. But allegiance and loyalty cannot be censored or severed. Our acknowledged leadership is more than [the] justly democratically chosen leadership of all the Palestinian people. It is the symbol of our national unity and identity, the guardian of our past, the protector of our present, and the hope of our future. Our people have chosen to entrust it with their history and the preservation of our precious legacy. This leadership has been clearly and unequivocally recognized by the community of nations, with only a few exceptions who had chosen for so many years shadow over substance. Regardless of the nature and conditions of our oppression, whether the disposition and dispersion of exile or the brutality and repression of the occupation, the Palestinian people cannot be torn asunder. They remain united—a nation wherever they are, or are forced to be.

And Jerusalem, ladies and gentlemen, that city which is not only the soul of Palestine, but the cradle of three world religions, is tangible even in its claimed absence from our midst at this stage. It is apparent, through artificial exclusion from this conference, that this is a denial of its right to seek peace and redemption. For it, too, has suffered from war and occupation. Jerusalem, the city of peace, has been barred from a peace conference and deprived of its calling. Palestinian Jerusalem, the capital of our homeland and future state, defines Palestinian existence, past, present, and future, but itself has been denied a voice and an identity. Jerusalem defies exclusive possessiveness or bondage. Israel's annexation of Arab Jerusalem remains both clearly illegal in the eyes of the world community, and an affront to the peace that this city deserves.

We come to you from a tortured land and a proud, though captive people, having been asked to negotiate with our occupiers, but leaving behind the children of the intifada and a people under occupation and under curfew who enjoined us not to surrender or forget. As we speak, thousands of our brothers and sisters are languishing in Israeli prisons and detention camps, most detained without evidence, charge, or trial, many cruelly mistreated and tortured in interrogation, guilty only of seeking freedom or daring to defy the occupation. We speak in their name and we say: Set them free. As we speak, the tens of thousands who have been wounded or permanently disabled are in pain. Let peace heal their wounds. As we speak, the eyes of thousands of Palestinian refugees, deportees, and displaced persons since 1967, are haunting us, for exile is a cruel fate. Bring them home. They have the right to return. As we speak, the silence of demolished homes echoes through the halls and in our minds. We must rebuild our homes in our free state.

And what do we tell the loved ones of those killed by army bullets? How do we answer the questions and the fear in our children's eyes. For one out of three Palestinian children under occupation has been killed, injured, or detained in the past four years. How can we explain to our children that they are denied education or schools are so often closed by the army fate? [sentence as heard] Or why their life is in danger for raising a flag in a land where even children are killed or jailed? What requiem can be sung for trees uprooted by army bulldozers? And most of all, who can explain to those whose lands are confiscated and clear waters stolen, a message of peace? Remove the barbed wire. Restore to the land and its life-giving water. The settlements must stop now. Peace cannot be waged while Palestinian land confiscated in myriad ways and the status of the occupied territories is being decided each day by Israeli bulldozers and barbed wire. This is not simply a position. It is an irrefutable reality. Territory for peace is a travesty when territory for illegal settlement is official Israeli policy and practice. The settlements must stop now.

In the name of the Palestinian people, we wish to directly address the Israeli people with whom we have had a prolonged exchange of pain: Let us share hope, instead. We are willing to live side by side on the land and the promise of the future. Sharing, however, requires two partners, willing to share as equals. Mutuality and reciprocity must replace domination and hostility for genuine reconciliation and coexistence under international legality. Your security and ours are mutually dependent as entwined as the fears and nightmares of our children. We have seen some of you at your best and at your worst. For the occupier can hide no secrets from the occupied, and we are witness to the toll that occupation has exacted from you and yours.

We have seen you agonize over the transformation of your sons and daughters into instruments of a blind and violent occupation. And we are sure that at no time did you envisage such a role for the children whom you thought would forge your future. We have seen you look back in deepest sorrow at the tragedy of your past, and look on in horror at the disfigurement of the victim-turned-oppressor. Not for this have you nurtured your hopes, dreams, and your offspring. This is why we have responded with solemn appreciation to those of you who came to offer consolation to our bereaved, to give support to those whose homes were being demolished, and to extend encouragement and counsel to those detained behind barbed wire and iron bars. And we have marched together, often choking together in the nondiscriminatory tear gas or crying out in pain as the clubs descended on both Palestinian and Israeli alike, for pain knows no national boundaries, and no one can claim a monopoly on suffering. We once formed a human chain around Jerusalem, joining hands and calling for peace. Let us today form a moral chain around Madrid and continue that noble effort for peace and a promise of freedom for our sons and daughters. Break through the barriers of mistrust and manipulated fears. Let us look forward in magnanimity and in hope.

To our Arab brothers and sisters, most of whom are represented here in this historic occasion, we express our loyalty and gratitude for their life-long support and solidarity. We are here together seeking a just and lasting peace, whose cornerstone is freedom for Palestine, justice for the Palestinians, and an end to the occupation of all Palestinian and Arab lands. Only then can we really enjoy together the fruits of peace, prosperity, security, and human dignity and freedom.

In particular, we address our Jordanian colleagues in our joint delegation: Our two peoples have a very special historic and geographic relationship. Together, we shall strive to achieve peace. We will continue to strive for our sovereignty, while proceeding freely and willingly to prepare the grounds for a confederation between the two states of Palestine and Jordan, which can be a cornerstone for our security and prosperity.

To the community of nations on our fragile planet, to the nations of Africa and Asia, to the Muslim world, and particularly to Europe, on whose southern and neighborly shores we meet today, from the heart of our collective struggle for peace, we greet you and acknowledge your support and recognition. You have recognized our rights and our government, and have given us real support and protection. You have penetrated the distorting mist of racism, stereotyping, and ignorance, and committed the act of seeing the invisible and listening to the voice of the silenced. Palestinians under occupation and in exile have become a reality in your eyes, and with courage and determination, you have affirmed the truth of our narrative. You have taken up our cause and our case, and we have brought you into our hearts. We thank you for caring and daring to know the truth, the truth which must set us all free.

To the cosponsors and participants in this occasion of awe and challenge, we pledge our commitment to the principle of justice, peace, and reconciliation based on international legitimacy and uniform standards. We shall persist in our quest for peace to place before you the substance and determination of our people, often victimized but never defeated. We shall pursue our people's right to self-determination to the exhilaration of freedom and to the warmth of the sun as a nation among equals.

This is the moment of truth. You must have the courage to recognize it and the will to implement it, for our truth can no longer be hidden away in the dark recesses of inadvertency or neglect. People of Palestine look at you with a straightforward, direct gaze, seeking to touch your heart, for you have dared to stir up hopes that cannot be abandoned. You cannot afford to let us down, for we have lived up to the values you espouse, and we have remained true to our cause.

We, the Palestinian people, made the imaginative leap in the Palestine National Council of November 1988, during which the Palestine Liberation Organization launched its peace initiative based on Security Council Resolution 242 and 338, and declared Palestinian independence based on Resolution 181 of the United Nations, which gave birth to two states in 1948, Israel and Palestine. December 1988, a historic speech before the United Nations in Geneva led directly to the launching of the Palestinian-American dialogue. Ever since then, our people have responded positively to every serious peace initiative and has done its utmost to ensure the success of this process. Israel, on the other hand, has placed many obstacles and barriers in the path of peace to negate the very validity of the process. Its illegal and frenzied settlement activity is the most glaring evidence of its rejectionism, the latest settlement being erected just two days ago. These historic decisions of the Palestine National Council wrench the course of history from inevitable confrontation and conflict towards peace and mutual recognition. With our own hands and in an act of sheer will, we have molded the shape of the future of our people. Our parliament has articulated the message of the people, with the courage to say yes to the challenge of history, just as it provided the reference in its resolutions last month in Algiers and in the Central Council meeting this month in Tunis to go forward to this historic conference. We cannot be made to bear the brunt of other people's noes. We must have reciprocity. We must have peace.

Ladies and Gentlemen: In the Middle East, there is no superfluous people outside time and place, but rather a state sorely missed by time and place. The state of Palestine must be born on the land of Palestine to redeem the injustice of the destruction of its historical reality and to free the people of Palestine from the shackles of their victimization.

Our homeland has never ceased to exist in our minds and hearts, but it has to exist as a state on all the territories occupied by Israel in the war of 1967 with Arab Jerusalem as its capital in the context of that city's special status and its nonexclusive character.

This state, in a condition of emergence, has already been a subject of anticipation for too long, should take place today rather than tomorrow. However, we are willing to accept the proposal for a transitional stage provided interim arrangements are not transformed into permanent status. The time frame must be condensed to respond to the dispossessed Palestinians' urgent need for sanctuary and to the occupied Palestinians' right to gain relief from oppression and to win recognition of their authentic will.

During this phase, international protection for our people is most urgently needed. And the de jure application of the Fourth Geneva Convention is a necessary condition. The phases must not prejudice the outcome. Rather, they require an internal momentum and motivation to lead sequentially to sovereignty. Bilateral negotiations on the withdrawal of Israeli forces, the dissolution of Israeli administration, and the transfer of authority to the Palestinian people cannot proceed under coercion or threat in the current asymmetry of power. Israel must demonstrate its willingness to negotiate in good faith by immediately halting all settlement activity and land confiscation while implementing meaningful confidence-building measures.

Without genuine progress, tangible constructive changes and just agreements during the bilateral talks, multilateral negotiations will be meaningless. Regional stability, security, and development are the logical outcome of an equitable and just solution to the Palestinian question, which remains the key to the resolution of wider conflicts and concerns.

In its confrontation of wills between the legitimacy of the people and the illegality of the occupation, the intifada's message has been consistent: to embody the Palestinian state and to build its institutions and infrastructure. We seek recognition for this creative impulse which nurtures within it the potential nascent state.

We have paid a heavy price for daring to substantiate our authenticity and to practice popular democracy in spite of the cruelty of occupation. It was a sheer act of will that brought us here; the same will which asserted itself in the essence of the intifada as the cry for freedom, an act of civil resistance and people's participation and empowerment.

The intifada is our drive towards nation-building and social transformation. We are here today with the support of our people, who have given itself the right to hope and to make a stand for peace. We must recognize as well that some of our people harbor serious doubts and skepticism about this process. Within our democratic, social, and political structures, we have evolved a respect for pluralism and diversity and we shall guard the opposition's right to differ within the parameters of mutual respect and national unity.

The process launched here must lead us to the light at the end of the tunnel. And this light is the promise of a new Palestine—free, democratic, and respectful of human rights and the integrity of nature.

Self-determination, ladies and gentlemen, can neither be granted nor withheld at the will of the political self-interest of others. For it is enshrined in all international charters and humanitarian law. We claim this right; we firmly assert it here before you and in the eyes of the rest of the world. For it is a sacred and inviolable right which we shall relentlessly pursue and exercise with dedication and self-confidence and pride.

Let's end the Palestinian-Israeli fatal proximity in this unnatural condition of occupation, which has already claimed too many lives. No dream of expansion or glory can justify the taking of a single life. Set us free to reengage as neighbors and as equals on our holy land.

To our people in exile and under occupation, who have sent us to this appointment, laden with their trust, love, and aspirations, we say that the load is heavy and the task is great, but we shall be true. In the words of our great national poet Mahmud Darwish: *My homeland is not a suitcase, and I am no traveler.*

To the exiled and the occupied we say you shall return and you shall remain and we will prevail, for our cause is just. We will put on our embroidered robes and kafiyehs [traditional headdresses] in the sight of the world and celebrate together on the day of liberation.

Refugee camps are not fit for people who were raised on the land of Palestine in the warmth of the sun and freedom. The hail of Israeli bombs almost daily pouring down on our defenseless civilian population in the refugee camps of Lebanon is no substitute for the healing rain of the homeland. Yet, the international will had ensured their return in United Nation Resolution 194—a fact willfully ignored and unenacted. Similarly, all other resolutions pertinent to the Palestinian question beginning with Resolution 181, through Resolutions 242 and 338, and ending with Security Council Resolutions 681, have until now been relegated to the domain of public debate rather than real implementation. They formed a larger body of legality, including all relevant provisions of international law within which any peaceful settlement must proceed. If international legitimacy and the rule of law are to prevail and govern relations among nations, they must be respected and impartially and uniformly implemented. We as Palestinians require nothing less than justice.

Palestinians everywhere: Today we bear in our hands the precious gift of your love and your pain, and we shall set it down gently here before the eyes of the world and say there is a right here which must be acknowledged—the right to self-determination and statehood. There is strength and there is the scent of sacred incense in the air. Jerusalem, the heart of our homeland and the cradle of the soul, is shimmering through the barriers of occupation and deceit.

The deliberate violation of its sanctities is also an act of violence against the collective human, cultural, and spiritual memory and an aggression against its enduring symbols of tolerance, magnanimity, and respect for cultural and religious authenticity.

The cobbled streets of the old city must not echo with the discordant beat of Israeli military boots. We must restore to them the chant of the muezzin, the chimes of the church, the call of the ram, and the prayers of all the faithful calling for peace in the city of peace.

From Madrid let's light the candle of peace and let the olive branch blossom. Let's celebrate the rituals of justice and rejoice in the hymns of truth, for the awe of the moment is a promise to the future, which we all must redeem.

Palestinians will be free and will stand tall among the community of nations in the fullness of the pride and dignity which, by right, belongs to all people. Today, our people under occupation are holding high the olive branch of peace. In the words of Chairman 'Arafat in 1974 before the UN General Assembly: *Let not the olive branch of peace fall from my hands. Let not the olive branch of peace fall from the hands of the Palestinian people.* May God's mercy, peace, and blessings be upon you.

Prime Minister Yitzhak Rabin: Inaugural Speech (July 13, 1992)

. . . This government is determined to embrace every possible effort, pave every road, and do every possible and impossible thing for the sake of national and personal security, for the sake of peace and of preventing war, for the sake of eliminating unemployment, for the sake of aliyah and its absorption, for the sake of economic growth, to enhance the foundations of democracy and the rule of law, and for the sake of ensuring equality for all citizens, while upholding human rights.

We will change the national order of priorities. We know well that the road we are about to tread will be fraught with obstacles; crises will erupt, and there will be disappointment, tears, and pain. After all this is over, however, once we come to the end of this road, we will have acquired a strong country, a good country, a country in which we all share in the big efforts and are proud to be its citizens. As the poet Rahel put it: Will a concerted, stubborn, and persistent effort of a thousand arms not move mountains? The answer lies with us and is up to us.

. . . In the last decade of the 20th Century, the atlases and the history and geography books no longer depict reality. Walls of hatred have crumbled, borders have been erased, superpowers have collapsed, ideologies have broken down, countries have been born and passed away, and the gates have opened to immigration to Israel. It is our duty, both to ourselves and to our children, to see the new world as it is today, to examine the risks and explore the chances, and to do everything so that the State of Israel becomes part of the changing world. We are no longer an isolated nation, and it is no longer true that the entire world is against us. We must rid ourselves of the feeling of isolation that has afflicted us for almost 50 years. We must join the campaign of peace, reconciliation, and international cooperation that is currently engulfing the entire globe, lest we miss the train and be left alone at the station.

This is why the new government made its main goal to promote the attainment of peace for Israel and to launch vigorous steps to bring about the termination of the Arab-Israeli conflict. We will do this on the basis of recognition by the Arab countries and the Palestinians of Israel as a sovereign state and of its right to live in peace and security. We sincerely believe that this is possible, imperative, and will come to be. As the poet Saul Tchernichowsky wrote: Believe I in the future. Though it may be far off, the day will yet come when peace shall be spoken and nation will bless nation. I would like to believe that this day is not far off.

The government will propose to the Arab countries and to the Palestinians to pursue the peace negotiations based on the format consolidated at the Madrid conference. As a first step on the way to the permanent solution, we will discuss the implementation of autonomy in Judaea, Samaria, and the Gaza district. It is not our intention to waste valuable time. The first directive the government will issue to the negotiating teams will be to accelerate the talks and to conduct intensive deliberations between the sides.

Within a short period of time, we will reopen the talks to dampen the flame of hatred between the Palestinians and the State of Israel. As a first step, and in order to demonstrate our integrity and goodwill, I wish to invite the Palestinian-Jordanian delegation for an informal meeting here in Jerusalem, to hear them and to let them hear us, in order to create the proper atmosphere for a good partnership.

From this podium I want to send a message to you, the Palestinians in the territories: We have been destined to live together on the same piece of land in the same country. Our life proceeds alongside yours, with you, and against you. You have failed in the wars against us. A hundred years of bloody terror on your part only inflicted suffering, pain, and bereavement upon you. You have lost thousands of your sons and daughters, and you have constantly lost ground. For over 44 years you have been deluding yourselves, your leaders have been leading you by the nose with false-hoods and lies. They missed all the opportunities, they rejected all our proposed solutions, and they led you from one disaster to another. You, the Palestinians in the territories, living in miserable exile in Gaza and Khan Yunus and in the refugee camps in Nabulus and Hebron, you who have never in your lives known even one day of freedom and happiness: You had better listen to us, if only this time. We are offering you the most fair and realistic offer we can put forth today: autonomy, self-rule, with its advantages and limitations. You will not get all that you want. We, too, may not get everything we want. Once and for all, take your fate into your own hands. Do not once again miss the opportunity which may never recur. Take our proposal seriously, give it the seriousness it deserves to spare yourselves yet more suffering and bereavement. Enough of tears and blood!

Today the new government proposes to the Palestinians in the territories to give peace a chance and to stop all violent and terrorist activities during the autonomy negotiations. We know very well that the Palestinians are not of one mind and that some of them think differently, but the people have been suffering for years.

To the troublemakers in the territories we propose to drop the stones and the knives and await the outcome of the talks which may engender peace in the Middle East. If the Palestinians accept this proposal, we will pursue the talks. Nevertheless, we will deal with the territories as if there were no negotiations going on between us. Instead of stretching out a friendly hand, we will enforce all the measures to prevent terror and vi-olence. The choice is in the hands of the Palestinians in the territories.

We have lost our best sons and daughters in the struggle over this land and in the wars against the Arab armies. My longtime comrades in the IDF [Israel Defense Forces] and I, as a former military man who fought in Israel's wars, carry their memory in our hearts with great love. We share the grief of the families whose nights are sleepless and for whom all days of the year are one long memorial day, because only those who have lost their best friends can understand the feeling. Our heart also goes out to the disabled whose bodies are marked with the scars of war and terror. Even at this festive time, we do not forget the Israeli MIA's and POW's. We will continue to wage every possible effort to bring them back home. Our thoughts today, as always, are with their families.

Members of the House, we will continue to fight for our right to live here in peace and tranquility. No knife, stone, firebomb, or mine will stop us. The government being presented here today sees itself responsible for the security of each and every Israeli citizen, Jew and Arab alike, in the State of Israel, in Judaea, Samaria, and the Gaza Strip. We will strike hard and relentlessly at the terrorists and their henchmen. There will be no compromises in the war against terror. The IDF and the other security forces will prove to the bloodthirsty men that our lives are not expendable. We will take action to reduce hostile activities as much as possible and safeguard the personal safety of the inhabitants of Israel and the inhabitants of the territories while meticulously upholding the law and individual freedoms.

Members of the House, on your behalf, too, allow me to seize this occasion to convey our gratitude to the soldiers and commanders of the IDF, to the secret warriors of the Shin Bet, to the men of the Border Police and the Israel Police for the nights spent in pursuit and lying in ambush, for the days spent on guard and on the alert. On behalf of all of us, I shake your hand.

Members of the Knesset, the plan for Palestinian self-rule in Judaea, Samaria, and Gaza—the autonomy—included in the Camp David accords involves a five-year interim arrangement. No later than three years after its establishment, discussions will begin on the permanent solution. By definition, the very fact that this issue is being discussed arouses concern among those of us who chose to settle in Judaea, Samaria, and the Gaza district. I hereby inform you that the government, by means of the IDF and the other security forces, will be responsible for the security and welfare of the residents in Judaea, Samaria, and the Gaza Strip. At the same time, the government will avoid moves and acts that would disturb the proper conduct of the peace negotiations. We would like to emphasize that the government will continue to strengthen and build up Jewish settlement along the confrontation lines, due to their security importance, and in metropolitan Jerusalem.

This government, just like all its predecessors, believes there are no differences of opinion within this House concerning the eternalness of Jerusalem as the capital of Israel. Jerusalem, whole and united, has been and will remain the capital of the Israeli people under Israeli sovereignty, the place every Jew yearns and dreams of. The government is resolute in its position that Jerusalem is not a negotiable issue. The coming years, too, will witness the expansion of construction in metropolitan Jerusalem. Every Jew, both religious and secular, vows: If I forget thee, O Jerusalem, let my right hand wither! This vow unites all of us and certainly applies to me, being a native of Jerusalem.

The government will uphold the freedom of worship of members of all other faiths in Jerusalem. It will meticulously maintain free access to the holy sites of all faiths and sects and will make a normal and comfortable life possible for all those visiting and living in it.

Members of the Knesset, the winds of peace that have been blowing recently from Moscow to Washington, from Berlin to Beijing; the voluntary elimination of weapons of mass destruction; and the abrogation of military pacts have decreased the risks of war in the Middle East as well.

Nevertheless, this region—made up of Syria, Jordan, Iraq, and Lebanon —is still rife with dangers, which is why we will not make even the slightest concession on issues of security. As far as we are concerned, security comes even before peace.

Several countries in our region have recently stepped up their efforts to develop and export nuclear weapons. According to reports, Iraq was very close to possessing nuclear arms. Fortunately, the Iraqi nuclear capability was exposed in time and, according to various testimonies, it was affected and damaged in and after the Gulf war. The possibility that nuclear weapons may make their appearance in the Middle East in the next few years is a negative and very serious development from Israel's point of view. Already in its initial steps, the government—possibly with the cooperation of other countries—will give its attention to the foiling of every possibility that any of Israel's enemies should get a hold on nuclear weapons. For a long time, Israel has been ready for the danger of the existence of nuclear weapons. Nevertheless, this reality requires us to give additional thought to the urgent need to terminate the Arab-Israeli conflict and to attain peace with our neighbors.

Members of the House, from this moment on, the term peace process is no longer relevant. Starting today we will not talk of a process, but of making peace. In making peace, we would like to employ the good services of Egypt, whose late leader Anwar al-Sadat mustered the courage and had the wisdom to award his people and us the first peace treaty. The government will seek other ways to improve neighborly relations and to enhance the ties with Egypt and its president, Husni Mubarak.

I call on the leaders of the Arab countries to follow in the footsteps of Egypt and its presidents, to make the move that will bring peace to us and them. I invite the king of Jordan and the Syrian and Lebanese presidents to come here to this podium, here in Israel's Knesset in Jerusalem, and talk peace. I am willing to travel today, tomorrow, to Amman, Damascus, Beirut on behalf of peace, because there is no greater triumph than the triumph of peace. In wars, there are victors and vanquished. In peace, all are victors.

In making peace, we will also be joined by the United States, whose friendship and special closeness we sincerely appreciate and hold dear. We will spare no effort to tighten and improve the special relations we have with the only superpower in the world. Although we will receive its advice, the decisions will be ours only—of Israel as a sovereign and independent state.

Chairman Yasir Arafat: Speech on Fatah's Anniversary (December 31, 1992)

O revolutionaries in all the posts of the revolution, inside and outside the homeland; O masses of our fighting Palestinian people, O masses of our militant Arab nation, on such a day 28 years ago, the Palestinian people announced the start of the armed Palestinian revolution, which was ignited by the bullets of your pioneering movement—namely, the Fatah movement—on 1 January 1965. . . .

The road to victory and freedom, which our free men and revolutionaries are building day after day with their bare hands and pure blood, is the road to Palestine, which the faithful are longing for with their hearts.

Our people, O brothers and friends, are the active volcano in the Middle East which will only calm itself when one of the youths of the revolution and the intifada hoists the flag of your state over Jerusalem, and our homeland Palestine; an independent Palestine. . . .

Our battle to free the Palestinian will has been decided in favor of the Palestinian people, away from guardianship, dependence, and containment. The battle of the Palestinian will as expressed by the bullets of your leading movement, Fatah, early in 1965 was a hard and bitter one, but the few believers remained true to the oath and continued with resolve and strength.

The vanguard of your revolution, the Fatah movement, has proven that there is no going back on the jihad for Palestine, on the homeland, or on martyrdom. . . .

Masses of our glorious Arab nation. Ideological, political, and economic changes have swept our contemporary world. What was yesterday an established fact has today become something of the past. These changes have reached our region in the Middle East, bringing in the wake of their first wave the Gulf crisis and the Gulf war. This has dealt our Arab nation a great blow, hit Arab solidarity, and paralyzed the Arab position toward the Palestinian question, and as a result, lost us an historic opportunity to exploit those world changes for the national and the Palestinian interest. . . .

Then, my brothers, came the second wave, with the collapse of the Soviet Union and the domination by the single uni-polar American power over the fate of international politics.

This new world order brings great, real, and manifest dangers that pose a challenge for the Arab nation—peoples as well as states. These risks keep our nation bogged down in the whirlwind of the conflicts of the new world order. We either live or we will have to die, especially as Israel, world Zionism, and their allies are lying in wait for any serious Arab trend aimed at building our national destiny in light of the new world situation. . . .

We must stand by our brothers in Iraq—its people and its children, lift their siege and their suffering, and thwart the conspiracy being perpetrated against Iraq's territorial integrity and its unity. Likewise, the sanctions against Libya and its fraternal people must be lifted and their suffering must be brought to an end. And what about Somalia and our absence, as one Arab nation, when dealing with its problems, of which others have had to take charge? . . .

This is a clear declaration in the name of the entire nation: This land will remain Arab, will remain Arab, and will remain Arab. History will not register that the present generation of Palestinians squandered an atom of the soil of its homeland or of Jerusalem—or of Jerusalem.

Sons of our heroic Palestinian people, heroes in the positions of revolution, brothers, I want it to be clear to us all that the distance between us and the enemy at the negotiations table is too wide. . . .

Likewise, the distance is wide between us and the enemy in the field of conflict and the battle. But it is our political battle that covers our land and sanctities, and that will determine our fate and future. After more than a year since the start of the Madrid negotiations, which we attended despite the unjust conditions, our negotiators find themselves still at the same point at which they began. This is because the Israeli enemy is bent on maneuvering and not on negotiating. He tries to gain more time so that the conditions that forced him to sit face to face before the delegation of Palestine—the delegation of the owners of the land the enemy usurped and the land of the people he is persecuting and denies existence—may change. . . .

We have entered the negotiations in highly complicated Arab and international conditions and under unjust circumstances that are aimed at obstructing Palestinian participation. But thanks to our trust in ourselves and in our people, and our bold participation, we overcame the unjust conditions the Israeli enemy imposed.

International support for the Palestine right grew, and then came the Israeli elections, which brought the government of Yitzhaq Rabin, whom the U.S. Administration has given loan guarantees of $10 billion and guarantees for Israeli military supremacy. And so the Israeli Government continued with its policy of the iron fist, beatings, deportation, collective punishments, and crimes against our Islamic and Christian sanctities. The Israeli Government thus persisted in the confiscation of lands and the building of settlements for the new settlers in our land.

The policy of double dealing and measures that govern American attitudes toward the Arab-Israeli conflict have so far frustrated all opportunities for forcing the Israeli enemy to abide by the resolutions of international legitimacy and the withdrawal of its aggressor enemies from the Palestinian and Arab territories in implementation of these international resolutions, on whose basis the invitations to the Madrid peace conference were given, and for the implementation of which, talks were held in Washington and elsewhere.

The chronic fault in the pro-Israel U.S. stance alone explains the failure of the peace process in the Middle East. It is clear that successive American administrations make Israel a state above the law and above the resolutions of international legitimacy, and provide it with international protection and unlimited support.

Militant brothers, O sons of our brave intifadah, our Palestinian delegation, the delegation of the Palestinian people, the PLO delegation, from the premise of our national constants approved by our national and central councils tightly tied Palestinian flexibility with the Palestinian national constants. [sentence as heard] With what brothers? With the national constants. Thus it rejected the enemy's sayings and submissions. Our delegation held fast to our national constants and the resolutions of international legitimacy, especially UN Security Council Resolutions 242 and 338, because they are the terms of reference of the peace process, from the moment it started until its conclusion with Israeli withdrawal from all the Arab and Palestinian territories, including holy Jerusalem, and the implementation of the principle of land for peace and the legitimate rights of the Palestinian people, including our right to return, to self-determination, and to establish an independent state with Jerusalem as its capital, on the way to Palestinian-Jordanian confederation in accordance with the voluntary and free choice of the two fraternal peoples: The Palestinian and the Jordanian.

Israel remaining an aggressive state, above the law and international legitimacy, only opens the door before lasting wars and total chaos. Yes, this only opens the door before lasting wars and total chaos in the region, which harms all. . . .

More steadfastness, more all-out confrontations in the sixth year of our blessed intifada in the towns, villages, camps, streets, fields, and mountains. The battle for national deliverance has begun with these solid Palestinian human blocs, who fill our lands and defy the bullets of the Israeli occupation and ferocity with their strong and profound faith and deep-rooted will and great sacrifices, and with national unity our staunch shield in the melting pot of the PLO, the sole legitimate representative of our people and revolution. . . .

The Palestinian people remain the secure fence for the unity of the revolution and the unity of the PLO, and for preserving its national program and its future decisions with patience, wisdom, and persistence, and on the basis of democratic principles and democratic dialogue, common denominators, political and organizational programs approved by our national councils, in order to consolidate this national unity. Those democratic principles have foiled crude intervention in our internal affairs of our Palestinian house. Hence, from here and in this blessed year, the sixth year of our intifada and the 29th of our revolution, we renew the call to all the brothers active in the national field, from all political orientations, to consolidate this national unity. . . .

I say to those I love in the Israeli prisons and detention camps that the day of freedom is nigh. Your brothers have been pounding at the doors of the great prison and you are pounding at the walls of your prisons and detention camps. Your voices roar to the world. Be patient. Victory is from God. Victory needs no more than an hour's patience. . . .

Be patient. You are the spark that has inflamed anew the wrath of the masses of the Palestinian people in the face of the Israeli occupation. You are the free sons of this struggling people who have exposed the falsehood of Rabin and his Labor government with regard to the peace process. There will be no peace while you remain away from your homeland and kinsmen and your intifada. . . .

Your organization, the PLO, has acted on all fronts throughout the world to prevent the plot of the transfer—from the UN Security Council in New York to Europe, to Russia, to the Islamic and African summits at Dakar, to the Arab foreign ministers' conference in Cairo, to the Nonaligned Movement in Indonesia, to China, and to Japan. The action continues. . . .

Sons of the great Palestinian revolution, proud struggling people of Palestine, let the 29th year of the Palestine revolution and the sixth year of our blessed intifada be the year of challenge and victorious confrontation. What year, brothers? The year of challenge and victorious confrontation under the shadow of our solid national unity and the confidence of the PLO, our national unity, for routing the forces of Israeli dictatorship and the liberation of our Palestinian land and our holy Jerusalem.

Let us all stand like one man with one heart and one goal against our enemy, who occupies our land and homeland and sanctities.

The greater the darkness the closer the dawn!

Mahmoud Darwish: Resigning from the PLO Leadership (August 1993)

I will shock you. This organization, complete with its hierarchy and structure and figures and perhaps its content—this organization is finished. Yes, it is finished, and you must admit this and act accordingly. [You must] put all your imaginative resources to work to see what comes next and to nurture the infant that it [the PLO] has given birth to, whether some of us weep for it [the PLO] or others rejoice at its demise.

This organization is finished whether you go with the settlement to the end or drop out of the settlement now. The organization's remaining role is to sign the agreement with Israel. The moment it signs, it will be transformed into something else. What is this something else? Think about it as of now, and think of the fate of the cadres standing in the wind. . . .

We are approaching a grave decision relating to an imminent agreement with the Israeli government on Gaza and Jericho. When will this matter be discussed? When?

Some will say: Israel does not want to keep Gaza, and handing it over to the Palestinians solves an Israeli problem caused by the Gaza's unsolvable problems and caused by the intifada and by Israel's inability to annex because it wants to preserve Israel's Jewish character. Some will say that the Israeli-Palestinian agreement will eliminate the obstacle standing in the way of the Arab-Israeli peace train, and that the agreement will cool down the Arab-Israeli conflict and divide the Palestinian cause and the Palestinian people, and, and . . . All this is true, but we cannot say that Gaza and Jericho don't concern us. Whether the proposal promises us full self-government or incomplete independence, we must take our time studying it in order to avoid leaping into thin air, in order not to take risks. We must carefully examine the details and the principles before we take this step, and the examination must involve all the groups and trends of the Palestinian people.

Have we obtained answers to the questions, including the following questions:

Is this deal part of a comprehensive peace settlement . . . ?

Is it clear that this is the first stage of the implementation of [Security Council] Resolution 242 in accordance with a clear timetable linked with a clear commitment and a clear recognition that this land is occupied land?

Who will run this experimental self-government in Gaza and Jericho? The PLO, whose role is going to end? Or an elected council?

Will the PLO go there, or will its chairman, in his capacity as its chairman or the president of something else?

What are the parameters of the experimental interim stage? Will it be self-government if the experiment and the test are a success? And what if it fails? Here, allow me to warn that our current conditions and present structure provide a negative answer to this question.

Is there a clear bridge linking the interim stage with the final stage, to reassure us that the interim stage will not be the final one?

Is the popular base ready to plunge into this experiment? Or is it charged with dangerous, explosive elements?

Can we ignore the fears, real or contrived, that our Arab 'neighbors' are expressing about the agreement with our Israeli 'neighbors'?

What international economic guarantees are there that to make Gaza viable and build its infrastructure . . . ?

What forms of national self-expression will be allowed in resisting the occupation, which will remain there through general security, the settlements, the borders, the right of foreign representation, the crossings and the bridges and other forms of Israeli sovereignty?

Those questions make me think we are about to take an historic risk. I hope it works, but I have fears about its failure and its destructive national effects, which could lead to disaster.

My conscience will not tolerate participation in this adventurous decision as long as I cannot answer the questions posed. For that reason, I stand by my resignation from the decision-making body, placing myself at the disposal of the Palestinian people and their higher national interests.

Forgive me if I say that I am under no obligation to take part in this gamble. . . .

It is your right to ask me: Why [resign from the PLO Executive Committee] now? Why at this particular time?

Among the easy, ready-made charges: Isn't this abandoning ship?

I will respond immediately. . . . I don't see a ship now, if the ship is the PLO. Look around you carefully: its institutions, departments and bureaus are unoperational. They are up for auction.

It would be a crime to ignore the objective element in the crisis we are going through, but it is arrogant to ignore the subjective element. I am asking for no more than good management of the ending, in a manner that preserves people's dignity and humanity. We have taken two generations to their death in the project of liberation and independence, and it now appears as if we are abandoning them completely, leaving them to the winds of the new wilderness. No, the martyrs were not stupid, as some angry people are saying. The martyrs were right. They believed their blood and their nation. We are the ones to blame, we who have no answer to any question relating to their children. . . .

We see a ship's captain in a fluid image driven by a mysterious force towards an unknown fate at sea. On the shore, we see thousands of the martyrs' children waving to him: wait for us, or take us with you. . . .

We are bidding a chaotic farewell to an historic stage and entering another stage for which we have not prepared ourselves. This is the question that haunts me. . . .

Israel–PLO Declaration of Principles on Interim Self-Government Arrangements (September 13, 1993)

The Government of the State of Israel and the P.L.O. team (in the Jordanian-Palestinian delegation to the Middle East Peace Conference) (the

"Palestinian Delegation"), representing the Palestinian people, agree that it is time to put an end to decades of confrontation and conflict, recognize their mutual legitimate and political rights, and strive to live in peaceful coexistence and mutual dignity and security and achieve a just, lasting and comprehensive peace settlement and historic reconciliation through the agreed political process. Accordingly, the two sides agree to the following principles:

ARTICLE I

Aim of the Negotiations

The aim of the Israeli-Palestinian negotiations within the current Middle East peace process is, among other things, to establish a Palestinian Interim Self-Government Authority, the elected Council (the "Council"), for the Palestinian people in the West Bank and the Gaza Strip, for a transitional period not exceeding five years, leading to a permanent settlement based on Security Council Resolutions 242 and 338.

It is understood that the interim arrangements are an integral part of the whole peace process and that the negotiations on the permanent status will lead to the implementation of Security Council Resolutions 242 and 338.

ARTICLE II

Framework for the Interim Period

The agreed framework for the interim period is set forth in this Declaration of Principles.

ARTICLE III

Elections

1. In order that the Palestinian people in the West Bank and Gaza Strip may govern themselves according to democratic principles, direct, free and general political elections will be held for the Council under agreed supervision and international observation, while the Palestinian police will ensure public order.

2. An agreement will be concluded on the exact mode and conditions of the elections in accordance with the protocol attached as Annex I, with the goal of holding the elections not later than nine months after the entry into force of this Declaration of Principles.

3. These elections will constitute a significant interim preparatory step toward the realization of the legitimate rights of the Palestinian people and their just requirements.

Article IV

Jurisdiction

Jurisdiction of the Council will cover West Bank and Gaza Strip territory, except for issues that will be negotiated in the permanent status negotiations. The two sides view the West Bank and the Gaza Strip as a single territorial unit, whose integrity will be preserved during the interim period.

Article V

Transitional Period and Permanent Status Negotiations

1. The five-year transitional period will begin upon the withdrawal from the Gaza Strip and Jericho area.

2. Permanent status negotiations will commence as soon as possible, but not later than the beginning of the third year of the interim period, between the Government of Israel and the Palestinian people representatives.

3. It is understood that these negotiations shall cover remaining issues, including: Jerusalem, refugees, settlements, security arrangements, borders, relations and cooperation with other neighbors, and other issues of common interest.

4. The two parties agree that the outcome of the permanent status negotiations should not be prejudiced or preempted by agreements reached for the interim period.

Article VI

Preparatory Transfer of Powers and Responsibilities

1. Upon the entry into force of this Declaration of Principles and the withdrawal from the Gaza Strip and the Jericho area, a transfer of authority from the Israeli military government and its Civil Administration to the authorised Palestinians for this task, as detailed herein, will commence. This transfer of authority will be of a preparatory nature until the inauguration of the Council.

2. Immediately after the entry into force of this Declaration of Principles and the withdrawal from the Gaza Strip and Jericho area, with the view to promoting economic development in the West Bank and Gaza Strip, authority will be transferred to the Palestinians on the following spheres: education and culture, health, social welfare, direct taxation, and tourism. The Palestinian side will commence in building the Palestinian police force, as agreed upon. Pending the inauguration of the Council, the two parties may ne-

gotiate the transfer of additional powers and responsibilities, as agreed upon.

ARTICLE VII

Interim Agreement

1. The Israeli and Palestinian delegations will negotiate an agreement on the interim period (the "Interim Agreement")

2. The Interim Agreement shall specify, among other things, the structure of the Council, the number of its members, and the transfer of powers and responsibilities from the Israeli military government and its Civil Administration to the Council. The Interim Agreement shall also specify the Council's executive authority, legislative authority in accordance with Article IX below, and the independent Palestinian judicial organs.

3. The Interim Agreement shall include arrangements, to be implemented upon the inauguration of the Council, for the assumption by the Council of all of the powers and responsibilities transferred previously in accordance with Article VI above.

4. In order to enable the Council to promote economic growth, upon its inauguration, the Council will establish, among other things, a Palestinian Electricity Authority, a Gaza Sea Port Authority, a Palestinian Development Bank, a Palestinian Export Promotion Board, a Palestinian Environmental Authority, a Palestinian Land Authority and a Palestinian Water Administration Authority, and any other Authorities agreed upon, in accordance with the Interim Agreement that will specify their powers and responsibilities.

5. After the inauguration of the Council, the Civil Administration will be dissolved, and the Israeli military government will be withdrawn.

ARTICLE VIII

Public Order and Security

In order to guarantee public order and internal security for the Palestinians of the West Bank and the Gaza Strip, the Council will establish a strong police force, while Israel will continue to carry the responsibility for defending against external threats, as well as the responsibility for overall security of Israelis for the purpose of safeguarding their internal security and public order.

ARTICLE IX

Laws and Military Orders

1. The Council will be empowered to legislate, in accordance with the Interim Agreement, within all authorities transferred to it.
2. Both parties will review jointly laws and military orders presently in force in remaining spheres.

ARTICLE X

Joint Israeli-Palestinian Liaison Committee

In order to provide for a smooth implementation of this Declaration of Principles and any subsequent agreements pertaining to the interim period, upon the entry into force of this Declaration of Principles, a Joint Israeli-Palestinian Liaison Committee will be established in order to deal with issues requiring coordination, other issues of common interest, and disputes.

ARTICLE XI

Israeli-Palestinian Cooperation in Economic Fields

Recognizing the mutual benefit of cooperation in promoting the development of the West Bank, the Gaza Strip and Israel, upon the entry into force of this Declaration of Principles, an Israeli-Palestinian Economic Cooperation Committee will be established in order to develop and implement in a cooperative manner the programs identified in the protocols attached as Annex III and Annex IV.

ARTICLE XII

Liaison and Cooperation with Jordan and Egypt

The two parties will invite the Governments of Jordan and Egypt to participate in establishing further liaison and cooperation arrangements between the Government of Israel and the Palestinian representatives, on the one hand, and the Governments of Jordan and Egypt, on the other hand, to promote cooperation between them. These arrangements will include the constitution of a Continuing Committee that will decide by agreement on the modalities of admission of persons displaced from the West Bank and Gaza Strip in 1967, together with necessary measures to prevent disruption and disorder. Other matters of common concern will be dealt with by this Committee.

ARTICLE XIII

Redeployment of Israeli Forces

1. After the entry into force of this Declaration of Principles, and not later than the eve of elections for the Council, a redeployment of Israeli military forces in the West Bank and the Gaza Strip will take place, in addition to withdrawal of Israeli forces carried out in accordance with Article XIV.

2. In redeploying its military forces, Israel will be guided by the principle that its military forces should be redeployed outside populated areas.

3. Further redeployments to specified locations will be gradually implemented commensurate with the assumption of responsibility for public order and internal security by the Palestinian police force pursuant to Article VIII above.

ARTICLE XIV

Israeli Withdrawal from the Gaza Strip and Jericho Area

Israel will withdraw from the Gaza Strip and Jericho area, as detailed in the protocol attached as Annex II.

ARTICLE XV

Resolution of Disputes

1. Disputes arising out of the application or interpretation of this Declaration of Principles, or any subsequent agreements pertaining to the interim period, shall be resolved by negotiations through the Joint Liaison Committee to be established pursuant to Article X above.

2. Disputes which cannot be settled by negotiations may be resolved by a mechanism of conciliation to be agreed upon by the parties.

3. The parties may agree to submit to arbitration disputes relating to the interim period, which cannot be settled through conciliation. To this end, upon the agreement of both parties, the parties will establish an Arbitration Committee.

ARTICLE XVI

Israeli-Palestinian Cooperation Concerning Regional Programs

Both parties view the multilateral working groups as an appropriate instrument for promoting a "Marshall Plan", the regional programs and other programs, including special programs for the West Bank and Gaza Strip, as indicated in the protocol attached as Annex IV.

ARTICLE XVII

Miscellaneous Provisions

1. This Declaration of Principles will enter into force one month after its signing.

2. All protocols annexed to this Declaration of Principles and Agreed Minutes pertaining thereto shall be regarded as an integral part hereof.

ANNEX I

Protocol on the Mode and Conditions of Elections

1. Palestinians of Jerusalem who live there will have the right to participate in the election process, according to an agreement between the two sides.

2. In addition, the election agreement should cover, among other things, the following issues:

a. the system of elections;

b. the mode of the agreed supervision and international observation and their personal composition; and

c. rules and regulations regarding election campaign, including agreed arrangements for the organizing of mass media, and the possibility of licensing a broadcasting and TV station.

3. The future status of displaced Palestinians who were registered on 4th June 1967 will not be prejudiced because they are unable to participate in the election process due to practical reasons.

ANNEX II

Protocol on Withdrawal of Israeli Forces from the Gaza Strip and Jericho Area

1. The two sides will conclude and sign within two months from the date of entry into force of this Declaration of Principles, an agreement on the withdrawal of Israeli military forces from the Gaza Strip and Jericho area. This agreement will include comprehensive arrangements to apply in the Gaza Strip and the Jericho area subsequent to the Israeli withdrawal.

2. Israel will implement an accelerated and scheduled withdrawal of Israeli military forces from the Gaza Strip and Jericho area, beginning immediately with the signing of the agreement on

the Gaza Strip and Jericho area and to be completed within a period not exceeding four months after the signing of this agreement.

3. The above agreement will include, among other things:

a. Arrangements for a smooth and peaceful transfer of authority from the Israeli military government and its Civil Administration to the Palestinian representatives.

b. Structure, powers and responsibilities of the Palestinian authority in these areas, except: external security, settlements, Israelis, foreign relations, and other mutually agreed matters.

c. Arrangements for the assumption of internal security and public order by the Palestinian police force consisting of police officers recruited locally and from abroad (holding Jordanian passports and Palestinian documents issued by Egypt). Those who will participate in the Palestinian police force coming from abroad should be trained as police and police officers.

d. A temporary international or foreign presence, as agreed upon.

e. Establishment of a joint Palestinian-Israeli Coordination and Cooperation Committee for mutual security purposes.

f. An economic development and stabilization program, including the establishment of an Emergency Fund, to encourage foreign investment, and financial and economic support. Both sides will coordinate and cooperate jointly and unilaterally with regional and international parties to support these aims.

g. Arrangements for a safe passage for persons and transportation between the Gaza Strip and Jericho area.

4. The above agreement will include arrangements for coordination between both parties regarding passages:

a. Gaza—Egypt; and

b. Jericho—Jordan.

5. The offices responsible for carrying out the powers and responsibilities of the Palestinian authority under this Annex II and Article VI of the Declaration of Principles will be located in the Gaza Strip and in the Jericho area pending the inauguration of the Council.

6. Other than these agreed arrangements, the status of the Gaza Strip and Jericho area will continue to be an integral part of the West Bank and Gaza Strip, and will not be changed in the interim period.

ANNEX III

Protocol on Israeli-Palestinian Cooperation in Economic and Development Programs

The two sides agree to establish an Israeli-Palestinian Continuing Committee for Economic Cooperation, focusing, among other things, on the following:

1. Cooperation in the field of water, including a Water Development Program prepared by experts from both sides, which will also specify the mode of cooperation in the management of water resources in the West Bank and Gaza Strip, and will include proposals for studies and plans on water rights of each party, as well as on the equitable utilization of joint water resources for implementation in and beyond the interim period.

2. Cooperation in the field of electricity, including an Electricity Development Program, which will also specify the mode of cooperation for the production, maintenance, purchase and sale of electricity resources.

3. Cooperation in the field of energy, including an Energy Development Program, which will provide for the exploitation of oil and gas for industrial purposes, particularly in the Gaza Strip and in the Negev, and will encourage further joint exploitation of other energy resources. This Program may also provide for the construction of a Petrochemical industrial complex in the Gaza Strip and the construction of oil and gas pipelines.

4. Cooperation in the field of finance, including a Financial Development and Action Program for the encouragement of international investment in the West Bank and the Gaza Strip, and in Israel, as well as the establishment of a Palestinian Development Bank.

5. Cooperation in the field of transport and communications, including a Program, which will define guidelines for the establishment of a Gaza Sea Port Area, and will provide for the establishing of transport and communications lines to and from the West Bank and the Gaza Strip to Israel and to other countries. In addition, this Program will provide for carrying out the necessary construction of roads, railways, communications lines, etc.

6. Cooperation in the field of trade, including studies, and Trade Promotion Programs, which will encourage local, regional and interregional trade, as well as a feasibility study of creating free trade zones in the Gaza Strip and in Israel, mutual access to these zones, and cooperation in other areas related to trade and commerce.

7. Cooperation in the field of industry, including Industrial De-

velopment Programs, which will provide for the establishment of joint Israeli-Palestinian Industrial Research and Development Centers, will promote Palestinian-Israeli joint ventures, and provide guidelines for cooperation in the textile, food, pharmaceutical, electronics, diamonds, computer and science-based industries.

8. A program for cooperation in, and regulation of, labor relations and cooperation in social welfare issues.

9. A Human Resources Development and Cooperation Plan, providing for joint Israeli-Palestinian workshops and seminars, and for the establishment of joint vocational training centers, research institutes and data banks.

10. An Environmental Protection Plan, providing for joint and/ or coordinated measures in this sphere.

11. A program for developing coordination and cooperation in the field of communication and media.

12. Any other programs of mutual interest.

ANNEX IV

Protocol on Israeli-Palestinian Cooperation Concerning Regional Development Programs

1. The two sides will cooperate in the context of the multilateral peace efforts in promoting a Development Program for the region, including the West Bank and the Gaza Strip, to be initiated by the G-7. The parties will request the G-7 to seek the participation in this program of other interested states, such as members of the Organisation for Economic Cooperation and Development regional Arab states and institutions, as well as members of the private sector.

2. The Development Program will consist of two elements:

    a) An Economic Development Program for the West Bank and the Gaza Strip.

    b) A Regional Economic Development Program.

A. The Economic Development Program for the West Bank and the Gaza strip will consist of the following elements:

(1) A Social Rehabilitation Program, including a Housing and Construction Program.

(2) A Small and Medium Business Development Plan.

(3) An Infrastructure Development Program (water, electricity, transportation and communications, etc.)

(4) A Human Resources Plan.

(5) Other programs.

B. The Regional Economic Development Program may consist of the following elements:

(1) The establishment of a Middle East Development Fund,

as a first step, and a Middle East Development Bank, as a second step.

(2) The development of a joint Israeli-Palestinian-Jordanian Plan for coordinated exploitation of the Dead Sea area.

(3) The Mediterranean Sea (Gaza)—Dead Sea Canal.

(4) Regional Desalinization and other water development projects.

(5) A regional plan for agricultural development, including a coordinated regional effort for the prevention of desertification.

(6) Interconnection of electricity grids.

(7) Regional cooperation for the transfer, distribution and industrial exploitation of gas, oil and other energy resources.

(8) A Regional Tourism, Transportation and Telecommunications Development Plan.

(9) Regional cooperation in other spheres.

3. The two sides will encourage the multilateral working groups, and will coordinate towards their success. The two parties will encourage intersessional activities, as well as pre-feasibility and feasibility studies, within the various multilateral working groups.

Agreed Minutes to the Declaration of Principles on Interim Self-Government Arrangements

Any powers and responsibilities transferred to the Palestinians pursuant to the Declaration of Principles prior to the inauguration of the Council will be subject to the same principles pertaining to Article IV, as set out in these Agreed Minutes below.

B. Specific Understandings and Agreements

ARTICLE IV

It is understood that:

1. Jurisdiction of the Council will cover West Bank and Gaza Strip territory, except for issues that will be negotiated in the permanent status negotiations: Jerusalem, settlements, military locations, and Israelis.

2. The Council's jurisdiction will apply with regard to the agreed powers, responsibilities, spheres and authorities transferred to it.

ARTICLE VI (2)

It is agreed that the transfer of authority will be as follows:

(1) The Palestinian side will inform the Israeli side of the names of the authorised Palestinians who will assume the powers, authorities and responsibilities that will be transferred to the Palestinians according to the Declaration of Principles in the following fields: education and culture, health, social welfare, direct taxation, tourism, and any other authorities agreed upon.

(2) It is understood that the rights and obligations of these offices will not be affected.

(3) Each of the spheres described above will continue to enjoy existing budgetary allocations in accordance with arrangements to be mutually agreed upon. These arrangements also will provide for the necessary adjustments required in order to take into account the taxes collected by the direct taxation office.

(4) Upon the execution of the Declaration of Principles, the Israeli and Palestinian delegations will immediately commence negotiations on a detailed plan for the transfer of authority on the above offices in accordance with the above understandings.

ARTICLE VII (2)

The Interim Agreement will also include arrangements for coordination and cooperation.

ARTICLE VII (5)

The withdrawal of the military government will not prevent Israel from exercising the powers and responsibilities not transferred to the Council.

ARTICLE VIII

It is understood that the Interim Agreement will include arrangements for cooperation and coordination between the two parties in this regard. It is also agreed that the transfer of powers and responsibilities to the Palestinian police will be accomplished in a phased manner, as agreed in the Interim Agreement.

ARTICLE X

It is agreed that, upon the entry into force of the Declaration of Principles, the Israeli and Palestinian delegations will exchange the names of the individuals designated by them as members of the Joint Israeli-Palestinian Liaison Committee.

It is further agreed that each side will have an equal number of members in the Joint Committee. The Joint Committee will reach decisions by agreement. The Joint Committee may add other technicians and experts, as necessary. The Joint Committee will decide on the frequency and place or places of its meetings.

ANNEX II

It is understood that, subsequent to the Israeli withdrawal, Israel will continue to be responsible for external security, and for internal security and public order of settlements and Israelis. Israeli military forces and civilians may continue to use roads freely within the Gaza Strip and the Jericho area.

September 9, 1993

Mr. Prime Minister,

The signing of the Declaration of Principles marks a new era in the history of the Middle East. In firm conviction thereof, I would like to confirm the following PLO commitments:

The PLO recognizes the right of the State of Israel to exist in peace and security.

The PLO accepts United Nations Security Council Resolutions 242 and 338.

The PLO commits itself to the Middle East peace process, and to a peaceful resolution of the conflict between the two sides and declares that all outstanding issues relating to permanent status will be resolved through negotiations.

The PLO considers that the signing of the Declaration of Principles constitutes a historic event, inaugurating a new epoch of peaceful coexistence, free from violence and all other acts which endanger peace and stability. Accordingly, the PLO renounces the use of terrorism and other acts of violence and will assume responsibility over all PLO elements and personnel in order to assure their compliance, prevent violations and discipline violators.

In view of the promise of a new era and the signing of the Declaration of Principles and based on Palestinian acceptance of Security Council Resolutions 242 and 338, the PLO affirms that those articles of the Palestinian Covenant which deny Israel's right to exist, and the provisions of the Covenant which are inconsistent with the commitments of this letter are now inoperative and no longer valid. Consequently, the PLO undertakes to submit to the Palestinian National Council for formal approval the necessary changes in regard to the Palestinian Covenant.

Sincerely,
Yasser Arafat
Chairman
The Palestine Liberation Organization

September 9, 1993

Mr. Chairman,

In response to your letter of September 9, 1993, I wish to confirm to you that, in light of the PLO commitments included in your letter, the Government of Israel has decided to recognize the PLO as the representative of the Palestinian people and commence negotiations with the PLO within the Middle East peace process.

Sincerely,
Yitzhak Rabin
Prime Minister of Israel

President Bill Clinton, Prime Minister Yitzhak Rabin, and Chairman Yasir Arafat: Speeches at the Signing of the Israel-PLO Declaration of Principles, September 13, 1993

President Bill Clinton

We have been granted the great privilege of witnessing this victory for peace. Just as the Jewish people this week celebrate the dawn of a new year, let us all go from this place to celebrate the dawn of a new era—not only for the Middle East but for the entire world.

The sound we heard today, once again as in ancient Jericho, was of trumpets toppling walls, the walls of anger and suspicion between Israeli and Palestinian, between Arab and Jew. This time, praise God, the trumpets herald not the destruction of that city but its new beginning.

Now let each of us here today return to our portion of that effort. Uplifted by the spirit of the moment, refreshed in our hopes and guided by the wisdom of the Almighty, who has brought us to this joyous day. Go in peace. Go as peacemakers.

Prime Minister Yitzhak Rabin

President Clinton, the President of the United States, your excellencies, ladies and gentlemen. This signing of the Israeli-Palestinian declaration of principles here today is not so easy, neither for myself as a soldier in Israel's wars, nor for the people of Israel, nor for the Jewish people in the Diaspora who are watching us now with great hope mixed with apprehension. It is certainly not easy for the families of the victims of the wars, violence, terror, whose pain will never heal, for the many thousands who defended our lives with their own and have even sacrificed their lives for our own. For them, this ceremony has come too late.

Today, on the eve of an opportunity for peace, and perhaps an end to violence and wars, we remember each and every one of them with everlasting love. We have come from Jerusalem, the ancient and eternal capital of the Jewish people. We have come from an anguished and grieving land. We have come from a people, a home, a family that has not known a single year, not a single month, in which mothers have not wept for their sons. We have come to try and put an end to the hostilities so that our children, and our children's children, will no longer experience the painful cost of war, violence and terror. We have come to secure their lives and to ease the sorrow and the painful memories of the past, to hope and pray for peace.

Let me say to you, the Palestinians, we are destined to live together on the same soil in the same land. We, the soldiers who have returned from battles stained with blood; we who have seen our relatives and friends killed before our eyes; we who have attended their funerals and cannot look into the eyes of their parents; we who have come from a land where parents bury their children: we who have fought against you, the Palestinians, we say to you today in a loud and a clear voice, enough of blood and tears. Enough!

We have no desire for revenge. We harbor no hatred towards you. We, like you, are people—people who want to build a home, to plant a tree, to love, live side by side with you in dignity, in affinity, as human beings, as free men. We are today giving peace a chance and saying again to you, "Enough." Let us pray that a day will come when we all will say farewell to arms. We wish to open a new chapter in the sad book of our lives together—a chapter of mutual recognition, of good neighborliness, of mutual respect, of understanding. We hope to embark on a new era in the history of the Middle East.

Today here in Washington at the White House, we will begin a new reckoning in the relations between peoples, between parents tired of war, between children who will not know war. President of the United States, ladies and gentlemen, our inner strength, our higher moral values have been derived for thousands of years from the Book of the Books, in one of which, Koheleth (Ecclesiastes), we read, "To every thing there is a season and a time to every purpose under heaven. A time to be born and time to die, a time to kill and a time to heal. A time to weep and a time to laugh. A time to love and a time to hate, a time of war and a time of peace." Ladies and gentlemen, the time for peace has come.

Chairman Yasser Arafat

In the name of God, the most merciful, the passionate, Mr. President, ladies and gentlemen, I would like to express our tremendous appreciation to President Clinton and to his administration for sponsoring this historic event which the entire world has been waiting for.

Mr. President, I am taking this opportunity to assure you and to assure the great American people that we share your values for freedom, justice and human rights—values for which my people have been striving.

My people are hoping that this agreement which we are signing today marks the beginning of the end of a chapter of pain and suffering which has lasted throughout this century.

My people are hoping that this agreement which we are signing today will usher in an age of peace, coexistence and equal rights. We are relying on your role, Mr. President, and on the role of all the countries which believe that without peace in the Middle East, peace in the world will not be complete.

Enforcing the agreement and moving toward the final settlement, after two years, to implement all aspects of U.N. resolutions 242 and 338 in all of their aspects, and resolve all the issues of Jerusalem, the settlements, the refugees and the boundaries will be a Palestinian and an Israeli responsibility. It is also the responsibility of the international community in its entirety to help the parties overcome the tremendous difficulties which are still standing in the way of reaching a final and comprehensive settlement.

Now as we stand on the threshold of this new historic era, let me address the people of Israel and their leaders, with whom we are meeting today for the first time, and let me assure them that the difficult decision we reached together was one that required great and exceptional courage.

We will need more courage and determination to continue the course of building coexistence and peace between us. This is possible and it will happen with mutual determination and with the effort that will be made with all parties on all the tracks to establish the foundations of a just and comprehensive peace.

Our people do not consider that exercising the right to self-determination could violate the rights of their neighbors or infringe on their security. Rather, putting an end to their feelings of being wronged and of having suffered an historic injustice is the strongest guarantee to achieve coexistence and openness between our two peoples and future generations. Our two peoples are awaiting today this historic hope, and they want to give peace a real chance.

Such a shift will give us an opportunity to embark upon the process of economic, social and cultural growth and development. And we hope that international participation in that process will be extensive as it can be. This shift will also provide an opportunity for all forms of cooperation on a broad scale and in all fields. . . .

I wish to thank the Russian Federation and President Boris Yeltsin. Our thanks also go to Secretary Christopher and Foreign Minister Kozyrev, to the government of Norway and to the Foreign Minister of Norway for the positive part they played in bringing about this major achievement. I extend greetings to all the Arab leaders, our brothers, and to all the world leaders who contributed to this achievement.

Ladies and gentlemen, the battle for peace is the most difficult battle of our lives. It deserves our utmost efforts because the land of peace, the land of peace yearns for a just and comprehensive peace.

Prime Minister Yitzhak Rabin: Speech to Parliament, September 21, 1993

Honorable President of the State, Mr. Speaker, distinguished Knesset: The government today submitted to the Knesset the declaration of principles about the interim arrangements on self-government for the Palestinians in the territories, as well as the letters exchanged between Israel and the PLO and the agenda for the negotiations between Israel and Jordan. All the documents pertaining to the issue have been placed before the members of the House, and there is no other, secret agreement. Everything is out in the open and aboveboard. The government will ask for the Knesset's endorsement and will regard the Knesset's decision as a vote of confidence in the government and its resolutions.

Distinguished Knesset, in three days every Jew, wherever he may be, will observe the sanctity of Yom Kippur. On this day of national and personal reckoning, as the sun sets and we say the concluding prayer, millions of Jews in every corner of the earth, from Casablanca and Buenos Aires to Melbourne and Qiryat Shemona, will utter the prayer: As you close the gates, open them anew because a new day has dawned.

The Israeli government today believes that with the beginning of the new year, a gate has opened—a gate of peace, a gate of blessing. As the prayer goes: Bestow peace, good, blessings, life, favor and grace, charity and mercy upon us and all the people of Israel. On the eve of Yom Kippur 5754, the Israeli government presents the Israeli people with a chance for peace and, perhaps, for an end to the wars, violence, and terror. In the high holidays prayers we also say: who will live and who will die, who will perish and who will not, who will die by water, fire, or sword.

On this bitter day twenty years ago, we felt death by fire and sword on our flesh and skin. All of us, both religious and secular, left-wing or right-wing, Jewish and non-Jewish citizens of Israel experienced one of the toughest hours in our history as a state. In the sands of the Chinese Farm in the Sinai Peninsula, on the cliffs of the Mount Hermon on the Golan Heights, IDF soldiers in the regular army and in the reserves, our best sons, used their bodies to block the waves of tanks and columns of soldiers that threatened our existence. In the battle to defend our lives and homes against the Egyptian and Syrian armies, 2,569 IDF soldiers and officers fell.

Today, too, twenty years later, we anguish over the deaths of our dear ones and we share in the sorrow of the bereaved families, whose pain does not abate or the scars of their tragedy heal as years go by. On the eve of Yom Kippur, our hearts are with them, and so it will be forever.

Distinguished Knesset, the Yom Kippur War taught us as well as our enemies the limitations of military power and the possibilities entailed in a political solution. In the wake of the disengagement agreements we signed with Egypt and Syria, the interim agreement we signed with Egypt, and the IDF's withdrawal from Egypt and the heart of Syria, we knew and we know to this day long years of peace, quiet, and tranquility in those two cores of fire and war. Thanks to the determination and initiative of the late Prime Minister Menahem Begin—and here with us is the Honorable President of the State, who was a full partner to it—the Israeli government signed the first and unprecedentedly important peace treaty with Egypt. As for the Israeli-Syrian border, quiet and security have prevailed for almost twenty years, and are enjoyed by the population of the Golan Heights.

Mr. Speaker, distinguished Knesset, for over 100 years we have been seeking to build ourselves a home in the only place on earth that was and will be our home: here, in the land of Israel. For over 100 years we have been seeking to live here in peace and tranquility, to plant a tree, to pave a road. For over 100 years we have been seeking good relations with our neighbors, a life without fear and dread. For over 100 years we have been dreaming and fighting. In 100 years of colonization, this land experienced a great deal of suffering and blood. We who came back home after 2,000 years in exile, after the Holocaust which sent the best of the Jewish people to the crematoriums, we who look for a harbor in the storm, a place to rest our head, we stretched out our hand to our neighbors, but this hand was rejected time and again. Time and again it was rejected, but our soul did not tire of seeking peace. Our life in this suffering land was accompanied by salvos of fire, mines, and grenades. We planted and they uprooted, we built and they destroyed, we defended and they attacked. Almost every day we buried our dead. One hundred years of terror and war harmed us, but it did not destroy our dream. We dreamed of peace for 100 years.

Distinguished Knesset, when it assumed office over a year ago, this government decided to put an end to the terror and war, to try to build a new world in the state, at home, in the family which did not know even one year or one month of its life in which mothers did not cry for their sons. This government decided to put an end to the hatred so that our children and grandchildren will no longer suffer the painful price of wars, terror, and violence. This government decided to safeguard their lives and security, to ease the pain and horrible memories, to pray and hope for peace. When we presented the government to the Knesset over a year ago, we said—and I quote: This government is determined to do everything in its power, to forge any path, to do everything possible and impossible for the sake of national and personal security, for the sake of peace and preventing war. We said then—and I quote: The road we will tread will be fraught with obstacles, crises, disappointments, tears, and pain. After all these, however, when we come to the end of this road, we will have a strong country, a good country, a country in which we all share in the big effort and whose citizens we are proud to be.

We said then: The new government shares the current feeling among the people that this is an hour of great opportunities, and we will do everything not to miss the opportunities. We said then: We owe it to ourselves and our children to see the new world as it is, to study the dangers, check out the chances, and do everything so that the State of Israel becomes part of the changing world. We must rid ourselves of the feeling of isolation that gripped us for almost a quarter of a century. We must join the international march of peace, reconciliation, and cooperation that is currently storming across the entire globe. Otherwise, we will be the last and only ones waiting behind at the station.

We said then that the main goal of the new government will be to promote the making of peace and to take feverish steps to bring about the end of the Arab-Israeli conflict. We will do that on the basis of the Arab states' and the Palestinians' recognition of Israel as a sovereign state and of its right to live in peace and security. We sincerely believe that this is possible and imperative, and that it will come.

Members of the Knesset, we said then the following words—and I quote: The government will propose to the Arab states and the Palestinians to pursue the peace negotiations based on the format consolidated in the Madrid conference as the first step on the way to a permanent solution. We will discuss the implementation of autonomy in Judea, Samaria, and the Gaza District. We do not intend to waste precious time. Within a short period of time, we will open and pursue the talks in order to lower the flame of hostility between the Palestinians and the State of Israel.

The day we presented our government we also said: Holding such negotiations on the issue worry those among us who chose to settle in Judea, Samaria, and the Gaza District. I hereby inform you that this government, by means of the IDF and the other security forces, will be responsible for the security and welfare of the inhabitants of those areas.

On the question of Jerusalem, we said that this government, just like all its predecessors, believes there are no differences of opinion in this House over the eternalness of Jerusalem as Israel's capital. United and unified Jerusalem is not negotiable and will be the capital of the Israeli people under Israel's sovereignty and the subject of every Jew's yearnings and dreams for ever and ever.

Members of the Knesset, fourteen months ago we presented an IOU to the Knesset, the voters, and the Israeli people. We promised to try to bring peace to this land. In the time that has elapsed since then, we did not close any doors or miss any opportunity. We checked out every crack and hint. We did not forestall any chance of attaining peace or interim arrangements that would offer a normal life to both peoples in this land.

We conducted negotiations with the delegations of Syria, Lebanon, Jordan, and the Palestinians. During the negotiations, and in fact from their beginning, it transpired that the only address for negotiations with the Palestinians was PLO-Tunis. We could have behaved like ostriches; we could have lied to ourselves and buried our heads in the sand. We could have claimed that Faisal Husseini, Hanan Ashrawi, and others represent the residents of the territories while ignoring the real party that stood behind them. We decided not to behave in this manner. We knew very well who stood behind them, and the Israeli public is also perfectly aware of this. We have no desire to deny the fact that this is a merciless terrorist organization, an organization that dispatched the terrorists who murdered the children in Avivim and Ma'alot, who shot the guests in Tel Aviv's Savoy Hotel, who attacked the innocent victims riding the bus on the Tel Aviv-Haifa coastal road, and who committed hundreds of other acts of murder and terror. This organization has shed the blood of hundreds of our beloved citizens: the blood of Smadar Haran's family in Nahariyya; the blood of 'Ofra and Tal Moses, members of the family of Abie Moses from Alfey Menashe; the blood of innocent people whose only fault was being Jewish.

Knesset members, we cannot choose our neighbors and our enemies, including the cruelest of them. We must deal with what we have: the PLO, which has fought against us and against whom we fought. Today we are looking for a way to achieve peace together with this organization. We can shut all the doors, cease any attempt to achieve peace. Morally, we are entitled not to sit at the negotiating table with the PLO, not to shake the hands of those who have wielded knives or pulled the trigger. We could have rejected the proposals of the PLO with disgust, in which case we would have unwittingly been among those responsible for the continuation of the vicious circle in which we have been forced to live so far: war, terrorism, and violence.

We chose to adopt another way, one which offers a chance and hope. We decided to recognize the PLO as the representative of the Palestinian people to the negotiations in the framework of the peace talks. We have known, and we still know, what a heavy load we are carrying from the past. We took this step only after the PLO undertook, in its letters to the prime minister, the following: recognition of Israel's right to live in peace and security and a commitment to settle any future controversy by peaceful means and through negotiations. The PLO has undertaken to denounce and put an end to terrorism and violence in Israel, in the territories, and elsewhere. I want to say here that since the agreements were signed, the PLO has not carried out even one act of terrorism. The PLO has undertaken to enforce an end to terrorism and violence by its members and to punish the violators. The PLO has undertaken to renounce the clauses of the Palestinian Covenant that negate Israel's right to exist and the peace process and to bring about their formal cancellation by the pertinent institution.

In Washington, Foreign Minister Shimon Peres signed on Israel's behalf the declaration of principles agreement for the interim period only. This agreement, which permits the Palestinians to run their affairs, safeguards the following issues for Israel: Unified Jerusalem remains under Israel's rule, and the body that will run the lives of the Palestinians in the territories will have no authority over it. The Israeli settlements in Judea, Samaria, and Gaza will remain under Israel's rule without any change whatsoever in their status. The authority of the Palestinian council will not apply to any Israeli in the areas of Judea, Samaria, and Gaza. The IDF will continue to bear overall responsibility for the security of the Israeli settlements in the territories, the security of every Israeli staying in the territories, and for external security—namely, for the defense of the current confrontation lines along the Jordan River and for the Egyptian border. The IDF will deploy in all areas of Judea, Samaria, and the Gaza District on the basis of these missions. All the issues pertaining to the permanent arrangement will be put off for the negotiations that will begin two years after the date stipulated in the agreement, while preserving the Israeli government's freedom to determine its positions regarding the permanent solution. This means that the declaration of principles leaves all the options open on this issue.

The agreement on the interim period in Gaza and Jericho will be implemented before the establishment of the elected Palestinian council, which will direct the affairs of the Palestinians in Judea, Samaria, and the Gaza Strip. The council will be established only after we agree with the Palestinians about its structure, composition, and functions. The target date for elections is nine months after the declaration of principles goes into effect. Israel will regard the Gaza-Jericho First stage as a sort of test of the Palestinians' ability to implement the agreement on the declaration of principles.

I would like to repeat here what I said in Washington last week—and I quote: We are destined to live together on the same soil, in the same land. We, the soldiers who have returned from the battles stained with blood; we, who have seen our relatives and best friends killed before our eyes; we, who have attended their funerals and cannot look into the eyes of their parents and their orphans; we, who have come from a land where parents bury their children; we, who have fought against you, the Palestinians; we say to you today in a loud and clear voice: enough of blood and tears, enough. We harbor no hatred towards you. We have no desire for revenge. We, like you, are people who want to build a home, to plant a tree, to love, to live with you side by side, in dignity, in empathy, as human beings, as free men. Today we are giving peace a chance and saying to you in a clear voice: enough, no more.

Mr. Speaker, distinguished Knesset, we have no intention or desire to hide the truth from the Knesset members and the Israeli public. In addition to the great advantages, the expected peace also harbors dangers. We are aware of these dangers and will do everything necessary to minimize them. At the same time, we believe the risks are calculated and will not harm Israel's security and existence. In any event, the might of the IDF—the best army in the world—is available for our use if, God forbid, we are faced with such a challenge. Today we are looking forward to the good chances, to days without worries and nights without fears, to a developing economy and a prosperous society. If and when the long-desired peace arrives, our lives will completely change. We will no longer live only by our swords.

On the eve of the New Year, after 100 years of violence and terrorism, after wars and suffering, today there is a good chance to open a new chapter in Israel's history. There is a chance for putting an end to tears. Flower buds and new horizons are opening up for the Israeli economy and society. Above all, I want to tell you that this is a victory for Zionism, which is now recognized by its most adamant and bitter enemies. There are chances for good relations with our neighbors, for an end to the bereavement which has afflicted our homes, for an end to war.

President Hafiz al-Asad: Reaction to Israel-PLO Agreement, October 1, 1993

The PLO was the Arab party pressing most for coordination among Arab parties. We have also stood for coordination, because we thought intra-Arab coordination could propel the peace process forward toward its objectives and firm up the steps leading in that direction. So, meetings to coordinate Arab moves were held between the bilateral rounds. The foreign ministers of the Arab states involved in the peace process used to meet to assess the previous round and devise tactics that might advance the peace process in the next round. In addition, the Arab delegations that held talks with the Israeli teams in Washington used to meet every week or so to compare notes. Each party, then, had a picture of how and what the others were doing. Thus, the Arabs moved in tandem toward a common objective.

All of a sudden, we hear that a secret agreement was reached between some PLO members and Israel. It turns out that the agreement was worked out in many months of secret negotiations, when, meanwhile, Arab states were meeting at the levels I have noted. The Palestinian side was engaged in talks with Israel, without the coordination it had pressed for. To my mind, this is not their best option, nor the best route to the establishment of peace. Yet, we decided not to obstruct the agreement. We said this is up to the Palestinian people and their organizations. However, no one should expect us to wax enthusiastic over a secret agreement concluded behind our backs. . . .

. . . What is the justification for the unilateral decision that has been taken? We are all together. We all participated in the preliminary talks that laid the foundations of the Madrid conference. But, suddenly, one party began following a separate path. As we have always done, we will continue to urge and hope that the Palestinian Arab people regain their legitimate rights.

I said we decided not to obstruct the agreement. I did not say we will obstruct those who oppose it. We will not obstruct it, although we are not satisfied with it, especially since it deviates from the consensus. . . .

It is not our specialty, responsibility, or right to repress those who oppose this agreement or those who oppose anything else. . . .

We must carry on with the peace process that began in Madrid. . . .

If I struck the deal Arafat did, I would come up against many real problems. This has nothing to do with how the masses feel about Arafat or me. If I were to conclude such a deal, the Syrian people would conclude I had compromised my cause and abandoned the cause of another Arab people. . . . You know, there are those who paid with their lives for individual actions the masses perceived as not being in their best interests. I don't want to lead you to think I have just one individual in mind, but more than one.

Arafat and I and every Arab know that the masses will conduct themselves according to their perception of their leaders. This is not to be interpreted as encouragement on my part for such a course of action; nor do I see it as a solution; if anything, it will further complicate matters. This is my personal opinion.

We have repeatedly said that, many times. The Syrian delegation to the negotiations said that, and I, too, have said that in some statements. I said three elements should be dealt with, although they are classified under the title of peace. They are withdrawal, peace, and security. We should discuss all these. Each side will attain what we all agree is its right, and which will provide security and peace of mind for it. We know peace has its requirements. We do not expect to take what we believe to be our right while others do not take theirs. We also believe we should take our rights and give others their rights. . . .

As long as this occupation remains, its results, including the boycott, must remain. I heard some statements by Israelis, including Peres while he was at the United Nations. In his statements, both in the U.N. General Assembly and to the press, he says, effectively: Why are you Arabs boycotting us? You have been saying the Palestine question is the core of the conflict. Here we are now, we have reached an agreement. It seems to me he is either insulting the intelligence of the others, specifically the Arabs, or he wants to fill the occasion, or the paper he is reading, with any words. Of course, we have said, and we still say, that the Palestine question is the core of the conflict. It is the core of the conflict in that it was the starting point of hostility. Hence, we called it the core of the conflict, but it is not the conflict. The Palestine question is the core of the conflict, but it is not the conflict. The Israelis know they have fought states. All the wars that were fought between Arabs and Israel were wars with states bordering Palestine. As a result of these wars, the core of the conflict that started in Palestine expanded to mean that every occupied Arab territory has become the core of the conflict.

Hani al-Hassan: Opposition to the Israel-PLO Accord, October 1993*

I personally thought from the outset that the letter of invitation to the October 1991 Madrid peace conference would only lead to the consecration of Israeli control over Palestinian land and the Palestinian people. In my view, what happened now amounts to the consecration of this control.

Indeed, Israel did recognize the PLO, but only after stripping the organization of all that it represents. The PLO which Israel has recognized is one that has submitted to Israeli demands. It is no longer the PLO that embodies the Palestinian people's aspirations to independent statehood after a full Israeli withdrawal from the West Bank and Gaza Strip and upholds the rights of the Palestinian refugees.

The Palestinian negotiator knows full well that Israel has no intention of withdrawing to the pre-June 1967 borders, and the proposed accord is therefore aimed at deceiving the Palestinian people.

Israel's intention to keep 20 percent of the West Bank in addition to East Jerusalem when a permanent solution is supposed to be in place five

---

* Interview with *Mideast Mirror*, October 9, 1993

years down the line was spelled out during Palestinian-Israeli "security talks" held in London in late 1992. . . .

At another secret PLO-Israel meeting, this one in Cairo around two months ago, Israeli Environment Minister Yossi Sarid made clear to Nabil Shaath, an Arafat adviser, that even his own Meretz faction supported the official Israeli position on Jerusalem (that it will remain Israel's undivided capital) and that the Jerusalem issue can only be discussed from a religious angle. Hence East Jerusalemites who will take part in elections to the proposed Palestinian Council will do so as candidates or electors from other West Bank towns.

Those who concluded the accord with Israel, agreeing to stop the intifada, are banking on the Jewish state's good will. The accord treats the occupied lands as disputed territories and is a recipe for the establishment of a federation between the State of Israel and a Palestinian "entity." PLO negotiators Abu-Mazen and Ahmad Krai (Abu-Ala'a) were told as much during the Oslo talks. That is how Israel plans to keep its army in the West Bank even if a Palestinian "entity" emerges there.

As to the refugee issue, it was decided at the last meeting in Oslo that the multilateral committee on refugees would deal with seven areas none of which features UN Resolution 194 calling for the repatriation or compensation of 1948 refugees. This is a step towards ending the refugee issue and striking it off the United Nations' agenda.

That is why we, the 1948 exiles, categorically reject what is happening. The PLO leaders who concluded the deal with Israel have all but buried the refugees' right of return.

This is why someone like myself oppose what is happening now—even though I do not belong to the school of rejectionism and fully belong to the school of political settlements. But settlements are based on balance, whereas the proposed solution is one imposed by Israel as the victor.

As Israeli Prime Minister Yitzhak Rabin's remarks after he recognized the PLO indicate, proponents of the Gaza-Jericho deal have been entrusted with the task of punishing anyone who resorts to violence. It is strange that a Palestinian leader should undertake to stop the resistance in, say, Nablus or Hebron (on the West Bank) which will remain under Israeli occupation for at least five years. Hence Gaza-Jericho advocates will be the allies of the Israeli security forces over the next five years.

It is true that we will get a handful of billions of dollars and that we will build power stations in Gaza and a sewage system on the West Bank. But this is not what the PLO is about.

West Bank–Gaza Palestinian Leaders: Memorandum to Chairman Yasir Arafat, November 1993

Mr. President of Palestine and Chairman of the PLO Executive Committee; Members of the PLO Executive Committee:

Greetings from Palestine:

Since the signing of the Declaration of Principles and the mutual recognition agreement between the PLO and the Israeli Government, the Palestinian people, together with their national forces, have been facing a new situation that has imposed new challenges. This is because the Declaration of Principles is an event that separates a militant stage, which aimed at underscoring Palestinian presence on the political map of the region and the world, from another militant stage that moves toward a greater and more advanced achievement; namely, the setting up of an independent Palestinian state on the land of Palestine by Palestinian hands.

Your Excellency the President: We assume that our Palestinian people, together with their national forces, have studied the agreement in terms of preambles, texts, and prospects as the various national institutions did in order to endorse it constitutionally through the PLO Executive Committee and the PLO Central Council. However, the agreement has produced an opposition that has different principles and objectives. And this is natural in an arena which pioneered the entrenching of democratic dialogue and relations among its forces as the only way to govern national life in the various fields.

The signatories to this memorandum believe that the Palestinian-Israeli agreement is a decisive political event which should be dealt with in a positive and responsible way in order to develop what is positive in it and besiege what is negative.

In light of all this, we declare:

First, our total affiliation with our people's potentials to build our new entity on the ground;

Second, our commitment to the PLO and its legitimate institutions as the sole representative of the Palestinian people and the national framework to which there is no alternative in order to organize and lead the national potentials toward achieving all the national legitimate objectives of the Palestinian people.

Proceeding from this, and in order to benefit from our democratic right of taking the initiative to propose ideas and procedures which are important and vital in this qualitative stage of our national struggle, we reiterate the following:

First: We are not satisfied with the political leadership's method of work in this stage, either in terms of running the difficult and delicate negotiations with the Israeli side or in terms of the preparations to embark on the stage of national construction in the interim period. It is obvious to everybody that the political leadership is practicing its role in a manner that is close to improvisation and without prior preparation for the necessary practical steps toward embodying the national interests through a planned implementation of our obligations to what was signed.

Second: The political leadership has not made sufficient effort to invigorate the required national dialogue whether on the level of the national forces, which adopted the agreement as an opportunity that would provide serious possibilities to proceed toward our national objectives, or on the level of the principled opposition to the agreement. Our national traditions require that we expeditiously launch such dialogue and work seriously to render it a success. The objective is to create a reasonable level of national harmony that will entrench Palestinian national security and create a healthy atmosphere for further mobilization toward the new tasks of the Palestinian people.

Third: The political leadership failed to present the agreement in an objective way to the Palestinian people so that this people would be aware of the prospects and potentials of their present and future moves. Consequently, this increased the confusion, ambiguity, and concern, particularly when the Palestinian people receive various and contradictory interpretations, not only on the level of the PLO and Israel, but also within the PLO itself.

Fourth: If we return to the statements and comments of the majority who voted, during the recent meeting of the PLO Central Council, in favor of the Declaration of Principles agreement, we will find that their support was on condition that the leadership performance will develop, Palestinian potentials will be mobilized, Palestinian skills and expertise will be exploited in the best way possible, and that the peace process will be dealt with as a militant process, not an administrative or bureaucratic one. As many of the PLO Central Council members said, whether the result of the Declaration of Principles agreement will be good or bad for the Palestinian people, and whether it will pave the way for national independence and an independent state, or whether it will consecrate the occupation, this result will be basically decided through the materialization of the previous conditions.

While we present these general remarks as a first step, we ask the political leadership to shoulder its responsibilities in dealing with the negative aspects in a manner that guarantees a balanced, viable, and responsible performance during the next stage.

Based on this, we present the following urgent demands:

1. The political leadership should set up specialized councils in all fields of political action, whether on the level of building the

new entity or on the level of organizing moves in the Arab and international arenas.

2. The political leadership should appeal to all specialists in various sectors to join these councils and their working groups, whether through planning or implementation. In order to regulate this great process, a department should be set up in the PLO assigned with following up this issue and working out the appropriate action frameworks.

3. Adopting the principle of professional and political efficiency in forming the working groups, establishments, negotiating committees, and other bodies, and abandoning the fractional mentality and appeasement at the expense of efficiency.

4. Working out an integrated negotiating plan that is based on the Declaration of Principles and that ensures integration and harmony of the working groups and the various negotiating teams.

5. Forming a mini-leadership team to lead the entire negotiating process, supervise and follow it up, and coordinate between the various committees and groups.

6. Forming the Palestinian Development and Reconstruction Council according to certain specifications that ensure sound performance, planning, follow up and monitoring, and the credibility of our people with the donor countries and in order to develop the infrastructure of our national economy. Any delay in the formation of this council will waste more time and weaken the credibility of the Palestinians with the international parties that assist our people.

7. Completing the work of the Legal Committee assigned with drafting the bylaw of the Palestinian national authority (the constitutional document) in a manner that emphasizes its democratic nature and commitment to all principles contained in the Palestinian Declaration of Principles. This constitutional document should then be presented for broad deliberations by the Palestinian people as soon as possible.

8. The political leadership should immediately form a higher leadership authority that will start a national dialogue and work for the continuation and success of this dialogue. The political leadership should benefit from its previous mistakes in this respect, since the committees that used to be formed did not work with sufficient seriousness.

9. Setting up a higher planning, consulting, and guidance authority of experts that operates alongside the Executive Committee and assists it in carrying out its major tasks in this stage.

While making such a proposal, we are not undermining the role and jurisdiction of the first executive authority. We present these proposals because we know how this authority has been adversely affected by the resignation of some of its members and the possibility that others may resign or freeze their membership. . . .

The signatories: Dr. Haydar 'Abd al-Shafi, Bashir al-Barghuthi, Ibrahim Abu 'Ayyash, Dr. Anis Fawzi al-Qasim, Tawfiq Abu Bakr, Dr. Taysir 'Aruri, Samih 'Abd al-Fattah, known as Abu Hisham, Lawyer 'Ali al-Safarini, Faysal Hurani, Lawyer Muhammad 'Ayyash Milham, Nabil 'Amr, the Reverend Ibrahim 'Ayyad, Dr. Mundhir Salah, Dr. 'Izz al-Din al-Manasirah, and Ghazi al-Sa'di.

President Hafiz al-Asad and President Bill Clinton: Statement on Their Meeting, January 16, 1994

President Asad

I wish to express my deep satisfaction for what these talks have effected in terms of U.S. determination to do all it can in order to bring the peace process to its desired objective—the objective of establishing a just and comprehensive peace in the region through the implementation of UN Security Council Resolutions 242, 338, and 425 as well as the principle of land for peace.

In this respect, I appreciate the fact that not withstanding the great importance that President Clinton attaches to the internal affairs of his country, he has attached a special importance as a full partner and honest intermediary to helping the parties reach a comprehensive peace that is in the interest not only of the peoples of the region, but also the people of the world at large.

Today's meeting between President Clinton and myself came to crown a number of exchanges and telephone communications between us over the last year. I hope that our meeting today will contribute to the realization of the aspirations of the peoples in the region; mainly, that this new year will be the year of achieving a just and comprehensive peace which puts an end to the tragedies of violence and wars endured by them for several decades.

During our meeting, I had the opportunity to stress to President Clinton Syria's firm commitment to the principles and bases of the peace process and our strong conviction that peace cannot be genuine and lasting unless it is comprehensive and based on the principles of international legitimacy and justice. This means endeavoring to reach a just solution on all tracks.

Historical evidence, both past and present, has proved that separate peace and partial solutions are not conducive to the establishment of real peace in the region. In this regard, I would like to express my satisfaction that President Clinton himself has committed to the objective of comprehensive peace.

On this basis, we have agreed to work together for successful efforts aimed at putting an end to the Arab-Israeli conflict and at reaching a genuine and comprehensive peace that enables the peoples of the region to focus on development, progress, and prosperity.

This meeting has also provided us with the opportunity to exchange views on a number of issues, including those related to bilateral relations between our countries. We have agreed that the noble objective toward which we are working requires a qualitative move in these relations.

We have also discussed questions related to the regional situation as well as all matters that might constructively contribute to the achievement of security and stability in the Middle East. Syria seeks a just and comprehensive peace with Israel as a strategic choice that secures Arab rights; ends the Israeli occupation; and enables all peoples in the region to live in peace, security, and dignity. In honor we fought; in honor we negotiate; and in honor we shall make peace. We want an honorable peace for our people and for the hundreds of thousands who paid their lives in defense of their countries and their rights.

There is hardly a home in Syria in which there is no martyr who has fallen in defense of his country, nation, and Arab pride. For the sake of all those, for our sons, daughters, and families, we want the peace of the brave—a genuine peace which can survive and last, a peace which secures the interests of each side and renders to all their rights. If the leaders of Israel have sufficient courage to respond to this kind of peace, the new era of security and stability in which normal peaceful relations among all shall dawn anew.

President Clinton

I believe you could tell from that statement that I have just completed a constructive and encouraging meeting with President Asad. From the first days of my Administration, the achievement of a comprehensive peace between Israel and its Arab neighbors, based on Security Council Resolutions 242 and 338 and the principle of territory for peace, has been one of my highest foreign policy objectives.

In pursuit of that priority, I have always viewed Syria's involvement as critical. That is why, from the outset of our Administration, I have engaged President Asad in regular correspondence by telephone and letter, and why I am now pleased to have had this opportunity to hear, personally, President Asad's views about how best to make this a year of breakthroughs on all fronts.

During our meeting, I told President Asad that I was personally committed to the objective of a comprehensive and secure peace that would produce genuine reconciliation among the peoples of the Middle East. I told him of my view that the agreement between Israel and the PLO constitutes an important first step by establishing an agreed basis for resolving the Palestinian problem. I also told him that I believe Syria is the key to the achievement of an enduring and comprehensive peace that finally will put an end to the conflict between Israel and her Arab neighbors.

President Asad, as you have just heard, shares this objective—not just an end to war, but the establishment of real and comprehensive peace with Israel that will ensure normal, peaceful relations among good neighbors.

Crucial decisions will have to be made by Syria and Israel if this common objective is to be achieved. That is why President Asad has called for a peace of the brave. And it is why I join him now in endorsing that appeal. Accordingly, we pledged today to work together in order to bring the negotiations that started in Madrid over two years ago to a prompt and successful conclusion.

Critical issues remain to be resolved, especially the question of relating withdrawal to peace and security. But as a result of our conversation today, I am confident that we laid the foundations for real progress in the negotiations between heads of delegation that will begin again next week in Washington.

President Asad and I also discussed the state of relations between the United States and Syria and agreed on the desirability of improving them. This requires honestly addressing the problems in our relationship. Accordingly, we've instructed the Secretary of State and the Syrian Foreign Minister to establish a mechanism to address these issues in detail and openly.

For too long, the Middle East has been denied the benefits of peace. And yet, it is within our power to create the conditions that will enable Israeli and Arab, Muslim, Christian, and Jew to live together in peace. Today's meeting was an important step toward fulfilling that vision. We have a lot of work to do, but we are closer to our goal.

Israel-PLO: Cairo Agreement, March 4, 1994

The Government of the State of Israel and the Palestine Liberation Organization (hereinafter "the PLO"), the representative of the Palestinian people;

PREAMBLE

WITHIN the framework of the Middle East peace process initiated at Madrid in October 1991;

REAFFIRMING their determination to live in peaceful coexistence, mutual dignity and security, while recognizing their mutual legitimate and political rights;

REAFFIRMING their desire to achieve a just, lasting and comprehensive peace settlement through the agreed political process;

REAFFIRMING their adherence to the mutual recognition and commitments expressed in the letters dated September 9, 1993, signed by and exchanged between the Prime Minister of Israel and the Chairman of the PLO;

REAFFIRMING their understanding that the interim self-government arrangements, including the arrangements to apply in the Gaza Strip and the Jericho Area contained in this Agreement, are an integral part of the whole peace process and that the negotiations on the permanent status will lead to the implementation of Security Council Resolutions 242 and 338;

DESIROUS of putting into effect the Declaration of Principles on Interim Self-Government Arrangements signed at Washington, D.C., on September 13, 1993, and the Agreed Minutes thereto (hereinafter "the Declaration of Principles"), and in particular the Protocol on withdrawal of Israeli forces from the Gaza Strip and the Jericho Area;

HEREBY AGREE to the following arrangements regarding the Gaza Strip and the Jericho Area:

ARTICLE I

Definitions

For the purpose of this Agreement:

a. The Gaza Strip and the Jericho Area are delineated on Map Nos. 1 and 2 attached to this Agreement;

b. "the Settlements" means the Gush Katif and Erez settlement areas, as well as the other settlements in the Gaza Strip, as shown on attached Map No. 1;

c. "the Military Installation Area" means the Israeli military installation area along the Egyptian border in the Gaza Strip, as shown on Map No. 1; and

d. The term "Israelis" shall also include Israeli statutory agencies and corporations registered in Israel.

ARTICLE II

Scheduled Withdrawal of Israeli Military Forces

1. Israel shall implement an accelerated and scheduled withdrawal of Israeli military forces from the Gaza Strip and from the Jericho Area to begin immediately with the signing of this Agreement. Israel shall complete such withdrawal within three weeks from this date.

2. Subject to the arrangements included in the Protocol concerning withdrawal of Israeli military forces and security arrangements attached as Annex I, the Israeli withdrawal shall include evacuating all military bases and other fixed installations to be handed over to the Palestinian Police, to be established pursuant to Article IX below (hereinafter "the Palestinian Police").

3. In order to carry out Israel's responsibility for external security and for internal security and public order of Settlements and Israelis, Israel shall, concurrently with the withdrawal, redeploy its remaining military forces to the Settlements and the Military Installation Area, in accordance with the provisions of this Agreement. Subject to the provisions of this Agreement, this redeployment shall constitute full implementation of Article XIII of the Declaration of Principles with regard to the Gaza Strip and the Jericho Area only.

4. For the purposes of this Agreement, "Israeli military forces" may include Israeli police and other Israeli security forces.

5. Israelis, including Israeli military forces, may continue to use roads freely within the Gaza Strip and the Jericho Area. Palestinians may use public roads crossing the Settlements freely, as provided for in Annex I.

6. The Palestinian Police shall be deployed and shall assume responsibility for public order and internal security of Palestinians in accordance with this Agreement and Annex I.

ARTICLE III

Transfer of Authority

1. Israel shall transfer authority as specified in this Agreement from the Israeli military government and its Civil Administration to the Palestinian Authority, hereby established, in accordance with Article V of this Agreement, except for the authority that Israel shall continue to exercise as specified in this Agreement.

2. As regards the transfer and assumption of authority in civil spheres, powers and responsibilities shall be transferred and as-

sumed as set out in the Protocol concerning civil affairs attached as Annex II.

3. Arrangements for a smooth and peaceful transfer of the agreed powers and responsibilities are set out in Annex II.

4. Upon the completion of the Israeli withdrawal and the transfer of powers and responsibilities as detailed in Paragraphs 1 and 2 above and in Annex II, the Civil Administration in the Gaza Strip and the Jericho Area will be dissolved and the Israeli military government will be withdrawn. The withdrawal of the military government shall not prevent it from continuing to exercise the powers and responsibilities specified in this Agreement.

5. A Joint Civil Affairs Coordination and Cooperation Committee (hereinafter ''the CAC'') and two Joint Regional Civil Affairs Subcommittees for the Gaza Strip and the Jericho Area respectively shall be established in order to provide for coordination and cooperation in civil affairs between the Palestinian Authority and Israel, as detailed in Annex II.

6. The offices of the Palestinian Authority shall be located in the Gaza Strip and the Jericho Area pending the inauguration of the Council to be elected pursuant to the Declaration of Principles.

ARTICLE IV

Structure and Composition of the Palestinian Authority

1. The Palestinian Authority will consist of one body of 24 members which shall carry out and be responsible for all the legislative and executive powers and responsibilities transferred to it under this Agreement, in accordance with this Article, and shall be responsible for the exercise of judicial functions in accordance with Article VI, subparagraph 1.b of this Agreement.

2. The Palestinian Authority shall administer the departments transferred to it and may establish, within its jurisdiction, other departments and subordinate administrative units as necessary for the fulfillment of its responsibilities. It shall determine its own internal procedures.

3. The PLO shall inform the Government of Israel of the names of the members of the Palestinian Authority and any change of members. Changes in the membership of the Palestinian Authority will take effect upon an exchange of letters between the PLO and the Government of Israel.

4. Each member of the Palestinian Authority shall enter into office upon undertaking to act in accordance with this Agreement.

ARTICLE V

Jurisdiction

1. The authority of the Palestinian Authority encompasses all matters that fall within its territorial, functional and personal jurisdiction, as follows:

a. The territorial jurisdiction covers the Gaza Strip and the Jericho Area territory, as defined in Article I, except for Settlements and the Military Installation Area.

Territorial jurisdiction shall include land, subsoil and territorial waters, in accordance with the provisions of this Agreement.

b. The functional jurisdiction encompasses all powers and responsibilities as specified in this Agreement. This jurisdiction does not include foreign relations, internal security and public order of Settlements and the Military Installation Area and Israelis, and external security.

c. The personal jurisdiction extends to all persons within the territorial jurisdiction referred to above, except for Israelis, unless otherwise provided in this Agreement.

2. The Palestinian Authority has, within its authority, legislative, executive and judicial powers and responsibilities, as provided for in this Agreement.

3. a. Israel has authority over the Settlements, the Military Installation Area, Israelis, external security, internal security and public order of Settlements, the Military Installation Area and Israelis, and those agreed powers and responsibilities specified in this Agreement.

b. Israel shall exercise its authority through its military government, which, for that end, shall continue to have the necessary legislative, judicial and executive powers and responsibilities, in accordance with international law. This provision shall not derogate from Israel's applicable legislation over Israelis in personam.

4. The exercise of authority with regard to the electromagnetic sphere and airspace shall be in accordance with the provisions of this Agreement.

5. The provisions of this Article are subject to the specific legal arrangements detailed in the Protocol Concerning Legal Matters attached as Annex III. Israel and the Palestinian Authority may negotiate further legal arrangements.

6. Israel and the Palestinian Authority shall cooperate on matters of legal assistance in criminal and civil matters through the legal subcommittee of the CAC.

ARTICLE VI

Powers and Responsibilities of the Palestinian Authority

1. Subject to the provisions of this Agreement, the Palestinian Authority, within its jurisdiction:

a. has legislative powers as set out in Article VII of this Agreement, as well as executive powers;

b. will administer justice through an independent judiciary;

c. will have, inter alia, power to formulate policies, supervise their implementation, employ staff, establish departments, authorities and institutions, sue and be sued and conclude contracts; and

d. will have, inter alia, the power to keep and administer registers and records of the population, and issue certificates, licenses and documents.

2. a. In accordance with the Declaration of Principles, the Palestinian Authority will not have powers and responsibilities in the sphere of foreign relations, which sphere includes the establishment abroad of embassies, consulates or other types of foreign missions and posts or permitting their establishment in the Gaza Strip or the Jericho Area, the appointment of or admission of diplomatic and consular staff, and the exercise of diplomatic functions.

b. Notwithstanding the provisions of this paragraph, the PLO may conduct negotiations and sign agreements with states or international organizations for the benefit of the Palestinian Authority in the following cases only: (1) economic agreements, as specifically provided in Annex IV of this Agreement; (2) agreements with donor countries for the purpose of implementing arrangements for the provision of assistance to the Palestinian Authority; (3) agreements for the purpose of implementing the regional development plans detailed in Annex IV of the Declaration of Principles or in agreements entered into in the framework of the multilateral negotiations; and (4) cultural, scientific and educational agreements.

c. Dealings between the Palestinian Authority and representatives of foreign states and international organizations, as well as the establishment in the Gaza Strip and the Jericho Area of representative offices other than those described in subparagraph 2.a. above, for the purpose of implementing the agreements referred to in subparagraph 2.b. above, shall not be considered foreign relations.

ARTICLE VII

Legislative Powers of the Palestinian Authority

1. The Palestinian Authority will have the power, within its jurisdiction, to promulgate legislation, including basic laws, laws, regulations and other legislative acts.

2. Legislation promulgated by the Palestinian Authority shall be consistent with the provisions of this Agreement.

3. Legislation promulgated by the Palestinian Authority shall be communicated to a legislation subcommittee to be established by the CAC (hereinafter "the Legislation Subcommittee"). During a period of 30 days from the communication of the legislation, Israel may request that the Legislation Subcommittee decide whether such legislation exceeds the jurisdiction of the Palestinian Authority or is otherwise inconsistent with the provisions of this Agreement.

4. Upon receipt of the Israeli request, the Legislation Subcommittee shall decide, as an initial matter, on the entry into force of the legislation pending its decision on the merits of the matter.

5. If the Legislation Subcommittee is unable to reach a decision with regard to the entry into force of the legislation within 15 days, this issue will be referred to a Board of Review. This Board of Review shall be comprised of two judges, retired judges or senior jurists (hereinafter "Judges"), one from each side, to be appointed from a compiled list of three Judges proposed by each.

In order to expedite the proceedings before this board of review, the two most senior Judges, one from each side, shall develop written informal rules of procedure.

6. Legislation referred to the Board of Review shall enter into force only if the Board of Review decides that it does not deal with a security issue which falls under Israel's responsibility, that it does not seriously threaten other significant Israeli interests protected by this Agreement and that the entry into force of the legislation could not cause irreparable damage or harm.

7. The Legislation Subcommittee shall attempt to reach a decision on the merits of the matter within 30 days from the date of the Israeli request. If this Subcommittee is unable to reach such a decision within this period of 30 days, the matter shall be referred to the Joint Israeli-Palestinian Liaison Committee referred to in Article XV below (hereinafter "the Liaison Committee"). This Liaison Committee will deal with the matter immediately and will attempt to settle it within 30 days.

8. Where the legislation has not entered into force pursuant to paragraphs 5 or 7 above, this situation shall be maintained pending

the decision of the Liaison Committee on the merits of the matter, unless it has decided otherwise.

9. Laws and military orders in effect in the Gaza Strip or the Jericho Area prior to the signing of this Agreement shall remain in force, unless amended or abrogated in accordance with this Agreement.

ARTICLE VIII

Arrangements for Security and Public Order

1. In order to guarantee public order and internal security for the Palestinians of the Gaza Strip and the Jericho Area, the Palestinian Authority shall establish a strong police force, as set out in Article IX below. Israel shall continue to carry the responsibility for defense against external threats, including the responsibility for protecting the Egyptian border and the Jordanian line, and for defense against external threats from the sea and from the air, as well as the responsibility for overall security of Israelis and Settlements, for the purpose of safeguarding their internal security and public order, and will have all the powers to take the steps necessary to meet this responsibility.

2. Agreed security arrangements and coordination mechanisms are specified in Annex I.

3. A joint Coordination and Cooperation Committee for mutual security purposes (hereinafter "the JSC"), as well as three joint District Coordination and Cooperation Offices for the Gaza district, the Khan Younis district and the Jericho district respectively (hereinafter "the DCOS") are hereby established as provided for in Annex I.

4. The security arrangements provided for in this Agreement and in Annex I may be reviewed at the request of either Party and may be amended by mutual agreement of the Parties. Specific review arrangements are included in Annex I.

ARTICLE IX

The Palestinian Directorate of Police Force

1. The Palestinian Authority shall establish a strong police force, the Palestinian Directorate of Police Force (hereinafter "the Palestinian Police"). The duties, functions, structure, deployment and composition of the Palestinian Police, together with provisions regarding its equipment and operation, are set out in Annex I, Article III. Rules of conduct governing the activities of the Palestinian Police are set out in Annex I, Article VIII.

2. Except for the Palestinian Police referred to in this Article

and the Israeli military forces, no other armed forces shall be established or operate in the Gaza Strip or the Jericho Area.

3. Except for the arms, ammunition and equipment of the Palestinian Police described in Annex I, Article III, and those of the Israeli military forces, no organization or individual in the Gaza Strip and the Jericho Area shall manufacture, sell, acquire, possess, import or otherwise introduce into the Gaza Strip or the Jericho Area any firearms, ammunition, weapons, explosives, gunpowder or any related equipment, unless otherwise provided for in Annex I.

ARTICLE X

Passages

Arrangements for coordination between Israel and the Palestinian Authority regarding the Gaza-Egypt and Jericho-Jordan passages, as well as any other agreed international crossings, are set out in Annex I, Article X.

ARTICLE XI

Safe Passage Between the Gaza Strip and the Jericho Area

Arrangements for safe passage of persons and transportation between the Gaza Strip and the Jericho Area are set out in Annex I, Article IX.

ARTICLE XII

Relations Between Israel and the Palestinian Authority

1. Israel and the Palestinian Authority shall seek to foster mutual understanding and tolerance and shall accordingly abstain from incitement, including hostile propaganda, against each other and, without derogating from the principle of freedom of expression, shall take legal measures to prevent such incitement by any organizations, groups or individuals within their jurisdiction.

2. Without derogating from the other provisions of this Agreement, Israel and the Palestinian Authority shall cooperate in combating criminal activity which may affect both sides, including offenses related to trafficking in illegal drugs and psychotropic substances, smuggling, and offenses against property, including offenses related to vehicles.

ARTICLE XIII

Economic Relations

The economic relations between the two sides are set out in the Protocol on Economic Relations signed in Paris on April 29, 1994 and the Appendices thereto, certified copies of which are attached as Annex IV, and will be governed by the relevant provisions of this Agreement and its Annexes.

ARTICLE XIV

Human Rights and the Rule of Law

Israel and the Palestinian Authority shall exercise their powers and responsibilities pursuant to this Agreement with due regard to internationally-accepted norms and principles of human rights and the rule of law.

ARTICLE XV

The Joint Israeli-Palestinian Liaison Committee

1. The Liaison Committee established pursuant to Article X of the Declaration of Principles shall ensure the smooth implementation of this Agreement. It shall deal with issues requiring coordination, other issues of common interest and disputes.

2. The Liaison Committee shall be composed of an equal number of members from each Party. It may add other technicians and experts as necessary.

3. The Liaison Committee shall adopt its rules of procedure, including the frequency and place or places of its meetings.

4. The Liaison Committee shall reach its decisions by Agreement.

ARTICLE XVI

Liaison and Cooperation with Jordan and Egypt

1. Pursuant to Article XII of the Declaration of Principles, the two Parties shall invite the Governments of Jordan and Egypt to participate in establishing further Liaison and Cooperation Arrangements between the Government of Israel and the Palestinian Representatives on the one hand, and the Governments of Jordan and Egypt on the other hand, to promote cooperation between them. These arrangements shall include the constitution of a Continuing Committee.

2. The Continuing Committee shall decide by agreement on the modalities of admission of persons displaced from the West Bank and the Gaza Strip in 1967, together with necessary measures to prevent disruption and disorder.

3. The Continuing Committee shall deal with other matters of common concern.

ARTICLE XVII

Settlement of Differences and Disputes

Any difference relating to the application of this Agreement shall be referred to the appropriate coordination and cooperation mechanism established under this Agreement. The provisions of Article XV of the Declaration of Principles shall apply to any such difference which is not settled through the appropriate coordination and cooperation mechanism, namely:

1. Disputes arising out of the application or interpretation of this Agreement or any subsequent agreements pertaining to the interim period shall be settled by negotiations through the Liaison Committee.

2. Disputes which cannot be settled by negotiations may be settled by a mechanism of conciliation to be agreed between the Parties.

3. The Parties may agree to submit to arbitration disputes relating to the interim period, which cannot be settled through conciliation. To this end, upon the agreement of both Parties, the Parties will establish an Arbitration Committee.

ARTICLE XVIII

Prevention of Hostile Acts

Both sides shall take all measures necessary in order to prevent acts of terrorism, crime and hostilities directed against each other, against individuals falling under the other's authority and against their property, and shall take legal measures against offenders. In addition, the Palestinian side shall take all measures necessary to prevent such hostile acts directed against the Settlements, the infrastructure serving them and the Military Installation Area, and the Israeli side shall take all measures necessary to prevent such hostile acts emanating from the Settlements and directed against Palestinians.

ARTICLE XIX

Missing Persons

The Palestinian Authority shall cooperate with Israel by providing all necessary assistance in the conduct of searches by Israel within the Gaza Strip and the Jericho Area for missing Israelis, as well as by providing information about missing Israelis. Israel shall cooperate with the Palestinian

Authority in searching for, and providing necessary information about, missing Palestinians.

ARTICLE XX

Confidence-Building Measures

With a view to creating a positive and supportive public atmosphere to accompany the implementation of this Agreement, and to establish a solid basis of mutual trust and good faith, both Parties agree to carry out confidence-building measures as detailed herewith:

1. Upon the signing of this Agreement, Israel will release, or turn over, to the Palestinian Authority within a period of 5 weeks, about 5,000 Palestinian detainees and prisoners, residents of the West Bank and the Gaza Strip. Those released will be free to return to their homes anywhere in the West Bank or the Gaza Strip. Prisoners turned over to the Palestinian Authority shall be obliged to remain in the Gaza Strip or the Jericho Area for the remainder of their sentence.

2. After the signing of this Agreement, the two Parties shall continue to negotiate the release of additional Palestinian prisoners and detainees, building on agreed principles.

3. The implementation of the above measures will be subject to the fulfillment of the procedures determined by Israeli law for the release and transfer of detainees and prisoners.

4. With the assumption of Palestinian Authority, the Palestinian side commits itself to solving the problem of those Palestinians who were in contact with the Israeli authorities. Until an agreed solution is found, the Palestinian side undertakes not to prosecute these Palestinians or to harm them in any way.

5. Palestinians from abroad whose entry into the Gaza Strip and the Jericho Area is approved pursuant to this Agreement, and to whom the provisions of this Article are applicable, will not be prosecuted for offenses committed prior to September 13, 1993.

ARTICLE XXI

Temporary International Presence

1. The Parties agree to a temporary international or foreign presence in the Gaza Strip and the Jericho Area (hereinafter "the TIP"), in accordance with the provisions of this Article.

2. The TIP shall consist of 400 qualified personnel, including observers, instructors and other experts, from 5 or 6 of the donor countries.

3. The two Parties shall request the donor countries to establish a special fund to provide finance for the TIP.

4. The TIP will function for a period of 6 months. The TIP may extend this period, or change the scope of its operation, with the agreement of the two Parties.

5. The TIP shall be stationed and operate within the following cities and villages: Gaza, Khan Younis, Rafah, Deir al-Balah, Jabalya, Absan, Beit Hanun and Jericho.

6. Israel and the Palestinian Authority shall agree on a special Protocol to implement this Article, with the goal of concluding negotiations with the donor countries contributing personnel within two months.

ARTICLE XXII

Rights, Liabilities and Obligations

1. a. The transfer of all powers and responsibilities to the Palestinian Authority, as detailed in Annex II, includes all related rights, liabilities and obligations arising with regard to acts or omissions which occurred prior to the transfer. Israel will cease to bear any financial responsibility regarding such acts or omissions and the Palestinian Authority will bear all financial responsibility for these and for its own functioning.

b. Any financial claim made in this regard against Israel will be referred to the Palestinian Authority.

c. Israel shall provide the Palestinian Authority with the information it has regarding pending and anticipated claims brought before any court or tribunal against Israel in this regard.

d. Where legal proceedings are brought in respect of such a claim, Israel will notify the Palestinian Authority and enable it to participate in defending the claim and raise any arguments on its behalf.

e. In the event that an award is made against Israel by any court or tribunal in respect of such a claim, the Palestinian Authority shall reimburse Israel the full amount of the award.

f. Without prejudice to the above, where a court or tribunal hearing such a claim finds that liability rests solely with an employee or agent who acted beyond the scope of the powers assigned to him or her, unlawfully or with willful malfeasance, the Palestinian Authority shall not bear financial responsibility.

2. The transfer of authority in itself shall not affect rights, liabilities and obligations of any person or legal entity, in existence at the date of signing of this Agreement.

ARTICLE XXIII

Final Clauses

1. This Agreement shall enter into force on the date of its signing.

2. The arrangements established by this Agreement shall remain in force until and to the extent superceded by the Interim Agreement referred to in the Declaration of Principles or any other agreement between the Parties.

3. The five-year Interim Period referred to in the Declaration of Principles commences on the date of the signing of this Agreement.

4. The Parties agree that, as long as this Agreement is in force, the security fence erected by Israel around the Gaza Strip shall remain in place and that the line demarcated by the fence, as shown on attached Map No. 1, shall be authoritative only for the purpose of this Agreement.

5. Nothing in this Agreement shall prejudice or preempt the outcome of the negotiations on the Interim Agreement or on the Permanent Status to be conducted pursuant to the Declaration of Principles. Neither Party shall be deemed, by virtue of having entered into this Agreement, to have renounced or waived any of its existing rights, claims or positions.

6. The two Parties view the West Bank and the Gaza Strip as a single territorial unit, the integrity of which will be preserved during the Interim Period.

7. The Gaza Strip and the Jericho Area shall continue to be an integral part of the West Bank and the Gaza Strip, and their status shall not be changed for the period of this Agreement. Nothing in this Agreement shall be considered to change this status.

8. The Preamble to this Agreement, and all Annexes, Appendices and Maps attached hereto, shall constitute an integral part hereof.

Prime Minister Yitzhak Rabin and Chairman Yasir Arafat: Speeches at the Signing of the Cairo Agreement, March 4, 1994

Prime Minister Yitzhak Rabin

We witnessed, you witnessed, the world witnessed the tip of the iceberg of problems that we shall have to overcome in the implementation of even the first phase of the Declaration of Principles [DOP]. To overcome 100 years of animosity, suspicion, bloodshed, it's not so simple. There is an opposition on both sides to what we are doing today, and it will require a lot, a lot on both sides to make sure that we will succeed and achieve peaceful coexistence and, in addition to the coexistence, to bring a permanent solution.

Today we signed the Gaza-Jericho First agreement, which is the first phase of implementation. It's a very daring project, and we are committed by signature today to make sure that it will work. We will achieve our goals; we will be able to overcome all these problems.

In 1889, 105 years ago, Avraham Jablonsky, a blacksmith, was murdered in his clay hut in Wadi Khalil. Avraham Jablonsky was the first victim in the history of the Jewish settlement in Eretz Yisra'el in modern times. He was the first victim of the bloody conflict between us and the Palestinian people since our return to the land of our forefathers after 2,000 years of exile. Since Avraham Jablonsky's death, the experience of our grandparents, parents, ourselves, and even our children and grandchildren has been almost solely one of blood and bereavement. For 100 years, this blood gave us no rest. What did we want? We wanted to return to the land of our forefathers, to the land of the Bible. We wanted a homeland; we wanted a home; we wanted a safe haven; we wanted a place to call our own; we wanted to live as all men live, to be like other nations. We wanted to live.

The war for the land of our forefathers took our best sons and daughters. It drained us of spiritual and physical energies and channeled our entire spiritual and physical existence to paths we did not want, to paths of pain. We deplore that. Even in our most difficult times, our hearts ached at the sights of devastation, hatred, and death. Even in our most bitter moments, we knew that the tears of a bereaved mother from within our midst are no different from the tears of another bereaved mother; that they are equally piercing and painful in any family; that the cries of despair are the same even when uttered in other languages.

We decided to try to put an end to this terrible circle of pain. We decided to look ahead at a different future. On 13 September 1993, on the White House lawn in Washington, we decided to embark on a new road. Tomorrow we will begin implementing the DOP. The DOP and its implementation—in Gaza and Jericho, at this point—is designed to attain a dual purpose: to enable the Palestinian authority to administer the lives of the Palestinians and to uphold public law and order in their places of residence. Our goal is to uphold security for Israelis wherever they may be, particularly in the wake of the change that is scheduled to take place in Gaza and Jericho. If the security of the Israelis is not ensured and if the Palestinians are not given new hope, the goal of the agreement will not be attained.

A great deal depends on the Palestinians. We are embarking on this new road with a lot of hope and with strong will, and we know that it entails wonderful chances as well as serious risks. We are convinced that both peoples can live on the same strip of land, every man under his vine and under his fig tree, as the Biblical prophets envisioned; to give this land, the land of stones and graves, the taste of milk and honey it deserves.

At this hour, I appeal to the Palestinian people and say to them: Palestinian neighbors, 100 bloody years have instilled in us hatred for each other. For 100 years, we wanted to see you dead and you wanted to see us dead. We killed you and you killed us. Thousands of our graves and yours dot the mountains and the valleys, and they are painful landmarks in your history and ours. Today, you and we are extending our hands in peace. Today we are opening a new account. The Israeli people expect you not to let them down. Let the new hope flourish. It is not easy to forget the past, but let us try to overcome the rancors and obstacles in order to open a new, unique, and historic horizon; an opportunity which may never recur for a different life, a life that is not fraught with fear, a life that is not fraught with hatred, a life that does not involve the frightened eyes of children, a life that does not entail pain, a life in which we will build a home, plant a vineyard, and live to a ripe old age alongside our fellow men. . . .

On a spring day of 1994, two weeks ago, the late Second Lieutenant Shahar Simani was murdered. He was 21 years old and a resident of Ashqelon. His bullet-riddled body was found by the roadside on the way to Jerusalem. A thread of blood links the Israeli people from the murder of Avraham Jablonsky, the blacksmith, 105 years ago to the murder of 2d. Lt. Shahar Simani two weeks ago. I pray: May Shahar Simani be the last fatality among all of us, Israelis and Palestinians.

The new hope we are taking with us as we leave this place is immeasurable. There is no limit to our goodwill, to the will to see a historic reconciliation between two peoples that have lived so far by their swords. In the alleyways of Khan Yunus and on the outskirts of Ramat Gan, in the houses of Gaza, in the squares of Hadera, Rafah, and 'Afula, a new reality is being born today. One hundred years of the Palestinian-Israeli conflict and millions of people who want to live are watching us. May God be with us.

Chairman Yasir Arafat

In the name of every Palestinian man and woman, I look with great confidence and hope at our brothers and our people's friends who are participating in this historic occasion and I think of those who could not come. I thank them all and stress to them that our people today in the West Bank, Gaza, holy Jerusalem, and in all the diaspora are looking more than ever toward your role so that this first step in Gaza and Jericho will become the real start for completing the peace process, guaranteeing our Palestinian people's legitimate rights, achieving justice and equality by ending the occupation of our Palestinian territories, and building the Palestinian future based on democracy, development, and progress, a future linked with the tradition of its glorious Arab nation. . . .

The withdrawal from Gaza and Jericho is the prelude; it opens the door to removing the entire óccupation and to establishing new relations between our peoples, Prime Minister Rabin, between our Israeli and Palestinian peoples, for the sake of our children and yours.

Completing this step required Herculean courage after long periods of war and violence. The coming stage will require still greater courage, a thorough insight, real farsightedness, and firm patience so that we can establish a firm and unshakable peace, the peace of the bold.

The Palestinian people have lived on their land throughout history. They helped to create civilization and raise the voice of peace, the voice of the only all-powerful God, the creator, the lord of the universe and of the three heavenly religions, calling for praising God's blessings, giving, and his name on this sacred land.

The people of Palestine, based on their deep historical heritage, today express their loyalty to the just and comprehensive peace. Thus our people demonstrated faithfulness to the heritage of their successive generations; to the sweat of the Palestinian people, mixed as it is with the soil of the earth; to the Palestinian maker's determination to build life and let it flourish; and to the creativity of the Palestinian intellectual, who always believes that history will never go off its track no matter how much time passes.

Our people, gentlemen, have struggled long to see the beginning of the peace era. For peace to be achieved, our people offered dear sacrifices. To achieve this recognition of our national rights, the eyes of bereaved mothers and of children who were raised to know that love and loyalty to the homeland are the highest values of life looked forward. Also looking forward to this were the prisoners, whose hope of freedom, for themselves and for their people, is renewed every day, and the refugee camp residents, who never lost confidence that a new era of freedom would come.

Nothing has gone in vain. Alive and great nations make their wounds, the sacrifice of their martyrs, and their long suffering the motives for the future and the banners for building a new era based on justice under the shadow of tolerance and coexistence among the three religions of Judaism, Christianity, and Islam over centuries.

We have offered a great deal to reach this day. We confronted patiently and persistently every hindrance and doubt and we always thought that every step in the peace negotiations, despite all the pain, was a move away from the era of war and violence nearer to the era of equal rights and the implementation of international legitimacy. While today we celebrate the signing of the first step, we must all realize that all those concerned about peace, including our people at home and in the diaspora, measure the seriousness of this step by one criterion: honest and precise implementation and the change it will make to the reality on the ground. It is the right of our people and of everybody concerned with genuine peace to point to the measures isolating holy Jerusalem from its surroundings and preventing the Palestinians from entering it and the other sacred Islamic and Christian places. These measures obstruct life in the city, paralyze its economy, and separate the sons of the same family.

All this is incompatible with the spirit of the just and real peace, with the course of equality, justice, and human rights that we are aspiring to adopt as the basis for free and positive relations between the two neighboring peoples, as Mr. Peres said, between the Palestinian and Israeli peoples. The suffering of the city of Hebron following the bloody massacre cannot continue. It is still suffering encirclement and siege both inside and outside it.

The continuation of the settlement and the attempt to impose the fait accompli in Jerusalem and in other areas conflict with the essence, clauses, and the short and long-term objectives of the peace process.

The boldness of peace prompts me today to adopt the policy of frankness on peace without which we cannot end the age of confrontation and start the age of constructive and real cooperation. The Arab peoples and millions of Muslims and Christians will observe our practical steps tomorrow to pass judgment on the possibility of coexistence and of opening a new chapter in normal relations. All those who want the success of the Palestinian-Israeli peace experiment realize the importance of the great steps facing this peace, including the settlements, the refugee problem, holy Jerusalem, and the need to solve it later, as we agreed, so as to help create a new era of protecting the future of the entire region and ensuring openness between their peoples and countries on the basis of respect for the rules and resolutions of international legitimacy.

Ladies and gentlemen, I am confident today that the Palestinian people will receive this new stage with a desire to provide a real opportunity for building real peace with the same desire it has for its national identity and its independent national being. Our people extends its hand to the Israeli people to start this era and end the whirlpool of violence for the sake of our real interests today and the interests of our coming generations.

Coexistence is possible. It is inevitable. It is our common fate to live together as neighbors governed by the rules of justice, democracy, and national and human dignity.

Hatred, bigotry, and extremism will only lead to more squandering of our creative and brilliant resources. We are proposing the alternative today, namely equality, joint building, and respect for every people's right and independent choice and security.

Today again I also address our great Arab nation, leaders and peoples, on the threshold of the first step of the return to the homeland and stress to them that their pain, sacrifice, and determination to uphold our Palestinian people's national legitimate rights prompt us today to strengthen our fraternal ties in every field so that peace for Palestine will, as always, be a peace for all the Arabs.

Yes, gentlemen, our peace is a peace for our Arab nation. It is a peace for Israel, for the Middle East region, for the whole world. Yes, it is a peace for the whole world.

O God, you are peace, peace comes from you, and peace is for you. Blessed are you God, full of majesty, bounty, and honor. Glory to God in the highest, peace on earth, and goodwill toward men. Peace be with you.

Prime Minister Yitzhak Rabin: Speech to Parliament, April 18, 1994

Last week, we celebrated the forty-sixth anniversary of the establishment of the State of Israel and its independence. Today, we return to our regular lives, but we are all permitted to look back with pride—and forward, with great hope.

Forty-six difficult years of struggle for life, and of building an economy and society have brought about the great accomplishments of the State of Israel. Despite its deficiencies, it is today one of the more enchanting and beautiful countries of the world; one of those in which it is good to live. I want to take advantage of this opportunity, of the opening of the Knesset's summer session, to again congratulate the citizens of Israel on the occasion of Independence Day.

The last Independence Day took place in the shadow of the terrorist attacks, and of the most recent attack—just before the Memorial Day siren. Five civilians and soldiers died in the explosion of a bomb at the central bus station in Hadera.

The bomb was planted by a degenerate murderer, a member of Hamas, who apparently chose to perish with his innocent victims. This House, the entire country, joins in the mourning and agony of the bereaved families . . . to offer our condolences for their suffering. This House, the Government, also wishes a speedy recovery to the wounded.

Last September, we embarked on a new path. We set forth on an honest attempt to turn a page of history that is fraught with the blood of both Jews—later Israelis—and Palestinians. We decided not to deal with past accounts. We decided to overcome the accumulations of hatred and blood. We decided to try and create a new and better future for both peoples who have been summoned to the same tract of land by fate and history.

We came with a desire to make peace and I must tell you, members of Knesset, that we also found a willingness for peace on the other side, that of the Palestinians—who have also known great suffering for generations. Both we and the Palestinians knew that we would not receive everything we wanted. The Palestinians will not get everything they want. That is the nature of negotiations. That is the nature of compromise. That is the nature of peace.

The negotiations with the Palestinians on "Gaza-Jericho first" continue even today and, in my opinion, we are at an advanced stage. I hope that it will be possible to conclude the negotiations in a short time.

It is our current assessment that, shortly after the agreement is signed, IDF forces and other security branches will be able to conclude their redeployment—I mean in the wake of the Gaza-Jericho negotiations—and the attempt to create peaceful co-existence with the Palestinians will be tested.

I say: I am waiting for this moment when I will feel more comfortable as Defense Minister, not sending IDF soldiers to patrol in metropolitan Gaza City—which contains 250,000 Palestinians, in refugee camps, in Khan Yunis, in Rafiah, in Dir al-Balah.

I want to add: In the wake of reports that have been published—true or not—I wish to clarify that any PLO agreement or accord with Hamas on the possibility of continuing Hamas terror with the approval of the PLO will prevent the achievement of an agreement and its implementation.

This Government, which promised to make every effort for peace, also intends to continue talks with Syria, Lebanon and Jordan.

Towards the end of April and the beginning of May, the bilateral talks in Washington will resume, and Secretary of State Warren Christopher will apparently come to the region to prepare for the talks—in order to enable progress toward the signing of a peace treaty between us and the neighboring countries.

At the peace talks, and as of today, we have still not discovered an appropriate measure of openness and flexibility on the part of the Syrians which would enable a breakthrough and a substantive discussion with respect to a peace agreement. Even the efforts of our American friends, who so want to see peace come to our region, have been unsuccessful.

At the same time, the position of the current government is known. We are making a great effort so that the precedent of the price we paid for peace with Egypt—comprehensive withdrawal, the removal of any Israeli presence—will not be repeated as a condition for achieving peace with Syria. Still, we are seriously preparing for the negotiations and working on various possibilities relating to the character of peace, the depth of the withdrawal on the Golan Heights, security arrangements and the phases for the implementation of peace—so that there will be time to examine the normalization before completing the withdrawal from the Golan Heights as well as what we will require from our friend the United States in the wake of peace. If and when we reach a viable agreement with the

Syrians, and should it require a significant withdrawal, we will call a referendum. The people, and nobody else, will decide.

The negotiations with Lebanon are connected to the negotiations with Syria, and we know that Beirut will not lift a finger without the approval of Damascus. Despite this, we repeat—even today—our offer to the authority in Beirut. We have proposed that, in the first phase, the Lebanese military be deployed up to the northern border of the security zone. For six months, it must prove its ability to maintain total calm and to disarm Hizballah in southern Lebanon. If this is proven and total quiet reigns on the northern border of the security zone, we will begin peace negotiations that I hope will continue for three months. We will be prepared to withdraw to the international border between Lebanon and Israel on three conditions: full peace and normalization; appropriate security arrangements; and, of course—our commitment to the SLA and the residents of southern Lebanon—the integration of the SLA within the Lebanese army and a guarantee to residents of southern Lebanon that they will not be harmed.

In the negotiations with Jordan, a resolution is possible. But, unfortunately, I get the impression that it will not come before an agreement with Syria, the big brother who watches over all.

I want to tell the truth. For twenty-seven years, we have controlled another people that does not want our rule. For twenty-seven years, the Palestinians—who now number 1,800,000—have risen in the morning and cultivated a burning hatred for us as Israelis and as Jews. Every morning, they awake to a difficult life and it is partly our fault . . . but not completely. It cannot be denied: The continued rule of a foreign people who does not want us has a price. There is first of all a painful price, the price of constant confrontation between us and them.

For six and one-half years, we have witnessed a popular Palestinian uprising against our rule—the intifada. They are trying, through violence and terror, to harm us, to cause us casualties and to break our spirit.

I would like to present some data, provided to me by the IDF. Since the beginning of the uprising, 219 Israelis have been killed, murdered; 68 were security forces personnel and 151 were civilians. A heavy price.

It is difficult for me to recall the War of Independence. In the brigade which I had the privilege to command, in the battle for besieged Jerusalem and the road to Jerusalem, during six months, from one of the ten Haganah brigades which became the Israel Defense Forces, the same number of people fell. One of the outstanding commanders of the brigade and of the IDF, MK Rafael Eitan, is sitting here, and he certainly remembers this. One of 10 brigades, from slightly more than 600,000 civilians. Not one of those people's spirit was broken then. No one rejoiced over the blood.

Our wounded: 7,872, of whom 5,062 were security force personnel and 2,810 were civilians.

1,045 Palestinians have been killed by our forces, those of the IDF and the security branches. 69 have been killed by Israeli civilians. 922 Palestinians have been killed by their own people. 99 have been killed in unknown circumstances. 21 have blown themselves up while handling explosives. A total of 2,156.

Palestinians wounded, according to IDF figures: 18,967. I estimate that at least 25,000 have been wounded. Between 120,000 and 140,000 have been detained and imprisoned.

These are the figures of the struggle over the past six and a half years.

What are the possibilities which face us after twenty-seven years of ruling—and I do not want to use other terms—a different entity than us: religiously, politically, nationally, another people?

The first possibility is to perpetuate the situation as it is, to make proposals with no partner—there never were, and there is no settlement without a partner. To try and eternalize the rule of another people, to continue on a course of never-ending violence and terrorism, which will bring about a political impasse.

Governments of Israel, all Governments of Israel—certainly since the Yom Kippur War—have well-understood the danger contained in freezing the situation. Accordingly, all the governments have sought the second option. The second option is to try and find a political solution. The first phase—in separation agreements. The Government of Menachem Begin went this way, with the peace agreement with Egypt. The Government of Yitzhak Shamir also went this way, in consenting to the Madrid peace conference. We have also gone this way since the Oslo discussion and the Washington signing.

Today, peace seems closer than ever. There is a chance, a great chance, to put an end to wars, to one hundred years of terror and blood, one hundred years of animosity. When we embarked on the journey to peace, we knew that it would be impossible to erase one hundred years of hatred with one signature. We knew that it would be impossible to alter concepts and education from the moment of birth. We knew that this peace would have enemies. We knew there would be people and organizations—whose very existence is founded on hostility between peoples—that would continue to enflame passions to the best of their abilities.

On the Palestinian side, the opposition to peace is led by Hamas along with Islamic Jihad, the rejectionist organizations. The emissaries of this organization have carried out most of the recent acts of terror and murder, some of them in suicide operations. Over the past two or three years, we have encountered radical Islamic terror reminiscent of Hizballah, which was created in Lebanon and carried out attacks—including suicide attacks.

There is no end to the goals of Hamas and other terrorism—every citizen, every Israeli in the territories and within the Green Line, every bus and every home is a target for its murderous intentions.

And, without separating the two populations, the current situation creates endless possibilities for the Hamas murderers. According to our estimate, about 40,000 vehicles move about daily in Judea, Samaria and Gaza. Tens of thousands of soldiers and civilians move about on the roads. IDF soldiers safeguard hundreds of vehicles in the territories, mostly buses, every day.

Hundreds of thousands, Jews and Arabs, thousands of vehicles are intermingled each day. One population within the other.

There are endless possibilities of moving for the territories to Israel. Fewer from Gaza, more from Judea and Samaria. Thousands of hidden and exposed paths lead from the territories into Israel. We cannot hermetically seal the territory.

We are making every effort to ensure the security of Israeli citizens—Jews and Arabs—within the Green Line zone territories, everywhere. I reveal to the Knesset today that a significant part of the standing force of the IDF is now engaged in missions protecting and defending Israeli citizens everywhere.

In this situation, where Hamas has endless targets, it embarks on operations of murder—declaring that its foremost aim is to murder Israelis. And, politically, to destroy the peace talks, not to allow them to

At first, Hamas murderers operated against the Israeli residents of Judea, Samaria and the Gaza Strip. The political intent of Hamas members was that the Israeli residents of Judea, Samaria and Gaza—who were harmed by terror—would demonstrate and act against the Israeli government, in an effort to halt peace efforts.

When this attempt was unsuccessful, and we continued our peace efforts, Hamas directed its primary effort to attacks against the Israeli population within the sovereign territory of Israel, including united Jerusalem.

Since 1 January 1994, twenty-three Israeli civilians, Jews and Arabs, have been killed. Twenty of them were killed within sovereign Israel, including united Jerusalem. Three were killed in the territories.

It is no secret how sensitive we are to casualties, and the Hamas murderers are trying to break us through attacks—with knives, explosive devices, shots from ambushes, car bombs.

They have no chance. We already learned about knives during the bloody incidents of the 1930s. We already learned about car bombs during the War of Independence. We learned about buses filled with bloodshed: in Ma'aleh Akrabim, in Avivim, on the coastal road. We learned about massacres in Ma'alot, and we learned about massacres at the airport in Lod, at the Savoy Hotel, in Kfar Yuval, in Kiryat Shmona, in Misgav Am, in Nahariya. Time and again. We are not panicked. It is painful, but we recover and continue. Even acts of terrorism will not stop the peace convoy.

It is difficult for me to determine that the extent of the risk to our security has increased of late, in the wake of the despicable massacre committed by the Jewish murderer from Hebron. Even though Arab terror had one thousand reasons and excuses to harm us, this man came and added some.

We have found that one of the concentrations of Hamas activity is in Jordan. We are convinced that the Jordanian security authorities are aware of this and, nevertheless, they have enabled information and operational activities in Amman.

Thus, we have seen fit to warn the Jordanian authorities about the continuation of Hamas activity there, and we expect that the King will act against the Hamas murderers—who will attempt to challenge and bring down his regime and rule there as well.

We have also taken a series of measures, including strengthening the terms of closure. We are aware of the suffering being caused to residents of the territories as a consequence of the closure, but we have no other choice. If we wish to live, we must be stricter. And, if reality requires us to do so, we will be even stricter.

And above all, IDF forces, the GSS, the Israel Police and Border Police officers are engaged in an all-out war against all those continuing the violence and terror. There is no limitation to the activity of these forces against terrorism and violence, obviously within the framework of the law.

The Hizballah terrorist organization is also a partner to in the effort to destroy the chance for peace. The Lebanon war did not eradicate terror from Lebanon. Hizballah is the leader in attacks on IDF and SLA forces in the security zone and, sometimes, even against targets in Israel. IDF and SLA soldiers guarantee that northern communities and residents will lead normal lives.

From this platform, I wish to offer my heartfelt praise to IDF commanders and IDF soldiers, to the Israel Police and the Border Police, and particularly to members of the GSS, who are playing a significant role in the difficult war on the murderous terrorism waged by the enemies of Israel and of peace.

This is the situation for now. The path to peace is laid with our good intentions, and with their murderous attacks. It may be even more difficult; we may not manage to prevent more terror attacks. But peace will be victorious.

Prime Minister Yitzhak Rabin: Speech on Accepting the UNESCO Peace Prize, July 6, 1994

For over a hundred years, we have fought over the same strip of land: the country in which we, the sons of Abraham, have been fated to live together. Both peoples, Israelis and Palestinians, have known suffering, pain, and bereavement.

Now the fanfares and festivals are over. Now the vapors of euphoria are slowly settling into grains of dust, and the echoes of celebration are being scattered by the hot southern wind. Now the flags have been folded, the trumpets silenced, the stages dismantled—now, the more difficult, more dangerous part has come. And both sides must calculate their steps slowly, with prudence and care. For a century of hatred does not dissolve suddenly, with a handshake in Washington. All the bloodshed can't be covered by the beating of drums. Peace will be built slowly, day by day, through modest deeds, and countless spontaneous details. It will be built, step by step, by people.

From now on, the making of peace is not a matter for spotlights, for elegant halls, and ball gowns. From now on, the baking sun in Jericho and Na'ama, in Khan Yunis and Netzer Hazani, will replace the spotlights in Washington, Cairo, and Paris. The handshakes on the lawn in Washington, the stage in Cairo, and here in Paris must be repeated by the residents of Gaza and Ashkelon, of Jericho and Ma'ale Adumim. What we have acknowledged here in this beautiful setting in Paris must be transferred to the markets in Gaza, where Israelis will buy fruit from Palestinian vendors.

Peace will be tasted in the Palestinian coffee poured into the cups of Israeli friends. It will be heard in the applause of Israeli audiences for the performance of a Palestinian theater troupe, and in the jeers of the rival soccer fans when Khan Yunis plays against Tel Aviv.

Peace will be seen when an Israeli driver yields the right of way to his Palestinian counterpart—vice versa: when a Palestinian policeman gives a ticket to an Israeli driver—and the other way around. Peace lies in the grin of an Israeli doctor delivering Palestinian newborn, and in the smile of a Palestinian lifeguard toward Israeli bathers on the beach.

That, ladies and gentlemen, is peace.

We are going along slowly and cautiously, one step at a time, because the enemies of peace are even more numerous than we imagine. Because extremists on both sides are lying in wait for us, and we—Israelis and Palestinians, alike—must not fail. At every step, we must think, consider, we—Israelis and Palestinians, alike—must not fail. At every step, we must think, consider, weigh, check, and beware.

We are in a hurry because we have waited over a hundred years for this day, in Gaza and Jerusalem, in Jericho and Netanya, in Rafiah and Rosh Pinah.

We are in a hurry to spare another Israeli mother weeping tears of pain and another Palestinian mother from shedding bitter sobs.

We are in a hurry in order to see a light in the eyes of neighbors who, until now, have never seen a single day of freedom and joy. We are hastening in order to hike, drive, tour, and enjoy life in every corner of this land.

We are in a hurry so that children can be born into a new world—a world where 'hostility' and 'war' are just dead words, found only in the dictionary.

We are in a hurry, Ladies and Gentlemen—and therefore we are proceeding slowly. We are moving very carefully. For not all of us will have another chance. . . .

Ladies and Gentlemen, peace is an abstract concept. Prime Ministers tend to see the essential things—the 'big picture'—and it's said that they don't have time for details. I translate peace into people: men and women, flesh and blood, with names and addresses. Sometimes when I have to make a decision, there are certain people I think of, and I contemplate their fate.

There was a family in Israel that symbolizes, in our eyes, the bond of generations to the Land of Israel, Jewish moral and cultural values, a return to the soil after two thousand years of exile, security, and the dream of peace.

The mother of the family, Rachel Kaplan was the daughter of the Chief Rabbi of Jerusalem—the offspring of a family deeply rooted, for generations, between the Western Wall—the walls of the Old City—and the new city of Jerusalem, the City of Peace.

The father, Yisrael, came to the land that had been promised to the Patriarch Abraham, the father of the Jewish People, from exile in Poland. Hundreds of thousands came like him, and after him, from seventy countries of dispersion, and set down roots in their ancient home.

Avner was the eldest son of Rachel and Yisrael Kaplan. He chose to settle the land and to work the soil as a way of life as another expression of the Jewish ties to the Land of Israel. Avner Kaplan died in a fire in his house, on Kibbutz Tel Katzir, facing the Golan Heights.

Yossi was the Kaplan's second son. He chose defense as a way of life and served as an outstanding officer in the paratroops. Yossi was killed while in pursuit of terrorists in the Jordan Valley. He entered a cave where a woman was sitting with her baby. A moral man, a humanist whom circumstances had made into a tough soldier, Yossi believed her when she said that she was alone. But when he turned to leave, he was shot by the man hiding there. That's how Yossi Kaplan died.

Yoni was their third son. He chose university studies and army service. Although he was entitled to be exempt from combat, because of the death of his brothers, he did not waive his right to serve on the front line, the vanguard of attack. Yoni Kaplan was killed in the bitter fighting against the Egyptian Army in the Yom Kippur War.

The mother of this wonderful family, Rachel, was struck down by cancer.

The father, Yisrael, died of a broken heart over the loss of his sons, one after the other.

There remains the fourth, last son: Amiram Kaplan.

For your sake, Amiram—for you, for our children and their children, we are moving toward peace. We are proceeding slowly, and we shall hurry to bring it to you. That is our vow to you.

Israel-Jordan: The Washington Agreement, July 26, 1994

A. After generations of hostility, blood, and tears and in the wake of years of pain and wars, His Majesty King Hussein and Prime Minister Yitzhak Rabin are determined to bring an end to bloodshed and sorrow. It is in this spirit that His Majesty King Hussein of the Hashemite Kingdom of Jordan and Prime Minister and Minister of Defense, Mr. Yitzhak Rabin of Israel, met in Washington today at the invitation of President William J. Clinton of the United States of America. The initiative of President William J. Clinton constitutes an historic landmark in the United States untiring efforts in promoting peace and stability in the Middle East. The personal involvement of the president has made it possible to realize agreement on the content of this historic declaration. The signing of this declaration bears testimony to the president's vision and devotion to the cause of peace.

B. In their meeting, His Majesty King Hussein and Prime Minister Yitzhak Rabin have jointly reaffirmed the five underlying principles of their understanding on an Agreed Common Agenda designed to reach the goal of a just, lasting, and comprehensive peace between the Arab States and the Palestinians, with Israel.

1. Jordan and Israel aim at the achievement of just, lasting, and comprehensive peace between Israel and its neighbors and at the conclusion of a Treaty of Peace between both countries.

2. The two countries will vigorously continue their negotiations to arrive at a state of peace, based on Security Council Resolutions 242 and 338 in all their aspects, and founded on freedom, equality and justice.

3. Israel respects the present special role of the Hashemite Kingdom of Jordan in Moslem holy shrines in Jerusalem. When negotiations on the permanent status will take place, Israel will give high priority to the Jordanian historic role in these shrines. In addition,

the two sides have agreed to act together to promote interfaith relations among the three monotheistic religions.

4. The two countries recognize their right and obligation to live in peace with each other as well as with all states within secure and recognized boundaries. The two states affirmed their respect for and acknowledgment of the sovereignty, territorial integrity, and political independence of every state in the area.

5. The two countries desire to develop good neighborly relations of cooperation between them to ensure lasting security and to avoid threats and the use of force between them.

C. The long conflict between the two states is now coming to an end. In this spirit, the state of belligerency between Jordan and Israel has been terminated.

D. Following this declaration and in keeping with the Agreed Common Agenda both countries will refrain from actions or activities by either side that may adversely affect the security of the other or may prejudice the final outcome of negotiations. Neither side will threaten the other by use of force, weapons, or any other means against each other and both sides will thwart threats to security resulting from all kinds of terrorism.

E. His Majesty King Hussein and Prime Minister Yitzhak Rabin took note of the progress made in the bilateral negotiations within the Jordan-Israel track last week on the steps decided to implement the sub-agendas on borders, territorial matters, security, water, energy, environment, and the Jordan Rift Valley.

In this framework, mindful of items of the Agreed Common Agenda (borders and territorial matters) they noted that the boundary subcommission has reached agreement in July 1994 in fulfillment of part of the role entrusted to it in the subagenda. They also noted that the subcommission for water, environment, and energy agreed to mutually recognize, as the role of their negotiations, the rightful allocations of the two sides in Jordan River and Yarmouk River waters and to fully respect and comply with the negotiated rightful allocations, in accordance with agreed acceptable principles with mutually acceptable quality.

Similarly, His Majesty King Hussein and Prime Minister Yitzhak Rabin expressed their deep satisfaction and pride in the work of the trilateral commission in its meeting held in Jordan on Wednesday, July 20, 1994, hosted by the Jordanian Prime Minister, Dr. Abdessalam Majali, and attended by Secretary of State Warren Christopher and Foreign Minister Shimon Peres. They voiced their pleasure at the association and commitment of the United States in this endeavor.

F. His Majesty King Hussein and Prime Minister Yitzhak Rabin believe that steps must be taken to both overcome psychological barriers and to break with the legacy of war. By working with optimism towards the dividends of peace for all the people in the region, Jordan and Israel are determined to shoulder their responsibilities towards the human dimension of peace making. They recognize imbalances and disparities are a root cause of extremism which thrives on poverty and unemployment and the degradation of human dignity. In this spirit, His Majesty King Hussein and Prime Minister Yitzhak Rabin have today approved a series of steps to symbolize the new era which is row at hand:

1. Direct telephone links will be opened between Jordan and Israel.

2. The electricity grids of Jordan and Israel will be linked as part of a regional concept.

3. Two new border crossings will be opened between Jordan and Israel—one at the southern tip of Akaba-Eilat and the other at a mutually agreed point in the North.

4. In principle, free access will be given to third country tourists traveling between Jordan and Israel.

5. Negotiations will be accelerated on opening an international air corridor between both countries.

6. The police forces of Jordan and Israel will cooperate in combating crime with emphasis on smuggling and particularly drug smuggling. The United States will be invited to participate in this joint endeavor.

7. Negotiations on economic matters will continue in order to prepare for future bilateral cooperation, including the abolition of all economic boycotts.

All these steps are being implemented within the framework of regional infrastructural development plans and in conjunction with the Jordan-Israel bilaterals on boundaries, security, water and related issues and without prejudice to the final outcome of the negotiations on the items included in the Agreed Common Agenda between Jordan and Israel.

G. His Majesty King Hussein and Prime Minister Yitzhak Rabin have agreed to meet periodically or whenever they feel necessary to review the progress of the negotiations and express their firm intention to shepherd and direct the process in entirety.

H. In conclusion, His Majesty King Hussein and Prime Minister Yitzhak Rabin wish to express once again their profound thanks and appreciation to President William J. Clinton and his administration for their untiring efforts in furthering the cause of peace, justice, and prosperity for all the peoples of the region.

King Hussein and Prime Minister Yitzhak Rabin: Speeches on Signing the Washington Agreement, July 26, 1994

King Hussein

We in Jordan have always sought a bold peace. We have been conscious of our responsibilities towards the coming generations to ensure that they will have the certainty of leading a dignified and fulfilled life. We have sought a peace that can harness the creative energies to allow them to realize their true potential and build their future with confidence, devoid of fear and uncertainty. None of this can be achieved without establishing a direct dialogue at the highest level of leadership.

This meeting in Washington, at the invitation of President Clinton, represents the beginning of a new phase in our common journey towards peace between Jordan and Israel. It is a milestone on the road toward comprehensive peace in our region. This meeting was preceded by a trilateral Jordanian-American-Israeli meeting at which my brother, Crown Prince Hassan, represented myself and the Hashemite Kingdom of Jordan, and Foreign Minister Shimon Peres represented Israel.

The trilateral working group was established under an agreement completed at the meeting hosted by President Clinton at the White House in October 1993.

Following my recent visit to the United States, in light of the status of negotiations, I decided to share with my people the realities affecting our search for peace. In a meeting with members of our parliament, I addressed the entire Jordanian nation. I have been rewarded by their approval and support. Their expression of confidence has always been the foremost consideration in my life. All of Jordan is here with me today.

We also remember today the three generations of gallant Jordanians and so many others who sacrificed themselves for the cause of Palestine. Every household in Jordan has sent a son to answer the Arab call. Many have not returned. Their sacrifice has made it possible for me to be here today.

My family has also paid a heavy price. My great grandfather, the leader of the great Arab revolt for freedom, independence and unity, lies buried next to the blessed Al Aqsa Mosque in Jerusalem. I was by the side of my grandfather, King Abdallah, at the doors of Al Aqsa Mosque when he was martyred. He was a man of peace who gave his life for this ideal. I have pledged my life to fulfilling his dream. He, too, is here today.

Mr. Speaker, at our meeting today I hope you will find a clear message to the American nation and to the world.

We are, together, committed to work tirelessly, to banish forever the abnormal conditions which have dominated our people's lives. We want normality and humanity to become the prevailing order.

Although we have labored for so long under conditions of hostility, I am certain that we can see these conditions for what they are: emblems of an unnatural and sinister state. We have all known the portents of the state—the fear of death, the silence of isolation—and we have all felt the fear that has mesmerized us, preventing us from moving forward to create together a bright future for the coming generations. What we are witnessing today, God willing, is a progression from a state of war to a state of peace.

These unique circumstances allow us to take bold steps. Our meeting now represents a revolt against all that is unnatural. It is unnatural not to have direct and open meetings between our respective officials and their leaders in order to grapple with all aspects of the conflict and, God willing, to resolve them. It is unnatural not to wish to bridge this gulf across which we have all paid a shattering toll in blood and tears, the waste of our youth, and the grief of our forefathers. We have suffered this loss together, and it will leave its impact on all of us far into the future.

The two Semitic people, the Arabs and the Jews, have endured bitter trials and tribulations during the journey of history. Let us resolve to end this suffering forever and to fulfill our responsibilities as leaders of our peoples and our duty as human beings towards mankind. I come before you today fully conscious of the need to secure a peace for all the children of Abraham. Our land is the birthplace of the divine faiths and the cradle of the heavenly messages to all humanity.

I also come before you today as a soldier who seeks to bear arms solely in the defense of his homeland, a man who understands the fears of his neighbors and who wishes only to live in peace with them, a man who wishes to secure democracy, political pluralism and human rights for his nation.

I come before you today encouraged in the knowledge that the prime minister of Israel and his government have responded to the call for peace. They have recognized the Palestinian people and their rights and are negotiating with their chosen leadership in accordance with United Nations Security Council Resolutions 242 and 338.

For our part, we will never forget Palestine, not for a moment. We in Jordan were the first to shoulder our responsibility, and we were the most adversely affected by the legacy of the Palestinian tragedy. And still our people in Jordan remain one united family irrespective of their origins, sharing equally, free to choose our political future and destiny.

My religious faith demands that sovereignty over the holy places in

Jerusalem reside with God, and God alone. Dialogue between the faiths should be strengthened. Religious sovereignty should be accorded to all believers of the three Abrahamic faiths in accordance with their religions, and this way Jerusalem will become the symbol of peace and its embodiment as it must be for both Palestinians and Israelis when their negotiations determine the final status of Arab East Jerusalem.

I come before you today fully confident that progress will be made on the Syrian-Israeli and Lebanese-Israeli tracks of the peace process and towards achievement of comprehensive peace. . . .

The state of war between Israel and Jordan is over.

We have accepted United Nations Security Council Resolution 338, which calls for negotiations between the parties concerned under appropriate auspices to establish a just and durable peace in the Middle East. We have accepted United Nations Security Council Resolution 242, which sought acknowledgement of the sovereignty, territorial integrity and political independence of every state in the area and thereby to live in peace within secure and recognized boundaries, free from threats or acts of force.

I want to reaffirm, without any reservation, that we, together with other parties concerned, have exercised our sovereign right to make peace.

We are moving forward and tackling, one by one, all the problems listed in our common agenda. We have great faith in our joint progress towards the ultimate goal, the culmination of all our efforts, a Jordanian-Israeli peace treaty.

In this we take courage from the words of God in his holy book, the Koran, that if they should be inclined to make peace, do thou incline towards it also, and put thy trust in Allah. Surely it is he who is all hearing, all knowing.

I value the long friendship between Jordan and the United States inherited from the era of my grandfather. I have strived over 34 years since the presidency of Dwight Eisenhower to ensure that it be honest and true.

It has been a friendship built on mutual respect and common interests, and I am proud to remind how we stood shoulder to shoulder during the long years of the Cold War. And now, together we share a great hope to establish a lasting peace in the Middle East.

We believe that an enduring partnership for cooperation and development between Jordan and the United States is essential to the realization of this dream. We aim to build a better future under peace, to change the pattern of life for our people from despair and hopelessness to honor and dignity. We want to fashion a new commonwealth of hope on our ancient soil. We want all voices to be heard in shaping a new regional order. If we are to achieve our aims, all of us must be given the opportunity and the tools to play our part in this historic endeavor.

The creative drive of our region has been crippled by the conflict. The healing hand of the international community is now essential. It should never be forgotten that peace resides ultimately not in the hands of governments but in the hands of the people, for unless peace can be made real to the men, women and children of the Middle East, the best efforts of negotiators will come to naught.

I have come before you today to demonstrate that we are ready to open a new era in our relations with Israel. With the help and cooperation of this august body, the peace we all want can be achieved. With your help, I am certain that the imbalances between our societies can be remedied and that the sources of frustration and enmity can be eradicated. It is in this spirit and with these hopes that I share this platform with Prime Minister Yitzhak Rabin.

Prime Minister Yitzhak Rabin

Each year, on Memorial Day for the Fallen of Israel's Wars, I go to the cemetery on Mount Herzl in Jerusalem. Facing me are the graves and headstones, the colorful flowers blooming on them—and thousands of pairs of weeping eyes. I stand there, in front of the large silent crowd—and read in their eyes the words of The Young Dead Soldiers—as the famous American poet Archibald MacLeish entitled the poem from which I take these lines:

> *"They say:*
> *Whether our lives and our deaths*
> *were for peace and a new hope,*
> *or for nothing,*
> *we cannot say;*
> *it is you who must say this".*

We have come from Jerusalem to Washington because it is we who must say, and we are here to say: Peace is our goal. It is peace we desire.

With me here in this House today are my partners in this great dream. Allow me to refer to some Israelis who are here with me, here with you:

• Amiram Kaplan, whose first brother was killed in an accident, whose second brother was killed in pursuit of terrorists, whose third brother was killed in war, and whose parents died of heartbreak. And today he is a seeker of peace.
• Moshe Sasson, who, together with his father, was an emissary to the talks with King Abdallah and to other missions of peace. Today he is also an emissary of peace.
• With me, a classmate of mine, Chana Rivlin of Kibbutz Gesher, which faces Jordan, who endured bitter fighting and lost a son in war. Today she

looks out her window onto Jordan, and wants the dream of peace to come true.

• Avraham Daskal, almost 90 years old, who worked for the Electric Company in Trans-Jordan and was privileged to attend the celebrations marking King Hussein's birth, is hoping for peace in his lifetime.

• And Dani Matt, who fought against Jordan in the War of Independence, was taken prisoner of war, and devoted his life to the security of the State of Israel. He hopes that his grandchildren will never know war.

• Mrs. Penina Herzog, whose husband wove the first threads of political ties with Jordan.

With us here in this hall are:

• Mr. Gabi Kadosh, the mayor of Eilat, which touches the frontier with Jordan and will be a focus of common tourism.

• And Mr. Shimon Cahaner, who fought against the Jordanians, memorializes his fallen comrades, and hopes that they will have been the last to fall.

• And Mr. Talal al-Krienawi, the mayor of a Bedouin town in Israel, who looks forward to renewing the friendship with their brothers in Jordan,

• And Mr. David Coren, a member of a kibbutz which was captured by the Jordanians in 1948, who awaits the day when the borders will be open.

• And Dr. Asher Susser, a scholar who has done research on Jordan throughout his adult life.

• And Dr. Sharon Regev, whose father was killed while pursuing terrorists in the Jordan Valley, and who yearns for peace with all his heart.

Here they are before you. All of them wanted to come. Here they are, people who never rejoiced in the victories of war, but whose hearts are now filled with joy in peace.

I have come here from Jerusalem on behalf of those thousands of bereaved families—though I haven't asked their permission. I stand here on behalf of the parents who have buried their children; of the children who have no fathers; and of the sons and daughters who are gone, but return to us in our dreams. I stand here today on behalf of those youngsters who wanted to live, to love, to build a home.

I have come from Jerusalem in the name of our children, who began their lives with great hope—and are now names on graves and memorial stones; old pictures in albums; fading clothes in closets.

Each year as I stand before the parents whose lips are chanting "Kaddish", the Jewish memorial prayer, ringing in my ears are the words of Archibald MacLeish, who echoes the plea of the young dead soldiers:

"They say: We leave you our deaths.
Give them their meaning".

Let us give them meaning. Let us make an end to bloodshed. Let us make true peace. Let us today be victorious in ending war.

The debate goes on: Who shapes the face of history?—leaders or circumstances?

My answer to you is: We all shape the face of history. We, the people. We, the farmers behind our plows, the teachers in our classrooms, the doctors saving lives, the scientists at our computers, the workers on the assembly lines, the builders on our scaffolds.

We, the mothers blinking back tears as our sons are drafted into the army; we, the fathers who stay awake at night worried and anxious for our children's safety. We, Jews and Arabs. We, Israelis and Jordanians. We, the people, we shape the face of history.

And we, the leaders, hear the voices, and sense the deepest emotions and feelings of the thousands and the millions, and translate them into reality.

If my people did not desire peace so strongly, I would not be standing here today. And I am sure that if the children of Amman, and the soldiers of Irbid, the women of Saltt and the citizens of Aqaba did not seek peace, our partner in this great quest, the King of Jordan, would not be here now, shaking hands, calling for peace.

We bear the responsibility. We have the power to decide. And we dare not miss this great opportunity. For it is the duty of leaders to bring peace and well-being to their peoples. We are graced with the privilege of fulfilling this duty for our peoples. This is our responsibility.

The complex relations between Israel and Jordan have continued for a generation. Today, so many years later, we carry with us good memories of the special ties between your country, your Majesty, and mine, and we carry with us the grim reminders of the times we found ourselves at war. We remember the days of your grandfather, King Abdallah, who sought avenues of peace with the heads of the Jewish people and the leaders of the young State of Israel.

There is much work before us. We face psychological barriers. We face genuine practical problems. Walls of hostility have been built on the River Jordan which runs between us. You in Amman, and we in Jerusalem, must bring down those barriers and walls, must solve those concrete problems. I am sure that we will do it.

Yesterday we took a giant step towards a peace which will embrace it all: borders and water, security and economics, trade without boycotts, tourism and environment, diplomatic relations. We want peace between countries, but above all, between human beings.

Beyond the ceremonies, after the festivities, we will move on to the negotiations. They will not be easy. But when they are completed, a wonderful, common future awaits us. The Middle East, the cradle of the great monotheistic civilizations—Judaism, Christianity, and Islam; the Middle East, which was a valley of the shadow of death, will be a place where it is a pleasure to live.

We live on the same stretch of land. The same rain nourishes our soil; the same hot wind parches our fields. We find shade under the same fig tree. We savor the fruit of the same green vine. We drink from the same well. Only a 70-minute journey separates these cities—Jerusalem and Amman—and 46 years. And just as we have been enemies, so can we be good and friendly neighbors.

Since it is unprecedented that in this joint meeting two speakers are invited, allow me to turn to His Majesty.

Your Majesty, We have both seen a lot in our lifetime. We have both seen too much suffering. What will you leave to your children? What will I leave to my grandchildren? I have only dreams: to build a better world —a world of understanding and harmony, a world in which it is a joy to live. This is not asking too much.

The State of Israel thanks you: thanks you for accepting our hand in peace; for your political wisdom and courage; for planting new hope in our hearts, in the hearts of your subjects, and the hearts of all peace-loving people. And I know that you enjoy the highest esteem of the United States—this great America which is helping the bold to make a peace of the brave. . . .

I do so because no words can express our gratitude to you and to the American people for your generous support, understanding, and cooperation which are beyond compare in modern history. Thank you, America. God bless America.

Tomorrow I shall return to Jerusalem, the capital of the State of Israel and the heart of the Jewish people. Lining the road to Jerusalem are rusting hulks of metal—burnt-out, silent, cold. They are the remains of convoys which brought food and medicine to the war-torn and besieged city of Jerusalem 46 years ago.

For many of Israel's citizens, their story is one of heroism, part of our national legend. For me and for my comrades-in-arms, every scrap of cold metal lying there by the wayside is a bitter memory. I remember it as though it were just yesterday.

I remember them. I was their commander in war. For them this ceremony has come too late. What endures are their children, their comrades, their legacy.

Allow me to make a personal note. I, military I.D. number three-zero-seven-four-three, retired general in the Israel Defense Forces in the past, consider myself to be a soldier in the army of peace today. I, who served my country for 27 years as a soldier, I say to you, Your Majesty, the King of Jordan, and I say to you, American friends:

Today we are embarking on a battle which has no dead and no wounded, no blood and no anguish. This is the only battle which is a pleasure to wage: the battle for peace.

Tomorrow, on the way up to Jerusalem, thousands of flowers will cover the remains of those rusting armored vehicles, the ones that never made it to the city. Tomorrow, from those silent metal heaps, thousands of flowers will smile to us with the word peace: "shalom."

In the Bible, our Book of Books, peace is mentioned, in its various idioms, 237 times. In the Bible, from which we draw our values and our strength, in the Book of Jeremiah, we find a lamentation for Rachel the Matriarch. It reads:

> *"Refrain your voice from weeping, and your eyes from tears:*
> *for their work shall be rewarded, says the Lord."*

I will not refrain from weeping for those who are gone. But on this summer day in Washington, far from home, we sense that our work will be rewarded, as the prophet foretold.

The Jewish tradition calls for a blessing on every new tree, every new fruit, on every new season. Let me conclude with the ancient Jewish blessing that has been with us in exile, and in Israel, for thousands of years:

"Blessed are You, O Lord, who has preserved us, and sustained us, and enabled us to reach this time."

Israel-Jordan Peace Treaty: October 1994

PREAMBLE

The government of the Hashemite Kingdom of Jordan and the government of the State of Israel:

Bearing in mind the Washington Declaration, signed by them on 25 July 1994 and which they are both committed to honor.

Aiming at the achievement of a just, lasting, and comprehensive peace in the Middle East based on Security Council resolutions 242 and 318 in all their aspects;

Bearing in mind the importance of maintaining and strengthening peace based on freedom, equality, justice, and respect for fundamental and human rights: thereby overcoming psychological barriers and promoting human dignity;

Reaffirming their faith in the purposes and the principles of the Charter of the United Nations and recognizing their right and obligation to live in peace with each other as well as with all states, within secure and recognized boundaries;

Desiring to develop friendly relations and cooperation between them in accordance with the principles of international law governing international relations in times of peace;

Desiring as well to ensure lasting security for both their states and, in particular, to avoid threats and the use of force between them;

Bearing in mind that in their Washington Declaration of 25 July 1994, they declared the termination of the state of belligerency between them;

Deciding to establish peace between them in accordance with this treaty of peace;

Have agreed as follows:

ARTICLE 1—ESTABLISHMENT OF PEACE

Peace is hereby established between the Hashemite Kingdom of Jordan and the State of Israel (the parties) effective from the exchange of the instruments of ratifications of this treaty.

ARTICLE 2—GENERAL PRINCIPLES

The parties will apply between them the provisions of the Charter of the United Nations and the principles of international law governing relations among states in times of peace. In particular:

a. They recognize and will respect each other's sovereignty, territorial integrity, and political independence.

b. They recognize and will respect each other's right to live in peace within secure and recognized boundaries.

c. They will develop good neighborly relations of cooperation between them to ensure lasting security, will refrain from the threat or use of force against each other, and will settle all disputes between them by peaceful means.

d. They respect and recognize the sovereignty, territorial integrity, and political independence of every state in the region.

e. They respect and recognize the pivotal role of human development and dignity in regional and bilateral relationships.

f. They further believe that within their control, involuntary movements of persons in such a way as to adversely prejudice the security of either party should not be permitted.

ARTICLE 3—INTERNATIONAL BOUNDARY

a. The international boundary between Israel and Jordan is delimited with reference to the boundary definition under the Mandate as is shown in Annex I (a), on the mapping materials attached thereto and coordinates specified therein.

b. The boundary, as set out in Annex I (a), is the permanent, secure, and recognized international boundary between Israel and

Jordan, without prejudice to the status of any territories that came under Israeli military government control in 1967.

c. The parties recognize the international boundary, including the territorial waters and airspace, as inviolable, and will respect and comply with them.

d. The demarcation of the boundary will take place as set forth in the Appendix I to Annex I (a) and will be concluded no later than nine months after the signing of the treaty.

e. It is agreed that where the boundary follows a river, in the event of natural changes in the course of the flow of the river as described in Annex I (a), the boundary shall follow the new course of the flow. In the event of any other changes, the boundary shall not be affected unless otherwise agreed.

f. Immediately upon the exchange of the instruments of ratification of this treaty, each party will deploy on each side of the international boundary as defined in Annex I (a).

g. The parties shall, upon the signature of the treaty, enter into the negotiations to conclude, within nine months, an agreement on the delimitation of their maritime boundary in the Gulf of Akaba.

h. Taking into account the special circumstances of the Bakura/ Naharayim area, which is under Jordanian sovereignty, with Israeli private ownership rights, the parties agreed to apply the provisions set out in Annex I (b).

i. With respects to the Tzofar area the provisions set out in Annex I (c) will apply.

ARTICLE 4 — SECURITY

1. a. Both parties, acknowledging that mutual understanding and cooperation in security-related matters will form a significant part of their relations and will further enhance the security of the region, take upon themselves to base their security relations on mutual trust, advancement of joint interests and cooperation, and to aim towards a regional framework of partnership in peace.

b. Towards that goal, the parties recognize the achievements of the European Community and European Union in the development of the Conference on Security and Cooperation in Europe (CSCE) and commit themselves to the creation, in the Middle East, of a CSCME (Conference on Security and Cooperation in the Middle East).

This commitment entails the adoption of regional models of security successfully implemented in the post World War era (along the lines of the Helsinki process) culminating in a regional zone of security and stability.

2. The obligations referred to in this article are without prejudice

to the inherent right of self-defense in accordance with the United Nations Charter.

3. The parties undertake, in accordance with the provisions of this article, the following:

a. To refrain from the threat or use of force or weapons, conventional, non-conventional, or of any other kind, against each other or of other actions or activities that adversely affect the security of the other party;

b. To refrain from organizing, instigating, inciting, assisting, or participating in acts or threats of belligerency, hostility, subversion, or violence against the other party;

c. To take necessary and effective measures to ensure that acts or threats of belligerency, hostility, subversion, or violence against the other party do not originate from, and are not committed within, their territory (hereinafter the term ''territory'' includes the airspace and territorial waters), or through or over their territory.

4. Consistent with the era of peace and with the efforts to build regional security and to avoid and prevent aggression and violence, the parties further agree to refrain from the following:

a. Joining or in any way assisting, promoting, or cooperating with any coalition, organization, or alliance with a military or security character with a third party, the objectives or activities of which include launching aggression or other acts of military hostility against the other party, in contravention of the provisions of the present treaty;

b. Allowing the entry, stationing, and operating on their territory, or through it, of military forces, personnel, or material of a third party, in circumstances which may adversely prejudice the security of the other party.

5. Both parties will take necessary and effective measures, and will cooperate in combating terrorism of all kinds. The parties undertake:

a. To take necessary and effective measures to prevent acts of terrorism, subversion, or violence from being carried out from their territory or through it, and to take necessary and effective measures to combat such activities and all their perpetrators;

b. Without prejudice to the basic rights of freedom of expression and association, to take necessary and effective measures to prevent the entry, presence and operations in their territory of any group or organization, and its infrastructure, which threatens the security of the other party by the use or incitement to the use of violent means;

c. To cooperate in preventing and combating cross-boundary infiltrations.

6. Any question as to the implementation of this article will be

dealt with through a mechanism of consultation which will include a liaison system, verification, supervision, and where necessary, other mechanisms, and higher level consultation. The details of the mechanism of consultation will be contained in an agreement to be concluded by the parties within three months of the exchange of the instruments of ratification of this treaty.

7. To work as a matter of priority and as soon as possible in the context of the multilateral working groups on arms control and regional security, and jointly, toward the following:

a. The creation in the Middle East of a region free from hostile alliances and coalitions;

b. The creation of a Middle East free from weapons of mass destruction, both conventional and non-conventional, in the context of a comprehensive, lasting, and stable peace, characterized by the renunciation of the use of force, reconciliation, and goodwill.

ARTICLE 5—DIPLOMATIC AND OTHER BILATERAL RELATIONS

1. The parties agree to establish full diplomatic and consular relations and to exchange resident ambassadors within one month of the exchange of the instruments of ratification of this treaty.

2. The parties agree that the normal relationship between them will further include economic and cultural relations.

ARTICLE 6—WATER

With the view to achieving a comprehensive and lasting settlement of all the water problems between them:

1. The parties agree mutually to recognize the rightful allocations of both of them in Jordan River, Yarmuk River waters, and Arab/Arava ground water in accordance with the agreed acceptable principles, quantities, and quality as set out in Annex II, which shall be fully respected and complied with;

2. The parties, recognizing the necessity to find a practical, just, and agreed solution to their water problems and with the view that the subject of water can form the basis for the advancement of cooperation between them, jointly undertake to ensure that the management and development of their water resources do not, in any way, harm the water resources of the other party;

3. The parties recognize that their water resources are not sufficient to meet their needs. More water should be supplied for their use through various methods, including projects of regional and international cooperation;

4. In light of paragraph 2A, with the understanding that the

cooperation in water-related subjects would be to the benefit of both parties, and will help alleviate their water shortages, and that water issues along their entire boundary must be dealt with in their totality, including the possibility of trans-boundary water transfers, the parties agreed to search for ways to alleviate water shortages and to cooperate in the following fields:

a. Development of existing and new water resources increasing the water availability, including on a regional basis, as appropriate, and minimizing wastage of water resources through the chain of their uses;

b. Prevention of contamination of water resources;

c. Mutual assistance in the alleviation of water shortages;

d. Transfer of information and joint research and development in water-related subjects, and review of the potentials for enhancement of water resources development and use;

5. The implementation of both countries' undertakings under this article is detailed in Annex II.

ARTICLE 7—ECONOMIC RELATIONS

1. Viewing economic development and prosperity as pillars of peace, security, and harmonious relations between states, peoples, and individual human beings, the parties, taking note of understandings reached between them, affirm their mutual desire to promote economic cooperation between them, as well as within the framework of wider regional economic cooperation.

2. In order to establish this goal, the parties agree to the following:

a. To remove all discriminatory barriers to normal economic relations, to terminate economic boycotts directed at each other, and to cooperate in terminating boycotts against each other by third parties;

b. Recognizing that the principle of free and unimpeded flow of goods and services should guide their relations, the parties will enter into negotiations with a view to concluding agreements on economic cooperation, including trade and the establishment of a free trade area, investment, banking, industrial cooperation, and labor, for the purpose of promoting beneficial economic relations, based on principles to be agreed upon, as well as on human development considerations on a regional basis. These negotiations will be concluded no later than six months from the exchange the instruments of ratification of the treaty;

c. To cooperate bilaterally, as well as in multilateral forums, toward the promotion of their respective economies and of their neighborly economic relations with other regional parties.

ARTICLE 8—REFUGEES AND DISPLACED PERSONS

1. Recognizing the massive human problems caused by both parties by the conflict in the Middle East, as well as the contribution made by them towards the alleviation of human suffering. The parties will seek to further alleviate those problems arising on a bilateral level.

2. Recognizing that the above human problems caused by the conflict in the Middle East cannot be fully resolved on the bilateral level, the parties will seek to resolve them in appropriate forums, in accordance with international law, including the following:

(a) In the case of displaced persons, in a quadripartite committee together with Egypt and the Palestinians;

(b) In the case of refugees,

(i) in the framework of the work of the Multilateral Group on Refugees;

(ii) in negotiations, in a framework to be agreed, bilateral or otherwise, in conjunction with and at the same time as the permanent status negotiations pertaining to the territories referred to in Article 3 of this treaty.

3. Through the implementation of agreed United Nations programs and other agreed international economic programs concerning refugees and displaced persons, including assistance to their settlement.

ARTICLE 9—PLACES OF HISTORICAL AND RELIGIOUS SIGNIFICANCE

1. Each party will provide freedom of access to places of religious and historical significance.

2. In this regard, in accordance with the Washington Declaration, Israel respects the present special role of the Hashemite Kingdom of Jordan in Moslem holy shrines in Jerusalem. When negotiations on the permanent status will take place, Israel will give high priority to the Jordanian historic role in these shrines.

3. The parties will act together to promote interfaith relations among the three monotheistic religions, with the aim of working towards religious understanding, moral commitment, freedom of religious worship, and tolerance and peace.

ARTICLE 10—CULTURAL AND SCIENTIFIC EXCHANGES

The parties, wishing to remove biases developed through periods of conflict, recognize the desirability of cultural and scientific exchanges in all fields, and agree to establish normal cultural relations between them. Thus, they shall, as soon as possible and not later than nine months from the exchange of the instruments of ratification of this treaty, conclude the negotiations on cultural and scientific agreements.

ARTICLE 11—MUTUAL UNDERSTANDING AND GOOD NEIGHBORLY RELATIONS

1. The parties will seek to foster mutual understanding and tolerance based on shared historic values, and accordingly undertake:

a. To abstain from hostile or discriminatory propaganda against each other, and to take all possible legal and administrative measures to prevent the dissemination of such propaganda by any organization or individual present in the territory of either party;

b. As soon as possible, and not later that three months from the exchange of the instruments of ratification of this treaty, to repeal all adverse or discriminatory references and expressions of hostility in their respective legislation;

c. To refrain in all government publications from any such reference or expressions;

d. To ensure mutual enjoyment by each other's citizens of due process of law within their respective legal systems and before their courts.

2. Article 1 (a) is without prejudice to the right to freedom of expression as contained in the International Covenant on Civil and Political Rights.

3. A joint committee shall be formed to examine incidents where one party claims there has been a violation of this article.

ARTICLE 12—COMBATING CRIME AND DRUGS

The parties will cooperate in combating crime, with an emphasis on smuggling, and will take all necessary measures to combat and prevent such activities as the production of, as well as the trafficking in illicit drugs, and will bring to trial perpetrators of such acts. In this regard, they take note of the understandings reached between them in the above spheres, as per Annex III and undertake to conclude all relevant agreements no later than nine months from the date of the exchange of the instruments of ratification of this treaty.

ARTICLE 13—TRANSPORTATION AND ROADS

Taking note of the progress already made in the area of transportation, the parties recognize the mutuality of interest in good neighborly relations in the area of transportation and agree to the following means to promote relations between them in this sphere:

a. Each party will permit the free movement of nationals and vehicles of the other into and within its territory according to the general rules applicable to nationals and vehicles or other states. Neither party will impose discriminatory taxes or restrictions on the free movement of persons and vehicles from its territory to the territory of the other;

b. The parties will open and maintain roads and border-crossings between their countries and will consider further road and rail links between them;

c. The parties will continue their negotiations concerning mutual transportation agreements in the above and other areas, such as joint projects, traffic safety, transport standards and norms, licensing of vehicles, land passages, shipment of goods and cargo, and meteorology, to be concluded not later than six months from the exchange of the instruments of ratification of this treaty;

d. The parties agree to continue their negotiations for a highway to be constructed and maintained between Egypt, Israel, and Jordan near Eilat. . . .

ARTICLE 14—FREEDOM OF NAVIGATION AND ACCESS TO PORTS

. . . 3. The parties consider the Strait of Tiran and the Gulf of Akaba to be international waterways open to all nations for unimpeded and non-suspendable freedom of navigation and overflight. The parties will respect each other's right to navigation and overflight for access to either party through the Strait of Tiran and the Gulf of Akaba.

ARTICLE 15—CIVIL AVIATION

1. The parties recognize as applicable to each other the rights, privileges, and obligations provided for by the multilateral aviation agreements to which they are both party. . . .

ARTICLE 16—POSTS AND TELECOMMUNICATIONS

The parties take note of the opening between them, in accordance with the Washington Declaration, of direct telephone and facsimile lines. Postal links, the negotiations on which having been concluded, will be activated upon the signature of this treaty. The parties further agree that normal wireless and cable communication and television relay services by cable, radio, and satellite, will be established between them, in accordance with all relevant international conventions and regulations. The negotiations on these subjects will be concluded not later than nine months from the exchange of the instruments of ratification of this treaty.

ARTICLE 17—TOURISM

The parties affirm their mutual desire to promote cooperation between them in the field of tourism. . . .

ARTICLE 19—ENERGY

1. The parties will cooperate in the development of energy resources, including the development of energy-related projects, such as the utilization of solar energy.

2. The parties, having concluded their negotiations on the interconnecting of their electric grids in the Eilat-Akaba area, will implement the interconnecting upon the signature of this treaty. The parties view this step as a part of a wider bi-national and regional concept. They agree to continue their negotiations as soon as possible to widen the scope of their interconnected grids. . . .

ARTICLE 20—RIFT VALLEY DEVELOPMENT

The parties attach great importance to the integrated development of the Jordan Rift Valley area, including joint projects in the economic, environmental, energy-related, and tourism fields. Taking note of the terms of reference developed in the framework of the trilateral Israel-Jordan-US economic committee towards the Jordan Rift Valley Development Master nPlan . . . they will vigorously continue their efforts towards the completion of planning and towards implementation. . . .

Prime Minister Yitzhak Rabin, Chairman Yasir Arafat, and Foreign Minister Shimon Peres: Speeches Accepting the Nobel Peace Prize, December 1994

Yitzhak Rabin

At an age when most youngsters are struggling to unravel the secrets of mathematics and the mysteries of the Bible; at an age when first love blooms; at the tender age of sixteen, I was handed a rifle so that I could defend myself.

That was not my dream. I wanted to be a water engineer. I studied in an agricultural school and I thought being a water engineer was an important profession in the parched Middle East. I still think so today. However, I was compelled to resort to the gun.

I served in the military for decades. Under my responsibility, young men and women who wanted to live, wanted to love, went to their deaths instead. They fell in the defense of our lives.

In my current position, I have ample opportunity to fly over the State of Israel, and lately over other parts of the Middle East as well. The view from the plane is breathtaking; deep-blue seas and lakes, dark-green fields, dune-colored deserts, stone-gray mountains, and the entire countryside peppered with white-washed, red-roofed houses.

And also cemeteries. Graves as far as the eye can see. Hundreds of cemeteries in our part of the world, in the Middle East—in our home in Israel, but also in Egypt, in Syria, Jordan, Lebanon. From the plane's window, from the thousands of feet above them, the countless tombstones are silent. But the sound of their outcry has carried from the Middle East throughout the world for decades.

Standing here today, I wish to salute our loved ones—and past foes. I wish to salute all of them—the fallen of all the countries in all the wars; the members of their families who bear the enduring burden of bereavement; the disabled whose scars will never heal. Tonight, I wish to pay tribute to each and every one of them, for this important prize is theirs. . . .

Of all the memories I have stored up in my seventy-two years, what I shall remember most, to my last day, are the silences: The heavy silence of the moment after, and the terrifying silence of the moment before.

As a military man, as a commander, as a minister of defense, I ordered many military operations. And together with the joy of victory and the grief of bereavement, I shall always remember the moment just after taking such decisions: the hush as senior officers or cabinet ministers slowly rise from their seats; the sight of their receding backs; the sound of the closing door; and then the silence in which I remain alone.

That is the moment you grasp that as a result of the decision just made, people might go to their deaths. People from my nation, people from other nations. And they still don't know it.

At that hour, they are still laughing and weeping; still weaving plans and dreaming about love; still musing about planting a garden or building a house—and they have no idea these are their last hours on earth. Which of them is fated to die? Whose picture will appear in the black frame in tomorrow's newspaper? Whose mother will soon be in mourning? Whose world will crumble under the weight of the loss?

As a former military man, I will also forever remember the silence of the moment before: the hush when the hands of the clock seem to be spinning forward, when time is running out and in another hour, another minute, the inferno will erupt.

In that moment of great tension just before the finger pulls the trigger, just before the fuse begins to burn; in the terrible quiet of the moment, there is still time to wonder, to wonder alone: Is it really imperative to act? Is there no other choice? No other way?

"God takes pity on kindergartners," wrote the poet Yehudah Amichai, who is here with us this evening—and I quote his:

"God takes pity on kindergartners, Less so on the schoolchildren, And will no longer pity their elders, Leaving them to their own, And sometimes they will have to crawl on all fours, Through the burning sand, To reach the casualty station, Bleeding."

For decades, God has not taken pity on the kindergartners in the Middle East, or the schoolchildren, or their elders. There has been no pity in the Middle East for generations.

I was a young man who has now grown fully in years. And of all the memories I have stored up in my seventy-two years, I now recall the hopes.

Our people have chosen us to give them life. Terrible as it is to say, their lives are in our hands. Tonight, their eyes are upon us and their hearts are asking: How is the power vested in these men and women being used? What will they decide? Into what kind of morning will we rise tomorrow? A day of peace? Of war? Of laughter? Of tears?

A child is born in an utterly undemocratic way. He cannot choose his father and mother. He cannot pick his sex or color, his religion, nationality or homeland. Whether he is born in a manor or a manger, whether he lives under a despotic or democratic regime is not his choice. From the moment he comes, close-fisted, into the world, his fate—to a large extent—is decided by his nation's leaders. It is they who will decide whether he lives in comfort or in despair, in security or in fear. His fate is given to us to resolve—to the governments of countries, democratic or otherwise.

Just as no two fingerprints are identical, so no two people are alike, and every country has its own laws and culture, traditions and leaders. But there is one universal message which can embrace the entire world, one precept which can be common to different regimes, to races which bear no resemblance, to cultures that are alien to each other.

It is a message which the Jewish people has carried for thousands of years, the message found in the Book of Books: "Therefore take good heed of yourselves"—or, in contemporary terms, the message of the sanctity of life.

The leaders of nations must provide their peoples with the conditions —the infrastructure, if you will—which enables them to enjoy life: freedom of speech and movement; food and shelter; and most important of all: life itself. A man cannot enjoy his rights if he is not alive. And so every country must protect and preserve the key element in its national ethos: the lives of its citizens.

Only to defend those lives, we can call upon our citizens to enlist in the army. And to defend the lives of our citizens serving in the army, we invest huge sums in planes and tanks, and other means. Yet despite it all, we fail to protect the lives of our citizens and soldiers. Military cemeteries in every corner of the world are silent testimony to the failure of national leaders to sanctify human life.

There is only one radical means for sanctifying human life. The one radical solution is a real peace.

The profession of soldiering embraces a certain paradox. We take the best and the bravest of our young men into the army. We supply them with equipment which costs a virtual fortune. We rigorously train them for the day when they must do their duty—and we expect them to do it well. Yet we fervently pray that that day will never come—that the planes will never take off, the tanks will never move forward, the soldiers will never mount the attacks for which they have been trained so well.

We pray that it will never happen, because of the sanctity of life.

History as a whole, and modern history in particular, has known harrowing times when national leaders turned their citizens into cannon fodder in the name of wicked doctrines: vicious Fascism, terrible Nazism. Pictures of children marching to slaughter, photos of terrified women at the gates of the crematoria must loom before the eyes of every leader in our generation, and the generations to come. They must serve as a warning to all who wield power.

Almost all regimes which did not place the sanctity of life at the heart of their worldview, all those regimes have collapsed and are no more. You can see it for yourselves in our own time.

Yet this is not the whole picture. To preserve the sanctity of life, we must sometimes risk it. Sometimes there is no other way to defend our citizens than to fight for their lives, for their safety and freedom. This is the creed of every democratic state.

In the State of Israel, from which I come today; in the Israel Defense Forces, which I have had the privilege to serve, we have always viewed the sanctity of life as a supreme value. We have never gone to war unless a war was forced on us.

The history of the State of Israel, the annals of the Israel Defense Forces, are filled with thousands of stories of soldiers who sacrificed themselves—who died while trying to save wounded comrades; who gave their lives to avoid causing harm to innocent people on their enemy's side.

In the coming days, a special commission of the Israel Defense Forces will finish drafting a Code of Conduct for our soldiers. The formulation regarding human life will read as follows, and I quote:

"In recognition of its supreme importance, the soldier will preserve human life in every way possible and endanger himself, or others, only to the extent deemed necessary to fulfill this mission.

"The sanctity of life, in the point of view of the soldiers of the Israel Defense Forces, will find expression in all their actions."

For many years ahead—even if wars come to an end, after peace comes to our land—these words will remain a pillar of fire which goes before our camp, a guiding light for our people. And we take pride in that.

We are in the midst of building the peace. The architects and the engineers of this enterprise are engaged in their work even as we gather here tonight, building the peace, layer by layer, brick by brick. The job is difficult, complex, trying. Mistakes could topple the whole structure and bring disaster down upon us.

And so we are determined to do the job well—despite the toll of murderous terrorism, despite the fanatic and cruel enemies of peace.

We will pursue the course of peace with determination and fortitude. We will not let up. We will not give in. Peace will triumph over all its enemies, because the alternative is grimmer for us all. And we will prevail.

We will prevail because we regard the building of peace as a great blessing for us, for our children after us. We regard it as a blessing for our neighbors on all sides, and for our partners in this enterprise—the United States, Russia, Norway—which did so much to bring the agreement that was signed here, later on in Washington, later on in Cairo, that wrote a beginning of the solution to the longest and most difficult part of the Arab-Israeli conflict: the Palestinian-Israeli one. We thank others who have contributed to it, too.

We wake up every morning, now, as different people. Peace is possible. We see the hope in our children's eyes. We see the light in our soldiers' faces, in the streets, in the buses, in the fields. We must not let them down. We will not let them down.

I stand here not alone today, on this small rostrum in Oslo. I am here to speak in the name of generations of Israelis and Jews, of the shepherds of Israel—and you know that King David was a shepherd; he started to build Jerusalem about 3,000 years ago—the herdsmen and dressers of sycamore trees, and as the Prophet Amos was; of the rebels against the establishment, as the Prophet Jeremiah was; and of men who went down to the sea, like the Prophet Jonah.

I am here to speak in the name of the poets and of those who dreamed of an end to war, like the Prophet Isaiah.

I am also here to speak in the names of sons of the Jewish people like Albert Einstein and Baruch Spinoza, like Maimonides, Sigmund Freud and Franz Kafka.

And I am the emissary of millions who perished in the Holocaust, among whom were surely many Einsteins and Freuds who were lost to us, and to humanity, in the flames of the crematoria.

I am here as the emissary of Jerusalem, at whose gates I fought in the days of siege; Jerusalem which has always been, and is today, the eternal capital of the State of Israel and the heart of the Jewish people, who pray toward Jerusalem three times a day.

And I am also the emissary of the children who drew their visions of peace; and of the immigrants from St. Petersburg and Addis Ababa.

I stand here mainly for the generations to come, so that we may all be deemed worthy of the medal which you have bestowed on me and my colleagues today.

I stand here as the emissary today—if they will allow me—of our neighbors who were our enemies. I stand here as the emissary of the soaring hopes of a people which has endured the worst that history has to offer and nevertheless made its mark—not just on the chronicles of the Jewish people but on all mankind.

With me here are five million citizens of Israel—Jews, Arabs, Druze and Circassians—five million hearts beating for peace, and five million pairs of eyes which look at us with such great expectations for peace.

I wish to thank, first and foremost, those citizens of the State of Israel, of all the generations, of all the political persuasions, whose sacrifices and relentless struggle for peace bring us steadier closer to our goal.

I wish to thank our partners—the Egyptians, the Jordanians, and the Palestinians, that are led by the Chairman of the Palestinian Liberation Organization, Mr. Yasir Arafat, with whom we share this Nobel Prize—who have chosen the path of peace and are writing a new page in the annals of the Middle East.

I wish to thank the members of the Israeli government, but above all my partner the Foreign Minister, Mr. Shimon Peres, whose energy and devotion to the cause of peace are an example to us all. . . .

Allow me to close by sharing with you a traditional Jewish blessing which has been recited by my people, in good times and bad ones, as a token of their deepest longing:

"The Lord will give strength to his people; the Lord will bless his people—and all of us—in peace."

Chairman Yasir Arafat

In the name of God, the merciful, the compassionate. "But if the enemy incline toward peace, do thou also incline toward peace, and trust in God." [Koranic quotation]

Since my people entrusted me with the hard task of searching for our lost home, I have been filled with warm faith that those who carried their keys in the diaspora as they carry their own limbs, and that those who endured their wounds in the homeland and maintained their identity will be rewarded by return and freedom for their sacrifices. I have also been filled with faith that the arduous trek on the long path of pain will end in our home's yard.

As we celebrate together the first sight of the crescent of peace, I, at this podium stare into the open eyes of the martyrs within my conscience. They ask me about the national soil and their vacant seats there. I conceal my tears from them and tell them: How true you were; your generous blood has enabled us to see the holy land and to take our first steps in a difficult battle, the battle of peace, the peace of the brave.

As we celebrate together, we invoke the powers of creativity within us to reconstruct a home destroyed by war, a home overlooking our neighbor's, where our children will play with their children and will compete in picking flowers. Now, I have a sense of national and human pride in my Palestinian Arab people's patience and sacrifice, through which they have established an uninterrupted link between the homeland, history and the people, adding to the old legends of the homeland an epic of hope. For them, for the children of those good-natured and tough people, who are made of oaks and dews, of fire and sweat, I present this Nobel Prize, which I will carry to our children, who have a promise of freedom, security and safety in a homeland not threatened by an invader from outside or an exploiter from inside.

I know that this highly indicative prize has not been granted to me and my partners, Israel's Prime Minister Yitzhak Rabin and Foreign Minister Shimon Peres, to crown a mission that we have fulfilled, but to encourage us to complete a path which we have started with larger strides, deeper awareness, and more honest intentions. This is so we can transfer the option of peace, the peace of the brave, from words on paper to practices on the ground, and so we will be worthy of carrying the message that both our peoples and the world and human conscience have asked us to carry. Like their Arab brethren, the Palestinians, whose cause is the guardian of the gate of the Arab-Israeli peace, are looking forward to a comprehensive, just, and durable peace on the basis of land for peace and compliance with international legitimacy and its resolutions.

Peace, to us, is a value and an interest. Peace is an absolute human value which will help man develop his humanity with freedom that cannot be limited by regional, religious, or national restrictions. It restores to the Arab-Jewish relationship its innocent nature and gives the Arab conscience the opportunity to express—through absolute human terms—its understanding of the European tragedy of the Jews. It also gives the Jewish conscience the opportunity to express the suffering of the Palestinian peoples which resulted from this historical intersection and to find an echo for this suffering in the pained Jewish soul. The pained people are more capable than others of understanding the suffering of other people.

Peace is an interest because, in an atmosphere of just peace, the Palestinian people will be able to achieve their ambitions for independence and sovereignty, to develop their national and cultural existence through relations of good neighborliness, mutual respect, and cooperation with the Israeli people. Peace will enable the Israeli people to define their Middle East identity and to enjoy economic and cultural openness toward their Arab neighbors, who are eager to develop their region, which was kept by the long war from finding its real position in today's world in an atmosphere of democracy, pluralism, and prosperity.

As war is an adventure, peace is also a challenge and a gamble. If we do not fortify peace to stand against storms and wind, and if we do not support it and strengthen it, the gamble will then be exposed to blackmail, perhaps to fall. Therefore, I call on my partners in peace on this high platform to expedite the peace process, achieve early withdrawal, pave the road for elections, and to move to the second stage in record time, so that peace will grow and become a firm reality.

We have started the peace process based on land for peace, on UN Resolutions 242 and 338, and on the other international resolutions calling for achieving the legitimate rights of the Palestinian people. While the peace process has not yet reached its target, the new atmosphere of confidence and the modest achievements of the first and second year of the peace process are promising. Therefore, the parties are urged to abandon their reservations, facilitate measures, and achieve the remaining goals, foremost of which are transferring powers and taking steps toward an Israeli withdrawal in the West Bank and the settlements. This will finally lead to a comprehensive withdrawal and will enable our society to build its infrastructure and utilize its status, heritage, knowledge, and awareness to formulate our new world.

In this context, I call on Russia and the United States, sponsors of the peace process, to accelerate the steps of this process, to take part in its formulation and to overcome its obstacles. I urge Norway and Egypt, in their capacity as hosts to the Palestinian-Israeli agreement, to continue their good initiative, which started from Oslo and reached Washington and Cairo. Oslo, as well as the names of the other states that have been hosting the multilateral talks, will remain shining names linked to the peace of the courageous. I also urge all countries, foremost of which are the donor countries, to make their contributions quickly to enable the Palestinian people to overcome their economic and social problems, to rebuild themselves and to establish their infrastructure. Peace cannot grow and the peace process cannot be entrenched unless their necessary material conditions are met.

I then urge my partners in peace to view the peace process in a comprehensive and strategic way. Confidence alone cannot make peace, but only recognizing the rights, together with confidence, can make peace. Encroaching on rights generates a sense of injustice, keeps the fire under the ashes, and will push peace to a dangerous point and toward quicksand that may destroy it. We view peace as a strategic option, rather than a tactical option influenced by temporary calculations of loss and profit. The peace process is not only a political one, but also an integrated process in which national awareness and economic, scientific, and technological development play an important role. The interaction of cultural, social, and creative elements also play basic roles in strengthening the peace process.

I view all this as I recall the difficult peace march, in which we have covered only a short distance. We should have courage and move as far as possible to cover the greater distance based on just and comprehensive peace and to absorb the strength of creativity which is contained in the deeper lesson of peace.

As long as we have decided to coexist and live in peace, then we should coexist on a solid basis that can last through all time and that is acceptable to the future generations. In this context, full withdrawal from the West Bank and the Gaza Strip requires deep discussions about the settlements that cut through geographic and political unity, prevent free movement between the areas of the West Bank and the Strip, and create hotbeds of tension that conflict with the spirit of peace, which we want to be free of anything that spoils its purity.

As for Jerusalem, it is the spiritual home of Christians, Muslims, and Jews. To Palestinians, it is the city of cities. The Jewish shrines in the city are our shrines, the same as the Islamic and Christian shrines. So let us make Jerusalem an international symbol of this spiritual harmony, this cultural brightness, and this religious heritage of humanity as a whole.

There is an urgent task that activates the peace mechanism and enables it to overcome the problem that is troubling hearts, the question of prisoners. It is important to release them so smiles can return to their children, their mothers, and their wives. Let us together protect this little baby from the winter's winds, and let us provide it with the milk and honey it deserves in the land of milk and honey in the land of Salim, Ibrahim, Isma'il, and Ishaq—the holy land, the land of peace.

Finally, I again congratulate my partners in peace—Israeli Prime Minister Yitzhak Rabin and Israeli Foreign Minister Simon Peres—for winning the Nobel Peace Prize. . . . I emphasize to you that we will discover ourselves through peace more than we did through confrontation and conflict. I am certain that Israelis will find themselves through peace more than they did in war.

Glory to God in the highest, and on Earth peace, and good will toward men.

Foreign Minister Shimon Peres

I am pleased to be receiving this prize together with Yitzhak Rabin, with whom I have labored for long years for the defense of our country and with whom I now labor together in the cause of peace in our region. This is a salute to his daring leadership.

I believe it is fitting that the prize has been awarded to Yasir Arafat. His quitting the path of confrontation in favor of the path of dialogue has opened the way to peace between ourselves and the Palestinian people, to whom we wish all the best in the future. . . .

From my earliest youth, I have known that while obliged to plan with care the stages of our journey, we are entitled to dream, and keep dreaming, of its destination. A man may feel as old as his years, yet as young as his dreams. The laws of biology do not apply to sanguine aspiration.

I was born in a small Jewish town in White Russia. Nothing Jewish remains of it. From my youngest childhood, I related to my place of birth as a mere way station. My family's dream, and my own, was to live in Israel, and our voyage to the port of Jaffa was a dream that came true. Had it not been for this dream and this voyage, I would probably have perished in the flames, as did so many of my people, among them most of my own family.

I went to school at an agricultural youth village in the heart of Israel. The village and its fields were enclosed by barbed wire which separated their greenness from the bleakness of the enmity all around. In the morning, we would go out to the fields with scythes on our backs to harvest the crop. In the evening, we went out with rifles on our shoulders to defend our lives. On Shabbat we would go out to visit our Arab neighbors. On Shabbat, we would talk with them of peace, though the rest of the week we traded rifle fire across the darkness!

From the Ben Shemen Youth village, my comrades and I went to Kibbutz Alumot in the Lower Galilee. We had no houses, no electricity, no running water. But we had a magnificent view and a lofty dream: to build a new, egalitarian society that would ennoble each of its members.

Not all of it came true, but not all of it went to waste. The part that came true created a new landscape. The part that did not come true resides in our hearts to this very day.

For two decades, in the Ministry of Defense, I was privileged to work closely with a man who was and remains, to my mind, the greatest Jew of our time. From him I learned that the vision of the future should shape the agenda for the present; that you can overcome obstacles by dint of faith; that you may feel disappointed—but never despair. And above all, I learned that the wisest consideration is the moral one. David Ben-Gurion has passed away, yet his vision continues to flourish: to be a singular people, to live at peace with our neighbors.

The wars we fought were forced upon us. Thanks to the Israel Defence Forces, we won them all, but we did not win the greatest victory that we aspired to: release from the need to win victories.

We proved that aggressors do not necessarily emerge as the victors, but we learned that victors do not necessarily win peace.

It is no wonder that war, as a method of conducting human affairs, is in its death throes, and that the time has come to bury it.

The sword, as the Bible teaches us, consumes flesh, but it cannot provide sustenance. It is not rifles but people who triumph, and the conclusion from all the wars is that we need better people, not better rifles—to avoid wars, to win peace.

There was a time when war was fought for lack of choice. Today peace is the "no-choice" option for all of us. The reasons for this are profound and incontrovertible. The sources of material wealth and political power have changed. No longer are they determined by the size of territory won by war. Today they are a consequence of intellectual potential, obtained principally by education.

Israel, essentially a desert country, has achieved remarkable agricultural yields by applying science to its fields, without expanding its territory or its water resources.

Science must be learned; it cannot be conquered. An army that can occupy knowledge has yet to be built. And that is why armies of occupation are passé. Indeed, even for the defense of the country you cannot rely on the army alone. Territorial frontiers are no obstacle to ballistic missiles, and no weapon can shield a nation from a nuclear device. Today, the battle for survival must be based on political wisdom and moral vision no less than on military might.

Science, technology, information are—for better or for worse—universal, not national. They are universally available. Their availability is not contingent on color of skin or place of birth. Past distinctions between West and East, North and South, have lost their importance in the face of a new distinction: between those who move ahead in pace with new opportunities, and those who lag behind.

Countries used to divide the world into their friends and foes. No longer.

The foes now are universal—poverty, famine, religious radicalization, desertification, drugs, proliferation of nuclear weapons, ecological devastation. They threaten all nations, just as science and information are the potential friends of all nations.

Classical diplomacy and strategy were aimed at identifying enemies and confronting them. Now they have to identify dangers, global and local, to tackle them before they become disasters.

As we leave a world of enemies, as we enter a world of dangers, the future wars which may break out will not be, probably, the wars of the strong against the weak for conquest, but the wars of the weak against the strong for protest.

The Middle East must never lose pride in having been the cradle of civilization. But though living in the cradle, we cannot remain infants forever.

Today as in my youth, I carry dreams. I would mention two: the future of the Jewish people and the future of the Middle East.

In history, Judaism has been far more successful than the Jews themselves. The Jewish people remained small, but the spirit of Jerusalem—the capital of Jewish life, the city holy and open to all religions—went from strength to strength. The Bible is to be found in hundreds of millions of homes. The moral majesty of the Book of Books has been undefeated by the ups and downs of history.

Moreover, time and again, history has succumbed to the Bible's immortal ideas. The message that the one, invisible God created man in His image, and hence there are no higher and lower orders of man, has fused with the realization that morality is the highest form of wisdom and, perhaps, of beauty and courage, too.

Slings, arrows, gas chambers can annihilate man, but they cannot destroy human values, the dignity and freedom of the human being.

Jewish history presents an encouraging lesson for mankind. For nearly four thousand years, a small nation carried a great message. Initially, the nation dwelt in its own land; later, it wandered in exile. This small nation swam against the tide and was repeatedly persecuted, banished, downtrodden. There is no other example in all history—neither among the great empires nor among their colonies and dependencies—of a nation, after so long a saga of tragedy and misfortune, rising up again, shaking itself free, gathering together its dispersed remnants, and setting out anew on its national adventure. Defeating doubters within and enemies without. Reviving its land and its language. Rebuilding its identity, and reaching toward new heights of distinction and excellence.

The message of the Jewish people to mankind is that faith and moral vision can triumph over all adversity.

The conflicts shaping up as our century nears its close will be over the content of civilization, not over territory. Jewish culture has lived over many centuries; now it has taken root again in its own soil. For the first time in our history, some five million people speak Hebrew as their native language. That is both a lot and a little: a lot, because there have never been so many Hebrew-speaking people; but a little, because a culture based on five million people can hardly withstand the pervasive, corrosive effect of the global television culture.

In the five decades of Israel's existence, our efforts have focused on re-establishing our territorial center. In the future, we shall have to devote our main effort to strengthen our spiritual center. Judaism—or Jewishness—is a fusion of belief, history, land, and language. Being Jewish means to belong to a people that is both unique and universal. My greatest hope is that our children, like our forefathers, will not make do with the transient and the sham, but will continue to plow the historic Jewish furrow in the fields of human spirit, that Israel will become the center of our heritage, not merely a homeland for our people; that the Jewish people will be inspired by others, but at the same be to them a source of inspiration.

The second dream is about the Middle East. In the Middle East most people are impoverished and wretched. A new scale of priorities is needed, with weapons on the bottom and regional market economy at the top. Most inhabitants of the region—more than sixty percent—are under the age of eighteen. The Middle East is a huge kindergarten, a huge school. A new future can be and should be offered to them. Israel has computerized its education and has achieved excellent results. Education can be computerized throughout the Middle East, allowing young people, Arabs and others, to progress not just from grade to grade but from generation to generation.

Israel's role in the Middle East should be to contribute to a great, sustained regional revival:

A Middle East without wars, without enemies, without ballistic missiles, without nuclear warheads.

A Middle East in which men, goods and services can move freely without the need for customs clearance or police licenses.

A Middle East in which every believer will be free to pray in his own language—Arabic, Hebrew, Latin, or whatever language he chooses—and in which the prayers will reach their destination without censorship, without interference, and without offending anyone.

A Middle East in which nations strive for economic equality and encourage cultural pluralism.

A Middle East where young men and women can attain university education. A Middle East where living standards are in no way inferior to those in the world's most advanced countries—may I say, a Middle East very much like Scandinavia.

A Middle East where waters flow to slake thirst, to make crops grow and deserts bloom, in which no hostile borders bring death, hunger, despair, or shame.

A Middle East of competition, not of domination. A Middle East in which men are each other's hosts, not hostages.

A Middle East that is not a killing field, but a field of creativity and growth.

A Middle East that honors so much its history, that it strives to add to it new noble chapters.

A Middle East which will serve as a spiritual and cultural focal point for the entire world.

While thanking you, for the Prize, thanking the many people in uniform and civil dress in many nations, for arriving to this moment of happiness and hope, I believe that all of us remain committed to the process. I thank my family, that stood behind me for such a long journey, and are convinced as I am that this is the best option.

We have reached the age where dialogue is really the only way to run the world.